FOURTH EDITION

OUR ORIGINS

4th

EDITION

OUR ORIGINS

DISCOVERING PHYSICAL ANTHROPOLOGY

CLARK SPENCER LARSEN

THE OHIO STATE UNIVERSITY

W. W. NORTON & COMPANY
NEW YORK · LONDON

W. W. NORTON & COMPANY has been independent since its founding in 1923, when William Warder Norton and Mary D. Herter Norton first published lectures delivered at the People's Institute, the adult education division of New York City's Cooper Union. The firm soon expanded its program beyond the Institute, publishing books by celebrated academics from America and abroad. By midcentury, the two major pillars of Norton's publishing program—trade books and college texts—were firmly established. In the 1950s, the Norton family transferred control of the company to its employees, and today—with a staff of four hundred and a comparable number of trade, college, and professional titles published each year—W. W. Norton & Company stands as the largest and oldest publishing house owned wholly by its employees.

Editor: Jake Schindel
Assistant Editor: Rachel Goodman
Development Editor: Sunny Hwang
Project Editors: Rachel Mayer and Caitlin Moran
Associate Director of Production: Benjamin Reynolds
Marketing Manager, Anthropology: Katie Sweeney
Associate Director of Digital Media: Tacy Quinn
Associate Editor, Emedia: Mary Williams
Editorial Assistant, Emedia: Sarah Rose Aquilina
Photo Editor: Stephanie Romeo
Photo Researcher: Elyse Rieder
Permissions Manager: Megan Schindel
Permissions Clearing: Bethany Salminen
Text Designer: Jillian Burr
Art Director: Rubina Yeh
Composition and page layout: Brad Walrod
Illustrations: Imagineering—Toronto, ON
Manufacturing: LSC Communications—Kendallville, IN

Fourth Edition

Library of Congress Cataloging-in-Publication Data
Names: Larsen, Clark Spencer.
Title: Our origins : discovering physical anthropology / Clark Spencer Larsen, The Ohio State University.
Description: Fourth edition. | New York : W.W. Norton & Company, [2017] |
    Includes bibliographical references and index.
Identifiers: LCCN 2016053370 | ISBN 9780393284904 (pbk.)
Subjects: LCSH: Physical anthropology.
Classification: LCC GN50.4 .L37 2017 | DDC 599.9—dc23 LC record available at https://lccn.loc.gov/2016053370

W. W. Norton & Company, Inc., 500 Fifth Avenue, New York, N.Y. 10110-0017
www.wwnorton.com
W. W. Norton & Company Ltd., Castle House, 75/76 Wells Street, London W1T 3QT

1 2 3 4 5 6 7 8 9 0

To Chris and Spencer,
with my deepest thanks for their help,
encouragement, and (unwavering) patience

In memory of Jack Repcheck
(January 13, 1957–October 14, 2015)
Editor, writing mentor, and friend

ABOUT THE
AUTHOR

CLARK SPENCER LARSEN is a native of Nebraska. He received his B.A. from Kansas State University and M.A. and Ph.D. from the University of Michigan. Clark's research is in bioarchaeology, skeletal biology, and paleoanthropology. He has worked in North America, Europe, and Asia. His current fieldwork is in Turkey, Italy, and the United States. He has taught at the University of Massachusetts, Northern Illinois University, Purdue University, and the University of North Carolina. Since 2001, he has been a member of the faculty at The Ohio State University, where he is Distinguished Professor of Social and Behavioral Sciences. He teaches introductory physical anthropology, osteology, bioarchaeology, and paleoanthropology. Clark has served as president of the American Association of Physical Anthropologists and as editor-in-chief of the *American Journal of Physical Anthropology*. He is a member of the National Academy of Sciences and a Fellow of the American Association for the Advancement of Science. In addition to *Our Origins*, he has authored or edited 35 books and monographs, including *Bioarchaeology: Interpreting Behavior from the Human Skeleton*, *Skeletons in Our Closet*, *Advances in Dental Anthropology*, and *A Companion to Biological Anthropology*.

BASIC TABLE OF CONTENTS

TABLE OF CONTENTS

CHAPTER 6   Biology in the Present: The Other Living Primates   167

PART II The Past: Evidence for the Present   231

CHAPTER 8 Fossils and Their Place in Time and Nature   233

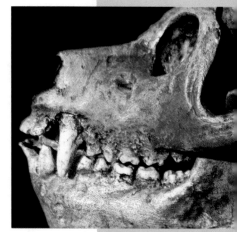

CHAPTER 11 The Origins and Evolution of Early *Homo*   353

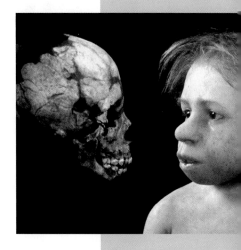

CHAPTER 13 The Past 10,000 Years: Agriculture, Population, Biology   445

PART III The Future: The Shape of Things to Come   481

CHAPTER 14 Evolution: Today and Tomorrow   483

TWO-PAGE SPREADS

TO THE INSTRUCTOR

How This Book Can Help Your Students Discover Physical Anthropology

It Is about Engagement

Teaching is about engagement—connecting the student with knowledge, making it real to the student, and having the student come away from the course with an understanding of core concepts. *Our Origins: Discovering Physical Anthropology* seeks to engage the student in the learning process. Engaging the student is perhaps more of a challenge in the study of physical anthropology than in the study of other sciences, mainly because the student has likely never heard of the subject. The average student has probably taken a precollege course in chemistry, physics, or biology. Physical anthropology, though, is rarely mentioned or taught in precollege settings. Commonly, the student first finds out about the subject when an academic advisor explains that physical anthropology is a popular course that fulfills the college's natural science requirement.

Once taking the course, however, that same student usually connects quickly with the subject because so many of the topics are familiar—fossils, evolution, race, genetics, DNA, monkeys, forensic investigations, and origins of speech, to name a few. The student simply had not realized that these separately engaging topics come under the umbrella of one discipline, the subject of which is the study of human evolution and human variability.

Perhaps drawn to physical anthropology because it focuses on our past and our present as a species, the student quickly sees the fundamental importance of the discipline. In *Discover* magazine's 100 top stories of 2009, 18 were from physical anthropology. Three topics from the field were in the top 10, including the remarkable new discovery of our earliest human ancestor, *Ardipithecus.* So important was this discovery that *Science,* the leading international

professional science journal, called it the "Breakthrough of the Year" for 2009. The discussions in this textbook of topics familiar and unfamiliar give the student stepping-stones to science and to the centrality of physical anthropology as a window into understanding our world. Whether the students find the material familiar or unfamiliar, they will see that the book relates the discipline to human life: real concerns about human bodies and human identity. They will see themselves from an entirely different point of view and gain new awareness.

In writing this book, I made no assumptions about what the reader knows, except to assume that the reader—the student attending your physical anthropology class—has very little or no background in physical anthropology. As I wrote the book, I constantly reflected on the core concepts of physical anthropology and how to make them understandable. I combined this quest for both accuracy and clarity with my philosophy of teaching; namely, engage the student to help the student learn. Simply, teaching is about engagement. While most students in an introductory physical anthropology class do not intend to become professional physical anthropologists, some of these students become interested enough to take more courses. So this book is written for students who will not continue their study of physical anthropology, those who get "hooked" by this fascinating subject (a common occurrence!), and those who now or eventually decide to become professionals in the field.

The book is unified by the subject of physical anthropology. But equally important is the central theme of science—what it is, how it is done, and how scientists (in our case, anthropologists) learn about the natural world. I wrote the book so as to create a picture of who humans are as organisms, how we got to where we are over the past millions of years of evolution, and where we are going in the future in light of current conditions. In regard to physical anthropology, the student should finish the book understanding human evolution and how it is studied, how the present helps us understand the past, the diversity of organisms living and past, and the nature of biological change over time and across geography. Such knowledge should help the student answer questions about the world. For example, How did primates emerge as a unique group of mammals? Why do people look different from place to place around the world? Why is it important to gain exposure to sunlight yet unsafe to prolong that exposure? Why is it unhealthy to be excessively overweight? Throughout their history, what have humans eaten, and why is it important to know?

I have presented such topics so that the student can come to understand the central concepts and build from them a fuller understanding of physical anthropology. Throughout the book, I emphasize hypothesis testing, the core of the scientific method, and focus on that process and the excitement of discovery. The narrative style is personalized. Often I draw on my own experiences and those of scientists I know or am familiar with through their teaching and writing, to show the student how problems are addressed through fieldwork or through laboratory investigations.

Scientists do not just collect facts. Rather, they collect data and make observations that help them answer questions about the complex natural world we all inhabit. Reflecting this practice, *Our Origins: Discovering Physical Anthropology* is a collection not of facts for the student to learn but of answers to questions that help all of us understand who we are as living organisms and our place in the world. Science is a way of knowing, it is a learning process, and it connects our lives with our world. In these ways, it is liberating.

How the Book Is Organized

The book is divided into three parts. After an introductory overview of anthropology and physical anthropology, part I presents the key principles and concepts in biology, especially from an evolutionary perspective. This material draws largely on the study of living organisms, including humans and nonhuman primates. Because much of our understanding of the past is drawn from what we have learned from the present, this part lays the foundation for the presentation in part II—the past record of primate and human evolution. In putting the record of the living up front, this book departs from the style of most other introductory physical anthropology textbooks, which start out with the earliest record and end with the living. This book takes the position that most of what we learn about the past is based on theory and principles learned from the living record. Just as all of Charles Darwin's ideas were first derived from seeing living plants and animals, much of our understanding of function and adaptation comes from living organisms as models. Therefore, this book views the living as the window onto what came before—the present contextualizes and informs our understanding of the past. It is no mistake, then, that *Our Origins* is the title of the book. The origins of who we are today do not just lie in the record of the past, but are very much embodied in the living. Our origins are expressed in our physical makeup (bones, teeth, and muscles), in our behavior, and in so many other ways that the student taking this course will learn about from this book and from you. You can teach individual chapters in any order, and that is partly because each

chapter reinforces the central point: we understand our past via what we see in the living.

Part II presents evidence of the past, covering more than 50 million years of primate and human evolution. Most textbooks of this kind end the record of human evolution at about 25,000 years ago, when modern *Homo sapiens* evolved worldwide. This textbook also provides the record since the appearance of modern humans, showing that important biological changes occurred in just the past 10,000 years, largely relating to the shift from hunting and gathering to the domestication of plants and animals. Food production was a revolutionary development in the human story, and part II presents this remarkable record, including changes in health and well-being that continue today. A new subdiscipline of physical anthropology, bioarchaeology, is contributing profound insights into the past 10,000 years, one of the most dynamic periods of human evolution. During this period, a fundamental change occurred in how humans obtained food. This change set the stage for our current environmental disruptions and modern living conditions.

Part III explores the record of continued evolution and discusses the impact of new developments, such as global warming, the alarming global increase in obesity, and the rise of health threats such as newly emerging infectious diseases, of which there is little understanding and for which scientists are far from finding cures. This part looks at the implications of these developments for evolution and for humans' future on Earth.

Changes in the Fourth Edition

Reflecting the dynamic nature of physical anthropology, there are numerous revisions and updates throughout this new, fourth edition of *Our Origins: Discovering Physical Anthropology*. These updates serve to provide content on the new and cutting-edge developments in the discipline, to give new ways of looking at older findings, and to keep the book engaging and timely for both you and your students. Although the core principles of the book remain the same, namely the focus on evolution, the revisions throughout the book present new insights, new discoveries, and new perspectives. Other changes are intended to give added focus and clarity and to increase the visual appeal that supports the pedagogy of engagement and learning:

- **New content on race and human variation.** The new edition provides answers to fundamental questions about race in America. This fourth edition explains that while race is a social reality, there is no meaningful biological basis for categorizing human variation. Therefore, while governmental and other institutions use categories to describe "race," the categories are not biologically informed.
- **New content on the globalization of diet.** The traditional low-fat, high-protein diet in many settings around the world is rapidly shifting to a high-fat, high-carbohydrate diet, resulting in an epidemic of obesity globally. This has important consequences for world health in the twenty-first century.
- **New content on rapidly emerging infectious diseases.** New infectious diseases—such as those caused by Ebola, bird flu, and, most recently, Zika—are emerging owing to the evolutionary

changes taking place in the viruses and in the human hosts. We are learning how that evolution occurs, and how understanding this evolution offers a very practical foundation for mitigating these life-threatening events.

- **New content on epigenetics.** The new edition explores the remarkable advances in our understanding of the human genome and the role of environment in modifying the way that DNA is regulated and expressed (but without modifying the DNA itself). Some of these modifications taking place well before birth can have long-term health consequences.

- **New content on primate social behavior.** Anthropologists are learning much more about social interactions between members of primate groups, and just how critical social behavior is for the well-being and functioning of social units.

- **New content on the genomes of hominins.** Analysis of ancient DNA of Neandertals reveals the presence of alleles for modern human disease. New analysis of ancient DNA from Kennewick Man and other Paleoamericans reveals a clear genetic link between the earliest humans in the Western Hemisphere with modern Native Americans.

- **New content on fossil primate discoveries.** A newly discovered fossil New World monkey pre-dates the earliest known fossil New World monkey by as much as 10 million years.

- **New content on fossil hominin discoveries.** New discoveries of *Ardipithecus* extend the lineage back to more than 6 million years ago, taking us closer to the divergence of the great apes and hominins. In South Africa, cavers exploring the Rising Star Cave system discovered hundreds of skulls, teeth, and bones, all representing at least 15 early hominins. Named *Homo naledi*, this species is represented by the largest assemblage of early hominins in a single site in Africa. Its study is full of surprises and is expanding the scope of our understanding of human origins and human evolution. Excavations on Flores Island, where the famous "Hobbit" (*Homo floresiensis*) fossils were found, landed a new surprise: a dwarf hominin that may be the ancestor of *H. floresiensis*. Re-dating of *H. floresiensis* takes it back in time to at least 60,000 yBP.

- **Anthropology Matters and How Do We Know? boxes.** New boxes highlight exciting and relevant new developments in physical anthropology, including work at the "Body Farm" for developing the field of forensic anthropology; the Ebola virus and how knowledge of its evolution helps us combat the disease; new findings from genomics and the origins and evolution of modern humans and their migrations; the meaning of race and what anthropology brings to the discussion of this controversial topic; new developments in primate conservation; the exciting discovery and study of *Homo naledi*; bone chemistry and its application to the study of diets in past human populations, both long extinct and recent; and the earliest evidence of warfare and what human skeletons tell us about violence and conflict.

- **New content on dramatic changes in the world's climate today.** We are living at a time of rapidly changing climate, involving global warming. New content in this edition makes the case that we may be living in a wholly new epoch, what many scientists are calling the "Anthropocene." New content in the final chapter of *Our Origins* focuses on the effects of climate change happening in the world around us today.

- **Revision of content to enhance clarity.** There is a continued focus on understanding core concepts, with considerable attention given to cell biology, genetics, DNA, race and human variation, primate taxonomy, locomotion, and dating methods. Like previous editions, I paid careful attention to the clarity of figure captions. The figure captions do not simply repeat text but rather offer the student additional details relevant to the topic and occasional questions about concepts that the figures convey.

- **Greatly enhanced art program.** The new edition contains more than 100 new or revised figures, often using a new "photorealistic" style. The book adds several full-color two-page spreads developed by Mauricio Antón, a world-renowned artist with expertise in representing past life in wonderful visual presentations.

- **InQuizitive.** InQuizitive is a new online formative and adaptive learning tool that includes a variety of question types featuring the vibrant, detailed, and photorealistic art from the text, as well as the accompanying suite of animations. Answer-specific feedback for every question helps students work through their mistakes, and InQuizitive personalizes students' quizzing experience to target the areas they need help with most.

- **Updated Evolution Review sections.** At the end of each chapter, an Evolution Review section summarizes material on evolution in each chapter and includes assignable questions about concepts and content. Suggested answers appear in the Instructor's Manual and the Interactive Instructor's Guide.

- **New teaching and learning tools.** Consistent with the highly visual nature of physical anthropology, the instructor media package has been greatly expanded. Please see the complete listing that starts on page xxv. The Update PowerPoint Service features a new minilecture that will be posted to the Norton Instructor's site each semester on the latest discoveries in the discipline.

Aids to the Learning Process

Each chapter opens with a *vignette* telling the story of one person's discovery that relates directly to the central theme of the chapter. This vignette is intended to draw your students into the excitement of the topic and to set the stage for the Big Questions that the chapter addresses.

Big Question learning objectives are introduced early in the chapter to help your students organize their reading and understand the topic.

Concept Checks are scattered throughout each chapter and immediately follow a major section. These aids are intended to help your students briefly revisit the key points they have been reading.

Locator Maps are placed liberally throughout the book. College-level instructors tend to hope that students have a good sense of geography, but like a lot of people who do not look at places around the world on a daily basis, students often need reminders about geography. In recognition of this, locator maps in the book's margins show the names and locations of places that are likely not common knowledge.

Photorealistic Art You Can "Touch": Designed to give students an even better appreciation for the feel of the discipline, the art program has been substantially reworked. Now most illustrations of bones and skeletons have an almost photorealistic feel, and most primates were redrawn for a high degree of realism. This book helps your students visualize what they are reading about by including hundreds of images, many specially prepared for the book. These illustrations tell the story of physical anthropology, including key processes, central players, and important concepts. As much thought went into the pedagogy behind the illustration program as into the writing of the text.

Definitions are also presented in the text's margins, giving your students ready access to what a term means in addition to its use in the associated text. For convenient reference, defined terms are signaled with boldface page numbers in the index.

A **How Do We Know?** box in each chapter discusses in more detail how a particular scientist went about the process of discovery.

An **Anthropology Matters** box in each chapter makes the important point that what we learn from this discipline has practical applications of broader significance in the "real" world. Students will come away from each box with a sense of how the material affects them.

At the end of each chapter, **Answering the Big Questions** presents a summary of the chapter's central points organized along the lines of the Big Questions presented at the beginning of the chapter. In addition, I have added to the Chapter Review at the end of each chapter a new Study Quiz, asking a handful of key questions that I ask my own students.

The study of evolution is the central core concept of physical anthropology. The **Evolution Review** section at the end of each chapter discusses topics on evolution featured in the chapter and asks questions that will help the student develop a focused understanding of content and ideas.

InQuizitive is our new online assessment service featuring visual, conceptual, and reading assessments keyed to the Big Question learning objectives, several of which are highlighted for your convenience at the end of each chapter. InQuizitive helps you track and report on your students' progress and make sure they are better prepared for class.

Join me now in engaging your students in the excitement of discovering physical anthropology.

Tools for Teaching and Learning

The *Our Origins* teaching and learning package provides instructors and students with all the tools they need to visualize anthropological concepts, learn key vocabulary, and test knowledge.

For Instructors

New InQuizitive New InQuizitive online assessment is available for use with *Our Origins*, Fourth Edition, featuring engaging assignments with focused feedback. InQuizitive includes drag-and-drop and other image-based questions designed to help students better understand the core objectives of each chapter. Further questions on the reading help you check if students have worked through the chapter material. Designed to be intuitive, accessible, and easy to use, InQuizitive makes it a snap to assign, assess, and report on student performance and help keep your class on track.

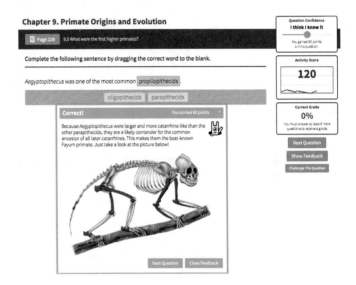

Student Access Codes for InQuizitive InQuizitive comes at no charge with all new books in any format (paperback, looseleaf, ebook, or custom). If students need to purchase a stand-alone access code for InQuizitive, they can do so at an affordable price at digital.wwnorton.com/ourorigins4.

New Interactive Instructor's Guide Find all the resources you need to create a rich and engaging course experience in one place with the new Interactive Instructor's Guide: iig.wwnorton/ourorigins4/full. Easily search by keyword, topic, or chapter to find and download videos, animations, in-class activity suggestions, PowerPoints, and more on this new site.

Coursepacks Available at no cost to professors or students, Norton Coursepacks for online or hybrid courses come in a variety of formats, including all versions of Blackboard. With just a simple download from wwnorton.com/instructors, instructors can bring high-quality Norton digital media into a new or existing online course. Content includes review and quiz questions designed for the distance or blended learning environment. Norton animations and videos are also made available to integrate in your classes, including the new Anthropology Matters videos. Additionally, if InQuizitive will be in use, contact the local Norton representative to learn about our easy integration options for a single sign-on and gradebook experience with your Coursepack.

New Animations Animations of key concepts from the text are available to instructors and students in several ways, including via the Coursepack, the Interactive Instructor's Guide, and at wwnorton.com/instructors and digital.wwnorton.com/ourorigins4. These are brief, easy to use, and great for explaining concepts either in class or as a self-study tool.

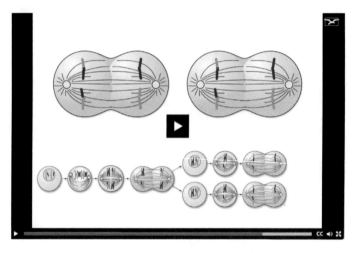

New Anthropology Matters and How Do We Know? Videos New original videos accompany a selection of Anthropology Matters and How Do We Know? features from the text. An icon indicates when a video is available. Each two- to three-minute video further enhances the content while inspiring students to learn more and understand the significance of what they are studying. Instructors can obtain the videos through the Interactive Instructor's Guide, wwnorton.com/instructors, or via the Coursepack. Students can view the videos via the Coursepack or digital.wwnorton.com/ourorigins4.

Update PowerPoint Service To help cover what is new in the discipline, each semester Norton will provide a new set of supplemental lectures, notes, and assessment material covering current and breaking research. Prepared by Laurie Reitsema (University of Georgia), this material will be available for download at wwnorton.com/instructors and in the Interactive Instructor's Guide.

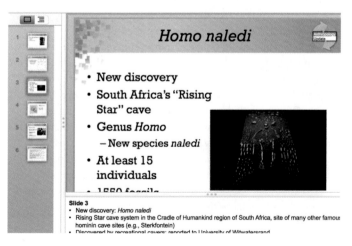

Lecture PowerPoint Slides and Art Slides Designed for instant classroom use, these slides prepared by Melissa Torpey (University of North Carolina Wilmington) using art from the text are a great resource for your lectures. All art from the book is also available in PowerPoint and JPEG formats. Download these resources from wwnorton.com/instructors or from the Interactive Instructor's Guide.

Prepare for Class with the *Our Origins* Instructor's Manual Prepared by Susan Kirkpatrick Smith (Kennesaw State University), this resource provides lecture ideas, discussion topics, suggested reading lists for instructors and students, and suggested answers to Evolution Review questions.

Quickly and Easily Create Tests with the *Our Origins* Test Bank Prepared by Greg Laden, this test bank contains multiple-choice and essay questions for each chapter. It is downloadable from Norton's Instructor's site and available in Word, PDF, and *ExamView® Assessment Suite* formats. Visit **wwnorton.com/instructors.**

Ebook: Same Great Book, a Fraction of the Price! An affordable and convenient alternative, Norton ebooks retain the content and design of the print book and allow students to highlight and take notes with ease, print chapters as needed, read online or offline, and search the text. Instructors can even take notes in their ebooks that can be shared with their students.

Who Helped

I owe much to the many people who made this book possible, from the planning and writing of the first and second editions, and now this fourth edition. First and foremost, I thank my wife, Christine, and son, Spencer, who helped in innumerable ways. They were my captive audience: without protest, they listened to my ideas at the dinner table, on family trips, and in other places where we probably should have been talking about other things. Chris read many drafts of chapters and gave great advice on when and where to cut, add, or rethink. I thank my parents, the late Leon and Patricia Larsen, who introduced me to things old and sparked my interest in the human past.

Jack Repcheck first approached me about writing a textbook on introductory physical anthropology. His power of persuasion, combined with my own interest in the discipline and its presentation to college students, was instrumental in reeling me in and getting the project off the ground. Jack and others at W. W. Norton & Company made the process of writing the book a great experience in all ways, from writing to publication. On the first edition, I began work with editors John Byram and then Leo Wiegman. I am indebted to Pete Lesser, who took on the project after Leo. Pete gave direction on writing and production, provided very helpful feedback on presentation and pedagogy, and orchestrated the process of review, revision, and production—all without a hitch. Under Pete's guidance, the first edition became the most widely used textbook in physical anthropology. Jack Repcheck continued the project in preparation for the second edition. The preparation of the third edition was overseen by editor Eric Svendsen. His advice and guidance were central to seeing the book come to fruition. The current fourth edition has benefited from Eric's continued review and input and was completed with the guidance and support of Jake Schindel. Tacy Quinn has spearheaded the development of new media for this edition including InQuizitive. Mary Williams and Sarah Rose Aquilina do an excellent job developing the core supplement package for each edition. Kurt Wildermuth edited the entire manuscript for the first three editions. Sunny Hwang has now taken Kurt's place and has especially helped with revision in the end-of-chapter material and the online supplements program. His skill as an editor and staying on top of content from beginning to end added enormously to the book's presentation and readability. Caitlin Moran, Rachel Mayer, and Rachel Goodman were instrumental in producing these pages and directing a wide variety of editing issues. I welcome Katie Sweeney, who crafted an expert marketing and promotional campaign. Ben Reynolds guided the process of production from beginning to end. I am also grateful to Mauricio Antón for his wonderful illustrations of six "big events" of human evolution in chapter 1; the rendition of the Taï Forest primates as a microcosm of primate adaptation in chapter 6; the Eocene, Oligocene, and Miocene primates and their habitats in chapter 9; and his reconstructions of *Ardipithecus* in chapter 10. Greg Laden's timely and efficient revision of the Test Bank is much appreciated. Susan Kirkpatrick Smith provided quality work on the Instructor's Manual and Interactive Instructor's Guide. Laurie Reitsema produces our valuable Update PowerPoints each semester. Thanks to Melissa Torpey for her capable work on the Lecture PowerPoint Slides.

With the input of instructors and focus group attendees who are included in the reviewer list, we have created an extensive new media and assessment suite for the fourth edition. However, my thanks for extensive work in developing InQuizitive and our new animations go to Tracy Betsinger of SUNY Oneonta, Ashley Hurst, Kristina Killgrove of University of West Florida, Greg Laden, Joanna Lambert of the University of Colorado, and Heather Worne of University of Kentucky, with further thanks to contributors Jaime Ullinger, Quinnipiac University, and Nancy Cordell, South Puget Sound Community College. And thanks to Sandra Wheeler of University of Central Florida, Ellen Miller of Wake Forest University, Bonnie Yoshida of Grossmont College, Jacqueline Eng of Western Michigan University, Jeremy DeSilva of Dartmouth College, K. Elizabeth Soluri of College of Marin, and again Nancy Cordell of South Puget Sound Community College for their important feedback and reviews of these resources.

There are a number of new boxes (Anthropology Matters and How Do We Know?) in this new edition of *Our Origins*. I especially thank the following anthropologists who helped with providing material and advice: Lee Berger, Tracy Betsinger, Doug Crews, Rachel Caspari, Agustín Fuentes, Scott McGraw, Hannah Morris, Erin Riley, and Karen Strier. In addition, the online interviews feature Rachel Caspari, Scott McGraw, Hannah Morris, Erin Riley, Karen Strier, Sarah Tishkoff, and Tiffiny Tung. For her leading role and considerable effort in seeing these amazing presentations completed, I am indebted to Tacy Quinn.

Thanks go to former and current graduate students and faculty colleagues at Ohio State University who helped in so many ways. I offer a very special thanks to Tracy Betsinger, who assisted in a number of aspects of the book as well as the Coursepack. For the first edition, she read drafts of chapters at various stages and helped in figure selection, in glossary compilation, and as a sounding board in general for ideas that went into the book. For the second edition, she offered very helpful suggestions for revisions. Thanks to Jaime Ullinger, who provided the content and data for the box on PTC tasting. Tracy, Jaime, Jim Gosman, Dan Temple, Haagen Klaus, and Josh Sadvari read parts or all of the manuscript and offered great advice. For all four editions, I had many helpful discussions with Scott McGraw and Dawn Kitchen about primate behavior, evolution, and taxonomy. Scott also provided advice on the production of the two-page spreads on both primate diversity and eagle predation in the Taï Forest, Ivory Coast (chapters 6 and 7). John Fleagle provided valuable support reviewing details in most of the new primate illustrations, in particular the two-page spreads, and every new piece of art was reviewed by Arthur Durband, Andrew Kramer, and Sandra Wheeler. Doug Crews gave advice on the complexities of primate (including human) biology and life history. Haagen Klaus provided materials for and help with the two-page spread on the biological consequences of the agricultural revolution and many other helpful comments and suggestions for revision. Barbara Piperata advised me on key aspects of modern human biology and nutrition science, and Dawn Kitchen provided discussion and help on the fundamentals of primate communication and how best to present it. Josh Sadvari was indispensable in the creation of the Evolution Review sections at the end of each chapter. Ellen Mosley-Thompspn and John Brookeadvised me on climate change and its role in our rapidly changing world. Likewise, Mary Beth Cole developed terrific student review questions for each chapter.

Over the years, I have had helpful conversations with my teachers, colleagues, and students about areas of their expertise, and these people have influenced the development of the book in so many ways. I am grateful to Patricia J. O'Brien and Milford H. Wolpoff, my respective undergraduate and graduate advisors. Both were instrumental in developing my interest in science and the wonderful profession I work in. I thank Barry Bogin, Kristen Hawkes, Jim O'Connell, David Thomas, Bob Kelly, Jerry Milanich, Bruce Smith, Kris Gremillion, Bonnie McEwan, Matt Cartmill, Dale Hutchinson, Chris Ruff, Simon Hillson, Michael Schultz, Sam Stout, Doug Ubelaker, Dan Sellen, Clark Howell, Rick Steckel, Phil Walker, John Relethford, Mark Weiss, Margaret Schoeninger, Karen Rosenberg, Lynne Schepartz, Fred Smith, Brian Hemphill, Bruce Winterhalder, Meg Conkey, Desmond Clark, Erik Trinkaus, Katherine Russell, Vin Steponaitis, Mark Teaford, Richard Wrangham, Jerry Rose, Mark Cohen, William Bass, Loring Brace, Stanley Garn, Frank Livingstone, Phil Gingerich, T. Dale Stewart, Larry Angel, Mike Finnegan, Harriet Ottenheimer, Marty Ottenheimer, Roberto Frisancho, Randy Susman, Karen Strier, Joanna Lambert, Jim Hijiya, Cecil Brown, Bill Fash, Rich Blanton, Henry Wright, James Griffin, Bill Jungers, David Frayer, Bill Pollitzer, George Armelagos, Jane Buikstra, Elwyn Simons, Steve Churchill, Neil Tubbs, Bob Bettinger, Tim White, Dean Falk, Owen Lovejoy, Scott Simpson, David

Carlson, Alan Goodman, Bill Dancey, Debbie Guatelli-Steinberg, Clark Mallam, and Chris Peebles.

The book benefited from the expertise of many anthropologists and other experts. I especially acknowledge the following reviewers for their insights, advice, and suggestions for revision of the text and creation of the support package:

Sabrina Agarwal, University of California, Berkeley
Paul Aiello, Ventura College
Lon Alterman, North Carolina State University
Tara Devi Ashok, University of Massachusetts Boston
Diana Ayers-Darling, Mohawk Valley Community College
Gerald Bacon, Coconino Community College
Philip de Barros, Palomar College
Thad Bartlett, University of Texas, San Antonio
Cynthia Beall, Case Western Reserve University
Owen Beattie, University of Alberta
Daniel Benyshek, University of Nevada, Las Vegas
Tracy Betsinger, College at Oneonta, State University of New York
Deborah Blom, University of Vermont
Amy Bogaard, Oxford University
Günter Bräuer, University of Hamburg
Margaret Bruchez, Blinn College
Emily Brunson, University of Washington
Victoria Buresch, Glendale Community College
Jessica Cade, University of California, Riverside
Maria Leonor Cadena, Fullerton College
Benjamin Campbell, University of Wisconsin, Milwaukee
Isabelle Champlin, University of Pittsburgh, Bradford
Joyce Chan, California State University, Dominguez Hills
Chi-hua Chiu, Kent State University
David Clark, Catholic University of America
Raffaella Commitante, California State University, Fullerton
Nancy Cordell, South Puget Sound Community College
Robert Corruccini, Southern Illinois University
Herbert Covert, University of Colorado
Fabian Crespo, University of Louisville
Douglas Crews, Ohio State University
Alejandra Estrin Dashe, Northwestern Health Sciences University
Eric Delson, Lehman College, City University of New York
Jeremy DeSilva, Boston University
Katherine Dettwyler, University of Delaware
Joanne Devlin, University of Tennessee
William Duncan, East Tennessee State University
Arthur Durband, Texas Tech University
Marta Alfonso Durruty, Kansas State University
Phyllisa Eisentraut, Santa Barbara City College
Jacqueline Eng, Western Michigan University
Paul Erickson, St. Mary's University
Becky Floyd, Cypress College
Susan Ford, Southern Illinois University
David Frayer, University of Kansas
Renee Garcia, Saddleback College

Daniel Gebo, Northern Illinois University
Victoria Giambrone, Oakton Community College
Rebecca Gibson, American University
Anne Grauer, Loyola University of Chicago
Mark Griffin, San Francisco State University
Michael Grimes, Western Washington University
Nanda B. Grow, Texas A&M University
Gregg Gunnell, Duke University
Lesley Harrington, University of Alberta
Cory Harris, Orange County Community College, State University of New York
Ryan P. Harrod, University of Alaska Anchorage
Lauren Hasten, Las Positas College
John Hawks, University of Wisconsin, Madison
Carrie Healy, University of Arkansas
Samantha Hens, California State University, Sacramento
James Hingham, New York University
Madeline Hinkes, San Diego Mesa College
Homes Hogue, Ball State University
Brigitte Holt, University of Massachusetts Amherst
Ashley Hurst
Nina Jablonski, Pennsylvania State University
Karin Enstam Jaffe, Sonoma State University
Gabriela Jakubowska, Ohio State University
Gail Kennedy, University of California, Los Angeles
Dawn Kitchen, Ohio State University
Haagen Klaus, George Mason University
Sam Kobari, San Diego State University
Andrew Kramer, University of Tennessee
Greg Laden
Joanna Lambert, University of Texas at San Antonio
Patricia Lambert, Utah State University
Cari Lange, Ventura College
Sang-Hee Lee, University of California, Riverside
Ginesse Listi, Louisiana State University
Michael Little, Binghamton University
Chris Loeffler, Irvine Valley College
Marilyn R. London, University of Maryland
Sara Lynch, Queens College, City University of New York
Lorena Madrigal, University of South Florida
Ann Magennis, Colorado State University
Stephen Marshak, University of Illinois, Urbana-Champaign
Debra Martin, University of Nevada, Las Vegas
Thomas McDade, Northwestern University
William McFarlane, Johnson County Community College
Scott McGraw, Ohio State University
Matthew McIntyre, University of Central Florida
Rachel Messinger, Moorpark College
Ellen Miller, Wake Forest University
Leonor Monreal, Fullerton College
Ellen Mosley-Thompson, Ohio State University
Michael Muehlenbein, Indiana University
Jennifer Muller, Ithaca College
Dawn Neill, California State Polytechnic University, San Luis Obispo

Elizabeth Newell, Elizabethtown College

Wesley Niewoehner, California State University, San Bernardino

Kevin Nolan, Ball State University

Rachel Nuger, Hunter College, City University of New York

Dennis O'Rourke, University of Utah

Janet Padiak, McMaster University

Elizabeth Pain, Palomar Community College

Amanda Wolcott Paskey, Cosumnes River College

Sandra Peacock, University of British Columbia

Michael Pietrusewsky, University of Hawai'i

Michael Pilakowski, Butte College

Deborah Poole, Austin Community College

Leila Porter, Northern Illinois University

Frances E. Purifoy, University of Louisville

Ryan Raaum, Lehman College, City University of New York

Mary Ann Raghanti, Kent State University

Lesley M. Rankin-Hill, University of Oklahoma

Jeffrey Ratcliffe, Pennsylvania State University, Abington

Marcia Regan, Hamline University

Laurie Reitsema, University of Georgia

Melissa Remis, Purdue University

Robert Renger, Ventura College

Erin Riley, San Diego State University

Paul Roach, Century College

Michael Robertson, Los Angeles Harbor College

Charles Roseman, University of Illinois

Karen Rosenberg, University of Delaware

John Rush, Sierra College

Joshua Sadvari, Ohio State University

Melissa Schaefer, University of Utah

Sarah A. Schrader, University of California, Santa Cruz

Timothy Sefczek, Ohio State University

Beth Shook, California State University, Chico

Sara Shrader, University of California, Santa Cruz

Lynette Leidy Sievert, University of Massachusetts

Scott W. Simpson, Case Western Reserve University

Pete Sinelli, University of Central Florida

Cynthia Smith, Ohio State University

Fred Smith, Illinois State University

Richard Smith, Washington University

Sara Smith, Delta College

Sarah Kirkpatrick Smith, Kennesaw State University

Lilian Spencer, Glendale Community College

James Stewart, Columbus State Community College

Marissa Stewart, Ohio State University

Sara Stinson, Queens College, City University of New York

Christopher Stojanowski, Arizona State University

Margaret Streeter, Boise State University

Karen Strier, University of Wisconsin, Madison

Nancy Tatarek, Ohio University

Linda Taylor, University of Miami

Lonnie Thompson, Ohio State University

Victor Thompson, University of Georgia

Christopher Tillquist, University of Louisville

Melissa Torpey, University of North Carolina, Wilmington

Sebina Trumble, Hartnell College

Lisa Valkenier, Berkeley City College

Dennis Van Gerven, University of Colorado, Boulder

Patricia Vinyard, University of Akron

Ronald Wallace, University of Central Florida

Brittany Walter, University of South Carolina

David Webb, Kutztown University

Daniel Wescott, Texas State University

Jessica Westin, Pennsylvania State University

Adam Wetsman, Rio Hondo College

Sandra Wheeler, University of Central Florida

Tim White, University of California, Berkeley

Janet Wiebold, Spokane Community College

Caleb Wild, Mira Costa College

Leslie Williams, Utah State University

Sharon Williams, Purdue University

Milford Wolpoff, University of Michigan

Thomas Wynn, University of Colorado, Colorado Springs

Thanks, everyone, for your help! Lastly, a very special thanks goes to all of the faculty around the globe who adopted the previous three editions of *Our Origins* for their introductory physical anthropology classes. I am also grateful to the hundreds of students who connected with the book—many of whom have written me with their comments. Please continue to send me your comments (Larsen.53@osu.edu).

Columbus, Ohio
July 1, 2016

TO THE STUDENT

Physical Anthropology Is about Discovering Who We Are

Thinking Like an Anthropologist

Who are we? Where do we come from? Why do we look and act the way we do? This book is a journey that addresses these and other big questions about us, *Homo sapiens.* This journey emphasizes humans' discovery of the fascinating record of our diversity and of our evolution, a record that serves as a collective memory of our shared biological presence on Earth. From here to the end of the book, I will share with you all kinds of ideas that add up to our current understanding of human beings as living organisms. Along the way, you will experience scientific breakthroughs such as the Human Genome Project and forensics (you might even watch *CSI* and *Bones* in a whole new way). You will gain new understandings of phenomena such as race and human diversity, global warming and its impact on our evolution and our well-being, the origins of human violence, global disease, and the growing worldwide obesity epidemic. Like an anthropologist tackling important questions, you will discover places on nearly every continent and come to see what life was like millions of years before the present, before the emergence and evolution of humans.

Neither your instructor nor I can expect you as an introductory student to understand all the developments in physical anthropology. Both of us can, however, present you with a clear and concise framework of the field. By the time you are finished reading this book and completing this course, you will have a solid background in the basic tenets of the discipline. This knowledge will help you understand your place in nature and the world that we—more than 7 billion of us and growing—live in. The framework for developing your understanding of physical anthropology is the scientific method, a universal approach to understanding the very complex natural world. You should not assume that this book and this course are about only knowing the right answers, the "facts" of physical anthropology. Rather, they are also about seeing how physical anthropologists know what they know—understanding the scientific method. So as you read, keep in mind the key questions that scientists try to answer, their processes and methods for finding the answers, and the answers themselves.

In writing this book, I have focused on the big questions in physical anthropology, how scientists have tackled them, and what key discoveries have been made. I have not shied away from identifying the scientists who made these discoveries—real people, young and old, from all over the world. Whether you need to learn all these individuals' names and what they contributed to the growth of physical anthropology and to our knowledge of human evolution and variation is up to your instructor. But in the introductory physical anthropology class that I teach, I encourage my students to learn about the people behind the ideas. By seeing the field through these people's eyes, you can start thinking like an anthropologist.

Seeing Like an Anthropologist

Thinking like an anthropologist includes seeing what anthropologists see. We anthropologists are constantly looking at things—fossilized human teeth, ancient DNA, excavated stone tools, primate skeletons, and much more—and using what we see to understand biology in the past and in the present. The photos and drawn art throughout this book have been chosen to help you see what anthropologists see. I strongly encourage you to pay close attention to the visuals in the book and their captions because much of our anthropological understanding is in the art program.

The Structure of the Book and Resources

The book is divided into three parts. After an overview of anthropology and physical anthropology (chapter 1), part I provides the basic context for how we understand human (and our nonhuman primate relatives') biology in the present (and how that helps us understand the past). From this section of the book you should come away with an understanding of evolution and the biology associated with it. Evolution as an idea has a long history (chapter 2). You will need to fully grasp the meaning and power of this theory, which explains humans' biological variation today and in the past. Part I also has the important job of providing you with an understanding of genetics (chapters 3 and 4). This information is a central part of the evidence for evolution, from the level of the molecule to the level of the population.

Part I also looks at the biology of living people, that of the other living primates, and the variation among primate species. I am keen on debunking the common notion that there are discrete categories—races—of human beings (chapter 5). In fact, nothing about the biology of people, present or past, indicates that we can be divided into distinct groups. After looking at how environment and culture help shape the way humans look and behave, I will look similarly at nonhuman primates (chapters 6 and 7). Because nonhuman primates' appearances are much more categorical than humans' are, nonhuman primate appearance lends itself to classification or taxonomy. In these chapters, we will look at what nonhuman primates do in the wild, what they are adapted to, and especially the environment's role in shaping their behavior and biology. By looking at living people and living nonhuman primates, we will be better equipped to understand the biological evidence drawn from the past.

Part II examines the processes and evidence physical anthropologists and other scientists use to understand the past (chapter 8), the evolution of prehuman primate ancestors that lived more than 50 million years ago (chapter 9), and both the emergence of our humanlike ancestors and their evolution into modern humans (chapters 10, 11, and 12). Contrary to popular (and some scientific) opinion, human evolution did not stop when anatomically modern people first made their appearance in various corners of the globe. Rather, even into the past 10,000 years a considerable amount of biological change has occurred. Anthropologists have learned that agriculture, which began some 10,000 years ago, has been a fundamental force behind population increase. The downside of this shift to new kinds of food and the resulting population increase was a general decline in health. The later section of part II (chapter 13) explores the nature and cause of biological change, including the changes associated with health and well-being that led to the biological and environmental conditions we face today.

Part III (chapter 14) looks at the future of our species. Humans continue to undergo biological change—some of it genetic, some not. To understand nongenetic biological change, we will look closely at how modern technologies and diets are profoundly affecting human appearance and contributing to behavioral change. Technologies and diets are helping produce new diseases, new threats to animal and plant diversity, and a planet that is in some ways becoming a less desirable place to live. In particular, global warming's evolving threat is among the most important issues of our day and will prove even more important in the future. Chapters 1–13 will enable us to consider how humans can cope and thrive when faced with such daunting challenges.

For every chapter, we have developed additional, helpful online tools so you can further study and understand the concepts. Visit digital.wwnorton.com/ourorigins4 to access animations and videos, free of charge. You can also access InQuizitive here for engaging, game-like, online questions with answer-specific feedback. InQuizitive personalizes the questions you receive, based on how you answer and express confidence along the way, to ensure that you understand all of the Big Questions.

With this book in hand and our goals—thinking and seeing like anthropologists—in mind, let us set off on this exciting journey. Consider it a voyage of discovery, on which our shipmates include your instructor and your fellow students. If we work hard and work together, we will find perhaps the most interesting thing on Earth: ourselves.

FOURTH EDITION

OUR ORIGINS

The Georgia coast was a focal point for Spanish colonization in the sixteenth and seventeenth centuries. European colonization set in motion changes in human living conditions that eventually affected human biology on a global scale.

1

What Is Physical Anthropology?

BIG QUESTIONS

1. **What is anthropology?**
2. **What is physical anthropology?**
3. **What makes humans so different from other animals?**
4. **How do physical anthropologists know what they know?**

In the heat of the midday summer sun, our boat slowly made its way across the five miles of water that separate mainland Georgia from St. Catherines Island, one of a series of barrier islands dotting the Atlantic seaboard. Today, the island is covered by dense vegetation typical of the subtropical American South—palmettos and other palm trees, pines, hickories, and live oaks—and is infested with a wide array of stinging, burrowing, and biting insects. It is hard to imagine that this setting was once a focal point of the Spanish colonial "New World," representing the northernmost extension of Spain's claim on eastern North America (**Figure 1.1**). This was the location of the Roman Catholic church and mission Santa Catalina de Guale, where several hundred Indians and a dozen Spaniards lived and worked during the late 1500s and most of the 1600s.

What could possibly have motivated my field team and me to work for months under a blazing sun, fighting insects? Like any scientific investigation, our fieldwork was motivated by specific questions that we keenly wanted to answer. Buried in the sands of St. Catherines were the mortal remains—skeletons—of the native people who had lived at this long-abandoned place. These remains held answers to

FIGURE 1.1

Spanish Mission Sites Spanish colonization relied on the establishment of missions north and west of St. Augustine, Florida, along the coast of Georgia and the panhandle of northern Florida. These sites, such as Mission Santa Catalina de Guale (on St. Catherines Island), provide insight into what the missions might have looked like (inset). Researchers have reconstructed the lifestyles of the Indians and the Spanish colonizers who inhabited the sites: by studying their skeletons, the researchers assessed how the inhabitants changed biologically after colonization.

questions about the biology of modern people. Native Americans had lived in this area of the world for most of the past 10,000 years. We wanted to know about their biological evolution and variation: How had these people changed biologically over this time span? What caused these changes? What circumstances led to the changes that we hoped to identify and interpret?

When we first set foot on St. Catherines Island in the summer of 1982 to begin our work at Mission Santa Catalina, we were excited about our project, but little did we realize just what a spectacular scientific journey we were undertaking. The skeletons we sought turned out to provide wonderfully rich biological details about a little-understood region of the world, especially relating to the health and behavioral consequences of European contact on native peoples. In setting up the research project, I had envisioned that our findings would prove to be a microcosm of what had unfolded globally—in the Americas, Asia, Africa, and Australia—during the previous 500 years of human history. During this period, significant biological changes had taken place in humans. Some of these changes were evolutionary—they resulted in genetic change. Other biological changes, nonevolutionary ones, reflected significant alterations in health and lifestyle, alterations that had left impressions on the skeletons we studied. Such study—of genetic and nongenetic changes—here and elsewhere in the world has proved fundamental to understanding human biology in the early twenty-first century.

Like any scientific investigation, the research project at Mission Santa Catalina did not develop in a vacuum. Prior to our work there, my team and I had devoted nearly a decade to studying hundreds of skeletons we had excavated from the region that predated the arrival of the Spaniards. We had learned from archaeological evidence that before AD 1000 or so, the people there ate exclusively wild animals, fish, and wild plants—they were hunters and gatherers. Never settling into one place for any period of time, they moved from place to place over the year, hunting animals, fishing on the coastline, and collecting plants. Then, their descendants—the later prehistoric ancestors of the mission Indians—acquired corn agriculture, becoming the first farmers in the region. These people did lots of fishing, but farming produced the mainstay of their diet. This major shift in lifestyle led to the establishment of semipermanent villages. In comparison with the hunter-gatherers living before AD 1000, the later agricultural people were shorter, their skulls and limb bones were smaller, and they had more dental disease and more infections. All of this information—scientific discoveries about the prehistoric people, their biological changes, and their adaptations—set the stage for our return to the island to study the people who lived at Santa Catalina, the descendants of the prehistoric hunter-gatherers and later farmers. From our study of their remains, we learned that after the Spaniards' arrival, the native people worked harder, became more focused on producing and eating corn, and their health declined. The combination of declining quality of life and new diseases introduced by the Spaniards led to the native people's extinction in this area of North America.

The research just described is one small part of the broader discipline known as *physical anthropology*. My work concerns life on the Atlantic coast of the southeastern United States, but physical anthropologists explore and study *everywhere* humans and their ancestors lived. This enterprise covers a lot of ground and a lot of time, basically the entire world and the past 50 million years or so! The territorial coverage of physical anthropology is so widespread and so diverse because the field addresses broad issues, seeking to understand human evolution—*what* we were in the past, *who* we are today, and *where* we will go in the future. Physical anthropologists seek answers to questions about *why* we are what we are as biological organisms. How we answer these questions is oftentimes difficult. The questions, though, motivate physical anthropologists to spend months in the subtropics of coastal Georgia, learning about an extinct native people; in the deserts of central Ethiopia, finding and studying the remains of people who lived hundreds, thousands, or even millions of years ago; or at the high altitudes of the Andes, studying living people and their responses and long-term adaptation to low oxygen and extreme cold, to name just a few of the settings you will learn about in this book. In this chapter, we will explore in more detail the nature of physical anthropology and its subject matter.

1.1 What Is Anthropology?

When European explorers first undertook transcontinental travel (for example, Marco Polo into Asia in the late 1200s) or transoceanic voyages to faraway lands (for example, Christopher Columbus to the Americas in the late 1400s and early 1500s), they encountered people that looked, talked, dressed, and behaved very differently from themselves. When these travelers returned to their home countries, they described the peoples and cultures they saw. Building on these accounts, early scholars speculated on the relationships between humans living in Europe and those encountered in distant places. Eventually, later scholars developed new ideas about other cultures, resulting in the development of the discipline of anthropology.

Anthropology is the study of humankind, viewed from the perspective of all people and all times. As it is practiced in the United States, it includes four branches or sub-disciplines: **cultural anthropology, archaeology, linguistic anthropology,** and **physical anthropology,** also called **biological anthropology (Figure 1.2).**

Cultural anthropologists typically study present-day societies in non-Western settings, such as in Africa, South America, or Australia. Culture—defined as learned behavior that is transmitted from person to person—is the unifying theme of study in cultural anthropology.

Archaeologists study past human societies, focusing mostly on their material remains—such as animal and plant remains and places where people lived in the past. Archaeologists are best known for their study of material objects—**artifacts**—from past cultures, such as weaponry and ceramics. Archaeologists study the processes behind past human behaviors; for example, why people lived where they did, why some societies were simple and others complex, and why people shifted from hunting and gathering to agriculture beginning more than 10,000 years ago. Archaeologists are the cultural anthropologists of the past—they seek to reassemble cultures of the past as though those cultures were alive today.

artifacts Material objects from past cultures.

Linguistic anthropologists study the construction and use of language by human societies. **Language**—defined as a set of written or spoken symbols that refer to things (people, places, concepts, etc.) other than themselves—makes possible the transfer of knowledge from one person to the next and from one generation to the next. Popular among linguistic anthropologists is a subfield called **sociolinguistics,** the investigation of language's social contexts.

sociolinguistics The science of investigating language's social contexts.

Physical (or biological) anthropologists study all aspects of present and past human biology. As we will explore in the next section, physical anthropology deals with the evolution of and variation among human beings and their living and past relatives.

No anthropologist is expected to be an expert in all four branches. Anthropologists in all four areas and with very different interests, however, acknowledge the diversity of humankind in all contexts. No other discipline embraces the breadth of the human condition in this manner. In fact, this remarkably diverse discipline differs from other disciplines in its commitment to the notion that, unlike other animals, humans are biocultural—both biological and cultural beings. Anthropologists are interested in the interrelationship between biology and culture. Anthropologists call this focus the **bio-cultural approach.** Anthropology also differs from other disciplines in emphasizing a broad comparative approach to the study of biology and culture, looking at all people (and their ancestors) and all cultures in all times and all places. They are interested in people and their ancestors, wherever or whenever they lived. Simply, you are studying a field that is holistic, unlike any you have studied before.

biocultural approach The scientific study of the interrelationship between what humans have inherited genetically and culture.

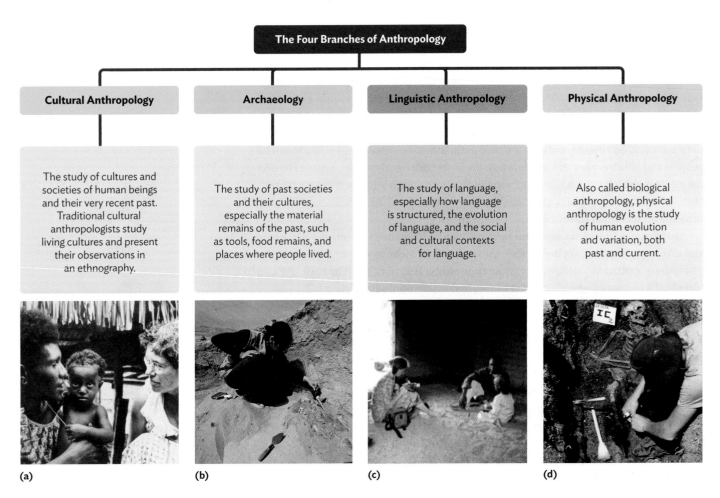

The Four Branches of Anthropology

Cultural Anthropology	Archaeology	Linguistic Anthropology	Physical Anthropology
The study of cultures and societies of human beings and their very recent past. Traditional cultural anthropologists study living cultures and present their observations in an ethnography.	The study of past societies and their cultures, especially the material remains of the past, such as tools, food remains, and places where people lived.	The study of language, especially how language is structured, the evolution of language, and the social and cultural contexts for language.	Also called biological anthropology, physical anthropology is the study of human evolution and variation, both past and current.

(a)   (b)   (c)   (d)

FIGURE 1.2

The Four Branches of Anthropology **(a)** *Cultural anthropologists,* who study living populations, often spend time living with cultural groups to gain more intimate perspectives on those cultures. The American anthropologist Margaret Mead (1901–1978), one of the most recognizable names in cultural anthropology, studied the peoples of the Admiralty Islands, near Papua New Guinea. **(b)** *Archaeologists* study past human behaviors by investigating material remains that humans leave behind, such as buildings and other structures. This archaeologist examines remnants from a pyramid in the ancient sacred city of Caral, Peru. **(c)** *Linguistic anthropologists* study all aspects of language and language use. Here, Leslie Moore, a linguistic anthropologist working in a Fulbe community in northern Cameroon, records as a teacher guides a boy in memorizing Koranic verses. **(d)** *Physical anthropologists* study human evolution and variation. Some physical anthropologists study skeletons from the past to investigate evolution and variation throughout human history. Those working in **forensic anthropology**, a specialty within physical anthropology, examine skeletons to identify who they were in life. Such an identification may be of a single person or of thousands. For example, the forensic anthropologist pictured here was called on to help identify the estimated 30,000 victims of Argentina's "Dirty War," which followed the country's 1976 coup.

1.2 What Is Physical Anthropology?

The short answer to this question is, *Physical anthropology is the study of human biological evolution and human biocultural variation.* Two key concepts underlie this definition.

Number one, every person is a product of evolutionary history, or all the biological changes that have brought humanity to its current form. The remains of humanlike beings, or **hominins,** indicate that the earliest human ancestors, in Africa, date to sometime around 6–8 million years ago (mya). Since that time, the physical appearance of hominins and their descendants, including modern humans, has changed dramatically. Our physical appearance, our intelligence, and everything else that makes us

hominins Humans and humanlike ancestors.

distinctive biological organisms evolved in our predecessors, whose genes led to the species we are today. (Genes and species are among the subjects of chapters 3 and 4.)

Number two, each of us is the product of his or her own individual life history. From the moment you were conceived, your biological makeup has been determined mostly by your genes. (The human **genome**—that is, all the genetic material in a person—includes some 20,000–25,000 genes.) Your biological makeup is also strongly influenced by your environment. *Environment* here refers not just to the obvious factors such as climate but to everything that has affected you—the physical activities you have engaged in (which have placed stress on your muscles and bones), the food you have eaten, and many other factors that affect overall health and well-being. Environment also includes social and cultural factors. A disadvantaged social environment, such as one in which infants and children receive poor-quality nutrition, can result in negative consequences such as poor health, reduced height, and shortened life expectancy. The Indian child who lived after the shift from foraging to farming on the Georgia coast ate more corn than did the Indian child who lived in the same place before AD 1000. Because of the corn-rich diet, the later child's teeth had more cavities. Each child's condition reflects millions of years of evolution as well as more immediate circumstances, such as diet, exposure to disease, and the stresses of day-to-day living.

genome The complete set of genetic information—chromosomal and mitochondrial DNA—for an organism or species that represents all of the inheritable traits.

WHAT DO PHYSICAL ANTHROPOLOGISTS DO?

Physical anthropologists routinely travel to places throughout the United States and around the world to investigate populations. Some physical anthropologists study living people, while others study extinct and living species of our nearest biological relatives, **primates** such as lemurs, monkeys, and apes. I am among the physical anthropologists who travel to museum collections and archaeological localities to study past societies. When I tell people outside the field what I do for a living, they often think physical anthropology is quite odd, bizarre even. Frequently they ask, "Why would anyone want to study dead people and old bones and teeth?" Everyone has heard of physics, chemistry, and biology; but the average person has never heard of this field. Compared to other areas of science, physical anthropology is small. But smallness does not make it unimportant. It is practical and significant, providing answers to fundamental questions that have been asked by scholars and scientists for centuries, such as *Who are we as a species? What does it mean to be human? Where did we come from?* Moreover, physical anthropology plays a vital role in addressing questions that are central to our society, sometimes involving circumstances that all of us wish had never come about. For example, the tragedy that Americans identify as 9/11 called immediately for the assistance of specialists from forensic anthropology.

primates A group of mammals in the order Primates that have complex behavior, varied forms of locomotion, and a unique suite of traits, including large brains, forward-facing eyes, fingernails, and reduced snouts.

The discipline as practiced in the United States began in the first half of the twentieth century, especially under the guidance of three key figures: Franz Boas for American anthropology generally (see "How Do We Know: Franz Boas Invents Anthropology, American Style"); Czech-born Aleš Hrdlička, who started the professional scientific journal and professional society devoted to the field; and Earnest Hooton, who trained most of the first generation of physical anthropologists. While the theory and methods of physical anthropologists today have changed greatly since the early 1900s, the same basic topics first envisioned by these founders form what we do.

Physical anthropologists study all aspects of human biology, specifically looking at the evolution and variation of human beings and their living and past relatives. This focus on biology means that physical anthropologists practice a *biological science*. But they also practice a *social science,* in that they study biology within the context of culture and behavior. Depending on their areas of interest, physical anthropologists might

FRANZ BOAS INVENTS ANTHR

The origins of academic anthropology in the United States go back to the late 1800s. More than anyone else, Franz Boas (1858–1942) pulled together the various scholarly themes that give the discipline its distinctive identity in the United States.

German by birth and by education, Boas attended graduate school, majoring in physics and geography. He was expected to know a lot about a lot of different things. By the time he received his Ph.D. from the University of Kiel in 1881, he had developed a passionate interest in studying other cultures, drawing the conclusion that human societies were best understood from as many angles as possible, including the cultural side (culture, technology, and society) and the biological side (variation, physical characteristics, and adaptation). He was also trained to observe the natural world and to record it in detail, not just to collect facts but to answer questions. This perspective grew from his exposure to senior scholars with interdisciplinary approaches and to scientists who focused on empirical, measurable evidence. Among his teachers was the leading European anthropologist of the nineteenth century, Rudolf Virchow (1821–1902).

In the late spring of 1883, Boas left his hometown of Minden, Germany, for his first anthropological expedition, to spend a year observing the Inuit (Eskimos) living on Baffin Island in the eastern Arctic of North America. His education and training had convinced him that he needed to find out as much as he could on the cultural and biological sides of the human condition, in this case as they applied to the Inuit. This endeavor was a central element of the birth of anthropology in the United States.

Franz Boas aboard the *Germania* in 1883 on his expedition to Baffin Island.

Boas's objective in his fieldwork was simple. In his own words, he wanted to research "the simple relationships between the land and the people." His work represented a fundamental development in the history of anthropology because it brought together different perspectives, seeking to understand the Inuit's living and past cultures, language, and biology. Today, these emphases comprise the four main branches of anthropology: cultural anthropology, archaeology, linguistic anthropology, and physical anthropology.

OPOLOGY, AMERICAN STYLE

Boas, here dressed and equipped for Arctic exploration, sought to learn how the Inuit people interacted with their environment and how the environment affected their biology. He also studied their language and material culture during this yearlong, physically and emotionally taxing expedition.

After Boas moved to the United States, he served as one of the first scientific curators of anthropology at the American Museum of Natural History in New York City during the 1890s. Over the next half-century, he taught full-time at Columbia University, instilling in his students a central tenet of anthropology: we learn about cultures, societies, and peoples' biology via *direct* observation and *careful* attention to detail. Boas trained the first generation of American academic anthropologists, all leaders in the field: Ruth Benedict, Margaret Mead, Edward Sapir, Alfred Kroeber, Robert Lowie, and Melville Herskovits, to name a few. He was also an important force in founding one of the primary professional organizations, American Anthropological Association, and its journal, *American Anthropologist,* and played leading roles in the founding of other anthropological organizations, including the American Association of Physical Anthropologists, the professional organization of physical anthropologists in the United States. By basing his research and his teaching on questions such as *How do we know?,* Boas laid the foundation for scientific anthropology: reliance on the scientific method, with its focus on the collection of evidence, for addressing hypotheses and answering questions about past and living people.

Boas has left a lasting legacy, and his approach to understanding the human condition continues to influence anthropology today. For physical anthropology, he was a strong proponent of the idea of the plasticity of human biology, observing physical changes from one generation to the next. His most important legacy is his commitment to the idea of cultural relativism, namely that we must look at the values, behaviors, and beliefs from the point of view of the people and the culture being studied. All anthropologists today can look back on when they were first exposed to the idea. I well recall my own "ah ha" moment in the introduction to cultural anthropology course I took when I was an undergraduate, realizing that it isn't just other cultures that have different perspectives; others in my own culture may have different points of view as well. Boas celebrated human diversity in all ways—culturally, socially, and biologically.

FIGURE 1.3

A Sample of What Physical Anthropologists Do **(a)** Human remains excavated at Badia Pozzeveri, a medieval church cemetery in Tuscany, Italy, provide a window through which to view health and living conditions in Europe. **(b)** Geneticists analyze samples of human DNA for various anthropological purposes. DNA studies are used to determine how closely related humans are to other primate species, to examine human origins, and to determine individual identities. **(c)** A human biologist records the physical activities of a lactating woman (right, weaving basket) living in a rural community in the eastern Amazon, Brazil. These data will be used to calculate the woman's energy expenditure and to understand how she copes with reproduction's great energy demands. **(d)** In a lab, a forensic anthropologist measures and assesses human bones. If the bones came from a contemporary grave, this forensic information might help to identify the victim. If the bones belonged to a past population, physical anthropologists might use these data to gain insight into the population's health and lifestyle. **(e)** Laboratory investigations of human ancestors' bones help paleoanthropologists to determine where these ancestors fit in the human family tree. **(f)** Primatologists, such as the British researcher Jane Goodall (b. 1934), study our closest living relatives, nonhuman primates. The behavior and lifestyle of chimpanzees, for example, help physical anthropologists to understand our evolutionary past.

examine molecular structure, bones and teeth, blood types, breathing capacity and lung volume, genetics and genetic history, infectious and other types of disease, origins of language and speech, nutrition, reproduction, growth and development, aging, primate origins, primate social behavior, brain biology, and many other topics dealing with variation in both the living and the dead—sometimes the very long dead (**Figure 1.3**).

In dealing with such topics, physical anthropologists apply methods and theories developed in other disciplines as well as in their own as they answer questions that help us understand who we are, a point that I will raise over and over again throughout this book. The very nature of their discipline and their constant borrowing from other disciplines mean that physical anthropologists practice an *interdisciplinary science.* For example, they might draw on the work of geologists who study the landforms and layering of deposits of soil and rock that tell us when earlier humans lived. Or they might obtain information from paleontologists, who study the evolution of life-forms in the distant past and thus provide the essential context for understanding the world in which earlier humans lived. Some physical anthropologists are trained in chemistry, so they can analyze the chemical properties of bones and teeth to determine what kinds of foods were eaten by those earlier humans. Or to learn how living humans adapt to reduced-oxygen settings, such as in the high altitudes of the Peruvian Andes, physical anthropologists might work with physiologists who study the ability of the lungs to absorb oxygen. The firm yet flexible identity of their science allows physical anthropologists to gather data from other disciplines in order to address key questions. Questions drive what they do.

1.3 What Makes Humans So Different from Other Animals? The Six Steps to Humanness

Human beings clearly differ from other animals. From humanity's earliest origin (about 6–8 mya, when an apelike primate began walking on two feet) to the period beginning about 10,000 years ago (when modern climates and environments emerged after what is commonly known as the Ice Age), six key attributes developed that make us unique. These attributes are bipedalism, nonhoning chewing, complex material culture and tool use, hunting, speech, and dependence on domesticated foods (**Figure 1.4**). The first development represents the most profound physical difference between humans and other animals, namely the manner in which we get around: we are committed to **bipedalism,** that is, walking on two feet. The next development was the loss of a large, honing canine tooth, like the one that apes typically use to shred their food (mostly plants), replaced by the simple **nonhoning canine,** with which we process food in ways unique to humans. (I will talk more about that in chapter 10.) Our ancestors' honing canine disappeared because they developed the ability to make and use tools for processing food.

Today, our species completely depends on **culture**—and especially material culture—for its day-to-day living and its very survival. Culture is a complex human characteristic that facilitates our survival by enabling us to adapt to different settings. **Material culture** is the part of culture that is expressed as objects that humans use to manipulate environments. For example, hammers and nails are forms of material culture that enable us to make cabinets, tables, and countless other forms of material culture.

bipedalism Walking on two feet.

nonhoning canine An upper canine that, as part of a nonhoning chewing mechanism, is not sharpened against the lower third premolar.

material culture The part of culture that is expressed as objects that humans use to manipulate environments.

The Six Big Events of Human Evolution

BIPEDALISM, NONHONING CHEWING, DEPENDENCE ON MATERIAL CULTURE, SPEECH, HUNTING, AND DOMESTICATION OF PLANTS AND ANIMALS

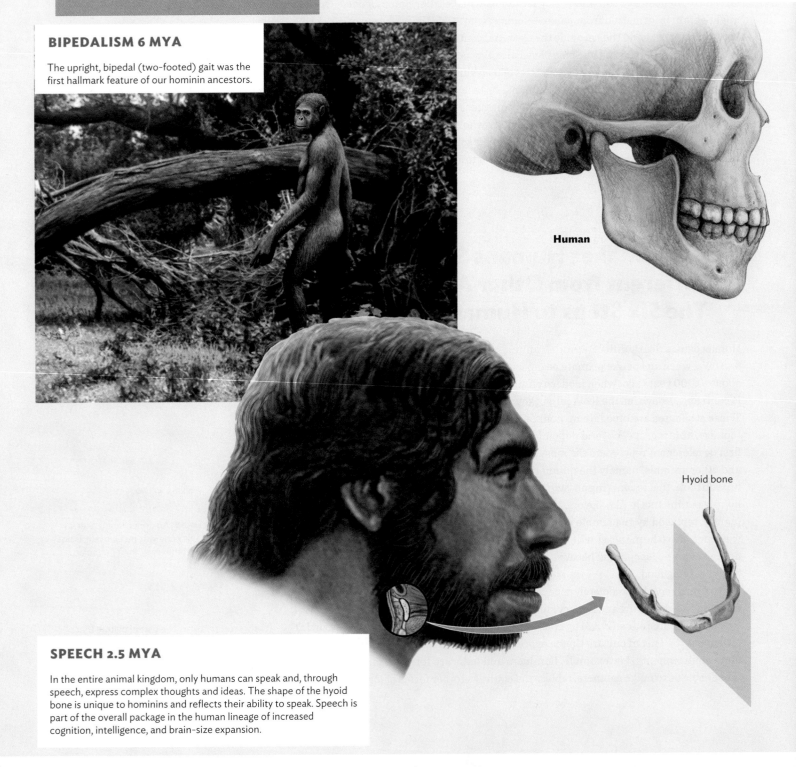

NONHONING CHEWING 5.5 MYA

Humans' nonhoning chewing complex (below) lacks large, projecting canines in the upper jaw and a diastema, or gap, between the lower canine and the third premolar.

Human

BIPEDALISM 6 MYA

The upright, bipedal (two-footed) gait was the first hallmark feature of our hominin ancestors.

Hyoid bone

SPEECH 2.5 MYA

In the entire animal kingdom, only humans can speak and, through speech, express complex thoughts and ideas. The shape of the hyoid bone is unique to hominins and reflects their ability to speak. Speech is part of the overall package in the human lineage of increased cognition, intelligence, and brain-size expansion.

The chewing complex of apes such as gorillas (below) has large, projecting upper canines and a diastema in the lower jaw to accommodate them.

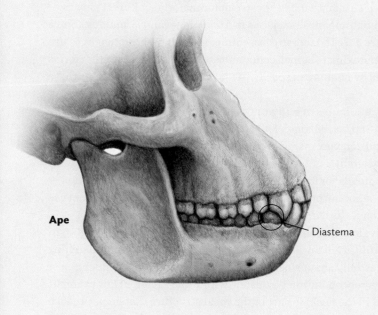

Ape

Diastema

MATERIAL CULTURE AND TOOLS 3.3 MYA

Humans' production and use of stone tools is one example of complex material culture. The tools of our closest living relatives, the chimpanzees, do not approach the complexity and diversity of modern and ancestral humans' tools

HUNTING 1 MYA

Humans' relatively large brains require lots of energy to develop and function. Animal protein is an ideal source of that energy, and humans obtained it for most of their evolution by eating animals they hunted. To increase their chances of success in hunting, humans employed tools they made and cooperative strategies.

DOMESTICATED FOODS 11,000 YEARS AGO

In recent evolution—within the last 10,000 years or so—humans domesticated a wide variety of plants and animals, controlling their life cycles and using them for food and other products, such as clothing and shelter.

FIGURE 1.5

First Tools The earliest stone tools date to 3.3 mya and are associated with early human ancestors in East Africa. The example shown here is from Lomekwi, West Turkana, Kenya. This tool likely had various functions, including the processing of plants and meat for food.

The material remains of past cultures go back hundreds of thousands of years, to the first simple tools made from rocks 3.3 mya (**Figure 1.5**). Material culture today makes our lifestyles possible. Can you imagine your life without it? We could survive without modern additions to material culture, such as cars, computers, television sets, plumbing, and electricity, as our ancestors did before the past century. But what about living without basic material culture, such as shelter and clothing, especially in climates where it can be very, very cold in the winter? Without material culture, how would any of us get food? The answer to both questions is simple: we could not make it without some forms of technology—to regulate temperature, to acquire food, and so on. Some societies are much less technologically complex than others, but no society functions without any technology.

Anthropologists and animal behaviorists have shown that human beings are not, however, the only type of animal that has or can employ material culture. Primatologists have observed some chimpanzee societies in Africa, for example, making simple tools from twigs (**Figure 1.6**). In laboratories, chimpanzees have been taught to use physical symbols that approximate human communication. Still, these and other forms of material culture used by nonhuman species are nowhere near as complex as those created by humans.

The other three key attributes of humanness—hunting, speech, and dependence on domesticated foods—appeared much later in human evolution than bipedalism, nonhoning chewing, and complex material culture and tool use. *Hunting* here refers to the social behavior whereby a group of individuals, adult men in general, organize themselves to pursue animals for food. This behavior likely dates back to a million or more years ago. Some nonhuman primates organize to pursue prey, but they do not use tools or travel long distances as humans distinctively do when they hunt.

An equally distinctive human behavior is speech. We are the only animal that communicates by talking. Unfortunately for research purposes, recording-and-listening technology was invented only about a century ago. For information about long-past speech, anthropologists rely on indirect evidence within the skeleton. For example, the hyoid bone (located in the neck) is part of the vocal structure that helps produce words. The unique appearance of the human hyoid helps anthropologists conjecture about the origins of speech.

FIGURE 1.6

Toolmaking Once thought to be a uniquely human phenomenon, toolmaking has been observed in chimpanzees, the closest biological relatives of humans. As seen here, a chimpanzee has modified a twig to scoop termites from nests. Other chimpanzees have used two rocks as a hammer and anvil to crack open nuts. More recently, gorillas were seen using a stick to test the depth of a pool of water they wanted to cross. Tool use such as this likely preceded the first identified tools (see Figure 1.5).

FIGURE 1.7

Social Learning Father teaching his son traditional wood-carving in Ubud, Bali, Indonesia. Social learning provides a means of accumulating and maintaining knowledge over many generations.

The most recently developed unique human behavior is the domesticated manner in which we acquire our food. About 10,000–11,000 years before the present (yBP), humans began to raise animals and grow plants. This development led to our current reliance on domesticated species. This reliance has had a profound impact on human biology and behavior and represents a fundamental part of our biological evolution.

Human beings' unique behaviors and survival mechanisms, and the anatomical features related to them, arose through the complex interaction of biology and culture. Indeed, our ancestors' increasing dependence on culture for survival has made us *entirely* culture-dependent for survival. The behaviors that are unique to humans—speech, tool use, and dependence on culture—are also related to the fact that humans are very smart. Our remarkable intelligence is reflected in our abilities to think and interact in the ways we do (and take for granted), to communicate in complex ways, and to accomplish diverse tasks on a daily basis to survive. Our brains are bigger and have more complex analytical skills than the brains of both other primates and animals in general. These biological advantages enable us to figure out complex problems, including how to survive in a wide range of environments.

The American anthropologist Robert Boyd and his colleagues argue that while humans are the smartest animals, in no way are we individually smart enough to acquire all the complex information necessary to survive in any particular environment. Today and through much of human evolution, our species has survived owing to our complex culture, including tool use and other technology, practices, and beliefs. For hundreds of thousands of years, humans have had a record of unique ways of learning from other humans. Retaining new knowledge, we pass this information to our offspring and other members of our societies, and this process extends over many generations (**Figure 1.7**). That is, **social learning** makes it possible for humans to accumulate an amazing amount of information over long time periods.

In the chapters that follow, you will be looking at these processes and behaviors—the particulars of physical anthropology—from a biocultural perspective. It is the unique and phenomenal interplay between biology, culture, and behavior that makes us human.

social learning The capacity to learn from other humans, enabling the accumulation of knowledge across many generations.

1.4 How We Know What We Know: The Scientific Method

How do physical anthropologists and other scientists make decisions about what their subject matter means? More specifically, how do we know what we know about human evolution and human variation? Like all other scientists, physical anthropologists carefully and systematically observe and ask questions about the natural world around them. These observations and questions form the basis for identifying problems and gathering evidence—**data**—that will help answer questions and solve problems; that is, fill gaps in scientific knowledge about how the natural world operates. These data are used to test **hypotheses,** possible explanations for the processes under study. Scientists observe and then reject or accept these hypotheses. This process of determining whether ideas are right or wrong is called the **scientific method** (**Figure 1.8**). It is the foundation of science.

Science (Latin *scientia,* meaning "knowledge"), then, is more than just knowledge of facts about the natural world. Science is also much more than technical details. Certainly, facts and technical details are important in developing answers to questions, but facts and technical skills are not science. Rather, science is a *process* that provides new discoveries that connect our lives with the world we live in—it is a way of knowing through observation of natural phenomena. This repeated acquisition results in an ever-expanding knowledge base, one built from measurable, repeatable, and highly tangible observations. In this way, science is **empirical,** or based on observation or experiment. After the systematic collection of observations, the scientist develops a **theory**—an explanation as to why a natural phenomenon takes place. For many non-scientists, a theory is simply a guess or a hunch; but for a scientist, a theory is not just some stab at an explanation. Rather, a theory is an explanation grounded in a great deal of evidence, or what a lawyer calls the "evidentiary record." A scientist builds a case by

hypotheses Testable statements that potentially explain specific phenomena observed in the natural world.

scientific method An empirical research method in which data are gathered from observations of phenomena, hypotheses are formulated and tested, and conclusions are drawn that validate or modify the original hypotheses.

empirical Verified through observation and experiment.

FIGURE 1.8

The Scientific Method: How We Know What We Know Physical anthropologists employ the scientific method to draw understanding about the natural world around us. Starting with observations of natural phenomena, they develop a hypothesis that will predict an outcome. They test the hypothesis with additional observations, which either support or reject the hypothesis.

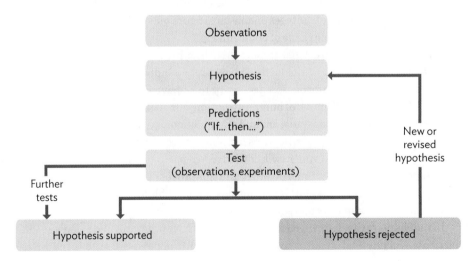

identifying incontrovertible facts. To arrive at these facts, the scientist examines and reexamines the evidence, putting it through many tests.

The scientist thus employs observation, documentation, and testing to generate hypotheses and, eventually, to construct a theory based on those hypotheses. Hypotheses *explain* observations, *predict* the results of future investigation, and *can be refuted* by new evidence.

For example, the great English naturalist Charles Robert Darwin (1809–1882) developed the hypothesis that the origin of human bipedalism was linked to the shift from life in the trees to life on the ground (**Figure 1.9**). Darwin's hypothesis was based on his own observations of humans walking, other scientists' then-limited observations of nonhuman primate behavior, and other scientists' **anatomical** evidence, or information about structural makeup drawn from dissections, in this case of apes. Darwin's hypothesis led to an additional hypothesis—itself based on evidence accumulated over the following decades, and widely believed for the subsequent century and a half—that the first hominins arose in the open grasslands of Africa from some apelike animal that was formerly **arboreal**; that is, had once lived in trees (**Figure 1.10**).

Support for Darwin's hypothesis about human origins—and in particular the origin of bipedal locomotion—began to erode in 2001, when a group of scientists discovered early hominins, from 5.2 to 5.8 mya, in the modern country of Ethiopia. Contrary to expectation and accepted wisdom, these hominins had lived not in grasslands but in woodlands (**Figure 1.11**). Moreover, unlike modern humans, whose fingers and toes are straight because we are fully **terrestrial**—we live on the ground (**Figure 1.12**)—the early hominins had slightly curved fingers and toes. The physical shape and appearance

FIGURE 1.9
Charles Darwin George Richmond painted this portrait of Darwin in 1840.

terrestrial Life-forms, including humans, that live on land versus living in water or in trees.

FIGURE 1.10
Grasslands Darwin hypothesized that the earliest hominins originated in grasslands similar to this one (Serengeti Plain, Tanzania, East Africa). Recent studies refute the notion that hominins originated in grassland habitats.

THE FORENSIC ANTH

Body Decomposition at the Body Farm

Forensic anthropologists have arguably one of the toughest jobs, as it usually involves the not especially pleasant circumstance of identifying decomposing bodies. The remains of deceased persons present grim images in their various stages of decay, but it is the process and timing of decomposition in these deceased persons that provide crucial information for solving murders.

WATCH THE VIDEO

www.digital.
wwnorton.com/
ourorigins4

Recognizing the potential of human remains to answer fundamental questions about time since death, William M. Bass—one of the world's leading forensic anthropologists—established the University of Tennessee's Anthropological Research Facility in 1980 and began asking relatives of deceased persons to donate the bodies to the research facility. Indeed, whenever Bass's unique facility comes up in conversation with forensic scientists, it is often referred to as the "Body Farm."

Whatever would possess an anthropologist to undertake such an ambitious project? Bass came up with the idea because at the time, there had been very little substantive research on body decomposition, at least the kind of research that would stand up in a court of law or under the scrutiny of science. Bass's own lack of knowledge about decomposition was underscored when he was called to look at human remains from a disturbed Civil War–era burial site in Tennessee. On arrival at the burial site, he saw a decaying body whose excellent state of preservation appeared to represent that of someone who died recently. In his mind, Bass had a routine forensic case on his hands. On closer examination, however, it turned out the body was associated with

the headstone of a Civil War officer buried in the cemetery in 1864. The officer's body was remarkably well-preserved because after his death he had been embalmed and then interred in an airtight, cast-iron casket. Bass realized then and there that the field of forensic science and its practitioners, himself included, needed to develop an experimental record of body decomposition, focusing on circumstances that influence decay of body tissues. The key goal would be the ability to estimate time since death, a central element of crime-scene investigations.

With the support of his university administration, Bass began to pull together the necessary resources to establish the facility and to seek donors who would be willing to donate the bodies of loved ones. Although only a few bodies were donated in the first few years after the opening of the facility, once it became known to the public that Bass's project would have significant importance in solving murders, body donations began to come into the facility by the hundreds each year.

What happens to the bodies once they arrive at the facility? This is determined by the particular "experiment"—focusing on a specific aspect of decomposition—that they are needed for. Some of the bodies are placed directly on the ground, whereas others are placed in closed containers or in water, or are buried. Some of the bodies are placed on the ground surface in the winter when colder temperatures are known to slow down the decomposition process, whereas others are placed on the ground surface in the summer when decomposition is accelerated by high heat and humidity. What is the demographic composition of the more than 2,000 donated bodies? The bodies are of European (91%), African (7%), and Hispanic (2%) ancestry, and 70% are male and 30% are female. All bodies are well documented, including information such as family history, age, sex, ancestry, medical history, cause of death, habitual activities, and life events.

Decomposition—the central focus of studies at the Body Farm—consists of two main processes: **autolysis** and **putrefaction**. Autolysis is a kind of "self-digestion" in which the high-carbon-dioxide environment within the decomposing body results in breakdown of the cells of the body. This process starts just a few days after death. Putrefaction is the result of the activity of microorganisms, especially bacteria, in the breakdown of tissues. The rate of decomposition is strongly linked to temperature, humidity, availability of oxygen, exposure to sunlight, soil acidity and chemistry, and insect and animal activity.

What are the practical applications of the studies of decomposition at the facility? Some of the remains that I encounter in my own field research in **bioarchaeology** in various parts of the world include skeletal remains that show evidence of disarticulation of joints—such as those between hand bones or foot bones. I and other bioarchaeologists want to know how much time after death it takes for the soft tissue holding various skeletal elements together to decompose. Law enforcement agencies, including local police, want to know when death occurred for bodies involved in

murder investigations. For bioarchaeologists, these are scientific concepts that contribute to our understanding of past peoples. But for law enforcement, answers to questions about decomposition address real problems surrounding the tragic deaths of relatives and friends.

Today, owing to the study of these processes and the

experimental conditions carefully monitored on a daily basis (for example, temperature), the stages and rates of decomposition are now far better known than when William Bass first established the facility. Bioarchaeologists who study ancient remains are now on much more solid footing in understanding both the process and the circumstances of death and decomposition. And law enforcement officials can re-create much more accurate timelines for murder investigations based on the condition of bodies. *Anthropology matters!*

Students at the Body Farm. Studies of body decomposition in a controlled setting provide an essential forensic science tool for evaluating body decomposition in uncontrolled settings. This research has contributed to understanding time since death, an important element of criminal investigations.

FIGURE 1.11

Forests Scientific findings have revealed that, in fact, the earliest hominins lived in wooded settings, perhaps like this locality in East Africa (Great Rift Valley, Lake Manyara National Park, Tanzania).

morphology Physical shape and appearance.

scientific law A statement of fact describing natural phenomena.

(what physical anthropologists call **morphology**) of the hominins' finger and toe bones indicate a lot of time spent in trees, holding on to branches, moving from limb to limb. These findings forced scientists to reject Darwin's hypothesis, to toss out what had been a fundamental tenet of physical anthropology.

This story does not end, however, with the understanding that the earliest hominins lived in forests. Instead, this new hypothesis generated new questions. For example, why did the earliest hominins arise in a wooded setting, and why did they "come out of the woods" as time went on? Later in this book, we will consider these questions. For now, the point is that science is a self-correcting approach to knowledge acquisition. Scientists develop new hypotheses as new findings are made. Scientists use these hypotheses to build theories. And like the hypotheses that underlie them, theories can be modified or even replaced by better theories, depending on findings made through meticulous observation. As new observations are made and hypotheses and theories are subjected to the test of time, science revises its own errors.

A **scientific law** is a statement of irrefutable truth of some action or actions occurring in the natural world. Among the few scientific laws, the well-known ones are the laws of gravity, thermodynamics, and motion. But scientific truth seldom gets finalized into law. Rather, truth is continually developed—new facts are discovered and new understandings about natural phenomena are made. Unlike theories, scientific laws do not address the larger questions as to why a natural action or actions take place.

As my crew and I traveled to St. Catherines Island, we were intent on discovering new facts and forming new understandings about the prehistoric farmers' descendants who were first encountered by Spaniards in the late 1500s. These facts and understandings would enable us to test hypotheses about human evolution and human variation. Once we completed the months of arduous fieldwork and the years of laboratory investigations on the remains that fieldwork uncovered, we would have some answers. The scientific method would guide us in providing insights into this part of the human lineage—human beings' most recent evolution—and how our species came to be what it is in the early twenty-first century.

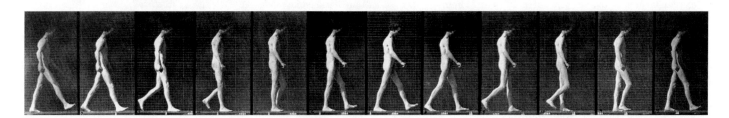

FIGURE 1.12

Bipedalism These 1887 photographs by Eadweard Muybridge capture the habitual upright stance of humans. Other animals, such as chimpanzees, occasionally walk on two feet; but humans alone make bipedalism their main form of locomotion. As Darwin observed, this stance frees the hands to hold objects. What are some other advantages of bipedalism?

CHAPTER 1 REVIEW

ANSWERING THE BIG QUESTIONS

1. **What is anthropology?**
   - Anthropology is the study of humankind. In two major ways, it differs from other sciences that study humankind. First, anthropology views humans as both biological and cultural beings. Second, anthropology emphasizes a holistic, comparative approach, encompassing all people at all times and all places.
   - The four branches of anthropology are cultural anthropology (study of living cultures), archaeology (study of past cultures), linguistic anthropology (study of language), and physical anthropology.

2. **What is physical anthropology?**
   - Physical (or biological) anthropology is the study of human biology, specifically of the evolution and variation of humans (and their relatives, past and present).
   - Physical anthropology is an eclectic field, deriving theory and method both from within the discipline and from other sciences that address important questions about human evolution and human variation.

3. **What makes humans so different from other animals?**
   - Humans living today are the product of millions of years of evolutionary history and their own personal life histories.
   - Humans have six unique physical and behavioral characteristics: bipedalism, nonhoning chewing, complex material culture and tool use, hunting, speech, and dependence on domesticated foods.

4. **How do physical anthropologists know what they know?**
   - Physical anthropologists derive knowledge via the scientific method. This method involves observations, the development of questions, and the answering of those questions. Scientists formulate and test hypotheses that they hope will lead to theories about the natural world.

KEY TERMS

anatomical
anthropology
arboreal
archaeology
artifacts
autolysis
bioarchaeology
biocultural
 approach
biological
 anthropology
bipedalism
cultural
 anthropology
culture
data
empirical
forensic
 anthropology
genome

hominins
hypotheses
language
linguistic
 anthropology
material culture
morphology
nonhoning canine
physical
 anthropology
primates
putrefaction
scientific law
scientific method
social learning
sociolinguistics
terrestrial
theory

STUDY QUIZ

1. **A physical anthropologist would be most likely to study**
   a. learned and shared behaviors in a current human society.
   b. material remains from a past human society.
   c. the evolution of humans or other primates.
   d. the construction and cultural context of human language.

2. **What is influenced both by genes and by environmental factors.**
   a. Cultural behavior
   b. Biological makeup
   c. Spoken language
   d. Individual genome

3. **Which is *not* unique to humans?**
   a. large, honing canine teeth specialized for shredding food
   b. reliance on bipedalism for locomotion
   c. dependence on material culture and tools to survive
   d. spoken language for communication with other individuals

4. **In the scientific method, a theory is supported by**
   a. initial guesses and impressions.
   b. the collection of facts about a phenomenon.
   c. the creation of a hypothesis.
   d. rigorous testing of hypotheses.

5. **Franz Boas helped establish that human societies**
   a. are influenced both by biology and by culture.
   b. represent a biological evolution from simple to complex.
   c. are equivalent to nonhuman primate societies.
   d. cannot be studied using the scientific method.

EVOLUTION REVIEW

PHYSICAL ANTHROPOLOGY AS SCIENCE

Synopsis Anthropology is a holistic discipline in that it views humankind from the perspectives of all people and all eras. Anthropology is also an interdisciplinary science in that it both draws on and influences research in many related fields. Physical anthropology is one of the four subfields (along with cultural anthropology, archaeology, and linguistic anthropology) that make up anthropology as both a biological and a social science. The two main concepts that define physical anthropology are human biological evolution and human biocultural variation. By use of the scientific method, physical anthropologists study many different aspects of living humans, modern and extinct nonhuman primates, and fossil hominins, among other lines of research. Through all of these different ways of gathering knowledge about the human condition, physical anthropologists ultimately address research questions related to the two broad themes of evolution and variation.

Q1. Define the biocultural approach—a hallmark of physical anthropology.

Q2. Focusing on Figure 1.4, "The Six Big Events of Human Evolution," identify which two of these events were caused primarily by biological changes in humans and which four were caused by changes in both human biology and human culture.

Q3. Over time, has culture had a large or small effect on human evolution? Focusing on Figure 1.4, briefly explain your answer.

Q4. As a species, humans are unique in the degree to which culture influences our evolution. Consider Figure 1.4 again. How might aspects of human culture have affected the evolution of other species, such as livestock or wild animals?

Q5. Many nonscientists often critique evolution as "just a theory." What does it mean for evolution to be a theory in the context of the scientific method? How does the study of evolution illustrate the interdisciplinary nature of physical anthropology?

Hint What other scientific fields might contribute data that are used to test hypotheses related to biological evolution?

ADDITIONAL READINGS

Larsen, C. S., ed. 2010. *A Companion to Biological Anthropology*. Chichester, UK: Wiley-Blackwell.

Molnar, S. 2005. *Human Variation: Races, Types, and Ethnic Groups*. Upper Saddle River, NJ: Prentice Hall.

Moore, J. A. 1999. *Science as a Way of Knowing: The Foundations of Modern Biology*. Cambridge, MA: Harvard University Press.

Spencer, F., ed. 1997. *History of Physical Anthropology: An Encyclopedia*. New York: Garland.

Stocking, G., ed. 1974. *The Shaping of American Anthropology, 1883–1911: A Franz Boas Reader*. New York: Basic Books.

Some Periodicals in Anthropology

Physical anthropology: *American Journal of Human Biology, American Journal of Physical Anthropology, American Journal of Primatology, Evolutionary Anthropology, Human Biology, International Journal of Paleopathology, Journal of Human Evolution, Yearbook of Physical Anthropology*.

Archaeology: *American Antiquity, Antiquity, Archaeology, Journal of Archaeological Science, Latin American Antiquity, World Archaeology*.

Cultural anthropology: *American Anthropologist, Cultural Anthropology*.

General anthropology: *American Anthropologist, Annual Review of Anthropology, Current Anthropology*.

PART I

THE PRESENT

Foundation for the Past

Some physical anthropologists learn about human evolution by studying living primates, including humans. Other physical anthropologists learn about human evolution by investigating the past, now represented mostly by fossilized bones and fossilized teeth. Together, living and past enable us to understand evolution in the largest context. The fossil record provides us with the history of humans and of humanlike ancestors, while the living record provides the essential picture through which to view that history. Charles Darwin, the pioneering force behind our knowledge about evolution and natural selection, developed his ideas by studying living plants and animals. He had the extraordinary insight to realize that his theories and hypotheses applied to past organisms. For Darwin, living organisms were key to interpreting the past because they displayed evidence of evolution's elements and mechanics. In the same way, living organisms provide insights—into fundamental forces such as reproduction, DNA synthesis, protein synthesis, and behavior—that are not available, at least in the same way, within the past record. Part I of this book lays out observations and principles based on the study of living populations, the essential background for understanding evolution. Part II then digs into the past, into the study of ancestors whose descendants are present in the world (all of us now living) and of those evolutionary lineages that did not survive.

The living primates—such as, here, orangutans and humans—have much in common, biologically and behaviorally. Their study provides essential context for understanding variation and evolution, now and in the past.

Charles Darwin's observations provided the groundwork for his theory of natural selection, the basis of his 1859 book, *On the Origin of Species*.

Evolution

CONSTRUCTING A FUNDAMENTAL SCIENTIFIC THEORY

BIG QUESTIONS

1. **How did the theory of evolution come to be?**

2. **What was Darwin's contribution to the theory of evolution?**

3. **What has happened since Darwin in the development of our understanding of evolution?**

The nineteenth century was the century of scientific collecting. During the 1800s, the world discovered itself through collections. Expeditions large and small—involving scientists, explorers, and adventurers—crossed the continents and investigated landmasses around the globe. These teams collected hundreds of thousands of samples: plants, animals, rocks, and preserved remains (or **fossils**—the subject of chapter 8). If it seemed worth picking off the ground or exposing in some other fashion, it was fair game. This kind of work, on one of these international expeditions, helped lay the foundation for the most important biological theory, arguably among the half-dozen most important scientific theories—the theory of evolution.

In 1831, a 22-year-old Englishman and recent graduate of Cambridge University, Charles Darwin, was appointed the naturalist for a five-year voyage around the world on the ship HMS *Beagle* (**Figure 2.1**). Imagine that as your first job right out of college! Young Mr. Darwin, who was trained in medicine and theology, accepted a very difficult task. He was to collect, document, and study the natural world—plants and animals, especially—everywhere the ship harbored.

(a)

(b)

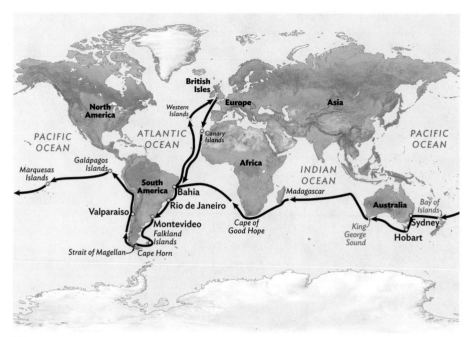

(c)

FIGURE 2.1

Darwin's Voyage **(a)** Charles Darwin ca. 1855, about 25 years after he set out on HMS *Beagle*. **(b)** In this illustration, the ship is passing through the Strait of Magellan, during the South American stretch of **(c)** its worldwide journey, whose ports of call are here mapped.

fossils Physical remains of part or all of once-living organisms, mostly bones and teeth, that have become mineralized by the replacement of organic with inorganic materials.

species A group of related organisms that can interbreed and produce fertile, viable offspring.

habitat The specific area of the natural environment in which an organism lives.

natural selection The process by which some organisms, with features that enable them to adapt to the environment, preferentially survive and reproduce, thereby increasing the frequency of those features in the population.

By the end of that voyage, Darwin had amassed a wonderfully comprehensive collection of plants, insects, birds, shells, fossils, and lots of other materials. The specimens he collected and the observations he made about the things he saw on that trip would form the basis of his lifetime of research. His discoveries would do no less than shape the future of the biological sciences, including physical anthropology. His ideas would provide the key to understanding the origin and evolution of life itself.

Soon after returning home from the voyage, Darwin began to formulate questions about the origins of plants and animals living in the many lands he and his shipmates had explored. His most prominent observations concerned the physical differences, or variation, between and among members of **species,** or like animals and like plants. He articulated the phenomenon best in his notes on finches that live in the Galápagos, a small cluster of islands 965 km (600 mi) off the coast of Ecuador (**Figure 2.2**). Not only did these birds differ from island to island, but even within a single island they seemed to vary according to **habitat,** or surroundings. For example, finches living on an island's coast had a different beak shape from finches living in an island's interior (**Figure 2.3**). These observations raised two questions for Darwin: *Why* were the birds different from island to island and from habitat to habitat? *How* did different species of finches arise? After years of study, Darwin answered these questions with an idea called "descent with modification," or the theory of evolution.

Darwin also came to realize that the variations in physical characteristics of the different species of finches and other organisms were adaptations—physical characteristics that enhance an organism's ability to survive and reproduce. Darwin recognized many other adaptations in the natural world, and he concluded that adaptation was the crux of evolution. To connect these processes, he coined the term **natural selection.** According to this principle, biological characteristics that enhance survival increase in frequency from generation to generation. Members of a population endowed with these characteristics produce more offspring that survive to reproductive age than members that are not endowed with these characteristics. Natural selection is thus the primary driver of evolution. Recognizing that the different species of finches all derived from a single common ancestor that had originated in

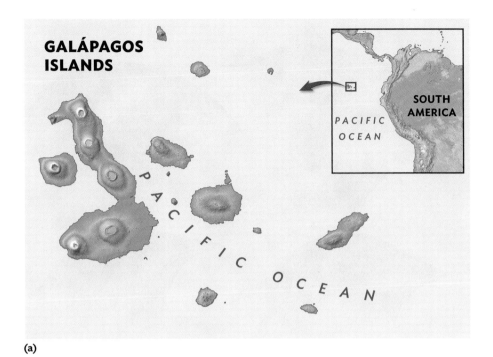

GALÁPAGOS ISLANDS

SOUTH AMERICA

PACIFIC OCEAN

PACIFIC OCEAN

(a)

(b)

(c)

(f)

(d)

(e)

FIGURE 2.2

Galápagos Islands **(a)** An archipelago off the coast of Ecuador, South America, the Galápagos consists of 13 major volcanic islands and numerous smaller islands and islets. **(b–f)** These islands are well known for their many **endemic**, or native, species, such as the 13 species of Galápagos finches, also known as Darwin's finches, that are found only at this location.

endemic Refers to a characteristic or feature that is natural to a given population or environment.

South America, Darwin also postulated the process of **adaptive radiation:** out of one species branch multiple closely related species.

Darwin regarded evolution as simply biological change from generation to generation. Many evolutionary biologists today limit their definition of evolution to genetic change only. However, nongenetic developmental change—biological change occurring within an individual's lifetime—can give an adaptive advantage (or disadvantage) to an individual or individuals within a population. Moreover, genes control developmental processes, which likewise influence other genes.

In subsequent chapters, we will further explore these and other aspects of evolution. Although the core of this book is human evolution, or how human biology came to be, understanding human evolution requires understanding the term *evolution* as it applies to all living organisms. In this chapter, we will take a historical approach to the term and the theory behind

adaptive radiation The diversification of an ancestral group of organisms into new forms that are adapted to specific environmental niches.

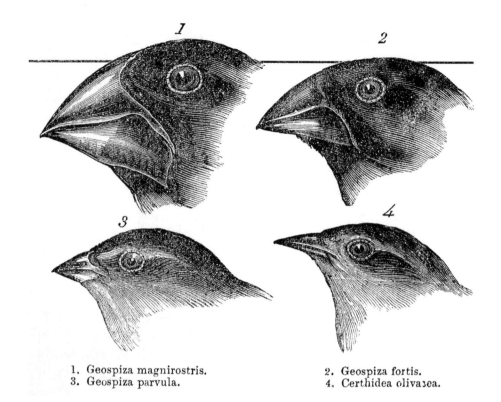

1. Geospiza magnirostris.
2. Geospiza fortis.
3. Geospiza parvula.
4. Certhidea olivasea.

FIGURE 2.3

Darwin's Finches Darwin studied the physical variation in finches living on different islands of the Galápagos. Among other attributes, he studied beak shape, which varied from island to island. Eventually, Darwin related each beak shape to diet, especially to the texture of food and how the food was acquired. Finches with larger beaks typically consumed harder foods, such as seeds and nuts, while finches with smaller beaks ate softer foods, such as berries. Darwin concluded that each finch species had adapted to the particular environment and food resources of its island.

it. After reading about its intellectual history before Darwin, Darwin's contribution, and developments since Darwin, you should have a clear idea of what physical anthropologists and other evolutionary biologists mean by *evolution*.

FIGURE 2.4

James Hutton Hutton (here depicted ca. 1790) founded modern geology with his theory of Earth's formation. Hutton realized that the same natural processes he observed in Scotland had occurred in the past.

2.1 The Theory of Evolution: The Context for Darwin

Before Darwin's time, Western scientists' understanding of Earth and the organisms that inhabit it was strongly influenced by religious doctrine. In the Judeo-Christian view, the planet was relatively young, and both its surface and the life-forms on it had not changed since their miraculous creation. By the late 1700s, scientists had realized three key things about the world and its inhabitants: Earth is actually quite ancient, its surface is very different from what it was in the past, and plants and animals have changed over time. These realizations about the natural world provided the context for Darwin's theory of evolution.

To generate his theory, Darwin drew on information from five scientific disciplines: geology, paleontology, taxonomy and systematics, demography, and what is now called evolutionary biology. **Geology** is the study of Earth, especially with regard to its composition, activity, and history. This discipline has demonstrated the great age of our planet and the development of its landscape. **Paleontology** is the study of fossils. This discipline has detailed past life-forms, many now extinct. **Taxonomy** is the classification of past and living life-forms. This discipline laid the foundation for **systematics,** the study of biological relationships over time. **Demography** is the study of population, especially with regard to birth, survival, and death and the major factors that influence these three key parts of life. **Evolutionary biology** is the study of organisms and their changes. By investigating the fundamental principles by which evolution operates, Darwin founded this discipline. In the following sections, we will look at these fields in more detail.

Geology: Reconstructing Earth's Dynamic History

We now know that our planet is 4.6 billion years old and that over time its surface has changed dramatically. If you had espoused these ideas in, say, the late 1600s, you would not have been believed, and you would have been condemned by the church because you had contradicted the Bible. According to a literal interpretation of the Bible, Earth is a few thousand years old and its surface is static. The Scottish scientist James Hutton (1726–1797) became dissatisfied with the biblical interpretation of the planet's history (**Figure 2.4**). He devoted his life to studying natural forces, such as wind and rain, and how they affected the landscape in Scotland. Hutton inferred from his observations that these forces changed Earth's surface in the past just as they do in the present. Wind and rain created erosion, which provided the raw materials—sand, rock, and soil—for the formation of new land surfaces. Over time, these surfaces became stacked one on top of the other, forming layers, or strata, of geologic deposits (**Figure 2.5**). From the (very long) time it took for these strata to build up, he calculated Earth's age in the millions of years. This was a revolutionary, indeed heretical, realization.

Hutton's idea—that the natural processes operating today are the same as the natural processes that operated in the past—is called **uniformitarianism.** Few paid much attention to Hutton's important contribution to our understanding of Earth's history until the rediscovery of the idea by the Scottish geologist Charles Lyell (1797–1875; **Figure 2.6**). Lyell devoted considerable energy to thinking and writing about uniformitarianism and its implications for explaining the history of our planet. His calculations of how long it would have taken for all known strata to build up created a mountain of evidence, an undeniable record, that Earth was millions of years old. Hutton and Lyell, relying on empirical evidence and personal observation to develop their ideas and to test clear hypotheses about the natural world, had revised the timescale for the study of past life.

Paleontology: Reconstructing the History of Life on Earth

For hundreds of years, people have been finding the preserved—that is, fossilized—remains of organisms all over the world (see also the full discussion of fossils in chapter 8). To test his hypothesis that fossils are the remains of past life, the English scientist Robert Hooke (1635–1703) studied the microscopic structure of fossil wood. After observing that the tissue structure of the fossil wood was identical to the tissue structure of living trees, Hooke concluded that the fossil wood derived from once-living trees (**Figure 2.7**).

The potential of fossils to illuminate the past was demonstrated by the French naturalist and zoologist Georges Cuvier (1769–1832). Cuvier dedicated himself to learning the anatomy, or structural makeup, of many kinds of animals (**Figure 2.8**). Pioneering what we now call paleontology and comparative anatomy, he applied his extensive knowledge of comparative anatomy to fossils. By doing so, he reconstructed the physical characteristics of past animals—their appearance, physiology, and behavior.

FIGURE 2.5

Geologic Strata The succession of strata from oldest at the bottom to youngest at the top (as here, in Utah's Bryce Canyon) marks the formation of new land surfaces over time.

uniformitarianism The theory that processes that occurred in the geologic past are still at work today.

FIGURE 2.6

Charles Lyell Lyell (here depicted ca. 1845) rediscovered Hutton's work and the idea of uniformitarianism. Lyell's research, based on examinations of geologic strata, confirmed Hutton's estimate of Earth's very old age.

FIGURE 2.7

Robert Hooke **(a)** Hooke did pioneering biological research using a very simple microscope. He was the first to identify cells; in fact, he coined the term *cell*. **(b)** This illustration of cork wood cells appeared in Hooke's *Micrographia* (1667), the first major book on microscopy. His examinations of cells like this enabled Hooke to determine that fossils represented past life-forms.

(a)   **(b)**

Although not very accurate by today's standards, these efforts provided early tools for understanding past life-forms as once-living organisms. Through detailed reconstructions, Cuvier demonstrated that fossils found in geologic strata in France were the remains of animals that had gone extinct at some point in the remote past. Cuvier's work provided the first basic understanding of the history of life, from the earliest forms to recent ones.

Cuvier observed that each stratum seemed to contain a unique set of fossils. What happened to the animals represented by each set, each layer? Cuvier concluded that they must have gone extinct due to some powerful catastrophe, such as an earthquake

FIGURE 2.8

Georges Cuvier **(a)** One of Cuvier's most important contributions to science was the concept of extinction. Here, Cuvier is depicted examining a fish fossil. **(b)** In his 1796 paper on fossil and living elephants, Cuvier suggested that mammoth remains—such as those shown here, from one of his many publications— represented a species different from any living elephant species, and, therefore, mammoth remains were from a species that had gone extinct. This idea was revolutionary because the common perception was that God had created all species, none of which had ever gone extinct.

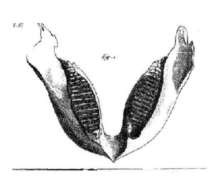

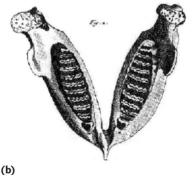

(a)   **(b)**

or a volcanic eruption. He surmised that after each catastrophe, the region was vacant of all life and was subsequently repopulated by a different group of animals moving into it from elsewhere. This perspective is called **catastrophism**.

We now know that Earth's history does not consist of sequential catastrophes and resulting extinctions. Past catastrophes, such as the extinction of the dinosaurs at around 65 mya, have profoundly affected the direction of evolution, but they were not the leading factor in evolution.

However, such events are rare and do not explain even the sequence of fossils Cuvier observed, mostly in the region called the Paris Basin. In addition to confirming that fossils were the remains of life in the distant past, Cuvier revealed that the most recent geologic strata contain mostly mammals and earlier geologic strata contain mostly reptiles, including the dinosaurs.

Taxonomy and Systematics: Classifying Living Organisms and Identifying Their Biological Relationships

In the pre-Darwinian world, most scientists who studied life-forms realized the importance of developing a taxonomy—a classification of life-forms—for identifying biological relationships. Early efforts at taxonomy took a commonsense approach. Animals were placed within major groups such as dogs, cats, horses, cattle, and people. Plants were placed within major groups such as trees, shrubs, vines, and weeds.

As late as the seventeenth century, scientists generally believed that species were immutable. In their view, life had changed very little, or not at all, since the time of the single Creation. Thus, early taxonomists were not motivated by an interest in evolution. Rather, they were motivated by their desire to present the fullest and most accurate picture of the Creator's intentions for His newly created world. To construct the best possible taxonomy, the English naturalist John Ray (1627–1705) advocated personal observation, careful description, and consideration of plants' and animals' many attributes. Ray's attention to detail laid the groundwork for later taxonomy, especially for the binomial nomenclature (two-name) system developed by the Swedish naturalist Carl von Linné (1707–1778). Von Linné, better known by his Latinized name, Carolus Linnaeus, gave each plant and animal a higher-level **genus** (plural, **genera**) name and a lower-level species (plural is also **species**) name (**Figure 2.9**). A single genus could include one or more species. For example, when Linnaeus named human beings *Homo sapiens*—*Homo* being the genus, *sapiens* being the species—he thought there were species and subspecies of living humans (an idea discussed further in chapter 5). The presence of more than one level in his taxonomy acknowledged different degrees of physical similarity. Today, we recognize that *sapiens* is the one living species in the genus *Homo*.

Linnaeus presented the first version of his taxonomy in his book *Systema Naturae* (1735), or *System of Nature.* As he revised the taxonomy—his book would eventually go through 10 editions—he added more and more levels to the hierarchy. He classified groups of genera into orders and groups of orders into classes. For example, he named one order "Primates"—the group of mammals that includes humans, apes, monkeys, and prosimians. Since the eighteenth century, this taxonomic system has evolved into multiple levels of classification, going from the subspecies at the bottom to the kingdom at the top (**Figure 2.10**).

Like Ray, Linnaeus was committed to the notion that life-forms were static, fixed at the time of the Creation. In later editions of his book, he hinted at the possibility that some species may be related to each other because of common descent, but he never developed these ideas. His taxonomy is still used today, although viewed with a much stronger sense of present and past variation. The system's flexibility aided evolutionary

FIGURE 2.9

Carolus Linnaeus Linnaeus, a botanist, zoologist, and physician, is known for his contributions to the system of classification used today by all biological scientists, including physical anthropologists. He is also a founder of modern ecology.

TAXONOMIC CATEGORY	TAXONOMIC LEVEL	COMMON CHARACTERISTICS
Kingdom	Animalia	Mobile multicellular organisms that consume other organisms for food and develop during an embryo stage.
Subkingdom	Eumetazoa	All major animals (except sponges) that contain true tissue layers, organized as germ layers, which develop into organs in humans.
Phylum	Chordata	Group of vertebrate and invertebrate animals that have a notochord, which becomes the vertebral column in humans and other primates.
Subphylum	Vertebrata	Animals with vertebral columns or backbones (including fish, amphibians, reptiles, birds, and mammals).
Superclass	Tetrapoda	Vertebrate animals with four feet or legs, including amphibians, birds, dinosaurs, and mammals.
Class	Mammalia	Group of warm-blooded vertebrate animals that produce milk for their young in mammary glands. They have hair or fur and specialized teeth.
Subclass	Theria	Group of mammals that produce live young without a shelled egg (including placental and marsupial mammals).
Order	Primates	Group of mammals specialized for life in the trees, with large brains, stereoscopic vision, opposable thumbs, and grasping hands and feet.
Suborder	Haplorhini	Group of primates, including monkeys, apes, humans, and tarsiers. They have in general long life cycles and are relatively large-bodied.
Infraorder	Anthropoidea	Group of haplorhines, including humans, apes, and monkeys.
Parvorder	Catarrhini	Group of anthropoids, including humans, apes, and Old World monkeys.
Superfamily	Hominoidea	Group of anthropoids, including humans, great apes, lesser apes, and humanlike ancestors. They have the largest bodies and brains of all primates.
Family	Hominidae	Great apes, humans, and humanlike ancestors.
Subfamily	Homininae	Chimpanzees, humans, and humanlike ancestors
Tribe	Hominini	Commonly called "hominins," this level includes humans and humanlike ancestors, all of which are obligate bipeds.
Genus	*Homo*	Group of hominins including modern humans, their direct ancestors, and extinct relatives (e.g., Neandertals). They have the largest brains in the Hominini.
Species	*sapiens*	Modern and ancestral modern humans. They have culture, use language, and inhabit every continent except Antarctica.
Subspecies	*sapiens*	Modern humans alone.

FIGURE 2.10

The Place of Humans in Linnaeus's Taxonomy Linnaeus's system organized living things into various levels of hierarchical classification. Kingdom, at the top of the taxonomy, is the largest classification. The five kingdoms of the natural world—animals, plants, fungi, protists, monera—include all living organisms. Through descending taxonomic levels, each group's size gets progressively smaller. For example, there are fewer organisms in a genus than there are in a phylum. Additionally, these classifications reflect the relationships of organisms to one another. For example, organisms within a genus are more closely related than are those from different genera.

biologists in their study of biological diversity, and the focus on taxonomic relationships over time is now called *systematics.*

Demography: Influences on Population Size and Competition for Limited Resources

After returning to England and while developing his ideas on natural selection, Darwin read the works of all the great scientists of the time. Probably the most important influence on his ideas was *An Essay on the Principle of Population,* by the English political economist Thomas Malthus (1766–1834). First published in 1798, Malthus's book made the case that an abundance of food—enough to feed anyone born—would allow the human population to increase geometrically and indefinitely. In reality, the *Essay* argued, there simply is not enough food for everyone born, so population is limited by food supply (**Figure 2.11**). Who survives to reproductive age? Those who can successfully compete for food. Whose children thrive? Those of survivors who manage to feed their offspring. Applying Malthus's demographic ideas to human and nonhuman animals, Darwin concluded that some members of any species successfully compete for food because they have some special attribute or attributes. That an individual characteristic could facilitate survival was a revelation!

Evolutionary Biology: Explaining the Transformation of Earlier Life-Forms into Later Life-Forms

By the late 1700s, a handful of scientists had begun to argue that, contrary to religious doctrine, organisms are not fixed—they change over time, sometimes in dramatic ways. Simply, life evolved in the past and evolution is an ongoing, undirected process. Building on this concept, the French naturalist Jean-Baptiste de Monet (1744–1829),

(a)

FIGURE 2.11

Thomas Malthus **(a)** Malthus, the founder of demography, theorized that population size was limited by food supply. **(b)** London's crowded conditions influenced Malthus's view that an insufficient food supply causes some people to fall into poverty, while others are able to acquire the resources they need to thrive.

(b)

better known by his title, Chevalier de Lamarck, speculated that plants and animals not only change in form over time but do so for purposes of self-improvement. Lamarck believed that in response to new demands or needs, life-forms develop new anatomical modifications, such as new organs. His central idea—that when life-forms reproduce, they pass on to their offspring the modifications they have acquired to that point—is called *Lamarckian inheritance of acquired characteristics,* or **Lamarckism** (**Figure 2.12**). We now know Lamarck's mechanism for evolution to be wrong—offspring do not inherit traits acquired by their parents—but his work was the first major attempt to develop a theory built on the premise that living organisms arose from precursor species. Lamarck was also convinced that humans evolved from some apelike animal.

Lamarckism First proposed by Lamarck, the theory of evolution through the inheritance of acquired characteristics in which an organism can pass on features acquired during its lifetime.

(a)

FIGURE 2.12

Jean-Baptiste Lamarck **(a)** Lamarck developed an early theory of evolution involving the inheritance of acquired characteristics. Although his mechanism of evolution was wrong, Lamarck's recognition of the dynamic nature of life in the past made an important contribution to the development of evolutionary theory. **(b)** According to the classic (though incorrect) example of Lamarckism, giraffes stretched to reach food at the tops of trees, their necks grew as a result, and they passed on these long necks to their offspring.

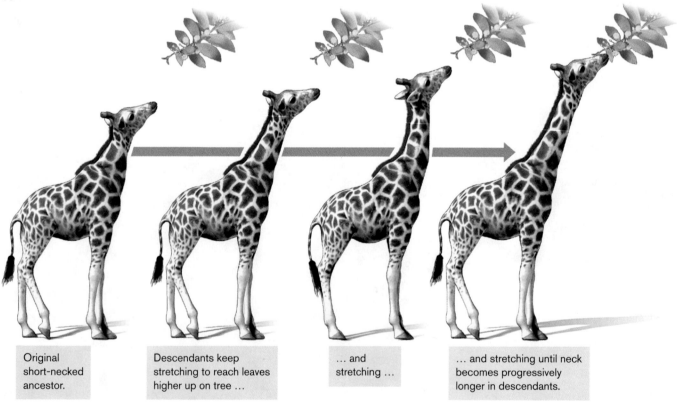

Original short-necked ancestor.

Descendants keep stretching to reach leaves higher up on tree …

… and stretching …

… and stretching until neck becomes progressively longer in descendants.

(b)

Darwin Borrows from Malthus

Five of Malthus's observations inspired Darwin's principle of natural selection.

Observation 1

For most organisms, every pair of parents produces multiple (sometimes many) offspring.

Observation 2

For most organisms, the population size remains the same. No increase occurs over time.

Observation 3

Population is limited by the food supply.

Observation 4

Members of populations compete for access to food.

Observation 5

No two members of a species are alike in their physical attributes—variation exists.

Theory: Evolution by Means of Natural Selection

Individuals having variation that is advantageous for survival to reproductive age produce more offspring (and more offspring that survive) than do individuals lacking this variation.

Among the other scholars who believed that life had changed over time was the English physician, naturalist, and poet Erasmus Darwin (1731–1802), grandfather of Charles Darwin. Like Lamarck, he hypothesized about the inheritance of characteristics acquired thanks to wants and needs; but he, too, was wrong about the mechanism for change.

2.2 The Theory of Evolution: Darwin's Contribution

Darwin's remarkable attention to detail enabled him to connect his voluminous reading with his personal observations from the *Beagle* voyage. For example, while in Chile, Darwin had observed firsthand the power of earthquakes in shaping the landscape. Hutton's and Lyell's uniformitarianism led him to recognize that the accumulation of such catastrophes over a long period of time explains, at least in part, the appearance of

CATASTROPHES

THEIR "IMPACT" ON EVOLUTION

Georges Cuvier believed that in the past, catastrophes had wiped out life on a regular basis. Extinction, he thought, explained why every geologic stratum had its own apparently unique assemblage of fossils. He also believed that catastrophes and extinctions had made it impossible for life-forms to change over time. In the post-Darwinian world, however, as the discovery of more and more geologic strata and fossils made clear that organisms had evolved, scientists came to believe that catastrophes do not affect evolution. Or do they affect it?

Paleontologists have long debated why the composition of plant and animal life changed so remarkably at about 65 mya, the end of the Mesozoic era and the beginning of the Cenozoic (see chapter 8 for a full discussion of geologic time). Why, for example, did the dinosaurs, which had existed for some 150 million to 200 million years, disappear within an eyeblink of geologic time? In 1980, the father–son physicist–geologist team of Luis Alvarez (1911–1988) and Walter Alvarez (b. 1940) proposed that some kind of major catastrophe took place at the time of the Cretaceous–Tertiary (K–T) boundary, wiping out most life-forms.[1] The small minority of scientists who accepted the Alvarezes' hypothesis were labeled "Cuvier-style catastrophists," and their ideas were summarily dismissed. Little evidence supported the notion of a K–T catastrophe.

In 1991, geologists discovered an enormous crater made about 65 mya by the impact of a giant bolide (an extraterrestrial object such as a meteor, meteorite, or comet) centered at the present-day village of Chicxulub on the Yucatán Peninsula in southern

A giant crater in Mexico indicates that 65 mya, an enormous extraterrestrial object crashed on Earth. Did the impact produce a catastrophe at the Cretaceous–Tertiary (K–T) boundary?

IN THE PAST

Mexico. Evidence for the worldwide effect of this impact has convinced most geologists. Around the world, for example, geologic deposits dating to 65 mya include chemically altered rocks and iridium, an extraordinarily rare element found only in extraterrestrial objects. The crater's size indicates that the bolide was at least 10 km (6 mi) wide, large enough to have produced a sufficiently massive impact.

The Alvarezes hypothesized that the impact resulted in mass deaths around the globe. The giant tsunamis, or tidal waves, following the impact of such a large body slamming into Earth would have destroyed life along coastlines worldwide. In addition, an enormous dust cloud would have been created, enveloping Earth, shutting out sunlight, and greatly inhibiting photosynthesis. The cooling of the globe's surface would have essentially stopped the food chain, as massive extinctions brought about a lack of prey and vice versa.

NORTH AMERICA

Coastline at the end of the Cretaceous (65 mya)

0   300 mi

0   500 km

ATLANTIC OCEAN

GULF OF MEXICO

CUBA

Chicxulub crater

Yucatán Peninsula

PACIFIC OCEAN

SOUTH AMERICA

Once the dust had settled and the atmosphere had cleared, the stage would have been set for the appearance and evolution of new kinds of plants and animals—thousands of them. In fact, paleontologists have shown that mammals, which had existed before as a very minor part of the animal world, diversified around the world in this (theoretically) new environment. Primates were among the mammals that proliferated.

Catastrophes do not determine the larger body of evolutionary change. However, events such as the giant bolide impact 65 mya represent part of the unpredictability and bad luck that contribute to evolution. Cuvier was not all wrong—catastrophes have played a role in the history of life on Earth.

[1] The Cretaceous–Tertiary boundary is about 66 mya, marking a fundamental shift in many kinds of plants and animals. It is referred to as the K–T boundary, K being the traditional abbreviation for "Cretaceous."

Today, as this map shows, the crater is partly underwater; 65 mya, however, the coastline was much farther from the impact site. The site was identified by Alan R. Hildebrand, a graduate student studying geologic formations of the Cretaceous–Tertiary (K–T) period.

Pre-Darwinian Theory and Ideas: Groundwork for Evolution

Charles Darwin first presented his theory of evolution in his book *On the Origin of Species* (1859). Based on years of personal observation and of study, this unifying biological theory drew on geology, paleontology, taxonomy and systematics, and demography.

Scientist	Contribution (and Year of Publication)	Significance
James Hutton	Calculated Earth's age as millions of years (1788)	Provided geologic evidence necessary for calculating time span of evolution
Charles Lyell	Rediscovered and reinforced Hutton's ideas (1830)	Provided more geologic evidence
Robert Hooke	Proved that fossils are organisms' remains (1665)	Revealed that fossils would provide the history of past life
Georges Cuvier	Extensively studied fossils (1796)	Revealed much variation in the fossil record
John Ray	Pioneered taxonomy based on physical appearance (1660)	Created the first scientific classification of plants and animals
Carolus Linnaeus	Wrote *Systems of Nature* (1735)	Presented the binomial nomenclature taxonomy of plants and animals
Thomas Malthus	Founded demography: only some will find enough food to survive (1798)	Provided the concept of characteristics advantageous for survival
Jean-Baptiste de Lamarck	Posited characteristics acquired via inheritance (Lamarckism) (1809)	Provided the first serious model of physical traits passing from parents to offspring
Erasmus Darwin	Also posited characteristics (determined by wants and needs) acquired via inheritance (1794)	Advanced the notion that physical changes occurred in the past

the present-day landscape. This understanding of Earth's remarkably dynamic geologic history laid the groundwork for Darwin's view of evolution as a long, gradual process.

That process, he saw, could be reconstructed through the fossil record. He had read carefully Cuvier's studies of fossils, and in South America he saw fossils firsthand. Some of these fossils resembled living animals native to South America, such as the armadillo, ground sloth, and llama. This evidence strongly suggested that an earlier species had transformed into the modern species, most likely through a succession of species over time. Drawing on Malthus's ideas about reproduction, population, and variation, Darwin wrote, "it at once struck me that under these circumstances [that is, specific environmental conditions] favorable variations would tend to be preserved and unfavorable ones to be destroyed. The result of this would be the formation of new species." Another revelation.

Darwin hypothesized that surviving offspring had attributes advantageous for acquiring food. Because these offspring survived, the frequency of their advantageous characteristics increased over time. Meanwhile, as environmental conditions

(a)

(b)

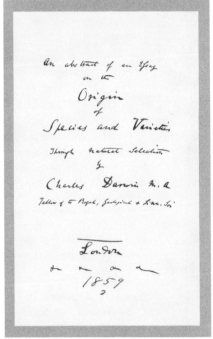

(c)

FIGURE 2.13

Writing a Masterpiece **(a)** Darwin wrote most of *On the Origin of Species* at his beloved home, Down House, in Kent, England. **(b)** He generally worked in his study there. **(c)** The title page of the manuscript, written in Darwin's own hand, reads "An Abstract of an Essay on the Origin of Species and Varieties through Natural Selection, by Charles Darwin, Fellow of the Royal, Geographical, and Linnean Soc., London, 1859."

changed—such as when rainfall decreased—offspring lacking adaptive attributes suited to their survival in the new environment died off. Building on these observations and their implications, Darwin deduced that natural selection was the primary mechanism of evolution. Over a long period of time, through generations' adaptation to different environments and different foods, a common ancestor gave rise to related species. Darwin's hypothesis was revolutionary, undermining the mid-nineteenth-century consensus that species were fixed types in a defined natural order of life. Now, species would have to be considered as populations with no predetermined limit on variation.

Darwin's background research had begun in the 1830s. It was not until 1856, however—fully two decades after his voyage around the world—that Darwin had gathered enough evidence and developed his ideas enough to begin writing his great work about evolution by means of natural selection, *On the Origin of Species* (**Figure 2.13**). His colleagues had warned him that if he did not write his book soon, someone else might receive credit for the idea. Indeed, in 1858, Darwin received from the English naturalist and explorer Alfred Russel Wallace (1823–1913) a letter and a 20-page report outlining Wallace's theory of evolution by means of natural selection (**Figure 2.14**). Independently from Darwin, Wallace had arrived at most of the same conclusions that Darwin had. Both men had been aware of their shared interest in the subject, and both men formulated their theories independently. Concerned that Wallace would publish first, Darwin completed *Origin* over the next 15 months and published it in London in 1859. Who, then, "discovered" natural selection, the key mechanism that explains evolution? Some argue that Wallace should be given primary credit for the theory; however, because Wallace had not amassed the extensive body of evidence needed to support the theory, Darwin is generally recognized as the discoverer (**Figure 2.15**).

Darwin and Wallace made monumental discoveries, but neither man could come up with a compelling explanation of the physical mechanisms by which evolution takes place. That is, what mechanisms result in evolutionary change? Half a continent away, a series of novel experiments led to the discovery of these biological mechanisms, paving the way for remarkable new insights into evolution.

FIGURE 2.14

Alfred Russel Wallace Although Darwin often gets sole credit for the development of the theory of evolution through natural selection, Wallace (here depicted ca. 1860) contributed substantially to evolutionary theory. Wallace was the leading authority on the geographic distribution of animals, for example, and was the first to recognize the concept of warning coloration in animals. In addition, he raised the issue of human impact on the environment a full century before it became a concern for the general public.

2.15

Timeline:
DARWIN'S THEORY OF EVOLUTION

Darwin's theory did not arise out of a vacuum. It arose from Darwin's experiences, the people he knew and respected, his interests in living plants and animals, and his dogged commitment to tracking down answers to questions about the natural world we live in.

3 | **DARWIN SEES THE WORLD, 1831–36**

As the *Beagle* made landfall at the rainforests, deserts, and mountains of South America, Darwin recorded detailed observations. He read the geology pioneer Charles Lyell's book *Principles of Geology* and became taken with Lyell's ideas about uniformitarianism, that the Earth is very old and that landmasses are constantly changing, rising, and falling.

SKELETON OF THE MEGATHERIUM. Page 106.

A prodigious collector, Darwin shipped back to England thousands of shells, bones, fossils, animal skins, and preserved plants. On the coast of Argentina, he excavated a fossil bed of megafauna, including the remains of an extinct giant sloth, noting the strong similarity between the fossils and living forms. On the Galápagos Islands, he saw tortoises, lizards, and mockingbirds (now known as Darwin's finches).

In organizing his notes, during the voyage home, he wrote that the variation in birds represented varieties of the same general kind of bird and concluded that species are not stable.

1 | **DARWIN GROWS UP, 1809–25**

Darwin belonged to a wealthy, cultured family and was raised to respect hard work and education. As a boy, he loved to walk through the countryside around his home in rural England, to think, and to speculate about the natural world around him. During these years, he began to study the variation of plants and animals.

2 | **DARWIN GOES TO COLLEGE, 1825–31**

While attending medical school at the University of Edinburgh, Darwin was drawn to natural history and became interested in marine invertebrates. He learned about Jean-Baptiste Lamarck's hypothesis that species change over time. A lecture by the American painter and ornithologist John James Audubon encouraged his interest in birds and wildlife. He left the University of Edinburgh for Cambridge University, where he continued to pursue natural history.

While collecting natural specimens on his own, Darwin studied with the English geology, archaeology, and botany pioneer John Stevens Henslow. Henslow introduced Darwin to the English geology pioneer Adam Sedgwick, who took him on a field trip to learn survey techniques. Henslow recommended that Darwin read the German pioneer naturalist Alexander von Humboldt's book on explorations in South America. In fact, Henslow was so impressed with Darwin's intellectual and personal abilities that he recommended him to serve as naturalist aboard HMS *Beagle*. Darwin enthusiastically accepted the position.

4 DARWIN RETURNS HOME AND DEVELOPS HIS IDEAS, 1837–55

In 1837, Darwin wrote that all forms of life had "transmuted" from a single life-form. He noted that fossils represent animals previous to living descendants, that some of the past forms went extinct, and that species evolve rather than being created. In 1838, Darwin read the work of the pioneer demographer and economist Thomas Malthus, who argued that the human population was too large to be supported by current resources. Darwin thought that, in the same way, weak plants and animals died off. Those with some kind of advantage—biological characteristics best suited for a particular setting—survived and produced offspring.

Realizing that his ideas would be challenged, Darwin decided not to publish them during his lifetime. To Lyell, the eminent geographical botanist Joseph Dalton Hooker, and the eminent biologist Thomas Henry Huxley, he showed a 230-page essay stating the ideas behind and some of the evidence for natural selection in particular and evolution in general. Darwin spent the next 15 years in his beloved rural home, Down House, preparing a major treatise on evolution. He studied barnacles and seed dispersions. He bred pigeons and studied the variations in their bones over generations.

5 DARWIN INTRODUCES HIS IDEAS TO THE WORLD, 1855–59

Alfred Russel Wallace had heard of Darwin and, having also read Malthus, drew the same conclusion about the driving force of natural selection and the mutability of species. Wallace's scientific paper "On the law which has regulated the introduction of new species" suggested that he might "scoop" Darwin, who was encouraged by colleagues to finish a big book that would present all his findings and theories. In 1858, Darwin and Wallace presented brief papers to the Linnean Society of London and published them later that year. Darwin abandoned his plan to finish the big book. Instead, he published a shorter version, *On the Origin of Species by Means of Natural Selection*. The book sold out immediately, beginning the modern era of biology and its affiliated sciences, including what would later become known as physical anthropology.

6 DARWIN'S LATER LIFE AND HIS IMPACT, 1859–82

For the next two decades, Darwin continued to gather data to support his theory. With a few exceptions, his ideas were accepted widely by the scientific community and viewed as fundamental to understanding the natural world. As a result, scientists came to see evolution as the source of life. The idea that all life, including humans and other primates, is related by descent provided the basis for some of the most important scientific discoveries and applications over the next century and a half. Later scientists' discoveries of the fossil record and, subsequently, the DNA revolution confirmed and expanded this remarkably powerful theory, which explains life and the world around us.

2.3 Since Darwin: Mechanisms of Inheritance, the Evolutionary Synthesis, and the Discovery of DNA

Mechanisms of Inheritance

Having articulated and supported his theory of evolution by means of natural selection, Darwin turned to the next fundamental question about natural selection: How do the traits that are being selected for (or against) pass from parent to offspring? Like other scientists of his day, Darwin believed that each body part contained invisible particles called **gemmules.** Darwin hypothesized that representative gemmules for all body parts resided in the reproductive organs. During fertilization, each parent contributed his or her gemmules to the potential offspring. The father's and the mother's gemmules then intermingled to form the characteristics observed in their progeny. Called **blending inheritance,** this process was a popular notion at the time.

Unknown to Darwin, research elsewhere in Europe was calling into question the idea of blending inheritance. In 1865, just six years after the publication of *On the Origin of Species,* Gregor Mendel (1822–1884), an Augustinian monk living in a monastery in what is now Brno, Czech Republic, published in an obscure local scientific journal the results of his work on inheritance (**Figure 2.16**). Mendel had spent the previous eight years crossbreeding different varieties of garden pea plants. Over the course of his experiments, he grew some 28,000 plants. These plants enabled him to identify and carefully observe seven characteristics, or traits, that were especially informative about breeding and its outcome over generations (**Figure 2.17**). From his results, Mendel inferred that a *discrete* physical unit was responsible for each characteristic. This unit passed from parent to offspring, and in this way the characteristic was inherited. In fact, the discrete unit could be traced through generations, and its passage (the inheritance) was determined by mathematical laws.

Mendel also discovered that the garden peas' traits did not blend. For example, plants and their offspring were either tall or short. Over time, the short plants diminished in frequency and eventually disappeared. Later scientists determined that the physical unit of inheritance—now known as a gene—has two subunits, one from the father and one from the mother, each called an **allele.** Each allele is either **dominant** or **recessive.** In garden peas, the allele for tallness is dominant and the allele for shortness is recessive. If one parent provides a "tall" allele (T) and the other parent provides a "short" allele (t), then the offspring having one of each allele (Tt) would be tall because of the presence of the "tall" allele—the dominant allele is physically expressed, whereas the recessive allele is hidden. The pure strain for tall (TT) includes one tall maternal allele (T) and one tall paternal allele (T). The pure strain for short (tt) includes one short maternal allele (t) and one short paternal allele (t) (**Figure 2.18**).

While Darwin's theory generated immediate excitement in the scientific community and among the public and was supported by leading scientists of the time such as Thomas Henry Huxley (**Figure 2.19**), Mendel's crucial discovery (now known as **Mendelian inheritance**) went unnoticed. His writing was not widely distributed, and his work was simply ahead of its time. But in 1900, three scientists working independently—the German botanist Carl Erich Correns (1864–1933), the Austrian botanist Erich Tschermak von Seysenegg (1871–1962), and the Dutch botanist Hugo de Vries (1848–1935)—discovered Mendel's research and replicated his findings. The

gemmules As proposed by Darwin, the units of inheritance, supposedly accumulated in the gametes so they could be passed on to offspring.

blending inheritance An outdated, disreputed theory that the phenotype of an offspring was a uniform blend of the parents' phenotypes.

allele One or more alternative forms of a gene.

dominant Refers to an allele that is expressed in an organism's phenotype and that simultaneously masks the effects of another allele, if another one is present.

recessive An allele that is expressed in an organism's phenotype if two copies are present but is masked if the dominant allele is present.

Mendelian inheritance The basic principles associated with the transmission of genetic material, forming the basis of genetics, including the law of segregation and the law of independent assortment.

FIGURE 2.16

Gregor Mendel Mendel, the father of modern genetics, was a Christian monk by profession but a scientist by nature. His observations provided the foundation for our understanding of genetics (the subject of chapters 3 and 4).

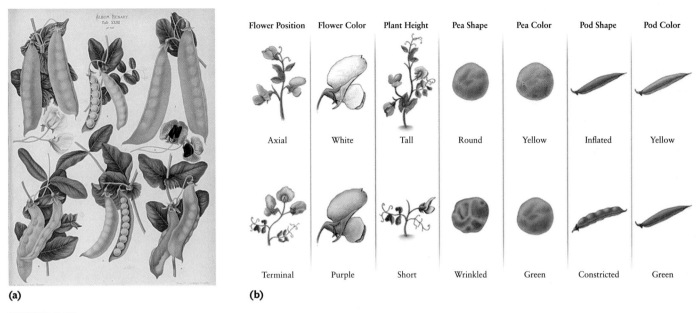

FIGURE 2.17

Mendel's Peas **(a)** This illustration—from the 1876 catalog of one of Mendel's seed suppliers—shows **(b)** the seven characteristics Mendel studied, each of which had two variants. Flower position, for example, could be axial or terminal, while flower color could be white or purple.

Danish botanist Wilhelm Ludvig Johannsen (1857–1927) called the pair of alleles (for example, *TT, Tt, tt*) the **genotype** and the actual physical appearance (tall, short) the **phenotype**.

Mendel's theory of inheritance forms the basis of the modern discipline of genetics (the subject of chapters 3 and 4). It makes clear that the physical units—the genes and the two component alleles of each gene—responsible for physical attributes are located in the reproductive cells: eggs and sperm. When microscope technology improved in the late nineteenth century, the cell structure and the units of inheritance were defined (see chapter 3).

Beginning in 1908, the American geneticist Thomas Hunt Morgan (1866–1945) and his associates bred the common fruit fly in experiments that built on Mendel's pea breeding. All genes, they discovered, are transmitted from parents to offspring in the ratios identified by Mendel. The genes are on **chromosomes,** and both the hereditary material and its carriers are duplicated during reproductive cell division (**Figure 2.20**).

The Evolutionary Synthesis, the Study of Populations, and the Causes of Evolution

The combination of Darwin's theory of evolution and Mendel's theory of heredity resulted in an **evolutionary synthesis.** Darwin's theory provided the mechanism for one cause of evolution (natural selection), and Mendel's theory showed how traits are passed on systematically and predictably (Mendelian inheritance). The melding of natural selection and Mendelian inheritance led biologists to ask further questions about evolution, specifically about the origins of particular genes, genetic variation in general, and change in physical characteristics over time. *Why* do some genes increase in frequency, some decrease in frequency, and some show no change? *How* do completely new genes appear? These questions and a focus on population—viewed as the

genotype The genetic makeup of an organism; the combination of alleles for a given gene.

phenotype The physical expression of the genotype; it may be influenced by the environment.

chromosomes The strand of DNA found in the nucleus of eukaryotes that contains hundreds or thousands of genes.

evolutionary synthesis A unified theory of evolution that combines genetics with natural selection.

population genetics A specialty within the field of genetics; it focuses on the changes in gene frequencies and the effects of those changes on adaptation and evolution.

mutation A random change in a gene or chromosome, creating a new trait that may be advantageous, deleterious, or neutral in its effects on the organism.

gene flow Admixture, or the exchange of alleles between two populations.

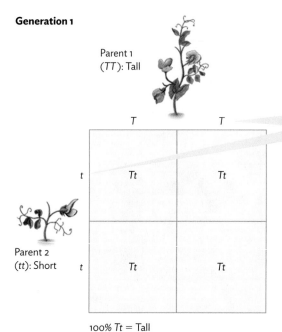

Generation 1

Parent 1 (*TT*): Tall

Parent 2 (*tt*): Short

100% *Tt* = Tall

If the tallness allele is expressed as *T* and the shortness allele is expressed as *t*, the pure strain for tall is *TT* (one *T* is the maternal allele, the other *T* is the paternal allele), and the pure strain for short is *tt* (one *t* is the maternal allele, and the other *t* is the paternal allele).

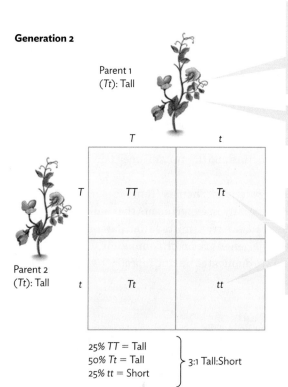

Generation 2

Parent 1 (*Tt*): Tall

Parent 2 (*Tt*): Tall

25% *TT* = Tall
50% *Tt* = Tall
25% *tt* = Short
} 3:1 Tall:Short

When a *Tt* plant is crossbred with a *Tt* plant, one allele must come from the father (paternal) and one allele (maternal) must come from the mother, thereby producing a *Tt* offspring.

Because *T* is dominant, the offspring is tall.

When the offspring from two *Tt* parental plants are bred, the offspring's alleles independently redistribute, producing about equal numbers of the four possible combinations of *T* and *t* alleles: *TT, Tt, tT,* and *tt*.

Thus, three of the four plants (75%) will be tall owing to the dominance of the *T* allele and one plant (25%) will be short owing to the recessiveness of the *t* allele. Note, however, that 25% of the offspring are tall with two dominant tall alleles (*TT*), while 50% are tall with one of each allele (*Tt*).

FIGURE 2.18
Mendel's Genetics

gene pool—provided the basis for a newly emerging field in evolutionary biology called **population genetics** (among the subjects of chapter 4).

Natural selection, the guiding force of evolution, could operate only on variation that already existed in a population. How did new variation—new characteristics—arise in a population? Through his experiments with fruit flies, Morgan showed that a new gene could appear as a result of spontaneous change in an existing gene. This kind of genetic change is called **mutation** (**Figure 2.21**). The only source of new genetic material, mutation is a second cause of evolution.

Gene flow, a third cause of evolution, is the diffusion, or spread, of new genetic material from one population to another of the same species. In other words, via reproduction, genes from one gene pool are transferred to another gene pool. Take, for example, the gene that causes sickle-cell anemia (this disorder is discussed extensively in chapter 4). Among West African blacks, it has a frequency of about 10%. Among American whites, it has a frequency of 0%. Because West African blacks and their descendants have long reproduced with American whites, the frequency among people descended from both West African blacks and American whites of the gene that causes sickle-cell anemia is approximately 5%, halfway between that of the two original populations. Over time, as the two populations have mixed, gene flow has decreased genetic difference.

Genetic drift, a fourth cause of evolution, is random change in the frequency of alleles; that is, of the different forms of a gene. Such change affects a small population more powerfully than it affects a large population (**Figure 2.22**). Over time, it increases the genetic difference between two genetically related but not interbreeding populations.

By the mid-twentieth century, the four causes of evolution—natural selection, mutation, gene flow, and genetic drift—were well defined, thanks to a synthesis of ideas drawn from the full range of sciences that deal with biological variation. In effect, evolutionary

FIGURE 2.19

Thomas Henry Huxley Huxley (1825–1895), an English biologist, was known as "Darwin's bulldog" because he so forcefully promoted Darwin's theory of evolution by natural selection. Among Huxley's contributions to evolutionary theory was the concept that humans evolved from an apelike animal.

genetic drift The random change in allele frequency from one generation to the next, with greater effect in small populations.

(a) (b)

FIGURE 2.20

Thomas Hunt Morgan **(a)** In 1933, Morgan was awarded the Nobel Prize in Physiology or Medicine, largely for demonstrating that chromosomes carry genetic material in the form of genes. **(b)** A micrograph shows chromosomes of Morgan's research subject, the common fruit fly (*Drosophila melanogaster*).

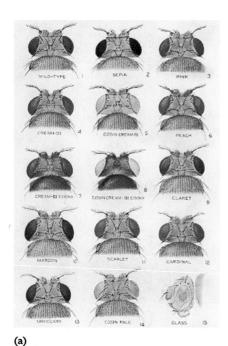

(a)

(b)

(c)

FIGURE 2.21

Fruit Fly Mutations **(a)** Thomas Hunt Morgan's research on fruit flies focused on a variety of mutations, including eye color. This image shows the normal, or wild-type, eye color as well as several possible mutations. Morgan first observed mutation when a white-eyed offspring appeared within a strain of red-eyed flies. **(b)** The normal fruit fly has two wings, while **(c)** the four-wing mutation has two wings on each side.

synthesis unified the branches of biology and its affiliated sciences, including genetics, taxonomy, morphology, comparative anatomy, paleontology, and the subject of this book, physical anthropology. Similarly, evolution unites living and past worlds. All organisms are related through common descent, and organisms more closely related than others share a more recent common ancestor.

DNA: Discovery of the Molecular Basis of Evolution

Once chromosomes were recognized as the carriers of genes, scientists sought to understand the structure of **deoxyribonucleic acid (DNA),** the chemical that makes up chromosomes. In 1953, the American geneticist James Watson (b. 1928) and the British biophysicist Francis Crick (1916–2004) published their discovery that DNA molecules have a ladderlike, double-helix structure. Crucial to their discovery was the work of the British X-ray crystallographer Rosalind Franklin (1920–1958), who used a special technique, X-ray diffraction, to produce high-quality images of DNA. The combined efforts of Franklin, Watson, and Crick opened up a whole new vista for biology by helping explain how chromosomes are replicated (**Figure 2.23**).

Analysis of the DNA from a wide variety of organisms, including primates, has provided both new perspectives on biological relationships and a molecular "clock" with which to time the branches of evolution (based on the similarity of species within those branches). In addition, DNA analysis has begun to shed light on a growing list of illnesses such as viral and bacterial infections, cancer, heart disease, and stroke (**Figure 2.24**).

Little did Darwin realize just what a powerful foundation his evolutionary theory would build for science, ushering in modern biology and its allied disciplines, including physical anthropology. Long after his death, Darwin's search for the biological mechanisms involved in evolution would continue to inspire scientists. The questions Darwin and his colleagues asked, especially about how physical attributes

deoxyribonucleic acid (DNA) A double-stranded molecule that provides the genetic code for an organism, consisting of phosphate, deoxyribose sugar, and four types of nitrogen bases.

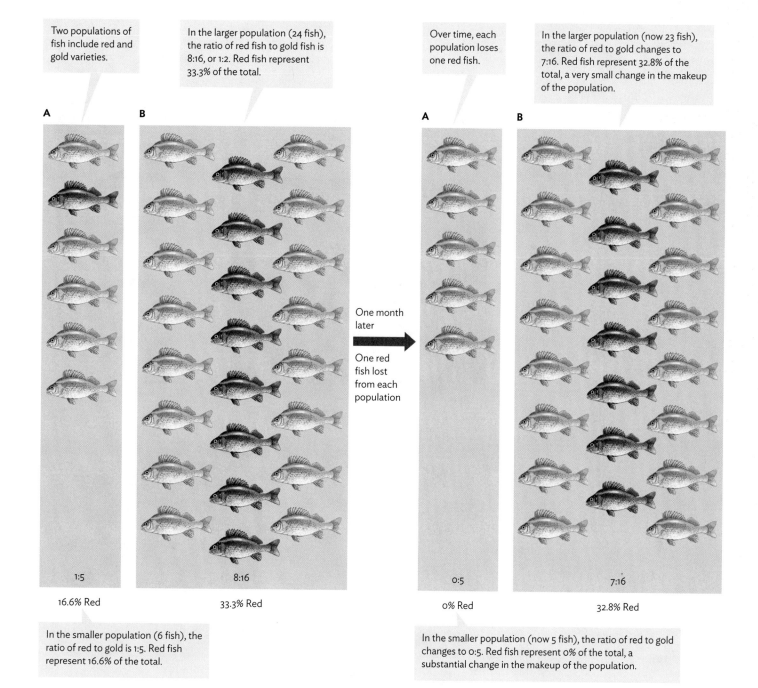

Two populations of fish include red and gold varieties.

In the larger population (24 fish), the ratio of red fish to gold fish is 8:16, or 1:2. Red fish represent 33.3% of the total.

Over time, each population loses one red fish.

In the larger population (now 23 fish), the ratio of red to gold changes to 7:16. Red fish represent 32.8% of the total, a very small change in the makeup of the population.

A B   A B

One month later

One red fish lost from each population

1:5 8:16   0:5 7:16

16.6% Red 33.3% Red   0% Red 32.8% Red

In the smaller population (6 fish), the ratio of red to gold is 1:5. Red fish represent 16.6% of the total.

In the smaller population (now 5 fish), the ratio of red to gold changes to 0:5. Red fish represent 0% of the total, a substantial change in the makeup of the population.

FIGURE 2.22

Genetic Drift's Effects on Small and Large Populations

pass from parents to offspring, laid the foundation for the study of inheritance—the science of genetics—and eventually the DNA revolution. Darwin would have been impressed.

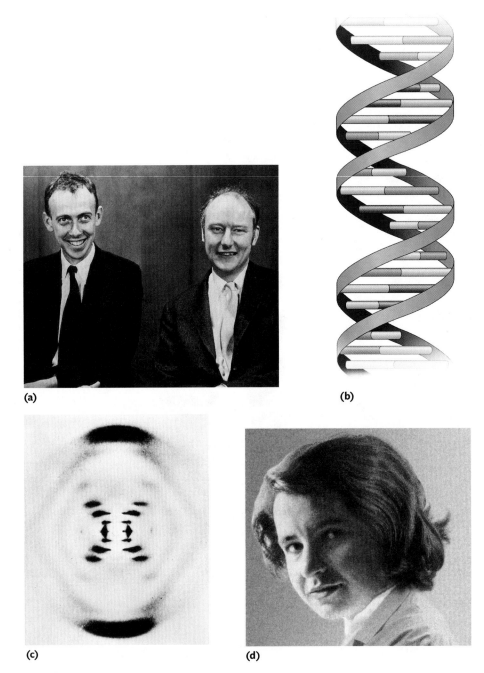

FIGURE 2.23

Discovery of DNA **(a)** In 1962, James Watson (left) and Francis Crick (right) were awarded a Nobel Prize for their 1953 discovery of **(b)** DNA's double-helix structure. **(c)** Watson and Crick had worked with X-ray diffraction photographs taken in 1953 by **(d)** Rosalind Franklin. Franklin's death in 1958 made her ineligible to receive the Nobel Prize with Watson and Crick because Nobels are not awarded posthumously.

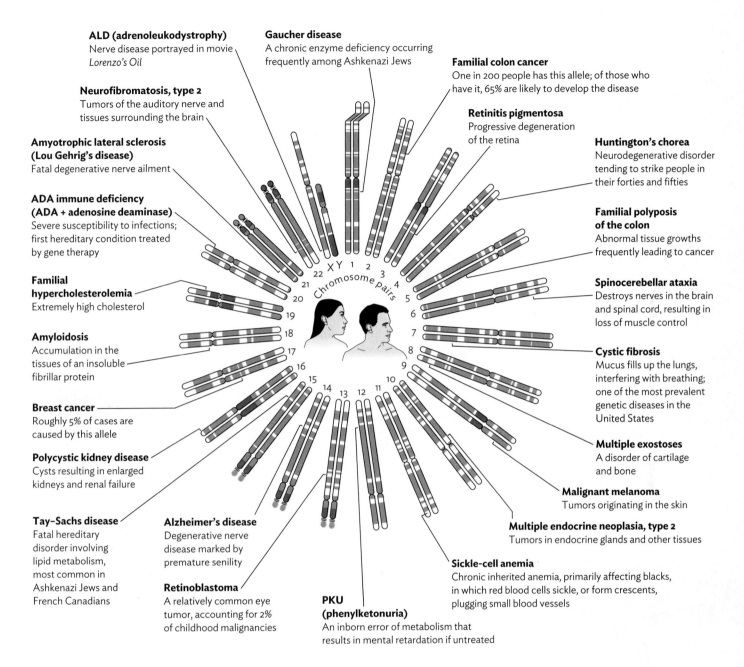

ALD (adrenoleukodystrophy)
Nerve disease portrayed in movie *Lorenzo's Oil*

Gaucher disease
A chronic enzyme deficiency occurring frequently among Ashkenazi Jews

Familial colon cancer
One in 200 people has this allele; of those who have it, 65% are likely to develop the disease

Neurofibromatosis, type 2
Tumors of the auditory nerve and tissues surrounding the brain

Retinitis pigmentosa
Progressive degeneration of the retina

Amyotrophic lateral sclerosis (Lou Gehrig's disease)
Fatal degenerative nerve ailment

Huntington's chorea
Neurodegenerative disorder tending to strike people in their forties and fifties

ADA immune deficiency (ADA + adenosine deaminase)
Severe susceptibility to infections; first hereditary condition treated by gene therapy

Familial polyposis of the colon
Abnormal tissue growths frequently leading to cancer

Familial hypercholesterolemia
Extremely high cholesterol

Spinocerebellar ataxia
Destroys nerves in the brain and spinal cord, resulting in loss of muscle control

Amyloidosis
Accumulation in the tissues of an insoluble fibrillar protein

Cystic fibrosis
Mucus fills up the lungs, interfering with breathing; one of the most prevalent genetic diseases in the United States

Breast cancer
Roughly 5% of cases are caused by this allele

Multiple exostoses
A disorder of cartilage and bone

Polycystic kidney disease
Cysts resulting in enlarged kidneys and renal failure

Malignant melanoma
Tumors originating in the skin

Tay–Sachs disease
Fatal hereditary disorder involving lipid metabolism, most common in Ashkenazi Jews and French Canadians

Multiple endocrine neoplasia, type 2
Tumors in endocrine glands and other tissues

Alzheimer's disease
Degenerative nerve disease marked by premature senility

Sickle-cell anemia
Chronic inherited anemia, primarily affecting blacks, in which red blood cells sickle, or form crescents, plugging small blood vessels

Retinoblastoma
A relatively common eye tumor, accounting for 2% of childhood malignancies

PKU (phenylketonuria)
An inborn error of metabolism that results in mental retardation if untreated

Chromosome pairs
22 X Y 1 2 3 4 5 6 7 8 9 10 11 12 13 14 15 16 17 18 19 20 21

FIGURE 2.24

DNA Chromosomes in Medical Research Researchers for the Human Genome Project, which works to identify all human genes, have identified the location of hundreds of genes that control or influence a variety of diseases and disorders. For example, cystic fibrosis is located on chromosome 7 of the human genome. The identification of gene location will facilitate early detection and treatment for many diseases.

EBOLA: THE EVOLU

WATCH
THE VIDEO

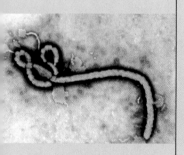

www.digital.
wwnorton.com/
ourorigins4

The Ebola virus has probably been around for a very long time, but it wasn't identified until 1976 near the Ebola River in the Democratic Republic of the Congo. Four of the five species of the virus cause Ebola disease in humans. All five species have caused the disease in other primates.

From the tiniest virus to the largest mammal, evolution is happening all around us, all the time. A great example is virus evolution. Virus evolution is due primarily to mutation, one of the four causes of evolution (see chapter 4). Viruses are amazing in their speed of evolution, adapting readily to their animal or human hosts.

Like the pathogens that cause a number of other infectious diseases affecting humans today—such as tuberculosis, rabies, infection by antibiotic-resistant "superbugs," AIDS, Lyme disease, and SARS—the Ebola virus (*Ebolavirus zaire ebolavirus*, or EBOV) originated in animals, then evolved in animal host populations, and then passed on to humans. Zoonosis—the transfer of pathogens from animals to humans—has been part of the story of evolution for millions of years. Ebola disease, however, is relatively new, with the first known outbreak occurring in humans in 1976 in Sudan and Zaire (present-day Democratic Republic of the Congo).

The 1976 Ebola outbreak was of considerable concern, largely owing to its very high fatality rate. Of the 600 or so people who contracted the disease, 71% who had hemorrhagic fever symptoms died. Since then, outbreaks of similar size continued off and on. But none of the outbreaks reached the severity of the 2014–2015 epidemic that swept through West Africa, especially in the countries of Guinea, Liberia, and Sierra Leone. The outbreak likely began as a zoonotic event, when the virus jumped from a bat to a two-year-old boy playing in and around roost tree of an infected bat. The boy died just four days after showing symptoms in December 2013. Within a month following his death, his sister, mother, and grandmother contracted the virus (probably due to the local practice of communally washing the corpse prior to burial) and died. By mid-2015, 27,560 cases

had been reported in the region, and there were 11,236 reported deaths.

Humans are not the only primates to suffer losses from Ebola. Based on censuses of gorilla and chimpanzee populations in protected and unprotected areas in West Africa, mortality rates due to Ebola reached staggering figures amounting to thousands of gorillas and chimpanzees. During the 2002–2003 epidemic alone, it is estimated that 5,000 gorillas—roughly half the study population—died in one study area alone. An estimate compiled for the Jane Goodall Institute indicated that in total, at least one-third of the chimpanzee and gorilla populations in West Africa were obliterated over the past few decades of disease peaks. Combined with illegal hunting and other factors such as habitat fragmentation and destruction in West Africa, the populations and social groups in various settings are now either fully wiped out or reduced to small remnant populations.

The mechanisms of genetic change in a virus are fundamental to the development of vaccines used to fight the disease it causes. And fortunately for humans, the genetics of the Ebola virus have been mapped and vaccines developed. For chimpanzees, however, it has been a different story. Due to the reclassification of captive chimpanzees as "endangered" by the U.S. Fish and Wildlife Service, it is not possible to do fundamental medical research on them, including development of vaccines that could potentially protect the members of their species now living in wild settings in Africa.

TION OF A CRISIS

The high death rate in humans, chimpanzees, and gorillas reveals an extraordinarily high **virulence** of the Ebola **pathogen**. Authorities speculate that the high virulence of the virus in the 2014–2015 outbreak may be due to the virus mutating faster than in previous outbreaks. The great fear was that if the virus was not contained in a timely manner, the disease would spread quickly into other parts of Africa and around the world, owing to its virulence. Indeed, it takes only one carrier traveling by plane from Africa to the United States to introduce the virus to North America. Fortunately, only four confirmed cases of Ebola were reported in the United States during the 2014–2015 outbreak. Although a frightening **epidemic** in Africa, Ebola did not turn into a **pandemic** due to a number of factors. With new technology and the ability to characterize the viral genome from victims, it was possible to map the progression and spread of the Ebola virus, showing how it moved from place to place, all within a period of weeks. In essential ways, evolution is at the core of understanding health threats from pathogens.

Disease in human society is not just about biology. Soon after the World Health Organization declared that the Ebola outbreak was a *Public Health Emergency of International Concern*, doctors, nurses, and other health-care workers went to West Africa to assist with the crisis. Medical anthropologists also arrived, bringing their expertise in health care and understanding of social context. For example, to slow the spread of the virus, state-enforced quarantines had been quickly established. American medical anthropologist Paul Farmer pointed out that while quarantine will slow the transmission of the disease, it also means that the quarantined communities would soon be without the supplies and services to treat the sick and dying. Indeed, the predicted depletion of medical supplies, food, and water occurred in the areas hardest hit by the crisis, likely contributing to at least some deaths. Most of the same communities included in the quarantines had long experienced the ill effects of colonial domination and state corruption, viewing Western health-care agencies as simply "more of the same" when it came to inequality and poor access to food, nutrition, and a healthy environment. Unfortunately, the effect of this is continued elevated mortality in some settings. It is this social context combined with the biology of disease that makes anthropology such a central discipline for understanding the broad picture of Ebola and other infectious diseases. *Anthropology matters!*

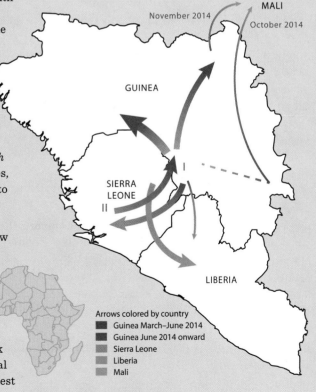

Arrows colored by country
- Guinea March–June 2014
- Guinea June 2014 onward
- Sierra Leone
- Liberia
- Mali

The spread of Ebola in 2014 was rapid and deadly. The map shows the location of the first outbreak in Sierra Leone (I), from which the disease spread throughout the country and to Guinea, Mali, and Liberia. Within a few months, evolution of the virus resulted in the appearance of a new lineage of Ebola (II), which spread into Liberia and throughout Guinea.

CHAPTER 2 REVIEW

ANSWERING THE BIG QUESTIONS

1. **How did the theory of evolution come to be?**

   - In developing his theory of evolution by means of natural selection, Darwin drew on geology, paleontology, taxonomy and systematics, demography, and what is now called evolutionary biology.
   - Scientists working in these disciplines had shown that
     —Earth is quite old and has changed considerably over time
     —fossils represent the remains of once-living, often extinct organisms and thus provide a record of the history of life
     —life evolves over time
     —groups of related species help clarify evolutionary history
     —the number of adults in a population tends to remain the same over time

2. **What was Darwin's contribution to the theory of evolution?**

   - Darwin's key contribution was the principle of natural selection. Three principles allowed him to deduce that natural selection is the primary driver of evolution:
     —the number of adults in a population tends to remain the same over time even though, for most organisms, parents tend to produce multiple and sometimes many offspring
     —variation exists among members of populations
     —individuals having variation that boosts survival and reproduction increase in relative frequency over time

3. **What has happened since Darwin in the development of our understanding of evolution?**

   - Gregor Mendel discovered the principles of inheritance, the basis for our understanding of how physical attributes are passed from parents to offspring.
   - Mendel's revelation that attributes are passed as discrete units, which we now know as genes, laid the groundwork for our understanding of cell biology and chromosomes, and eventually for the field of population genetics.
   - We now know that evolution—genetic change in a population or species—has one or more of four causes: natural selection, mutation, gene flow, and genetic drift.
   - We now know that each chromosome in an organism's cells consists of DNA molecules. DNA is the blueprint for all biological characteristics and functions.

KEY TERMS

adaptive radiation
allele
blending inheritance
catastrophism
chromosomes
demography
deoxyribonucleic acid (DNA)
dominant
endemic
epidemic
evolutionary biology
evolutionary synthesis
fossils
gemmules
gene flow
genetic drift
genotype
genus
geology
habitat
Lamarckism
Mendelian inheritance
mutation
natural selection
paleontology
pandemic
pathogen
phenotype
population genetics
recessive
species
systematics
taxonomy
uniformitarianism
virulence

STUDY QUIZ

1. **Which idea did *not* help Darwin form his theory of evolution?**

   a. Earth is very old, and its past organisms are preserved as fossils.
   b. Physically similar organisms tend to be closely related.
   c. Organisms compete for limited resources to survive to reproduce.
   d. Parents get new traits through their actions and pass them to offspring.

2. **Which observation supports the principle of natural selection?**

   a. Populations generally remain the same size over time.
   b. Individuals within a population vary in their physical traits.
   c. Trait variants that help organisms survive to reproduce become more common in a population over time.
   d. Whole populations are routinely wiped out by catastrophes.

3. **How would Lamarckism explain why the giraffe has a long neck?**

   a. A giraffe's neck grows as it stretches to reach food, and this trait is passed on to offspring.
   b. Giraffes with long necks survive to reproduce at higher rates.
   c. Giraffes have always had long necks because species do not change.
   d. All short-necked giraffes went extinct because of a natural disaster.

4. **Today we know that _____ pass on traits.**

   a. gemmules
   b. genes
   c. amino acids
   d. phenotypes

5. **The evolutionary synthesis combines natural selection with**

   a. genetics.
   b. paleontology.
   c. taxonomy.
   d. geology.

EVOLUTION REVIEW

PAST, PRESENT, AND FUTURE OF A FUNDAMENTAL SCIENTIFIC THEORY

Synopsis The theory of evolution forms the foundation of all the biological sciences, including physical anthropology. Although Charles Darwin is the most famous contributor to the formulation of this theory, his innovative idea of natural selection was partly influenced by the work of scientists across a number of disciplines, including geology, paleontology, taxonomy, and demography, and what is now called evolutionary biology. The work of Gregor Mendel, rediscovered years after his death, provided a genetic basis for the evolutionary processes envisioned by Darwin and showed how evolution can occur in the natural world. Darwin's principle of natural selection and Mendel's principles of inheritance are intertwined in the modern evolutionary synthesis, the framework by which physical anthropologists address research questions related to human biological evolution and biocultural variation.

Q1. Darwin's principle of natural selection laid the foundations for all future biological thinking and discoveries. However, other scientists before Darwin argued in favor of biological evolution. Who is credited with one of the first major attempts to explain the process of evolutionary change through time? What is the erroneous mechanism hypothesized by this scientist to be a driving force of evolution?

Q2. Before the discoveries of Gregor Mendel, Darwin hypothesized that the characteristics of the father and mother intermingled in the offspring. What was this idea called at the time? What discovery, first made by Mendel and later by scientists such as Thomas Hunt Morgan, proved this hypothesis to be wrong?

Q3. Darwin was inspired by the idea of the demographer Thomas Malthus that population is limited by food supply. How is this idea a concern for human populations today? What steps might be taken to address this issue in the future?

Q4. Darwin originally did not publish his theory of evolution by means of natural selection as he was well aware of the controversy it would generate. More than 150 years later, and backed by massive amounts of evidence spanning many scientific disciplines, evolution remains a subject of controversy among the general public. Why has evolution always been the subject of fierce debate?

Q5. Darwin gathered information from of geology, paleontology, taxonomy, demography, and evolutionary biology to develop his theory of evolution, which includes the ideas of variation and natural selection. What are the five most important ideas from these other fields (described in this chapter) that contributed to Darwin's development of his theory?

ADDITIONAL READINGS

Alvarez, W. 1997. *T. rex and the Crater of Doom.* Princeton, NJ: Princeton University Press.

Berra, T. M. 2009. *Charles Darwin: The Concise Story of an Extraordinary Man.* Baltimore: Johns Hopkins University Press.

Bowler, P. J. 2003. *Evolution: The History of an Idea.* Berkeley: University of California Press.

Carroll, S. B. 2009. *Remarkable Creatures: Epic Adventures in the Search for the Origins of Species.* Boston: Houghton Mifflin Harcourt.

Gould, S. J. 1992. *Ever since Darwin: Reflections on Natural History.* New York: Norton.

Huxley, R. 2007. *The Great Naturalists.* New York: Thames & Hudson.

Repcheck, J. 2003. *The Man Who Found Time: James Hutton and the Discovery of the Earth's Antiquity.* Cambridge, MA: Perseus Publishing.

Stott, R. 2012. *Darwin's Ghosts: The Secret History of Evolution.* New York: Spiegel & Grau.

Wilson, E. O. 2006. *From So Simple a Beginning: Darwin's Four Great Books [Voyage of the H.M.S. Beagle, The Origin of Species, The Descent of Man, The Expression of Emotions in Man and Animals].* New York: Norton.

On the surface, a human being and a chimpanzee might not seem to have much in common; however, they share 98% of their DNA. Chimpanzees are humans' closest living relatives, and both primates often have similar facial expressions, emotions, and body movements. In these and many other ways, these two primates share a considerable amount of biology.

3

Genetics
REPRODUCING LIFE AND PRODUCING VARIATION

BIG QUESTIONS

1. **What is the genetic code?**
2. **What does the genetic code (DNA) do?**
3. **What is the genetic basis for human variation?**

There is a revolution going on in science: the discovery of DNA and the identification of its molecular structure have brought about a "DNA revolution." At no time in history have humans learned so much so quickly about the biology of plants and animals. In addition to bringing about developments in agriculture and food production, medicine, and other areas that affect billions of people every day, the information derived from DNA has transformed a number of scientific disciplines. Consider forensic science, where fingerprints and blood types were once the primary evidence. Thanks to DNA, far smaller samples—of tissue, bone, hair, and blood—can be used to identify victims' remains and to identify criminals with far greater accuracy. DNA in samples saved from old crime scenes has helped free scores of individuals convicted of crimes they had not committed. Beyond forensics, DNA analysis has helped determine family relationships. It has helped genealogists reach into the past to chart ancestry. It has even been used to detect the presence of diseases, such as leprosy and syphilis, in ancient skeletons. Given the long and growing list of ways in which DNA can be used, no wonder former US president Bill Clinton referred to the human DNA sequence, right after it was presented to the public in 2003, as "the most important, most wondrous map ever produced by mankind."

When I studied introductory biology in college in the early 1970s, knowledge of DNA was just a tiny fraction of what it is today. Evolution was understood in terms of entire organisms and their biological history. Now, DNA provides us with the information—a whole new window—whereby we can *see* how organisms are put together and *what* is actually evolving. Powerful stuff! In anthropology, it has meant new insights into primate and human evolution. Before we can tie together the growing strands of DNA and evolution, though, we need to back up and examine the foundational work in genetics—the study of heredity.

Although the great nineteenth-century biologists discussed in chapter 2 knew a lot about variation in species, they did not fully understand how this variation is produced or how it is transmitted from parents to offspring. For example, how do an organism's attributes grow from a fertilized egg? The answers to questions about variation—its origin and continuation—lie in the cell, its structures, and the myriad functions it performs from conception through full maturity. And governing each cell is the genetic code.

3.1 The Cell: Its Role in Reproducing Life and Producing Variation

The cell is the basic unit of life for all organisms (**Figure 3.1**). Every organism has at least one cell (that is the baseline definition of an organism). Organisms having cells with no internal compartments are called **prokaryotes.** These were likely the first life on Earth, appearing about 3.5 billion years ago (bya). Today, the prokaryotes are

prokaryotes Single-celled organisms with no nuclear membranes or organelles and with their genetic material as a single strand in the cytoplasm.

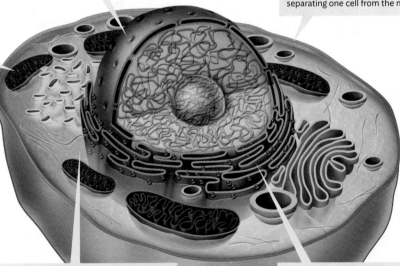

The *nucleus* is the largest organelle in a cell. It houses one copy of nearly all the genetic material, or DNA, of that organism. It is covered by a nuclear membrane, or nuclear envelope, which keeps the contents of the nucleus separate from the rest of the cell.

The *cell membrane* is a semipermeable membrane surrounding the entire cell, separating one cell from the next.

The *mitochondrion* is considered the "powerhouse" of the cell, because it generates most of the energy. The number of mitochondria per cell varies by tissue type and by organism.

The *cytoplasm* is fluid that fills the cell and maintains the cell's shape. Organelles are suspended in the cytoplasm, which can also store chemical substances. The extranuclear DNA is in the mitochondria.

The *endoplasmic reticulum* is an organelle that usually surrounds the nucleus. It plays an especially important role in protein synthesis (a process discussed later in this chapter).

FIGURE 3.1

Cells and Their Organelles This illustration depicts the many components of cells found in plants and animals. Among the components are *organelles*, specialized parts analogous to organs.

single-cell bacteria. Organisms with internal compartments separated by membranes are called **eukaryotes.** The membranes enclose the two main parts of individual cells, the **nucleus** and the **cytoplasm,** between which various communications and activities happen (**Figure 3.2**). Eukaryotes evolved much later than prokaryotes, appearing

eukaryotes Multicelled organisms that have a membrane-bound nucleus containing both the genetic material and specialized organelles.

nucleus A membrane-bound structure in eukaryotic cells that contains the genetic material.

cytoplasm The jellylike substance inside the cell membrane that surrounds the nucleus and in which the organelles are suspended.

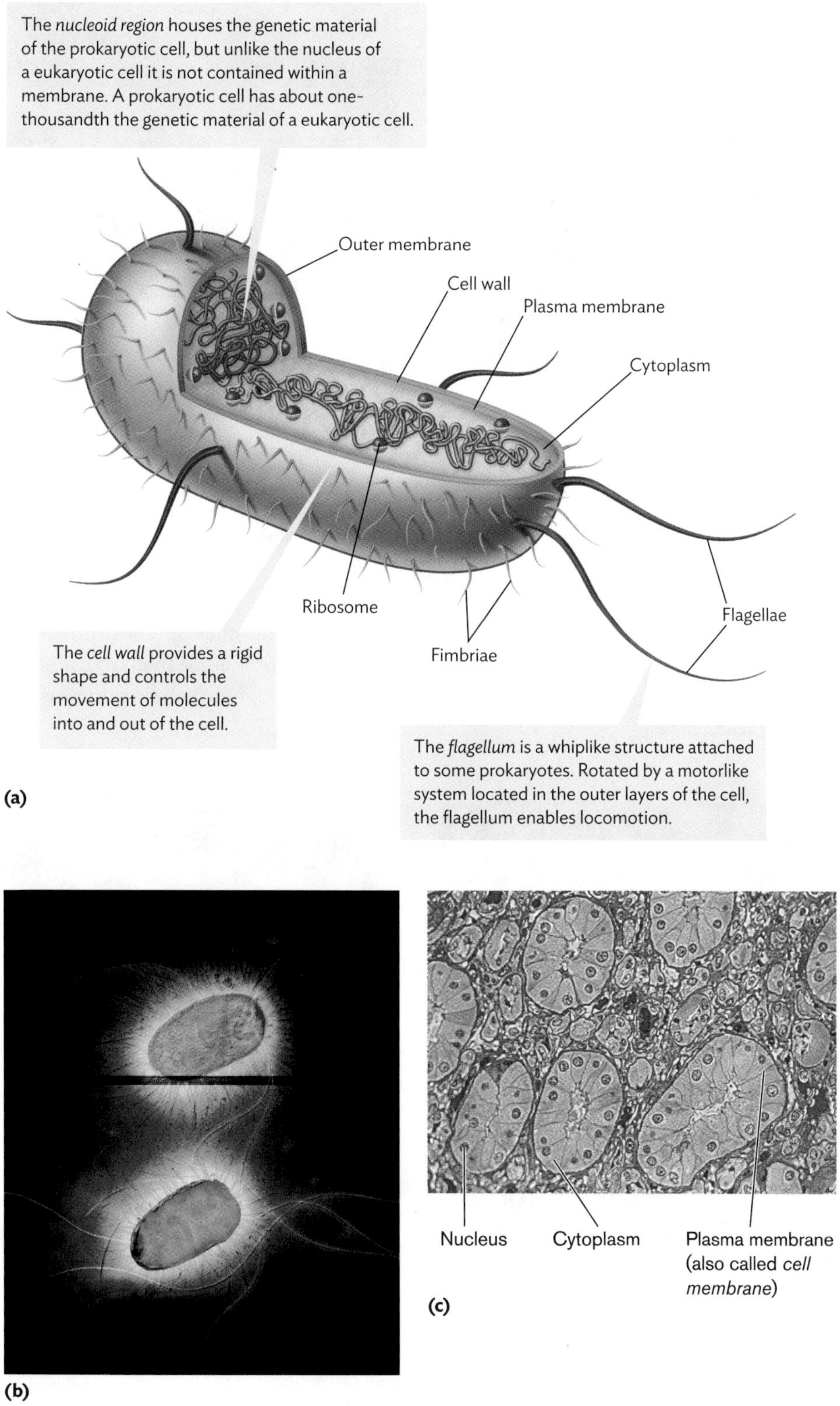

The *nucleoid region* houses the genetic material of the prokaryotic cell, but unlike the nucleus of a eukaryotic cell it is not contained within a membrane. A prokaryotic cell has about one-thousandth the genetic material of a eukaryotic cell.

Outer membrane
Cell wall
Plasma membrane
Cytoplasm
Ribosome
Flagellae
Fimbriae

The *cell wall* provides a rigid shape and controls the movement of molecules into and out of the cell.

The *flagellum* is a whiplike structure attached to some prokaryotes. Rotated by a motorlike system located in the outer layers of the cell, the flagellum enables locomotion.

(a)

(b)

Nucleus   Cytoplasm   Plasma membrane (also called *cell membrane*)

(c)

FIGURE 3.2

Prokaryotes and Eukaryotes (a) The many types of bacteria that we encounter in our daily lives are prokaryotic cells like this one. **(b)** For example, *Escherichia coli* (*E. coli*), two single cells of which are shown here, is a bacterium that aids digestion in the intestines of mammals, including humans. **(c)** This image shows the eukaryotic cells of a primate's kidney.

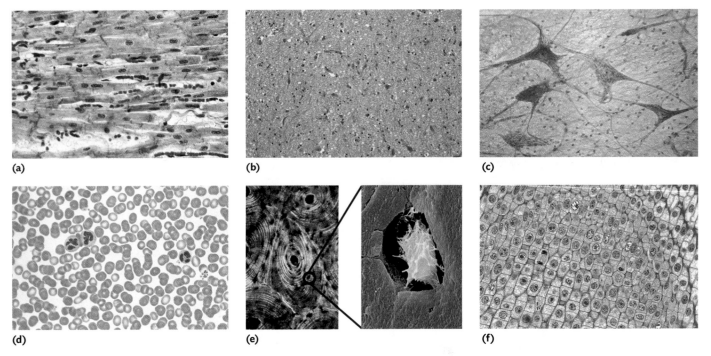

(a)   **(b)**   **(c)**

(d)   **(e)**   **(f)**

FIGURE 3.3

Somatic Cells Somatic cells in different tissues have different characteristics, but most somatic cells share a number of features. With the exception of red blood cells, somatic cells have a nucleus, which contains a complete copy of the organism's DNA. As a result, throughout the organism's body there are millions of copies of that DNA. Note the nuclei in these images of human anatomy: **(a)** a heart muscle, **(b)** brain tissue, **(c)** motor neurons (nerve cells), **(d)** red blood cells (the larger cells are white blood cells, and the small dots are platelets), **(e)** osteocyte (bone cell), **(f)** skin cells.

some 1.2 bya. Their quite complex structures require enormous amounts of energy to survive and reproduce. As they did in the past, eukaryotes come in many different forms, ranging from single-cell yeasts to large, complex, multicellular organisms, such as us.

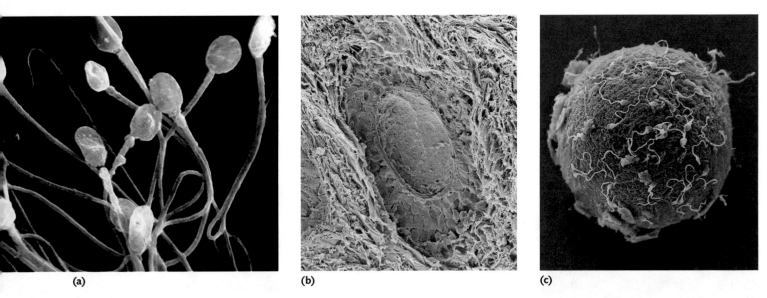

(a)   **(b)**   **(c)**

FIGURE 3.4

Gametes **(a)** Human male sex cells (sperm) have heads and tails; the tails are responsible for the sperm's motility. **(b)** A human female sex cell (ovum, in blue) is developing at the center of this ovarian follicle, or cavity. Once the egg reaches full maturity, it will be released at ovulation. If it is not fertilized by a sperm, the egg will be shed through menstruation. **(c)** Only one of the sperm surrounding this ovum will penetrate the external membrane and fertilize the ovum.

In all animals and plants, there are two types of eukaryotic cells. **Somatic cells**, also called *body cells*, compose most tissues, such as bone, muscle, skin, brain, lung, fat, and hair (**Figure 3.3**). **Gametes** are the sex cells, sperm in males and ova (or eggs) in females (**Figure 3.4**). The root of somatic cell and gamete production is in the chromosomes, located in the nucleus of each cell. In humans, somatic cells are **diploid**, having 46 chromosomes, whereas gametes are **haploid** with 23 chromosomes (**Figure 3.5**).

somatic cells Diploid cells that form the organs, tissues, and other parts of an organism's body.

gametes Sexual reproductive cells, ova and sperm, that have a haploid number of chromosomes and that can unite with a gamete of the opposite type to form a new organism.

diploid A cell that has a full complement of paired chromosomes.

haploid A cell that has a single set of unpaired chromosomes; half of the number of chromosomes as a diploid cell.

Camel: 70

Guinea pig: 64

Salamander: 24

Housefly: 12

Apple: 34

Potato: 48

Petunia: 14

Algae: 148

Ring-tailed lemur: 56

Black-and-white colobus monkey: 44

Orangutan: 48

(b)

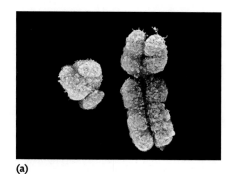

(a)

FIGURE 3.5

Chromosomes **(a)** To get an idea of the incredibly minute size of chromosomes, consider that this pair has been magnified 35,000 times. If a penny (approximately 2 cm, or .8 in, in diameter) were magnified 35,000 times, it would be approximately .7 km, or .44 mi, in diameter. **(b)** An organism's complexity is not related to its number of chromosomes, as this comparison illustrates. While humans have 46 chromosomes, other primates have more (for example, ring-tailed lemurs) or fewer (for example, black-and-white colobus monkeys).

3.2 **The DNA Molecule: The Genetic Code**

The chemical that makes up each chromosome, DNA, is the body's genetic code. Because chromosomal DNA is contained in the nucleus of the cell, it is referred to as nuclear DNA, or nDNA (**Figure 3.6**). Within each chromosome, DNA molecules form sequences, or codes, that are templates for the production of proteins or parts of proteins in the body. Each protein has a specific function, and collectively the proteins determine all physical characteristics and govern the functions of all cells, tissues, and organs. Each DNA sequence, each protein-generating code, is a gene; and the complete set of genes is the **genome**.

Although the number of chromosomes varies according to species (see Figure 3.5), all organisms share much the same genome. Chimpanzees have two more chromosomes than humans, but the DNA in chimpanzees and in humans is about 98% identical. Even the DNA in baker's yeast is 45% similar to human DNA. Within any organism, nDNA is **homoplasmic,** meaning it is the same in each and every cell—the DNA in a skin cell matches the DNA in a bone cell. (An exception to the rule is mature red blood cells, which have no nuclei and, hence, no nuclear DNA.)

A small but significant amount of DNA is contained in tiny organelles, called **mitochondria,** within each cell's cytoplasm (**Figure 3.7**). These structures use oxygen to turn food molecules, especially sugar and fat, into **adenosine triphosphate (ATP),** a high-energy molecule that powers cells and, in turn, powers every tissue in the body. The number of mitochondria in a cell varies according to the cell's activity level. For example, the cells in highly active body tissues, such as muscles, contain far more mitochondria than do cells in relatively inactive tissues, such as hair.

The mitochondrial DNA (mtDNA), a kind of miniature chromosome containing 37 genes, is inherited just from the mother. That is, the mtDNA comes from the ovum. Each of us, then, carries our mother's mtDNA, she carries or carried her mother's mtDNA, and so on for generation after generation. In theory, a maternal lineage, or **matriline,** can be traced back hundreds of thousands of years. (Ancient matrilines in fossil hominins are discussed in chapter 10.) Unlike nDNA, mtDNA is **heteroplasmic,** meaning it can differ among different parts of a person's body or even within the same kinds of cells.

genome The complete set of genetic information—chromosomal and mitochondrial DNA—for an organism or species that represents all the inheritable traits.

homoplasmic Refers to nuclear DNA, which is identical in the nucleus of each cell type (except red blood cells).

mitochondria Energy-producing (ATP) organelles in eukaryotic cells; they possess their own independent DNA.

adenosine triphosphate (ATP) An important cellular molecule, created by the mitochondria and carrying the energy necessary for cellular functions.

matriline DNA, such as mitochondrial DNA, whose inheritance can be traced from mother to daughter or to son.

heteroplasmic Refers to a mixture of more than one type of organellar DNA, such as mitochondrial DNA, within a cell or a single organism's body, usually due to the mutation of the DNA in some organelles but not in others.

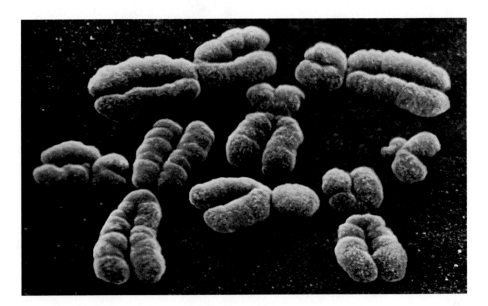

FIGURE 3.6

Nuclear DNA The cell's nucleus houses most of the body's DNA, in very long pieces called *chromosomes*. The different sizes of the human chromosomes reflect the relative amount of DNA in each.

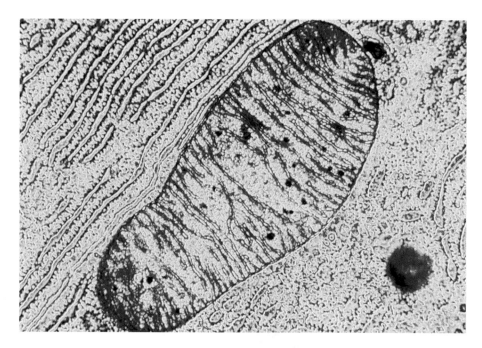

FIGURE 3.7

Mitochondrion Almost every cell includes mitochondria, sometimes thousands of them; they are known as the "powerhouses of the cell," and they are thought to have evolved from a free-living type of bacteria. The footprintlike shape pictured here is a single mitochondrion.

DNA: The Blueprint of Life

The DNA molecule is the blueprint of life. It serves as the chemical template for *every* aspect of biological organisms. As Watson and Crick discovered, the molecule has a right-twisted, double-helix structure (see "DNA: Discovery of the Molecular Basis of Evolution" in chapter 2). Understanding this structure is key to understanding the growth of any organism and the transmission of genes from parents to offspring. The starting point for looking at the DNA molecule in any detail is to unravel a chromosome and look at a tiny segment of it under supermagnification. Its helical, ladderlike structure consists of two uprights and many rungs. The uprights of the structure are made up of alternating sugar and phosphate molecules, while the rungs are composed of paired nitrogen bases linked by a weak hydrogen bond (**Figure 3.8**).

On each side of the ladder, every unit of sugar, phosphate, and nitrogen base forms a single **nucleotide** (**Figure 3.9**). While the sugar and phosphate are the same throughout DNA, the base can be **adenine** (A), **thymine** (T), **guanine** (G), or **cytosine** (C). Owing to the bases' unvarying chemical configurations, adenine and thymine always pair with each other and guanine and cytosine always pair up. In other words, apart from the rare errors in matching, adenine and thymine are **complementary bases** and guanine and cytosine are complementary bases. This means that if on one side of the ladder the sequence is ATGCAG, on the other side the sequence will be complementary, TACGTC. This predictability of base pairings ensures the high reliability of one key function of the DNA molecule, that of self-reproduction. Anthropologists and geneticists investigate the many thousands of single DNA base pairings that produce genetic differences between individuals. Known as **single nucleotide polymorphisms** (**SNPs,** pronounced "snips"), these pairings are spread uniformly throughout the genome. Groups of SNPs play a critical role in determining various attributes, such as hair color and blood type (see "Polymorphisms: Variations in Specific Genes" later in this chapter).

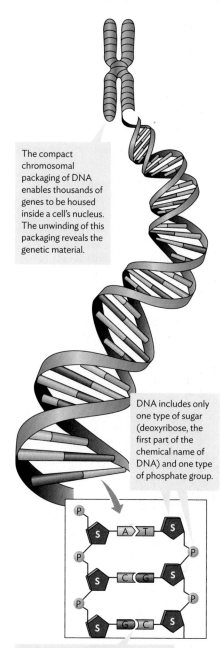

The compact chromosomal packaging of DNA enables thousands of genes to be housed inside a cell's nucleus. The unwinding of this packaging reveals the genetic material.

DNA includes only one type of sugar (deoxyribose, the first part of the chemical name of DNA) and one type of phosphate group.

DNA includes four different types of nitrogen bases. A gene is a specific and unique sequence of these bases.

FIGURE 3.8
The Structure of DNA

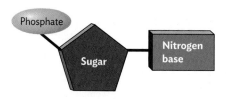

FIGURE 3.9

Nucleotide A nucleotide is the building block of DNA and is made up of a phosphate group, a sugar, and a single nitrogen base.

3.3 The DNA Molecule: Replicating the Code

replication The process of copying nuclear DNA prior to cell division, so that each new daughter cell receives a complete complement of DNA.

mitosis The process of cellular and nuclear division that creates two identical diploid daughter cells.

meiosis The production of gametes through one DNA replication and two cell (and nuclear) divisions, creating four haploid gametic cells.

zygote The cell that results from a sperm's fertilization of an ovum.

One function of the DNA molecule is to replicate itself. **Replication** takes place in the nucleus and is part of cell division, leading to the production of new somatic cells (**mitosis**) or the production of new gametes (**meiosis**). Replication thus results in continued cell production, from the single-celled **zygote** (the fertilized egg) to two cells, then four cells, and so on, to the fully mature body with all of its many different tissues and organs—within which cells are continually dying and being replaced.

In replication, DNA makes *identical* copies of itself, going from one double-stranded parent molecule of DNA to two double strands of daughter DNA. This means that where there was one chromosome, now there are two (**Figure 3.10**).

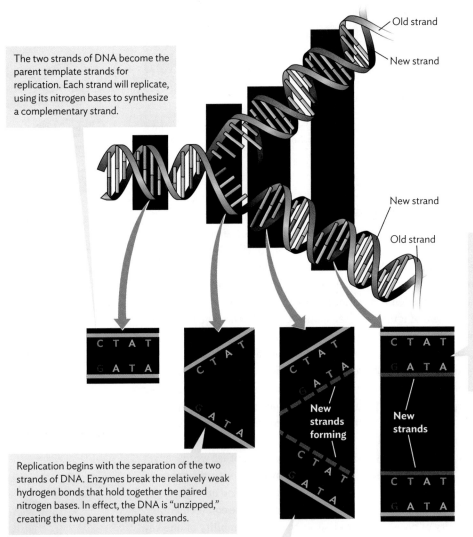

The two strands of DNA become the parent template strands for replication. Each strand will replicate, using its nitrogen bases to synthesize a complementary strand.

Old strand

New strand

New strand

Old strand

When all the nitrogen bases of the parent strands are paired with (formerly free-floating) nucleotides, replication is complete. There are now two complete DNA molecules, each consisting of one parent strand and one new strand.

C T A T
G A T A

C T A T
G A T A

C T A T
G A T A
New strands forming
C T A T
G A T A

C T A T
G A T A
New strands
C T A T
G A T A

Replication begins with the separation of the two strands of DNA. Enzymes break the relatively weak hydrogen bonds that hold together the paired nitrogen bases. In effect, the DNA is "unzipped," creating the two parent template strands.

Each parent strand serves as a template for the creation of a new complementary DNA strand. The exposed, unpaired nitrogen bases on the parent strands attract complementary free-floating nucleotides. The nitrogen bases of these nucleotides form hydrogen bonds with the existing nitrogen bases; for example, a free-floating nucleotide with a cytosine base will attach itself to a guanine base.

FIGURE 3.10
The Steps of DNA Replication

Chromosome Types

Within somatic cells, chromosomes occur in **homologous,** or matching, pairs (**Figure 3.11**). Each pair includes the father's contribution (the paternal chromosome) and the mother's contribution (the maternal chromosome). These nonsex chromosomes are called **autosomes**.

The **karyotype,** or complete set of chromosomes, includes all of the autosomes and one pair of **sex chromosomes,** so called because they determine an individual's biological sex. Females have two X chromosomes, and males have one X and one Y chromosome. The Y chromosome contains a small amount of genetic material, which determines only male characteristics (**Figure 3.12**). The interaction of gametes

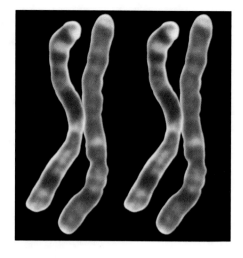

FIGURE 3.11

Chromosome Pairs Homologous chromosomes are virtually identical in their physical and chemical structure. Each pair of chromosomes has the same genes, but the pair may have different alleles for specific genes.

homologous Refers to each set of paired chromosomes in the genome.

autosomes All chromosomes, except the sex chromosomes, that occur in pairs in all somatic cells (not the gametes).

karyotype The characteristics of the chromosomes for an individual organism or a species, such as number, size, and type. The karyotype is typically presented as a photograph of a person's chromosomes that have been arranged in homologous pairs and put in numerical order by size.

sex chromosomes The pair of chromosomes that determine an organism's biological sex.

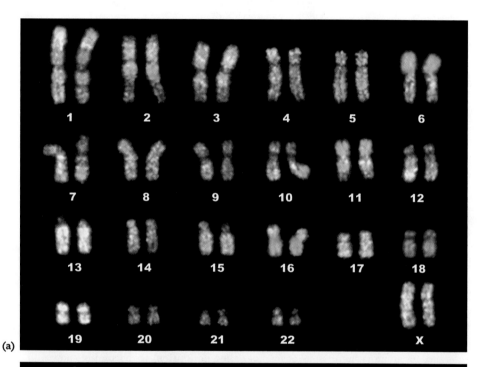

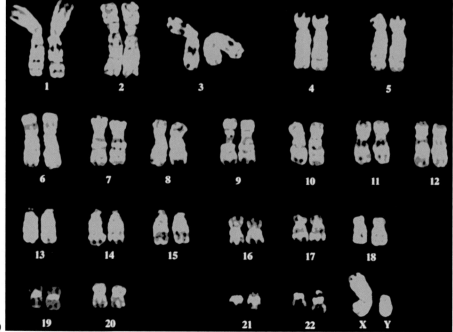

FIGURE 3.12

Karyotype **(a)** Contained within each somatic cell, the human karyotype typically consists of 46 chromosomes of various sizes in 23 pairs. Of those 23, one pair determines the person's sex. Here, the label "X" means that these sex chromosomes are both Xs and thus belong to a human female. **(b)** In this karyotype, the pair labeled "XY" belongs to a human male.

GENOMICS AND HU

Answers to Fundamental Questions

The advances in our understanding of the human genome have grown enormously in the twenty-first century. Scientists have mapped the 3 billion base pairs that make up the human genome, pinpointing the locations of the genes of the specific proteins that control the multitude of structures and functions in the human body.

WATCH
THE VIDEO

www.digital.
wwnorton.com/
ourorigins4

This work came out of the 13-year-long *Human Genome Project* (1990–2003), an international collaboration involving hundreds of scientists focused on discovering and mapping all human genes. In the decade following that pioneering research, we have taken advantage of this global reference for human genetic variation, which was developed by sequencing the genomes of more than 2,500 individuals representing 26 different populations from around the world. And this global reference is growing as labs all over the world map more and more individuals, sequencing samples derived from both living people and the remains of those long dead. These mapping projects focus on genetic variation, providing tools to assess and understand a range of issues dealing with human evolution, health, migration, and population history.

From these collected sequences, we have learned that each of us has our own set of base pairs, which are mostly unique from generation to generation. Your parents have essentially the same genome as you, as will your children. However, what makes your genome slightly different from your parents' genomes is that you have about 200 **de novo mutations.** These mutations are those occurring in the egg or sperm of one of your parents or in the fertilized egg that develops in your mother. Unlike the genetic variation you inherited from your parents, de novo mutations may have a great-

er tendency to be more deleterious (harmful), perhaps because they have been less subject to natural selection over the course of human evolution.

In addition to the identification of specific genes, the functions and interactions of all genes (an area of science called **genomics**) are becoming known. This newfound knowledge is giving unprecedented opportunities for the diagnosis of a range of diseases having a genetic basis. At present, owing to the precise information available about the human genome, the identification of specific genetic variants provides the basis for developing genetic tests. But first, the science has to take place to find the genes behind the disease. One such disease that currently affects millions of people and costs billions of dollars is osteoporosis, commonly known as "fragile bone disease." We know that bone mineral density is a highly heritable condition and key predictor of fractures due to osteoporosis. Simply, persons with low bone mineral density are more prone to osteoporosis and fractures than persons with relatively high bone mineral density. In 2015, geneticist Hou-Feng Zheng and his team identified, in European-descent populations, genetic variants located near the *EN1* gene that play a role in determining an individual's bone mineral density. In particular, their pioneering study shows very clear association between a number of alleles near the *EN1* gene and low

MAN EVOLUTION

risk of fracture. This work lays the ground work for genetic testing.

In an anthropological context, in addition to understanding genetic diseases, the very fine-grained genetic details we now have in hand make it possible to address long-standing questions about where ancestors originated. For example, where did native peoples of Australia and the Americas come from? For these continents, the histories of native groups are points of heated debate but are critical for developing answers to questions about human evolution in general and the origins and evolution of native peoples in particular. From the archaeological record alone, the answers to these questions are vague. We know what the first tools look like on both continents, and we more or less know the dates of these artifacts (see chapter 12). Moreover, there are some phenotypic traits that allow anthropologists to link broad phenotypes from different continents. Ultimately, genomic data has allowed us to refine our hypotheses about the patterns of human migration and evolution. In the past few years, anthropological genomicists have developed methods for extracting the genome sequences from the remains of native peoples from Australia and the Americas. For example, paleogeneticist Eske Willerslev and his team at the Natural History Museum of Denmark have reconstructed the genome sequence of a DNA sample derived from an Australian Aboriginal man's hair from the early twentieth century. Comparisons of sequences from a wide range of populations from around the world show that the original founding population of Australia derived from Asia and that they were part of an early expansion from East Asia dating to about 62,000–75,000 yBP. This genetics-based date is also consistent with absolute dating methods based on the earliest human remains from Australia (see chapter 12). The genomic record reveals that today's Australian Aborigines are the descendants of the original founding population, making them one of the oldest populations to continually occupy the same region outside of Africa.

Most anthropologists agree that the founding ancestors of modern-day Native Americans came to North America via the Bering Land Bridge from Siberia. However, there has been considerable disagreement among anthropologists regarding the timing and pattern of migration. Was it a wavelike affair, with multiple migrations forming different founding groups and descent populations, or was it a few events or even a single event that originated *all* Native Americans and their descendants, including those living today? As with Australia, this is a critical question relating to broad patterns of human evolution as well as the identification of the history of native peoples and descent groups, such as specific tribes. Willerslev's team has analyzed the genomes of 31 living native individuals from the Americas, Siberia, and the Pacific region, 23 genomes from skeletal remains from archaeological sites, and single nucleotide polymorphisms from 79 living native individuals from South America, North America, and Siberia. The analysis shows that all modern Native Americans from North and South America derive from a single wave of migration, coming across the Bering Land Bridge no earlier than 23,000 yBP. At some point around 13,000 yBP, the founding population divided, forming a southern branch leading to Native Americans in southern North America and Central and South America, and a northern branch representing Athabascans and Native Americans in northern North America.

These ambitious projects provide anthropologists and other scientists with a remarkable set of tools for reconstructing the origins and evolution of modern people, and for addressing poorly resolved issues about the timing of divergence from ancestral populations, the number of migrations, and the relationships between past and present peoples. *Anthropology matters!*

The newly explored genomic record of the population history of native peoples of the Americas facilitates increased understanding of the timing of founding events and the appearance of modern-day groups. The record indicates one migration into the Americas sometime after 23,000 yBP, forming the founding population of all native people in the Western Hemisphere.

during fertilization determines the combination of chromosomes in the offspring. If an X-carrying sperm fertilizes an egg (which always carries an X), the offspring will be female. If a Y-carrying sperm fertilizes an egg, the offspring will be male. Therefore, the male parent's gamete determines the sex of his offspring because the Y chromosome is present in males only; it is passed from father to son.

The Y chromosome can be highly informative about paternity over many generations. This **patriline** is in part analogous to the matriline-based mtDNA, which is passed on only by females. However, mtDNA goes to all of a woman's children, whereas the Y chromosome is passed only to a man's son.

patriline DNA whose inheritance can be traced from father to son via the Y chromosome.

3.4 Mitosis: Production of Identical Somatic Cells

An organism starts life as a single cell, the zygote, which then produces identical copies of itself many, many times. A single human zygote, for example, eventually results in more than 10 trillion cells, each having the *exact* same DNA (**Figure 3.13**). Here, the

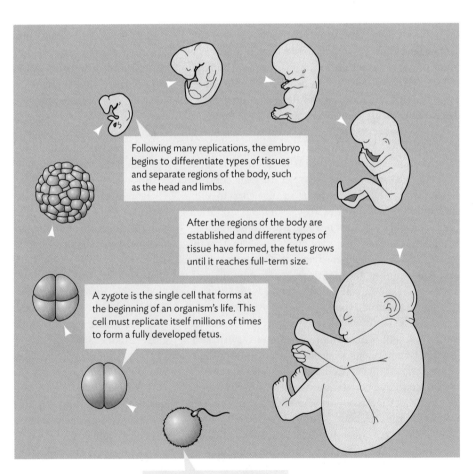

Following many replications, the embryo begins to differentiate types of tissues and separate regions of the body, such as the head and limbs.

After the regions of the body are established and different types of tissue have formed, the fetus grows until it reaches full-term size.

A zygote is the single cell that forms at the beginning of an organism's life. This cell must replicate itself millions of times to form a fully developed fetus.

Fertilization occurs when one sperm penetrates the outer membrane of the ovum, or egg.

FIGURE 3.13

Prenatal Development The stages of human development from fertilization to a full-term infant.

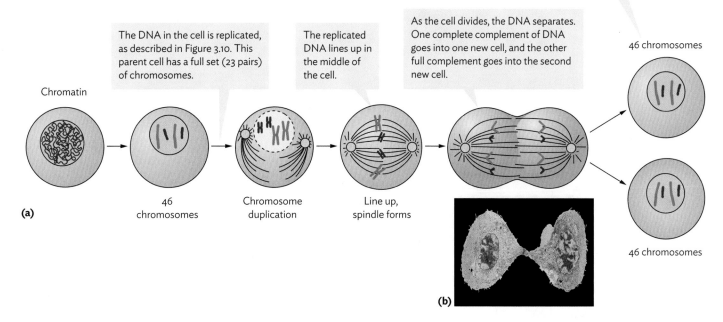

The DNA in the cell is replicated, as described in Figure 3.10. This parent cell has a full set (23 pairs) of chromosomes.

The replicated DNA lines up in the middle of the cell.

As the cell divides, the DNA separates. One complete complement of DNA goes into one new cell, and the other full complement goes into the second new cell.

Each new cell has a full set of DNA, with 23 pairs of chromosomes.

Chromatin

46 chromosomes

Chromosome duplication

Line up, spindle forms

46 chromosomes

46 chromosomes

(a)

(b)

FIGURE 3.14

Mitosis **(a)** The steps of mitosis in humans. **(b)** A human skin cell undergoing mitosis, dividing into two new daughter cells.

production of identical daughter cells from an original parental cell—mitosis—involves one DNA replication followed by *one* cell division (**Figure 3.14**). In this kind of cell division, a **diploid cell**—a cell having its organism's full set of chromosomes—divides to produce two cells, each of which also has the full set of chromosomes.

diploid cell A cell that has a full complement of paired chromosomes.

free-floating nucleotides Nucleotides (the basic building block of DNA and RNA) that are present in the nucleus and are used during DNA replication and mRNA synthesis.

PALEOGEN

ANCIENT DNA OPENS NEW WINDOWS ON THE PAST

Imagine if we could look at ancient organisms' DNA to understand their evolution. In fact, new technology is enabling anthropological geneticists to extract DNA routinely from the tissues (mostly bones and teeth) of ancient remains.

This emerging field, called **paleogenetics**, has been made possible by the development of **polymerase chain reaction (PCR)**, a method of amplifying a tiny sequence of DNA for study by incrementally increasing the sizes of a billion copies made from a single template of DNA. PCR has opened new windows onto the genetics of ancient populations, including the identification of sex chromosomes, the documentation of diseases, and the isolation of unique repetitions of DNA segments. It has yielded insight into the genetic dissimilarity of Neandertals and modern humans, and it has enabled exploration into population origins and movements (both subjects are among the topics of chapter 12).

Anthropologists have long speculated about the origins of Native Americans (where they came from is another subject of chapter 12). Key to understanding their origins is their genetic diversity. Studies have revealed that the haplogroups of mtDNA—A, B, C, and D—in living Native Americans are quite similar to

In an underwater cave in Mexico, scuba divers and archaeologists discover a skeleton that dates to among the oldest in the Americas, with genetic links to today's Native Americans.

ETICS

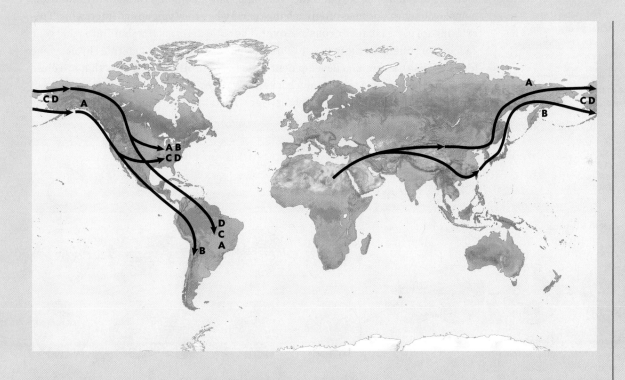

By examining the distribution of haplogroups A, B, C, and D in North and South America and in eastern Asia, researchers have estimated that Native Americans arrived in the Western Hemisphere between 15,000 and 40,000 yBP. The presence of the same haplogroups in the northeastern part of Asia suggests that Native Americans originated from this area.

the haplogroups of their ancestors. This resemblance strongly suggests that Native Americans' genetic structure is quite old. Based on current assumptions about mutation rates in mtDNA, anthropologists and geneticists have estimated that people arrived in the Americas sometime between 15,000 and 40,000 yBP, earlier than what is documented in the archaeological record (among the subjects of chapter 13). But a new variant of haplogroup D, discovered in the DNA of a 10,300-year-old skeleton from Alaska by paleogeneticist Brian Kemp and his collaborators, suggests that

the molecular clock may be off and that humans first arrived in the New World around 13,500 yBP, a date that jibes well with the archaeological evidence.

In addition, the presence of all four haplogroups and their variants in the skeletons of Native Americans dating to before 1492 tells us that the widespread decline of the Native American population after Columbus's arrival did not reduce their genetic, and therefore biological, diversity. Native Americans living today are likely as diverse genetically as were their ancestors living hundreds and thousands of years ago.

3.5 Meiosis: Production of Gametes (Sex Cells)

The genetic code is transmitted from parents to offspring via the female and male gametes. Gametes, remember, have only half the chromosomes that are in somatic cells—they are **haploid,** containing one chromosome from each pair. Unlike mitosis, the production of these cells—meiosis—does not result in identical copies of the parent cell and the parent cell's DNA. Meiosis involves one DNA replication followed by *two* cell divisions (**Figure 3.15**).

Meiosis plays a critical role in the inheritance of biological characteristics and the variation seen in offspring. Because each gamete contains just one chromosome from a homologous pair and just one sex chromosome, during reproduction each parent contributes only half of his or her genetic material. For example, in your somatic cells, each homologous pair includes one chromosome from your mother and one chromosome from your father. Whether a particular gamete, on the other hand, contains your mother's chromosome or your father's chromosome is completely random. In addition, homologous chromosomes often exchange parts when they pair up and intertwine. This exchange of parts is called **crossing-over.** The outcome of such reshuffling is that gene variants originally on the maternal chromosome are now on the paternal chromosome (or vice versa), a common development called **recombination.** Genes that are close together on a chromosome are much less likely to recombine. These units or blocks of genetic material are called **haplotypes.** Geneticists prefer to study haplotypes because

recombination The exchange of genetic material between homologous chromosomes, resulting from a cross-over event.

haplotypes A group of alleles that tend to be inherited as a unit due to their closely spaced loci on a single chromosome.

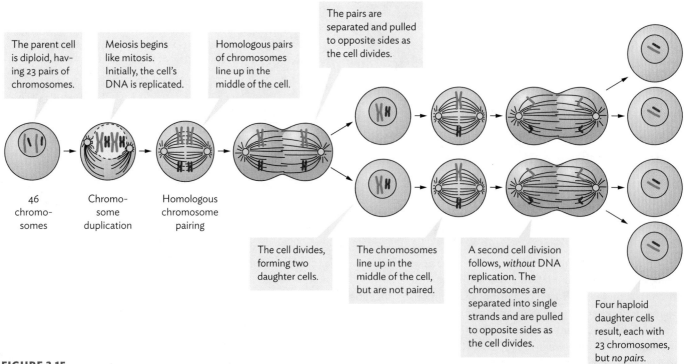

The parent cell is diploid, having 23 pairs of chromosomes.

Meiosis begins like mitosis. Initially, the cell's DNA is replicated.

Homologous pairs of chromosomes line up in the middle of the cell.

The pairs are separated and pulled to opposite sides as the cell divides.

46 chromosomes

Chromosome duplication

Homologous chromosome pairing

The cell divides, forming two daughter cells.

The chromosomes line up in the middle of the cell, but are not paired.

A second cell division follows, *without* DNA replication. The chromosomes are separated into single strands and are pulled to opposite sides as the cell divides.

Four haploid daughter cells result, each with 23 chromosomes, but *no pairs.*

FIGURE 3.15

Meiosis The steps of meiosis in humans. Compare this process to mitosis, shown in Figure 3.14.

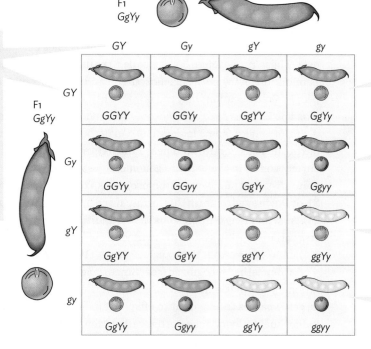

F1
GgYy

This Punnett square shows all possible combinations of two different genes, pod color and seed color:
G = green pod
g = yellow pod
Y = yellow seed
y = green seed

Because both parents have two different alleles for both traits, there are 16 possible combinations.

F1
GgYy

	GY	Gy	gY	gy
GY	GGYY	GGYy	GgYY	GgYy
Gy	GGYy	GGyy	GgYy	Ggyy
gY	GgYY	GgYy	ggYY	ggYy
gy	GgYy	Ggyy	ggYy	ggyy

Of the 16 combinations, nine have green pods and yellow seeds. The genotypes vary and include: GGYY, GGYy, GgYY, GgYy.

Three of the resulting combinations have green pods and green seeds. They have one of two genotypes: GGyy or Ggyy.

Three of the resulting combinations have yellow pods and yellow seeds. There are two possible genotypes: ggYY or ggYy.

One of the resulting combinations has yellow pods and green seeds, with the genotype ggyy.

(a)

The small chromosomes have a gene that determines hair color: red represents brown hair, and blue represents blond hair.

The large chromosomes have a gene that determines eye color: red represents brown eyes, and blue represents blue eyes.

Alternatively, following the first cell division of meiosis, one cell has genes for brown eyes and blond hair, while the second has genes for blue eyes and brown hair.

Following the first cell division of meiosis, one cell has genes for brown eyes and brown hair, while the second cell has genes for blue eyes and blond hair.

The four daughter cells, or gametes, follow suit: two gametes have genes for brown eyes and brown hair, while the other two gametes have genes for blue eyes and blond hair.

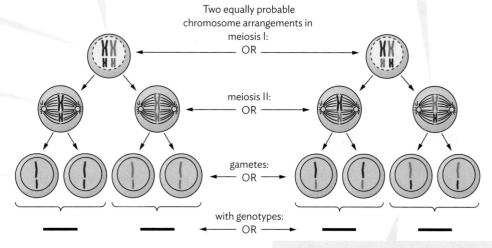

Two equally probable chromosome arrangements in meiosis I:
OR

meiosis II:
OR

gametes:
OR

with genotypes:
OR

Again, the four daughter cells, or gametes, follow suit: two gametes have genes for brown eyes and blond hair, while the other two gametes have genes for blue eyes and brown hair.

(b)

FIGURE 3.16

Law of Independent Assortment Through his research with pea plants, Mendel formulated several laws pertaining to inheritance. **(a)** His second law, the law of independent assortment, asserts that traits linked to different chromosomes are inherited independently from one another. **(b)** Hair color, for example, is inherited independently from eye color.

haplogroups A large set of haplotypes, such as the Y-chromosome or mitochondrial DNA, that may be used to define a population.

translocations Rearrangements of chromosomes due to the insertion of genetic material from one chromosome to another.

nondisjunctions Refers to the failure of the chromosomes to properly segregate during meiosis, creating some gametes with abnormal numbers of chromosomes.

monosomy Refers to the condition in which only one of a specific pair of chromosomes is present in a cell's nucleus.

trisomy Refers to the condition in which an additional chromosome exists with the homologous pair.

law of independent assortment Mendel's second law, which asserts that the inheritance of one trait does not affect the inheritance of other traits.

amino acids Organic molecules combined in a specific sequence by the ribosomes to form a protein.

essential amino acids Those amino acids that cannot be synthesized in the body; they must be supplied by the diet.

structural proteins Proteins that form an organism's physical attributes.

regulatory proteins Proteins involved in the expression of control genes.

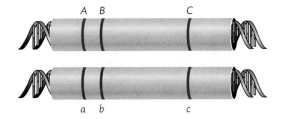

FIGURE 3.17

Linkage Because alleles A, B, and C are on the same chromosome, they have a better chance of being inherited as a unit than of being combined and inherited with alleles a, b, and c, which are together on a separate chromosome and thus also have a good chance of being inherited as a unit. Meanwhile, because they are close together, alleles A and B (like alleles a and b) stand a better chance of being inherited together than do alleles B and C (like alleles b and c). If, for example, eye color and hair color were on the same chromosome, especially if they were close together on that chromosome, they would most likely *not* be inherited separately with all the combinations examined in Figure 3.16.

they do not recombine and are passed on for many generations, potentially hundreds, over time. Groups of related haplotypes, called **haplogroups,** are an important tool for studying both long-term evolution and populations' histories.

In rare instances, nonhomologous chromosomes exchange segments during meiosis. These rare exchanges are called **translocations.** The most common form in humans, involving both chromosome 13 and chromosome 14, affects about 1 in 1,300 people. Translocations may cause infertility, Down syndrome (when one-third of chromosome 21 joins onto chromosome 14), and a number of diseases, including several forms of cancer (some leukemias). On occasion, chromosome pairs fail to separate during meiosis or mitosis. These **nondisjunctions** result in an incorrect number of chromosomes in the person's genome. A loss in number of chromosomes is a **monosomy.** A gain in number of chromosomes is a **trisomy,** the most common being trisomy 21, or Down syndrome (in this form, caused by an extra or part of an extra chromosome 21). As with many chromosomal abnormalities, the age of the mother determines the risk of the offspring's having Down syndrome. For 20- to 24-year-old mothers, the risk is 1/1,490. It rises to 1/106 by age 40 and 1/11 beyond age 49.

As Mendel had recognized (see "Since Darwin: Mechanisms of Inheritance, the Evolutionary Synthesis, and the Discovery of DNA" in chapter 2), each physical unit (that is, gene) passes from parent to offspring independently of other physical units. This independent inheritance—often called Mendel's **law of independent assortment** (**Figure 3.16**)—applies to genes from *different* chromosomes. However, what happens when genes are on the *same* chromosome? Because meiosis involves the separation of chromosome pairs (homologous chromosomes), genes on the same chromosome, especially ones near each other on that chromosome, have a greater chance of being inherited as a package. They are less subject to recombination. This gene linkage—the inheritance of a package of genes (such as haplotypes) from the same chromosome (**Figure 3.17**)—is an exception to Mendel's law of independent assortment.

3.6 Producing Proteins: The Other Function of DNA

In addition to replicating itself, DNA serves as the template for protein synthesis. Proteins are the complex chemicals that make up tissues and bring about the functions, repair, and growth of tissues (**Table 3.1**). While some work within cells—for example, the enzymes that unzip DNA during replication—others, such as hormones, work within the whole body. Proteins consist of **amino acids,** of which there are 20 (**Table 3.2**, p. 76). Each kind of protein is defined by its particular combination and number of linked amino acids. Most of the human body is composed of proteins, and the body produces 12 of the amino acids. The other eight, also called **essential amino acids,** come from particular foods.

Two main categories of proteins are constantly being synthesized. **Structural proteins** are responsible for physical characteristics, such as hair form, eye color, tooth size, and basic bone shape (**Figure 3.18**). The other category, **regulatory** (also called *functional*) **proteins,** includes enzymes, hormones, and antibodies. Enzymes regulate activities within cells, hormones regulate activities between cells, and antibodies are key to fighting infections.

Table 3.1 The Seven Types of Proteins

Name	Function	Examples
Enzymes	Catalyze chemical reactions	Lactase—breaks down lactose in milk products
Structural Proteins	Give structure or support to tissues	Keratin—hair; collagen—bone
Gas Transport Proteins	Carry vital gases to tissues	Hemoglobin—oxygen
Antibodies	Part of immune system	Anti-A and anti-B in ABO blood system
Hormones	Regulate metabolism	Insulin—regulates metabolism of carbohydrates and fats
Mechanical Proteins	Carry out specific functions or work	Actin and myosin—help muscles contract
Nutrients	Provide vital nutrients to tissues	Ovalbumin—main protein of egg whites

Protein synthesis is a two-step process (**Figure 3.19**). The first step, **transcription,** takes place mostly in the cell's nucleus. The second, **translation,** takes place in the cytoplasm. Transcription starts out just like the first step of DNA replication: a double strand of parental DNA unzips. Rather than producing daughter strands of DNA, the now-exposed bases in the DNA molecule serve as a single template for another kind of nucleic acid, **ribonucleic acid (RNA).** RNA has the same nitrogen bases as

transcription The first step of protein synthesis, involving the creation of mRNA based on the DNA template.

translation The second step of protein synthesis, involving the transfer of amino acids by tRNA to the ribosomes, which are then added to the protein chain.

ribonucleic acid (RNA) A single-stranded molecule involved in protein synthesis, consisting of a phosphate, ribose sugar, and one of four nitrogen bases.

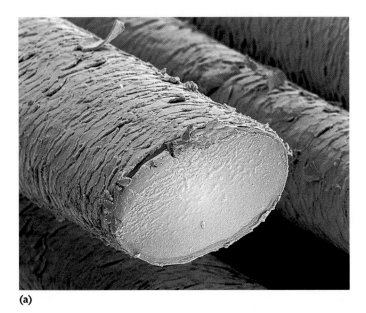

(a)

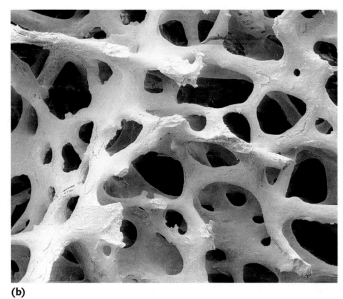

(b)

FIGURE 3.18

Structural Proteins While culture and environment strongly influence the development of biological structures, those structures are initially determined by structural proteins. Two important structural proteins are keratin and collagen. **(a)** In humans, keratin is the primary component of hair (pictured here), skin, and fingernails. In other mammals and in amphibians, birds, and reptiles, it also contributes to structures such as hooves, antlers, claws, beaks, scales, and shells. **(b)** Collagen is the most abundant protein in humans and other mammals and is essential for connective tissues, such as bone (pictured here), cartilage, ligaments, and tendons. In addition, collagen strengthens the walls of blood vessels and, along with keratin, gives strength and elasticity to skin. In its crystalline form, collagen is found in the cornea and lens of the eye.

3.19

Protein Synthesis

As in DNA replication, transcription begins with enzymes "unzipping" the DNA. Unlike replication, however, transcription uses only one strand of DNA.

DNA template

mRNA strand

··· T A C T C ···

··· A U G A G ···

Once the DNA strands have opened, messenger RNA (mRNA) attaches free-floating RNA nitrogen bases to the exposed, unpaired DNA nitrogen bases.

(b)

Completed mRNA strand

··· A U G A G U G G A U A G ···

Transcription, which occurs in the nucleus, involves the creation of mRNA from one strand of DNA.

After the mRNA strand is completed, it leaves the nucleus and goes to the ribosomes, in the cytoplasm.

Once completed, the DNA closes back up, and the mRNA strand leaves the nucleus and goes to one of the ribosomes on the endoplasmic reticulum.

(a)

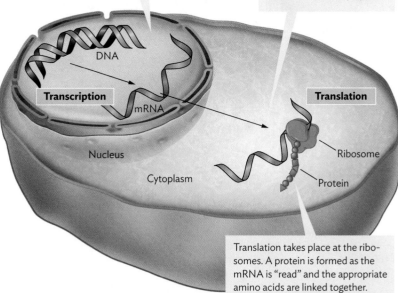

DNA

Transcription

mRNA

Translation

Nucleus

Cytoplasm

Ribosome

Protein

Translation takes place at the ribosomes. A protein is formed as the mRNA is "read" and the appropriate amino acids are linked together.

Moves out of nucleus to ribosomes in cytoplasm

FIGURE 3.19

Protein Synthesis **(a)** As this overview of protein synthesis shows, transcription occurs mostly within the cell's nucleus, and translation follows at the ribosomes. **(b)** Here, the steps of protein synthesis are diagrammed for a hypothetical protein. **(c)** At the top is a computer model of a tRNA molecule, and below that is a diagram of the molecule.

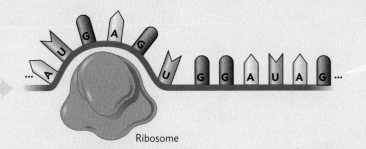

Translation begins as the mRNA binds to a ribosome. In effect, the "message" carried by the mRNA is "translated" by a ribosome.

Ribosome

Translation

at ribosome

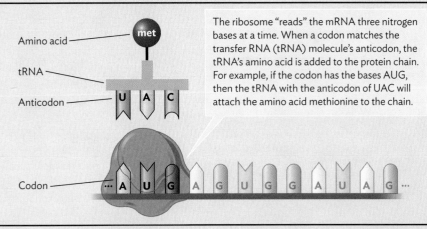

Amino acid

tRNA

Anticodon

Codon

The ribosome "reads" the mRNA three nitrogen bases at a time. When a codon matches the transfer RNA (tRNA) molecule's anticodon, the tRNA's amino acid is added to the protein chain. For example, if the codon has the bases AUG, then the tRNA with the anticodon of UAC will attach the amino acid methionine to the chain.

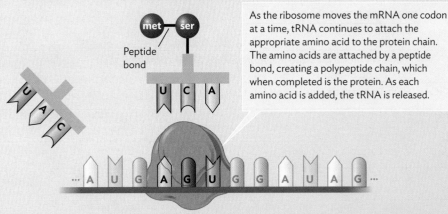

Peptide bond

As the ribosome moves the mRNA one codon at a time, tRNA continues to attach the appropriate amino acid to the protein chain. The amino acids are attached by a peptide bond, creating a polypeptide chain, which when completed is the protein. As each amino acid is added, the tRNA is released.

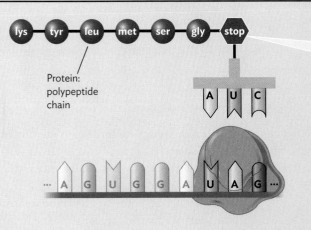

Protein: polypeptide chain

Eventually, a "stop" codon is reached, which indicates that the protein is completed. The mRNA leaves the ribosome, and the protein is released.

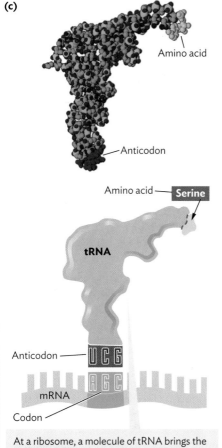

(c)

Amino acid

Anticodon

Amino acid — Serine

tRNA

Anticodon — UCG

mRNA — AGC

Codon

At a ribosome, a molecule of tRNA brings the anticodon for each codon on the mRNA. The tRNA carries its anticodon on one end and the associated amino acid on the other.

Table 3.2 The 20 Amino Acids

Amino Acid	DNA Triplet Code	Function	Sources
Alanine (ala)	CGA, CGG, CGT, CGC	Used in the production of glucose	Meat, poultry, dairy products
Arginine (arg)	GCA, GCG, GCT, GCC, TCT, TCC	Induces growth hormone release from pituitary gland	Chocolate, flour, dairy products
Asparagine (asn)	TTA, TTG	Used by central nervous system to maintain equilibrium	Plant proteins (e.g., asparagus), dairy products, poultry
Aspartic acid (asp)	CTA, CTG	Promotes mineral uptake in intestinal tract	Sugarcane, dairy products, beef
Cysteine (cys)	ACA, ACG	Promotes iron absorption	Meat, garlic, dairy products
Glutamic acid (glu)	CTT, CTC	Works as a neurotransmitter	Meat, poultry, fish, dairy products
Glutamine (gln)	GTT, GTG	Carrier of urinary ammonia	Red meat, fish, beans
Glycine (gly)	CCA, CCG, CCT, CCC	Works as a neurotransmitter	Fish, meat, beans
Histidine (his)	GTA, GTG	Detoxifies chemicals in the liver	Bananas, grapes, meat, dairy products
Isoleucine (ile)*	TAA, TAG, TAT	Helps to rebuild muscle tissue	Eggs, poultry, cereal grains, dairy products
Leucine (leu)*	AAT, AAC, GAA, GAG, GAT, GAC	Involved in energy release from muscles during work	Whole grains, dairy products
Lysine (lys)*	TTT, TTC	Stimulates secretion of gastric juices in digestion	Cereal grains, fish
Methionine (met)*	TAC	Prevents fat deposits in liver	Fruits, vegetables, nuts
Phenylalanine (phe)*	AAA, AAG	Increases blood pressure in hypotension (low blood pressure)	Dairy products, legumes
Proline (pro)	GGA, GGG, GGT, GGC	Helps in repair of muscle and tendons	Meat
Serine (ser)	AGA, AGG, AGT, AGC, TCA, TCG	Takes part in metabolism	Meat, dairy products
Threonine (thr)*	TGA, TGG, TGT, TGC	Takes part in metabolism	Poultry, fish, beans
Tryptophan (trp)*	ACC	Aids in blood clotting	Oats, dairy products, red meat, poultry
Tyrosine (tyr)	ATA, ATG	Aids in formation of thyroid hormones	Soy products, poultry
Valine (val)*	CAA, CAG, CAT, CAC	Aids in building of muscles	Fish, poultry, beans

*Essential amino acid.

uracil One of four nitrogen bases that make up RNA; it pairs with adenine.

messenger RNA (mRNA) The molecules that are responsible for making a chemical copy of a gene needed for a specific protein, that is, for the transcription phase of protein synthesis.

ribosomes The organelles attached to the surface of the endoplasmic reticulum, located in the cytoplasm of a cell; they are the site of protein synthesis.

ribosomal RNA (rRNA) A fundamental structural component of a ribosome.

DNA, except that **uracil** (U) replaces thymine (T). Uracil always matches with adenine (A), while guanine (G) continues to pair with cytosine (C).

Only one of the two DNA strands serves as the template for the production of RNA. This strand attracts free-floating RNA nucleotides. The strand of RNA—now called **messenger RNA (mRNA)**—then splits off from the DNA template, leaves the nucleus, and moves into the cytoplasm.

In the translation step, the mRNA attaches itself to structures called **ribosomes.** The mRNA is a "messenger" because (in the form of its own open bases) it carries the code for the protein being synthesized from the nucleus to the ribosomes. Ribosomes are made up of another kind of ribonucleic acid, **ribosomal RNA (rRNA).** Once the mRNA is attached to the ribosome, the transcription step of protein synthesis is complete.

Floating in the cytoplasm is yet another kind of ribonucleic acid, **transfer RNA (tRNA)**. tRNA occurs as triplets, or **anticodons,** that seek complementary triplet strands of mRNA, known as **triplets** or **codons.** For example, a triplet of AUC mRNA would pair with the complementary UAG tRNA. The three bases of the tRNA triplet represent a specific amino acid (see Table 3.2).

As the tRNA strand builds off the mRNA template, the amino acids are chemically linked together by a **peptide bond,** resulting in a chain of amino acids. A chain of these peptide bonds is called a **polypeptide.** Although a single polypeptide may function as a protein, in many cases multiple polypeptides must bind together and fold into a three-dimensional structure to form a functional protein. For example, hemoglobin, a molecule found on the surface of red blood cells, is composed of two pairs of polypeptide chains. Once the protein has formed, it breaks away from the tRNA and commences with its task, either structural or functional.

All of the DNA involved in protein synthesis is **coding DNA,** the molecular segments encoded for particular proteins. The total length of DNA in humans is about 3 billion nucleotides. Each of the 20,000 or so genes has about 5,000 nucleotides, so (according to the math) only about 3% of the DNA contains protein-coding material. Thus, most human DNA is **noncoding DNA.** Often interspersed with coding DNA

transfer RNA (tRNA) The molecules that are responsible for transporting amino acids to the ribosomes during protein synthesis.

anticodons Sequences of three nitrogen bases carried by tRNA, they match up with the complementary mRNA codons, and each designates a specific amino acid during protein synthesis.

triplets Sequences of three nitrogen bases each in DNA, known as codons in mRNA.

codons The sequences of three nitrogen bases carried by mRNA that are coded to produce specific amino acids in protein synthesis.

peptide bond Chemical bond that joins amino acids into a protein chain.

polypeptide Also known as a protein, a chain of amino acids held together by multiple peptide bonds.

coding DNA Sequences of a gene's DNA (also known as exons) that are coded to produce a specific protein and are transcribed and translated during protein synthesis.

noncoding DNA Sequences of a gene's DNA (also known as introns) that are not coded to produce specific proteins and are excised before protein synthesis.

The Two Steps of Protein Synthesis

The second function of DNA is to synthesize proteins, which are responsible for all the structures and functions of the body.

Step		Activity
1.	Transcription (nucleus)	The parental strand of DNA unzips, exposing two daughter strands of DNA.
		Free-floating RNA nucleotides match one exposed daughter strand of DNA.
		The strand of messenger RNA (mRNA) moves out of the nucleus and into the cytoplasm.
2.	Translation (cytoplasm)	The mRNA attaches to a ribosome in the cytoplasm.
		Triplets of transfer RNA (tRNA), with exposed bases and each carrying an amino acid specific to its set of three bases, recognize and bind with complementary base pairs of mRNA.
		The amino acids, linked by peptide bonds, form a chain called a polypeptide.
		The protein forms, either as a single polypeptide or as multiple polypeptides bound together.

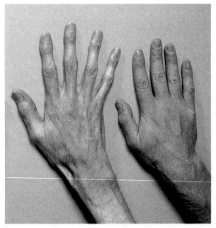

(a)

(b)

FIGURE 3.20

Marfan Syndrome **(a)** The hand on the right shows normal finger growth. The hand on the left has much longer and thinner fingers due to Marfan syndrome, a hereditary disorder of the regulatory genes that control connective tissue. As a result of Marfan syndrome, uncontrolled bone growth leads to long and thin fingers and toes, long and thin arms and legs, and increased stature. Organs such as the lungs and heart can also be negatively affected. **(b)** In the 1960s, a scientific paper asserted that US president Abraham Lincoln (1809–1865) was afflicted with Marfan syndrome. This still-controversial assessment was based entirely on Lincoln's unusual tallness and the length of his limbs.

from one end of the chromosome to the other, this noncoding DNA was long thought to have no function and was referred to as "junk DNA." However, non-protein-coding DNA is now known to have considerable regulatory functions throughout the genome; specifically, regulation of gene activities by helping to turn them on or off. New work on the genome suggests that 80% of the noncoding DNA is functional in some manner, containing instructions for proteins such as which genes a cell uses and when or determining if a cell becomes a bone cell or a brain cell. In protein synthesis, the noncoding DNA is cut out before translation. Recent studies by anthropological geneticists have suggested that noncoding DNA located close to genes that control brain function may have a role in the overall wiring of the brain cells to each other. Most research, however, focuses on the DNA that codes for particular body structures or particular regulatory functions. This DNA makes up the two main types of genes: structural and regulatory.

3.7 Genes: Structural and Regulatory

Structural genes are responsible for body structures, such as hair, blood, and other tissues. **Regulatory genes** turn other genes on and off, an essential activity in growth and development. If the genes that determine bones, for example, did not turn off at a certain point, bones would continue to grow well beyond what would be acceptable for a normal life **(Figure 3.20)**.

Chickens have the genes for tooth development, but they do not develop teeth because those genes are permanently turned off. Humans have a gene for total body hair coverage, but that gene is not turned on completely. The human genes for sexual maturity turn on during puberty, somewhat earlier in girls than in boys. Finally, regulatory genes can lead to lactose intolerance in humans (among the topics of chapter 4). In this instance, the gene that produces lactase—the enzyme for the digestion of milk—is turned off for most human populations around the world after weaning, usually by about age four. However, most humans of northern European and East African descent have inherited a different regulatory gene, which creates lactase persistence. A person who lacks this gene and eats dairy products experiences great gastrointestinal discomfort. A person who retains the gene is able to digest lactose owing to the persistence of lactase, thus enjoying the nutritional benefits of milk.

An organism's form and the arrangement of its tissues and organs are determined by regulatory genes called **homeotic (*Hox*) genes.** These master genes guide, for example, the embryological development of all the regions of an animal's body, such as the head, trunk, and limbs (**Figure 3.21**). This means that in the process of development, particular sets of *Hox* genes are turned on in a particular sequence, causing the correct structure or part of a structure to develop in each region. Until recently, scientists thought that the genes that control the development of the key structures and functions of the body differed from organism to organism. We now know, however, that the development of various body parts in complex organisms—such as the limbs, eyes, and vital organs—is governed by the *same* genes. *Hox* genes were first found in fruit flies, but research has shown that a common ancestral lineage has given organisms—ranging from flies to mice to humans—the same basic DNA structure in the key areas that control the development of form. Flies look like flies, mice look like mice, and humans look like humans because the *Hox* genes are turned on and off at different places and different times during the development process.

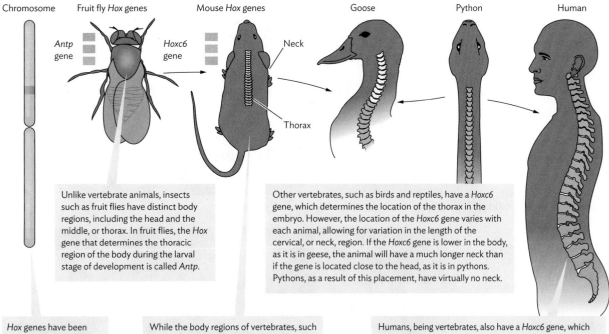

Chromosome   Fruit fly *Hox* genes   Mouse *Hox* genes   Goose   Python   Human

Antp gene

Hoxc6 gene

Neck

Thorax

Unlike vertebrate animals, insects such as fruit flies have distinct body regions, including the head and the middle, or thorax. In fruit flies, the *Hox* gene that determines the thoracic region of the body during the larval stage of development is called *Antp*.

Other vertebrates, such as birds and reptiles, have a *Hoxc6* gene, which determines the location of the thorax in the embryo. However, the location of the *Hoxc6* gene varies with each animal, allowing for variation in the length of the cervical, or neck, region. If the *Hoxc6* gene is lower in the body, as it is in geese, the animal will have a much longer neck than if the gene is located close to the head, as it is in pythons. Pythons, as a result of this placement, have virtually no neck.

Hox genes have been identified in all animals, plants, and fungi. They are found as a unique cluster known as the *Hox* cluster or *Hox* complex.

While the body regions of vertebrates, such as mice, are not as distinct as those of flies and other insects, *Hox* genes determine their body regions during embryological development. The *Hoxc6* gene in mice delimits the thoracic region, which is indicated by the thoracic vertebrae.

Humans, being vertebrates, also have a *Hoxc6* gene, which determines the location of the thoracic region. Humans have a neck of intermediate length when compared to geese and pythons; the *Hoxc6* gene is closer to the head in humans than in geese, but is lower than in pythons. The *Hoxc6* gene is responsible not just for determining the location of the thorax; in humans, this gene determines the development of the entire thoracic region, including mammary glands.

FIGURE 3.21

Homeotic (Hox) Genes Discovered in 1983 by Swiss and American researchers, these regulatory genes are coded to produce proteins that turn on many other genes, in particular those that determine the regions of the body during prenatal development. Without these genes, or if there are mutations in these genes, body development may be altered. For example, a mutation in the *Hox* genes of a fruit fly can cause a leg instead of an antenna to grow from the head. The gray refers to the thorax location for the four vertebrates, the *Hoxc6* gene.

3.8 Polymorphisms: Variations in Specific Genes

Along each chromosome, a specific gene has a specific physical location, or **locus** (plural, *loci*). This locus is of intense interest to geneticists, especially in understanding the appearance and evolution of genetic variation (among the topics of chapter 4). Alleles, the genetic subunits (see "Mechanisms of Inheritance" in chapter 2), are slightly different chemical structures at the same loci on homologous chromosomes. That is, they are simply chemically alternative versions of the same gene. Some genes have only one allele, while others have 20 or more.

Human blood type is one genetic trait with different alleles. Each person has one of four blood types—A, B, AB, or O—and these four types compose the ABO blood group system, first discovered in 1900 (**Figure 3.22**). Because it has two or more variants, a genetic trait such as this one is called a **polymorphism** (Greek *poly*, meaning "many"; Greek *morph*, meaning "form"). Each person has one *A, B,* or *O* allele on one chromosome

locus The location on a chromosome of a specific gene.

polymorphism Refers to the presence of two or more alleles at a locus and where the frequency of the alleles is greater than 1% in the population.

FIGURE 3.22

Antibody–Antigen System When a person receives a blood transfusion, the transfused blood must have the same blood type as the recipient's own to avoid an antibody–antigen reaction. **(a)** Each red blood cell has structures on its surface, known as **antigens**, that identify the cell as being type A, B, AB, or O. If the wrong type of blood is given to a person, the body's immune system recognizes the new antigens as foreign. Special proteins called **antibodies** are then produced in the blood in response to the "invaders." **(b)** The antibodies attach themselves to the foreign antigens, causing agglutination, or clumping, of the blood cells. Because the coagulated blood cannot pass through blood vessels properly, the recipient's tissues do not receive the blood they need. If not treated, the person might die.

For all the blood types in the ABO blood group system, **Table 3.3** shows the antigens, antibodies, and acceptable and unacceptable blood types in transfusions. For example, type A blood, which can result from *AO* alleles or *AA* alleles, has A antigens on its surface and anti-B antibodies, which will react with B or AB blood. (Genotypes and phenotypes are defined and discussed later in this section.)

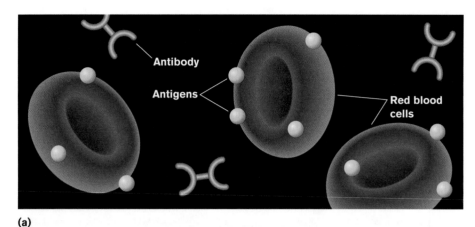

(a)

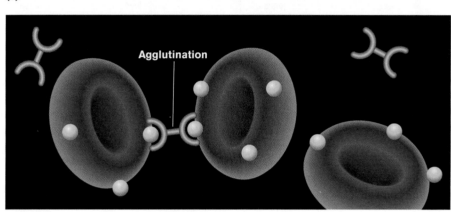

(b)

Table 3.3 The ABO Blood Group System

Phenotypes	Genotypes	Antigens	Antibodies	Unacceptable Blood Types	Acceptable Blood Types
A	AO, AA	A	Anti-B	B, AB	A, O
B	BO, BB	B	Anti-A	A, AB	B, O
AB	AB	A, B	None	None (universal recipient)	A, B, AB, O
O	OO	None (universal donor)	Anti-A, anti-B	A, B, AB	O

antigens Specific proteins, on the surface of cells, that stimulate the immune system's antibody production.

antibodies Molecules that form as part of the primary immune response to the presence of foreign substances; they attach to the foreign antigens.

law of segregation Mendel's first law, which asserts that the two alleles for any given gene (or trait) are inherited, one from each parent; during gamete production, only one of the two alleles will be present in each ovum or sperm.

of the homologous pair and another *A, B,* or *O* allele on the other chromosome of that pair. The combination determines the person's blood type.

Although Mendel did not know about chromosomes, he recognized that physical units of inheritance—which we now know to be the genes—segregate in a very patterned fashion. That is, his experiments with garden peas showed that the father contributes one physical unit and the mother contributes the other. This is Mendel's **law of segregation (Figure 3.23)**. For example, a person with blood type AB will pass on either an *A* or a *B* allele to a child but not both. The other allele will come from the other parent. This discovery was revolutionary because it explained how new variation arises in reproduction.

Some of the most exciting contemporary DNA research has revealed a whole new array of genetic markers. Showing a tremendous amount of variation within and

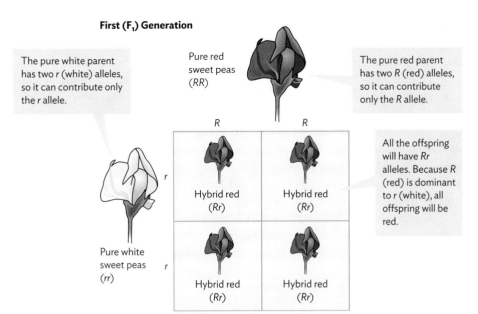

First (F₁) Generation

Pure red
sweet peas
(*RR*)

The pure white parent
has two *r* (white) alleles,
so it can contribute only
the *r* allele.

The pure red parent
has two *R* (red) alleles,
so it can contribute
only the *R* allele.

Pure white
sweet peas
(*rr*)

R   R

r   Hybrid red
(*Rr*)   Hybrid red
(*Rr*)

r   Hybrid red
(*Rr*)   Hybrid red
(*Rr*)

All the offspring
will have *Rr*
alleles. Because *R*
(red) is dominant
to *r* (white), all
offspring will be
red.

100% *Rr* = red

Second (F₂) Generation

Hybrid
red (*Rr*)

Each parent is a
hybrid, with one *R*
allele and one *r* allele.

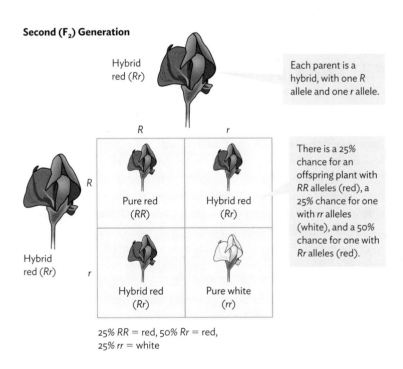

R   r

R   Pure red
(*RR*)   Hybrid red
(*Rr*)

r   Hybrid red
(*Rr*)   Pure white
(*rr*)

Hybrid
red (*Rr*)

There is a 25%
chance for an
offspring plant with
RR alleles (red), a
25% chance for one
with *rr* alleles
(white), and a 50%
chance for one with
Rr alleles (red).

25% *RR* = red, 50% *Rr* = red,
25% *rr* = white

FIGURE 3.23

Law of Segregation Mendel's first law, the
law of segregation, declares that the mother
and father contribute equally to an offspring's
genetic makeup. For each gene, a person
has two alleles (which can be the same or
different). One allele is from the person's
mother, and one is from the person's father.

Remember that meiosis (see Figure 3.15)
creates four gametes, each of which has only
one set of chromosomes and no pairs. Each
gamete, having this one set, can pass on only
one allele for each gene. If the gamete that the
father contributes to fertilization has the allele
for brown hair, for example, that is the only
allele the father will contribute to the offspring.
The other allele, for brown or a different color,
will come from the mother.

between human populations, these SNPs are known from well over 1 million sites on
the human genome. Closer examination of the human genome has also revealed that
DNA segments are often repeated, sometimes many times and for no apparent reason.
These repeated sections, or **microsatellites,** are highly individualistic, forming a
unique DNA signature for each person. Microsatellites have quickly become the most
important tool for individual identification, and they have proved especially valuable
in forensic science. For example, they have been used to identify victims of the 9/11
attacks as well as genocide and mass-murder fatalities in the Balkans, Iraq, Mexico,
and Argentina.

microsatellites Also called *short tandem
repeats* (STRs); refers to sequences of repeated
base pairs of DNA, usually no more than two
to six. If repeated excessively, they are often
associated with neurological disorders, such as
Huntington's chorea.

homozygous Refers to the condition in which a pair of alleles at a single locus on homologous chromosomes are the same.

heterozygous Refers to the condition in which a pair of alleles at a single locus on homologous chromosomes are different.

codominance Refers to two different alleles that are equally dominant; both are fully expressed in a heterozygote's phenotype.

Genotypes and Phenotypes: Genes and Their Expression

The two alleles, whether they are chemically identical (for example, *AA*) or chemically different (for example, *AO*), identify the genotype—the actual genetic material in the pair of homologous chromosomes. Chemically identical alleles are called **homozygous.** Chemically different alleles are called **heterozygous.** When alleles are heterozygous, the dominant one will be expressed in the phenotype—the visible manifestation of the gene. For example, individuals who are *AA* or who are *AO* have the same phenotype—A expresses dominance over *O*, and both individuals are blood type A. The recessive allele is not expressed. When you know simply that a person's blood type is A, you cannot tell whether that person's genotype is *AA* or *AO*. Rather, the blood type refers to the phenotype and not the genotype. If the person is *AO*, then the *O* allele is hidden because that allele is recessive. For the recessive allele to be expressed, each of the homologous chromosomes must have the recessive allele. For example, the alleles for type O blood are *OO*. For a person to have type O blood, both alleles in the pair of homologous chromosomes have to be *O*.

Sometimes alleles exhibit **codominance,** where neither chemically different version dominates the other. In the ABO blood group system, the *A* and *B* alleles are codominant and both are expressed. If someone has type AB blood, you know that person's phenotype and genotype.

3.9 The Complexity of Genetics

After the discovery of how the genetic code works (see chapter 2), the general impression about genes was that they simply represented specific locations of DNA coded to produce specific proteins. Much of the field of genetics, including anthropological genetics, was based on this "one gene–one protein" model. However, physical anthropologists, geneticists, and the many other disciplines interested in understanding the relationship between genes and their physical expression have learned that the relationship is considerably more complex than previously thought. Unlike PTC tasting (see pp. 102–103), many physical and behavioral traits are **polygenic**, affected by genes at many more loci than one or two. For example, adult human height is determined by hundreds of SNPs, many of which have been recently identified by geneticists. Similarly, neurodevelopmental disorders, such as autism spectrum disorder and attention-deficit-hyperactivity disorder, are highly heritable, but in a complex fashion involving interactions of various loci.

polygenic Refers to one phenotypic trait that is affected by two or more genes.

pleiotropy A single gene can have multiple effects.

On the other hand, **pleiotropy** may be operating, whereby a single gene can have multiple effects. One classic example of a pleiotropic effect is Marfan syndrome (see Figure 3.20). This condition is a dominant collagen disorder caused by a gene on chromosome 15. Collagen is a major protein, representing 25%–35% of all protein in the body. Because collagen is found in so many types of body tissues—for example, skeletal, visual, and cardiovascular—this single gene's effects are pervasive throughout the body. In fact, most complex traits are both polygenic and pleiotropic (**Figure 3.24**).

Adding to the complexity of the genome is the role of environment in influencing its physical manifestations. That is, we are seeing the importance of environment as an influence in genomic programming. In humans, thousands of complex phenotypes—such as birth weight, height, skin color, head form, tooth size, and eye shape—have multiple genetic components and are influenced by environmental factors. Many other complex phenotypes—such as autism spectrum disorder and other behavioral and

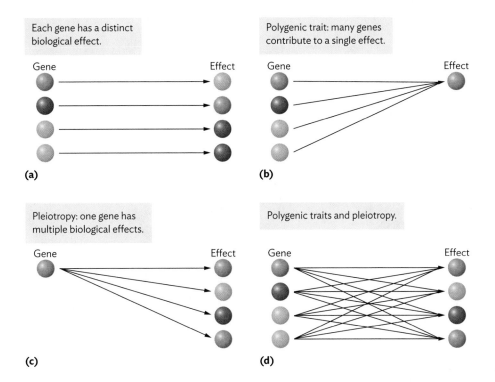

Each gene has a distinct biological effect.

Gene   Effect

(a)

Polygenic trait: many genes contribute to a single effect.

Gene   Effect

(b)

Pleiotropy: one gene has multiple biological effects.

Gene   Effect

(c)

Polygenic traits and pleiotropy.

Gene   Effect

(d)

FIGURE 3.24

Polygenic Traits and Pleiotropic Genes **(a)** Mendel's simple rules of inheritance **(b)** do not apply when one trait is affected by many genes. Eye color, for example, is determined by at least three genes. Because this trait is polygenic, some children's eye colors are very different from those of their parents. **(c)** Pleiotropic genes affect more than one physical trait. The *PKU* allele, for example, affects mental abilities and the coloration of hair and skin. A person who inherits this allele will have the disease phenylketonuria, in which a missing enzyme leads to mental retardation as well as reduced hair and skin pigmentation. **(d)** One trait can be affected by several genes, and each of those genes can affect several other traits as well.

cognitive disorders—probably have environmental influences. Scientists have long understood that environment plays an important role in the physical manifestations of various aspects of one's genome. For example, environmental factors affecting the mother can also affect the developing fetus. If the fetus is female, then those offspring resulting from her developing ova may also be affected. In this way, environmental factors operating at a given point in time can affect the health and well-being of not just the immediate offspring but also subsequent generations. Such **epigenetic** effects represent potentially heritable changes in behavior or biology but without altering the DNA sequence. In other words, the sequence of base pairs remains fully intact, but the changes owing to environmental circumstances modify the way that DNA is regulated and expressed, without modifying the DNA itself.

A new and exciting area of research is showing that epigenetic mechanisms occurring within cells may be activated by a variety of behavioral and environmental factors. In this regard, regulation of DNA in the offspring may be altered because of epigenetic phenomena, resulting in birth defects and other negative outcomes. These outcomes are due to **methylation**, a process in which a methyl group, a chemical, attaches to the DNA (**Figure 3.25**). In this process, methylation represses or fully stops gene expression, which may result in profound outcomes for offspring. Methylation can

epigenetic Refers to chemical changes in the genome affecting how the underlying DNA is used in production of proteins, but without altering the DNA sequences.

methylation The attachment of a methyl group, a simple chemical, to DNA at certain sites throughout the genome.

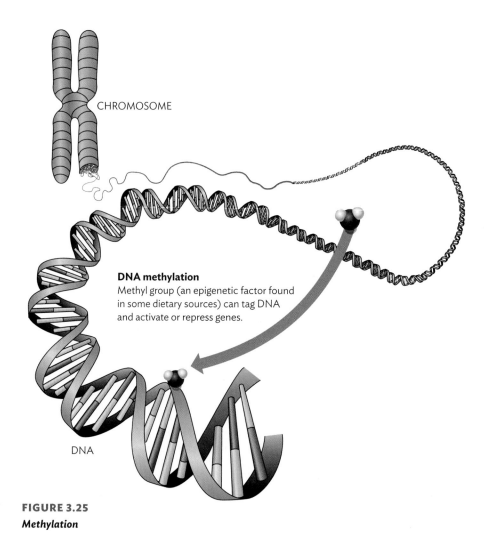

DNA methylation
Methyl group (an epigenetic factor found in some dietary sources) can tag DNA and activate or repress genes.

DNA

FIGURE 3.25
Methylation

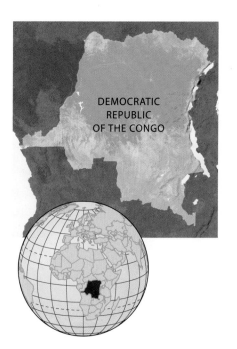

DEMOCRATIC REPUBLIC OF THE CONGO

be activated by various factors such as exposure to temperature extremes or environmental chemicals, disease, poor nutrition, and a variety of behaviors such as smoking, alcohol consumption, and inactivity.

The interaction between the environment and the genes of the mother and her offspring, from conception to birth, has considerable impact on the normal growth of the fetus as well as risk for disease after birth. Indeed, obesity and some birth defects, common diseases, and cancers appear to be influenced by epigenetic factors. For example, key nutrients—including vitamins A, B$_3$, C, and D—play roles in regulating DNA. An insufficiency of these nutrients is linked to diabetes, atherosclerosis, and cancer. By investigating the epigenetics of health and behavior, scientists have opened up a pathway toward understanding factors that influence parent and offspring health. In short, researchers have shown how environment interacts with the genome across generations. These discoveries have begun to revolutionize our understanding of the effects of environment on the genome, underscoring the role of environmental circumstances—both positive and negative—in health.

The emerging record of epigenetics is revealing that gene expression can be influenced in profound ways by social circumstances. For example, American anthropological geneticist Connie Mulligan has found a probable link between stress and gene expression in mothers and their offspring in the Democratic Republic of the Congo, where communities have been subjected to warfare and violence for many years. In these settings, there is clear evidence of an association between war-related stress and genetic changes in infants, such as in the *NR3C1* gene, the gene located on chromosome 5 that codes for a protein associated with newborn birth weight. Similarly, exposure of the fetus to maternal stress associated with intimate partner violence and other violence-related stressors has been identified with changes in the *NR3C1* gene. These findings support the notion that various factors relating to exposure of the mother to violence may be important methylation factors across generations.

The DNA revolution has made it possible to understand in much greater detail the underlying principles of inheritance laid out so eloquently by Gregor Mendel a century and a half ago. In presenting the great breadth of knowledge about how genetic variation is transmitted from parents to offspring and the growing understanding of the impact of environment on the genome, this chapter has laid the groundwork for the topic of the next chapter, the study of genetic change in populations.

CHAPTER 3 REVIEW

ANSWERING THE BIG QUESTIONS

1. What is the genetic code?

- The genetic code is DNA, packaged in chromosomes.
- Nuclear DNA provides most of the genetic code.

2. What does the genetic code (DNA) do?

- DNA serves as the chemical template for its own replication and for the creation of proteins.
- DNA replication is the first step in producing new cells.
  —Mitosis produces two identical somatic cells. In humans, each has 46 chromosomes in 23 homologous pairs.
  —Meiosis produces four gametes. In humans, each has 23 chromosomes.
- Proteins are combinations of amino acids. They compose the entire body and determine all of its functions, from conception through maturity.
  —The two categories of proteins are governed by two corresponding gene types: structural and regulatory.

3. What is the genetic basis for human variation?

- A gene is a linear sequence of nucleotides that codes for specific bodily structures and functions. Each gene has a particular locus on each chromosome.
- Each pair of homologous (like) chromosomes consists of a paternal chromosome and a maternal chromosome.
- An individual's genotype, or actual genetic composition, is based on two alleles, one from the father and one from the mother. Alleles can be chemically identical or chemically different. The genotype is expressed physically as a phenotype.
- Most physical characteristics are determined by more than one gene (polygenic), and some genes can have multiple effects (pleiotropy).
- Epigenetics, the study of environmental effects on gene function, is yielding revolutionary insights into how biological and cultural circumstances impact inheritance.

KEY TERMS

amino acids
autosomes
codominance
codons
complementary bases
crossing-over
diploid
epigenetic
gametes
genome
haploid
haplotypes
heterozygous
homeotic (*Hox*) genes
homologous
homozygous
karyotype
law of independent assortment
law of segregation
locus

meiosis
microsatellites
mitochondria
mitosis
nondisjunctions
nucleotide
pleiotropy
polygenic
polymorphism
recombination
regulatory genes
replication
ribonucleic acid
ribosomes
sex chromosomes
single nucleotide polymorphisms
somatic cells
structural genes
transcription
translation
translocations
zygote

STUDY QUIZ

1. **Which is *true* about gametes (sex cells)?**
   a. Gametes are diploid.
   b. Gametes are produced through mitosis.
   c. Gametes pass the genetic code from parent to offspring.
   d. Gametes are found in every tissue of the body.

2. **What process is necessary for both mitosis and meiosis to occur?**
   a. DNA replication
   b. recombination
   c. crossing-over
   d. translocation

3. **Which is *not* a role played by a type of RNA in protein synthesis?**
   a. mRNA (messenger RNA) transcribes the DNA template.
   b. rRNA (ribosomal RNA) makes up ribosomes, which translate the genetic code into protein.
   c. tRNA (transfer RNA) pairs RNA bases with amino acids.
   d. pRNA (protein RNA) is the product of chemically linked amino acids.

4. **For a Mendelian trait that is not codominant, an individual with a heterozygous genotype will express**
   a. the dominant phenotype.
   b. the recessive phenotype.
   c. a blend of the dominant phenotype and the recessive phenotype.
   d. no phenotype for that trait.

5. **Human height is affected by many genes, so it is a _____ trait.**
   a. pleiotropic
   b. codominant
   c. polygenic
   d. epigenetic

EVOLUTION REVIEW

INSIGHTS FROM GENETICS

Synopsis DNA is often described as a genetic blueprint because it encodes the plan for an organism's traits and ensures that these traits are passed on to future generations. One of the major functions of the DNA molecule is replication: creating identical copies of itself. The reliability of this process influences evolution by making variation heritable; that is, traits will be passed on to offspring, who will be similar to their parents. A second major function of DNA is directing protein synthesis, which is how genotype (genetic code) is translated to phenotype (physical expression of this code). Protein synthesis is the basis for the traits that allow organisms to interact with their environment and undergo natural selection. Molecular genetics can be complex. Many traits are polygenic (influenced by more than one gene), and many genes are pleiotropic (operating on more than one trait). Furthermore, epigenetic (environmental, nongenetic) phenomena can alter DNA regulation and phenotype without altering the DNA sequence itself. Thus, genetics both complicates and illuminates our understanding of human variation and evolution.

Q1. What are the two types of cell division? How does each type affect individual genetic variation?

Q2. What is recombination? How does the effect of recombination differ from that of mutation?

Q3. Given our growing knowledge of humans from a genetic perspective, why is it still important for physical anthropologists to study physical remains (for example, bones and teeth) when testing hypotheses about evolution and variation among ourselves and our closest living and fossil relatives?

Hint Think about the types of remains available for living and fossil organisms and about how genetics is related to physical characteristics.

Q4. Consider various human characteristics, such as height, weight, skin color, head form, and eye shape. Are the phenotypic expressions of these characteristics discontinuous (able to be assigned to discrete categories) or continuous (on a continuum rather than separable into discrete categories)? What might they tell us about the mechanisms behind human variation?

Q5. Epigenetic phenomena are environmental factors that affect the way DNA is regulated and may affect future generations. How do epigenetic phenomena differ from Lamarckian inheritance of acquired characteristics (discussed in chapter 2)?

Hint Compare the heritability of characteristics involved in epigenetics and Lamarckism.

ADDITIONAL READINGS

Carey, N. 2012. *The Epigenetics Revolution: How Modern Biology Is Rewriting Our Understanding of Genetics, Disease, and Inheritance.* New York: Columbia University Press.

Kaestle, F. A. 2010. Paleogenetics: Ancient DNA in anthropology. Pp. 427–441 in C. S. Larsen, ed. *A Companion to Biological Anthropology.* Chichester, UK: Wiley-Blackwell.

Mielke, J. H., L. W. Konigsberg, and J. H. Relethford. 2006. *Human Biological Variation.* New York: Oxford University Press.

Portugal, F. H. and J. S. Cohen. 1977. *A Century of DNA: A History of the Discovery of the Structure and Function of the Genetic Substance.* Cambridge, MA: MIT Press.

Relethford, J. H. 2003. *Reflections of Our Past: How Human History Is Revealed in Our Genes.* Boulder, CO: Westview Press.

Sapolsky, R. M. 2004. Of mice, men, and genes. *Natural History* May: 21–24, 31.

Sykes, B. 2001. *The Seven Daughters of Eve: The Science That Reveals Our Genetic Ancestry.* New York: Norton.

Weiss, M. L. and J. Tackney. 2012. An introduction to genetics. Pp. 53–98 in S. Stinson, B. Bogin, and D. O'Rourke, eds. *Human Biology: An Evolutionary and Biocultural Perspective,* 2nd ed. Hoboken, NJ: Wiley-Blackwell.

The key driver of evolution is natural selection. Members of species having genetic variation that enhances survival to reproductive age will tend to live to reproductive age. In the leafy sea dragon, for example, there is selection for genes controlling for pigmentation and other attributes of body phenotype. These phenotypes make it difficult for predators to see this animal. This "visual" selection is commonplace worldwide now, as it must have been in the past.

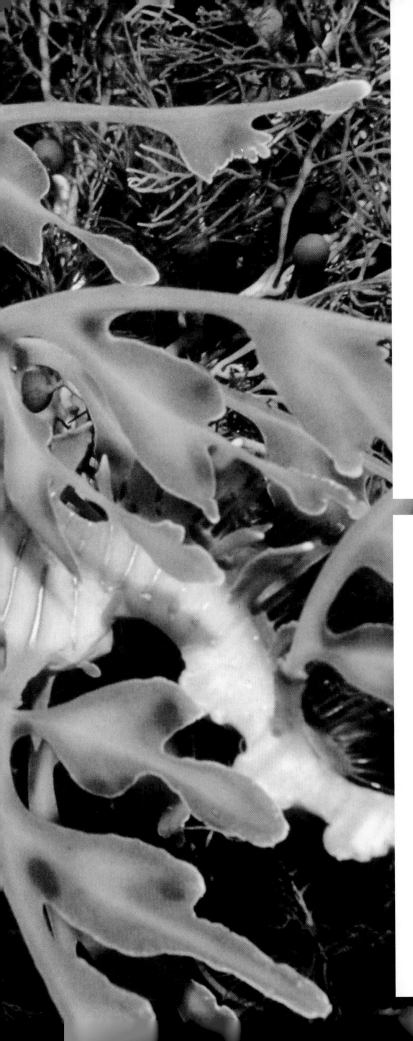

4

Genes and Their Evolution

POPULATION GENETICS

BIG QUESTIONS

1. **What causes evolutionary (genetic) change?**

2. **How is evolutionary (genetic) change measured, and how is the cause determined?**

One of the great stories about genetics comes not from a research program of a famous scientist in charge of a large laboratory filled with technicians, graduate students, and postdoctoral fellows and funded by a multimillion-dollar grant, but rather from a student with a simple hypothesis and a passionate interest in testing a hypothesis. At Oxford University in the late 1940s, a 20-something Anthony Allison was finishing his coursework in basic sciences and was about to start his clinical medical training. Allison had grown up in Kenya; his interest in anthropology reflected his intellectual curiosity, but his desire to become a doctor was motivated by an ambition to help improve native Kenyans' quality of life. While at Oxford, he was exposed to the ideas of the English scientists R. A. Fisher and J. B. S. Haldane and the American scientist Sewall Wright, pioneers of the new field of population genetics and advocates of the novel idea that gene frequencies were tied to natural selection.

After a bout of malaria, Allison decided to help Kenyans (and other peoples) by seeking a cure for this disease. In 1949, he joined an expedition to document blood groups and genetic traits in native Kenyans. On this expedition, Allison discovered that in areas affected by malaria, especially along Kenya's coast (southeast) and near Lake

Victoria (southwest), a remarkably high 20%–30% of the population carried the gene for sickle-cell anemia. But in the highlands (west), where there was no malaria, less than 1% of the people carried the gene. In what he described as a "flash of inspiration," he hypothesized that individuals with the sickle-cell allele were resistant to malaria and that natural selection was operating on the gene. But how? he wondered.

Before pursuing these ideas, Allison completed his medical education. In 1953, with just enough money to buy passage back to Kenya and for food and simple lodging, he spent a year researching the relationship between malaria and sickle-cell anemia. He generated lab and field data, looking at malaria infection rates in people with and without the sickle-cell allele. His results showed that carriers of the gene are much more likely to survive malaria than are noncarriers. Natural selection was favoring the carriers.

The next year, Allison published three landmark scientific articles in rapid succession, laying out the proof for his hypothesis. Gene frequencies *are* tied to natural selection: carriers of the sickle-cell allele survive longer and produce more offspring than do noncarriers. In Allison's words, "disease is an agent of natural selection." Although his ideas met with strong skepticism, eventually Allison's hypothesis was accepted by most scientists. His research enabled generations of geneticists and anthropologists to further investigate genes and their evolution, all of these researchers asking why some gene frequencies remain the same while others change over time.

Human populations exhibit some remarkable biological differences, and the science of genetics helps biologists answer questions about those differences. The questions and the answers are founded on Darwin's discovery that phenotypes—the physical manifestations of genes—change over time. In addition, Mendel's research on garden peas revealed how the inheritance of genes produces variation in phenotypes. These two revolutionary scientific discoveries inform our understanding of biological variation and its evolution.

Before considering this chapter's big questions, we need to look at populations and species, the units that evolutionary biologists work with.

4.1 Demes, Reproductive Isolation, and Species

To show how genetic variation is produced, the previous chapter focused on the individual and the transmission of genes from parents to offspring. When physical anthropologists and geneticists study the genetics of individuals, they focus on the reproductive population, or **deme:** members of a species that produce offspring. That is, evolution is about groups of organisms that have the potential to reproduce. When physical anthropologists talk about populations, they often refer to the **gene pool,** which is all the genetic material within a population. When geneticists talk about the gene pool, they are even more specific, referring to all the variation within a specific genetic locus. For example, some people carry the sickle-cell allele and some do not.

The concept of the breeding population is also central to the definition of *species.* A species is composed of all the populations (and their individual members) that are capable of breeding with each other and producing viable (fertile) offspring. Species, therefore, are defined on the basis of **reproductive isolation (Figure 4.1).** In biological terms, if two populations are reproductively isolated, members of one population cannot interbreed with members of the other. Reproductive isolation is largely related

deme A local population of organisms that have similar genes, interbreed, and produce offspring.

gene pool All the genetic information in the breeding population.

reproductive isolation Any circumstance that prevents two populations from interbreeding and exchanging genetic material, such as when two populations are separated by a large body of water or a major mountain range.

(a)

FIGURE 4.1

Reproductive Isolation **(a)** This map depicts
the distribution of two related bird species:
(b) ostriches are found in Africa, while **(c)**
emus are found in Australia. These two
species share a common ancestor, but the
ocean between the two groups prevented
them from interbreeding for thousands of
years. Eventually, this geographic isolation led
to reproductive isolation and two separate
species.

(b)　　　　　　　　　　　　　　　　**(c)**

to geographic isolation. If two populations of the same species become isolated, such
as by a mountain range or a large body of water, enough genetic differences could accumulate for two entirely different species to emerge.

In the living world, we can observe members of a species to verify that they can
produce offspring. Obviously, we cannot do this with fossils. Rather, we have to infer
reproductive isolation in fossil populations on the basis of geographic distance and the
physical resemblance between fossils. Fossil remains that share the same characteristics in morphology of teeth and bones likely represent members of the same species
(**Figure 4.2**). (This important concept will inform the discussion of primate evolution
in chapters 9–13. Fossils are the subject of chapter 8.)

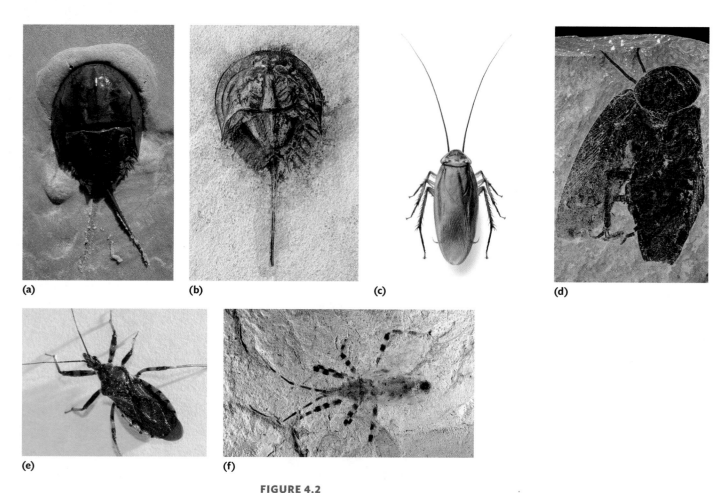

(a) (b) (c) (d)

(e) (f)

FIGURE 4.2

Living Fossils Fossilized remains might represent animals and plants that lived thousands or millions of years ago, but a number of such organisms have counterparts that live today. Compare the forms of the following organisms: **(a)** living horseshoe crab and **(b)** fossil of *Mesolimulus walchii,* the ancestor to the modern horseshoe crab; **(c)** living cockroach and **(d)** a 49 million–year-old fossil cockroach; **(e)** living Assassin bug (Ruduriidae) and **(f)** 50 million-year-old fossil Assassin bug (Ruduriidae).

microevolution Small-scale evolution, such as changes in allele frequency, that occurs from one generation to the next.

macroevolution Large-scale evolution, such as a speciation event, that occurs after hundreds or thousands of generations.

equilibrium A condition in which the system is stable, balanced, and unchanging.

Population genetics (see "The Evolutionary Synthesis, the Study of Populations, and the Causes of Evolution" in chapter 2) is the study of changes in genetic material—specifically, the change in frequency of alleles (genes). Genes are the records from which evolution is reconstructed, both over the course of a few generations (**microevolution**) and over many generations (**macroevolution; Figure 4.3**). Geneticists strive to *document* genetic change and to explain *why* it occurred. Such documentation and explanation are the central issues of evolutionary biology. Population geneticists, physical anthropologists, and other evolutionary biologists tend to focus on genetic change over time. For example, if a trait in a population has two alleles, *A* and *a,* and the parent generation is 60% *A* and 40% *a* and the next generation is 65% *A* and 35% *a,* scientists would want to know why the evolution occurred—why the frequency of the *A* allele increased in the population.

Just as interesting, however, are instances in which frequency does not change over time; that is, when the frequencies of a population's alleles for a particular trait are in a state of **equilibrium.** For example, in areas of West Africa where malaria is common, the frequency of the sickle-cell allele remains relatively constant. What factors—forces of evolution—account for deviations from equilibrium?

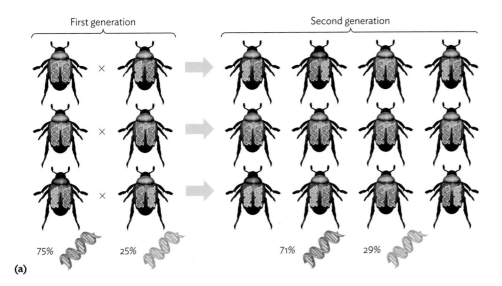

(a)

First generation | Second generation

75%   25%   71%   29%

FIGURE 4.3

Microevolution and Macroevolution (a)
Microevolution is change in gene frequency over a few generations. For example, the beetles in this diagram have either of two colors, represented by two alleles. In the first generation, 75% of the color alleles are green and 25% are brown. In the second generation, 71% of the color alleles are green and 29% are brown. Thus, the frequencies of the green and brown alleles have undergone a microevolutionary change. **(b)** Macroevolution is substantial change over many generations—the creation of new species. For example, over 60 million years, the eohippus—a small, dog-sized animal with multitoed feet that inhabited rainforests—evolved into the modern horse. Among the species' large-scale changes were increases in overall body size and height as well as the loss of toes. Horses' single-toed hooves enable them to run more efficiently in the open grasslands they naturally inhabit.

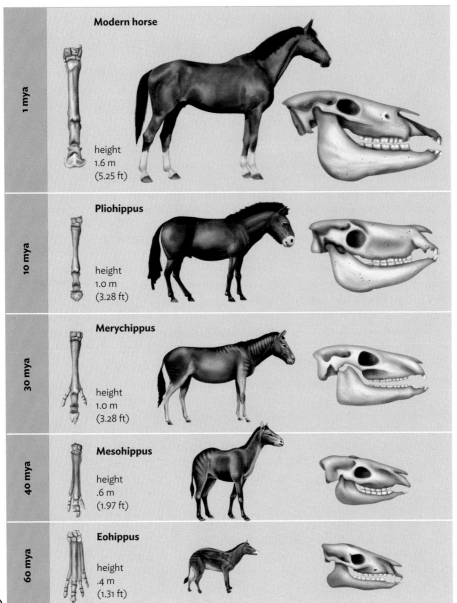

(b)

Modern horse
height 1.6 m (5.25 ft)
1 mya

Pliohippus
height 1.0 m (3.28 ft)
10 mya

Merychippus
height 1.0 m (3.28 ft)
30 mya

Mesohippus
height .6 m (1.97 ft)
40 mya

Eohippus
height .4 m (1.31 ft)
60 mya

GOT MILK? THE LCT

Lactose Tolerance and Lactase Persistence

Lactose is a complex sugar composed of the linked simple sugars glucose and galactose. Animals obtain it by consuming milk and milk products, and they digest it with lactase (technically called lactase-phlorizin hydrolase), an enzyme produced in the cells lining the wall of the small intestine. The enzyme breaks down the lactose into its two sugar components.

As noted in chapter 3 (see "Genes: Structural and Regulatory"), most children and adults around the world—especially in native populations across Asia, Africa, Australia, southern Europe, and both North and South America—experience a decline in lactase activity after weaning, generally around age four. As a result, people lose the ability to digest lactose. If lactose-intolerant individuals drink milk or eat ice cream, for example, they feel discomfort in the digestive tract.

A very uncommon ability to digest lactose, known as lactase persistence, is inherited as an autosomal dominant gene, *LCT*, with the three genotypes *PP* (homozygous for lactase persistence), *RR* (homozygous for lactase nonpersistence), and *PR* (heterozygous for lactase persistence but having intermediate output of the enzyme). The gene coded to produce the enzyme is on chromosome 2. Some 77% of European Americans and only 14% of African Americans have the *LCT* gene, and most human populations around the globe approach the African American frequency.

Nutritional anthropologists have documented some interesting exceptions to the widespread loss of lactase production in humans, and this evidence suggests that natural selection favors the persistence. There are remarkably high proportions of lactase persistence in three regions of the world, including western Europe, with especially high frequency in the Baltic and North Sea areas; West Africa; and a band encompassing far eastern Africa to the Indian subcontinent. In all three geographic settings, populations generally have elevated lactase activity their entire lives. And all these populations have long histories of animal husbandry and milk consumption.

The American cultural geographer Frederick Simoons has hypothesized that the ability to digest lactose reflects these peoples' histories. According to this model, the primitive (unevolved) condition is lactase deficiency after weaning. However, with the domestication of animals (among the topics of chapter 13), which began at the end of the Pleistocene era (on geologic time, see chapter 8), natural selection began to favor lactase persistence in human groups that depended on animal milk as a protein source. In short, wherever their ancestors did not raise cattle or other milk animals, humans are not able to metabolize lactose.

Research undertaken by the American molecular anthropologist Sarah Tishkoff and colleagues suggests that the *LCT* gene is a mutation that arose independently in northern Europe and East Africa. Tishkoff and colleagues speculate that the mutation and the strong natural selection for it occurred within the past 7,000 years, but DNA analysis of a half-dozen or so skeletons dating to about that time suggests

PHENOTYPE

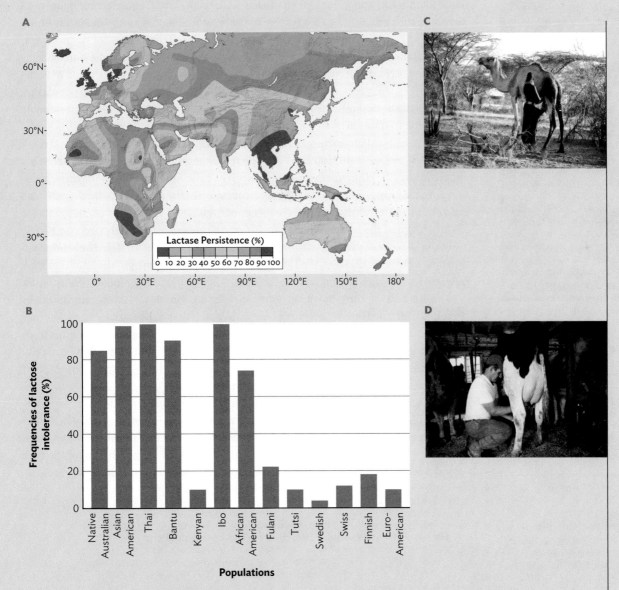

A

B

Frequencies of lactose intolerance (%)

Populations

Native Australian, Asian American, Thai, Bantu, Kenyan, Ibo, African American, Fulani, Tutsi, Swedish, Swiss, Finnish, Euro-American

C

D

the shift occurred somewhat later. In any case, like the sickle-cell allele, lactase persistence is one of the most powerful signals of natural selection known in humans. The anthropology of lactase deficiency explains a condition that affects billions of people today. *Anthropology matters!*

(a)

(b)

FIGURE 4.4

Godfrey Hardy and Wilhelm Weinberg (a) Hardy and **(b)** Weinberg independently discovered the equilibrium that bears their names and is still used in population genetics. This equilibrium, worked out in a simple Punnett square, is used to assess whether gene frequencies have changed from one generation to the next. It can also be used to estimate the genotype frequencies of the subsequent generation.

Hardy–Weinberg law of equilibrium A mathematical model in population genetics that reflects the relationship between frequencies of alleles and of genotypes; it can be used to determine whether a population is undergoing evolutionary changes.

4.2 Hardy–Weinberg Law: Testing the Conditions of Genetic Equilibrium

In 1908, Godfrey Hardy (1877–1947), an English mathematician, and Wilhelm Weinberg (1862–1937), a German obstetrician, independently recognized that some alleles are in a state of equilibrium (**Figure 4.4**). If no mutation or natural selection or gene flow occurs, if the population is large, if mating is random, and if all members of the population produce the same number of offspring, then genotype frequencies at a single gene locus will remain the same after one generation. Moreover, the equilibrium frequencies will be a function of the allele frequencies at the locus. This is called the **Hardy–Weinberg law of equilibrium.** In the simplest case (**Table 4.1**), a single locus has A (dominant) and a (recessive) alleles, with respective frequencies of p and q. In assessing the population as a whole, it is assumed that males and females have both alleles. The Hardy–Weinberg law predicts the genotype frequencies for the next generation after one mating, where p^2 is the genotype frequency for the AA homozygous alleles, $2pq$ is the genotype frequency for the Aa (heterozygous) alleles, and q^2 is the genotype frequency for the aa homozygous alleles. In other words, the total population (100%) should be the sum of the frequencies of three genotypes, expressed by the simple mathematical equation $p^2 + 2pq + q^2 = 1$. If a hypothetical population were 60% A ($p = .6$) and 40% a ($q = .4$), then the genotype frequencies in the next generation would work out to $AA = .36$, $Aa = .48$, and $aa = .16$. The frequencies can be expressed as decimals or percentages, but they are expressed most often as decimals. Because the three genotypes are the only genotypes for the gene in question in the population, the frequencies must add up to 1, or 100%. So, if the frequency of AA is .36 (or 36%), the frequency of Aa is .48 (or 48%), and the frequency of aa is .16 (or 16%), together they add up to 1 (or 100%).

In the absence of evolution, the frequencies of the genotypes will in theory remain the same forever. In this way, the Hardy–Weinberg equilibrium hypothesizes that gene frequencies remain the same because no evolutionary change takes place (**Figure 4.5**).

By determining the genotype frequencies for a population at different points in time, however, the Hardy–Weinberg equation establishes expectations as to whether evolution is operating on a particular gene. If the genotype frequencies change from one generation to the next, the population is not in equilibrium—it is evolving. If the frequencies remain the same, the population is in equilibrium—the population is not evolving, at least with respect to the locus being studied.

What might cause a population to change its allele frequencies and go out of equilibrium? As discussed in chapters 2 and 3, genes are passed from generation to generation by interbreeding within populations in particular and among members of the same species in general, and genetic changes result from one or a combination of the four forces of evolution: mutation, natural selection, genetic drift, and gene flow.

Table 4.1 Punnett Square for Hardy–Weinberg Equilibrium

		Females	
		A (p)	a (q)
Males	A (p)	AA (p²)	Aa (pq)
	a (q)	Aa (pq)	aa (q²)

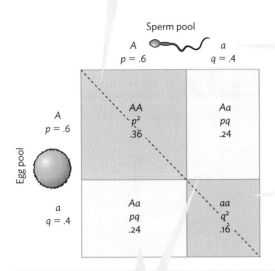

Approximately 36% of the offspring will have the genotype *AA*. The estimate is made by multiplying the male p (frequency of A allele = .6) with the female p (.6). Thus, $p \times p = p^2$, and $.6 \times .6 = .36$. The frequency of the *AA* genotype is represented by p^2.

Sperm pool

A a
$p = .6$ $q = .4$

A
$p = .6$

AA p^2 .36	*Aa* pq .24
Aa pq .24	*aa* q^2 .16

Egg pool

a
$q = .4$

The allele frequencies for males and females in this population are the same: p (frequency of A allele) is .6 and q (frequency of a allele) is .4.

Approximately 16% of the offspring will have the genotype *aa*. This estimate is made by multiplying the male q (frequency of a allele = .4) with the female q (.4). Thus, $q \times q = q^2$, and $.4 \times .4 = .16$. The frequency of the *aa* genotype is represented by q^2.

Approximately 48% of the offspring will have the genotype *Aa*. This estimate is made by multiplying the male p (.6) with the female q (.4) and the male q (.4) with the female p (.6). Thus, $p \times q = pq$ and $q \times p = qp$; $.6 \times .4 = .24$ and $.4 \times .6 = .24$. Because both $p \times q$ and $q \times p$ must be included, the two results are added together. $2pq = 2 \times .24$ (or $.24 + .24$) $= .48$. The frequency of the *Aa* genotype is represented by $2pq$.

FIGURE 4.5

Gene Frequencies in Equilibrium As this Punnett square illustrates, the Hardy–Weinberg equilibrium captures gene frequencies in a static moment, when no evolutionary change is taking place. Crossing the males (sperm pool) and females (egg pool) of the population produces theoretical genotype frequencies of the next generation.

Once evolutionary change takes place, the actual genotype frequencies will differ significantly from the theoretical genotype frequencies expressed in this Punnett square. For example, if the population later turns out to be 5% *AA*, 65% *aa*, and 30% *Aa*, an evolutionary force has most likely altered its genotype frequencies.

4.3 Mutation: The Only Source of New Alleles

During cell reproduction, DNA almost always replicates itself exactly. Sometimes, however, the replication process produces an error or a collection of errors in the DNA code. If the problem is not at once detected and corrected by a set of enzymes that monitor DNA, a mutation results. The mutation can be any heritable change in the structure or amount of genetic material.

Some of any person's DNA is noncoding (see "Producing Proteins: The Other Function of DNA" in chapter 3) and nonfunctional. For noncoding, nonfunctional DNA, mutations do not affect the individual's health, well-being, or survival. But a new sequence of *coding* DNA that results from mutation may have profound consequences, positive or negative. For example, the mutation might code the DNA for a protein with an altered or different function from that performed by the protein coded for in the original parent strand of DNA, or the mutation might create a sequence that results in either no protein or an abnormal protein (**Figure 4.6**). Mutations occur at random and can occur in any cell, but the ones with consequences for future generations take place in gametes. Gametes may transfer mutations to offspring, depending on what happens during meiosis in the parents. Regardless of their causes or outcomes, in the absence of gene flow (see "Gene Flow: Spread of Genes across Population Boundaries" later) *mutations are the only source of new genetic variation in a population.*

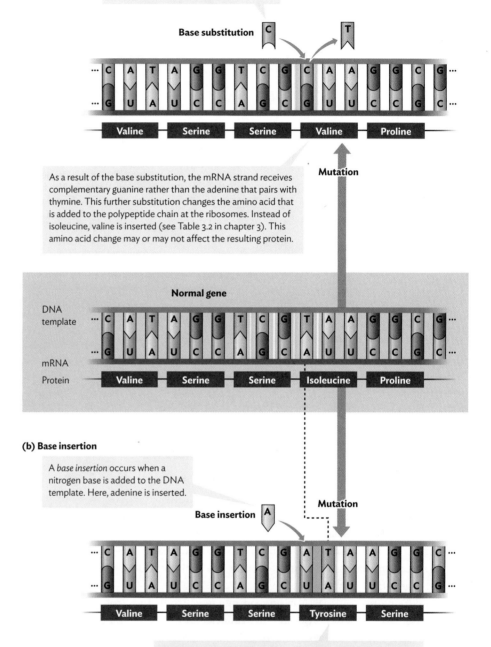

(a) Base substitution

A *base substitution*, the simplest kind of mutation, occurs when a single nitrogen base is substituted by another base. Here, thymine is being replaced by cytosine.

Base substitution C   T

Valine — Serine — Serine — Valine — Proline

Mutation

As a result of the base substitution, the mRNA strand receives complementary guanine rather than the adenine that pairs with thymine. This further substitution changes the amino acid that is added to the polypeptide chain at the ribosomes. Instead of isoleucine, valine is inserted (see Table 3.2 in chapter 3). This amino acid change may or may not affect the resulting protein.

Normal gene

DNA template

mRNA

Protein   Valine — Serine — Serine — Isoleucine — Proline

(b) Base insertion

A *base insertion* occurs when a nitrogen base is added to the DNA template. Here, adenine is inserted.

Base insertion A

Mutation

Valine — Serine — Serine — Tyrosine — Serine

The mRNA receives the appropriate complementary nitrogen base, uracil. When the mRNA reaches the ribosomes, the series of codons is changed because of the insertion. Instead of reading the correct AUU, the ribosomes read UAU, which codes for the amino acid tyrosine instead of isoleucine. Again, this amino acid change may or may not affect the resulting protein.

FIGURE 4.6

DNA Mutations During the transcription phase of protein synthesis, errors in the DNA template can affect the resulting protein. Two types of DNA mutation are illustrated in these diagrams: **(a)** base substitution and **(b)** base insertion.

Mutations involving incorrect base pairing are called **point mutations. A synonymous point mutation** creates an altered triplet in the DNA, but the alteration carries with it the original amino acid. Because the amino acid is the same, the protein formed is the same. A **nonsynonymous point mutation** results in a matchup that brings along a different amino acid. Such a mutation can have dramatic results for the individual carrying it. For example, a mutation on human chromosome 11 results in a GUG codon instead of a GAG codon. The GUG codon is encoded to produce the amino acid valine, whereas the GAG codon would have normally led to the production of glutamic acid. This substitution leads to the abnormal hemoglobin that results in sickle-cell anemia (discussed later in this chapter).

As a result of the shifting base pairs caused by base insertion, the reading frame of a gene is altered or stopped entirely. This **frameshift mutation** produces a protein having no function. Such a mutation usually involves a small part of the DNA sequence, often just a base pair or a relatively limited number of base pairs.

Other kinds of mutations can affect far more of the genome. **Transposable elements** are genes that can copy themselves to entirely different places along the DNA sequence. If such a gene inserts itself into another gene, it can fundamentally alter the other gene, doing real damage. If, as is strongly likely, the gene transposes itself to a noncoding area of the DNA sequence, little or no significant alteration will occur.

Large parts of DNA sequences or entire chromosomes can be affected by mutations. An entire piece of chromosome can be moved to another chromosome, can be placed differently on the same chromosome, or can be positioned in a chromosome backward. The effects of these mutations are highly variable and depend on the loci of the mutations.

In the most extreme mutations, entire chromosomes can be duplicated (a trisomy) or lost altogether (a monosomy). Examples of trisomies are Down syndrome, with its extra chromosome 21 (see "Meiosis: Production of Gametes [Sex Cells]" in chapter 3) and **Klinefelter's syndrome,** a common sex chromosome variant that appears in about 1 of 500–1,000 births (**Figure 4.7**).

point mutations Replacements of a single nitrogen base with another base, which may or may not affect the amino acid for which the triplet codes.

synonymous point mutation A neutral point mutation in which the substituted nitrogen base creates a triplet coded to produce the same amino acid as that of the original triplet.

nonsynonymous point mutation A point mutation that creates a triplet coded to produce a different amino acid from that of the original triplet.

frameshift mutation The change in a gene due to the insertion or deletion of one or more nitrogen bases, which causes the subsequent triplets to be rearranged and the codons to be read incorrectly during translation.

transposable elements Mobile pieces of DNA that can copy themselves into entirely new areas of the chromosomes.

Klinefelter's syndrome A chromosomal trisomy in which males have an extra X chromosome, resulting in an XXY condition; affected individuals typically have reduced fertility.

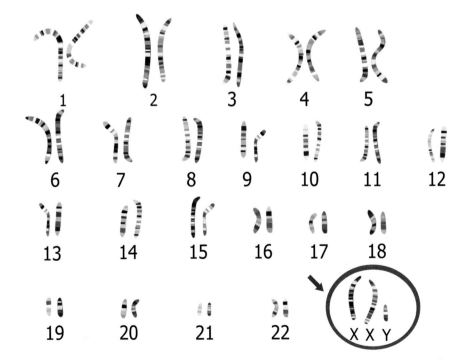

FIGURE 4.7

Klinefelter's Syndrome This karyotype belongs to a male human with Klinefelter's syndrome, a disorder that results from chromosome duplication. Only men receive the additional X chromosome that makes for a total of 47 chromosomes rather than the normal 46. This extra chromosome usually leads to sterility and can produce a range of physical effects, from a youthful, lanky appearance to a rounded, generally feminized body with gynecomastia (additional breast tissue).

FIGURE 4.8

Spontaneous Mutations Spontaneous mutations can affect only physical appearance or can have health consequences, sometimes extreme ones. **(a)** A mutation called *leucism* has made this American alligator white. On its head are some spots of alligators' normal, dark color. **(b)** The mutation that gives some cats white fur and blue eyes can also produce deafness and timidity. **(c)** Cheetahs normally have spotted coats, but a genetic mutation has produced stripes on this cheetah's back. **(d)** Mutations can affect the wing count, eye color, and eye placement of fruit flies. A mutation has given this fruit fly abnormally placed, or ectopic, eyes, one of which is visible here as the red area on the wing.

(a)

(b)

(c)

(d)

spontaneous mutations Random changes in DNA that occur during cell division.

induced mutations Mutations in the DNA resulting from exposure to toxic chemicals or to radiation.

mutagens Substances, such as toxins, chemicals, or radiation, that may induce genetic mutations.

All mutations fall into either of two types: **spontaneous mutations** have no known cause (**Figure 4.8**); **induced mutations** are caused by specific environmental agents, usually associated with human activity. These agents, or **mutagens,** are increasingly becoming known. For example, ionizing radiation (X-rays) and various toxic chemicals have been linked to mutations in animals and humans. Most mutations are spontaneous, however, and are simply DNA copying errors. The human mutation rate is higher in male sex cells (sperm) than in female sex cells (eggs) but is generally on the order one per million per nucleotide per generation. The human genome includes about 3 billion base pairs, about 1.5% of which code for proteins, so the average mutation rate in humans is .45 mutations in protein-coding genes per generation, or about one new, potentially significant mutation in every other person born.

For individuals, most mutations are relatively harmless, while a few may have profound consequences. For populations, mutations are inconsequential unless they offer selective adaptive advantages.

4.4 Natural Selection: Advantageous Characteristics, Survival, and Reproduction

Darwin's theory of evolution by means of natural selection provided the conceptual framework for understanding adaptation. That framework has become even more powerful over the past 150 years because it has allowed for many refinements. The principle of natural selection is based on Darwin's conclusion that individuals with advantageous characteristics will survive in higher numbers and produce more offspring than members of a population lacking advantageous characteristics. Natural selection, therefore, focuses on reproductive success, or **fitness.** In particular, fitness is defined as some measure of the propensity to contribute offspring to future generations, usually by the next generation. Fitness can be defined in reference to individuals in a population or to specific genotypes. For our purposes, fitness is defined on the basis of genotypes. This means that some genotypes have more (or less) fitness than other genotypes. The implication is that fitness differences can result in changes to allele frequencies. For example, if the genotype for darker coloring confers an adaptive advantage over the genotype for lighter coloring, the dark-color genotype will likely increase in frequency over time.

fitness Average number of offspring produced by parents with a particular genotype compared to the number of offspring produced by parents with another genotype.

Patterns of Natural Selection

Evolutionary biologists have identified three alternative patterns by which natural selection can act on a specific trait. **Directional selection** favors one extreme form of a trait—more children are produced by individuals who have that extreme trait, so selection moves in that direction. Human evolution, for example, has clearly favored larger brains (for more on these topics, see chapters 10 and 11). **Stabilizing selection** favors the average version of a trait. For example, living humans whose birth weights are in the middle of the range have a better chance of surviving and reproducing than do those born with the lowest and highest weights. In **disruptive selection,** the pattern of variation is discontinuous. Individuals at both extreme ends of the range produce more offspring than does the remainder of the population. Given enough time, this pattern can result in a speciation event as those in the middle fail to survive and reproduce and two new species arise at the extremes (**Figure 4.9**).

directional selection Selection for one allele over the other alleles, causing the allele frequencies to shift in one direction.

stabilizing selection Selection against the extremes of the phenotypic distribution, decreasing the genetic diversity for this trait in the population.

disruptive selection Selection for both extremes of the phenotypic distribution; may eventually lead to a speciation event.

Natural Selection in Animals: The Case of the Peppered Moth and Industrial Melanism

Examples of natural selection in animals are wide-ranging. Among them are animals that "blend in" with their surrounding habitat (**Figure 4.10**). Perhaps the best evidence ever documented of natural selection operating on a heritable trait concerns the peppered moth, *Biston betularia,* a species common throughout Great Britain (**Figure 4.11**). This moth is nocturnal, eating and breeding by night and attaching itself to trees, especially in the upper branches, during the day. Prior to the mid-1800s, all members of the species had a peppered appearance, their white coloring sprinkled with black. Trees throughout Great Britain were covered with lichen, and the moths' coloration provided excellent camouflage against the trees' variable-colored surface and thus protected the moths from their major predator, birds. In 1848, a naturalist exploring the countryside near Manchester, England, spotted a completely black variety of the moth.

HARDY–WEINBERG VIS

THE CASE OF PTC TASTERS VERSUS PTC NONTASTERS

Anthropologists have long been interested in taste discrimination because tasting plays a central role in determining what foods we eat. If you don't like a food because it doesn't taste good, then chances are you will avoid that food. (I still can't stand liver!) Understanding how tasting works is important for understanding dietary and ecological specializations in human populations. One commonly studied Mendelian trait is the ability to taste the chemical phenylthiocarbamide (PTC).

In 1931, the American chemist Arthur Fox discovered that he could taste PTC but that his coworkers could not. At first, he thought he had some weird condition not shared by others. However, he quickly learned that other people were "tasters" like him. Ever since his discovery, scientists have used the chemical to test genetic variation in the ability to taste. PTC is not found in any foods eaten by humans, but its chemical structure is similar to a number of compounds found in some fruits and vegetables that are related to and taste like PTC. Scientists do not know why some people are tasters and some are not, but there may be a selective advantage because tasting bitter things enables people to avoid eating toxic substances.

People able to taste PTC have the dominant allele, *T*. The recessive allele is *t*. So tasters are either homozygous, *TT*, or heterozygous, *Tt*. Nontasters are *tt*. In 2003, Un-kyung Kim and colleagues discovered that the ability to taste PTC is tied to one gene (*TAS2R38*) found on chromosome 7. That gene and the protein it is coded for result in tongue receptors that are able to taste PTC. The homozygous recessive, *tt*, produces differently shaped receptors, which do not respond to PTC.

Simple genetic markers like this one help illustrate how gene frequencies work. To demonstrate Hardy–Weinberg equilibrium frequencies, for example, graduate student Jaime Ullinger asked the 50 students enrolled in her introduction to physical anthropology class at The Ohio State University to take part in their own simple study. Each student placed a strip of paper containing the synthetic version of PTC toward the back of his or her tongue. After experiencing a bitter taste or no taste, each student recorded his or her phenotype (taster or nontaster) and potential genotype (again, tasters are *TT* or *Tt*; nontasters, *tt*).

Twenty-nine students were tasters, and 21 were nontasters. Ullinger and her students then used these phenotypes to determine hypothetical genotypes for the class. Using the Hardy–Weinberg law of equilibrium—where $p^2 + 2pq + q^2 = 100\%$ or 1, $p^2 = TT$, $2pq = Tt$, $q^2 = tt$, and $p + q = 1$—they first determined the genotype frequency for *tt*:

$$q = \sqrt{.42} = .65$$

The gene frequency for *t*, then, is simply the square root of .42, or .65. Because $p + q = 1$, the gene frequency of *T* (or *p*) is

$$p = 1 - q, \text{ or } p = .35$$

Therefore, given the assumptions of the Hardy–Weinberg law, $p = .35$ and $q = .65$. This means that of the 100 alleles in Ullinger's class of 50 students,

(a)

(b)

Some bitter-tasting foods, including grapefruit juice and broccoli, contain a chemical similar to PTC. This explains why some people are averse to drinking grapefruit juice or eating broccoli.

approximately 35 were dominant alleles (T) and 65 were recessive alleles (t). Ullinger and her students then calculated the number of students who were homozygous dominant and the number who were heterozygous dominant. The homozygous dominants (TT) are represented by p^2. In the class, $p^2 = (.35)(.35) = 12\%$. Therefore, approximately 12% of the class, or six students, were homozygous dominant. The heterozygous dominants (Tt) are the $2pq$ group, where $2pq =$ $(2)(.35)(.65) = 46\%$. For Ullinger's class, 23 (or 46% of 50) were heterozygotes.

Ullinger's class was of course not a deme, and it represented only one point in time. So, by this record alone, no one could say whether the PTC locus for the "population" has remained in a state of equilibrium. However, given equilibrium (no evolution), the frequencies Ullinger and her students determined for the class would remain unchanged indefinitely.

FIGURE 4.9

Types of Selection **(a) Top:** In the population represented here, smaller body size is more favorable than larger body size, so the frequency of smaller body size will increase thanks to directional selection. **Middle:** The fitness of individuals with smaller body sizes will be greater than that of individuals with larger body sizes. **Bottom:** Over time, the population's average body size will decrease.

(b) Top: In this population, medium body size is favored, so the frequency of medium body size will increase thanks to stabilizing selection. **Middle:** The fitness of individuals with medium body sizes will be much greater. **Bottom:** However, the population's average body size will remain relatively stable over time.

(c) Top: Here, owing to disruptive selection, the frequencies of small and large body sizes will increase, while the frequency of medium body size will decrease. **Middle:** The fitness levels are highest at the extremes and lowest in the middle. **Bottom:** Over time, the population will split between those with large bodies and those with small bodies.

(d) Top: In the absence of selection, the population will have a range of sizes. **Middle:** Fitness levels will vary independently of size. **Bottom:** The population's average body size will not change over time.

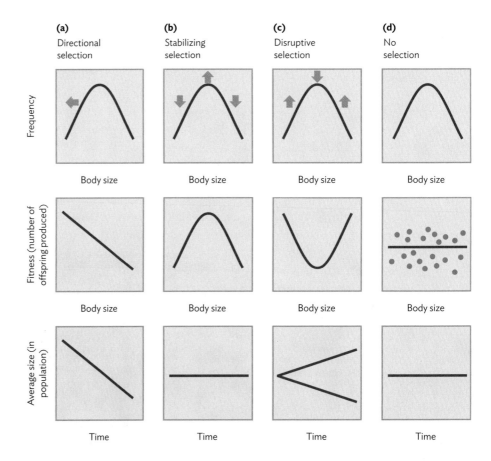

melanic Refers to an individual with high concentrations of melanin.

nonmelanic Refers to an individual with low concentrations of melanin.

A new species name, *Biston carbonaria,* distinguished this **melanic** (dark) form from the **nonmelanic** (light) form. The frequency of the melanic form remained relatively low for a couple of decades but climbed rapidly in the late nineteenth century. By the 1950s, 90% or more of peppered moths were melanic (**Figure 4.12**).

FIGURE 4.10

Leafy Sea Dragon As a result of natural selection, the leafy sea dragon looks just like the sea plants around it in its ocean setting.

This rapid increase in melanic frequency was a case of evolution profoundly changing phenotype. Directional selection had favored the melanic form over the nonmelanic form, and the melanic form exhibited a greater fitness. But what was this form's adaptive advantage?

The selecting factor was the Industrial Revolution. With the rise of industry throughout England and elsewhere in the middle to late nineteenth century, mills, fueled entirely by coal, spewed coal particles from smokestacks—50 tons per square mile per month, in some places—blackening the sky and covering the landscape. The trees survived this pollution onslaught, but the lichen covering the trees did not. The surfaces of the trees changed from light-colored to black, greatly altering the peppered moth's habitat. This pollution crisis provided a huge selective advantage for the melanic moths, which were now perfectly camouflaged against blackened trees. Nonmelanic moths became easy prey.

How did the genetics of this evolutionary change work? Breeding experiments revealed that, in a classic case of Mendelian genetics, the color difference between the two *Biston* species was determined by one locus. The nonmelanic variety had a genotype of *cc* (homozygous recessive), while the melanic variety was either heterozygous, *Cc*, or homozygous, *CC*. The dominant allele, *C*, likely first appeared as a mutation, perhaps in the first half of the nineteenth century or earlier, long before the first melanic moth was observed in 1848. The *C* allele may have been in the population, maintained by the mutation's reoccurrence. Recent estimates suggest that the frequency of the nonmelanic variety was only 1%–10% in polluted regions of England and no more than 5% around Manchester (**Figure 4.13**). Plugged into the Hardy–Weinberg equilibrium, this information in turn suggests that 46% of the population had the *CC* genotype, 44% had the *Cc* genotype, and 10% had the *cc* genotype (**Table 4.2**). Beginning in the late 1960s and early 1970s, the stricter pollution laws, changes in coal burning, and decline of mill-based industry in Great Britain profoundly affected the moth population, once again illustrating natural selection. That is, in areas that were no longer polluted, the frequency of *Biston carbonaria* dropped. In Manchester, for example, the frequency of the melanic moth decreased from 90% in 1983 to well under 10% in the late 1990s. Plugged into the Hardy–Weinberg equilibrium, these numbers reveal that the *CC* genotype decreased to 0.25%, the *Cc* genotype decreased to 9.5%, and the *cc* genotype increased to 90% (**Table 4.3**). This rapid evolutionary change reflected the return of the original coloration of the trees, which conferred a selective disadvantage—predation

FIGURE 4.11

Peppered Moths The genus *Biston* includes two species: *Biston betularia* (light) and *Biston carbonaria* (dark).

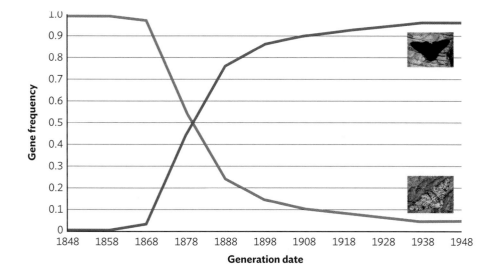

FIGURE 4.12

Changes in the Peppered Moth Gene Frequency The frequency of the melanic gene in peppered moths increased from 1848 through 1948. The frequency of the nonmelanic gene decreased during that same period.

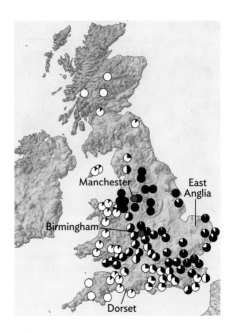

FIGURE 4.13

Melanic Moths This map of Great Britain illustrates melanic moths' prevalence there during the Industrial Revolution. Highly industrialized areas, such as Manchester, had almost no light moths, while rural, nonindustrial areas, such as Scotland (north) and southwestern England, had substantially more light moths, almost to the exclusion of dark moths. What would this map look like for the preindustrialization period?

Table 4.2 Moth Genotype Frequencies—Industrialization Period

Phenotype	Melanic	Nonmelanic
Phenotype Frequencies	.90	.10
Genotype	$CC + Cc$	cc
Genotype Frequencies	$p^2 + 2pq$	q^2

Allele Frequency* Calculations:

Step 1		$q^2 = .10\ (q^2 = f[cc])$
Step 2		$q = \sqrt{q^2} = \sqrt{.10} = .32$
Step 3	$p = 1 - q = 1 - .32 = .68$	

Genotype Frequency Calculations:

$$p^2 = f(CC) = .68^2 = .46$$

$$2pq = f(Cc) = 2 \times .68 \times .32 = .44$$

$$q^2 = f(cc) = .32^2 = .10$$

Check:	$p^2 + 2pq + q^2 = 1$
	$.46 + .44 + .10 = 1$

*f = frequency

Table 4.3 Moth Genotype Frequencies—Postindustrialization Period

Phenotype	Melanic	Nonmelanic
Phenotype Frequencies	.10	.90
Genotype	$CC + Cc$	cc
Genotype Frequencies	$p^2 + 2pq$	q^2

Allele Frequency* Calculations:

Step 1		$q^2 = .90\ (q^2 = f[cc])$
Step 2		$q = \sqrt{q^2} = \sqrt{.90} = .95$
Step 3	$p = 1 - q = 1 - .95 = .05$	

Genotype Frequency Calculations:

$$p^2 = f(CC) = .05^2 = .0025$$

$$2pq = f(Cc) = 2 \times .05 \times .95 = .095$$

$$q^2 = f(cc) = .95^2 = .90$$

Check:	$p^2 + 2pq + q^2 = 1$
	$.0025 + .095 + .90 = 1$

*f = frequency

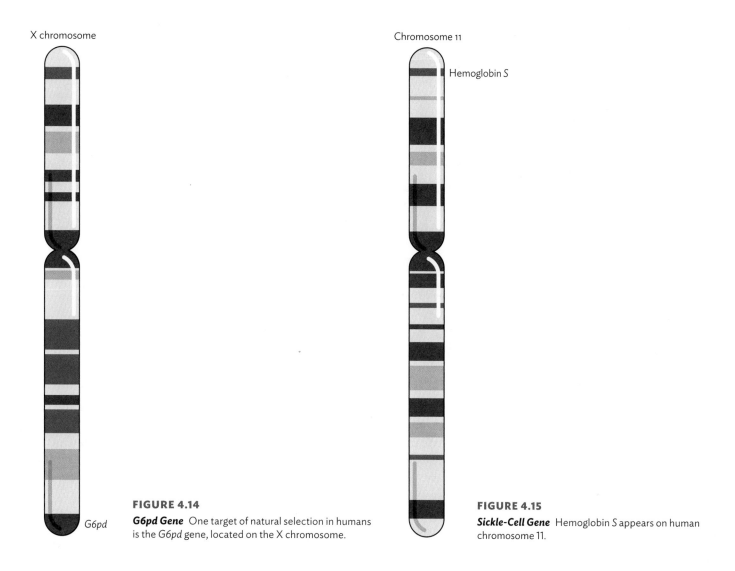

X chromosome

FIGURE 4.14

G6pd Gene One target of natural selection in humans is the *G6pd* gene, located on the X chromosome.

G6pd

Chromosome 11

Hemoglobin *S*

FIGURE 4.15

Sickle-Cell Gene Hemoglobin *S* appears on human chromosome 11.

visibility—on the melanic variety. This postscript adds even more power to the story of how natural selection brought about biological changes in the genus *Biston*.

Natural Selection in Humans: Abnormal Hemoglobins and Resistance to Malaria

The above case of industrial melanism is an example of **positive selection,** whereby an organism's biology is shaped by selection for beneficial traits. Natural selection for beneficial traits in humans is best understood by studying genes that control specific traits. Of the 90 or so different loci that are targets of natural selection (**Figure 4.14**), among the most compelling examples is the sickle-cell allele—the hemoglobin *S* (or simply *S*) allele—which causes **sickle-cell anemia** (**Figure 4.15**). Millions of people suffer from such **hemolytic anemias,** which involve the destruction of red blood cells. A low number of red blood cells can produce health problems because of the resultant lack of hemoglobin, the chemical in red blood cells that carries oxygen to all the body tissues. The *S* gene yields a specific kind of **abnormal hemoglobin.**

Sickle-cell anemia has been known since the early 1900s, and the genetics behind it was documented in the 1950s. The *S* gene is a simple base-pair mutation (**Figure 4.16**). Genetically, people with normal hemoglobin have the alleles *AA,* the homozygous

positive selection Process in which advantageous genetic variants quickly increase in frequency in a population.

sickle-cell anemia A genetic blood disease in which the red blood cells become deformed and sickle-shaped, decreasing their ability to carry oxygen to tissues.

hemolytic anemias Conditions of insufficient iron in the blood due to the destruction of red blood cells resulting from genetic blood diseases, toxins, or infectious pathogens.

abnormal hemoglobin Hemoglobin altered so that it is less efficient in binding to and carrying oxygen.

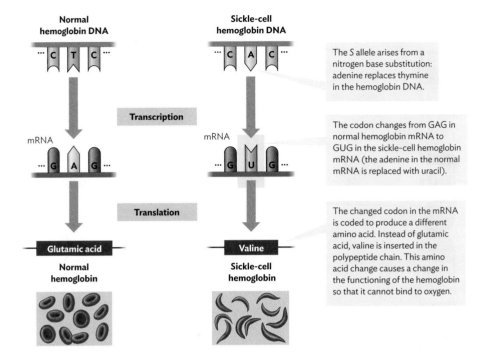

Normal hemoglobin DNA

··· C T C ···

Sickle-cell hemoglobin DNA

··· C A C ···

The *S* allele arises from a nitrogen base substitution: adenine replaces thymine in the hemoglobin DNA.

Transcription

mRNA
··· G A G ···

mRNA
··· G U G ···

The codon changes from GAG in normal hemoglobin mRNA to GUG in the sickle-cell hemoglobin mRNA (the adenine in the normal mRNA is replaced with uracil).

Translation

Glutamic acid

Normal hemoglobin

Valine

Sickle-cell hemoglobin

The changed codon in the mRNA is coded to produce a different amino acid. Instead of glutamic acid, valine is inserted in the polypeptide chain. This amino acid change causes a change in the functioning of the hemoglobin so that it cannot bind to oxygen.

FIGURE 4.16

Sickle-Cell Mutation Sickle-cell anemia begins with a single nitrogen base mutation—a base substitution. The abnormal hemoglobin that results is less efficient at binding oxygen and causes red blood cells to become sickle-shaped.

capillaries Small blood vessels between the terminal ends of arteries and the veins.

condition. People who carry the sickle-cell allele on one of the two homologous chromosomes only are *AS,* and people who have the homozygous form of the disease are *SS. AS* individuals are for all practical purposes normal in their survival and reproduction rates. There is no cure for sickle-cell anemia, and in the absence of modern medical treatment, some 80% of people who are *SS* die before the reproductive years, usually considerably earlier. The *SS* genotype results in many red blood cells having a sickle shape caused by the abnormal hemoglobin, in sharp contrast to the round appearance of red blood cells in people with normal hemoglobin (**Figure 4.17**). The abnormal shape of the cells prevents them from passing through the **capillaries,** the narrow blood vessels that form networks throughout tissues. When the clogging of capillaries cuts off the oxygen supply in vital tissues, severe anemia and death can result.

THE GEOGRAPHY OF SICKLE-CELL ANEMIA AND THE ASSOCIATION WITH MALARIA Beginning in the mid-twentieth century, the medical community observed that many people living in equatorial Africa—as many as 20%–30%—had the *S* gene. This finding represented a huge puzzle: as the gene was so bad for survival, why was its frequency so high? In other words, one would expect strong selection against this non-beneficial gene. The solution to the puzzle began to emerge with the discovery that high heterozygous (*AS*) frequencies appear in regions of Africa where malaria is endemic. In other words, where malaria—a potentially lethal parasitic infection in which the parasite is introduced to a human host by a mosquito—is always present, there is a high frequency of carriers of the gene (**Figure 4.18**). Moreover, *AS* people (sickle-gene carriers) die of malaria in far fewer numbers than do *AA* people.

As described at the beginning of this chapter, Anthony Allison discovered that in low-lying, wet areas of Kenya (where the number of mosquitoes was great and the rate of malaria was high), the frequency of the sickle-cell allele was considerably higher than in highland or arid areas. He developed the simple but elegant hypothesis that the infection and the genetic mutation were related. Individuals homozygous for normal hemoglobin (*AA*) were highly susceptible to dying from malaria; individuals homozygous for sickle-cell anemia (*SS*) did not survive to reproduce; however, individuals heterozygous for normal hemoglobin and the sickle-cell mutation (*AS*) either did not contract malaria or suffered a less severe malarial infection. That these frequencies were being maintained indicated that the *AS* heterozygote was a **balanced polymorphism.** It was also a fitness trade-off: carriers could pass on the sickle-cell allele, but they received immunity from malaria.

THE BIOLOGY OF SICKLE-CELL ANEMIA AND MALARIAL INFECTION Why do people who are heterozygous for the sickle-cell allele survive malaria or not contract it at all? Unlike *SS* red blood cells, *AS* red blood cells do not sickle under most conditions (that is, except when severely deprived of oxygen). They are, however, somewhat smaller than normal cells, and their oxygen levels are somewhat lower. For reasons not yet understood, the *AS* red blood cells are simply a poor host—a nonconducive living and reproduction environment—for the parasite that causes malaria **(Figure 4.19)**.

THE HISTORY OF SICKLE-CELL ANEMIA AND MALARIA In the late 1950s, the American physical anthropologist Frank B. Livingstone (1928–2005) sought to strengthen the case for natural selection by historically linking sickle-cell anemia and malaria. Livingstone asked two important questions: *Where and when did the sickle-cell allele first appear in equatorial Africa?* and *What conditions led to the allele being naturally selected?* He hypothesized that the Bantu, a group of peoples who speak Bantu languages, carried the mutation with them when they migrated southward from the region of Cameroon and Nigeria **(Figure 4.20)**. Prior to the Bantu's arrival, the region was a largely unbroken forest. Bantu populations introduced agriculture there, clearing large swaths of the forest for cultivation. The peoples' iron-working technology made possible the creation of tools for cutting down large trees, clearing and plowing fields, and planting crops—mostly yams and cassava.

Even under the best conditions, tropical forests are fragile ecosystems. Once their trees have been cleared and their fields have been planted, their relatively poor soil, which normally soaks up rainwater, becomes thin or disappears. Geologic evidence shows a dramatic increase in soil erosion in the region after the arrival of Bantu populations, due in large part to **anthropogenic** deforestation and the overall environmental impact of humans on the landscape. As a result of these erosive processes, pools of water collect and become stagnant, providing ideal conditions for the breeding of

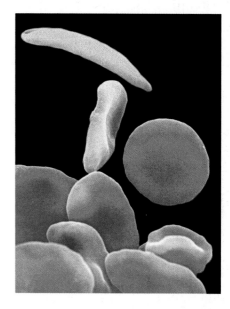

FIGURE 4.17

Sickle-Shaped Red Blood Cells This image shows normal red blood cells, which are round; a long, slender, sickle-shaped cell (at top); and other irregularly shaped cells. The abnormal cells are very fragile and easily damaged or destroyed.

balanced polymorphism Situation in which selection maintains two or more phenotypes for a specific gene in a population.

anthropogenic Refers to any effect caused by humans.

(a)

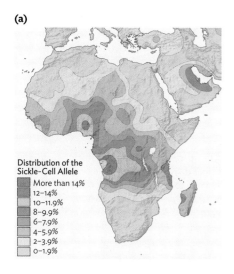

Distribution of the Sickle-Cell Allele

■ More than 14%
■ 12–14%
■ 10–11.9%
■ 8–9.9%
■ 6–7.9%
■ 4–5.9%
□ 2–3.9%
□ 0–1.9%

(b)

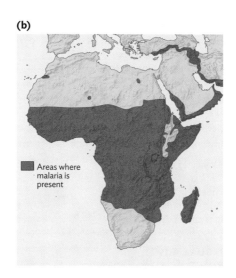

■ Areas where malaria is present

FIGURE 4.18

Distributions of the Sickle-Cell Allele and Malaria In equatorial Africa, **(a)** the distribution of the sickle-cell allele coincides with **(b)** areas of high malarial parasite concentration.

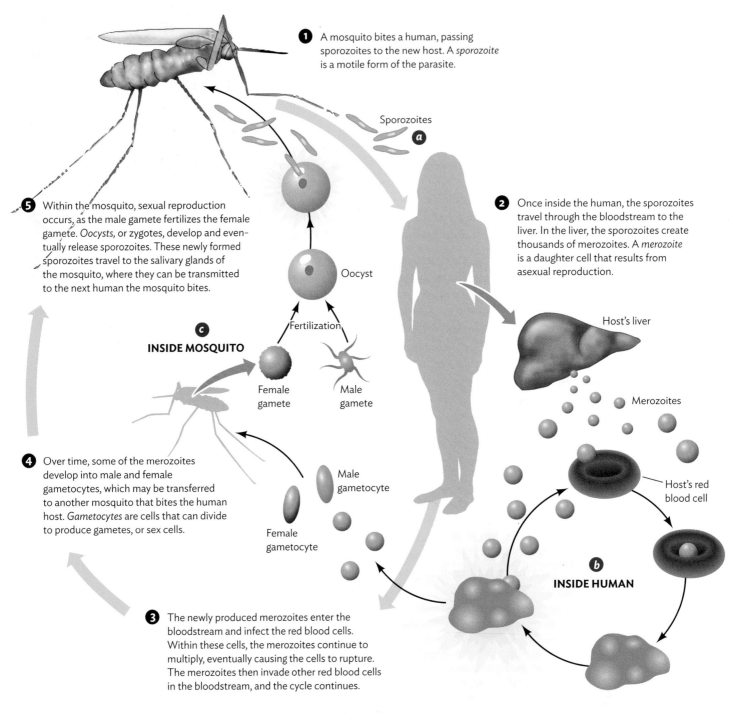

1 A mosquito bites a human, passing sporozoites to the new host. A *sporozoite* is a motile form of the parasite.

Sporozoites
a

5 Within the mosquito, sexual reproduction occurs, as the male gamete fertilizes the female gamete. *Oocysts,* or zygotes, develop and eventually release sporozoites. These newly formed sporozoites travel to the salivary glands of the mosquito, where they can be transmitted to the next human the mosquito bites.

2 Once inside the human, the sporozoites travel through the bloodstream to the liver. In the liver, the sporozoites create thousands of merozoites. A *merozoite* is a daughter cell that results from asexual reproduction.

Oocyst

Host's liver

c

INSIDE MOSQUITO

Fertilization

Female gamete

Male gamete

Merozoites

Host's red blood cell

b

INSIDE HUMAN

4 Over time, some of the merozoites develop into male and female gametocytes, which may be transferred to another mosquito that bites the human host. *Gametocytes* are cells that can divide to produce gametes, or sex cells.

Male gametocyte

Female gametocyte

3 The newly produced merozoites enter the bloodstream and infect the red blood cells. Within these cells, the merozoites continue to multiply, eventually causing the cells to rupture. The merozoites then invade other red blood cells in the bloodstream, and the cycle continues.

VACCINE TARGETS

a Sporozoite: The goal of sporozoite vaccines is to block parasites from entering or growing within human liver cells.

b Merozoite: Vaccines based on merozoite antigens lessen malaria's severity by hobbling the invasion of new generations of red blood cells or by reducing complications.

c Gametocyte: So-called altruistic gametocyte-based vaccines do not affect human disease but are designed to evoke human antibodies that derail parasite development within the mosquito.

FIGURE 4.19

The Spread of Malaria The life cycle of the malarial parasite, *Plasmodium falciparum,* takes place in two hosts: mosquito and human. Both hosts are needed if the parasite is to survive.

(a)

(b)

FIGURE 4.21

The Spread of Malaria As the Bantu cleared forests for agricultural fields, **(a)** pools of stagnant water **(b)** became an ideal breeding ground for mosquito larvae, which carried the malarial parasites.

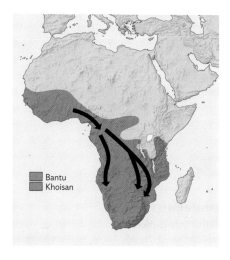

Bantu
Khoisan

FIGURE 4.20

The Ecology of Malarial Parasites Beginning by about 1000 BC, Bantu people began a series of migrations, originating in central Africa and pushing southward eventually into southern Africa. In addition to agriculture, they carried the mutation for the sickle-cell allele. Khoisan are the inhabitants of southern Africa encountered by Bantu as they spread southward.

parasite-carrying mosquitoes (**Figure 4.21**). This picture became clear to Livingstone as he developed his research: the newly created ecological circumstances fostered mosquito reproduction and the spread of malaria, and the growing host of humans made possible by agriculture-fueled population growth provided the food resources needed by the mosquitoes. The infectious disease gave those individuals with a very rare mutation—the sickle-cell allele—an adaptive advantage and the ability to survive and reproduce in these new environmental circumstances. Because of the advantage the heterozygous condition provides, the *S* allele was maintained and passed from generation to generation. For this reason, sickle-cell anemia predominantly affects those whose descendants came from the malarial environments in large parts of equatorial Africa. Outside of such malarial environments, the *S* allele never became advantageous.

OTHER HEMOGLOBIN AND ENZYME ABNORMALITIES Sickle-cell anemia turns out to be just one of a number of **hemoglobinopathies** and other genetic abnormalities in Africa, Asia, and Europe that provide a strong selective advantage in regions of endemic malaria (**Figure 4.22**). Heterozygous carriers of abnormal hemoglobins apparently make poor hosts for malarial parasites.

hemoglobinopathies A group of related genetic blood diseases characterized by abnormal hemoglobin.

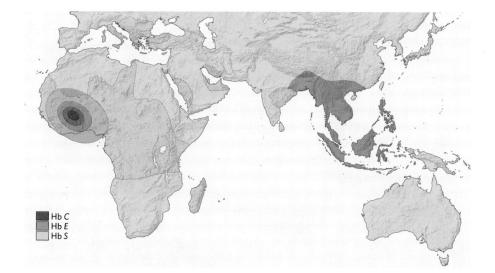

Hb C
Hb E
Hb S

FIGURE 4.22

Distribution of Hemoglobinopathies This map shows the distribution of hemoglobin *E* in Southeast Asia. People with hemoglobin *E* may have mild hemolytic anemia or other mild effects. Like hemoglobin *S*, hemoglobin *C* appears primarily in equatorial Africa. Like hemoglobin *E*, hemoglobin *C* has generally minor effects, most often mild hemolytic anemia.

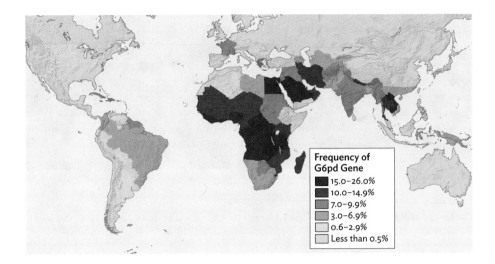

Frequency of G6pd Gene
- 15.0–26.0%
- 10.0–14.9%
- 7.0–9.9%
- 3.0–6.9%
- 0.6–2.9%
- Less than 0.5%

thalassemia A genetic blood disease in which the hemoglobin is improperly synthesized, causing the red blood cells to have a much shorter life span.

glucose-6-phosphate dehydrogenase (G6PD) An enzyme that aids in the proper functioning of red blood cells; its deficiency, a genetic condition, leads to hemolytic anemia.

Thalassemia, a genetic anemia found in Europe (especially in Italy and Greece), Asia, and the Pacific, reduces or eliminates hemoglobin synthesis. In some homozygous forms of the mutation, hemoglobin becomes clumped inside the red blood cells. The spleen then destroys the red blood cells, resulting in severe anemia. In the areas around the Mediterranean where the genetic frequency is highest—as high as 80%—the presence of malaria makes a strong case for a selective advantage for heterozygous individuals, for whom the condition and malaria are not lethal.

An association has long been recognized between deficiency of the enzyme **glucose-6-phosphate dehydrogenase (G6PD)** and malaria. A recessive hereditary mutation leads more males than females to lack the gene that is coded to produce this enzyme (see Figure 4.14). Without the G6PD enzyme, a person who takes sulfa-based antibiotics or eats fava beans risks the destruction of red blood cells, severe anemia, and occasionally death. Because of the connection with fava beans, this severe hemolytic disease is called *favism*. Its 130 genetic variants occur in high frequencies in some populations, the highest being 70% among Kurdish Jews (**Figure 4.23**). Heterozygous carriers have a strong selective advantage because they produce some of the enzyme but are protected from malaria (here again, the parasite cannot live in the abnormal red blood cells).

Analysis of genetic data by the anthropologist Sara Tishkoff indicates that the mutation for the disease arose between about 4,000 and 12,000 yBP, at the same time as the abnormal hemoglobins. Populations whose descendants did not encounter malaria do not have the G6PD mutation or abnormal hemoglobins. Today, for example, malaria appears throughout the tropical regions of the Americas, but Native Americans are 100% homozygous for normal alleles at the G6PD and hemoglobin loci. That these particular genes do not appear to have mutated in the New World strongly suggests that malaria was introduced to North and South America only after the Europeans' arrival. Indeed, the introduction of malaria and other Old World diseases—by either Spaniards or their African slaves—likely played an instrumental role in the precipitous decline in the native populations.

If malaria had been introduced in the Americas much earlier than the past few centuries—say thousands of years ago—and the mutations occurred, there might have been time for a natural selection to develop for the mutations. If the mutations did appear before the Europeans' arrival, however, they would have exhibited a clear selective disadvantage in the absence of malaria and been weeded out of the gene pool. Thus, red blood cell polymorphisms in the abnormal hemoglobin and G6PD loci reflect the fundamental interactions among environment, genes, and culture that have resulted in the modern human genome. The genes provide an important record about human evolution and the role of natural selection in shaping genetic variation.

4.5 Genetic Drift: Genetic Change Due to Chance

One of the four forces of evolution (see "The Evolutionary Synthesis, the Study of Populations, and the Causes of Evolution" in chapter 2), genetic drift is random change in allele frequency over time. Provided that no allele confers a selective advantage over another, a random change can lead to a change in gene frequency, such as one allele being lost and the other becoming fixated—or fixed, the only allele of its kind in the population. This force, this kind of change, makes possible the measuring of evolution as a statistical probability.

Coin tosses can demonstrate the effects of genetic drift (**Table 4.4**). Imagine that heads and tails are two alleles in a population. If there are only two members of the population (two coin tosses), there is a great chance that both will be heads. In effect, the "heads" allele will become fixed in the small population, while the "tails" allele will be lost. As the population size (number of coin tosses) increases, it becomes less likely that one allele will become fixed and the other lost. In very large populations (1 million coin tosses), both alleles may be present in equal proportions.

How does such statistical probability translate to populations? Now imagine that before the election of your student government you have been asked to predict the

Table 4.4 Heads versus Tails: Genetic Drift and Probability

Coin Tosses	Heads	Tails	Heads:Tails Ratio
2	2	0	2:0
10	4	6	4:6
50	22	28	11:14
100	55	45	11:9
200	199	201	199:201
500	253	247	253:247
1,000	501	499	501:499
5,000	2,500	2,500	1:1
10,000	5,000	5,000	1:1
100,000	50,000	50,000	1:1
500,000	250,000	250,000	1:1
1,000,000	500,000	500,000	1:1

FIGURE 4.24

Genetic Drift over Time The effects of genetic drift appear in this graph, which plots the frequencies over time (by generations) of one gene in three differently sized populations. Assume that population A is the smallest of the three and population C is the largest. At the start, each population has the gene at 50% frequency. Around 38 generations, population A has drifted significantly; the gene is fixed at 100% frequency, a 50% increase. At 50 generations, population B has also drifted. Its gene frequency has declined by 40%. Although the frequency in population C has changed over time, it is still approximately 50% after 50 generations, owing to the largeness of the population.

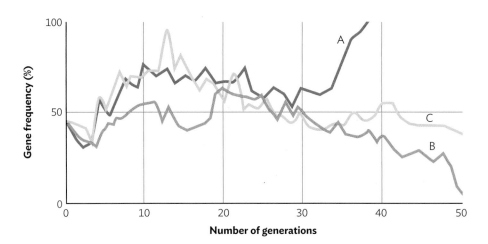

winners. The best way for you to predict would be to ask each voting-eligible student how he or she planned to vote. It is *highly* likely that the outcome of such a comprehensive poll would be close to the actual election results. The shortcomings of this approach might include the very large size of the target population. No one would interview, for example, 50,000 students! The second-best approach would be to select a sample, preferably a random sample that represented the entire student body. If you selected five students out of the 50,000, chances are very slim that those five would represent all the ethnic, national, regional, and economic backgrounds of the student body. In fact, chances are very high that this sample (.01% of the total population) would provide a voting outcome very different from the actual one. If you interviewed 500 students (1% of the population), the chances of representation would be much greater; and if you chose 5,000 students (10% of the population), they would be greater still. The larger the sample size, the greater the probability of an accurate prediction.

Variations in human populations work the exact same way, except that genetic drift operates over a period of time rather than at a single point. The probability of an allele's frequency changing in a relatively short period of time increases with decreasing

FIGURE 4.25

Genetic Drift in the Dunker Population Comparisons of ABO and MN blood type frequencies among Dunkers, Germans, and Americans reveal genetic drift. **(a)** Dunkers have a higher percentage of blood type A and lower percentages of blood types O, B, and AB than do Germans and Americans. **(b)** Dunkers have a higher percentage of blood type M and lower percentages of MN and N.

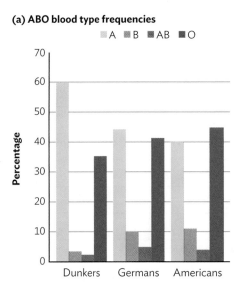

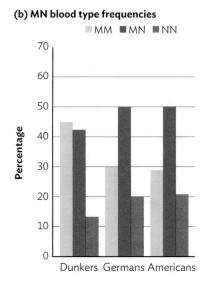

population size. The larger the population, the less divergence from the original gene frequency over time **(Figure 4.24)**.

How does this effect play out in real life? Among humans, for example, genetic drift might occur in a small group that is **endogamous,** discouraging reproduction outside the group. (An **exogamous** society extends reproduction outside its community.) Within such a group, the chances are great that the frequencies of genetic markers will differ from those of a larger population. When the Dunkers, a small religious sect that discourages outside marriage (and thus reproduction), first emigrated from Germany to Pennsylvania, in 1719, the group included just 28 members. Over the next few decades, several hundred more arrived in Pennsylvania; the breeding population remained quite small. Comparisons of contemporary blood type percentages among Dunkers, Germans, and Americans reflect significant changes in the Dunkers and a likely lack of change in the larger populations **(Figure 4.25)**. That is, blood type frequencies among Germans and Americans remain basically the same as they were in the 1700s. The Dunkers' original frequencies were probably much like those of the Germans, but the small Dunker population meant a much greater chance for genetic drift. The frequencies diverged dramatically over time simply due to chance.

Founder Effect: A Special Kind of Genetic Drift

Founder effect, one form of genetic drift, occurs when a small group (fewer than several hundred members) of a large parent population migrates to a new region and is reproductively isolated. The new region is either unoccupied or occupied by species with which the small group cannot breed. Because the founding population is so small, there is a very good chance that its genetic composition is not representative of the parent population's. Because of the founder effect, as the founding population grows its gene pool diverges even further from the source **(Figure 4.26)**. For example, around 12,000 yBP a very small number of individuals—perhaps just a few hundred—migrated from eastern Asia to North America (this movement is among the topics of chapter 12). Today, Native Americans have very high frequencies of type O blood—in many places the frequency is 100%—while eastern Asian populations have among the world's lowest frequencies of it **(Figure 4.27)**. This discrepancy strongly suggests that the original

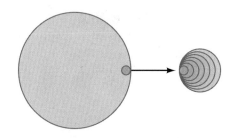

FIGURE 4.26

Founder Effect The large circle on the left represents a parent population, from which a very small proportion is removed to begin a new population. Over time, the founding population grows, and its gene pool looks less and less like that of the parent population.

endogamous Refers to a population in which individuals breed only with other members of the population.

exogamous Refers to a population in which individuals breed only with nonmembers of their population.

founder effect The accumulation of random genetic changes in a small population that has become isolated from the parent population due to the genetic input of only a few colonizers.

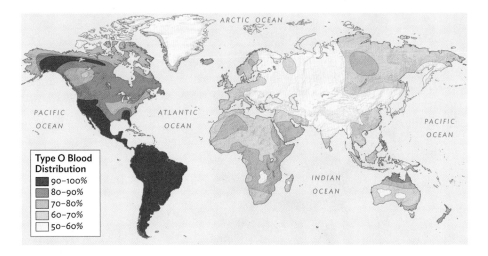

FIGURE 4.27

Type O Blood Distribution Native Americans in North and South America have much higher percentages of type O blood than do East Asians, with whom they share ancestors.

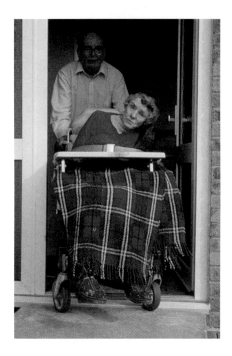

FIGURE 4.28

Huntington's Chorea The woman in the wheelchair suffers from Huntington's chorea, a degenerative genetic disorder.

Huntington's chorea A rare genetic disease in which the central nervous system degenerates and the individual loses control over voluntary movements, with the symptoms often appearing between ages 30 and 50.

east Asian immigrants, the founding "Native Americans," had a higher frequency of type O blood than their parent population had.

Founder effect has also been documented in several genetic diseases that affect humans. Among the best known is a type of microsatellite called **Huntington's chorea,** a genetic abnormality caused by an autosomal dominant gene (**Figure 4.28**). The gene is located on chromosome 4 at the locus that codes for the Huntington protein, and a person needs only one allele from a parent to have the disease. At the end of the normal gene is a sequence of three DNA bases, CAG (the code for valine). If the sequence is repeated numerous times, usually more than 35 times, the individual has the mutation. Huntington's chorea causes degeneration of parts of the brain that control body movement and abilities such as speech production, triggering involuntary jerky movements of the arms and legs as well as dementia. These multiple and debilitating symptoms normally do not manifest until late in life or after the reproductive years, usually after about age 40. Fortunately, the disease is quite rare, affecting only five to eight people per 100,000.

Huntington's chorea appears in very high frequencies, however, in communities around Lake Maracaibo, Venezuela—more than half the occupants of some villages have the disorder. To pinpoint the origin of the disease in this region, the American geneticist Nancy Wexler spent years tracking the genealogies of families living there (**Figure 4.29**). She found that everyone with the disease was descended from one woman who had lived 200 years earlier and carried the allele. This original carrier was not representative of her parent population, which would have had a much lower frequency of the allele. In accordance with the statistical probability, the genetic frequency had increased within the small population.

Why had such a debilitating disease not been removed from the gene pool via natural selection? Because the effects of the gene are not expressed until later in life, people might not have known they had the disease until after they had passed on the detrimental allele to their offspring.

Today, most human populations are not small and isolated, and they interbreed relatively freely with surrounding groups. Whenever interbreeding occurs across population boundaries, gene flow occurs.

FIGURE 4.29

Nancy Wexler Wexler, whose mother died of Huntington's chorea, here stands in front of a chart showing genetic histories she tracked in studying the disease.

4.6 Gene Flow: Spread of Genes across Population Boundaries

Another force of evolution, gene flow (or **admixture;** see "The Evolutionary Synthesis, the Study of Populations, and the Causes of Evolution" in chapter 2) is the transfer of genes across population boundaries. Simply, members of two populations produce offspring (**Figure 4.30**). The key determinant for the amount of gene flow is accessibility to mates—the less the physical distance between populations, the greater the chance of gene flow. While mutation increases genetic variation between two populations over time, gene flow decreases such variation. Anthropologists and geneticists have found that for many kinds of biological traits, ranging from cranial shapes to blood types to microsatellite DNA markers (see "Polymorphisms: Variations in Specific Genes" in chapter 3), similarity increases the closer one population is to another population.

Migration does not necessarily bring about gene flow. For example, when east Asians first migrated to North America (see "Founder Effect: A Special Kind of Genetic Drift" on p. 115), they reached a continental landmass where no humans had ever lived. Written records suggest that Vikings first traveled from Greenland to Newfoundland around AD 1000, but there is no evidence that they interbred with the native people. The first significant gene flow involving Native Americans and Europeans seems to have occurred when or soon after Christopher Columbus and his crew arrived in the New World in 1492. From that point on, gene flow in the Americas, North and South, has been extensive.

Gene flow and genetic variation are also highly influenced by social structure (**Figure 4.31**). Endogamous societies—for example, Australian aborigines—have relatively little genetic diversity because few individuals migrate into the community and thus little new genetic material is introduced. Exogamous societies have relatively high genetic diversity because proportionately more genetic material is brought into the gene pool.

admixture The exchange of genetic material between two or more populations.

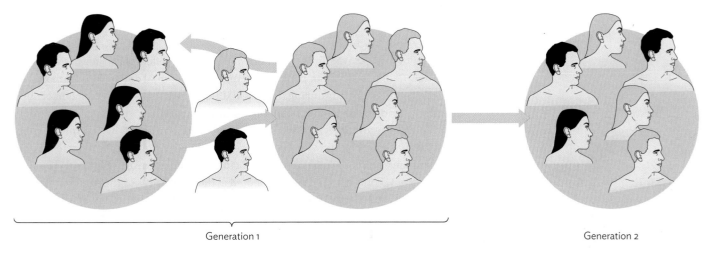

Generation 1   Generation 2

FIGURE 4.30

Gene Flow New genetic material can be introduced into a population through gene flow from another population. Say, for example, that a population in one place has genes for only brown hair. Members of that population interbreed with an adjacent population, which has genes for only blond hair. After interbreeding for a generation, both populations have genes for blond and brown hair. As a result, when people from either population interbreed with yet another population, they may contribute alleles for brown, blond, or both.

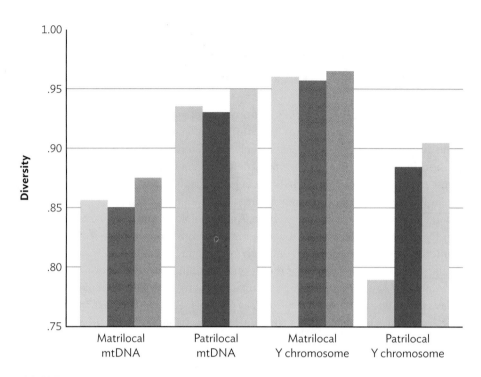

FIGURE 4.31

Social Structure in mtDNA and Y Chromosome Diversity In *patrilocal* societies, generally speaking, males stay in the birthplace, females migrate out, and female mates come from elsewhere. In *matrilocal* societies, females stay in the birthplace, males migrate out, and male mates come from elsewhere. To test the hypothesis that the out-migration of females and the out-migration of males produce different patterns of genetic diversity, the geneticist Hiroki Oota and colleagues studied six groups in Thailand, three of them patrilocal and three matrilocal. They found predictable patterns in the diversity of mtDNA and of Y chromosomes. Because mtDNA is passed from mother to daughter and son, the patrilocal groups showed high mtDNA variation (brought about by females moving into new villages) and the matrilocal groups showed low mtDNA variation (brought about by females remaining in place). Because the Y chromosome is passed from father to son, the patrilocal societies showed low Y chromosome variation (from males not migrating) and the matrilocal societies showed high Y chromosome variation (from males moving to new villages and introducing new Y chromosomes).

Gene flow has always affected human evolution, but its effects have increased greatly over time. Originally, human populations tended to be small and isolated (among the topics of chapter 13). Only during the past 10,000 years, with the development of agriculture and with major population increases, have humans had widespread interaction.

Specific genetic markers in living populations, such as the ABO blood group system, provide evidence of gene flow across large regions. For example, the frequencies of type B blood change gradually from eastern Asia to far-western Europe (**Figure 4.32**). This clinal—that is, sloping—trend was first noted in the early 1940s by the American geneticist Pompeo Candela, who made the case that the gradient from east to west reflects significant gene flow that occurred as Mongol populations migrated westward from AD 500 to 1500. That is, if Mongols had higher frequencies of the *B* allele, they might have passed on that allele as they interbred with local populations.

Subsequent data on blood groups, however, have revealed sharp distinctions in frequencies between adjacent populations. These distinctions suggest that, in addition to gene flow, genetic drift within small, isolated groups contributed to the frequency variations.

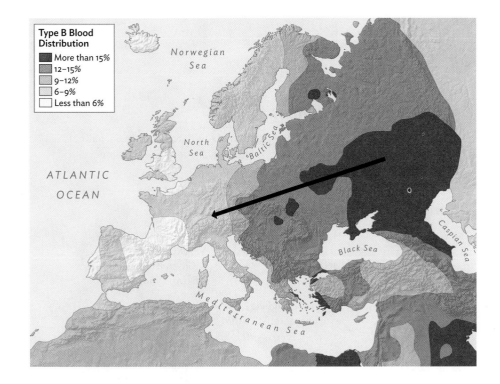

FIGURE 4.32

Type B Blood Distribution The frequency of blood type B ranges from 30% in eastern Asia to almost 0% in far-western Europe. The main factor contributing to this change was probably gene flow between populations in an east-to-west direction (shown by arrow).

Agriculture and Origins of Modern Europeans

Agriculture has existed in Europe since about 7,000 yBP. There, as in every place else where farming was either invented or adopted, its profound implications for society included the beginnings of cities, of complex social organization, of warfare, and of quality living conditions (all of these topics are discussed in chapter 13). How did agriculture get to Europe? Was it developed by the descendants of the hunter-gatherers who had lived there for hundreds of thousands of years? Or did some non-European group or groups bring the idea to Europe during the process of their migration? In 1925, the Australian archaeologist V. Gordon Childe (1892–1957) proposed that Europe's first farming communities (appearing in the Neolithic period; see chapters 8 and 13) were founded by Middle Eastern peoples who invaded Europe, replaced the hunter-gatherers there, and became the ancestors of today's Europeans.

In the 1970s, the Italian geneticist Luca Cavalli-Sforza and the American archaeologist Albert Ammerman countered Childe's hypothesis with a model of **demic diffusion**, framing the origin of agriculture as not invasion but rather gradual expansion and accompanying gene flow. In their model, Middle Eastern peoples invented farming in their homelands of Western Asia, then expanded and moved, interacting with, interbreeding with, and exchanging ideas about food production with local European populations. Ideas can spread without gene flow, as ideas about communication do today; but Cavalli-Sforza and Ammerman proposed that the spread of agriculture as a cultural innovation involved population spread.

What are the genetic implications of the two hypotheses? If Childe's hypothesis is correct, then both in past and present populations a strong genetic similarity should exist between Western Asian (what we sometimes call the "Middle East" or "Near East") and European populations. If Cavalli-Sforza and Ammerman's population spread hypothesis is correct, then genetic evidence should show some admixture and probably a gradient of gene frequencies from Western Asia into Europe.

demic diffusion A population's movement into an area previously uninhabited by that group.

What Causes Evolution?

Evolution is caused by one or a combination of four forces: mutation, natural selection, genetic drift, and gene flow. Although all four forces are important, natural selection accounts for most evolution.

Cause	Definition	Examples
Mutation	Heritable change in structure or amount of DNA	Sickle-cell anemia Huntington's chorea Klinefelter's syndrome Down syndrome
Natural Selection	Favoring of individuals with characteristics that enhance survival and reproduction	Sickle-cell anemia Industrial melanism Thalassemia G6PD deficiency Lactase deficiency
Genetic Drift	Genetic change due to chance	Klinefelter's syndrome Blood types Hemophilia Achromatopsia Porphyria
Gene Flow	Transfer of genes across population boundaries	Blood types

Although the genetic record initially showed some gradients of genetic trait frequencies from the Middle East into Europe, close inspection of the 95 genetic markers that Cavalli-Sforza and Ammerman analyzed revealed numerous contradictions that suggested weaknesses in their hypothesis. The record showed evidence of gene flow but not of uniform westward expansion.

Decades later, the remarkable increase in knowledge about human DNA has enabled scientists to revisit these two hypotheses. In particular, new findings about the mtDNA and Y chromosome lineages—matrilines and patrilines—in living people give detailed information about population history and a clear record of gene flow between Western Asia and Europe. The English geneticist Martin Richards and the Italian geneticist Ornella Semino have found that most European mtDNA and Y chromosome lineages likely extend to well before the origins of agriculture in Europe. That is, Europe's indigenous populations are descended from its pre-farming communities. However, study of the ancient DNA record from skeletons dating to 7000 yBP reveals the strong likelihood of significant gene flow from western modern-day Turkey in Western Asia to Europe. Turkish paleogeneticist Ayça Omrak and team analyzed the genetic sequences of a Neolithic skeleton from Anatolia (modern-day Turkey) and one from Europe. Their study documents similarities in the nuclear (genomic) DNA between the two regions.

This record of genetic admixture strongly suggests a network of population movement and gene flow connecting western Asia and Europe beginning in the Neolithic. Along with their genes, ancient Anatolians brought their farming practices to Europe, a key subsistence change that put into motion the spread of farming across the continent.

This chapter and the previous one have discussed inheritance, the genetic code, and genetic change in terms of evolution. Prior to the emergence of evolutionary approaches to the study of human variation, many scientists believed that human variation could be understood through discrete categories called *races*. The next chapter will address the study of biological diversity, the uses and misuses of biological classification, and the ways that variation in living people reflects adaptations to diverse and sometimes extreme environments across the earth.

CHAPTER 4 REVIEW

ANSWERING THE BIG QUESTIONS

1. What causes evolutionary (genetic) change?

- There are four forces of evolution: mutation, natural selection, genetic drift, and gene flow. These forces result in genetic change over time.
- Mutations are DNA coding errors involving permanent changes in the structure or amount of genetic material in cells. They are the only source of new genetic material.
- Only mutations in gametes can affect offspring, so they have greater importance for evolution than do mutations in somatic cells.
- During natural selection, population members with advantageous characteristics survive and reproduce in greater numbers than do members lacking the same characteristics. Allele frequencies can increase, decrease, or remain the same owing to natural selection.
- Advantageous characteristics can be visible physical attributes and/or invisible, biochemical attributes.

- Genetic drift is change in gene frequency due to chance. It is likelier within smaller populations.
- Gene flow is the transfer of genes across population boundaries.

2. How is evolutionary (genetic) change measured, and how is the cause determined?

- Deviation from the proportions of gene frequencies and genotype frequencies as defined by the Hardy–Weinberg law of equilibrium is used to measure evolutionary change.
- There is no apparent evolution of a gene in a population if there is no change in frequency over time.
- If gene frequency is changing, then evolution is likely occurring owing to one or more forces of evolution, but the Hardy–Weinberg law does not indicate which particular force (or forces) is the cause. The scientist examines the context for change, such as change in climate, migration of populations across territorial or geographic boundaries, introduction of new diseases, and change in diet.

KEY TERMS

admixture
anthropogenic
balanced
  polymorphism
deme
demic diffusion
directional
  selection
disruptive selection
endogamous
equilibrium
exogamous
fitness
founder effect
frameshift mutation
gene pool
G6PD
Hardy–Weinberg
  law of equilibrium
hemoglobinopathies
hemolytic anemias

Huntington's
  chorea
induced mutations
Klinefelter's
  syndrome
macroevolution
melanic
microevolution
mutagens
nonmelanic
nonsynonymous
  point mutation
point mutations
positive selection
reproductive
  isolation
sickle-cell anemia
stabilizing selection
synonymous point
  mutation
thalassemia
transposable
  elements

STUDY QUIZ

1. Mutation, natural selection, genetic drift, and gene flow can all

a. create new alleles that have never existed before.
b. increase reproductive success of individuals in a population.
c. change allele frequency in a population.
d. drive alleles to become lost or fixed in small populations.

2. A population at equilibrium according to the Hardy–Weinberg law

a. is rapidly evolving with respect to a given gene.
b. is not evolving with respect to a given gene.
c. is experiencing random changes in gene frequency.
d. must be either a small or a migrating population.

3. Evolutionary fitness measures

a. physical strength.

b. life span.
c. intelligence.
d. reproductive success.

4. Why is the heterozygous sickle-cell genotype common only in malarial regions?

a. The sickle-cell allele is a new mutation and will eventually spread worldwide.
b. Immunity to malaria outweighs the fitness.
c. The association of the sickle-cell allele and malaria is a random coincidence due to genetic drift.
d. Gene flow spread the sickle-cell allele only in malarial regions.

5. Reproductive isolation leads to

a. high rates of gene flow.
b. emergence of separate species.
c. induced mutations.
d. immunity to genetic drift.

EVOLUTION REVIEW

THE FOUR FORCES OF EVOLUTION

Synopsis Physical anthropologists carry out population genetics studies to measure the changes in genetic makeup (allele frequencies) from one generation to the next and to explain the evolutionary processes behind these changes. Researchers use the Hardy–Weinberg law to mathematically demonstrate whether or not a population is undergoing evolutionary change with respect to a particular trait. When there is no change in allele frequencies for a trait (and therefore no evolutionary change), the population is said to be in genetic equilibrium for that trait. Deviations from genetic equilibrium are brought about by the four forces of evolution: mutation, natural selection, genetic drift, and gene flow. Each of these four forces affects the level of genetic variation within a population and between populations in different ways, and any one or a combination of these forces may be acting on a population at any given time. Throughout our evolutionary history, humans have been and continue to be subject to the operation of these four forces. Physical anthropologists explain much of the variation observed among modern humans today within the specific context of one or more of these forces.

Q1. In the chapter, microevolution is defined as small-scale evolution that occurs over a few generations, while macroevolution is defined as large-scale evolution that occurs over many (hundreds or thousands) of generations. Microevolution can also be defined as changes occurring below the level of species (such as within or between populations), while macroevolution can also be defined as changes at the species level or above (family, class, order, etc.). Provide an example for each type of evolution. Considering these definitions and your examples, which one of the four forces of evolution will *not* be operating on groups undergoing macroevolution?

Hint Think about what defines a species.

Q2. Describe the three patterns of natural selection discussed in this chapter. Of these three, which pattern of selection would be most likely to eventually result in a speciation event?

Q3. Mutations can be either spontaneous (no known cause) or induced (caused by specific environmental agents). What are some environmental agents that could increase the rates of genetic mutations among humans today? What types of mutation have the potential to be the most significant from an evolutionary perspective?

Hint Think about how mutations are passed from one generation to the next.

Q4. Discuss the example of lactase persistence as it relates to human biocultural variation. Under what environmental conditions would those individuals carrying alleles for lactase persistence be favored, while their counterparts unable to produce this enzyme would be strongly selected against?

Hint Think about the ways this trait would contribute to greater fitness or reproductive success.

Q5. Provide at least one example each of a modern human population and nonhuman population in which genetic drift may be an especially important factor affecting variation and evolution.

Hint Think about whether genetic drift is more influential in smaller populations or larger populations.

ADDITIONAL READINGS

Kettlewell, H. B. D. 1973. *The Evolution of Melanism.* Oxford, UK: Oxford University Press.

Livingstone, F. B. 1958. Anthropological implications of sickle cell gene distribution in West Africa. *American Anthropologist* 60: 533–562.

Mielke, J. H., L. W. Konigsberg, and J. H. Relethford. 2010. *Human Biological Variation,* 2nd ed. New York: Oxford University Press.

Relethford, J. H. 2012. *Human Population Genetics.* Hoboken, NJ: Wiley-Blackwell.

Ridley, M. 2004. *Evolution,* 3rd ed. Malden, MA: Blackwell Science.

Modern human skin colors range from very light to very dark. If all the variants were lined up from lightest to darkest, it would be hard to determine the dividing lines between so-called racial categories. In fact, the number of racial categories differs by whom you ask, from three to 10 or more. Although skin color is an easily observable form of variation among humans, it is not the main form. Most of our variation as a species is invisible to the naked eye and does not divide up into discrete categories.

5

Biology in the Present

LIVING PEOPLE

BIG QUESTIONS

1. **Is race a valid, biologically meaningful concept?**

2. **What do growth and development tell us about human variation? What are the benefits of our life history pattern?**

3. **How do people adapt to environmental extremes and other circumstances?**

I was first introduced to the biology of living people in high school, when my biology teacher assigned the section on race in our textbook. From that reading and class discussion about it, I learned that in America race is complex and important, especially with regard to poverty and inequality. I also learned that, from a biological perspective, race is a useful way to classify human beings. The teacher informed the class that each human being belongs to one of three races: "Caucasoid," "Negroid," and "Mongoloid," referring respectively to Europeans and western Asians, Africans south of the Sahara Desert, and all other Asians and Native Americans. Simple.

Is racial categorization all that simple? Can human biological variation be classified? Is race a means of understanding why humans differ in appearance and biology around the world? If the answer to these questions is no, then is there a better way to comprehend the enormous variation among humans today? In addressing these questions in this chapter, I will show that race, as it was presented in my high school biology class, has deep historical roots going back centuries. These historical roots have led to a largely incorrect understanding of human biological variation, an incorrect understanding that persists to the present day.

In fact, race symbolizes the misperceptions that many Americans and others around the world have about human variation. Traits that are often seen as racial in origin are actually biological adaptations that have been strongly influenced by natural selection. As interpreted by anthropologists, human biological variation consists not of categories but of an evolutionary continuum. A key, underlying concept here is humans' flexibility toward their environmental circumstances, a process that begins before birth and continues through adulthood. The study of living human biology, then, emphasizes the enormous developmental flexibility that characterizes *Homo sapiens*. Simply, the popular perception is that race is biology. As you will explore in this chapter, race is *not* biology. Rather, human biological variation is driven by evolution.

5.1 Is Race a Valid, Biologically Meaningful Concept?

Brief History of the Race Concept

The idea of race—that human variation can be classified—is a recent invention. Early written records do not use the concept. For example, even though ancient Egyptians represented sub-Saharan Africans in their art, they never referred to the Africans' race. The Greek historian Herodotus (ca. 484–ca. 420 BC) traveled widely but never wrote about race. Similarly, the great Venetian historian and traveler Marco Polo (1254–1324), who saw more of the known world than anyone else of his day, recorded huge amounts of information about his sojourns in Asia without mentioning race.

The American physical anthropologist C. Loring Brace has argued that the race concept got its start in the fourteenth century, during the Renaissance. Before that time, people traveled gradually, either by walking or on horseback. A day's journey averaged 40 km (25 mi), over which travelers could observe subtle changes in human variation,

FIGURE 5.1

Christopher Columbus's Ships In 1492, on his voyage from Spain to what he thought was India but turned out to be the Americas, Columbus commanded a group of ships that included, as depicted at right, the now famous *Niña, Pinta,* and *Santa Maria*. Once ships and boats enabled explorers and other travelers to reach places that had been too far away to visit, people of different lands—who had different physical features—began to meet. Observations of physical and cultural differences led to notions of "us" versus "them," creating the foundation for the race concept.

such as in skin color, from place to place. When Renaissance-era travelers began covering long distances via oceangoing vessels, they also began categorizing people into discrete groups (**Figure 5.1**). In simply departing from seaports, covering vast bodies of water, and landing at their destinations, these travelers noted obvious and sometimes profound physical differences in people—say between western Europeans and equatorial Africans—without all the gradations that came between.

The early scientific articulation of the race concept—namely, that living humans could be lumped into different taxonomic groups—first emerged in the eighteenth century. By the 1700s, Europeans had encountered most of the biological diversity of the world's populations. Building on Linnaeus's taxonomy of organisms (see "Taxonomy and Systematics: Classifying Living Organisms and Identifying Their Biological Relationships" in chapter 2), the eminent German anatomist Johann Friedrich Blumenbach (1752–1840) developed a biological taxonomy of human races, which he published as his MD thesis at the University of Göttingen in 1775. Blumenbach based his taxonomy on human skin color and other physical traits, but mainly on features of the skull, such as the facial projection (**Figure 5.2**). After studying several hundred skulls he had collected from around the world, Blumenbach concluded that there were five races of people: Mongoloids, Malays, Ethiopians (Africans), American Indians, and Caucasoids. These types were static—they did not change over time. And while Blumenbach had focused on skulls, his racial taxonomy was subsequently applied to the living populations represented by those skulls. More than any other work, Blumenbach's study set the tone for the popular perception of human variation: that human beings come in categorical types called *races*.

Debunking the Race Concept

Franz Boas, the founder of American anthropology (see "How Do We Know? Franz Boas Invents Anthropology, American Style" in chapter 1), was among the first scientists to challenge the taxonomic approach to human biological variation. Specifically, he wanted to test the widely held notion that head shape and other so-called racial markers were static entities, essentially unchanging through time. In the early 1900s, he and his researchers studied some 18,000 immigrant families, calculating the cephalic index—the ratio of head length to head breadth—of parents born in Europe and of their children born in the United States (**Figure 5.3**). The results of this study revealed that the adults' and children's head shapes differed, not by a lot but by a degree that could be expressed mathematically. This finding undermined the idea, prevalent at the time, that racial types were innately stable. Because the differences that had been cited among various races were not immutable, Boas concluded that the race concept was invalid. Boas's work laid the foundation for a scientific focus on biological process rather than on typological classification.

Other social scientists in the early twentieth century were drawing similar conclusions regarding the lack of validity of racial categories. Contrary to the view held by most of the public, American sociologist and civil rights leader W. E. B. Du Bois argued that health differences between people of European descent and people of African descent in the United States were due to social inequality and not biology. The emerging understanding, simply put, was that race is a social construction.

So-Called Racial Traits Are Not Concordant

Single biological traits, such as cranial shape, had seemed to be a firm basis for racial categories partly because categorization is very easy when focusing on just one characteristic. What happens when human populations are grouped according to multiple

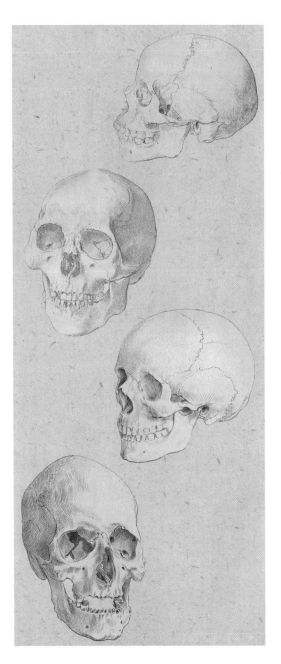

FIGURE 5.2

Blumenbach's Skulls Johann Blumenbach created a classification system for humans based on the shapes of crania he collected. Here, he has sketched the four skulls representing four of his five main groups: (from top to bottom) African (*Aethiopis*), Asian or Mongoloid (*Tungusae*), Caucasoid (*Georgianae*), and American Indian (*Americani illinoici*). This scheme as applied to living humans is still prevalent in the popular perception of human variation. Physical anthropologists have long discredited this classification scheme and other classification approaches to human variation.

FIGURE 5.3

Immigrant Family To test the hypothesis that head shapes change from one generation to the next, Franz Boas studied immigrant families in America like this one, photographed ca. 1888–1912. His conclusion—that cranial proportions were both inherited and influenced by environment—showed the biological malleability of human beings, a foundational principle in modern physical anthropology.

cline A gradual change in some phenotypic characteristic from one population to the next.

characteristics? In the early 1970s, the American geneticist R. C. Lewontin (b. 1929) tested the race concept by studying global genetic variation. If human races existed, most genetic diversity would be accounted for by them. Focusing on blood groups, serum proteins, and red blood cell enzyme variants, Lewontin found that the so-called races accounted for only about 5%–10% of the overall genetic diversity. In other words, most variation occurred *across* human populations regardless of "racial" makeup—human "races" have no taxonomic significance. Since Lewontin's study, many other genetic studies have reached the same conclusion.

Subsequent studies by other scientists—of wide-ranging characteristics such as genetic traits and cranial morphology—have all shown the same thing: so-called races account for a very small amount of biological variation. Multiple biological traits do not lead to clear-cut racial classifications because traits simply do not agree in their frequency or distribution. One trait might cut across human populations in one way, but another trait cuts across them in another way.

Human Variation: Geographic Clines, Not Racial Categories

If race is not a valid way to account for human diversity, how do we speak meaningfully about the enormous range of variation in all kinds of human characteristics around the globe? One important finding from physical anthropologists' study of human variation is that specific biological traits generally follow a geographic continuum, also called a **cline.** Think, for example, of two patterns discussed in chapter 4: first, the frequencies of type B blood changing gradually from eastern Asia to far-western Europe (see Figure 4.32 in chapter 4); second, the human gene that causes the disorder sickle-cell anemia, hemoglobin *S,* increasing in frequency in areas where the parasitic disease malaria is endemic and decreasing in frequency (to nearly zero) in areas where malaria is not endemic (see Figure 4.22 in chapter 4). Because living humans are a single, geographically diverse species, their variation is continuously distributed in ways like these—along various geologic continuums—rather than grouped in discrete categories.

Among the best examples of clinal variation are the skin pigmentations of living people. From equatorial to higher latitudes, skin color changes in a gradient from dark to light. Exceptions exist, such as the relatively dark skin of Native Americans in the Canadian Arctic, but the single strongest factor in determining skin pigmentation is exposure to ultraviolet radiation (see "Solar Radiation and Skin Color" later in this chapter).

One of the most important lessons that physical anthropologists have learned regarding race and human variation is how remarkably variable we are as a species. Yes, there is a common human genome, but each of us possesses biological variations that give us our own personal genetic signature. When we look at the genome at the *individual* level—the basis of the science of **personal genomics**—we see how impossible it is to place individuals in biological categories, or so-called races.

personal genomics The branch of genomics focused on sequencing individual genomes.

Maps of individual genomes are now available for thousands of persons around the globe, and some of the uniqueness of these genomes is due to their microsatellites. These repeated segments of DNA are so different from person to person that they have become an important tool for human identification—living and deceased—in forensic, archaeological, and other contexts (see chapter 3). But in circumstances where small populations have been relatively isolated, individuals can recombine microsatellites through sexual reproduction. Over time, continued population isolation results in the presence of common microsatellite characteristics that may no longer be unique to an individual. Using microsatellite analysis, it is possible to identify patterns of genetic variation within and between traditional ethnic groups. For example, in the United States, study of genomic variation of traditional ethnic groups (for example, African descent, European descent, East Asian descent) by geneticist Hua Tang and his research team revealed clear clusters of associated microsatellite markers corresponding to ethnicity. However, these clusters do not reveal biological categories but rather represent patterns of microsatellite variation resulting from social histories and migration patterns. That is, the same processes that produce clinal and other kinds of geographic-associated variation discussed in this chapter also produce the observed microsatellite clusters. And while this kind of microsatellite study is important in understanding genomic variation, the medical community can use microsatellite variation to identify specific genetic markers that indicate potential disease risk in individuals. Still in its preliminary stages, personal genomic research may lead to a better understanding of individual genetic markers that are linked with specific diseases and their associated health risks, and not with so-called races.

Human variation, then, cannot be subdivided into racial categories. As said best by the physical anthropologist Frank B. Livingstone, "There are no races, there are only clines." Human variation can be understood far more meaningfully in terms of **life history,** the biology of growth and development.

5.2 Life History: Growth and Development

Various factors, genetic and external, influence the human body's growth (increase in size) and development (progression from immaturity to maturity). DNA provides a blueprint that schedules growth, but environment and external events very much influence the actual development from conception through death.

IS RACE REAL?

If you asked the question "Is race real?" as part of an on-campus poll, nearly all would say with certainty that *yes*, race is real. Some might even go so far as to say, *of course race is real*. If those polled were then asked in what ways race is real, they would probably mention skin pigmentation as the lead diagnostic characteristic of one's racial identity. They would also probably tell you that all humans can be racially categorized, such as "white," "black," or "Asian." If pressed further, the majority in your poll would say that race as a biological category is very real indeed. But does this popular consensus mean that racial categories do, in fact, exist?

WATCH THE VIDEO

www.digital.
wwnorton.com/
ourorigins4

Physical anthropologists have long argued just the opposite: race as a biological concept is *not* real. So, why the disagreement between your poll and what anthropologists say about race? The answer to this question lies in the history of the race concept. The formal study of race and its strongly typological focus—that is, placing humans into discrete categories—has a long history in Western thought. Much of the discussion surrounding race can be traced to the German anatomist Johann Friedrich Blumenbach, who developed the five-race taxonomy (see page 127). In his classification scheme, first published in 1775, humans were typed into "subgroups" or "races" on the basis of their visible phenotypic characteristics. Blumenbach's main criteria were skin pigmentation, cranial form, and geography, although other characteristics were considered. The existing scientific community rapidly adopted this taxonomy, and it has remained a mainstay of human classification ever since. Even today, as it was in my own early education, this five-way taxonomy is still taught to schoolchildren worldwide (see the opening comments in this chapter about my experience).

The notion of race as biology is well entrenched in American society. Like many societies around the world, our society is highly racialized, meaning that most Americans view differences in skin pigmentation and other phenotypic variation as representing fundamental differences between peoples. Physical anthropologist Rachel Caspari argues that the typological thinking introduced by Blumenbach not only persists in modern society but extends across a wide range of sciences. Caspari further suggests that racial or typological thinking may be a natural human thought pattern, a mental construct for organizing variation that is hard-wired into all of our brains. In fact, Americans create categorizations of humans from observed traits in similar ways to other cultures and societies around the world. From a psychological perspective, such typological thinking may be why we are so tied to categorizing human variability. This also may explain why most people understand and fully accept other key scientific facts, such as why there is daylight and that the world is round, but are unable to accept the fact that race is not a valid biological concept.

Abundant biological evidence shows that racial taxonomies, as espoused by Blumenbach and handed

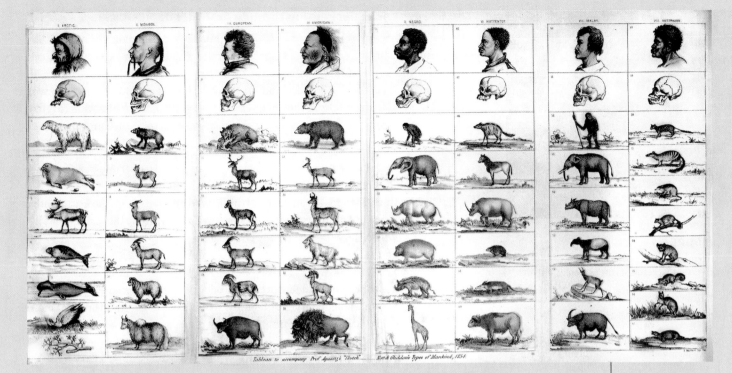

down through generations of scientists (and the public), are not accurate representations of how human biological variation is patterned. For example, a large and growing body of evidence exists showing very few genetic differences between human groups and no consistent pattern of genetic differences between what are popularly called races. The fact that the distribution of human genetic variation does not map onto the so-called races shows that race as commonly used is not a viable biological category. If races were real biologically, then what are called races would show distinctive and patterned genetic differences.

While anthropologists have long concluded that race has no *scientific* meaning, it certainly does not mean that race has no relevance. In reality, race is extremely relevant because of the biomedical consequences of uninformed lumping of persons into traditional categories. These are consequences that have real *social* meaning. In particular, think of the consequences for millions of Americans and others around the world who have experienced negative social outcomes because of or at least strongly influenced by their "race," including but not limited to income disparities, discrimination, and inequality that limits access to health care, nutrition, education, and other resources that promote well-being. The record is quite clear: in the United States, individuals deriving from certain descent groups have elevated death rates, more chronic diseases and various cancers, and an increased risk of injury. Considerable evidence also connects residential discrimination with low birth weight, infant mortality, tuberculosis, HIV infection, obesity, and cardiovascular disease. Unfortunately, these differences are typically biologized, often based on the assumption that these differences come from underlying genetic patterns (which they do not). In fact, these differences are environmentally based: strongly influenced by living conditions and not due to one's "race." Such ill-guided interpretations in society in general, and by a large swath of the health sciences in particular, shade the treatment and care of individuals assumed to have innate (genetic) attributes. For much of the general public and the scientific community, social inequality and poor health are unfairly dismissed as outcomes of inferior biology.

Today, considerable research funding is available for the study of population disparities in the social and medical sciences, which of course is a valuable development for society. However, the dependence on old, unfounded, centuries-old taxonomic models of race make the path toward addressing social inequality a rough one. We are responsible as a society to understand that human biological variation cannot be reduced to types and to understand the social and historical context of prejudice favoring one "race" over another. The bottom line: racial categories today are socially constructed boundaries that have no basis in biology in particular and science in general. Races don't exist—they are classification schemes that slow our pace toward improving the human condition.

Some authorities in the mid-nineteenth century believed that living humans and animals could be placed into distinctive biological types.

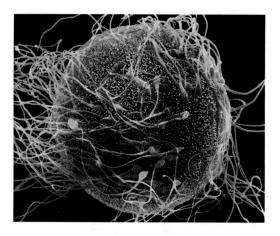

FIGURE 5.4

Fertilization Growth, in the form of mitoses that result in tissues, begins with the fertilization of an egg by a sperm. Of the many human sperm pictured here, only one will penetrate the ovum's outer layers.

prenatal stage The first stage of life, beginning with the zygote in utero, terminating with birth, and involving multiple mitotic events and the differentiation of the body into the appropriate segments and regions.

postnatal stage The second stage of life, beginning with birth, terminating with the shift to the adult stage, and involving substantial increases in height, weight, and brain growth and development.

lactation The production and secretion of milk from a female mammal's mammary glands, providing a food source to the female's young.

adult stage The third stage of life, involving the reproductive years and senescence.

stressors Any factor that can cause stress in an organism, potentially affecting the body's proper functioning and its homeostasis.

intrauterine Refers to the area within the uterus.

The Growth Cycle: Conception through Adulthood

The bodies of large mammals such as adult humans are made of more than 10 trillion cells, which are produced over the course of about 2^{38} mitoses (or cell divisions; see "Mitosis: Production of Identical Somatic Cells" in chapter 3). Mitoses result in all the various types of tissues (bone, blood, and muscle, for example) and organs (brain, stomach, heart, and so on), and they begin from the moment of fertilization (**Figure 5.4**). The human growth cycle, from embryo to fetus to child to adult, consists of three stages:

1. The **prenatal stage,** which includes the three periods, or trimesters, of pregnancy and ends with birth (forty weeks after conception)
2. The **postnatal stage,** which includes the *neonatal* period (about the first month), *infancy* (the second month to the end of **lactation,** usually by the end of the third year), *childhood* (ages 3–7, generally postweaning), the *juvenile* period (ages 7–10 for girls and 7–12 for boys), *puberty* (days or weeks), and *adolescence* (5–10 years after puberty)
3. The **adult stage,** which includes the reproductive period (from about age 20 to the end of the childbearing years, usually by age 50 for women and later for men) and *senescence* (the period of time after the childbearing years)

Prenatal Stage: Sensitive to Environmental Stress, Predictive of Adult Health

In humans, the prenatal stage, or pregnancy, lasts forty weeks. In the first trimester, or three-month period, the fertilized ovum multiplies into millions of cells. Distinctive cell groupings first represent different kinds of tissues, then give rise to the tissues, the organs, the brain, and the various physiological systems. By the end of the second month, the embryo is about 2.5 cm (1 in) long but is recognizably human. Because growth and development are at their most dynamic during this trimester, the embryo is highly susceptible to disruption and disease caused by mutation or environmental factors. Specific **stressors,** or potentially harmful agents, include the mother's smoking, consuming alcohol, taking drugs, and providing inadequate nutrition.

In the second trimester, the fetus mainly grows longer, from about 20.3 cm (8 in) at the end of the first month of this trimester to about 35.6 cm (14 in), or three-quarters the length of an average newborn.

The third trimester involves rapid weight growth and organ development. Humans are unique relative to other primates in having a very high percentage of body fat. This general pattern of humans producing fat babies may be related to the large brain of *Homo sapiens,* suggesting that the fat serves as a kind of energy "bank" or reserve supporting the high energy needs of the developing brain. During the final month, the lungs develop and most reflexes become fully coordinated. The fetus's wide range of movement includes the ability to grasp and to respond to light, sound, and touch.

This trimester culminates in birth, the profoundly stressful transition from the **intrauterine** environment to the external environment. Half of all neonatal deaths occur during the first 24 hours. Most of these deaths are caused by low birth weight (less than 2.5 kg, or 5.5 lb), which is generally linked to one or a combination of multiple stressors, such as maternal malnutrition, smoking, and excessive alcohol consumption. Because individuals of low socioeconomic status tend to be exposed to environmental stresses, their children are prone to low birth weights and early deaths. And a poor intrauterine environment predisposes the person to developing specific diseases later in life.

Postnatal Stage: The Maturing Brain, Preparing for Adulthood

Each of the six postnatal periods has a different **growth velocity,** or rate of growth per year (**Figure 5.5**). During infancy, the period of most rapid growth, the **deciduous** (or primary) **dentition** erupts through the gums (**Figure 5.6**). By the time an infant has completed weaning—when the infant shifts from consuming only milk provided by the mother to consuming external foods—all 20 deciduous teeth have erupted. The time of weaning varies, but the process is often finished by the end of the second or third year. **Motor skills** such as walking and running develop during the first two years. **Cognitive abilities** also progress rapidly during this time, reflecting the very rapid growth and development of the brain during infancy (**Figure 5.7**).

During childhood, general growth levels off, but the still rapidly growing brain requires the child to have a diet rich in fats, protein, and energy. The child learns behaviors important to later survival but still depends on adults for food and other resources. Because the child's dentition and digestive system are immature, adults sometimes prepare food that is soft and easy to chew. By age two, however, children normally can consume most adult foods.

By about age six, permanent teeth begin to replace primary teeth, and brain growth is completed (**Figure 5.8**). These hallmark developmental events occur nearly simultaneously, as they do in many other primate species. The eruption of the first permanent molar signals the ability to eat adult food, and very high nutritional requirements cease once the brain reaches its final weight.

During the juvenile years, growth slows. Although much learning occurs in childhood, the full-size brain makes possible formalized education and social learning.

Adolescence presents a number of profound biological developments. Sexual maturation commences with puberty, and its visible characteristics are the beginning of breast development and menstruation (**menarche**) in girls, the deepening of the voice and emergence of facial hair in boys, the development of secondary sexual characteristics (changes to genitals), and **sexual dimorphism** of girls' and boys' body sizes. Unlike other primates, humans experience increased growth velocity during this time. When nutrition is adequate and stressors are minimal, the adolescent growth spurt can add as much as 8.9 cm (3.5 in) to boys and somewhat less than 7.6 cm (3 in) to girls. Boys complete their growth later than girls, whose growth spurts peak earlier than those of boys. Growth spurts either do not happen or are minimized in very highly stressed populations, such as the Quechua Indians, who live at high altitudes in Peru and suffer from cold, overwork, malnutrition, and hypoxia (a condition discussed later in this chapter; see "High Altitude and Access to Oxygen").

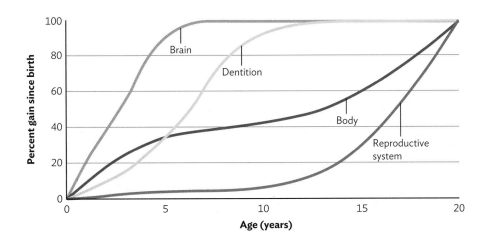

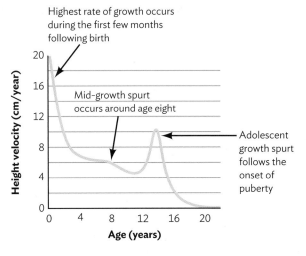

FIGURE 5.5

Human Growth Curve During postnatal life, a human grows at different rates. The highest rate of growth (on this graph, 20 cm/year) occurs during the first few months following birth. Growth velocity decreases through the rest of life, apart from a mid-growth spurt (here, approaching 7 cm/year) around age eight and an adolescent growth spurt (10 cm/year) following the onset of puberty.

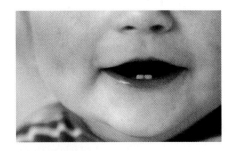

FIGURE 5.6

Deciduous Teeth Deciduous teeth, or baby teeth, form in the fetus and erupt shortly after birth.

FIGURE 5.7

Growth Curves of Body Tissues This chart shows the varying growth curves of the brain, body, dentition, and reproductive system in humans. The brain grows the fastest, reaching full cognitive development around age six. In fact, humans have such a large brain that much of it needs to be attained after birth; if the brain reached full size before birth, women would not be able to pass newborns' heads through their pelvic regions. Dentition has the next highest growth velocity (see Figures 5.6 and 5.8). The body grows more slowly and continues to grow until as late as 24 or 25 years of age. The reproductive system does not begin substantial growth and development until the onset of puberty, but it reaches completion around age 15–16 for girls.

CORONARY HEART DIS

Prenatal Origins of a Common Killer

For the most part, children recover from prenatal and early childhood illnesses and suffer no long-lasting effects. But the medical community is just now realizing that the early environment—even before birth—may have profoundly negative health consequences that last into adulthood. Adults who were stressed prenatally or in the first two years of childhood, from poor nutrition especially, tend to be smaller, more prone to disease, and shorter-lived than adults who were not stressed during this critical time of development.

The English nutrition scientist David Barker has studied the long-term implications of poor early health. Among other areas, he has investigated coronary heart disease and the factors that influence it, including the links between maternal and fetal health. Scientists have known for decades that particular cultural practices—cigarette smoking foremost—increase dramatically the risk of coronary heart disease. The traditional model for explaining coronary heart disease is based on adult lifestyles. If you smoke as an adult, for example, the model says you will develop coronary heart disease. Barker's findings indicate that while adult behaviors are important, the early events in a person's life—prenatal and early postnatal—better explain adult mortality due to coronary heart disease.

When laboratory animals are undernourished as fetuses, they suffer from altered metabolism, altered fat metabolism, high blood pressure, reduced body weight, and other factors that predispose them to coronary heart disease. Barker has hypothesized that poor fetal nutrition has similar long-lasting effects on adult

health, including heart disease. When he studied the lifetime body weights of 16,000 people from Hertford-shire, England, he found a direct and strong correlation between low birth weight and death from coronary heart disease. People who weighed less than 2.5 kg (5.5 lb) at birth died of coronary heart disease twice as frequently as people who weighed at least 3.4 kg (7.5 lb). Studies of other communities and populations revealed that small babies tend to become adults with higher blood pressure, higher serum cholesterol, and reduced glucose tolerance. Overall, poor health during the fetal period and early childhood sets an individual up for an increased susceptibility to adult disease and a reduced ability to maintain homeostasis (stability of organs and of physiological systems, further discussed later in this chapter; see "Adult Stage: Aging and Senescence").

If maternal health and fetal health do predict increased chances of chronic disease in the offspring, then this connection may also have multigenerational effects beyond the mother and her child. That is, poor maternal and prenatal nutrition likely affect

EASE STARTS EARLY

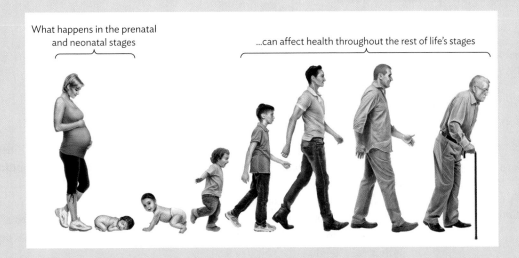

What happens in the prenatal and neonatal stages

...can affect health throughout the rest of life's stages

subsequent generations. Geneticists are learning that epigenetics—factors such as nutritional deprivation (see chapter 4) that regulate gene expression—play a crucial role in the health outcomes of future

generations. Beginning with the mother, nutritional stresses during important periods of growth and development, including the prenatal period, could be passed on to future generations. *Anthropology matters!*

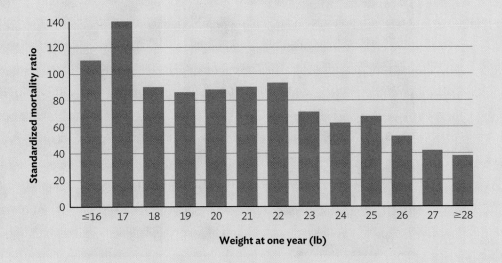

This graph helps illustrate David Barker's *fetal origins hypothesis*. The x-axis lists the weights of one-year-olds, increasing from left to right. The y-axis lists a mortality ratio that predicts the death rate from coronary heart disease. As weight increases, the mortality ratio (and death rate) decreases.

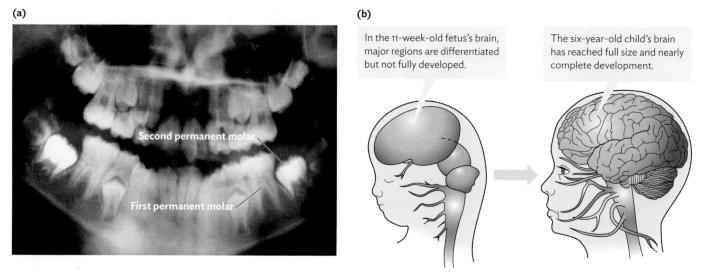

FIGURE 5.8

Molar Eruption and Brain Development **(a)** Permanent teeth form during the early years of life and begin to erupt around age six. In this X-ray image, the first permanent molars, called the six-year molars, have erupted. The second permanent molars, the 12-year molars, are still forming and will not erupt for another six years. The crowded anterior dentition, or front teeth, includes the deciduous teeth and new permanent teeth waiting to erupt and take their places. **(b)** Brain growth and development finish at around the same time as the full eruption of the first permanent molar.

epiphyses The end portions of long bones; once they fuse to the diaphyses, the bones stop growing longer.

diaphyses The main midsection, or shaft, portions of long bones; each contains a medullary cavity.

nonmineralized Refers to bone reduced to its organic component.

Prior to the completion of growth, the ends of the long bones—the humerus, radius, and ulna in the arm and the femur, tibia, and fibula in the leg—are separate growth centers called **epiphyses.** The epiphyses are separated from the main shaft, or **diaphysis,** by a growth plate containing cells that produce **nonmineralized** bone substance. As long as bone cells are producing bone substance and the epiphyses remain unfused, the long bone will continue to grow. The bone continually grows in width throughout life, but once the epiphyses have fused to the diaphyses, the growth in length stops and the individual's height is set (**Figure 5.9**).

Biologically, adulthood is signaled by the completion of sexual maturity, the reaching of full height, and the fusion of the epiphyses. The social maturity and behavioral

FIGURE 5.9

Long Bone Growth **(a)** This magnetic resonance image (MRI) of a child's knee shows the joining of the femur, or upper leg bone, with the tibia, or lower leg bone. Long bones like these begin as three separate bones—the diaphysis, or shaft, and two epiphyses, or ends—separated by growth plates. **(b)** In this photo of a child's knee joint, the epiphyses have not yet fused to the diaphyses. The line of union may be visible for several years after the attachment occurs; when it eventually disappears, the bone appears as a single element.

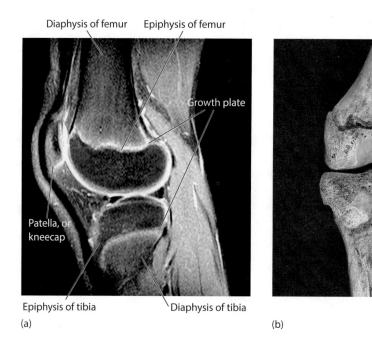

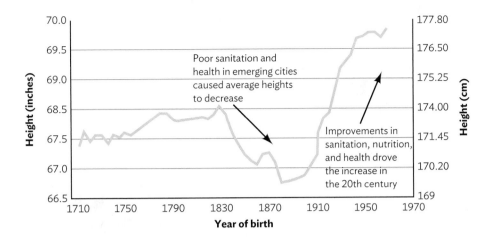

FIGURE 5.10

Changes in Height Beginning in the 1700s, the heights of soldiers, students, and slaves were routinely collected for identification or registration purposes. By combining these data with subsequent figures, Costa and Steckel discovered patterns of increase and decline in the heights of American-born males of European descent. From about 171.45 cm (67.5 in) in the early 1700s, heights rose to about 174 cm (68.5 in) around 1830, then sharply declined by 5.1 cm (2 in) over the next 50 years. After the late 1800s, heights increased by a few centimeters or about 2.5 inches during the twentieth century. Simply, the extraordinarily poor sanitation and health conditions in nineteenth-century cities resulted in increased disease, stress, and attenuated growth. The subsequent increase in Americans' heights reflected improvements in sanitation, nutrition, and health.

maturity associated with adulthood, however, are difficult to define. In fact, sociologists and social psychologists argue that social maturity is a lifelong process, developing earlier in some biologically mature individuals than in others.

While bone growth and epiphyseal fusion are influenced by genes and sex hormones (androgens and estrogens), the amount of growth and the terminal length of bones are strongly affected by environment, especially by nutrition and general health. Negative environmental effects in the present and in the historical past, such as downturns in nutrition, have been documented worldwide. The American economic historians Dora Costa and Richard Steckel have shown, for example, that between 1710 and 1970 substantial changes occurred in the heights of American males of European descent (**Figure 5.10**). Initially, a gradual increase in heights likely reflected improved living conditions and food availability. The sharp decline in heights around 1830 coincided with the urbanization trend. As people moved from rural, agricultural settings to overly crowded cities, they were exposed to more diseases that were easily passed from person to person. In addition, high population densities caused great accumulations of garbage and waste, which may have polluted water supplies and thus exposed people to more bacteria, viruses, and parasites that caused infection and disease. As living conditions improved at the beginning of the twentieth century, as trash removal became mandatory and sewers were constructed, height increased. Today, Americans' heights are among the greatest in the country's history, thanks to reliable food supplies, unpolluted water, and access to medical care.

This twentieth-century trend of increasing tallness, sometimes called a **secular trend,** has been noted in many other countries as well. Multiple factors have contributed to particular causes from place to place, but the collective increase in stature has resulted from improvements in disease control and nutrition. In wealthy nations, the increase in height has come to a stop or slowed considerably, most likely because growth has reached its genetic limit. In many less wealthy (and thus less healthy) nations, growth potential has not been reached, and growth periods are comparatively slow. For example, as the American anthropologist Barbara Piperata has documented, in Brazil's Amazon River basin the suboptimal nutrition and exposure to infectious disease have resulted in less-than-optimal growth **(Figure 5.11)**.

The growth and development of males, prenatally and postnatally, are more sensitive to environmental insult than are the growth and development of females. Human biologists have found much evidence of these differences in developing countries, but they have not been able to explain the mechanisms at work. In terms of evolution, it

secular trend A phenotypic change over time, due to multiple factors; such trends can be positive (e.g., increased height) or negative (e.g., decreased height).

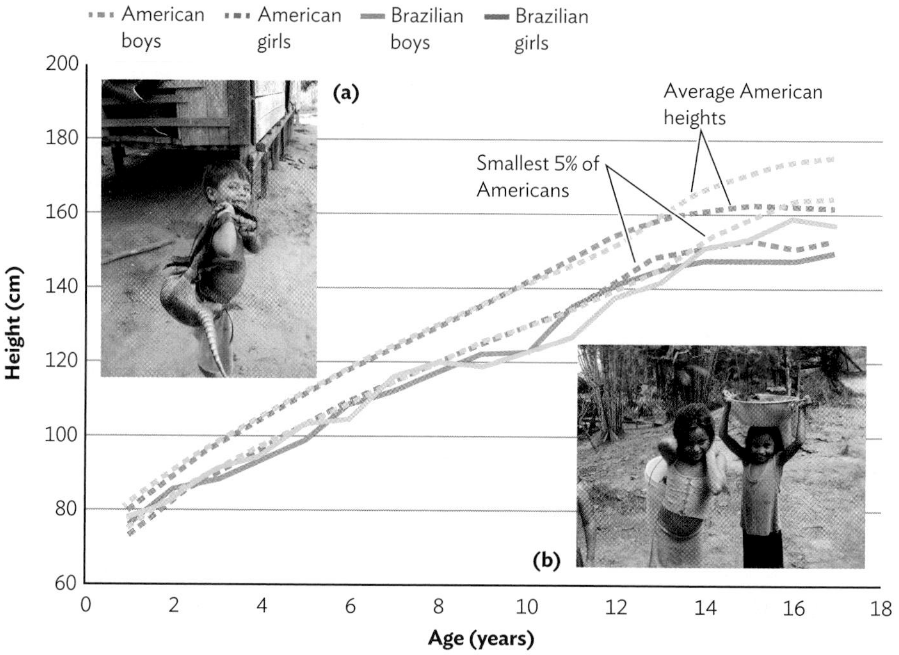

FIGURE 5.11

Height and Economically Disadvantaged Populations As this graph shows, some populations of **(a)** Brazilian boys and **(b)** Brazilian girls grow at rates less than those of the smallest 5% of American children. In countries such as Brazil, as in late-nineteenth-century America, poor environmental conditions have led to slowed growth and shorter adult height.

aging The process of maturation.

senescence Refers to an organism's biological changes in later adulthood.

homeostasis The maintenance of the internal environment of an organism within an acceptable range.

would make sense for females to have developed buffers from stress because females' roles in reproduction, including pregnancy and lactation, are much more demanding than the roles of males.

When a period of growth disruption occurs before adulthood, the resulting height deficit can be made up through rapid growth later on. In a long-term study of the Turkana in Kenya, growth has been documented to continue into early adulthood. Turkana children tend to be shorter than American children. However, growth among the Turkana extends well into their 20s, and Turkana adults are as tall as American adults. Few long-term growth studies have been done of nutritionally stressed populations, so we do not know about many other settings in which growth extends into adulthood. By and large, in areas of the world experiencing nutritional stress, adults are short owing to lifelong nutritional deprivation.

Adult Stage: Aging and Senescence

Throughout life, the body continually grows and develops—it is dynamic. By adulthood, its basic structure has been formed, so during this period most growth and development involve the replacement of cells and of tissues. In fact, over a person's lifetime nearly every cell and tissue in the body is replaced at least once every seven years. Indeed, your body is a very different one now than 10 years ago.

Aging basically means "becoming older," but it refers collectively to various social, cultural, biological, and behavioral events that occur over a lifetime yet do not by themselves increase the probability of death. **Senescence,** which accompanies aging, is a biological process characterized by a reduction in **homeostasis,** the body's ability to keep its organs and its physiological systems stable in the face of environmental stress. Senescing persons are increasingly susceptible to stress and death and have a decreased capacity to reproduce. For example, older adults produce less body heat than younger adults and hence are more uncomfortable in cold temperatures.

Whereas the previous life stages are generally predictable in their timing (mostly due to genetic programming), the chronology of senescence is highly variable but occurs in midlife. **Menopause,** the loss of ovarian function, is a key element of female senescence, marking the end of the reproductive phase and the end of childbearing. As a human biological universal, menopause usually occurs by age 50, but it varies by several years in different populations. Male senescence is different in that men normally produce sperm well into their 70s and 80s. However, the number of well-formed sperm and their motility decline by half after age 70. Male and female individuals older than 70 years, having lived through senescence, are considered elderly. These patterns of aging and senescence are unique to humans. That is, reproductive senescence is extremely rare in nonhuman primates. For all but a few species of nonhuman primates, fertility occurs throughout the adult life span. Where reproductive senescence has been found in nonhuman primates, it is present in very few individuals. American primatologist Susan Alberts and her research team found that just a few elderly individuals in three primate taxa were not fertile at the time of death: baboons, blue monkeys, and sifakas.

As discussed in chapter 3, bone loss is an effect of senescence that is universal in humans: after age 40, humans suffer increased bone porosity and reduction in bone mass. The increased susceptibility to bone fracture that comes with this loss is called **osteoporosis (Figure 5.12)**. In extreme cases, osteoporosis can weaken bone to the point that it easily fractures under small amounts of stress. This fragile nature commonly leads to fractures such as broken hips or to "compression" fractures of vertebrae, in which the bone simply cannot support the normal body weight and collapses. The collapse of several vertebrae can give the person a hunchback. Far more common in women than in men—because a loss of the hormone estrogen is linked to bone loss—osteoporosis shows less age variation than menopause does. Other factors that can predispose people to this condition are smoking, chronic diseases, and certain medications.

For every stage—from conception through senescence—humans (and other primates) have evolved strategies for enhancing their survival and reproductive potential, the prime movers of natural selection. In the next subsection, we will examine behaviors that are central to this adaptive success.

menopause The cessation of the menstrual cycle, signifying the end of a female's ability to bear children.

osteoporosis The loss of bone mass, often due to age, causing the bones to become porous, brittle, and easily fractured.

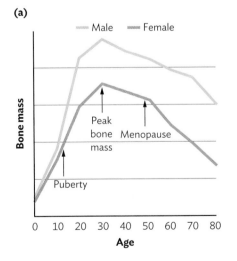

(a)

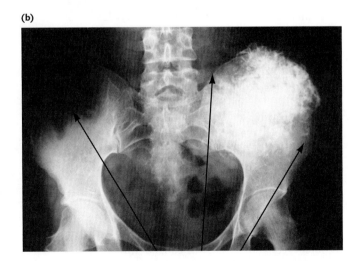

(b)

FIGURE 5.12

***Osteoporosis* (a)** As this graph shows, men and women reach their maximum bone mass around age 30. **(b)** The loss of bone mass becomes evident in the grayish areas of X-rays (arrows). The normal bone mass would be solid white.

LIFE ON THE

THE CASE OF THE EAST AFRICAN TURKANA PASTORALISTS

Anyone who sees the Great Rift Valley of East Africa, at least the first time, is struck by the raw beauty and remarkable harshness of the place. In the late 1970s, a group of American anthropologists and ecologists recognized that the region, on the western side of Kenya's Lake Turkana, was an ideal natural laboratory for studying human adaptation, especially how the native Turkana respond to this dry grassland's harshness and unpredictability.

The Turkana are nomadic pastoralists—they follow their livestock herds to new grazing grounds. From their livestock they acquire milk, meat, and blood, and they supplement this food through trading, hunting, gathering, and aid from the Kenyan government. These and other survival strategies have enabled the Turkana to prosper, expanding from their relatively small homeland to many more square miles of territory. Michael Little, Paul Leslie, and Rada and Neville Dyson-Hudson developed and carried out research plans to learn how the Turkana adapt to obtain key resources (primarily food), how their food choices and acquisition and overall lifestyle influence their health and well-being, and how their lifestyle affects the African savanna and its nonhuman occupants. An ambitious multidisciplinary research program, the South Turkana Ecosystem Project addressed fundamental issues about human behavior.

Spanning some two decades, the project eventually involved many scientists, graduate students, and others. To document how humans adapt to this marginal setting, Little and his collaborators collected a wide spectrum of data on health and quality of living that reflect responses to stress. They recorded what kinds of foods the Turkana ate; eating patterns; caloric intakes; body measurements (**anthropometry**) such as height, weight, and arm circumference of children

anthropometry Measurement of the human body.

Turkana advances to ca. 1850

Turkana advances to ca. 1900

Approximately 250,000 Turkana live in northwestern Kenya, which their people have inhabited for nearly 200 years. This map shows the Turkana's original homeland and their major migrations.

and adults; statistics about lactation and nursing; numbers of children born; ages at death; and various activities.

Analysis of these data showed that the Turkana have adapted, biologically and culturally, to their

MARGINS

The Turkana's lives are built around the care of domesticated livestock, including cattle, camels, and donkeys. Here, a Turkana man herds goats.

environment. Biologically, they have developed the body morphology typical of human groups adapted to hot climates: their linearity helps dissipate heat. Although the relative sparseness of their population minimizes the Turkana's effects on the environment, the environment has long-term consequences on the Turkana's growth and development, from childhood through adulthood. The study showed the profoundly positive impact of cultural buffering for the particularly vulnerable in times of shortfall. That is, in lean times, either seasonal or otherwise, the Turkana gave food preferentially to groups at the greatest risk of death, such as young children and pregnant or nursing women. This behavior had a clear biological outcome: the groups survived the deprivation and stress. That the Turkana also buffered postreproductive women supports the *grandmother hypothesis*; namely, that older women serve an important role of supporting herd owners and their families. The Turkana's recognition of older women's importance to long-term survival adds to scientists' growing understanding of the postreproductive years in terms of human adaptation and human evolution. The study thus had implications far beyond East Africa, for the Turkana's success underscores the notion that humans are remarkably flexible when dealing with marginal environments, as humans often do.

The project also illustrated the value of a multidisciplinary approach. Human biologists helped interpret the underlying biology of adaptation to stress, cultural anthropologists helped interpret the complexities of the culture and society, and ecologists helped interpret the environment and resources. Working as a team, these scientists provided new ways of looking at living people and their adaptations.

Evolution of Human Life History: Food, Sex, and Strategies for Survival and Reproduction

Two behaviors make possible the survival and adaptive success of humans and other primates: acquisition of food and reproduction. Unlike the other primates, humans acquire food and reproduce within the contexts of culture and society. For example, humans have created social institutions—especially kinship and marriage—and beliefs and rules supporting these institutions. Anthropologists are keenly interested in the relations between humans' sociocultural behaviors and the evolution of our unique life history, especially in comparison with other primates' life histories.

CONCEPT CHECK

Life History Stages in Humans: Prenatal, Postnatal, and Adult

A life history is the biological story—from conception to death—of an individual, a population, or a species. A life history provides insight into how energy is allocated to key events, such as reproduction, brain growth, and the care of offspring. It also sheds light on the interactions between genes and environment at crucial stages.

Stage	Period	Timing and Characteristics
Prenatal	First trimester	Fertilization to twelfth week; embryo development; organ development
	Second trimester	Fourth through sixth lunar months; rapid growth in length
	Third trimester	Seventh month to birth; rapid growth in weight and organ development
Postnatal	Neonatal	Birth to 28 days; first exposure to extrauterine environment; most rapid postnatal growth and development
	Infancy	Second month to 36 months; rapid growth; breast-feeding; deciduous tooth development; other milestones (e.g., walking); weaning at end of period
	Childhood	Three to seven years; moderate growth; eruption of first permanent molar; completion of brain growth
	Juvenile	Seven to 10 years (girls), seven to 12 years (boys); slower growth; self-feeding; cognitive transition in learning and increased ability to learn
	Puberty	Days to few weeks at end of juvenile years; activation of sexual development; marked increase in secretion of sex hormones
	Adolescence	Five- to ten-year period after puberty; growth spurt (earlier in girls than in boys); completion of permanent dental development and eruption; development of secondary sex characteristics; interest in adult social, sexual, and economic behaviors
Adult	Prime	Twenty years to end of reproductive years; stability in physiology, behavior, and cognition; menopause in women, commencing at about age 50
	Senescence	End of reproductive years to death; decline in function of many tissues and organs; homeostasis more easily disrupted than in earlier years; grandmother social behaviors

Source Adapted from Table 11.1 in B. Bogin and B. H. Smith. 2012. Evolution of the human life cycle. Pp. 515–586 in S. Stinson, B. Bogin, and D. O'Rourke, eds. *Human Biology: An Evolutionary and Biocultural Perspective*, 2nd ed. Hoboken, NJ: Wiley-Blackwell.

FIGURE 5.13
Grandmothering Postmenopausal women are often caregivers to children, frequently to their grandchildren. As more and more families have both parents working, child care by grandparents, and by grandmothers in particular, has become especially important.

PROLONGED CHILDHOOD: FAT-BODIED MOMS AND THEIR BIG-BRAINED BABIES
Humans have a relatively prolonged childhood. However, within this life period the spans of infancy and lactation are quite short. The mother's brief intensive child care allows her, theoretically, to have more births and to invest her resources among all her children.

The cost of this fertility advantage is the large amount of food the mother must provide for her children. The energy demands of the children's maturing brains require that this food be highly nutritious: rich in fats, protein, and energy. For only the first several years of a child's postnatal life can the mother provide these resources, via lactation, from her own stored body fats and other nutrients. Even during this period, a mother will begin to supplement the child's diet with other solids (at around four to six months).

GRANDMOTHERING: PART OF HUMAN ADAPTIVE SUCCESS Humans are also the only primates that experience prolonged postmenopausal survival at the other end of the life history. Some apes have a postmenopausal period, but it is briefer than that of humans. Ethnographic evidence from cultures around the world shows that postmenopausal women, most often grandmothers, play important roles in caring for children, provisioning food to children, and providing essential information about the world to various members of their social groups (**Figure 5.13**). Because older people can become key repositories of knowledge about culture and society, longevity may have a selective advantage in humans but not in other primates.

5.3 Adaptation: Meeting the Challenges of Living

Humans adjust remarkably well to new conditions and to challenges. As in other organisms, such adaptations—functional responses within particular environmental contexts—occur at four different levels. *Genetic* adaptation, as discussed in previous chapters, occurs at the population level via natural selection. Here, the biological change is inherited and is not reversible in a person (for example, someone with sickle-cell anemia). *Developmental* (or *ontogenetic*) adaptation occurs at the level of the individual during a critical period of growth and development, childhood especially. The capacity to make the change is inherited, but the change is not inherited and is not reversible. For example, children living at high altitudes develop greater chest size prior to reaching adulthood than that of children living at low altitudes. The expanded chest reflects the need for increased lung capacity in settings where less oxygen is available (discussed further later; see "High Altitude and Access to Oxygen"). *Acclimatization* (or *physiological* adaptation) occurs at the individual level, but unlike developmental adaptation it can occur anytime during a person's life. In this kind of adaptation, the change is not inherited and can be reversed. For example, exposure to sunlight for extended periods of time results in tanning (also discussed further later; see "Solar Radiation and Skin Color"). Lastly, *cultural* (or *behavioral*) adaptation involves the use of material culture to make living possible in certain settings. For example, wearing insulated clothing keeps people from freezing in extreme cold.

The American physical anthropologist Roberto Frisancho applies the term **functional adaptations** to the biological adjustments that occur within the individual's lifetime (that is, developmental adaptations and acclimatizations). Most functional adaptations are associated with extreme environmental conditions, such as heat, cold, high altitude, and heavy workload. Some of these conditions appear to have brought about genetic changes in humans. That is, over hundreds of generations humans have adapted to settings in which specific attributes enhance the potential for survival and reproduction. Skin pigmentation, for example, is related genetically to solar radiation exposure.

All adaptations have one purpose: *maintenance of internal homeostasis,* or maintenance of the normal functioning of all organs and physiological systems. Not to maintain homeostasis in body temperature, for example, or in oxygen accessibility or in strength of the bones of the skeleton has severe consequences for the individual, including work impairment and loss of productivity, decline in quality of life, and even death. The maintenance of homeostasis involves all levels of any organism's biology, from biochemical pathways to cells, tissues, organs, and ultimately the entire organism.

To determine how humans maintain internal homeostasis, anthropologists use indirect approaches and direct ones. *Indirect* approaches involve the study of populations in their natural environments, such as the Quechua Indians living in highland Peru or the Inuit living in Greenland. The observation of living populations as they engage in various activities in various settings provides great insight into functional adaptations, helping establish associations between specific biological attributes and environmental settings or circumstances. *Direct* approaches, by contrast, involve the replication of environmental conditions and of human responses to these conditions. In the course of such experiments, anthropologists determine cause-and-effect relationships, such as body response to temperature extremes.

Climate Adaptation: Living on the Margins

HEAT STRESS AND THERMOREGULATION Like all other mammals, humans are **homeothermic,** meaning they maintain a constant body temperature. A constant core temperature is essential for normal physiology, including brain function, limb function, and general body mobility. Humans can tolerate a body temperature higher than their normal 98.6 °F, but a body temperature above 104–107 °F for an extended period leads to organ failure and eventually death. Extremely hot weather can thus result in many

functional adaptations Biological changes that occur during an individual's lifetime, increasing the individual's fitness in the given environment.

homeothermic Refers to an organism's ability to maintain a constant body temperature despite great variations in environmental temperature.

deaths, such as in the summer of 2003, when at least 35,000 and perhaps as many as 50,000 people died in Europe during one of the hottest seasons ever recorded. Severe heat stress is experienced mostly in tropical settings, where it is hot much of the year, and during hot spells in temperate regions.

A body experiencing heat stress attempts to rid itself of internally and externally derived heat sources. Internal heat is produced by the body's metabolism, especially during activities involving movement, such as physical labor, walking, and running. External heat is derived from the air temperature. The initial physiological response to an elevated temperature is **vasodilation,** the dilation (expansion) of the blood vessels near the body's surface. By increasing the diameter of blood vessels, the body is able to move more blood (and associated heat) away from the body's core to the body's surface. The red face of a person who is in a hot environment is the visible expression of vasodilation.

Sweating is another response to heat. Sweat is mostly water produced by the eccrine glands, which are located over the entire body's surface. Evaporation of the thin layer of water on the skin results in cooling of the surface. Humans can sweat a remarkably high volume of water, and this physiological process is central to humans' long-term functional adaptation to heat.

Sweating is less effective in areas of the body having a dense hair cover than in areas of the body having little or no hair. This relationship suggests that sweating evolved as a thermoregulatory adaptation in association with the general loss of body hair. Humans' loss of body hair is unique among the primates, indicating that the thermoregulatory adaptation of hair loss and sweating occurred in human evolution only.

Humans have a strong capacity to adapt to excessive heat. Individuals who have not often experienced such heat are less able to conduct heat away from their cores and less able to sweat than are individuals living in hot climates. Individuals exposed for the first time to a hot climate, however, rapidly adjust over a period of 10–14 days. This adjustment involves a lowering of the body's core temperature, a lowering of the threshold for when vasodilation and sweating begin, and a reduction of the heart rate and metabolic rate. Overall, women are less able to tolerate heat than are men, in part due to a relatively reduced ability to move blood to the skin through vasodilation and the presence of greater body fat.

Human populations who have lived in hot climates for most of their history—such as native equatorial Africans and South Americans—have the same number of sweat glands as other populations. However, heat-adapted populations sweat less and perform their jobs and other physical functions better in conditions involving excessive heat than do non-heat-adapted populations.

BODY SHAPE AND ADAPTATION TO HEAT STRESS The relationship between body shape and temperature adaptation was first described in the 1800s by a combination of two biogeographic rules, one developed by the German biologist Carl Bergmann (1814–1865) and the other developed by the American zoologist Joel Allen (1838–1921). **Bergmann's rule** states that heat-adapted mammal populations will have smaller bodies than will cold-adapted mammal populations. Relative to body volume, small bodies have more surface area, facilitating more rapid heat dissipation. Conversely, large bodies have less surface area, thus conserving heat in cold climates (**Figure 5.14**). Consequently, human populations adapted to hot climates tend to have small and narrow bodies (discussed further in chapter 12). **Allen's rule** states that heat-adapted mammal populations will have long limbs, which maximize the body's surface area and thus promote heat dissipation, whereas cold-adapted mammal populations will have short limbs, which minimize the body's surface area and thus promote heat conservation.

vasodilation The increase in blood vessels' diameter due to the action of a nerve or of a drug; it can also occur in response to hot temperatures.

Bergmann's rule The principle that an animal's size is heat-related; smaller bodies are adapted to hot environments, and larger bodies are adapted to cold environments.

Allen's rule The principle that an animal's limb lengths are heat-related; limbs are longer in hot environments and shorter in cold environments.

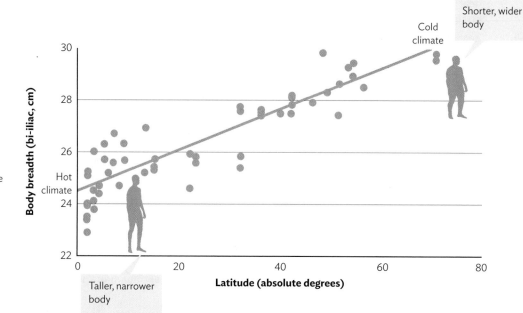

FIGURE 5.14

Bergmann's Rule This graph illustrates Carl Bergmann's biogeographic rule: as latitude increases (and temperature decreases), body breadth (as measured by bi-iliac breadth, or the maximum breadth between the pelvic bones) also increases. Bergmann's rule applies to all warm-blooded animals (including humans), which need to maintain a constant body temperature. Physically and physiologically, humans can adapt to a wide range of climates; but because humans are able to move about the earth, human body size may not strictly adhere to the latitude at which a person is living.

hypothermia A condition in which an organism's body temperature falls below the normal range, which may lead to the loss of proper body functions and, eventually, death.

vasoconstriction The decrease in blood vessels' diameter due to the action of a nerve or of a drug; it can also occur in response to cold temperatures.

Exceptions exist to Bergmann's and Allen's rules, but by and large these rules explain variation in human shapes that goes back at least 1.5 million years. Populations living in hot climates tend to have narrow bodies and long limbs. Populations living in cold climates tend to have wide bodies and short limbs. This long-term association between body shape and climate means that body shape is mostly a genetic adaptation. However, body shape also involves childhood developmental processes that respond to climatic and other stressors, such as poor nutrition. For example, poor nutrition during early childhood can retard limb growth, especially of the forearm and lower leg, resulting in shorter arms and legs. Ultimately, then, body shape and morphology reflect both evolutionary and developmental processes.

COLD STRESS AND THERMOREGULATION Severe cold stress is experienced mostly in places close to Earth's magnetic poles, such as the Arctic; at altitudes higher than 3 km (10,000 ft); and during cold spells in temperate settings. **Hypothermia,** or low body temperature, occurs in excessively cold air or immersion in cold water. During the great *Titanic* disaster in 1912, many hundreds of passengers and ship's crew members escaped the sinking vessel but died from hypothermia after floating in the northern Atlantic Ocean (28 °F) for two hours before rescue ships arrived.

Maintaining homeostasis against cold stress involves heat conservation and heat production. The human body's first response to cold stress is **vasoconstriction,** the constriction of the blood vessels beneath the skin. Decreasing the diameter of the blood vessels reduces blood flow and heat loss from the body's core to the skin. The chief mechanism for producing heat is shivering.

Humans adapt to cold, but the adaptation includes cultural and behavioral factors, practices that societies living in extremely cold settings pass from one generation to the next. That is, people teach their children how to avoid situations involving heat loss. They teach them what clothing to wear, what kinds of shelters to build, and how to keep the interiors of shelters warm. Cold-adapted cultures also know that alcohol consumption contributes to the loss of body heat, increasing the chances of hypothermia and death.

After being exposed to survivable cold for more than a few days, humans shiver less, produce more heat, and have higher skin temperatures. Overall, adjusting to cold means becoming able to tolerate lower temperatures—simply, feeling better in the cold.

To measure heat production, anthropologists take a specific kind of measurement called the **basal metabolic rate (BMR).** Indigenous people living in cold settings, such as the Indians at high altitudes in the Peruvian Andes, have a significantly higher BMR than that of other human populations. The Inuit are among the most studied populations on Earth, owing to their adaptation to the very cold, dry conditions in the Arctic Circle, where average winter temperatures range from –50 °F to –35 °F and even summer temperatures usually do not climb above 46 °F. In part, their high BMR is produced by their diet, which is high in animal protein and fat (about 9 calories per gram) and low in carbohydrates (about 3 calories per gram). Like most cold-adapted populations, however, the Inuit have adapted physiologically by developing a capacity for tolerating excessive cold. For example, their peripheral body temperatures, in the hands and feet, are higher than other peoples' because of a higher rate of blood flow from the body's core to the skin.

The Inuit conform to Bergmann's and Allen's rules, having large, wide bodies and short limbs. Moreover, they have developed a technology that conserves heat: their traditional housing focuses on insulation. For example, the walls of ice-constructed "igloos" include whale-rib rafters that are covered with alternating layers of seal skin and moss. Heat conductivity from a fire built beneath the main floor of the house serves to warm cold air as it rises, which is a simple but highly efficient way to heat a small interior environment.

SOLAR RADIATION AND SKIN COLOR One of the most profound environmental factors that humans deal with daily is solar radiation, or the sun's energy output, which plays a central role in the evolution and development of skin color (**Figure 5.15**). In daylight, skin—the largest organ and the most conspicuous feature of the human body, accounting for 15% of total body weight—is exposed to ultraviolet (UV) radiation, a component of solar radiation. The American anthropologists Nina Jablonski and George Chaplin have shown that the best predictor of skin color, as measured by **skin reflectance,** is UV radiation exposure. That is, the darkest skin (low skin reflectance) is associated with the highest levels of UV radiation, and the lightest skin (high skin reflectance) is associated with the lowest levels of UV radiation. UV radiation is highest at noon, during the summer, at the equator, and in higher altitudes, and skin becomes darker (more pigmented) at these times and in these settings. As a result, individuals living in low latitudes or equatorial regions of the globe have some of the darkest skin pigmentation because of the more direct and prolonged UV light throughout the year. As latitude increases, the amount of UV radiation decreases and so, too, does the amount of melanin in the skin; therefore, the lightest-skinned individuals are usually in the highest latitudes. In general, populations between 20°N latitude and 20°S latitude have the darkest skin **(Figure 5.16)**.

When first exposed to UV radiation, light skin reddens—the process commonly called *sunburn*. With ongoing exposure, the **melanocytes** increase the number and size of **melanin** granules. In addition, the outer layer of the epidermis thickens. This darkening—that is, tanning—and thickening serves to retard penetration of the epidermis and dermis by UV radiation, protecting the individual from sunburn and possibly cancer. Because melanin is a natural sunscreen, individuals with high melanin content receive the most protection. Thus, people with dark skin, such as in equatorial Africa, are able to tolerate more exposure to the sun than are those with light skin. Dark-skinned people have a **sun protection factor (SPF)** of 10–15; light-skinned people have an SPF of between 2 and 3. Around the world, populations with the most

basal metabolic rate (BMR) The rate at which an organism's body, while at rest, expends energy to maintain basic bodily functions; measured by the amount of heat given off per kilogram of body weight.

skin reflectance Refers to the amount of light reflected from the skin that can be measured and used to assess skin color.

melanocytes Melanin-producing cells located in the skin's epidermis.

melanin A brown pigment that determines the darkness or lightness of a human's skin color due to its concentration in the skin.

sun protection factor (SPF) The rating calculated by comparing the length of time needed for protected skin to burn to the length of time needed for unprotected skin to burn.

(a)

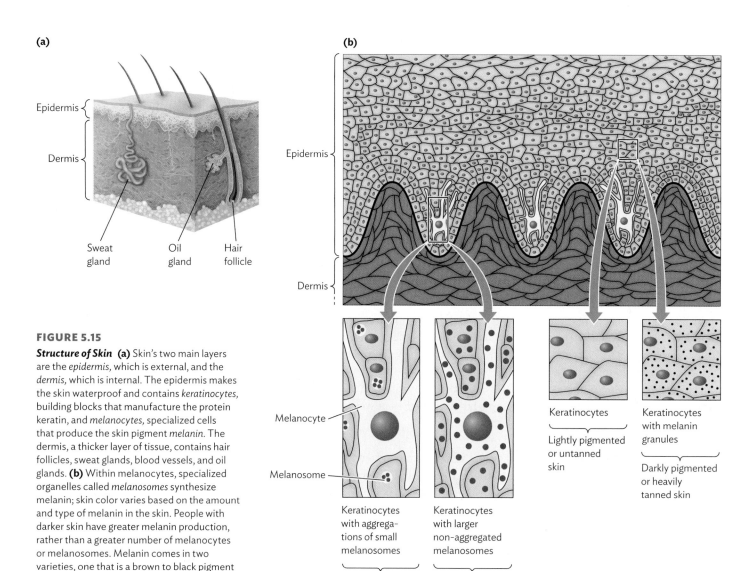

Epidermis

Dermis

Sweat gland

Oil gland

Hair follicle

(b)

Epidermis

Dermis

Melanocyte

Melanosome

Keratinocytes with aggregations of small melanosomes

Lightly pigmented or untanned skin

Keratinocytes with larger non-aggregated melanosomes

Darkly pigmented or heavily tanned skin

Keratinocytes

Lightly pigmented or untanned skin

Keratinocytes with melanin granules

Darkly pigmented or heavily tanned skin

FIGURE 5.15

Structure of Skin **(a)** Skin's two main layers are the *epidermis,* which is external, and the *dermis,* which is internal. The epidermis makes the skin waterproof and contains *keratinocytes,* building blocks that manufacture the protein keratin, and *melanocytes,* specialized cells that produce the skin pigment *melanin.* The dermis, a thicker layer of tissue, contains hair follicles, sweat glands, blood vessels, and oil glands. **(b)** Within melanocytes, specialized organelles called *melanosomes* synthesize melanin; skin color varies based on the amount and type of melanin in the skin. People with darker skin have greater melanin production, rather than a greater number of melanocytes or melanosomes. Melanin comes in two varieties, one that is a brown to black pigment and one that is a yellow to red pigment. Varying production of these two melanin pigments accounts for the wide range of skin color.

melanin have the fewest skin cancers and malignant melanomas. However, these effects occur largely during or after the late reproductive years, suggesting that skin cancer is not an element of natural selection.

SOLAR RADIATION AND VITAMIN D SYNTHESIS The body needs UV radiation for the synthesis of vitamin D, a steroid hormone that regulates calcium absorption and mineralization of the skeleton. Today, we obtain some vitamin D through fortified foods and by eating fatty fish such as salmon, but most vitamin D is produced in the skin. UV radiation in the form of UV photons penetrates the skin and is absorbed by a cholesterol-like substance, 7-dehydrocholesterol, in the epidermis (keratinocytes) and dermis (fibroblasts) layers (see Figure 5.15). This process produces a previtamin D that eventually converts to vitamin D, which is released from the skin and transported via the circulatory system to the liver and kidneys. There, more chemical reactions produce the active form of vitamin D. Without this form, the bones do not mineralize properly, resulting in a condition called *rickets* in children and *osteomalacia* in adults (**Figure 5.17**).

In addition to lower-limb deformation, a telltale sign of rickets in children is malformed pelvic bones. Both conditions result when poorly developed bone is unable

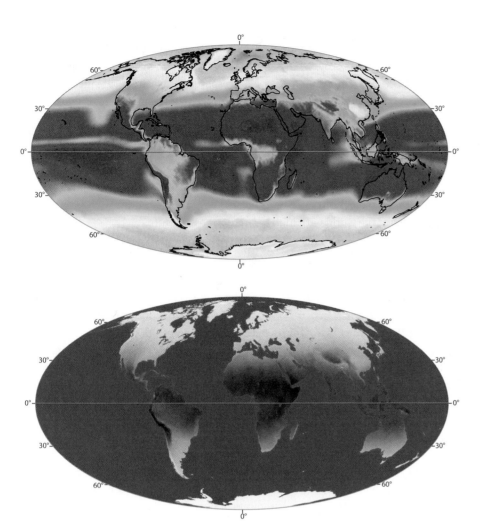

FIGURE 5.16

Skin Color Variation Humans inherit a certain amount of pigmentation, but exposure to solar radiation can alter skin color dramatically. Because melanin provides a protective barrier against UV radiation, the production of more melanin is an adaptation to areas with greater amounts of UV radiation. These maps show (top) how solar radiation shifts from the highest levels near the equator to the lowest levels at the poles and (bottom) how skin color varies from the darkest pigmentation at the equator to the lightest pigmentation at the poles.

to withstand the forces of body weight. Women who as children had rickets severe enough to affect the pelvic bones have trouble giving birth because the space for the fetus's passage during birth is restricted. Because a key element of natural selection is a greater number of births, this decreased reproductive capacity means that the trait—malformed pelvic bones caused by rickets—is disadvantageous.

Melanin, the primary influence on vitamin D synthesis, can be advantageous or nonadvantageous. That is, because melanin provides protection from solar radiation, substantial amounts of this pigment can inhibit vitamin D production. As a result, at high latitudes where there is less UV radiation, lighter skin, with less melanin, is favorable because it allows more solar radiation to be absorbed, enabling vitamin D production. In fact, as world populations today reveal, there is a strong correlation between distance of a population from the equator and degree of skin pigmentation: the closer a population is to the equator, the darker the skin pigmentation. Simply, skin needs to be dark enough to protect from UV radiation but light enough to allow solar radiation sufficient for vitamin D production.

The American physiologist William Loomis has hypothesized that as human ancestors moved out of Africa into the more northerly latitudes of Europe and elsewhere, their dark skin would not have produced enough vitamin D to bring about calcium absorption and skeletal development. Therefore, in those latitudes, natural selection strongly favored alleles for light skin. This scenario suggests that prior to 1 mya, all of our ancestors lived in what is now Africa and their skin was pigmented highly so that it would block dangerous UV radiation.

FIGURE 5.17

Rickets Photographed in Hungary in 1895, these children are suffering from rickets, a disorder in which poorly mineralized bones, especially the weight-bearing leg bones, become soft, are prone to fracture, and can warp or bow. Rickets was especially prevalent in the 1800s in Europe and America. In urban settings in particular, indoor work and air pollution decreased access to sunlight and exposure to UV radiation.

hypoxia Less than usual sea-level amount of oxygen in the air or in the body.

SOLAR RADIATION AND FOLATE PROTECTION Support for the evolution of skin pigmentation in humans is provided by the fundamental role of melanin in the protection of stored folate (folic acid) in our bodies. New research shows that folate is essential for the synthesis and repair of DNA and therefore directly affects cell division and homeostasis. Even very tiny deficiencies of folate have been linked to a range of health issues, including neural tube defects whereby the brain or spinal cord does not form properly, cleft palate, pregnancy loss, and reduced sperm production. Folate levels decline dramatically with exposure to high and prolonged levels of UV radiation. However, skin color and melanin production are key elements in protecting the body from folate depletion. Thus, natural selection would have played a key role in maintaining relatively dark skin in regions of the world with high UV-radiation exposure.

HIGH ALTITUDE AND ACCESS TO OXYGEN At high altitudes, generally defined as greater than 3,000 m (10,000 ft) above sea level, a fall in barometric pressure reduces the number of oxygen molecules. The primary environmental stress in such places is **hypoxia,** the condition in which body tissues receive insufficient amounts of oxygen (**Figure 5.18**). Secondary stresses include high UV radiation, cold, wind, nutritional deprivation, and the rigors of living in highly variable, generally rugged terrain.

The severity of hypoxia increases as a person moves higher, and the associated risk increases because all body tissues and physiological processes require an uninterrupted oxygen supply. Hypoxia results in mountain sickness, with headache, nausea, loss of appetite, fatigue, and breathlessness occurring at about 2,400 m (8,000 ft) during rest and about 1,900 m (6,500 ft) during physical activity. For some individuals living at sea level or in prehypoxic conditions who travel to high altitudes or otherwise experience hypoxia, mountain sickness becomes a life-threatening condition. For most people, the symptoms disappear within the first few days of exposure as the body begins to more efficiently use the reduced amounts of oxygen in the air and homeostasis is

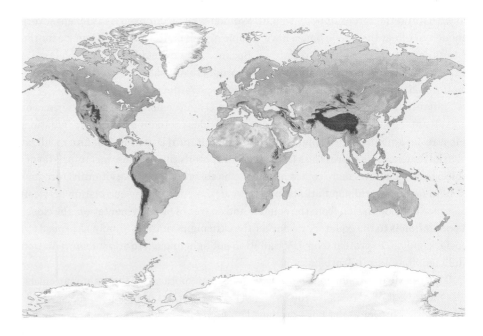

FIGURE 5.18

High Altitudes As this map shows, each continent except for Australia and Antarctica has at least one high-altitude area (shaded in red). A lack of oxygen is among the conditions to which humans must adapt at high altitudes.

restored. Extra red blood cells and oxygen-saturated hemoglobin are produced. The hemoglobin transports oxygen to body tissues, while an expansion in the diameter of arteries and of veins allows increased blood flow and increased access to oxygen.

Additional physiological changes represent a long-term response to hypoxia. A person who moved to the high-altitude settings of the Himalayas, for example, would function better there over time. A young child who moved there would, through the process of growth, develop greater lung volume and the ability to use oxygen more efficiently. Human populations who have lived at high altitudes for many generations—such as those in the Peruvian Andes—have larger chest cavities than those of populations at low altitudes, reflecting the high-altitude populations' inherited increases in lung volume. However, these populations are generally shorter than their low-altitude counterparts. Widespread growth retardation results from the increased energy required to live in cold environments with little oxygen and poor nutrition. But some biological attributes associated with living at high altitudes may offer selective advantages. For example, the American physical anthropologist Cynthia Beall and colleagues have found that Tibetan women with alleles for high oxygen saturation in their hemoglobin, a factor that enhances the body's access to oxygen, have more surviving children. Thus, hypoxia at high altitudes can be an agent of natural selection (**Figure 5.19**).

Nutritional Adaptation: Energy, Nutrients, and Function

MACRONUTRIENTS AND MICRONUTRIENTS Climate is only one key area in which humans adapt. We also adapt to diet, or the kinds of foods we eat, and nutrition, or the deriving of nutrients from those foods. Such adaptation is crucial to acquiring the necessary energy and nutrients for reproduction, growth, and development.

Each body function requires a certain amount of energy and particular nutrients, and a lack of energy or of nutrients can hamper body functions. Like many other primates (the other primates are discussed in chapter 6), humans are omnivorous, eating

FIGURE 5.19

Tibetan Farmers Tibetan farmers live in high-altitude areas and are shorter than Tibetans living in lowlands. Among the farmers' physical and physiological adaptations to their environment are large lungs, better lung function, and higher oxygen saturation in arteries.

Adaptation: Heat, Cold, Solar Radiation, High Altitude

Humans display both short-term adjustments and long-term adaptations to environmental extremes. These responses are crucial for maintaining homeostasis.

Setting	Exposure and Adaptation	Characteristics
Heat	First exposure	Vasodilation, profuse sweating; but effects reduce with continual exposure.
	Functional adaptation	Less sweating, normal work performance.
	Genetic adaptation	Narrow body, long limbs.
Cold	First exposure	Vasoconstriction, shivering; but effects reduce after continual exposure brings warmer skin temperature.
	Functional adaptation	Tolerance to cold and to lowering of skin temperature, metabolic rate higher than that of nonadapted populations, peripheral body temperature higher than that of nonadapted populations.
	Genetic adaptation	Large, wide body; short limbs.
Solar/UV radiation	First exposure	Reddening of skin (sunburn), followed by increased melanin production by melanocytes.
	Functional adaptation	Tanning, thickening of skin.
	Genetic adaptation	High melanin production (dark skin).
High altitude	First exposure	Hypoxia results in headache, nausea, loss of appetite, fatigue, and breathlessness; but symptoms disappear after a few days.
	Functional adaptation	Greater diameter of arteries and veins and greater relative blood flow to body tissues, greater lung volume, more efficient use of oxygen, larger chest size in some populations (reflecting greater lung volume).
	Genetic adaptation	High oxygen saturation in hemoglobin.

basal metabolic requirement The minimum amount of energy needed to keep an organism alive.

total daily energy expenditure (TDEE) The number of calories used by an organism's body during a 24-hour period.

macronutrients Essential chemical nutrients, including fat, carbohydrates, and protein, that a body needs to live and to function normally.

micronutrients Essential substances, such as minerals or vitamins, needed in very small amounts to maintain normal body functioning.

a wide range of both plants and animals. This dietary plasticity enhances our access to the nutrients we need for function and survival, and in terms of adaptability and evolution it reflects humans' unique combination of biology and culture.

Nutritionists have developed two sets of dietary recommendations: those based on energy requirements and those based on nutrient requirements. Measured in calories, the minimum energy needed to keep a person alive is called the **basal metabolic requirement.** A person needs additional energy for other functions, such as work and exercise, thermoregulation, growth, and reproduction (pregnancy and lactation). The **total daily energy expenditure (TDEE)** consists of the basal metabolic requirement plus all the other energy requirements, and we fulfill all these energy requirements by consuming specific **macronutrients** (carbohydrates, fats, and proteins) in food and **micronutrients** (vitamins and minerals) in food as well as in multivitamins. **Table 5.1** shows the daily minimum amounts of nutrients recommended in the United States.

Table 5.1 Dietary Reference Intakes for Selected Nutrients

Nutrient (Units)	Child 1–3 Years	Female 19–30 Years	Male 19–30 Years
Macronutrients			
Protein (g)	13	46	56
(% of calories)	5–20	10–35	10–35
Carbohydrate (g)	130	130	130
(% of calories)	45–65	45–65	45–65
Total fiber (g)	14	28	34
Total fat (% kcal)	30–40	20–35	20–35
Saturated fat (% kcal)	<10%	<10%	<10%
Linoleic acid (g)	7	12	17
(% kcal)	5–10	5–10	5–10
α-Linoleic acid (g)	0.7	1.1	1.6
(% kcal)	0.6–1.2	0.6–1.2	0.6–1.2
Cholesterol (mg)	<300	<300	<300
Minerals			
Calcium (mg)	500	1,000	1,000
Iron (mg)	7	18	8
Magnesium (mg)	80	310	400
Phosphorus (mg)	460	700	700
Potassium (mg)	3,000	4,700	4,700
Sodium (mg)	<1,500	<2,300	<2,300
Zinc (mg)	3	8	11
Copper (g)	340	900	900
Selenium (g)	20	55	55
Vitamins			
Vitamin A (g RAE)	300	700	900
Vitamin D (g)	5	5	5
Vitamin E (mg AT)	6	15	15
Vitamin C (mg)	15	75	90
Thiamin (mg)	0.5	1.1	1.2
Riboflavin (mg)	0.5	1.1	1.3
Niacin (mg)	6	14	16
Vitamin B_6 (mg)	0.5	1.3	1.3
Vitamin B_{12} (g)	0.9	2.4	2.4
Choline (mg)	200	425	550
Vitamin K (g)	30	90	120
Folate (g DFE)	150	400	400
USDA food pattern using goals as targets	1,000	2,000	2,400

RAE = retinol activity equivalent; AT = alpha-tocopherol; DFE = dietary folate equivalent.
Source United States Department of Agriculture, fnic.nal.usda.gov.

The lack of these essential vitamins and minerals, even those recommended in small amounts, can have devastating effects. For example, lack of folate in a pregnant woman can lead to neural tube defects, such as spina bifida, in the fetus. Many foods we commonly eat in the United States, such as cereal, bread, and milk, are fortified with some of these essential nutrients.

HUMAN NUTRITION TODAY The majority of human populations across the world are undernourished (consuming fewer than 2,000 calories per day), especially in developing nations in Africa, in South and Central America, and across large regions of Asia (**Figure 5.20**). Called the **nutrition transition,** in many settings of the world local populations have shifted from eating minimally refined, locally grown foods that generally provide sufficient calories and nutrients to eating highly processed foods that are high in saturated fats and sugar and low in fiber. American anthropologist Barry Bogin has documented the increasingly globalized diets of the Maya people of Mexico. In this setting, health has shown a precipitous decline owing to the shift to poor diets.

In the late twentieth century and the early twenty-first century, governments across the world have collaborated on increasing agricultural production to relieve famine and starvation. Currently, resources are directed at enhancing the nutritional attributes of key grains, particularly rice and corn. As a result of these international efforts, grains are more readily available and of better quality. This focus on grains has contributed, however, to a growing decline in the diversity of foods consumed by human populations, especially in nutritionally stressed settings. Increased agricultural production might help meet populations' caloric needs, but attention is shifting to increasing the availability of additional micronutrients—such as vitamin A, vitamins B_6 and B_{12}, vitamin D, iodine, iron, and zinc—through meat and other animal products.

Despite these efforts, the increasing trend of declining nutrition is having significant consequences for human populations around the world. Among the consequences of poor nutrition is the suppression of the immune system. Owing to poor living circumstances and poor sanitation conditions, meanwhile, undernourished populations are especially susceptible to the spread and maintenance of infectious disease. Thus, undernutrition and infection work hand in hand—each exacerbates the other, and the combination is much worse for the health and well-being of the individual than is either one alone.

Universally, undernourished populations experience stunted growth, resulting in shortness for age. The American economist David Seckler has hypothesized that shortness in height is an adaptation to reduced food supplies, one with no costs to individual health. The record shows quite the opposite, however: individuals who are undernourished typically have poor general functioning, reduced work capacity, ill health, and shortened life expectancy. Short individuals might require fewer calories and nutrients, but the associated health cost for them can be profound. Moreover, it is highly unlikely that undernourished populations' shortness is a genetic adaptation. Where energy and nutrition became adequate or abundant after periods of disruption and deprivation, body size rebounded. For example, in many countries, especially in Europe and Asia, World War II had a profoundly negative impact on growth. In the Netherlands, 1944 and 1945 were known as the "starving years." After the war, children and adults began growing again thanks to the return of adequate nutrition (**Figure 5.21**).

OVERNUTRITION AND THE CONSEQUENCES OF DIETARY EXCESS Much of the above discussion about nutrition focused on shortfalls and the consequences of not

nutrition transition Change in diet involving shift from traditional diet of low fat, cereals, and fiber to Western high fat, high carbohydrate, animal-source foods.

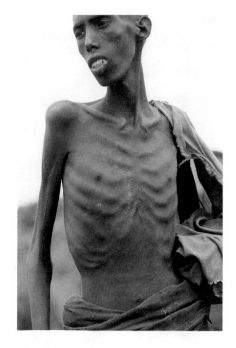

FIGURE 5.20

Malnutrition Malnutrition is a substantial problem in many parts of the world. Both of its forms—undernutrition, or insufficient consumption of calories and/or micronutrients, and overnutrition, or excessive consumption of calories and/or micronutrients—can have detrimental health consequences. Chronic undernutrition is a persistent problem for populations of many developing nations. This emaciated Somali man, for example, has not been able to consume enough food to sustain normal body weight.

FIGURE 5.21

Malnutrition and Height Height is a sensitive indicator of diet and health. During periods of insufficient nutrition, growth can be slowed or arrested, leading to reduced adult stature. If, however, proper nutrition is restored before adulthood, a recovery period can follow, during which growth "catches up" to where it should be. This graph shows the heights of boys and girls of various ages in Germany during and after World Wars I and II. During the wars, food shortages negatively affected growth in height. After the wars, food was more abundant and growth was not inhibited. What might account for the general increase in growth from 1910 through 1950?

getting enough of some nutrient or food or energy. Increasingly around the world, the problem is becoming just the opposite: too much food and too many of the wrong kinds of food. These dietary choices have their own negative consequences for health and well-being (**Figure 5.22**). In the United States, adults have increased their body weight by an average of 11 kg (24 lb) over the past four decades, and more than 50% of adults are overweight. The average weight of 6- to 11-year-old children increased from 29 kg (65 lb) in 1963–65 to 33 kg (74 lb) in 1999–2002. Today, 20% of American children are overweight or obese. Obesity was mostly unknown in the 1950s, but since the early

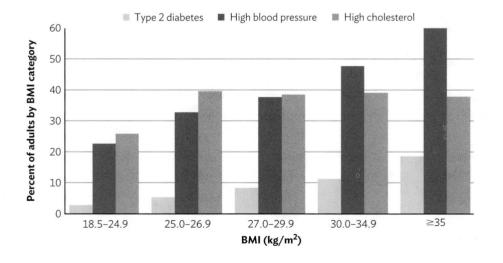

FIGURE 5.22

Overnutrition Like undernutrition, overnutrition has many negative consequences for health and well-being. As this graph shows, the risks of diabetes, high blood pressure, and high cholesterol increase substantially as BMI increases. BMI, or body mass index, is a statistical measure of weight according to height. A BMI between 18.5 and 24.9 indicates that a person has normal weight for his or her height. A BMI between 25 and 29.9 means "overweight," while 30 or above means "obese," where excess weight is so extreme that health and function are compromised.

LIFE IN AN OBESOGE

Understanding the Obesity Pandemic in an Evolutionary Perspective

On average, people in your generation are heavier than people in your parents' generation. Some of the average weight gains documented over the past 100 years or so are simply due to the fact that people are taller. But the trend of extra body weight is more alarming than that: most of the excessive weight is due to obesity—to people having considerably more adipose tissue, or body fat.

What is causing the remarkable rise in obesity, not only in the United States but around the world, and all within just the past several decades? By integrating the various lines of evolutionary, biological, and behavioral evidence, physical anthropologists are providing important answers to this question. The American physical anthropologist Leslie Sue Lieberman points out that modern lifestyles—characterized by the increased availability of cheap, high-calorie, energy-dense foods and labor-saving technology—has produced remarkable changes in body weight. In obesogenic environments, people are consuming more calories, engaging in fewer activities that require significant energy expenditure, and thus gaining body weight. The obesity pandemic, Lieberman argues, is best understood in terms of the disconnection between our lifestyles and our evolutionary history.

For 99% of human evolution, our hominin ancestors had a selective advantage for hunting and gathering. That is, our ancestors needed the suite of cognitive, behavioral, and physiological traits best suited for acquiring food and efficiently storing nutritional energy. These hominins were adapted to frequent shortages in the food supply. They hunted and gathered as much food as possible, limited only by what foods were available on the landscape and the technology used to acquire those foods. In very good times, our ancestors acquired and consumed more calories than they needed, and the excess calories were stored in their adipose tissues. When the food supply was low, their bodies drew upon these stored calories to meet energy requirements. Those hominins who possessed attributes that enhanced the maximum acquisition and consumption of food, coupled with the physiological means of storing energy for lean times, survived and reproduced in greater numbers than their counterparts lacking such attributes. These once-adaptive cognitive, behavioral, and physiological traits are still with us today. Now, however, these traits appear to be increasingly maladaptive, at least with respect to the obesogenic environment we currently inhabit.

Lieberman and other anthropologists speculate that there may have been little selection in our hominin ancestors for cognitive skills that document *portion size*, owing to the fact that the amount of food available to our hominin ancestors was controlled by the environment. In other words, ancient hominins were rarely able to acquire excessive quantities of foods. Compare that circumstance to the "supersized" portions of many

NIC WORLD

In 1996, India's first McDonald's opened in New Delhi. For religious reasons, no beef products are served, but high-fat foods such as french fries are readily available.

popular restaurant chains today. Furthermore, our modern obesogenic environment surrounds us with a diverse array of advertising visual cues, such as on television and on billboards. One iconic visual cue, for example, is the "golden arches" of McDonald's. These and numerous other visual cues tell us *when* it is time to eat and *what* is good to eat. Our enhanced sense of vision (accompanying a reduced sense of smell compared to earlier in our evolutionary history) draws us to these stimuli. In short, bigger portions and savvy advertising, combined with physiological and behavioral processes shaped over millions of years of our evolutionary past, are contributing to an increased prevalence of obesity.

Increased energy consumption and decreased activity may not be the entire story, however. The developmental biologists Felix Grün and Bruce Blumberg warn that exposure to industrial chemicals and organic pollutants during pregnancy can contribute to pathological weight gain in the child. In experimental studies of laboratory animals exposed to endocrine-disrupting chemicals found in various plastics and canned foods, the exposure caused the animals to increase their fat storage by increasing the number of fat cells. These chemicals have an epigenetic effect—they influence the gene regulators that turn on and off the genes controlling the development of fat cells. So important is this finding that the 2010 report by the US Interagency Task Force on Childhood Obesity presented to then-President Obama strongly advised that the potential effects of fat-promoting chemicals in early life should be a high research priority of the National Institutes of Health.

Scientists and others are rapidly providing answers to questions about obesity. Key for quelling the rise of obesity in children and adults across the globe will be concerted efforts aimed at improving nutrition, increasing physical activity, and understanding the potential role of environmental pollutants. The study of evolution has helped teach us these lessons.

1990s it has become a "growing" problem, not only in the United States but also in some areas of the Pacific, most of Europe and the Middle East, Latin America, and South Africa. The World Health Organization reported in 2015 that nearly 2 billion people globally are overweight.

The reasons for the remarkable increase in numbers of overweight and obese people are complex, but they basically boil down to the increased ability of our society to produce inexpensive food, most of which is high in fat, and advances in transportation technology, which provides greater access to cheap food sources. In general, people are consuming more at home and elsewhere. For example, the portions of food consumed in restaurants are vastly greater now than several decades ago. Calorie-dense pasta servings are as much as five times greater than US Department of Agriculture recommendations. In the past century, single servings of soft drinks more than tripled. More and more people, in other words, are expending less and less energy to consume a poor diet that is rich in calories and low in micronutrients (**Figure 5.23**). The combination of increased calorie consumption and reduced activity and energy expenditure is fueling the obesity pandemic.

As obesity rates have climbed, so have rates of **hypercholesterolemia,** or high cholesterol, a predisposing factor for coronary heart disease. The cholesterol levels of

hypercholesterolemia The presence of high levels of cholesterol in an organism's blood; this condition may result from the dietary consumption of foods that promote high cholesterol or through the inheritance of a genetic disorder.

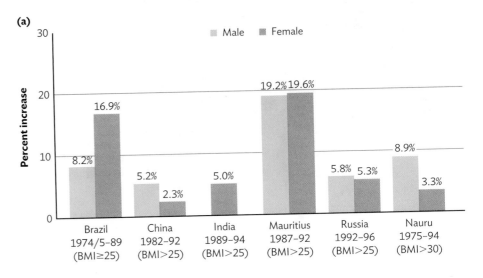

FIGURE 5.23

Obesity in Developing Countries While obesity is reaching epidemic levels in the United States, it is also becoming a problem in other countries. As Western culture, in general, and American fast food chains, in particular, move into developing countries, obesity follows. **(a)** In the past 30 years, many countries have had increasing percentages of their populations fall into the overweight and obese categories according to BMI. This graph shows the increasing obesity in six countries. Note: This study lacked data concerning Indian males. **(b)** This graph shows the percent change per year in obesity prevalence, based on the data in **(a)**.

traditional hunter-gatherers (and of our ancestors) averaged 125 mg/dl (milligrams per deciliter of blood), but the average level of Americans today well exceeds 200 mg/dl. The hunter-gatherers ate a lot of meat, just as we do, but the nondomesticated animals of 15,000 yBP contained very low levels of cholesterol-elevating saturated fatty acids, especially compared with the very high fat content of today's domesticated animals. In addition, hydrogenated vegetable fats and oils and very high levels of trans fatty acids contribute some 15% of the energy in the average American diet. Clearly, these changes in consumption are culturally influenced. That is, people learn to eat what they eat. This is an important characteristic of our evolution.

At the same time that the global epidemic of obesity is taking place, there is an epidemic of non-insulin-dependent diabetes mellitus, or **type 2 diabetes.** More than 100 million people suffer from the disease worldwide. Historically, type 2 diabetes was associated with overweight individuals older than 40. Since about 1990, however, more and more young adults and adolescents have been affected. The key elements of this complex disease are abnormally high blood glucose levels and excessive body weight, both of which result from excessive caloric consumption. Glucose, weight, and other biological signals prompt the pancreas to produce and secrete abnormal amounts of the hormone insulin. Eventually, insulin resistance develops at specific target tissues: muscle, fat, and the liver. The lack of insulin denies these target tissues key nutrients used for fuel and storage. This denial of nutrients is not the major health problem, however, because glucose—a necessary source of energy—is still stored as fatty acids in fat tissue. From the fat tissue, it is pushed into liver and muscle cells, so a person with type 2 diabetes typically becomes fatter and fatter.

The major health problem is that the extra glucose increases the blood's viscosity, and the thickened blood damages blood vessels in the kidneys, eyes, and extremities. In advanced stages of the disease, the kidneys function poorly, vision is reduced, and blood does not flow adequately to the hands, arms, feet, and legs. There is also a greater chance of cardiac disease and stroke.

Is there an adaptive component to the disease? In the early 1960s, the American geneticist James V. Neel noted the high percentages of type 2 diabetes among Native Americans. In the early twentieth century the disease had been virtually nonexistent in Native Americans, but after World War II it increased to the point of affecting more than half of some Native American tribes. Neel hypothesized a "thrifty genotype," one that during times of plenty stored energy efficiently in the form of glucose in fat tissue. For Native Americans, who lived a feast-or-famine lifeway, such a thrifty genotype for a rapid insulin trigger would have been a benefit. For populations that lived an abundant lifeway, the consequences of type 2 diabetes would have triggered a selection against the thrifty genotype.

Given the data in the 1960s, when only some populations around the world had type 2 diabetes, Neel's hypothesis made a lot of sense. Since that time, however, populations around the world have been experiencing an alarming increase in the disease, all in regions where people are becoming obese. Current projections indicate that by 2020, one-quarter of the US population will develop the disease. Little evidence supports the idea that some populations, such as Native Americans, have a thrifty genotype.

If genetic causes or susceptibilities do not explain the remarkable increase in type 2 diabetes, then why is there such a high frequency in some Native Americans, such as in the Pima of the American Southwest, where 50% of adults are afflicted? To understand the cause of the disease among Native American and other high-susceptibility groups, we need to view the disease in terms of nutritional history. Studies of populations show a strong association between poor maternal nutrition during pregnancy

type 2 diabetes A disease in which the body does not produce sufficient amounts of insulin or the cells do not use available insulin, causing a buildup of glucose in the cells.

Nutritional Adaptation

Food and the nutrition it provides are critical aspects of human life. Both undernourishment and overnourishment have negative consequences for all human populations.

Cause	Examples
Undernutrition	Too few calories and/or specific required nutrients; reduced growth, slower growth, susceptibility to infection, predisposition to adult disease (e.g., cardiovascular disease), and early adult death.
Overnutrition	Too many calories, resulting in excess stored fat (obesity); associated health risks include type 2 diabetes, osteoarthritis, hypertension, cardiovascular disease, stroke, and early adult death.

(usually leading to low-birth-weight babies) and development of type 2 diabetes among these offspring in later life. The American anthropologist Daniel Benyshek and his colleagues have made a strong case that Native Americans and other populations with a high incidence of type 2 diabetes share a common history of severe nutritional deprivation. Moreover, the effects of malnutrition are perpetuated for generations, even in subsequent generations no longer experiencing malnutrition. That is, the metabolism of children gestated under such conditions becomes permanently "programmed," in turn leading to comparable developmental programming effects in their children. Thus, the cycle can continue for generations.

In other Native American populations, such as those inhabiting the Aleutian Islands, Alaska, the incidence of type 2 diabetes is relatively low. Unlike native populations in the American Southwest, Aleutian Islanders do not have a history of severe malnutrition. During adulthood, too little activity and too many calories are risk factors for any population. But the impact of poor diet on the growing fetus is crucial for understanding the high prevalence of type 2 diabetes in humans today.

Workload Adaptation: Skeletal Homeostasis and Function

Homeostasis depends on the health of all the body's tissues, including the bone tissues. The skeleton must be maintained so that it can support the body and enable the body to move. Without this essential framework, where would tendons, ligaments, and muscles be attached and how would they get the leverage needed for their use?

The growth and development of bones are subject to a range of factors. Strongly controlled by genes, they are also affected by various physiological processes, disease, and nutrition. As discussed earlier, poor nutrition in childhood may result in short stature, both in children and in the adults they become. Various mechanical forces also affect

FIGURE 5.24

Framework of the Human Body Just as a building needs its framework, the human body needs the skeleton for support and rigidity. In addition to maintaining the body's shape and enabling its movement, the skeleton protects the many vital organs (such as by encasing the brain in the cranium). It makes possible the production of red blood cells (within the marrow cavities of bones). And it serves as a storage facility for minerals, which can be retrieved at any time (but which minerals would you expect to be stored in bone?).

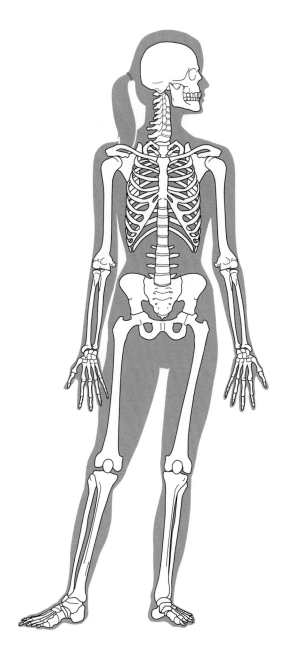

the growth and development of bones. The bones of the arms and legs, for example, are subject to bending and torsion, or twisting, whenever they are used. Bones' **rigidity,** or strength, is a functional adaptation to these forces, preventing fracture in the course of normal use (**Figure 5.24**). During growth and development, physical activity stimulates bone-forming cells, called **osteoblasts,** which produce **bone mass** where it is needed to maintain the rigidity of specific bones and bone regions. In the absence of physical activity, other cells, called **osteoclasts,** remove bone mass. A principle called **Wolff's Law** lays out the homeostatic balance of osteoblastic and osteoclastic activity, in which bone mass is produced where it is needed and taken away where it is not needed.

Wolff's Law also accounts for the remodeling of bone that occurs during life—the changing of certain bones' shapes as the result of particular activities. Because the movements of tendons, ligaments, and muscles put stress on individual bones, repetitive actions eventually can cause those bones to reinforce themselves by adding more material. Just as you need to reinforce a shelf if it starts to buckle under the weight it holds, so the body is likely to try preventing a bone from breaking under added weight or stress (**Figure 5.25**).

At the other end of the spectrum, people who are physically inactive—such as from partial or full immobilization—have less dense bones because osteoblasts are not stimulated to produce bone mass (**Figure 5.26**). The resulting decline in bone density may weaken the skeleton. For example, the skeletons of astronauts who have been in outer space for extended periods of time have remarkable loss in bone density. Around the world, children who are less physically active tend to have smaller and less developed bones than children who are more physically active. Children with less bone mass due to habitual physical *inactivity* become predisposed, as adults, to osteoporosis and fracture. Similarly, in one study of military recruits' leg bones, young men and women who had better-developed muscles and greater bone mass were less susceptible to fractures than were young men and women who had less-developed muscles and less bone mass.

Studying the larger picture of human variation, anthropologists have learned that highly physically active human populations—those that do lots of walking, lifting, carrying, or anything else that "stresses" the skeleton—have bones with optimum density. In addition, the diameters of long bones in populations with active lifestyles are greater than those in populations that are physically inactive. These greater diameters provide the bones with higher rigidity, increasing their ability to resist bending and torsion (this phenomenon is discussed further in chapter 12).

Excessive Activity and Reproductive Ecology

The biological benefits of physical activity are clear. Exercise improves physical fitness by contributing to bone strength, helping to lower blood pressure and cholesterol, increasing heart function and lung function, and so on. Exercise that becomes an excessive workload, however, can hinder female reproductive function, a crucial

rigidity (bone) Refers to the strength of bone to resist bending and torsion.

osteoblasts Cells responsible for bone formation.

bone mass The density of bone per unit of measure.

osteoclasts Cells responsible for bone resorption.

Wolff's Law The principle that bone is placed in the direction of functional demand; that is, bone develops where needed and recedes where it is not needed.

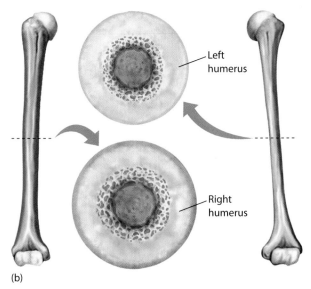

(a)

(b)

FIGURE 5.25

Skeletal Remodeling and Athletics The "playing" arms of athletes in certain sports undergo remodeling as a result of stress. **(a)** A baseball pitcher or a tennis player (such as, here, the professional player Amelie Mauresmo) typically has a dominant arm, which is used to a much greater degree than the nondominant arm. **(b)** The upper arm bone, or humerus, of the dominant arm is much stronger than that of the nondominant arm. In these cross sections, note the greater diameter of the right humerus.

factor in evolution. Many studies have shown that an excessive workload, such as regular intense aerobic exercise, can interrupt menstrual function, resulting in lower fertility. Even milder levels of physical activity have reduced the reproductive potential of some women. For example, a study of a large number of women from Washington State revealed that those who engage in more than an hour of exercise per day and whose body weights are 85% that of the average American woman are five to six times more likely to not be able to conceive within one year than women who do not exercise and have normal weight. Two important implications stand out from this and other studies on workload and ovarian function. First, human populations requiring heavy work by reproductive-age women will have reduced birthrates. Second, and in the larger picture of human adaptation and evolution, amount of work is an important selective factor—a population with relatively high fitness will likely not require excessive energy expenditure, at least for reproductive-age women.

Anthropologists have shown that the classification of humans into different types, or races, simply does not provide meaningful information about variation. While race may be an enduring social concept, it is not valid biologically. Understanding human variation in an evolutionary context—that is, understanding people's remarkable

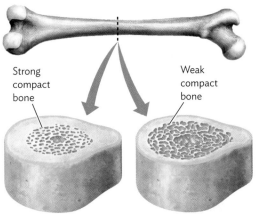

Strong compact bone

Weak compact bone

Healthy bone

Bone showing signs of osteoporosis

FIGURE 5.26

Bone Disuse When bones are not used routinely or for extended periods of time, bone density can decrease. Typically, the loss occurs on the inner surface of the bone, making the bone more fragile. The outer, compact bone becomes thinner as the bone marrow, or medullary cavity, in the middle increases in diameter. In this drawing, the osteoporotic bone, on the right, has a much thinner outer compact bone and a larger bone marrow cavity than those of the healthy bone.

adaptability to a wide range of environmental circumstances throughout the stages of growth, from conception through old age and senescence—is far more productive than attempting to classify different types of the human organism. Just as humans represent a continuum, so they are part of a larger continuum that includes their fellow primates, with whom they share a range of characteristics, many common adaptations, and much evolutionary history. As we will explore in the next chapter, the nonhuman primates provide an important record of adaptability and flexibility, one of the great success stories of mammalian evolution.

CHAPTER 5 REVIEW

ANSWERING THE BIG QUESTIONS

1. **Is race a valid, biologically meaningful concept?**
   - Race is a typological leftover that is neither a useful nor an appropriate biological concept.
   - Human variation is clinal. In general, traits do not correlate in their distribution.

2. **What do growth and development tell us about human variation? What are the benefits of our life history pattern?**
   - Differentiation and development of all the body organs occur during the prenatal stage of life.
   - The postnatal stage involves growth acceleration and deceleration. Childhood and adolescence are long events, in which individuals become physically and emotionally mature.
   - Reproductive senescence is unique to humans. Individuals older than 50 play important roles in the care of young and as sources of information.

3. **How do people adapt to environmental extremes and other circumstances?**
   - Some adaptations to the environment are genetic, whereas others occur within the individual's lifetime and either are inherited and are irreversible or are *not* inherited and are reversible. Biological change associated with all forms of adaptation occurs to maintain homeostasis.
   - Most functional adaptations—adaptations that occur during the individual's lifetime—have important implications for evolution.
   - Adaptations to UV radiation, high altitudes, and workloads are all seen in humans and can be subject to the forces of evolution. While many adaptations are beneficial, some can be disruptive, such as the negative effect of high levels of physical activity on female reproductive potential.
   - Undernutrition and obesity are not the result of adaptation—the body either receives adequate (or too much) nutrition or it does not. Nutritional deficiencies and overabundance both negatively affect health.

KEY TERMS

adult stage
aging
Allen's rule
anthropometry
basal metabolic rate (BMR)
basal metabolic requirement
Bergmann's rule
bone mass
cline
cognitive abilities
deciduous dentition
diaphysis
epiphysis
functional adaptations
homeostasis
homeothermic
hypothermia
hypoxia

lactation
life history
macronutrients
melanin
menarche
menopause
micronutrients
motor skills
nutrition transition
osteoporosis
postnatal stage
prenatal stage
rigidity (bone)
secular trend
senescence
sexual dimorphism
stressors
type 2 diabetes
vasoconstriction
vasodilation
Wolff's Law

STUDY QUIZ

1. **Which is true about race?**
   a. Racial traits change very suddenly across geographic regions.
   b. Racial categories explain a very high percentage of genetic variation.
   c. Race is socially constructed and is not a biological concept.
   d. Personal genomic research supports racial categories.

2. **Which is an example of a physiological adaptation to climate?**
   a. the loss of body hair in humans
   b. variation in the breadth and length of the body and limbs
   c. vasodilation of blood vessels in response to temperature
   d. the development of human technologies to conserve heat

3. **What *reproductive benefit* from reduced absorption of UV radiation could be driving natural selection for dark skin?**
   a. lower risk of sunburn
   b. lower risk of skin cancer
   d. increased vitamin D synthesis
   d. protection of stored folate

4. **Which is a developmental adaptation to high-altitude hypoxia?**
   a. alleles for hemoglobin with higher oxygen saturation
   b. growth of an expanded chest during childhood
   c. production of more red blood cells
   d. mountain sickness

5. **The *nutrition transition* refers to the**
   a. transition from hunting and gathering to agriculture.
   b. domestication of wild plants and animals.
   c. resumed growth of a formerly malnourished population.
   d. shift from eating local foods to highly processed foods.

EVOLUTION REVIEW

HUMAN VARIATION TODAY

Synopsis The biocultural approach of physical anthropology emphasizes that human evolution and variation are shaped by both biology and culture; that is, by both genetic factors and environmental factors. Physical anthropologists apply this concept in various ways. For instance, the relationship between the unique life history stages of humans and our sociocultural behaviors is an area of interest. Additionally, human populations across the globe vary in the ways that homeostasis (physiological equilibrium) is maintained, and such adaptations are a product of evolutionary processes operating over a wide range of environmental settings. The broad range of human adaptability—to life in hot and cold climates, among extremes of latitude and altitude, and with variable access to key nutrients—is a major contributor to the success of our species: humans survive and reproduce across a diverse array of environments worldwide.

Q1. Define Bergmann's rule and Allen's rule in relation to climate adaptation. What is one example of an environmental factor that can lead to the development of body-shape characteristics that deviate from those predicted by these two rules?

Q2. What is clinal variation? Identify two physiological effects of solar radiation that likely acted as selective pressures in shaping the pattern of clinal variation observed for human skin color.

Q3. In early life, human females are more highly buffered against environmental stresses than are human males. In addition, human females enter puberty, adolescence, and reproductive senescence earlier than human males do. Why are such features advantageous from an evolutionary standpoint?

Hint Focus on implications for fitness, or reproductive success.

Q4. In what ways have each of the four types of adaptation discussed in this chapter contributed to the ability of human populations to inhabit areas spanning the entire surface of the globe? Consider various factors, including climate and nutrition.

Hint Think about an extreme geographic setting. How might the ways that a resident maintains homeostasis differ from the ways a visitor maintains homeostasis?

Q5. Many scientists characterize the conditions of modern populations worldwide (but especially Western societies) as conducive to an obesity pandemic. Discuss the ways in which adaptive features from our evolutionary past may have become modern maladaptations.

Hint Think about the differences in nutritional resources and activity patterns between ourselves and our hominin ancestors.

ADDITIONAL READINGS

Barker, D. J. P. 1996. The origins of coronary heart disease in early life. Pp. 155–162 in C. J. K. Henry and S. J. Ulijaszek, eds. *Long-Term Consequences of Early Environment: Growth, Development and the Lifespan Developmental Perspective.* Cambridge, UK: Cambridge University Press.

Bogin, B. 1999. *Patterns of Human Growth*, 2nd ed. Cambridge, UK: Cambridge University Press.

Brace, C. L. 2005. *"Race" Is a Four-Letter Word: The Genesis of a Concept.* New York: Oxford University Press.

Frisancho, A. R. 1993. *Human Adaptation and Accommodation.* Ann Arbor: University of Michigan Press.

Jablonski, N. G. 2006. *Skin: A Natural History.* Berkeley: University of California Press.

Stinson, S., B. Bogin, and D. O'Rourke, eds. 2012. *Human Biology: An Evolutionary and Biocultural Perspective*, 2nd ed. Hoboken, NJ: Wiley-Blackwell.

Sussman, R. W. 2014. *The Myth of Race: The Troubling Persistence of an Unscientific Idea.* Cambridge, MA: Harvard University Press.

Yudell, M. 2014. *Race Unmasked: Biology and Race in the 20th Century.* New York: Columbia University Press.

Olive baboons (*Papio anubis*) from the Mole National Park, Ghana, are one of multiple species of baboons. These primates represent among the most successful and widespread adaptations in African monkeys. Some are adapted to open grasslands, whereas others are adapted to deserts and forest.

6

Biology in the Present

THE OTHER LIVING PRIMATES

BIG QUESTIONS

1. **Why study primates?**
2. **What is a primate?**
3. **What are the kinds of primates?**

Do you remember the first time you saw a primate (besides a human one, that is)?[1] I first saw a primate on a school trip to the Kansas City Zoo. My third-grade class and our teacher walked up to an enclosure containing several monkeys. I could not take my eyes off the faces of those animals. In so many ways, they looked just like us! Their eyes were on the fronts of their faces, they had different facial expressions, and they had grasping hands. For fear of retaliation from my fellow classmates, I did not point out the resemblances I saw between monkeys and people, including them. But I came away from that experience wondering why monkeys shared so many physical attributes with humans.

I did not think much about that trip to the zoo until I took my first physical anthropology class in college, 10 years later. My Introduction to Physical Anthropology professor explained that monkeys, like humans, are members of the order Primates and that one key unifying feature of all primates is forward-facing eyes. This feature is part of

---

[1] Throughout this chapter and the remainder of the book, *primate* or *primates* refers to nonhuman primates except where otherwise specified.

the generalized and arboreal adaptation that unites this amazing and diverse group of animals and indicates their common ancestry. Research by primatologists—scientists who study primates—had revealed one of the most impressive characteristics of primates: their marvelous ability to adapt to new or changing circumstances. My question was answered! Monkeys and humans share features because they share ancestry. They are not identical today because at some point in the remote past their ancestors diverged.

One key indicator of primates' adaptability is the fact that they are able to live almost anywhere—they inhabit many kinds of landscapes and widely diverse climates, ranging from the bitter cold of northern Japan to the humid tropics of Brazil (**Figure 6.1**). Anyone who has ever studied nonhuman primates for any length of time will tell you that they have other characteristics as impressive as their adaptability: their intelligence, their long lives, their variable diets, and their complex social behavior.

Primatologists come from a range of disciplines. Many are in anthropology departments in universities and colleges around the world, but primate studies are also part of disciplines such as biology, ecology, psychology, paleontology, anatomy, zoology, and genetics. In addition, animal and plant conservationists study primates as a barometer of broader species losses and extinctions. Many primates live in the tropics, which are disappearing by the hundreds of thousands of acres around the world annually, mostly due to forest clearing and encroachment by people; if primates are disappearing, then so are many other animals (a subject discussed further in chapter 14).

Among the practical applications for the study of primates are advances in medicine. Many types of primates have some of the same or closely related diseases as humans. In the past 50 years, millions of human lives have been saved around the world because of the study of diseases found in both primates and humans. For example, chimpanzees are susceptible to polio. The vaccine for polio, a once-dreaded disease that killed and debilitated millions around the world, was developed via primate research in the 1950s.

The physical and behavioral similarities between apes and humans provide important clues about the origins of humans (discussed further in chapter 9). The similarities between the muscles and bones of apes and of humans, for example, enable us to conjecture about what the common ancestor and the earliest hominin may have looked like. The study of primate behavior provides insights into our own behavior and perhaps even the origins of specific behaviors, such as cognition, parenting, social interactions, and (some argue) even conflict and warfare.

These diverse issues make the study of primates so interesting and important, far more than I imagined that day at the zoo. In this chapter, we will define the order Primates and discuss how primates are classified (taxonomy), where they live (ecology and geography), and their physical characteristics (anatomy). In the next chapter, we will look at key aspects of primates' social behavior, especially in the important linkage between social organization, ecology, and diet (socioecology). What you learn in this and the following chapter will provide the essential context for your understanding Part II of this book, which is about the evolution of primates and of humans.

6.1 **What Is a Primate?**

When Linnaeus first defined the order Primates in the eighteenth century (see "Taxonomy and Systematics: Classifying Living Organisms and Identifying Their Biological Relationships" in chapter 2), he did so purely for classification purposes and focused on descriptive traits. Physical anthropologists, however, define primates on the basis of behavioral, adaptive, or evolutionary tendencies. The eminent British anatomist Sir Wilfrid E. Le Gros Clark (1895–1971) identified three prominent tendencies:

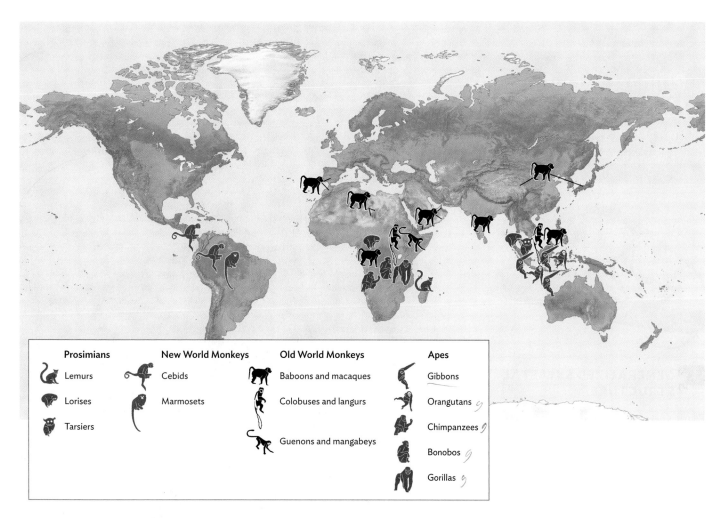

Prosimians
- Lemurs
- Lorises
- Tarsiers

New World Monkeys
- Cebids
- Marmosets

Old World Monkeys
- Baboons and macaques
- Colobuses and langurs
- Guenons and mangabeys

Apes
- Gibbons
- Orangutans
- Chimpanzees
- Bonobos
- Gorillas

FIGURE 6.1

Primate Distribution As shown on this map, primates inhabit every continent except Antarctica and Australia. New World primates live in North and South America, while Old World primates live in Europe, Africa, and Asia. Although they are often considered tropical animals that live in forested settings, primate species exist in a wide range of environments.

arboreal adaptation Adaptation to life in the trees

dietary plasticity A diet's flexibility in adapting to a given environment.

parental investment The time and energy parents expend for their offspring's benefit.

1. Primates are adapted to life in the trees—they express **arboreal adaptation** in a set of behaviors and anatomical characteristics that is unique among mammals.
2. Primates eat a wide variety of foods—they express **dietary plasticity**.
3. Primates invest a lot of time and care in few offspring—they express **parental investment**.

In addition to these tendencies, the physical and behavioral characteristics discussed in the subsections that follow identify primates as a separate order of mammals.

One thing that all anthropologists agree on when they talk about primates is the order's remarkable diversity. The panoramic view displayed in **Figure 6.2** provides a sense of that diversity. Depicted in the Taï Forest, in Ivory Coast, West Africa, are one kind of ape (chimpanzee), eight kinds of monkeys (black-and-white colobus, Campbell's, Diana, lesser spot-nosed, putty-nosed, red colobus, olive colobus, sooty mangabey), and three kinds of strepsirhines (potto, Demidoff's galago, Thomas's galago). All but the strepsirhines are active during the day. (The humans are, of course, primates as well. The eagle is an important predator of monkeys, especially the red colobus.)

Arboreal Adaptation—Primates Live in Trees and Are Good at It

Many animals—such as squirrels, nondomesticated cats, some snakes, and birds—have successfully adapted to living in trees. Primates, however, display a unique combination

6.2

Primate Adaptation in Microcosm:

THE TAI FOREST, IVORY COAST, WEST AFRICA

1 ⟩ GENERALIZED SKELETAL STRUCTURE

Primates have a generalized skeletal structure. The bones that make up the shoulders, upper limbs, lower limbs, and other major joints such as the hands and feet are separate, giving primates a great deal of flexibility when moving in trees. In this monkey skeleton, note the grasping hands and feet, the long tail, and the equal length of the front and hind limbs relative to each other.

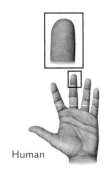

Human

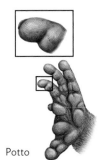

Potto

2 ⟩ ENHANCED TOUCH

Primates have an enhanced sense of touch. This sensitivity is due in part to the presence of dermal ridges (fingerprints and toe prints) on the inside surfaces of the hands and feet. The potto, a prosimian, has primitive dermal ridges, whereas the human, a higher primate, has more derived ridges, which provide better gripping ability.

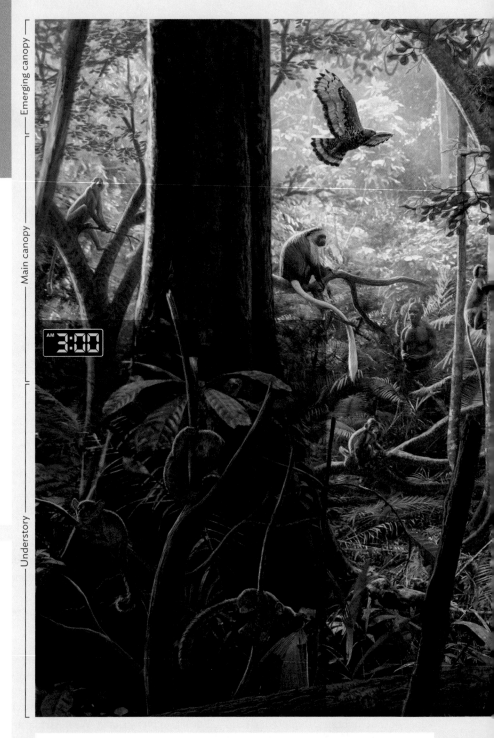

■ Black-and-white colobus	■ Human	■ Red colobus
■ Campbell's	■ Lesser spot-nosed	■ Sooty mangabey
■ Chimpanzee	■ Olive colobus	■ Thomas's galago
■ Demidoff's galago	■ Potto	■ Eagle
■ Diana monkey	■ Putty-nosed	

Taï Forest

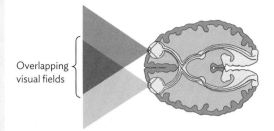

Overlapping visual fields

3 ◄ ENHANCED VISION

Primates have an enhanced sense of vision. Evolution has given primates better vision, including increased depth perception and seeing in color. The eyes' convergence provides significant overlap in the visual fields and thus greater sense of depth.

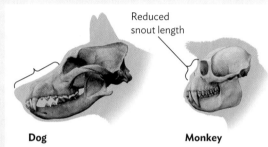

Reduced snout length

Dog   **Monkey**

4 ◄ REDUCED SMELL

Primates have a reduced sense of smell. The smaller and less projecting snouts of most primates indicate their decreased reliance on smell.

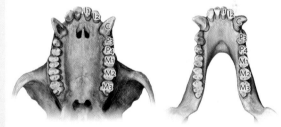

5 ◄ DIETARY VERSATILITY

Primates have dietary versatility. Part of the record of primate dietary adaptation is found in the teeth. The red colobus monkey dentition shown here is typical of a catarrhine dentition with a 2/1/2/3 dental formula. Note the differences in morphology of the four different tooth types: incisors (I_1, I_2), canines (C), premolars (P_3, P_4), and molars (M_1, M_2, M_3).

of specific arboreal adaptations. Even the few primates that spend all or most of their time on the ground have retained, over the course of their evolution, a number of features shared with an arboreal common ancestor.

PRIMATES HAVE A VERSATILE SKELETAL STRUCTURE Primates get around in trees using an unusually wide range of motions involving the limbs and body trunk. One has only to watch many of the primates perform their acrobatics in the forest canopy to appreciate this versatility, a function of the primate body's anatomy. That is, the bones making up the shoulders, limbs, hands, and feet tend to be separate. These separate bones are articulated at highly mobile joints.

Atop the list of separate bones is the collarbone (the clavicle), which acts as a strut, keeping the upper limbs to the sides of the body. The lower forelimb (the ulna and radius) and the fingers and toes (the phalanges) also have separate bones. The forearm rotates from side to side with relative ease, and the dexterity of the hands and feet is unparalleled among mammals.

One of the most important attributes of the primate hand is the **opposable** thumb—on either hand, the tip of the thumb can touch the tips of the other four fingers. Thus, the primate can grasp an object or manipulate a small one. Humans have the longest thumb, or pollex, among primates and therefore the greatest opposability (**Figure 6.3**). This elongated thumb is part of the unique adaptation of the human hand for what the English anatomist and evolutionary biologist John Napier calls the **power grip** and the **precision grip.** In the power grip, the palm grips an object, such as a hammer's handle, while the thumb and fingers wrap around it in opposite directions. In the precision grip, the thumb and one or more of the other fingers' ends provide fine dexterity, as when holding a screwdriver, picking up a small object (such as a coin), or writing with a pen or pencil. The American paleoanthropologist Randall Susman has identified in early hominins the anatomy that would have supported a power grip and a precision grip (discussed further in chapter 9).

Many primates also have opposable big toes (the halluces). Humans are not among these primates, mainly because of changes in the foot that took place when our prehuman ancestors shifted from quadrupedal locomotion to bipedalism (**Figure 6.4**).

opposable Refers to primates' thumb, in that it can touch each of the four fingertips, enabling a grasping ability.

power grip A fistlike grip in which the fingers and thumbs wrap around an object in opposite directions.

precision grip A precise grip in which the tips of the fingers and thumbs come together, enabling fine manipulation.

FIGURE 6.3

Grips and Opposable Thumbs Apes and humans have two kinds of grips: power and precision. **(a)** The power grip shown here, as a human holds a hammer, preceded the evolution of the precision grip. **(b)** The precision grip of apes is not nearly as developed as that of humans. **(c)** The finer precision grip of humans—in part due to the greater opposability of their thumbs—lets them finely manipulate objects.

(a) Power
grip (human)

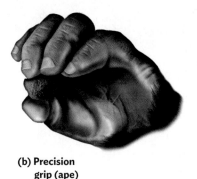

(b) Precision
grip (ape)

(c) Precision
grip (human)

(See also "What Makes Humans So Different from Other Animals? The Six Steps to Humanness" in chapter 1.) To walk or run, humans need all five toes firmly planted on the ground. The mobility of recent humans' toes has been even further reduced by the wearing of shoes.

The body trunk of primates is also distinctive. The backbone has five functionally distinct types of vertebrae—from top to bottom, the cervical, thoracic, lumbar, sacral (forming the sacrum of the pelvis), and coccyx vertebrae—which give primates a greater

(a)

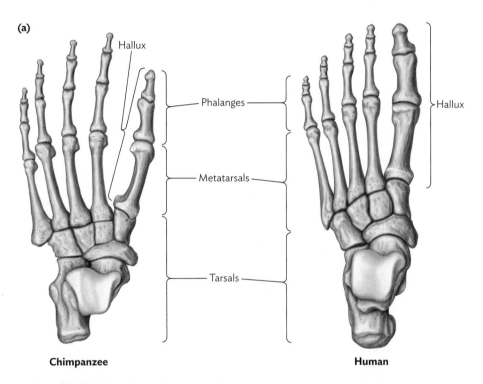

Chimpanzee   **Human**

(b)

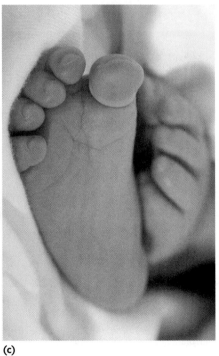

(c)

FIGURE 6.4

Opposable Big Toes Nonhuman primates' opposable big toes, like their opposable thumbs, enable their feet to grasp things such as tree branches. Humans lack this feature due to their adaptation to life on the ground. **(a)** Its curved hallux and large gap between the hallux and second toe make **(b)** the chimpanzee foot look more like a human hand (not shown) than like **(c)** a human foot.

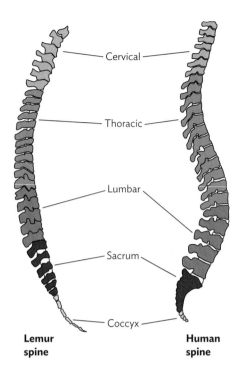

FIGURE 6.5

Primate Vertebrae The five types of vertebrae in primates, including lemurs and humans, create a flexible column allowing a wide range of movement. The cervical, thoracic, and lumbar vertebrae are the true, or movable, vertebrae, responsible for bending, twisting, and stretching. The sacral vertebrae are much less movable because they form part of the pelvis. In most nonhuman primates, the vertebrae of the coccyx form the tail; in humans, these vertebrae are reduced to three to five very short, fused segments. Notice, too, the *S*-shaped spine in humans versus the *C*-shaped spine in other primates, such as the lemur.

preadaptation An organism's use of an anatomical feature in a way unrelated to the feature's original function.

nocturnal Refers to those organisms that are awake and active during the night.

diurnal Refers to those organisms that normally are awake and active during daylight hours.

rhinarium The naked surface around the nostrils, typically wet in mammals.

range of movements than other animals have (**Figure 6.5**). The body trunk also tends to be vertically oriented, such as when the primate climbs, swings from tree limb to tree limb, or sits. The vertical tendency in a prehuman ancestor was an essential **pre-adaptation** to humans' bipedalism.

PRIMATES HAVE AN ENHANCED SENSE OF TOUCH The ends of the fingers and toes are highly sensitive in primates. This enhancement helps inform primates about texture and other physical properties of objects, such as potential food items. On the inside surfaces of the fingers and toes and on the palms and soles, respectively, of the hands and feet, the skin surface is covered with series of fine ridges called dermal ridges (fingerprints and toe prints). These ridges further enhance the tactile sense, and they increase the amount of friction, or resistance to slipping, when grasping an object, such as a tree branch. On the backs of the ends of the fingers and toes, most primates have flat nails instead of claws (**Figure 6.6**). (A few primates have specializations, such as a grooming claw on the second toe in lemurs and lorises.) Made of keratin, the strong protein also found in hair, flat nails may protect the ends of the fingers and toes. They may aid in picking up small objects. Most important, however, they provide broad support to the ends of the fingers and toes by spreading out the forces generated in the digits by gripping.

PRIMATES HAVE AN ENHANCED SENSE OF VISION The enhanced vision of primates stems from two developments in the order's evolutionary history. First, very early in primate evolution, the eyes rotated forward from the sides of the head to the front of the head (**Figure 6.7**). As a result, the two fields of vision overlapped, providing the primate with depth perception. (Along with convergence of the eyes, fully enclosed or partially enclosed eye orbits evolved.) Second, color vision evolved. Crucial for spotting insects and other prey within the surrounding vegetation, color vision likely evolved as early primates shifted from a **nocturnal** adaptation to a **diurnal** adaptation.

PRIMATES HAVE A REDUCED RELIANCE ON SENSES OF SMELL AND HEARING For most primates, enhanced vision led to greatly reduced senses of smell and hearing. Most primates have lost the **rhinarium** (the external wet nose, which most mammals

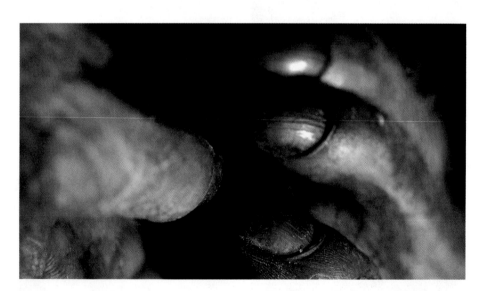

FIGURE 6.6

Flat Fingernails Finger pads with nail support help primates, such as this orangutan, securely hold tree branches that are smaller than their hands. By contrast, claws enable nonprimate mammals to dig into tree bark, an especially helpful ability when limbs or tree trunks are larger than the animals' paws.

(a)

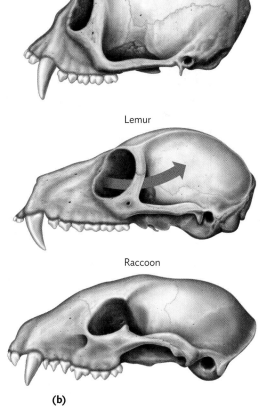

Gibbon

Lemur

Raccoon

(b)

FIGURE 6.7

***Primate Vision* (a)** Primates' forward-facing eyes enable depth perception, a vital adaptation to life in the trees that has a selective advantage beyond arboreal life. Consider what would happen if a primate attempted to leap from one branch to another without being able to determine the distance between the two branches. Now imagine a human leaping over a (relatively) narrow chasm without knowing how far to leap. **(b)** In most primates, such as the gibbon, the eye orbit is fully enclosed. In animals such as the lemur, a postorbital bar lines the back of the eye orbit but does not fully enclose it. In other animals, such as the raccoon, the eye orbit is open, with no bone enclosing it at the rear.

CONCEPT CHECK

What Makes Primates Good at Living in Trees?

Primates show a series of behavioral and anatomical tendencies that make them especially good at living in trees.

Characteristic	Features
Versatile skeletal structure emphasizing mobility and flexibility	Separation of bones in articular joints associated with mobility: clavicle, radius and ulna, wrist, opposable thumb, opposable big toe in many primates
	Five functionally distinct vertebral types: cervical, thoracic, lumbar, sacral, coccygeal
Enhanced sense of touch	Dermal ridges at ends of fingers and toes; nails instead of claws
Enhanced sense of vision	Convergence of eyes; color vision

(a)

(b)

FIGURE 6.8

Reduced Snout As primates have increased their reliance on vision, they have reduced their reliance on olfaction, the sense of smell. **(a)** Lemurs are among the few primates that have retained the rhinarium. **(b)** The snout of primates such as this Angola black-and-white colobus monkey has no rhinarium.

dental formula The numerical description of a species' teeth, listing the number, in one quadrant of the jaws, of incisors, canines, premolars, and molars.

FIGURE 6.9

Baboon Snout Baboons do not rely on olfaction. Their snout remains large because of oversized canines. (See also Figure 6.14.)

have) and the long snout. Some of the strepsirhines—the more primitive primates, such as lemurs and lorises—have retained the rhinarium, and they continue to rely on a well-developed sense of smell (**Figure 6.8**). The reduction in snout length resulted from a loss of internal surface area of the nasal passage, the location of the chemistry involved in smell. But some primates, such as baboons, later evolved a large and projecting snout to accommodate massive canine roots, especially in adult males (**Figure 6.9**).

Dietary Plasticity—Primates Eat a Highly Varied Diet, and Their Teeth Reflect This Adaptive Versatility

PRIMATES HAVE RETAINED PRIMITIVE CHARACTERISTICS IN THEIR TEETH One fundamental anatomical feature in primates that reflects their high degree of dietary diversity is the retention of primitive dental characteristics, especially of four functionally distinctive tooth types: incisors, canines, premolars, and molars (**Figure 6.10**). The mammalian ancestors of primates had these same tooth types and so must have eaten a range of foods.

PRIMATES HAVE A REDUCED NUMBER OF TEETH Because the numbers of the different types of teeth are the same in the upper and lower jaws and the left and right sides of the jaws, anthropologists record each primate species' **dental formula** with respect to one quadrant of the dentition. Primates' early mammalian ancestor, for example, had a dental formula of 3/1/4/3—three incisors, one canine, four premolars, and three molars—in one quadrant of its dentition. As indicated in **Table 6.1,** the Old World higher primates (anthropoids) have a dental formula of 2/1/2/3. Most New World primates have retained one more premolar and have a dental formula of 2/1/3/3. Some primates, such as tarsiers, have different numbers of teeth in the upper and lower jaws. Over the course of the order's evolution, primates' teeth have tended to reduce in number, thus the dental formula can be very useful in studies of ancestral primate species. For example, the ancestors of modern Old World monkeys had a dental formula of 2/1/2/3,

Table 6.1 Primate Dental Formulae

The major primate groups are distinguished dentally by the number of incisors, canines, premolars, and molars.

	Upper	Lower
Tarsiers	2.1.3.3	1.1.3.3
Lemurs	2.1.3.3	2.1.3.3 (although there is much variation with lemurs)
Lorises	2.1.3.3	2.1.3.3
New World Monkeys	2.1.3.2 *or* 2.1.3.3	2.1.3.2 *or* 2.1.3.3
Old World Monkeys	2.1.2.3	2.1.2.3
Apes and Humans	2.1.2.3	2.1.2.3

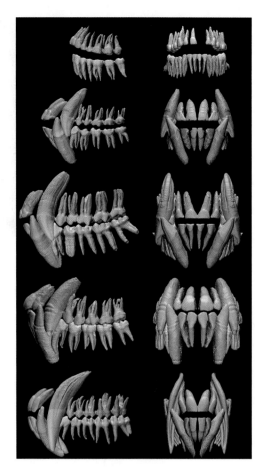

FIGURE 6.10

Primate Dentitions These five sets of dentitions represent, from top to bottom, human, chimpanzee, gorilla, orangutan, and baboon. Notice that humans do not have the large projecting canines evident in the other four dentitions. In the side view, the large upper canines fit into a diastema, or space, between the lower canines and the third premolars. Each time the jaws are closed, the upper canines are sharpened against the lower third premolars.

the same as today's Old World monkeys, and if fossilized remains of a primate ancestor have a dental formula of 2/1/3/3, the ancestor was likely related to New World monkeys, strepsirhines (lemurs, lorises, galagos), or perhaps tarsiers because these primates have retained the extra premolar.

PRIMATES HAVE EVOLVED DIFFERENT DENTAL SPECIALIZATIONS AND FUNCTIONAL EMPHASES The premolars and molars of primates have undergone little evolutionary change compared with those of other mammals. This evolutionary conservatism reflects the continued function of these teeth, especially of the molars: grinding and crushing food. Specialized attributes of some primates' teeth reflect particular food preferences. For example, some primates have high, pointed cusps on the occlusal, or chewing, surfaces of their molars, for puncturing and crushing insects. Others have crests on their molars, for shearing leaves. The many primates that eat fruit and seeds tend to have low, round cusps on their molars, for crushing and pulping.

The molars of monkeys, apes, and humans have distinctive occlusal surfaces (**Figure 6.11**). Old World monkeys have four cusps on upper and lower molars, with two of the cusps on the front and two of the cusps on the back of the tooth's occlusal surface. Each pair of cusps, front and back, is connected by an enamel ridge, or **loph.** This is called a **bilophodont** (meaning "two-ridge tooth") molar. Apes and humans have a lower molar with five separate cusps that are separated by grooves. A *Y*-shaped groove is dominant, with the fork of the *Y* directed toward the outside of the tooth. This is called a **Y-5** molar. Apes' and humans' upper molars generally have four cusps, separated by grooves.

While most primates' incisors are flat, vertically oriented, and used to prepare food before it is chewed by the premolars and molars, strepsirhines' lower incisors and canines are elongated, crowded together, and project forward. This specialized feature, a **tooth comb,** is especially useful for grooming (**Figure 6.12**).

The horizontally oriented canine is one of three different kinds of canines in primates. The small, vertical, incisor-shaped canine appears only in humans, and only in humans (and all their hominin ancestors) are the canines subject to wear at the tip of the tooth. The projecting, pointed canine is present in all monkeys and all apes. In Old World monkeys and apes, the canines are part of a **canine–premolar honing complex,** in which the upper canine fits in a space, or **diastema,** between the lower canine and lower third premolar. This configuration slices food, especially leaves and

loph An enamel ridge connecting cusps on a tooth's surface.

bilophodont Refers to lower molars, in Old World monkeys, that have two ridges.

Y-5 Hominoids' pattern of lower molar cusps.

tooth comb Anterior teeth (incisors and canines) that have been tilted forward, creating a scraper.

canine–premolar honing complex The dental form in which the upper canines are sharpened against the lower third premolars when the jaws are opened and closed.

diastema A space between two teeth.

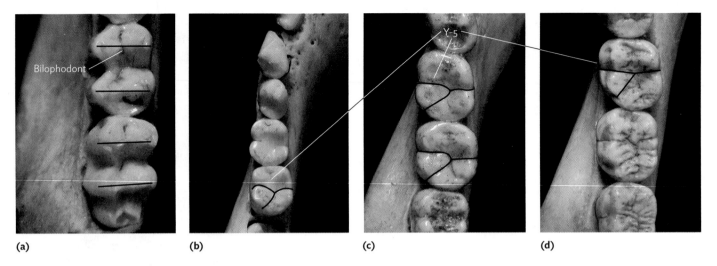

(a) (b) (c) (d)

FIGURE 6.11

Primate Molars The morphology of lower molars in primates has two main variants: Old World monkeys' bilophodont pattern, such as in **(a)** the colobus monkey; and apes' Y-5 pattern, such as in **(b)** the gibbon, **(c)** the chimpanzee, and **(d)** the orangutan. Like the dental formula, molar morphology can be used to determine whether fossilized remains of a primate represent an ancestor of Old World monkeys or of apes and humans.

sectorial (premolar) Refers to a premolar adapted for cutting.

other plants. When the primate chews, the movement of the back of the upper canine against the front of the lower first premolar creates and maintains a sharp edge on each of the two teeth (**Figure 6.13**).

The lower third premolar is **sectorial,** meaning that it has a single dominant cusp and a sharp cutting edge. The upper canine tends to be large, especially in males. In addition to its masticatory function, the large upper canine provides a strong social signal for establishing and maintaining dominance among male members of the primate society, such as in baboons (**Figure 6.14**). (In chapter 7, I talk more about dominance in primates, an important concept in social behavior.) The large upper canine is also displayed by adult males as a warning signal to potential predators.

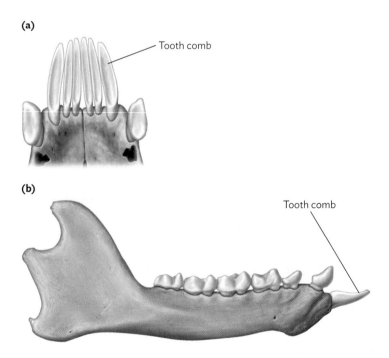

FIGURE 6.12

Tooth Comb Lemurs and lorises possess this unique morphology of lower incisors and canines—here seen from **(a)** above and **(b)** the side—useful for scraping and for grooming fur.

(a)

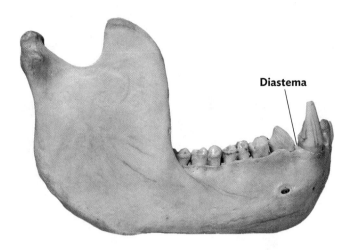

(b)

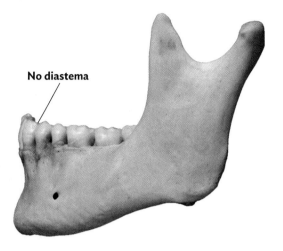

Diastema

No diastema

FIGURE 6.13

Honing Complex **(a)** In Old World monkeys and apes, the lower jaw has a diastema to accommodate the very large upper canines. **(b)** Humans lack such a space because they do not have large, projecting upper canines. Notice the different size and orientation of the canines in **(a)** and **(b)** and in Figure 6.12.

Thickness of tooth enamel varies across primate species. Orangutans and humans have thick enamel, whereas chimpanzees and gorillas have thin enamel. Thick enamel reflects an adaptation to eating tough, hard foods. Although humans today rarely eat hard foods, they have retained this primitive characteristic.

Parental Investment—Primate Parents Provide Prolonged Care for Fewer but Smarter, More Socially Complex, and Longer-Lived Offspring

Female primates give birth to fewer offspring than do other female mammals. A single female primate's births are spaced out over time—sometimes by several years in the

FIGURE 6.14

Canine Size In some primate species, such as baboons, the canines differ in size between males and females. Because the canines can be used as weapons, the fierce appearance of these large teeth serves to warn competitors and predators.

CONCEPT CHECK

What Gives Primates Their Dietary Flexibility?

Primates display a broad range of dietary adaptations. Although the teeth of strepsirhines and haplorhines have evolved specializations, such as the tooth comb in lemurs, the overall retention of a nonspecialized, primitive dentition reflects the order's diverse diet.

Characteristic	Features
Multiple tooth types	Incisors, canines, premolars, molars
Reduced number of teeth	Fewer incisors, premolars, and molars

FIGURE 6.15

Parental Investment Because a female primate generally expends so much energy in rearing each of her offspring, she generally will have few offspring. Here, a chimpanzee mother holds her baby.

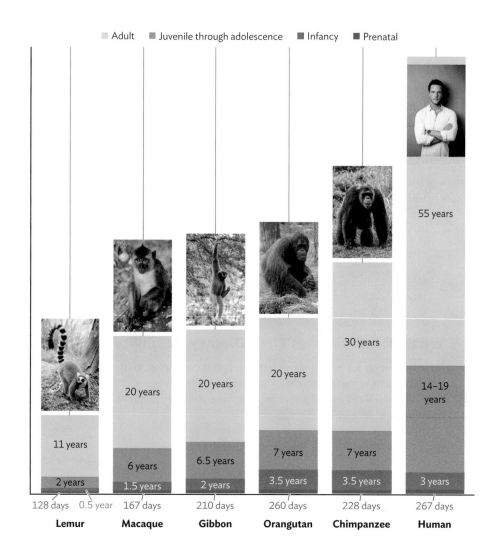

Adult ■ Juvenile through adolescence ■ Infancy ■ Prenatal

					55 years
				30 years	
	20 years	20 years	20 years		14–19 years
11 years					
			7 years	7 years	
2 years	6 years	6.5 years	3.5 years	3.5 years	3 years
	1.5 years	2 years			
128 days 0.5 year	167 days	210 days	260 days	228 days	267 days
Lemur	**Macaque**	**Gibbon**	**Orangutan**	**Chimpanzee**	**Human**

FIGURE 6.16

Growth Stages of Six Primates Lemurs and macaques have the shortest growth period; apes and humans have the longest. The longer growth period reflects the greater behavioral complexity in apes and humans than in lemurs and macaques.

cases of some apes. Primate mothers invest a lot of time and energy in caring for each of their offspring (**Figure 6.15**). By caring for their offspring, providing them with food, and teaching them about social roles and social behavior generally, primates increase the chances of their species' survival.

Primates have long growth and development periods, in part because of their high level of intelligence relative to other animals (**Figure 6.16**). That primates' brains are so large and complex reflects the crucial importance of intelligence—brainpower—in primate evolution (**Figure 6.17**). The back portion of the brain where visual signals are processed is expanded in primates, whereas the areas of the brain associated with smell (**olfactory bulb**) and hearing are considerably smaller than in other mammals. Among all primates, humans have the largest brain relative to body size and the most elaborate neural connections between different regions of the brain. This

olfactory bulb The portion of the anterior brain that detects odors.

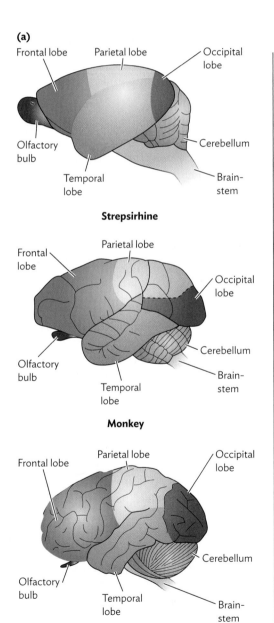

(a)

Strepsirhine

Monkey

Chimpanzee

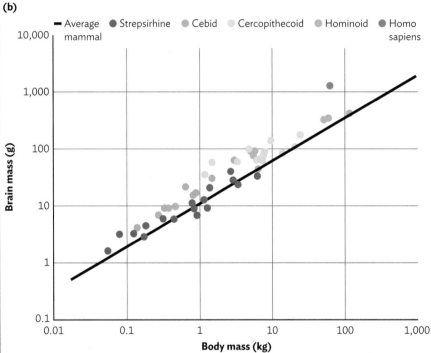

(b)

FIGURE 6.17

Primate Brain Morphology **(a)** The main regions of the brain are delineated in these drawings of primates' brains. The drawings are out of scale to show differences in anatomy. **(b)** As this graph shows, primates with the greatest body mass also have the greatest brain mass and thus the greatest intelligence. Most primates also have a larger brain relative to body size than the average mammal, a reflection of primates' higher intelligence. The *Homo sapiens* dot is way off the line because humans have a much bigger brain relative to body mass. The human brain is not just a large version of an ape's, monkey's, or strepsirhine's brain. Rather, during evolution, in addition to a size increase the human brain has undergone important qualitative and quantitative changes in some key regions. What are these changes, and how are they associated with behavior?

Primate Parenting

Compared with other mammals, primates display unique parenting characteristics. These relate to the fact that primate offspring are more intelligent and behaviorally complex than the offspring of other mammals.

Characteristic	Features
Fertility	Birth to relatively few offspring at a time, commonly just one
Birth interval	Relatively long period between births
Preadult care	Elongated and intensive

combination of greater mass and complexity provides humans with greater intelligence compared with other primates and has led humans to develop language and advanced culture.

6.2 What Are the Kinds of Primates?

grade Group of organisms sharing the same complexity and level of evolution.

clade Group of organisms that evolved from a common ancestor.

primitive characteristics Characteristics present in multiple species of a group.

Today, more than 200 taxa—number of species—of primates live in various parts of the world. If we count subspecies, there are more than 600 kinds of primates, from the mouse lemur, which weighs less than 0.5 kg (1 lb), to the gorilla, which weighs several hundred pounds. Primate biological diversity is reflected in two different classification systems. The long-standing approach, called *traditional* or *gradistic*, separates the order Primates into two suborders, the Prosimii (prosimians, or lower primates) and the Anthropoidea (anthropoids, or higher primates). This approach is based on **grades,** or levels of anatomical complexity, without consideration of identifying ancestral–descendant relationships. Physical anthropologists are increasingly using an alternative form of classification, which groups primates on the basis of lines of descent and identification of shared common ancestry (**Figure 6.18**). This *cladistic*, or *evolutionary* (sometimes called *phylogenetic*), approach uses anatomical and genetic evidence to establish the ancestral–descendant lines that link **clades.** This approach divides the order Primates into two clades (suborders): the Strepsirhini (or strepsirhines) and the Haplorhini (or haplorhines). The strepsirhines have retained **primitive characteristics,** such as the rhinarium and heightened sense of smell, and tend to have relatively specialized diets and behaviors. The haplorhines have the range of features that define primates as described earlier, but they have lost a number of primitive primate characteristics that strepsirhines have retained, such as the rhinarium.

The classification approaches—traditional/gradistic and evolutionary/cladistic—result in similar outcomes in the way primates are categorized (see Figure 6.19). The major difference is that the traditional approach groups tarsiers, a relatively specialized primate, with the prosimians. However, tarsiers share a number of **derived characteristics** with anthropoids, such as both lacking a rhinarium. Tarsiers' teeth are like higher primates'—their canines are large and projecting, the lower incisors are relatively small, and the upper central incisors are large. Many authorities argue that tarsiers share a common ancestor with anthropoids and not with the other prosimians (lorises, galagos, and lemurs) and should be considered part of a single (haplorhine) clade. Given the priority of and focus on evolution and not description in this book, I use the cladistic approach, placing the tarsiers with the anthropoids (monkeys, apes, and humans) in a haplorhine clade and the lorises, galagos, and lemurs in the strepsirhine clade (**Figure 6.19**).

There are two clades of haplorhines: the anthropoids and tarsiers. Anthropoids include catarrhines (Old World higher primates) and platyrrhines (New World higher primates): monkeys (cercopithecoids, or Old World monkeys, and ceboids, or New World monkeys), apes (hylobatids, or lesser apes, and nonhuman hominids, or great apes), and humans (**hominins**). Tarsiers have a number of primitive features, and they are highly specialized, especially with respect to having large, bulbous eyes for nocturnal vision. Rather than having four lower incisors, two on the left and two on the right, tarsiers have only two. Like some of the strepsirhines, they have retained three premolars on each side of the upper and lower jaws, giving them 34 teeth. Their name refers to the presence of two highly elongated tarsal bones in their feet. These long bones give extra leverage for leaping in search of prey, such as small birds. Tarsiers' eyes and eye sockets are enormous, reflecting their nocturnal adaptation (**Figure 6.20**). The smallness and relatively simple structure of their brain make it more similar to the brains of lemurs and lorises than to the brains of the higher primates.

Anthropoids are found in many places around the world, whereas tarsiers are restricted to a series of islands, especially Sulawesi, Borneo, and the Philippines. Both major clades of primates—strepsirhines and haplorhines—are hierarchically arranged, culminating at the bottom with genus and species (see Figure 6.19). Some

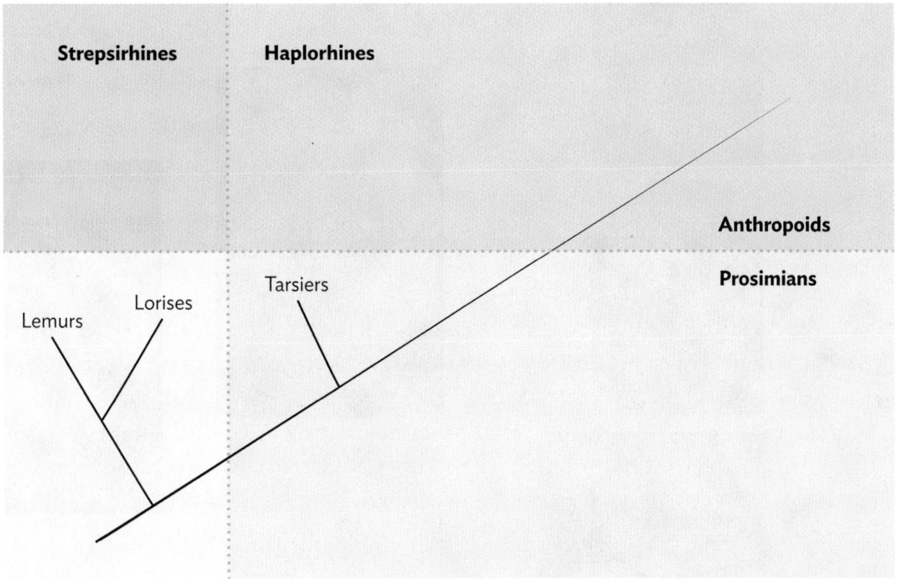

derived characteristics Characteristics present in only one or a few species of a group.

hominin Humans and humanlike ancestors.

FIGURE 6.18

Cladistic (Evolutionary or Phylogenetic) versus Gradistic (Traditional) Classification
According to the cladistic categorization (upper left), lemurs and lorises belong to the category strepsirhines, and anthropoids and tarsiers belong to the category haplorhines. By contrast, according to the gradistic categorization (right), lorises, lemurs, and tarsiers belong to the category prosimians, which is distinct from anthropoids.

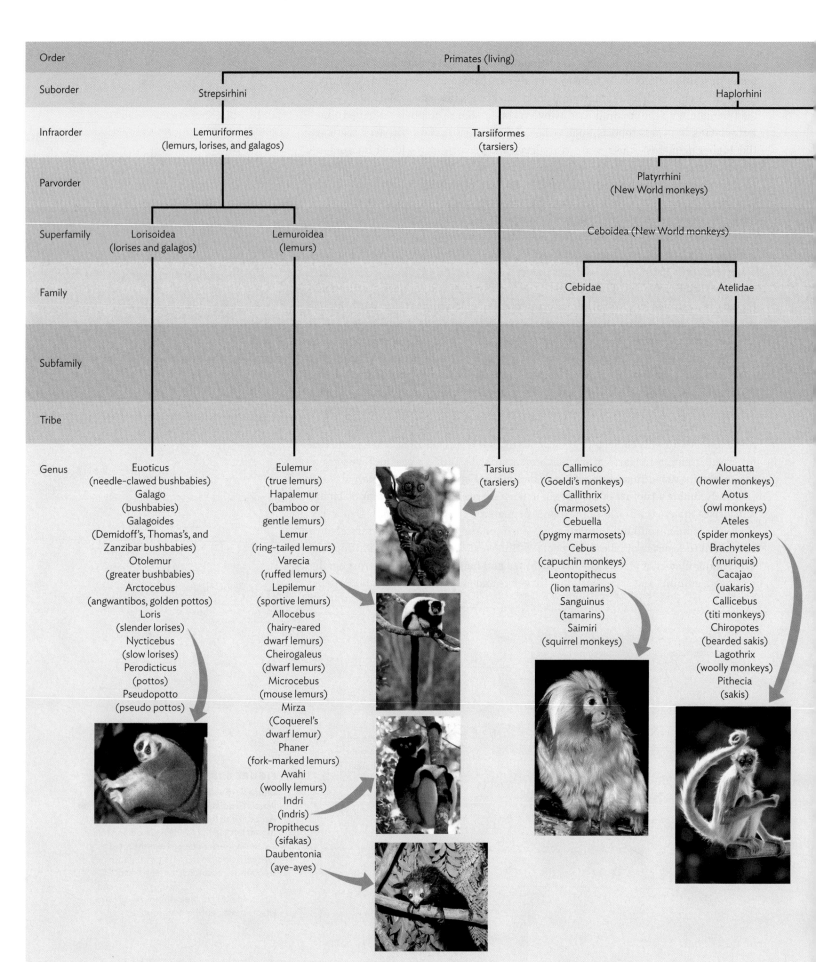

Order	Primates (living)				
Suborder	Strepsirhini		Haplorhini		
Infraorder	Lemuriformes (lemurs, lorises, and galagos)		Tarsiiformes (tarsiers)		
Parvorder				Platyrrhini (New World monkeys)	
Superfamily	Lorisoidea (lorises and galagos)	Lemuroidea (lemurs)		Ceboidea (New World monkeys)	
Family				Cebidae	Atelidae
Subfamily					
Tribe					
Genus	Euoticus (needle-clawed bushbabies) Galago (bushbabies) Galagoides (Demidoff's, Thomas's, and Zanzibar bushbabies) Otolemur (greater bushbabies) Arctocebus (angwantibos, golden pottos) Loris (slender lorises) Nycticebus (slow lorises) Perodicticus (pottos) Pseudopotto (pseudo pottos)	Eulemur (true lemurs) Hapalemur (bamboo or gentle lemurs) Lemur (ring-tailed lemurs) Varecia (ruffed lemurs) Lepilemur (sportive lemurs) Allocebus (hairy-eared dwarf lemurs) Cheirogaleus (dwarf lemurs) Microcebus (mouse lemurs) Mirza (Coquerel's dwarf lemur) Phaner (fork-marked lemurs) Avahi (woolly lemurs) Indri (indris) Propithecus (sifakas) Daubentonia (aye-ayes)	Tarsius (tarsiers)	Callimico (Goeldi's monkeys) Callithrix (marmosets) Cebuella (pygmy marmosets) Cebus (capuchin monkeys) Leontopithecus (lion tamarins) Sanguinus (tamarins) Saimiri (squirrel monkeys)	Alouatta (howler monkeys) Aotus (owl monkeys) Ateles (spider monkeys) Brachyteles (muriquis) Cacajao (uakaris) Callicebus (titi monkeys) Chiropotes (bearded sakis) Lagothrix (woolly monkeys) Pithecia (sakis)

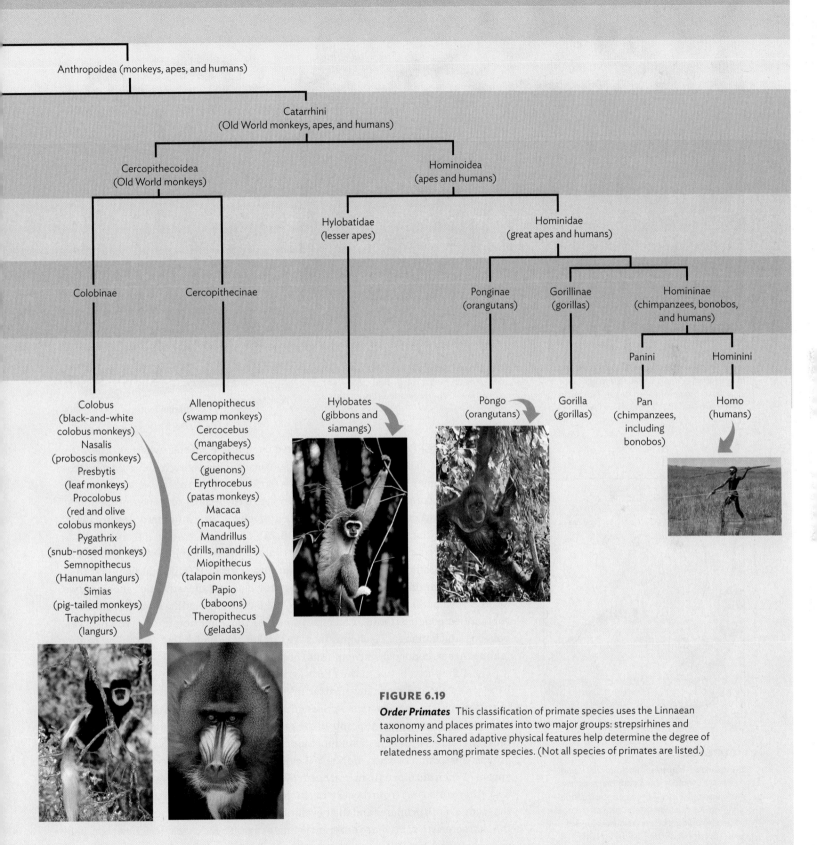

Anthropoidea (monkeys, apes, and humans)

Catarrhini
(Old World monkeys, apes, and humans)

Cercopithecoidea
(Old World monkeys)

Hominoidea
(apes and humans)

Hylobatidae
(lesser apes)

Hominidae
(great apes and humans)

Colobinae

Cercopithecinae

Ponginae
(orangutans)

Gorillinae
(gorillas)

Homininae
(chimpanzees, bonobos,
and humans)

Panini

Hominini

Colobus
(black-and-white
colobus monkeys)
Nasalis
(proboscis monkeys)
Presbytis
(leaf monkeys)
Procolobus
(red and olive
colobus monkeys)
Pygathrix
(snub-nosed monkeys)
Semnopithecus
(Hanuman langurs)
Simias
(pig-tailed monkeys)
Trachypithecus
(langurs)

Allenopithecus
(swamp monkeys)
Cercocebus
(mangabeys)
Cercopithecus
(guenons)
Erythrocebus
(patas monkeys)
Macaca
(macaques)
Mandrillus
(drills, mandrills)
Miopithecus
(talapoin monkeys)
Papio
(baboons)
Theropithecus
(geladas)

Hylobates
(gibbons and
siamangs)

Pongo
(orangutans)

Gorilla
(gorillas)

Pan
(chimpanzees,
including
bonobos)

Homo
(humans)

FIGURE 6.19

Order Primates This classification of primate species uses the Linnaean taxonomy and places primates into two major groups: strepsirhines and haplorhines. Shared adaptive physical features help determine the degree of relatedness among primate species. (Not all species of primates are listed.)

(a)

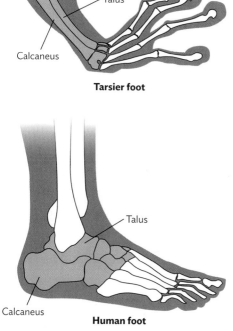

Talus

Calcaneus

Tarsier foot

Talus

Calcaneus

Human foot

(b)

FIGURE 6.20

Tarsier Eyes and Feet **(a)** Tarsiers are unique among prosimians in that their eyes have a fovea, a region of the retina that enables the sharp central vision needed for seeing details. This trait is unusual in nocturnal animals because dim light typically prevents them from seeing things that clearly. **(b)** Thanks to their elongated tarsals (shown in color), especially the talus and calcaneus bones, tarsiers are superb leapers.

FIGURE 6.21

Chimpanzee–Human Relationship As noted in chapter 3, humans and chimpanzees have approximately 98% of their genetic material in common. Perhaps we often seem as chimplike to them as chimps often seem humanlike to us. (*Brevity* © 2006. Dist. By ANDREWS MCMEEL SYNDICATION. Reprinted with permission. All rights reserved.)

genera are very diverse and are represented by multiple species, whereas others are not as diverse and have today just one species (for example, living humans). Among the hominoids, humans and African great apes (gorillas, chimpanzees, and bonobos) are more closely related to each other than they are to the Asian great apes (orangutans). In addition, DNA comparisons reveal that chimpanzees and humans are more closely related than either is to gorillas (**Figure 6.21**). Therefore, traditional and cladistic taxonomies produce somewhat different results for these primates (**Table 6.2**). The traditional classification includes three families: hylobatids (gibbons), pongids (great apes), and hominids (humans). By contrast, the cladistic classification includes two families, hylobatids (gibbons) and hominids (great apes, including humans), and three subfamilies, pongines (orangutans), gorillines (gorillas), and hominines (chimpanzees, bonobos, and humans). The hominines are further subdivided into two tribes: panins (chimpanzees, bonobos) and hominins (humans).

The differences between the major primate groups—for example, the differences between an ape and a monkey—matter, first, because they are a means of understanding the variation among primates. Second, the key characteristics of the different primate taxa appear at specific points in the evolutionary record. Paleontologists look for these characteristics in their study of the origins and evolution of the different primate groups. For example, when did the Y-5 molar, a defining characteristic of apes, first appear? When did bipedalism first occur? When did monkeys living in the New World first differ noticeably from those living in the Old World? Such questions are central to the study of both primates and their evolution. They can be answered only by knowing the characteristics unique to different primate taxa. These characteristics, then, help paleontologists and anthropologists reconstruct the evolutionary relationships and history of living species and their fossil ancestors. These evolutionary relationships, or

Table 6.2 Hominoid Classifications

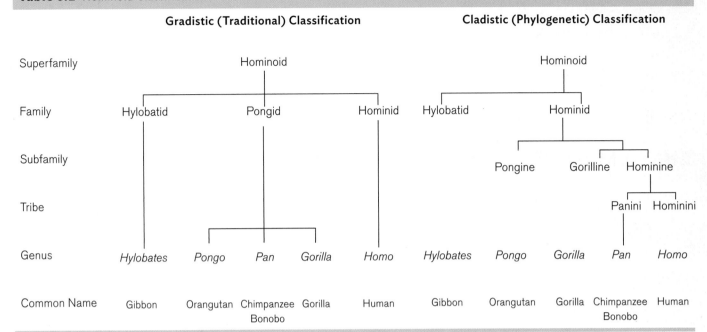

	Gradistic (Traditional) Classification				Cladistic (Phylogenetic) Classification				
Superfamily		Hominoid					Hominoid		
Family	Hylobatid	Pongid		Hominid	Hylobatid		Hominid		
Subfamily						Pongine	Gorilline	Hominine	
Tribe								Panini	Hominini
Genus	*Hylobates*	*Pongo*	*Pan*	*Gorilla*	*Homo*	*Hylobates*	*Pongo*	*Gorilla*	*Pan*	*Homo*
Common Name	Gibbon	Orangutan	Chimpanzee Bonobo	Gorilla	Human	Gibbon	Orangutan	Gorilla	Chimpanzee Bonobo	Human

phylogeny, are based on shared characteristics, including physical traits, genetics, and behavior. Organisms that share characteristics are more closely related than are organisms that do not share characteristics. For example, all mammals are homeothermic—all mammal species share this primitive trait. All apes have a sectorial complex—but humans lack this derived trait.

In addition, it is important to know about the physical differences between primate taxa because the variation in the living primates provides models for understanding the morphology, the behavior, and the adaptation in the evolutionary past. For example, the Y-5 lower molar pattern seen today in apes and humans first appeared in anthropoids 20–30 mya. This morphology indicates that apes originated at that time. (Humans have the pattern but evolved after apes.) Similarly, characteristics that define bipedalism in humans—long lower limbs and short upper limbs—first appeared 5 mya or so. When anthropologists find these anatomical characteristics in fossilized remains (fossils are the subject of chapter 8), they are able to identify the origins of humanlike ancestors. And knowing how those ancestors walked helps complete a timeline of adaptation.

The Strepsirhines

In acquiring food, strepsirhines rely heavily on their highly developed sense of smell. Reflecting this focus on smell, they have a rhinarium, enlarged nasal passages, scent glands, and a large olfactory bulb in the area in the front of the brain that controls the sense of smell. They also have the aforementioned tooth comb. Strepsirhines have nails at the ends of their fingers and toes, but the second toe has a toilet claw used primarily for grooming. Virtually all strepsirhines communicate with distinctive calls and mark their travel routes and territory with urine.

In evolutionary terms, the three strepsirhines—lemurs, lorises, and galagos—are among the most primitive primates (primate evolution is the subject of chapter 9). Many of the primitive characteristics seen in these primates have been around for many millions of years. There are a number of behaviors that the strepsirhines share

phylogeny The evolutionary relationships of a group of organisms.

HOW ADAPTABLE ARE

THE LEMURS OF ST. CATHERINES ISLAND

One of the hallmark features of primates is their remarkable adaptability, especially in new or changing circumstances. The primatologists Tim Keith-Lucas, Frances White, Lisa Keith-Lucas, and Laura Vick set out to test primate adaptability, in part to help make the case that captive primates can be successfully reintroduced to their natural habitats.

Mammal reintroduction programs are generally not very successful, but Keith-Lucas and his team had a hunch that primates would be an exception. As director of the St. Catherines Island Primate Research Program, located on one of the many barrier islands that dot the Atlantic coast of Georgia and Florida, Keith-Lucas was especially interested in demonstrating that a group of zoo-fed, zoo-habituated ring-tailed lemurs (*Lemur catta*) have the behavioral traits, both genetically programmed and learned, to adapt successfully to conditions in more natural habitats.

In 1985, a group of lemurs that had been housed in the close confines of enclosures at the Bronx Zoo in New York City were released on St. Catherines Island. About 16 km (10 mi) long and 4.8 km (3 mi) wide, St. Catherines is ideally suited for this natural experiment; the island is privately owned and only minimally occupied by humans. The island is subtropical and mostly forested, but its diverse habitats include salt marsh, open secondary forest, freshwater ponds, and limited grasslands.

Keith-Lucas correctly surmised that the animals could not just be let loose once they arrived on the island. Simply, none of the animals had the behavioral skills to survive: they would not be familiar with food sources, they had none of the predator-warning vocalizations, and they were out of shape—overweight, slow, and unable to climb trees. Therefore, before being released they were housed indoors for 10 weeks. There, they were fed dry monkey chow, canned primate food, vitamin supplements, and chopped fruit and vegetables. After the 10-week wait, the animals were released, and specific feeding sites were supplied on a regular basis with these same foods. For the next seven years, Keith-Lucas and his team observed the lemurs and recorded everything about them: each animal's behavior, location, level of activity, and foods eaten, both those supplied and those foraged from the natural habitat.

The team's massive data set—the only one of its kind for *Lemur catta*—showed that the lemurs' physical condition and level of activity changed in a matter of days. The animals lost excess weight and became much more physically active, more adept, and stronger. In addition, over time, the animals ventured farther and farther away from the original release site. They also demonstrated other natural behaviors completely missing in captivity. For example, for the first three weeks after release, none of the lemurs made a sound aside from some purrs and grunts. Then, after seeing a natural predator—a barred owl—one lemur made a loud call. Soon after that, the animals made other natural vocalizations. Especially exciting was the development of foraging as a central means of acquiring food, mostly the edible parts of plants (**Table 6.3**). After the first 10 months, both foraging time and variety of plants foraged increased significantly.

The results show that ring-tailed lemurs are

Although native to Madagascar, the lemurs shown here live on St. Catherines Island, Georgia, as part of a project aimed at preserving the species through the establishment of an independent breeding population.

PRIMATES?

Table 6.3 Plants Foraged by St. Catherines Island Lemurs

Plant	Part Eaten		Plant	Part Eaten	
Red bay	Leaves, fruit		Mulberry	Fruit	
Muscadine grape	Leaves, fruit		Myrtle	Leaves	
Hackberry	Leaves, fruit		Fig	Fruit	
Pine	Fruit, needles		Hickory	Bud scales	
Sparkleberry	Fruit		Cabbage palm	Fruit	
Live oak	Acorn nuts		Carolina laurel cherry	Fruit	
Southern magnolia	Petals		Dogwood	Fruit	
China berry	Fruit		Quince, Japanese plum	Fruit, buds, sap	

SOURCE Adapted from Keith-Lucas, T., F. J. White, L. Keith-Lucas, and L. G. Vick. 1999. Changes in behavior in free-ranging *Lemur catta* following release in a natural habitat. *American Journal of Primatology* 47:15–28.

adaptable: in the short term and the long term, these primates adjusted to a novel habitat. This finding is promising for future reintroduction programs. For example, on their native island of Madagascar, off southeastern Africa, lemurs are highly endangered. Should environmental conditions improve on Madagascar, perhaps this study could provide a template for reintroducing lemurs there.

FIGURE 6.22

Lemurs Lemurs show an extraordinary amount of variation. Shown here is a sampling of four genera of lemur: (a) mouse lemur (*Microcebus*), (b) sportive lemur (*Lepilemur*), (c) indri lemur (*Indri*), and (d) ringtailed lemur (*Lemur*). Some, such as the sportive lemur, are represented by numerous species.

(a)

(b)

(c)

(d)

in common, such as a focus on grooming and relatively simple social groupings. On the other hand, there is considerable variation in the biology and ecology of these highly diverse primates, associated with habitats and available foods, terrain, and climate.

Lemurs express the highest degree of diversity among primates today, so much so that they represent some 21% of primate genera worldwide (**Figure 6.22**). However, all of this remarkable diversity is highly constricted geographically. That is, lemurs are restricted to the large island of Madagascar off the southeast coast of Africa. Until humans first arrived on Madagascar, beginning around 2,000 years ago, many species of lemurs were present on the island, including the large *Megaladapis*, which reached 50 kg (110 lbs.) in adulthood (**Figure 6.23**). These and many other so-called subfossil lemurs are now extinct, owing mostly to human encroachment and exploitations of these primate species.

Today, there are about 100 taxa of lemurs, ranging from the tiny mouse lemur (*Microcebus berthae*), weighing only about 30 g (1 oz), to the indri (*Indri indri*), weighing around 9 kg (20 lbs). They are extraordinarily primitive, having very small brains relative to body size and enhanced sense of smell. Their high degree of anatomical diversity is also reflected in some species having relatively long hind limbs, an anatomical specialization used for leaping from tree branch to tree branch.

Lemurs are highly social, traveling in groups dominated by adult females. Reflecting their biological variation, lemurs have considerable dietary variation, with most depending on leaves and fruits, but with some having a relatively narrow diet. Lemurs

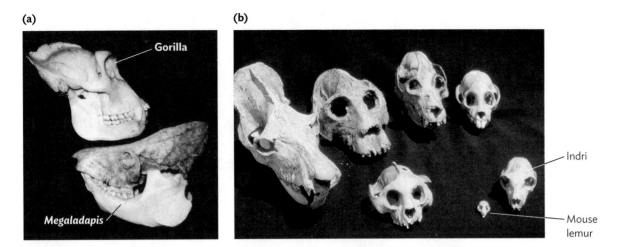

(a)

Gorilla

Megaladapis

(b)

Indri

Mouse
lemur

FIGURE 6.23

Megaladapis **(a)** The skull at the bottom of the photo belonged to a species of very large lemurs, the now extinct *Megaladapis*, on Madagascar. Skulls of *Megaladapis* were larger than a modern gorilla's, though *Megaladapis*'s body was smaller than a gorilla's. **(b)** In the right foreground, the skulls of a modern mouse lemur (middle) and an indri (right) represent the range of sizes in living lemurs. The crania in the back row and the skull to the left of the mouse lemur's show the range of sizes in extinct lemurs. The sizes of living and extinct lemurs overlap somewhat, but *Megaladapis*, the largest extinct lemur (far left), was substantially larger than any living lemur.

reflect the diversity of primates generally, with Madagascar serving as a kind of microcosm of environments globally, ranging from dense, tropical forest to open grasslands. Lemurs have successfully adapted to these diverse ecological contexts.

Owing to the continued expansion of human population on Madagascar, virtually all lemur taxa are threatened in some manner. Although a number of research centers are successful in breeding and maintaining populations, such as the Duke Lemur Center and on St. Catherines Island, Georgia (see *How Do We Know? How Adaptable Are Primates? The Lemurs of St. Catherines Island*), the degree of loss in their natural settings is alarming.

Lorises today are found in Southeast Asia, Sri Lanka, and Africa. Unlike the enormous variation seen in lemurs, lorises are less diverse and are represented by far fewer species (**Figure 6.24**). They are generally nocturnal and arboreal, in part making them difficult for primatologists to study their biology, behavior, and ecology. Unlike many other strepsirhines, lorises lack an external tail. The Sunda slow loris (*Nycticebus coucang*) is unique in having a toxic bite, whereby the primate licks its arm gland and the associated toxin is activated via mixing with its saliva. The toxin protects the adult and its infant from predators.

The very large, forward-facing eyes of lorises are an adaptation to their limitation to nocturnal activity. Their limbs are relatively long, but with some having specializations, such as opposability of the big toe with the other four toes, providing stability on branches and for acquisition of food. The Sunda slow loris has a long trunk, an anatomical adaptation for twisting around branches. Generally, multiple males compete for access to a single female. At dusk, lorises emerge from their nests. Over the course of the night, lorises interact regularly and sleep in groups. During the day, females and young sleep in groups. Food sources are limited primarily to insects.

Galagos (or bush babies) live in Africa. Like lorises, galagos feed and reproduce at night. Their most distinctive physical characteristics—very large, forward-facing eyes and very large eye orbits—reflect an adaptation that is exclusively nocturnal (**Figure 6.25**). They also have the specialized tooth comb. Their diet is highly insectivorous, but

FIGURE 6.24

Lorises Lorises are widespread, today found in Southeast Asia, Sri Lanka, and Africa. Unlike most primate taxa, these primates have a very small tail and do not leap. Shown here are (a) Sunda slow loris (*Nycticebus coucang*), (b) gray slender loris (*Loris lydekkerianus*), and (c) pygmy slow loris (*Nycticebus pygmaeus*).

FIGURE 6.25

Galagos The galagos, or bush babies, live in Africa and are exclusively nocturnal primates. There are multiple genera and species, including (a) bushbaby (*Galago senegalensis*), (b) southern lesser galago (*Galago moholi*), and (c) thick-tailed bushbaby (*Otolemur crassicaudatus*).

Monkey or Ape? Differences Matter

Differences between monkeys and apes track different evolutionary histories.

Characteristic	Monkey	Ape
Body size	Generally smaller	Generally larger
Posture/locomotion	Generally horizontal body trunk	Relatively vertical body trunk
Body trunk	Narrow	Broad
Tail	Has a tail	Lacks a tail
Lower molars	Bilophodont lower molar (cercopithecoids only)	Y-5 molar pattern
Brain	Relatively small	Relatively large
Growth	Relatively fast	Relatively slow
Interspecies variability	High	Low

includes occasional consumption of small animals and fruit. Like many other strepsirhines, the common social grouping includes an adult female and her young.

Perhaps most distinctive about galagos is their predilection to jumping upwards, often to heights exceeding 2 m (6 ft). Therefore, a considerable some 25% of their overall body mass is muscle in the hind limbs. Their remarkably powerful hind limbs facilitate movement over great distances in a short amount of time. The rapid travel is associated with both acquisition of food—such as fast moving insects—and fleeing from predators.

The Haplorhines

Haplorhines, the so-called higher primates, differ from strepsirhines in a number of important ways. In general, haplorhines have larger brains, are more dimorphic sexually in body size and other anatomical characteristics, and have fewer teeth (premolars, in particular) than strepsirhines. Moreover, unlike strepsirhines' eyes, haplorhines' eyes are convergent and enclosed by a continuous ring of bone. Haplorhines also see in color whereas strepsirhines see mostly in black and white.

The two parvorders of anthropoids—platyrrhines, or New World monkeys, and catarrhines—are named for the morphologies of their noses (**Figure 6.26**). Platyrrhine (from the Greek, meaning "broad-nosed") nostrils are round and separated by a wide nasal septum, the area of soft tissue that separates the nostrils. Catarrhine ("hook-nosed") nostrils are close together and point downward. (To understand nostril orientation, look at your own nostrils in a mirror. They should be directed downward, as you are a catarrhine.)

The one superfamily of platyrrhines is the ceboids. The two ceboid families, cebids

FIGURE 6.27

Prehensile Tails Atelines, such as muriquis or woolly spider monkeys (shown here), are the only primates with a fully prehensile tail. (Opossums and kinkajous are among the other mammals with a fully prehensile tail.) The prehensile tail is very muscular, and its undersurface has dermal ridges, like fingerprints and toe prints, that improve the tail's grip.

Platyrrhines
New World

Catarrhines
Old World

FIGURE 6.26

Platyrrhines versus Catarrhines In addition to their differently shaped noses, these two groups differ in their numbers of premolars: platyrrhines have six upper and six lower premolars, while catarrhines have four upper and four lower premolars.

prehensile tail A tail that acts as a kind of a hand for support in trees, common in New World monkeys.

and atelids, are widespread in Latin America, from southern Argentina to Mexico. Ceboids are arboreal, spending nearly all their time in trees. They use suspensory locomotion, in which all four limbs grasp on to branches and help move the body from one tree or branch to another. Within the atelids are two subfamilies, one of which, the atelines, is distinctive in that each of its four types (howler monkeys, spider monkeys, woolly monkeys, and woolly spider monkeys) has a **prehensile tail** (**Figure 6.27**). In addition to locomotion functions in the trees, the prehensile tail can be used to suspend the body from a branch so that the hands and feet can be used to feed. Ceboids have a diverse diet, ranging from insects (that is, they practice insectivory) to fruits (frugivory) and leaves (folivory). Smaller ceboids obtain protein from insects, whereas larger ones obtain it from leaves.

The Old World monkeys, cercopithecoids, are the most diverse and successful nonhuman primates. They inhabit a wide range of habitats throughout Africa and Asia but mostly live in the tropics or subtropics. Some are arboreal and some are terrestrial. Cercopithecoids have bilophodont upper and lower molars, a narrow face, a sitting pad on the rear, and a long body trunk that terminates with a nonprehensile tail. Their canines are highly dimorphic sexually—males' canines are larger than females' canines, sometimes considerably so.

Cercopithecoids are divided into two subfamilies: colobines and cercopithecines (**Figure 6.28**). Colobines are closely related, medium-sized primates with a long tail and a wide array of coloration. They are mostly arboreal and live in a variety of climates, though not in dry areas. Colobines are folivores, and their anatomical features have adapted to accommodate a diet rich in leaves. The high, pointed cusps of their molars shear leaves and thus maximize the amount of nutrition obtained from them. Conversely, cercopithecines have rounded, lower cusps on their molars as their diet is rich in fruit, which does not need as much processing to extract its nutrients. Colobines' large three- or four-chambered stomach, resembling a cow's stomach, contains microorganisms that break down cellulose, again to maximize the amount of nutrition

FIGURE 6.28

Old World Monkeys Colobines include **(a)** black-and-white colobus monkeys, **(b)** gray langurs, **(c)** proboscis monkeys, and **(d)** douc langurs. Cercopithecines include **(e)** mandrills, **(f)** De Brazza's monkeys, **(g)** olive baboons, and **(h)** vervet monkeys.

extracted from the leaves. By contrast, cercopithecines are often called "cheek-pouch monkeys" because inside each cheek they have a pouch that extends into the neck and serves as a kind of stomach. While foraging, they store food in their cheek pouches, which are especially useful when they need to gather food quickly in a dangerous area. Arboreal cercopithecines tend to have a longer tail, while terrestrial species have a short or no tail.

Colobines are receiving a lot of attention because some taxa are highly threatened. One colobine species, Miss Waldron's red colobus monkey, is the first primate to have gone extinct in the past five centuries.

The most studied cercopithecoids are the cercopithecines, which include baboons

MITIGATING END

Earlier in this chapter, I discussed the amazing diversity of the more than 600 taxa of primates alive today. Although the great apes—chimpanzees, gorillas, and orangutans—provide some of the most spectacular and iconic records of primate biology and behavior, there is so much more to the primate world, including the numerous and diverse species living in our own backyard in Latin America, extending from the tropics of Mexico to the temperate zones of southern South America.

WATCH THE VIDEO

www.digital.
wwnorton.com/
ourorigins4

But there is a dark side to the study of primates. The population explosion of the world's dominant primate, *Homo sapiens*, and our insatiable need for more and more natural resources from mining, lumber, and other extractive pursuits, and for more and more land for raising crops, is rapidly whittling away primate habitats and the animals inhabiting them. For most of recorded history, primates have been remarkably abundant. Even just a few decades ago, it seemed that primates of all sizes and shapes were safe—they certainly were not endangered. Within the past 30 or so years, however, that picture of primate security has changed for the worse, in large part owing to human encroachment. In fact, nearly *half* of primates today are on the International Union for Conservation of Nature's endangered species list.

That primates—our nearest kin—stay with us is critically important. These living primates provide essential records of evolution and behavior, crucial for understanding the place of humans in the present and past. If the world doesn't pay attention, these endangered species will disappear, and some within our lifetimes. How can primates be saved from extinction and threatened taxa taken off the endangered list? How can circumstances that might lead to extinction be mitigated?

Clearly, there are no simple answers to these questions. But there are successes that are built on sometimes highly local circumstances. One such success is the conservation and research project led by American primatologist Karen Strier, who has devoted her life's work to the study and protection of primates currently living in the once-extensive Atlantic Forest in the state of Minas Gerais in southeastern Brazil. Prior to human encroachment and deforestation, the northern muriqui (*Brachyteles hypoxanthus*) and its close relative, the southern muriqui (*Brachyteles arachnoides*), ranged widely in this vast region. Today, the forest itself is limited to relatively small, mostly discontinuous patches. Many of these forest patches are occupied by muriquis, but these populations nonetheless number fewer than a thousand individuals. Recognizing the vulnerability of these monkeys to deforestation and fragmentation, Strier began her study in 1982 with one group of the several hundred critically endangered individuals remaining in the government-protected Feliciano Miguel Abdala Reserve.

Given the long duration of the project, anthropologists now know a great deal about these primates—their behavior, habitat, reproduction, growth and development, and other social and physical characteristics. Importantly, the project has also focused on

ANGERMENT

The northern muriqui (*Brachyteles hypoxanthus*) living in the remaining patches of the once-massive Atlantic Forest of southeastern Brazil are among the most endangered primates in the world. Through a unique collaboration with landowners, governmental and nongovernmental agencies, scientists, and local communities, Karen Strier's long-term research and conservation efforts are helping to ensure the sustainability of these primate populations.

the social context of the primates' endangerment by involving landowners and surrounding communities in the efforts to preserve the muriquis. It is this acquired knowledge about their behavior and characteristics and communal involvement in helping them thrive that is laying the groundwork for the long-term survival plan for the northern muriquis. This plan is not just about providing protection for fragile habitats. It also includes other key elements, particularly having an informed understanding of the muriquis' strategy for survival and success. Strier and her team of students and colleagues have found that, like most primates, muriquis are superbly adaptable. For example, the protective environment offered by the reserve has resulted in a substantial increase in the population size. The downside of this increase in numbers is increased

pressure on food sources. The traditional arboreal foods of these arboreal primates are not sufficiently plentiful to support the increased population. The adaptive flexibility of the northern muriquis is revealed by their increasing focus on terrestrial foods, such that these once-exclusive tree-dwellers are now expanding their range to spend considerably more time on the ground in their quest for food. The northern muriquis are doing what primates do best: they are adapting.

The many lessons learned about the northern muriqui of Brazil and their long-term survival has meant increased sustainability for this species. The northern muriqui are not out of the woods yet, but Strier, her colleagues, and her students provide a model for how to keep them there for the long term. *Anthropology matters!*

and baboonlike monkeys (geladas, mandrills, macaques). Many cercopithecines live in the savannas of East Africa. Some of them have highly dexterous fingers, adapted for picking up small seeds from the ground. Because these primates live in habitats similar to those of early hominins (see chapter 10), they provide anthropologists

FIGURE 6.29

Great Apes and Lesser Apes The great apes—**(a)** chimpanzees, **(b)** bonobos, **(c)** orangutans, and **(d)** gorillas—tend to be larger than other primates. All but gorillas are smaller than humans, with whom they are highly similar genetically. While great apes have a variety of social groupings, lesser apes—**(e)** gibbons and (not pictured) siamangs—are unique in that they form pair bonds, in which one male, one female, and their offspring are the basic social unit.

with the means of understanding both the origins and evolution of early human social behavior and some physical attributes characteristic of primates living in open grasslands.

The hominoids are, in addition to humans, great apes and lesser apes (**Figure 6.29**). Humans live on every continent. Today, the only great ape that lives in Asia is the orangutan. The lesser apes live in Southeast Asia. The great apes of Africa—the chimpanzee, the closely related bonobo (or pygmy chimpanzee), and the gorilla—are restricted to small equatorial areas. All of these hominoids have large brains, broad faces, and premolars and molars with little occlusal surface relief. They all have a Y-5 lower molar pattern. All apes have the canine–premolar honing complex. None of the hominoids have an external tail.

All hominoids except humans—gibbons, siamangs, gorillas, chimpanzees, bonobos, and orangutans—have very long forelimbs (arms) compared with the hind limbs. The fingers and toes are also quite long, for grasping trees and branches of various shapes and sizes. These characteristics are important adaptations used in the forest in a range of suspensory postures and movements (**Figure 6.30**). Gibbons and siamangs are skilled **brachiators,** using their upper limbs to move from tree limb to tree limb. Chimpanzees, bonobos, and gorillas are efficient at various suspensory postures, but their large sizes—especially in adult males—lead them to spend significant amounts of time on the ground in feeding and in locomotion. They use a specialized form of quadrupedalism called knuckle-walking, in which the very strong arms are used to support the upper body weight while positioned on the backs of the fingers' middle phalanges. The knuckles bear the weight, while the fingers are flexed toward the palms (**Figure 6.31**).

In orangutans and gorillas, males have enormous masticatory muscles, which are accommodated by a large, well-developed sagittal crest, the ridge of bone running along the midline (mid-sagittal) plane of the skull. The sagittal crest is the terminal attachment site for the temporalis muscle (**Figure 6.32**). Gorillas devote considerable time to eating leaves and plant stems. In contrast, chimpanzees are omnivorous—they eat

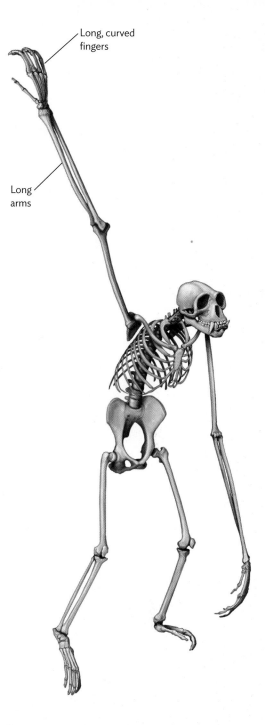

Long, curved fingers

Long arms

FIGURE 6.30

Suspensory Apes That the great apes and lesser apes regularly use suspensory locomotion can be seen in various features of their skeletal anatomy. For example, this gibbon's arms are long compared with its legs, its fingers and toes are long, and its fingers are curved and thus have enhanced grasping ability. If an ancestral primate's forelimbs were considerably longer than its hind limbs, the animal was likely suspensory.

FIGURE 6.31

Knuckle-Walking This unique type of quadrupedalism enables chimpanzees and gorillas, like the gorilla pictured here, to move very quickly. In contrast, orangutans typically use fist-walking, supporting their upper body weight on the palms, which are closed in fists.

(a)

(b)

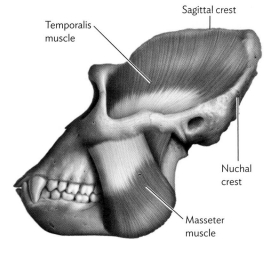

Sagittal crest

Temporalis muscle

Nuchal crest

Masseter muscle

FIGURE 6.32

Sagittal Crest **(a)** This ridge of bone is located at the sagittal suture along the midline of the cranium. **(b)** The more highly developed the sagittal crest is, the more highly developed the masticatory muscles are. This feature appears in gorillas and orangutans, as well as a variety of other animals, especially carnivores. It has been found in some human and primate ancestors.

CONCEPT CHECK

Strepsirhines and Haplorhines Differ in Their Anatomy and Senses

Strepsirhines tend to be more primitive than haplorhines.

Characteristic/ Adaptation	Strepsirhine Tendencies	Haplorhine Tendencies
Smell	More developed	Less developed
Vision	Nocturnal for many	Diurnal
Touch	Claws in some Less developed	Nails More developed
Diet	More specialized More teeth in some	More generalized Reduced number of teeth
Intelligence	Less developed Small brain	More developed Large brain

fruit, leaves, bark, insects, and meat, depending on the season, their habitat (ranging from dense rainforests to savanna-woodlands), and local tradition. When meat is not available, chimpanzees' body weight goes down, suggesting that they rely on animal sources for protein.

Humans' general body plan resembles that of the large-bodied apes of Africa, a fact that has been recognized since at least the middle of the nineteenth century, when Thomas Huxley wrote his famous treatise on primate anatomy and human evolution, *Man's Place in Nature* (Huxley's research is discussed further in chapter 10). Humans

FIGURE 6.33

Quadrupedalism versus Bipedalism Various morphological features differentiate these two forms of locomotion.

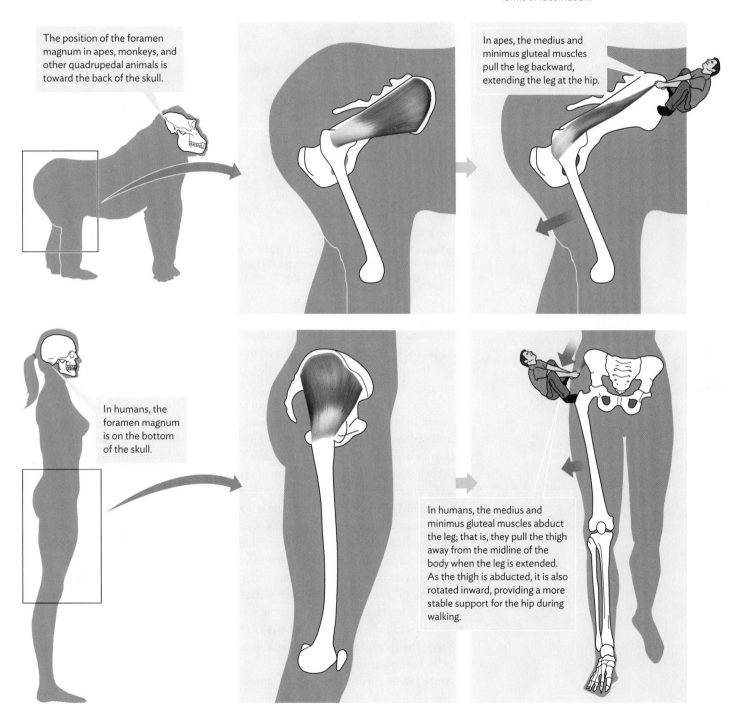

The position of the foramen magnum in apes, monkeys, and other quadrupedal animals is toward the back of the skull.

In apes, the medius and minimus gluteal muscles pull the leg backward, extending the leg at the hip.

In humans, the foramen magnum is on the bottom of the skull.

In humans, the medius and minimus gluteal muscles abduct the leg; that is, they pull the thigh away from the midline of the body when the leg is extended. As the thigh is abducted, it is also rotated inward, providing a more stable support for the hip during walking.

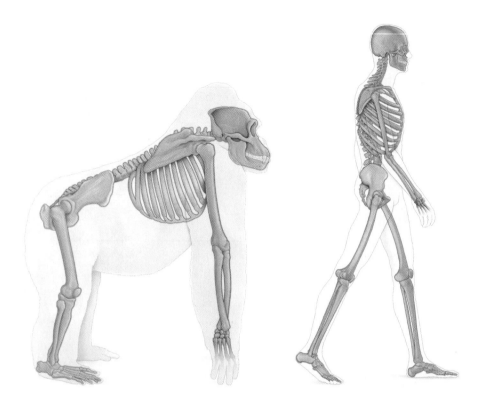

FIGURE 6.34

Limb Proportions In suspensory apes (left), the arms are long compared with the legs. In humans (right), the arms are relatively short because they are no longer used in locomotion. In addition, humans' fingers and toes are relatively shorter and straighter than apes', again as a result of bipedalism.

have several unique anatomical attributes, however, many of which are related to the fact that humans are the only obligate, or restrictedly, bipedal primate (see "What Makes Humans So Different from Other Animals? The Six Steps to Humanness" in chapter 1).

The skeletal indicators of bipedalism are found in the skull and the postcranial skeleton. In bipeds, the foramen magnum—the large opening for the passage of the spinal cord to the brain—is located at the bottom of the skull. The skull sits atop the body, whereas in quadrupeds the foramen magnum is located on the back of the skull and the skull is positioned on the front of the body. Many of the postcranial characteristics associated with bipedalism are in the pelvis. The pelvis of the human (the biped) is short and directed to the side of the body, whereas the pelvis of the ape (the quadruped) is long and directed to the back of the body. These differently shaped pelvises reflect the different positions and functions of two gluteal muscles—gluteus medius and gluteus minimus—which attach across the hip joints of both human and ape. In apes, these two muscles act as thigh straighteners, or extensors; but in humans, they abduct the thigh on the side of the hip that supports the body weight when a person walks. The muscles' contraction on the abducted side keeps the hip stable while the other leg swings forward (**Figure 6.33**). (Next time you walk, notice how only one foot is on the ground at any one time, and feel how on that side of your hip the gluteal muscles have contracted.)

Among the other anatomical differences between humans and apes are the relative lengths of the limbs, the curvature of the spine, and the angle of the femur in standing, walking, and running bipeds (**Figure 6.34**). In addition, unlike apes and monkeys, humans do not hone their canines and premolars. These differences are discussed more fully in chapter 10.

So far, we have concentrated on the anatomical differences among the different taxa of living primates. Of course, primates are not just about bones and teeth and other physical components. Like their anatomical variation, primates' behavioral variation reflects millions of years of evolution, during which adaptive strategies have enhanced the survival and reproduction of individuals and societies.

CHAPTER 6 REVIEW

ANSWERING THE BIG QUESTIONS

1. **Why study primates?**
   - Primates are physically and behaviorally similar to humans in numerous ways. For example, forward-facing eyes and grasping hands in both groups indicate a common ancestry.
   - Primates, including humans, are remarkably diverse, yet they all show ability to adapt to a wide range of circumstances.
   - Owing to biological similarities between primates and humans, the study of diseases in primates helps us understand and cure diseases in humans.
   - Primate diversity reflects the diversity of animal species. Reduction in primate diversity is a barometer of the "health" of the animal kingdom.

2. **What is a primate?**
   - Primates, an order of mammals, are best defined on the basis of their evolutionary trends: they are arboreal, have highly flexible diets, and invest a great deal of time in their young. Overall, they are generalized—primates have specialized in not specializing.

   - Their physical characteristics reflect primates' adaptation to life in the trees. A highly versatile body structure facilitates great mobility and manual dexterity. Vision is highly developed, but the senses of hearing and smell are greatly de-emphasized in most primate taxa.
   - Primates' highly varied diet is reflected in a generally nonspecialized dentition including functionally distinctive tooth types.
   - Primates' prolonged care for young reflects the fact that primates have a lot to teach, especially in the area of complex social behaviors.

3. **What are the kinds of primates?**
   - The more than 200 primate species living today are subdivided into two suborders: strepsirhines and haplorhines. Strepsirhines are the lesser, or lower, primates. Haplorhines are the higher primates. Tarsiers are included in the haplorhines but retain a significant suite of primitive characteristics.

KEY TERMS

arboreal adaptation
bilophodont
brachiators
canine–premolar honing complex
clade
dental formula
derived characteristics
diastema
dietary plasticity
diurnal
grade
hominin
loph
nocturnal
olfactory bulb
opposable
parental investment
phylogeny

power grip
preadaptation
precision grip
prehensile tail
primitive characteristics
rhinarium
sectorial (premolar)
tooth comb
Y-5

STUDY QUIZ

1. **Which is *not* an arboreal adaptation shared by most primates?**
   a. mobile joints connecting bones of the shoulders, limbs, hands, and feet
   b. an opposable thumb and often an opposable big toe
   c. dermal ridges and flat nails on fingertips
   d. rigidly connected, identical vertebrae in the backbone

2. **Which evolutionary adaptation provides primates with depth perception?**
   a. forward-facing eyes
   b. color vision
   c. loss of the rhinarium
   d. smaller olfactory bulb

3. **_____ retain more primitive characteristics than other primates,** such as a partially enclosed eye orbit.
   a. strepsirhines
   b. haplorhines
   c. platyrrhines
   d. catarrhines

4. **_____ have a dental formula of 2/1/2/3 and hook-shaped nostrils.**
   a. atelids
   b. catarrhines
   c. cebids
   d. platyrrhines

5. **Which feature is shared by both apes and Old World monkeys?**
   a. long tail
   b. lower molar morphology
   c. canine–premolar honing complex
   d. large bodies and brains

EVOLUTION REVIEW

OUR CLOSEST LIVING RELATIVES

Synopsis As a group, the members of the order Primates differ from other mammals in three key respects related to the evolutionary history that shaped their morphology and behavior. Primates are characterized by arboreal adaptations (associated with life in the trees), dietary flexibility (associated with the wide variety of foods that they eat), and parental investment (associated with offspring that require a large amount of care). Despite these key similarities among its members, perhaps the most remarkable feature of the order Primates is its immense diversity. Some primates are nocturnal, whereas others are diurnal. Some primates spend most of their time in the trees, whereas others spend a great deal of time on the ground. Some primates have specialized diets, whereas others might eat just about anything. The immense diversity among living primates was shaped by evolutionary forces over tens of millions of years, and this diversity reflects the interactions between species and their environmental settings.

Q1. Primates are characterized by adaptations for life in trees and for eating a broad diet. Provide two examples of primate adaptations for life in the trees and two examples of primate adaptations for eating a wide variety of foods.

Q2. Primates are also characterized by unique patterns of parental investment compared to other mammalian species. Describe three major features of primate parenting. What are the implications of these parenting features for intelligence, socialization, and fitness?

Q3. Compare and contrast the traditional/gradistic and evolutionary/cladistic approaches to primate classification. How do morphological and genetic features contribute to defining evolutionary (ancestral–descendant) relationships more accurately in the cladistic approach? Does the traditional/gradistic or evolutionary/cladistic scheme more accurately represent the similarities and differences between all members of the order Primates?

Hint See Table 6.2.

Q4. Discuss the ways in which evolutionary forces might operate to produce the huge amount of anatomical and behavioral diversity seen in the order Primates today. How does such diversity reflect the adaptability and evolutionary "success" of the order?

Hint Consider the ways in which different primates occupy distinct ecological niches.

Q5. As humans, we are obviously accustomed to thinking about most issues from a "people-centric" perspective. Pretend for a moment that you are a chimpanzee, gorilla, howler monkey, tarsier, ring-tailed lemur, or one of the many other nonhuman primate species discussed in this chapter. Which ecological and environmental factors have the greatest potential to affect the evolutionary future of your species? What types of adaptations might be most beneficial in response to these selective pressures?

ADDITIONAL READINGS

Aerts, P. 1998. Vertical jumping in Galago senegalensis: the quest for an obligate mechanical power amplifier. *Philosophical Transactions of the Royal Society of London* B 353:1607-1620.

Caldecott, J., and L. Miles, eds. 2005. *World Atlas of Great Apes and Their Conservation.* Berkeley: University of California Press.

Campbell, C. J., A. Fuentes, K. C. MacKinnon, M. Panger, and S. K. Bearder, eds. 2006. *Primates in Perspective.* New York: Oxford University Press.

Falk, D. 2000. *Primate Diversity.* New York: Norton.

McGraw, W. S. 2010. Primates defined. Pp. 222–242 in C. S. Larsen, ed. *A Companion to Biological Anthropology.* Chichester, UK: Wiley-Blackwell.

Nowak, R. M. 1999. *Walker's Primates of the World.* Baltimore: Johns Hopkins University Press.

Rowe, N. 1996. *The Pictorial Guide to the Living Primates.* Charlestown, RI: Pogonias.

Swindler, D. R. 1998. *Introduction to Primates.* Seattle: University of Washington Press.

At Gombe National Park, Tanzania, in 1965, one of her research subjects plays with Jane Goodall, who sometimes hid bananas for the chimpanzees beneath her shirt. A world-renowned primatologist, Goodall established the Jane Goodall Institute, dedicated to preserving wildlife worldwide. Projects spearheaded by the institute, such as sanctuaries in Africa for orphaned chimpanzees, provide opportunities for continued research and educational outreach, as well as jobs for local communities.

7

Primate Sociality, Social Behavior, and Culture

BIG QUESTIONS

1. **Why are primates social?**
2. **What is special about primate societies and social behavior?**
3. **How do primates acquire food?**
4. **How do primates communicate?**

Of all the scientists mentioned in this book so far, Jane Goodall (see Figure 1.3) may be the most famous. But when Goodall began doing what she most loves—observing primates and talking about them—about the only people who had heard of her were family and friends in her native England. Since childhood, Goodall had dreamed of living in Africa, and in 1957, after graduating from secretarial school and holding a series of odd jobs, she traveled with a friend to Kenya. Within two months, she had met the famous fossil hunter Louis Leakey (fossils are the subject of chapter 8; you will hear more about Leakey in chapter 10), who eventually employed her at the national museum in Nairobi.

Leakey was interested in human origins and had long thought that studying chimpanzees in the wild would be a window onto the behavior and social organization of early apes and humans. Other scientists, such as the American physical anthropologists Sherwood Washburn and Irven DeVore, were doing pioneering field studies of baboon behavior in Kenya, but Leakey thought that chimpanzees

Gombe National Park, Tanzania

would provide an even better understanding of the origins of ape and human social behavior. After getting to know the energetic and highly competent Goodall, he decided she was the right person to pursue this line of inquiry. She enthusiastically agreed to live among and study chimpanzees in Gombe, a remote area along the shores of Lake Tanganyika in western Tanzania. This venture would have been discouraging to most. No one had ever observed chimpanzees in the wild for an extended period or in the kind of detail needed to record behavior and draw conclusions. Moreover, living in the jungle was no easy undertaking—it was full of uncertainty and danger.

habituate Refers to the process of animals becoming accustomed to human observers.

The outcome proved even more amazing than Leakey might have imagined. A few months after reaching her field site in 1960, Goodall was able to **habituate** the chimpanzees to her presence, observe them for hours on end, and record their behaviors in unprecedented detail. Her findings bowled over the anthropological world. Chimpanzees proved highly intelligent, for example, and close social bonds existed between chimpanzee mothers and their offspring and between chimpanzee siblings. Goodall also discovered behaviors that other scientists found quite hard to believe, mainly because the behaviors did not fit expectations about the species. First, Goodall documented in words and on film how chimps made stick probes to harvest termites from termite nests and how they crumpled up leaves to make a kind of sponge, with which they soaked up rainwater from the crooks of trees and then squeezed the water into their mouths. That chimps used tools was an exciting discovery because it narrowed the perceived behavioral chasm between humans and apes, our closest living relatives. Second, Goodall discovered that chimpanzees regularly hunted other primates and animals. Chimps were not vegetarians!

A skilled scientist, formulating hypotheses, testing them with careful field observations, and drawing conclusions based on her observations, Goodall performed pioneering research that underscored the importance of the study of primates to understanding ourselves. Among her many accomplishments, Goodall documented key elements of primate societies and of primate social behavior in its broadest terms. This chapter considers primate social behavior, especially in the important linkage between learning, behavior, and socioecology (this latter term refers to the connections between social organization, ecology, and diet). Exciting new developments in the study of primates challenge long-held notions in the social and behavioral sciences that only humans have distinctive cultural traditions, and that knowledge of these traditions is socially transmitted.

Underlying much of what motivates primatologists to study primate social behavior is one central question: *Why are primates social?* To seek answers to this question, primatologists study primate societies all over the world with an eye toward social diversity and ways that primate societies are organized. To understand sociality in our nearest living relatives is to gain insight into the origins of sociality in we humans.

7.1 Primate Societies: Diverse, Complex, Long-Lasting

Diversity of Primate Societies

Primate societies are diverse in several ways. First, *primates express themselves socially through a range of behaviors*. Some of the more obvious behaviors include touching, hugging, mouthing, mounting, lip smacking, vocalizing, greeting, and grooming. Far more so than any other animal, primates use these social signals to express different kinds of relationships, many of them complex and reciprocal. These signals can serve as a kind of "currency" for items or activities they are interested in, such as grooming another individual to establish an alliance at the moment or in some future event.

Second, *many primate societies are complexly organized.* Within any primate group, individuals representing different kinships, ranks, ages, and sexes often form alliances.

Third, *primates form various social relationships for the long term.* Primates form relationships for immediate payoff (for example, access to food or to mates), but they also establish and maintain long-term alliances that at first glance do not appear to be beneficial, especially with regard to reproductive success and gaining access to food and other resources. For example, we might be surprised that chimpanzee males groom each other or travel together, as these entail forming social relationships with their rivals for food or mates. But males who frequently engage in these and other cooperative activities might later work together to compete, for food or mates, against other groups.

Primate Social Behavior: Enhancing Survival and Reproduction

The theory underlying the study of primate social behavior is simple. That is, as recognized by the American biologist Edward O. Wilson in his study of animals generally, primate social behavior is influenced by evolution. Basically, natural selection favors primate behaviors that enhance survival and reproduction. In this way, the genes of individuals who engage in those behaviors pass from generation to generation. Primatologists explore the relationships between specific social behaviors and reproductive fitness. Such behaviors may be purely natural or they may be learned. In other words, sometimes primates are not conscious of their actions, and other times they strategize, learning by observation and imitation. These extremely important processes are highly elaborated in primates.

Males and females have very different reproductive roles and very different life histories in adulthood. Males provide the sperm to produce offspring. Females provide the ova to conceive the young, grow the young within them, give birth, and nurse the young. Overall, females expend far more energy in the creation of and caring for offspring than males do. As a general rule for many animals, including primates, those members of the sex that expends less energy in this way (the males) compete more aggressively among themselves for sexual access to members of the sex that expends more energy (the females).

When male primates compete for females, whether they are competing singly or in groups, the males' bodies adapt. Sexual dimorphism in body size and in canine size is considerably higher in such societies than in societies where males do not compete. This difference reflects the fact that to compete for females successfully, males must be big and aggressive (**Figure 7.1**). In these societies, males are generally unrelated. In societies where males are related, live in the group in which they were born (the natal group), and compete with related males, sexual dimorphism tends to be lower than in groups where males disperse and compete with nonrelated males.

Finally, although all the life periods of primates are generally longer than those of other animals, humans have the longest life span of the primates (see Figure 6.16). The average human life lasts nearly 70 years, longer than that of the chimpanzee (44 years), the gibbon (30 years), the macaque (29 years), and the lemur (27 years). The American anthropologist and demographer Timothy Gage suggests that humans are the only primate to have "baby booms"; that is, variation in numbers of offspring in a population, fluctuating from small numbers to large numbers over time.

Primate Residence Patterns

Animals such as birds and nonprimate mammals tend to be regimented in their social structures and residence patterns. By contrast, individual primate species combine

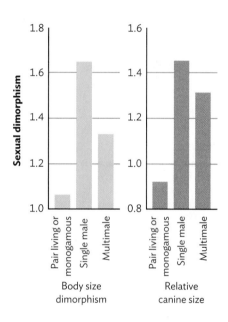

FIGURE 7.1

Competition and Sexual Dimorphism Among primates, as shown in these charts, sexual dimorphism in body size and in canine size is directly related to group composition. Here, a value of 1.0 indicates no sexual dimorphism. In primate species with monogamous pairs (such as gibbons), there is less competition for females and thus little sexual dimorphism. In primate species where a single male competes for multiple females (such as gorillas), there is substantial competition among males to hold the dominant position and thus great sexual dimorphism. In primate species where multiple males compete for multiple females (such as chimpanzees), the sexual dimorphism is not as extreme as in single-male groups.

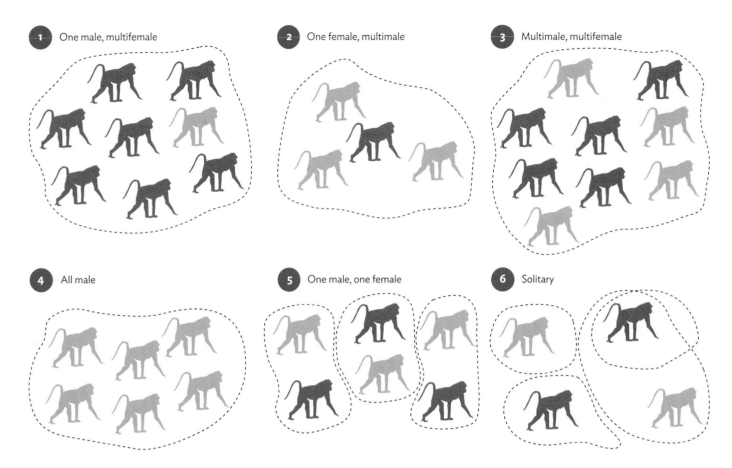

1. One male, multifemale
2. One female, multimale
3. Multimale, multifemale
4. All male
5. One male, one female
6. Solitary

FIGURE 7.2

Primate Residence Patterns Primates exhibit these six social groupings, which in many cases can change. In some species, for example, groups break apart if food is scarce and reunite when food becomes more ample.

polygynous Refers to a social group that includes one adult male, several adult females, and their offspring.

polyandrous Refers to a social group that includes one reproductively active female, several adult males, and their offspring.

monogamous Refers to a social group that includes an adult male, an adult female, and their offspring.

different patterns, and their social groups are strongly influenced by factors such as food availability, environment, and competition. Although it is thus exceedingly difficult to fully understand primate social behavior, primatologists have identified six main types of primate residence patterns (**Figure 7.2**):

1. *One male, multifemale*. This haremlike organization consists of one reproductive-age male, several mature females, and the immature offspring. The society is **polygynous,** meaning that the one male has more than one partner. Gorillas, orangutans, some howler monkeys, some langurs, and some Old World monkeys, such as gelada baboons, practice this social system.

2. *One female, multimale*. This group consists of one reproductive-age female, several mature males, and the immature offspring. The society is **polyandrous,** meaning that the one female mates with nonpolygynous males. The males often cooperate with the females in parenting activities. Only some New World monkeys practice this social system, and only rarely.

3. *Multimale, multifemale*. This group consists of many adults, male and female, and the offspring. Both sexes mate promiscuously. Competition for mates tends to be relatively low, especially among males. Many Old World monkeys, a few New World monkeys, and chimpanzees fit in this category.

4. *All male*. In some species, such as baboons, males form at least temporary groups, typically before joining or forming groups that include males and females. All-male groups commonly exist together with multimale, multifemale groups.

5. *One male, one female*. This group consists of an adult male, an adult female, and their immature offspring. Mating is typically **monogamous,** so each partner's

reproductive success is tied to that of the other, and the male invests a relatively large amount of time and energy in the young (for example, through protection and food acquisition). Gibbons, siamangs, two ceboids (owl monkeys and titi monkeys), and several species of strepsirhines practice this form of society.

6. *Solitary.* Solitary primates go it alone—rarely are these individuals seen with others. Interaction between adult males and adult females occurs only for sexual activity. Only orangutans and a few strepsirhines are solitary. An orangutan male has greater reproductive success if he maintains a territory with areas traversed by two or more females. Orangutan sexual dimorphism is predictably quite high—adult males are twice the size of adult females and have large canines, large cheek pads, and very loud calls over long distances. Males that have been relatively unsuccessful at competing for access to females tend to be more solitary than more successful males.

These categories of primate residence patterns capture only some of the variation primatologists have identified in social interactions. There is considerably more now understood about social behaviors that develop within individual primate taxa, reflecting the remarkable complexity of primate social interactions, even when comparing closely related taxa. For example, primatologists Amy Parish and Frans de Waal have documented key differences in social interactions among chimpanzees (*Pan troglodytes*) and bonobos (*Pan paniscus*). Whereas chimpanzee societies are male dominated, bonobo societies are largely female dominated. In the former, males regularly form bonds, whereas in the latter, female–female social bonds are far more commonplace. In addition, female–female sexual interactions occur regularly in bonobos, far more so than in chimpanzees.

Primate Reproductive Strategies: Males' Differ from Females'

Because reproduction makes very different demands on males and females in terms of energy expenditure and time investment, each sex has a different set of reproductive strategies and interests. As discussed earlier, with few exceptions the primary strategy of males is to physically compete for access to reproductively mature females, resulting in a strong degree of natural selection in males for both large bodies and large canines. This form of natural selection is called **sexual selection.** Another male strategy is **infanticide,** the killing of a nursing infant, primarily by a foreign male that has driven the single male out of a one-male, multifemale group. The American primatologist Sarah Blaffer Hrdy has hypothesized that the new male kills the nursing infant so that its mother stops lactating, resumes ovulation, and becomes sexually receptive to him. As a result, the new male enhances his reproductive fitness, largely at the expense of the previous male.

Whereas males compete with each other for mates, females compete with each other for resources that enable them to care for young. In various New World and Old World monkeys, including macaques and some baboons, the competition for resources happens within the context of stable dominance hierarchies. **Dominance** is key to how a primate acquires resources and access to mates. Specifically, a dominance hierarchy represents how individuals in a primate society are ranked relative to one another. For males, the alpha or most dominant male has successfully defeated all other males in a series of aggressive encounters. The second-rank male is in second rank because he has defeated all but the dominant male, and so on down the line to the least-dominant male, who has defeated no other male in an aggressive encounter. For females, hierarchical ranks usually pass from mother to daughter, and younger sisters usually rank higher than older sisters. The younger sister is protected more by the mother than

sexual selection The frequency of traits that change due to those traits' attractiveness to members of the opposite sex.

infanticide The killing of a juvenile.

dominance The ability to intimidate or defeat another individual in a pairwise or dyadic encounter.

Male and Female Reproductive Strategies

Reproductive strategies differ in male and female primates. Males compete for mates, but females both compete for resources and invest time and energy in the care of offspring.

Sex	Reproductive Strategy and Outcome
Males	*Behavior:* Physical competition for access to females
	Outcome: Selection for large body size and for large canines; selection for loud vocalization ability in some territorial primates
	Behavior: Sometime killing of nursing young (infanticide)
	Outcome: Suppressed lactation, resumption of ovulation, and receptiveness to new male partner
Females	*Behavior:* Acquisition of resources for raising young, usually in competition with other females
	Outcome: Higher-ranked females provide more resources than low-ranked females do

the older sister, therefore giving the younger sister a higher rank. The mother maintains her rank above all of them, except when the juvenile offspring become adults. In general, though, the higher the rank in primate societies, the greater the ability to acquire important resources, such as food. Higher-ranked females also tend to have more offspring, such as in gelada baboons in East Africa (**Figure 7.3**). In some primates, higher-ranked females have a greater number of offspring because they begin mating and producing offspring months before lower-ranked females. For example, dominant yellow baboons in Kenya start reproducing some 200 days before lower-ranked ones.

Primatologists have observed that some female primates are relatively more selective in choosing mates than are others, making the selection on the basis of characteristics such as disposition, physical appearance, and position in social hierarchy. Some adult females' social behaviors encourage support for and investment in their offspring by other members of the group. And some adult females protect their infants from aggression, as when they attempt to prevent infanticide.

The Other Side of Competition: Cooperation in Primates

Although competition and dominance are central to primate social behavior, primates are also highly cooperative social animals. About half the size of gorillas and not very dimorphic sexually, chimpanzees hunt in groups of cooperating males, often preying on juvenile monkeys such as red colobus. Chimpanzees also share food after a hunt. In the bonobo community, in contrast, it is the females that are highly cooperative among one another; males are far less so. Some primates issue warning calls to their social group when predators approach. Many primates also groom one another (**Figure 7.4**). In nonhuman primates, grooming involves one individual picking through the skin and

(a)

(b)

FIGURE 7.3

Grooming Among many primates, including (a) chimpanzees and (b) humans, grooming is one of the most important social bonding behaviors. While helping ensure proper hygiene and good health, it can also cement social bonds between individuals, resolve conflicts, and reinforce social structures or family links.

hair of another individual, removing insects or other foreign objects, sometimes eating these materials. Among this practice's functions are bonding two members of a social group, calming the primate being groomed, or appeasing that primate if he or she has a higher position in a dominance hierarchy.

Some cooperative behaviors are **altruistic,** in that they appear to reduce the reproductive fitness of the individuals performing them but enhance the recipients' reproductive fitness. For example, adult baboons might give warning calls to their social group or even attack predators and, in doing so, place themselves in jeopardy. Grooming, food sharing, and caregiving are also altruistic because one primate invests time and effort in another.

Why should a primate engage in altruistic behavior? Altruism seems not to be directed haphazardly but rather is directed primarily at relatives. According to the British evolutionary theorist William Hamilton's hypothesis of **kin selection,** the evolutionary benefits of an altruistic behavior to the kin group outweigh costs to the individual acting altruistically. A primate will most strongly and consistently act altruistically when living with relatives. This is particularly true among cercopithecoids, such as baboons and macaques, where females live mostly in the natal group, or in chimpanzees, where males live in the natal group. Wrangham has observed groups of cooperating related male chimpanzees attacking groups of male chimps unrelated to them. He has also observed groups of cooperating male chimps patrolling territorial boundaries. Such behaviors in living chimpanzees may be the best model for early hominin behavior and for the origins of human aggression.

Cooperation has many advantages, but it ultimately provides most primate taxa with their distinctive behavioral characteristic: primates live in social groups. And the primary reason for sociality is probably that while many primates are proficient predators, they are also preyed upon by a range of predators. The American primatologist Susanne Shultz and her associates suggest that the earliest primates were largely nocturnal and led a solitary existence. This understanding is suggested by the fossil record (see chapter 8) and by the fact that the nocturnal primates today are also the most primitive (many of the strepsirhines). As soon as primates began a diurnal

altruistic Refers to a behavior that benefits others while being a disadvantage to the individual.

kin selection Altruistic behaviors that increase the donor's inclusive fitness; that is, the fitness of the donor's relatives.

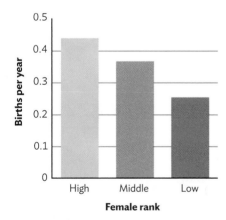

FIGURE 7.4

Female Dominance Hierarchy This graph compares the birthrates among high-, middle-, and low-ranked adult female gelada baboons. The higher the rank, the greater a female's access to resources and the more offspring she will bear.

CHIMPANZEE

A MODEL FOR ORIGINS OF HUMAN HUNTING

Humans are not the only primate cognitively sophisticated enough to undertake hunting. Research done separately by the primatologists Jane Goodall, Thomas Struhsaker, Craig Stanford, and Richard Wrangham has shown that chimpanzees skillfully and efficiently plan hunts as a means of acquiring meat for food.

Through her fieldwork in the early 1960s, Goodall had discovered that chimpanzees eat meat, disproving the popular belief that chimps, like their close cousins the gorillas, are strict vegetarians. Decades later, primatologists have concluded that meat is a regular and important part of chimpanzees' diet and that the red colobus monkey is the chimps' favored prey. Indeed, Struhsaker has documented a 90% decline in the red colobus population in the Kibale National Park, Uganda, owing to chimpanzee predation.

At Gombe National Park in Tanzania, Stanford and his colleagues have spent years tracking and watching chimpanzees. Their research has shown that when animal meat is low in supply, such as during the dry season, the chimps undergo significant weight loss. Hunting and meat eating, therefore, have a nutritional basis in these primates, for whom meat is a source of energy. Stanford and his team note that chimpanzees, like humans, tend to hunt in groups of males—upward of 35 males in some chimpanzee groups. For solitary chimps, the success rate for capturing monkeys is about 33%. When 10 or more chimps hunt together, the success rate is nearly 100%. The hunters share the meat with nonhunting females, and males most likely use access to meat as a means of gaining access to females. The number of males hunting at any particular time is directly proportional to the number of fertile females.

Because chimpanzees are humans' closest living relative, the chimps' hunting behavior may approximate early hominins' social behavior (early hominins are the subject of chapter 10).

Chimpanzees are omnivorous, consuming a wide variety of foods, including meat from various mammals. They appear to prefer and have the most success catching red colobus monkeys, particularly juveniles.

PREDATORS

The earliest hominins lived in forests, but the fossil record is not yet complete enough to say if they hunted red colobus monkeys (fossils are the subject of chapter 8).

Wrangham's field studies have shown that chimpanzee coalitions undertake war raids, going into neighboring territory to identify and then kill or brutally wound adult victims in other communities. Explanations for such behavior are complex, but Wrangham argues that aggressiveness is selected for in chimpanzees (and humans) to increase the group's dominance. Wrangham believes the case can be made that the common ancestor of chimpanzees and humans was violent and that violence seen in human males today is part of what defines us as a species.

However, the evidence of injuries deriving from violence emerges relatively late in hominin evolution. Evidence for trauma due to interpersonal aggression began to appear in hominin cranial fossils that mostly post-date 500,000 yBP. Moreover, the first clear evidence of warfare involving multiple aggressors and multiple deaths did not occur until after 10,000 years ago, a time of major population increase and when humans began living in sedentary communities (see *Anthropology Matters: First Warfare: The Massacre at Kilianstädten* in Chapter 13). It is quite possible that the aggressive behavior seen in all manner of primates, including humans, could have arisen independently in multiple taxa. However, as the work by Wrangham shows, the pattern of chimpanzee aggression is similar in some key respects to human aggression, suggesting an underlying evolutionary context for human behavior today.

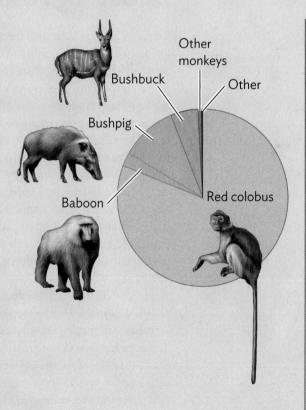

Bushbuck

Other monkeys

Other

Bushpig

Baboon

Red colobus

Also on the chimps' diet are other primates, such as baboons, and nonprimates, such as bushpigs and bushbucks.

lifestyle, they became subject to increased predation, which in turn placed an adaptive advantage on cooperative behavior and group living. Under circumstances of increased predation, primates' joining together to defend themselves from predators would seem to be an important form of cooperative behavior. While primatologists have observed the kinds of warning calls and direct physical defenses described above, however, the evidence of primates' protecting each other from predators is slim. It is difficult to directly observe predation, for example, because predators tend to be afraid of humans and they avoid primate groups being studied.

Many primates are preyed upon by large birds, such as eagles. Susanne Shultz and the American primatologist Scott McGraw have studied eagles' nests because the remains left in them—representative samples of "meals"—provide proxy information about what the eagles hunt and how often (**Figure 7.5**). The results show that predation rates are lower among larger primate groups than among smaller primate groups. Predation is a very strong selective pressure, and mutual cooperation—sociality—has been favored among primates because of the protection it provides. Sociality also provides access to mates, but the predation-related advantage of cooperation within a society is the underlying explanation for primates' living in social groups.

7.2 Getting Food

Primates acquire their food through a wide variety of foraging practices, which entail looking for food, then handling and processing the food for consumption. The American physical anthropologist Karen Strier estimates that on average, foraging can take up more than 50% of a primate's waking time. This burden is especially great on mothers. Not only do mothers need to eat food that will provide the energy for gestation and lactation, but they also need to look for food and then handle and process it for their young to consume. In a few primate species, the father is involved in caring for and providing food for the young, but generally the mother is the sole provider of her offspring's food. The American primatologist P. C. Lee estimates that in adult female primates, a mother's energy requirements are between two and five times higher than a nonmother's. For the female primate, success in caring for young, both before and after their birth, is very much tied to adequate nutrition. Females with good nutrition have young at an earlier age, have healthier young, experience shorter intervals between births, and live longer than those with suboptimal nutrition.

Three key factors contribute to a primate's success at feeding: quality, distribution, and availability of food. *Quality* refers to foods providing energy and protein that are readily digestible. Mature leaves and mature grasses, for example, are of relatively little value to many primates because the cellulose and dietary fiber are much harder to digest for nutrients than are the cellulose and dietary fiber of young leaves and young grasses. As discussed in chapter 6, sharp-crested teeth and compartmentalized stomachs have evolved in some primates, especially in leaf-eating monkeys. For example, folivorous Old World monkeys have sharp crests connecting the cusps on the fronts and backs of the occlusal surfaces of their bilophodont molars.

Distribution refers to the locations of food across the landscape. Ideally, the primate would have to expend relatively little energy to acquire food. In terms of evolution, behaviors that minimize the costs of acquiring food are selected for. Many primates focus on patches of food, such as a fruit-bearing tree or a group of such trees, whose fruit provides a ready and concentrated source of nutrients. However, a small patch will support only a relatively small group. All primates are able to adjust the size of the feeding group in relation to the amount of food available in a patch. Food *availability* can be highly fluid, depending on season and rainfall. The farther a region is from the equator, the more defined are its seasons and the less available are fruit and leaves, primates' main food sources. Thus, primates are generally restricted to equatorial regions.

Chimpanzees are enormously flexible in their ability to access preferred foods. Primatologist Karline Janmaat and colleagues have documented acquisition patterns of these ripe-fruit specialists in the Taï Forest, Ivory Coast (see Figure 7.5, p. 218). In this setting, chimpanzees strategically locate their nesting sites, increasing the likelihood that they will encounter trees bearing the best and most ripe fruit. Janmaat's study reveals that chimpanzees possess a mental map of food landscapes and display a strong sense of *where* the fruit-bearing trees are located and *when* the fruit will be ripe. In the group of chimpanzees they studied, a number of individuals built their evening nests directly on the route to a fruit-bearing tree. Moreover, these chimpanzees tended to rise earlier in the morning and increase their travel speed. Importantly, knowledge of the food landscape and planning gave these chimpanzees a competitive edge for acquiring the fruit, well ahead of other animals interested in the same foods. These findings make clear that chimpanzees in this setting apply their intelligence to acquiring food in a highly competitive landscape of the rainforest of West Africa. Moreover, there is increasing evidence to indicate that the memory of locations of fruit-bearing trees spans a period of years. The success of acquiring food is not limited to hearing, vision, or smell. Rather, it is a behavior that emphasizes memory over the long term.

7.3 Acquiring Resources and Transmitting Knowledge: Got Culture?

Primates and humans acquire food in vastly different ways. While primates can acquire food using only their bodies, humans depend on technology—material culture—to acquire food. But this distinction does not mean that primates have no material culture.

In the 1960s, Jane Goodall became the first to question that assumption when she observed adult chimps poking twigs into a termite hill, withdrawing them, and eating the termites that clung to the twigs (**Figure 7.6**). Goodall realized that one fundamental assumption about what it means to be human—namely, that material culture (and culture in general) is exclusive to human beings—seemed incorrect. Other scientists then realized that living chimpanzees' tool use may be the best model for understanding our prehuman ancestors' earliest cultures (among the topics of chapter 10).

Based on Goodall's research and a great deal of work since, anthropologists have identified three central features about chimpanzees' tool use. First, chimpanzees are extraordinarily intelligent and have the complex cognitive skills necessary for at least some kinds of behaviors that require learning and the ability to understand complex symbolization. The evidence for this ability is impressive, and it is growing. For example, chimpanzees are able to accomplish a number of complex behaviors for which visual acumen and ability to think abstractly are essential elements. In laboratory or otherwise controlled settings, humans have taught young chimpanzees to crack open nuts with stones. In turn, these chimpanzees

FIGURE 7.6

Chimpanzee Tool Use When "fishing" for termites (which are highly nutritious), a chimpanzee selects a branch or twig thin enough to pass through the holes of a termite nest, then removes all extra branches and leaves and inserts the twig into the nest. Simple and disposable, even primitive, tools like this might have been used by our ancestors long before the appearance of stone tools some 3.3 mya.

Primate Predation in the Taï Forest

Crowned Eagle Found throughout Africa south of the Sahara Desert, the crowned eagle (*Stephanoaetus corontus*) is among the most successful raptors in the world. This carnivore preys on a range of animals, including primates.

1 RAPTORS

Eagles, hawks, buzzards, falcons, and owls are predators known collectively as raptors, or birds of prey. Anthropologists, field ecologists, and other scientists have long been skeptical that primates could be preyed upon by these predators, owing to doubts about the birds being able to lift something as heavy as some primates off the ground. Extensive field studies have revealed, however, that small primates worldwide—indeed, most primates—are routinely and efficiently killed by raptors.

Some of our best understanding of primate predation is derived from the study of primate skeletal remains recovered from eagle nests, most of which are enormous. Study of the contents of these nests in the Taï Forest, Ivory Coast (see Figure 6.2, p. 170–171), provides important insight into not only what African crowned eagles hunt but also the manner in which the primates are killed and processed for food. In this setting, scientists have studied more than 1,200 bones from nests, representing about 35 species routinely preyed upon in this corner of West Africa. Some of these prey species weigh upwards of three to four times the size of the eagle predators. Anthropologists' study of the primate remains—sometimes numbering in the hundreds of bones—provides a remarkably complete story of predator–prey interactions.

2 PRIMATES

Which primates are the crowned eagles preying upon? Despite the fast movement and well-developed vocalized warnings of the Diana monkey and the inconspicuous nature of the Campbell's guenon, both species commonly fall victim to crowned eagle predation. Sooty mangabeys (*Cercocebus atys*), the largest cercopithecoid monkeys in the Taï Forest, are among the most common victims. Prior to her study, Susanne Shultz predicted that the sooty mangabeys' large body size and group-oriented social structure limited predation by even these highly aggressive birds. Her study revealed instead that raptors are fully able to prey upon primates weighing more than 11 kg (24.25 lb) and living in large groups. (The upper limit appears to be about 13 kg [29 lb]).

Campbell's Guenon The Campbell's guenon (*Cercopithecus campbelli*) has a distinctive yellow band across the brow and blue shading around the eyes. It is among the most common monkeys in West Africa. Although adapted to the shelter of the dark understory of the Taï Forest, the Campbell's guenon is choice prey for crowned eagles.

Diana Monkey The Diana monkey (*Ceropithecus diana*) is one of the most active monkeys in the Taï Forest. Diana monkeys have a highly visible black face framed by a striking white beard. They are noisy, fast moving, and on high alert for predators. Through their vocalized early detection of predators, they provide an important warning system to other primates in the vicinity.

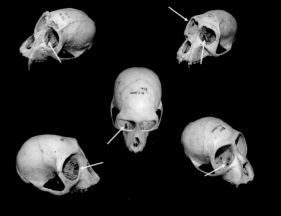

The study of these primate bones also shows that the eagles have a clear pattern of processing their prey. They first disable the primates by powerfully thrusting their sharp talons and beaks. The eagles then dismember their victims on the ground. They place portions of the flesh in nearby trees. Via forays from these cache sites, the eagles carry food to the nest for consumption by young eagles. The dismemberment of the prey's carcass explains why there are no complete skeletons of prey found in the nests or on the ground below the nests. It also means that transport of parts does not require the thrust to lift even the largest of the primates. These findings have important implications for the predation of primates generally, including ancient hominins. We now know that raptors prey on primates. This finding means that primate social behavior and social organization are almost certainly influenced by the behavior of birds of prey—and likewise were influenced in the distant past.

have taught other young chimpanzees to crack open nuts. Chimpanzees have also been shown how to use a sharp stone tool to cut a cord in order to gain access to food in a box. Similarly, they have been shown how to make simple stone tools, and they subsequently have passed on that behavior to relatives.

Second, in natural settings where chimpanzees have not been taught by humans, mothers have also shown their young how to use tools (**Figure 7.7**). Most of the tools chimpanzees produce are for acquiring and consuming food. Among the rare examples of primate tool use unrelated to food is that of chimpanzees in Gombe throwing stones as part of a dominance conflict between adult males. One of chimps' most fascinating food-based innovations, observed by the American primatologist Jill Pruetz, is the creation and use of a spearlike object—a trimmed, pointed twig—to skewer strepsirhines for food (**Figure 7.8**).

Third, tool production and tool use are sometimes highly localized. For example, although some adjacent chimpanzee groups in West Africa use stones to crack open hard-shelled nuts, this tool use has not been seen anywhere else in Africa.

While chimpanzees do not depend on material culture for survival—certainly not to the extent of living humans—they nonetheless use material culture. Laboratory experiments and natural-setting research from a range of places in Africa show that chimpanzees use several forms of tools and that not all forms occur in all chimpanzee groups. Perhaps local traditions are passed from generation to generation via social learning—parents pass the information to offspring, and the young share it with other young. In a very real sense, then, tool use in primates is an important form of social and cultural transmission. Moreover, the widespread nature of chimpanzee tool use suggests that it dates back to antiquity. Sites in Ivory Coast, West Africa, contain chimpanzee tools from 4,000 to 5,000 yBP, but tool use likely started earlier than that.

FIGURE 7.7

Chimpanzee Social Learning A chimpanzee juvenile watches its mother crack open palm nuts with a stone hammer and anvil in Guinea, West Africa.

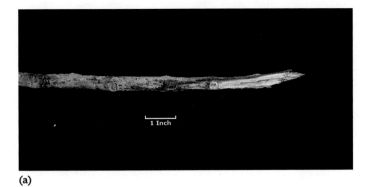

(a)

FIGURE 7.8

Chimpanzee Spears **(a)** A chimpanzee made this spear from a tree branch, sharpening one end with its teeth. **(b)** Chimpanzees who make such spears use them to thrust into the hollows of trees and kill bushbabies. Here, an adolescent female holds a dead bushbaby. This method is primates' first use of tools to hunt other mammals.

(b)

What about other primates? Field observations by the Swiss anthropologist Carel van Schaik and his associates show that, like chimpanzees, orangutans in Borneo and Sumatra habitually use probes to obtain insects for food. Across the Atlantic in South America, psychologist Dorothy Fragaszy and her research team have documented how some capuchin (*Cebus*) monkeys use stones to dig for food and to crack open nuts. The complexity here is far less than that of human technology, but these simple behaviors show that chimpanzees are not the only primates that interact with the environment through tools they make.

7.4 Vocal and Nonvocal Communication Is Fundamental Behavior in Primate Societies

All primates communicate vocally and nonvocally, behaviors that serve various functions. Some quiet vocal calls can be heard only by nearby group members, while some loud calls convey information over great distances and through dense vegetation. Scientists once believed that primate vocalizations were merely innate, emotional utterances produced involuntarily in response to stimuli. Therefore, these vocalizations could tell us nothing about the evolution of human language. Research has shown, however, that these vocal systems are actually rich and complex and largely under the callers' control. The study of primate vocal communication can give us insights into the selective pressures that may have shaped the evolution of language.

Translating Primate Communication: It's About the Context

To "translate" primates' calls, scientists first catalog a population's vocal repertoire. They then determine the contexts in which the members of that population produce the different vocalizations. Primate voices vary just as human voices do, but individuals in groups produce similar calls in categories.

ETHNOPRIMATOLOGY

Understanding Human-Nonhuman Primate Co-Adaptation and Conservation in Indonesia

Much of the record of primate conservation focuses on human impacts, especially on how these impacts are detrimental to primates. Mitigating the role that humans play in primate population decline is of course of fundamental importance.

WATCH THE VIDEO

www.digital.
wwnorton.com/
ourorigins4

On the other hand, it is becoming increasingly clear that a greater focus on the human and primate sympatric relationships—humans and primates coexisting in one place and in one time—is an essential element of conservation of primates. Anthropological primatologists are especially well equipped through their role as social scientists to recognize that conservation is designed by people, making it a social phenomenon involving the study of ecology, diet, and behavior of both humans *and* primates. American primatologists Erin Riley and Agustín Fuentes utilize the *ethnoprimatological* approach—the study of human and primate interactions ecologically and culturally—in order to develop a more informed approach to conservation.

There are many places in the world where humans and primates interact on a regular basis. Among these are various localities in Indonesia, where an enormous diversity of forest habitats supports both humans and primates. It is in this kind of setting where some of the most sought after trees in East Asia are routinely logged, producing a considerable part of Indonesia's economy. Moreover, the natural setting is being chipped away as agriculture is ramped up to feed Indonesia's rapidly increasing population. Indeed, Indonesia now ranks as the *fourth* highest population in the

world. It is also in this setting where there are more primates than anywhere in Asia, including at least 45 species representing five families—Lorisidae, Tarsiidae, Cercopithecidae, Hylobatidae, and Pongidae.

The Indonesian islands of Bali and Sulawesi present an excellent case in point on the very close interactions between humans and primates. Both of the island habitats generate a fundamental question having broad application: *How can we humans sustain this remarkable diversity of primates in such crowded (and increasingly so!) spaces involving overlapping use of food and other resources?* This is a critical question as we contemplate the future of natural settings and their occupants in the twenty-first century. Simply, primates will ultimately be lost unless a conservation solution can developed and applied to this growing crisis.

Riley and Fuentes utilized the ethnoprimatological approach to examine the conservation implications of the human-primate interface for the people and the primate taxa living on these islands today. The Bali macaques (*Macaca fascicularis*) live just about everywhere on Bali. Like many other primate taxa, these monkeys are highly adaptable, living in a diverse range of habitats, including coastal forests patches, dry scrubs, rainforests, temple and shrine localities, beaches, and even in the caldera of an active volcano. Temple and shrine settings are particularly beneficial to the Bali macaques because these sites are the central points where local people provide them with food. Owing to these provisioning practices, in part reflecting the local folklore emphasizing protection of primates, humans have artificially contributed to the growth of the local Bali macaque population. But, this is not necessarily a good thing for the Bali macaques. For example, it is highly likely that human influence on population growth of these primates has enhanced their exposure to intestinal parasites. This and other anthropogenic factors have a strong influence on the overall ecology of these primates. And just as Bali macaque behavior, ecology, and population size are influenced by humans, human behavior is influenced by the presence of monkeys in everyday life, and in some instances, livelihood. Indeed, the local tourist industry is at least in part dependent on the wellbeing of these monkeys.

Like Bali, Sulawesi is the locus of acceleration in the interactions between humans and primates, owing to increased logging, the development of cash crop agricultural economy, and the rapidly growing human population. In Central Sulawesi, Riley has been studying the interactions between humans and the Tonkean macaque (*Macaca tonkeana*), a cercopithecoid taxon protected in the Lore Lindu National Park. The park is also the home for indigenous humans—the Lindu—who are allowed by the Indonesian government to stay in the forest in order to maintain and harvest rice as well as engage in small-scale forest production and commercial tilapia fishing. The region is threatened by deforestation as cultivation of cash crops, such as cacao, intrudes along the forest margin. Thus, in contrast to Bali where the interface between primates and humans occurs in temples and religious sites, on the island of Sulawesi, the interface occurs where the forest and farm meets. But similar to Bali, there is a long-existing human-macaque folklore. The Lindu

people view Tonkean macaques as protectors of the local traditional law (*adat*). Their belief has translated into a taboo against any form of harm towards the Tonkean macaques in their shared space on the island. Owing to the respect Lindu have for the macaques, there is strong support for their primate neighbors.

In both Bali and Sulawesi, the positive synergy between humans and primates does not come without a cost. In both settings, primates routinely raid crops. However, the tolerance of the behavior remains high in both settings despite the destructive outcomes. The record for the Bali and Sulawesi macaque-human interactions demonstrates a social, cultural, and ecological context that must be understood in order to develop a best-practice for conservation of primates. To not understand the context is to not be in a position to develop strategies for protection and sustainability of primate health, wellbeing, and population size. Key in the ethnoprimatological approach is an understanding of the dynamic interconnections between humans and primates. This approach has broad meaning for the changing world today, especially in light of the fact that primates and their habitats are increasingly dominated by humans, in Indonesia and many other settings of the world. Although the contexts are different across the globe, development of conservation practices will be best served by understanding the social, ecological, and behavioral circumstances of both the humans and primates. We are all in this together. *Anthropology matters!*

Using an ethnoprimatological approach, Erin Riley (bottom) and Agustín Fuentes study the ecological and cultural interactions between humans and primates to better conserve populations of Bali macaques (top) and Tonkean macaques (center) in Indonesia.

FIGURE 7.9

Recording Alarm Calls Dawn Kitchen records chacma baboon alarm calls in Botswana. The lion prompting these calls is lying in the grass, about 75 m (250 ft) behind Kitchen.

Determining the context of a given call does not unequivocally prove that call's function. The use of playback experiments has revolutionized what scientists can say about a call's meaning, albeit only from the listener's perspective. In conducting such an experiment, the researchers record naturally occurring calls (**Figure 7.9**). They then use hidden speakers to broadcast call sequences to the primate group. In a classic example, the American primatologists Dorothy Cheney and Robert Seyfarth played the sound of an infant vervet monkey screaming to a group of mothers whose infants had all wandered off. Only the mother of that particular infant looked toward the hidden speaker, a finding that suggests females recognize the voices of their own infants. To Cheney and Seyfarth's surprise, however, the other females looked at the mother of the screaming infant. This finding gave the researchers insight into what primates "know" about each other. Their study laid the groundwork for a field of research in which scientists use carefully designed playback experiments to "interview" free-ranging primates about their social cognitive abilities.

In this way, researchers have determined that some quiet calls produced by primates mediate social encounters within a group. For example, Cheney, Seyfarth, and their colleagues, in studying chacma baboons in Botswana, found that a subordinate baboon was less likely to move away from a dominant animal if the dominant quietly "grunted" as it approached the subordinate. Conversely, if the dominant animal did not grunt, the subordinate would almost always move off. If the approaching dominant produced a "threat-grunt," a version of the call that indicates aggressive intent, the listener would likely flee rapidly.

Predator Alarms: In Defense of the Primate Society

Unlike quiet calls exchanged between nearby animals, the loudest calls in a primate species' repertoire transmit information over long distances and are typically produced during events such as an encounter with predators, an aggressive contest with another group, and one animal's separation from its group. In howler monkey societies, for example, adult males in different groups compete through their long, loud calls, warning potential competitors to stay off their turf. (Once you hear one of these bizarre calls, you understand why they are called "howlers.") The American primatologist Dawn Kitchen documented extremely loud choruses by male black howler monkeys in Belize. She found that the voices of individual callers within a group do not completely overlap during a chorus; thus, it is possible for listeners in another group to "count" the number of rivals they will face based on vocal cues alone. Howlers can assess the strength of opposing groups according to these criteria. Using playback experiments, Kitchen found that howler groups that thought they were outnumbered by invaders retreated, whereas groups that thought they outnumbered intruders not only vocalized in return but also advanced on the simulated rivals (**Figure 7.10**). Likewise, Kitchen found that during aggressive male–male competition in chacma baboons, the loud, repetitive call displays ("wahoos") produced by adult males reliably indicated the caller's physical condition. By judging each other's calls, rival baboons can assess an opponent's fighting ability and avoid a contest with a superior opponent.

Although primate vocalizations (such as the screams of an attack victim) can indicate a caller's emotional state, many also seem to convey information about the world around the caller. In the Taï Forest of the Ivory Coast, (see Figure 6.2), Diana monkeys produce two different loud alarm calls in response to predators, depending on whether

(a)   (b)

FIGURE 7.10

Primate Vocalizations **(a)** Male howler monkeys, such as the one in action here, are among the male primates that vocalize to protect their territories, their resources, and/or their females. Despite the name, howler monkeys roar more than howl, and their notorious calls can be heard over great distances. Howler monkeys are the loudest land animal and the second loudest of all animals, outdone only by the blue whale. **(b)** This chimpanzee is presenting a series of whoops, perhaps characterizing a food source. Chimpanzee vocalizations are diverse and difficult to interpret.

the predator is terrestrial (such as a leopard) or aerial (such as an eagle). Importantly, each type of predator requires a very different escape response from the Diana monkey. Using playback experiments, the Swiss primatologist Klaus Zuberbühler and his team found that listeners treat all sounds in the forest associated with one type of predator the same. For example, a leopard's growl produces the same response as the leopard alarm call of a male Diana monkey, despite the acoustic differences between these sounds. These and other experimental results suggest that primate calls can be functionally referential. That is, these calls convey semantic-like meaning, which makes them similar to human words, at least from the listener's perspective.

The variation in predator-specific vocalizations indicates that Diana monkeys have evolved an ability to modify their vocalizations and behavior based on the type of predator and the predator's attack strategy. For example, Diana monkeys issue loud alarm calls when they are confronted by "ambush" predators such as leopards or eagles, both of which are especially efficient hunters when they are able to surprise their prey. When "pursuit" predators such as chimpanzees or humans are also nearby, however, the Diana monkeys' loud alarm calls enable the predators to locate the monkeys. Zuberbühler found that Diana monkeys with a lot of exposure to chimpanzees respond more appropriately to playbacks of chimpanzee vocalizations—remaining silent and quietly moving away—than did monkeys with little chimpanzee experience. This finding strongly suggests that the perception of and response to certain vocalizations is learned.

Chimpanzee Vocalization: Labeling the World Around Them

Like monkeys, chimpanzees can label events and objects. They and many other primates have displayed food-associated vocalizations. In controlled laboratory studies of chimpanzees, Zuberbühler and his colleague Katie Slocombe found that chimpanzees express a specific kind of "rough grunt" when they see food. This grunt can vary in specific ways, depending on the type of food and how much the chimpanzee wants that food. Interpretations of distinctive sounds made by chimpanzees in field settings are beginning to provide new insights into how these apes communicate, insights going far beyond what can be learned in laboratory settings alone. The English primatologist Cathy Crockford and her associates have been studying chimpanzee communication

FIGURE 7.11

Chimpanzee Communication Research on animal communication with a habituated group of chimpanzees in the Budongo Forest in Uganda.

FIGURE 7.12

Monkey Alarm Calls Campbell's monkeys use specific alarm calls containing prefixes and suffixes.

in the Budongo Forest, Uganda. Their work shows that chimpanzee communication involves different combinations of sounds—grunts, pants, hoots, screams, barks, and other vocalizations—most of which have meaning for the individual that is vocalizing and for the intended audience. The work of Crockford and her colleagues shows that, as with most communication in other primates, understanding chimpanzee communication requires knowledge of both the vocalizations and their contexts. The vocalizations can be studied through recordings, but the contexts must be observed in the primates' natural setting (**Figure 7.11**). The natural environment provides critical clues to the meanings of vocalizations.

Because some calls within a species' repertoire vary so subtly that the human ear cannot easily differentiate them, the analysis of acoustic properties of vocal recordings (such as duration, amplitude, and frequency of a call) is a critical step in translating primate vocalizations. For example, the German scientist Julia Fischer and her colleagues found that female baboons produce two loud calls that are very similar: one when they encounter a predator and another when they are separated from their group. Using specially designed computer software, Fischer found that these two call types grade into each other along an acoustic continuum (in the same way that the words *fire* and *far* seem to overlap when spoken with a southern US accent). Furthermore, these subtle differences were detectable to baboons—adult females hearing the two call types during playback experiments responded strongly only to the alarm calls. These and other experiments suggest that, like humans, primates can perceive acoustically graded calls in discrete ways.

Primatologists are also learning that vocalizations have clear patterns, some of which bear a striking resemblance to the structural elements of human language. Humans change word structure to change meaning. One of the most important examples is what linguists call *affixation,* whereby a small unit is added at either the beginning (prefix) or the end (suffix) of the word stem (the part of the word that is never altered). Exciting new work by Zuberbühler and his group on Campbell's monkeys (**Figure 7.12**), also inhabitants of the Taï Forest, reveals that these primates use a kind of affixation by adding suffixes (similar in some respects to English speakers' changing the present tense of a verb to past tense by adding -*ed*). These researchers recorded a loud "krak" sound produced by adult male Campbell's monkeys that had seen a leopard in the area. Sharing the same forest, Diana monkeys and Campbell's monkeys have learned to respond to one another's alarm calls with their own alarm calls. However, when Campbell's monkeys issue a leopard alarm call in response to the leopard alarm call of Diana monkeys, they affix an "oo" sound to the warning call. This "krak-oo" alarm call indicates that they have heard the initial alarm call from a different primate taxa. These primates' altering of a stem term through the addition of a suffix is a very important discovery because it provides a strong parallel with human word construction. While human language is extremely complex and most of its characteristics are completely different from other animals' (including nonhuman primates') communication, this parallel suggests what the early hominins' first form of speech may have been like.

Humans routinely invent new vocalizations throughout their lives. In contrast, nonhuman primates appear to be basically preprogrammed, producing most of the calls typical of their species shortly after birth. However, as the Diana monkey example above illustrates, primates must still learn to use and to respond to these vocalizations appropriately. For example, vervet monkeys are susceptible to predation by raptors (birds of prey) and are born able to produce predator-specific alarm calls. Cheney and Seyfarth, in systematically recording the developmental changes in vocal usage among vervets living in Kenya, discovered that very young monkeys will produce these alarm calls in response to anything startling that appears in the sky—an actual raptor, a harmless songbird, even a falling leaf. As vervets age, they refine their call production, limiting it first to all raptors and finally, by the time they are adults, to only that subset of raptors large enough to prey on vervets. Likewise, until a vervet is about seven months old, before it reacts to alarm calls with an appropriate predator-escape response, it will look toward an adult or run toward its mother.

Gesturing Is Not Limited to Humans

Not all communication is vocal. Like humans, apes gesture with their hands, limbs, and bodies, and many of these behaviors are learned. Some 20 different gestures have been cataloged in siamangs, for example. Chimpanzees have been found to extensively and flexibly use gestural communication, even developing novel gestures in new situations. The primatologist Bill McGrew and his colleagues, while observing chimpanzees in Mahale National Park, Tanzania, were the first to note an unusual grooming technique, the *hand clasp*. The two participants face one another. Each one holds a hand up over its head and claps the other's hand, forming an *A*-frame, and each uses his or her free hand to pick parasites and other detritus off the other participant (**Figure 7.13**). Although this is the customary way to groom at Mahale, the nearby chimpanzees of Gombe National Park, Tanzania, do not groom in this manner, and these differences are not likely explained by ecological or genetic differences in the two populations. In addition to differences in grooming, chimpanzees show different kinds of vocalizations unique to specific groups and regions. These differences suggest that some vocal features may be transmitted through social learning. Group-specific patterns of grooming, gesturing, and vocalizing are just a sample of the many behaviors identified by primatologists

FIGURE 7.13

Hand Clasp Grooming The distinctive type of grooming depicted here has been observed only in groups of chimpanzees in Tanzania. Here, the paired chimpanzees grasp each other's wrist, while in other groups they grasp each other's hand. Such specific social customs are unique to individual groups of chimpanzees and thus must be learned within each group, a fundamental aspect of culture.

FIGURE 7.14

Chimpanzee Signing Student teacher Joyce Butler shows the famous chimpanzee Nim Chimpsky the American Sign Language sign configuration for "drank," and Nim imitates her.

that represent nonmaterial aspects of primate culture. In the larger picture, the great apes—especially chimpanzees—are the nonhuman primates with the highest degree of flexibility and most extensive use of material and nonmaterial culture.

Nonvocal Communication: Learning Signing

Although great apes lack the physical ability to produce human speech, the findings of several "ape language" research projects indicate that they have some of the rudimentary cognitive abilities necessary to understand human speech. Different groups of scientists have taught orangutan, gorilla, chimpanzee, and bonobo subjects to communicate with humans using either American Sign Language (**Figure 7.14**) or graphical symbols on computerized keyboards (lexigrams). While watching his mother being taught by Sue Savage-Rumbaugh and her colleagues, a captive bonobo named Kanzi spontaneously learned to use lexigrams (this process is in fact similar to the way human children learn to speak). Kanzi remains one of the most successful nonhuman users of such a symbolic communication system. He can understand English at the level of a two-year-old human, and he combines lexigrams in new ways according to a set of rules. The researchers argue that Kanzi's competence reflects an ancient history for a form of proto-grammar. Although such research has its share of critics, the ape language projects will continue to enrich what we know about the cognitive abilities of our closest living relatives, and they may shed light on the behaviors and linguistic abilities of our common ancestor.

This chapter has discussed primates' social behaviors, the methods that primates use for acquiring food, and the growing understanding of the essential role of material culture and nonmaterial culture and communication. All the information presented in this and the previous chapter lays the foundation for understanding the next part of this book, on roughly the past 50 million years of primate and human evolution.

CHAPTER 7 REVIEW

ANSWERING THE BIG QUESTIONS

1. **Why are primates social?**

   - Generally, primates that cooperate in social groups are better able to protect themselves from predators. The larger the group, the better the protection.
   - Living in social groups provides access to mates and enhances reproductive success.

2. **What is special about primate societies and social behavior?**

   - Primate societies range from solitary animals to complex multimale, multifemale groups. Most primates live in some kind of social group and do so on a long-term basis.
   - Male reproductive strategies emphasize competition between males for access to reproductive-age females. Female reproductive strategies emphasize care of young and access to food for mothers and their offspring.

3. **How do primates acquire food?**

   - Primates' wide variety of habitats require them to use a wide variety of food-foraging strategies.
   - Primates rely entirely on their bodies for acquiring and processing food for consumption. Humans rely on material culture to acquire and process food.
   - Some primates have material culture. They have displayed some learned behavior and cultural tradition, such as forms of social grooming, tool use, and vocalization that are unique to specific groups and regions.

4. **How do primates communicate?**

   - Primates communicate information through a wide variety of means, especially through vocalization.
   - Vocalizations serve a range of functions and vary in different contexts; they include the transmissions from one individual to another or one group to another.
   - Humans are the only primate to have speech, but use of symbols by apes in experimental contexts provides important insight into their cognitive abilities.

KEY TERMS

altruistic
dominance
habituate
infanticide
kin selection
monogamous
polyandrous
polygynous
sexual selection

STUDY QUIZ

1. **In primates, males and females primarily differ in**

   a. body and canine size.
   b. mode of locomotion.
   c. tool use.
   d. color.

2. **How do male and female primates differ in reproductive strategies?**

   a. Males and females of the same species usually have different residence patterns.
   b. Males compete for mates, while females compete for resources.
   c. Some males are part of dominance hierarchies, but females never are.
   d. Females typically commit infanticide when a new male enters the group.

3. **A primate's feeding success would be increased by**

   a. consuming large quantities of low-quality foods.
   b. living in a geographic region with widely distributed food sources.
   c. consuming a single type of food.
   d. memorizing locations and seasonal availability of food patches.

4. **Which statement is *false* regarding chimpanzee material culture?**

   a. Chimpanzees use tools in the wild.
   b. Chimpanzee tool use in the wild can be highly specific to a group.
   c. Chimpanzees can learn tool use from humans.
   d. Chimpanzees depend on tools to survive.

5. **Which feature of communication is found only in humans?**

   a. different vocalizations that refer to specific events or objects
   b. modifying vocalizations based on life experience
   c. using gestures or symbols
   d. physical ability to produce speech

EVOLUTION REVIEW

PRIMATE SOCIAL ORGANIZATION AND BEHAVIOR

Synopsis In addition to the wide variation of morphological characteristics present within the order Primates (see chapter 6), nonhuman primate species exhibit considerable diversity in social organization and behavior. Different primate species engage in various primary patterns of residence (social groupings), which influence the number of males, females, and juveniles present within the group at any one time. Within a species, males and females might have vastly different reproductive strategies, which can be associated with morphological and behavioral disparities between the two sexes. Primates also engage in cooperation, communication, and cultural behaviors, all of which vary drastically across this taxonomic order. As with their morphological characteristics, the immense diversity of behaviors among living primates has been shaped by the evolutionary histories of different species and continues to be shaped by environmental and social pressures.

Q1. List three ways in which reproductive strategies might differ among male and female primates of the same species. Describe the outcomes, in relation to morphology, behavior, and fitness, of these different reproductive strategies for both males and females.

Q2. Refer to Figure 7.1 and consider the following three primate species: bonobos, owl monkeys, and howler monkeys. Bonobos live in multimale, multifemale groups; owl monkeys in monogamous groups; and howler monkeys in one-male, multifemale (polygynous) groups. Based on their residence patterns, which of these species do you expect is the most sexually dimorphic in terms of body size and canine size, the least sexually dimorphic, and somewhere in between?

Q3. What kinds of advantages, in terms of evolutionary fitness, do cooperative behaviors provide among different species of nonhuman primates? Under what selective pressures would altruism (toward kin and nonkin) be likely to evolve?

Q4. Provide at least three examples (material or nonmaterial) from studies of chimpanzees or other nonhuman primates that fit the definition of *culture* (that is, learned behavior transmitted from individual to individual). Identify those that are likely adaptations that help the primate species survive and any that are more likely differences in behavior occurring between two populations for no apparent (or at least adaptive) reason.

Q5. In the strictest sense, *anthropology* is defined as "the study of humankind." Explain why studies of nonhuman primates are within the scope of physical anthropology. How can studies of nonhuman primate sociality and behavior enhance our understanding of our evolutionary past, and why are they important (and anthropological) in their own right?

ADDITIONAL READINGS

Cheney, D. L. and R. M. Seyfarth. 2007. *Baboon Metaphysics: The Evolution of a Social Mind.* Chicago: University of Chicago Press.

Goodall, J. 1986. *The Chimpanzees of Gombe: Patterns of Behavior.* Cambridge, MA: Harvard University Press.

Hart, D. and R. W. Sussman. 2005. *Man the Hunted: Primates, Predators, and Human Evolution.* Jackson, TN: Westview Press.

McGrew, W. C. 1998. Culture in nonhuman primates. *Annual Review of Anthropology* 27: 301–328.

Peterson, D. 2006. *Jane Goodall: The Woman Who Redefined Man.* New York: Houghton Mifflin.

Stanford, C. B. 2001. *The Hunting Apes.* Princeton, NJ: Princeton University Press.

Strier, K. B. 2011. *Primate Behavioral Ecology,* 4th ed. New York: Routledge, Taylor & Francis.

Visalberghi, E., Haslam, M., Spagnoletti, N., Fragaszy, D. (2013). Use of stone hammer tools and anvils by bearded capuchin monkeys over time and space: Construction of an archaeological record of tool use. *Journal of Archaeological Science,* 40, 8, 3222–3232.

Wrangham, R. and D. Peterson. 1996. *Demonic Males: Apes and the Origins of Human Violence.* New York: Houghton Mifflin.Pearson/ Prentice Hall.

PART II

THE PAST

Evidence for the Present

Living organisms have resulted from millions of years of both natural selection and other evolutionary forces. This living record has provided natural historians and biologists, Charles Darwin first and foremost, with important information about how evolution works and what forces are behind it. Fundamental as it is, however, the living record provides a limited picture of evolution, a record of just the *surviving* lineages. The other fundamental part of the evolutionary picture is found in the past, thanks to the fossil record, which portrays the lineages and extinct species that gave rise to living species. The focus of the remainder of this book—the fossil record—is the basis for documenting and interpreting biological history. Because fossils are the only source of evidence for what past organisms were like, where they lived, and how they behaved, living *and* past records are essential for understanding evolution—one is incomplete without the other.

Part II begins with a look at what fossils are and how they can be interpreted. Once this window onto the past has been opened, we will explore the diversity and abundance of primate species, starting with the first true primates (strepsirhines), followed by the origins and evolution of the first higher primates (haplorhines); then the appearance, evolution, and diversity of the first apes (hominoids); and, beginning around 6–7 mya, the origins and evolution of primitive, humanlike ancestors (hominins).

The past record of evolution comes from fossils. This record shows us what ancestral species looked like. For example, a 6-million-year sequence of fossils from the Middle Awash River valley in Ethiopia illustrates human evolution from *Ardipithecus*—the first bipeds—who lived 6 mya, to the earliest *Homo sapiens,* who lived more than 100,000 years ago. Just as important, the thousands of fossil remains of plants and animals found in this setting reveal details of the environment and ecology related to this lineage, whose evolution led to all of us now living around the globe. (Photo © 1996 David L. Brill, humanoriginsphotos.com)

The past record of evolution comes from fossils. For example, this 65-million-year old *Tyrannosaurus rex* fossil reveals that enormous carnivorous reptiles once roamed the plains of western North America. The fossil remains of plants and animals found around the world provide details of the environment and ecology of Earth through time, including the conditions that led to the evolution of modern humans.

8

Fossils and Their Place in Time and Nature

BIG QUESTIONS

1. **What are fossils?**

2. **What do fossils tell us about the past?**

3. **What methods do anthropologists and other scientists use to study fossils?**

Although Charles Darwin's theory of evolution was based mostly on his observations of living species, Darwin certainly knew about fossils. His extensive reading must have included the ancient Greek historian Herodotus, who had recognized the shells preserved in rock as the remains of organisms. Darwin was no doubt familiar with discoveries of fossils in the Americas. He even had a hand in prospecting for fossils in Argentina, noting in his journal that "the great size of the bones... is truly wonderful." He likely heard about discoveries in the United States, such as by the American president Thomas Jefferson (1743–1826), an avid fossil collector who reported on an extinct ground sloth found in Virginia (**Figure 8.1**). Darwin definitely knew the work of the French paleontologist Georges Cuvier (discussed in chapter 2), who had meticulously studied and published on the fossils of many different plants and animals around Paris.

Though Darwin and these other figures made important contributions to scientific and anthropological thought, none of these people fully appreciated the importance of fossils as a record of the past. Cuvier recognized the fact that fossils are the remains of once-living

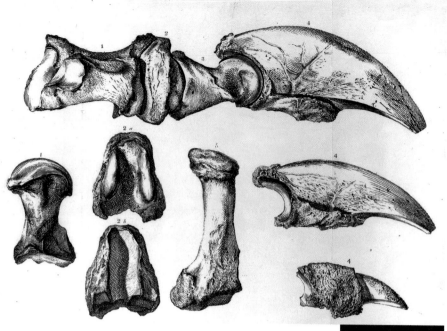

FIGURE 8.1

Megalonyx jeffersonii *Fossil Claws* In 1796, Thomas Jefferson (inset) discovered the bones of an extinct ground sloth. The paper he presented on his finding to the American Philosophical Society helped launch the field of vertebrate paleontology in America.

organisms. Darwin saw the significance of the similarity in features between living ground sloths and the extinct forms in Argentina. But the larger role of fossils in reconstructing the history of life and a time frame in which to place that history was not at the forefront of either Cuvier's or Darwin's thinking. In science, it sometimes takes one person with just the right combination of background, experience, and intellect to put together various lines of evidence and draw conclusions from this evidence that result in a breakthrough. The breakthrough that set the stage for fossils as a fundamental source of information about the past came not from a respected scientist but from an engineering surveyor with a remarkable attentiveness to detail and pattern. Unlike many of the great scientists of the eighteenth and nineteenth centuries, the Englishman William Smith (1769–1839) was born into a family of very modest means. At 18, he apprenticed as a surveyor, and he eventually worked for a coal-mining and canal-construction company. In the mines, he observed that layers of rock—**strata**—were always positioned the same way relative to each other. He deduced this pattern from the colors and other physical properties of each stratum. He also realized that each stratum contained a unique collection of fossils representing long-extinct life-forms. From these observations, he hypothesized that the relative positions of strata and the kinds of fossils found in the layers were the same throughout England. He called his hypothesis the *Principle of Faunal Succession,* and he tested it with a research program that correlated strata and fossils throughout Britain.

Smith was fired from his job in 1799, likely because of his distractions from his surveying work. Despite going into abject poverty and spending time in debtors' prison, he continued recording data across the country, ultimately producing in 1815 the first geologic map of the British Isles (**Figure 8.2**). What motivated him? Like the other scientists we have studied, Smith was motivated by questions about the natural world around him. And he believed that fossils provided an important record of past life and of time's passage. Although his passion

FIGURE 8.2

1815 Geologic Map of England, Wales, and Part of Scotland, by William Smith Using fossils and the physical characteristics of geologic strata, William Smith created this map of the British Isles, which measures some 2 m (6 ft) by 3 m (9 ft). Smith's methods laid the groundwork for how geologists and paleontologists understand Earth's landscape, reconstruct geologic history, and study the evolution of life worldwide.

was to produce a geologic map, he recognized the importance of fossils in the creation of a time frame for once-living organisms. The scientific world grew to realize what an important thing he had accomplished, and in the last years of his life Smith was recognized by the leading scientists of the time. Owing to his pursuit of answers to questions regarding the natural world, fossils became a means of documenting the evolution of life on Earth and a means of reconstructing geologic time.

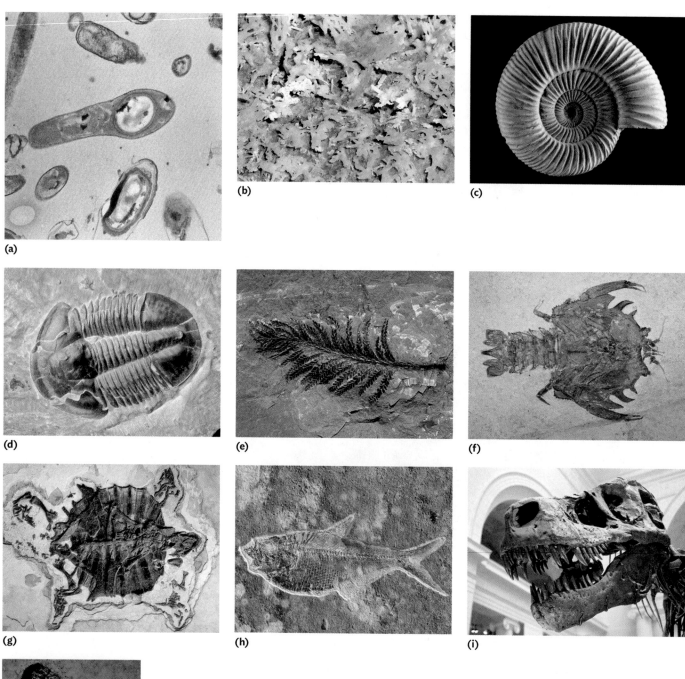

FIGURE 8.3

Kinds of Fossils Information about past organisms comes from various sources, such as **(a)** 250-million–year-old bacteria (*Bacillus permians*); **(b)** stromatolites, which resemble bacterial colonies that dominated life on Earth for more than 2 billion years; and fossils: **(c)** ammonite, **(d)** trilobite, **(e)** fern, **(f)** crab, **(g)** soft-shelled turtle, **(h)** fish, **(i)** *Tyrannosaurus* skeleton, and **(j)** Eocene primate, *Darwinius masillae.* Fossils like these have been found all over the world.

Fossils are the very heart of the study of evolution. They provide us with the only direct physical evidence of past life and its evolution, from the simple bacterial organisms that lived more than 3 billion years ago to the complex organisms that evolved later (**Figure 8.3**). The scientific study of fossils centers around two components: time and environment. Placement of fossils in time allows us to document *phylogeny*, or biological change and evolutionary relationships (see chapter 6). Placement of fossils in their environmental contexts helps us understand the factors that shaped the evolution of the organisms the fossils represent.

In this chapter, you will learn about the study of fossils, or paleontology, and the vast chronology within which scientists place the fossil record. You will also learn how paleontologists—the scientists who study fossils—determine how long ago organisms lived and what their environments were like. Paleontologists are the timekeepers of the past.

8.1 Fossils: Memories of the Biological Past

What Are Fossils?

Fossils (Latin *fossilis,* meaning "dug up") are the remains of once-living organisms. More specifically, they are the remains of organisms that have been wholly or partially transformed into rock through a long process of chemical replacement. In the replacement process, the minerals in bones and teeth, such as calcium and phosphorus, are very gradually replaced with rock-forming minerals like iron and silica.

Taphonomy and Fossilization

Fossils can derive from any body parts, but bones and teeth are by far the most common sources, providing more than 99% of the fossil record. Taphonomy—the study of what happens to an organism's remains—describes the multiple circumstances that must (and must not) occur for a dead organism to become a fossil (**Figure 8.4**). An organism will *not* become a fossil, for example, if its remains are left exposed for any length of time. If the remains are exposed for more than a day or so after death, scavengers such as dogs, wolves, or birds may eat the soft tissues. Maggots will quickly consume flesh. Once the flesh is gone, the bones of the skeleton will weather, break, or disappear. Because of the unlikelihood of a quick burial not brought about by humans, very few once-living organisms end up as fossils.

If an organism is buried soon after its death, such as under soil sediments deposited by water, the remains will be at least partly protected from scavengers. To become fossilized, however, the remains must stay in an oxygen-free (anoxic) environment, where scavengers cannot access the body and where bacterial activity and decomposition are limited.

Even in this ideal burial environment, other factors can lead to the decay or alteration of the remains. For example, groundwater or acidic soils can dissolve bones and teeth, and ground pressure or geologic activity can distort the appearance of any potential fossils.

Types of Fossils

Fossils are found in various types of rock, but most commonly in **sedimentary** rock, which is produced by water and wind carrying and then dropping tiny bits of rock, sand, and soil over time. In South Africa, for example, sediments were washed, blown,

sedimentary Rock formed when the deposition of sediments creates distinct layers, or strata.

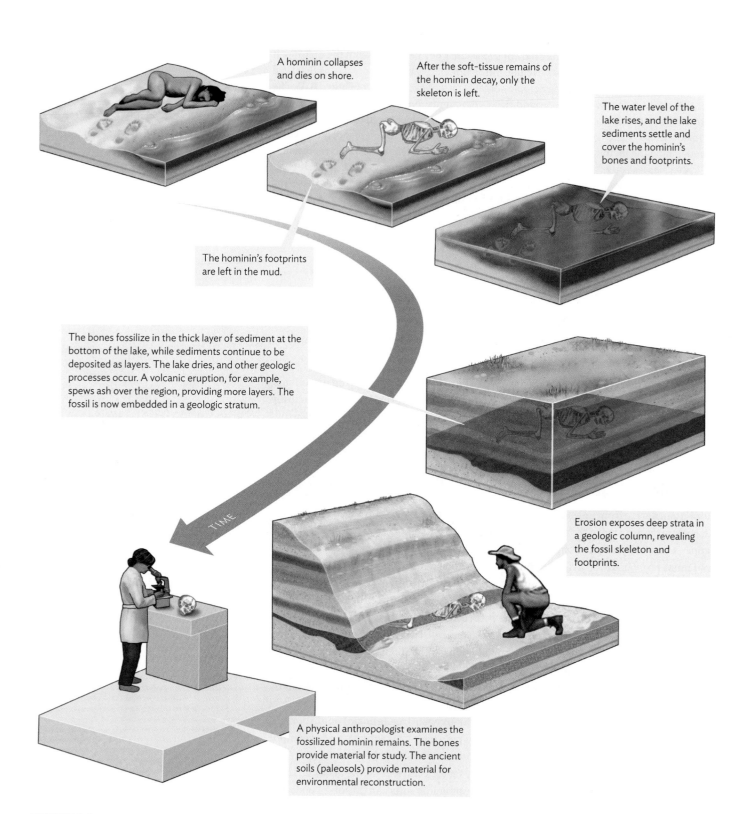

A hominin collapses and dies on shore.

After the soft-tissue remains of the hominin decay, only the skeleton is left.

The water level of the lake rises, and the lake sediments settle and cover the hominin's bones and footprints.

The hominin's footprints are left in the mud.

The bones fossilize in the thick layer of sediment at the bottom of the lake, while sediments continue to be deposited as layers. The lake dries, and other geologic processes occur. A volcanic eruption, for example, spews ash over the region, providing more layers. The fossil is now embedded in a geologic stratum.

TIME

Erosion exposes deep strata in a geologic column, revealing the fossil skeleton and footprints.

A physical anthropologist examines the fossilized hominin remains. The bones provide material for study. The ancient soils (paleosols) provide material for environmental reconstruction.

FIGURE 8.4
What Is in a Fossil? The Making of the Biological Past

or dropped into caves. Coincidentally, as the sediments built up, carnivores dropped the remains of animals, including early hominins, in the caves (**Figure 8.5**). Sediments subsequently buried the remains and filled the caves, preserving fossils for millions of years.

Fossilization has also occurred when volcanic activity has buried animal remains in volcanic ash. Occasionally, volcanic ash preserves footprints, such as the spectacular tracks left by three hominins around 3.5 mya at Laetoli, Tanzania (**Figure 8.6**).

Though fossils do not contain the original biological materials that were present in life, even fossils that are millions of years old preserve vestiges of the original tissue. DNA within this tissue can be used to identify genetic information. Also, chemicals within original bone tissue or tooth tissue may be used for dietary reconstruction. Chemical constituents of bone, for example, have been extracted from early hominins

(a) 2 mya

(b) Before excavation

(c) During excavation

FIGURE 8.5

South African Cave Taphonomy These cutaway figures show key aspects of the taphonomy of hominin remains in South African cave sites, 2 mya and today. Through the careful study of bone accumulations, the South African paleontologist Charles Kimberlin Brain realized that the early hominin bones as well as the bones of many other kinds of animals found in the caves were likely due to carnivore activity. **(a)** Carnivores such as leopards often take their prey into trees to feed. If such a tree hangs over an opening of a cave, the remains of the prey may fall into it when the animal has finished its meal. As the cave fills with bones and sediment, the remains become a part of the depositional process and are fossilized over time. **(b)** Paleontologists discover the strata with the fossils preserved from hundreds of thousands of years of deposition. One of the most famous hominin finds, the Taung child, was found in a South African cave (discussed further in chapter 10). **(c)** The excavation of Swartkrans Cave in South Africa has provided important hominin fossils. The grid over the evacuation is used to map fossils and artifacts. (Photo © 1985 David L. Brill, humanoriginsphotos.com)

THE FOSSIL

THE TIMING AND TEMPO OF EVOLUTION

The fossil record enables us to conjecture about what past plants and animals were like. But when substantial numbers of fossils exist for a particular setting and spread across periods, they also enable us to test hypotheses about the timing and tempo of evolution. Ever since Charles Darwin articulated his ideas about the rate of evolution in his *Origin of Species,* paleontologists and others interested in long-term biological change had agreed with Darwin that evolution is a gradual process.

Primates and primatelike ancestors have been evolving for more than 60 million years. Many fossil primate taxa have been identified, especially in North America, Europe, and Asia. In Wyoming's Bighorn Basin, a group of primates known as the *omomyids* is especially well documented (discussed further in chapter 9). Fossils ranging over about 2 million years show a gradual compaction of the front teeth in the lower jaw, including the first and second incisors (I1, I2), the canine (C), and the second and third premolars (P2, P3). Note how the second premolar (P2 in the oldest jaw) disappears and the incisors and canine decrease in size.

More than a century after the publication of Darwin's classic, two young American paleontologists, Niles Eldredge and Stephen Jay Gould, observed something interesting in the fossils of some invertebrate species. They noted long periods of evolutionary stasis in the exoskeletons, or outer coverings, of animals such as trilobites. These static periods were interrupted at times by rapid evolutionary change. Eldredge and Gould distinguished this punctuated equilibrium, or rapid change between long static periods, from gradualism, or long, slow change.

The fossil record for trilobites, studied by Eldredge and Gould, supports the hypothesis that evolutionary change can occur quite rapidly. In a complete succession of geologic strata in Wyoming's Bighorn Basin, however, the American vertebrate paleontologists Tom Bown and Kenneth Rose have documented the gradual evolution of the teeth and size of early Eocene primates. Over about 2 million years, these North American primates lost teeth and became smaller. Bown and

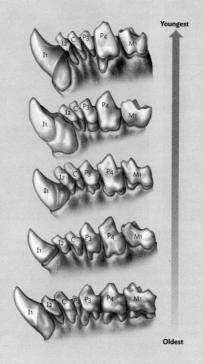

Rose's findings support Darwin's gradual-evolution hypothesis.

Which hypothesis is correct, punctuated equilibrium or gradualism? Likely, both are. The many differences between invertebrates and mammals could alone explain the differences in tempo of evolution. The differences between the invertebrates studied by Eldredge and Gould and the primates studied by Bown and Rose may have been increased by the different habitats occupied by these animals. As both patterns of evolution are supported by the fossil records, the speed of evolutionary change appears to be influenced by local, geographic factors. Some settings may promote rapid change, while others promote a gradual change as climate and other shifts occur over long time spans. Rather than representing alternative models for how evolution works, slow and rapid change may be part of the same overall record of evolution, an adaptive process that can fluctuate or be constantly slow, depending on external factors.

RECORD

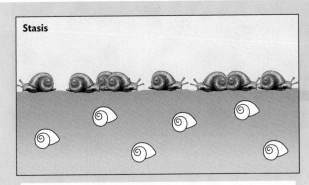

Stasis

During a static period, this snail population experiences little change to the form of its exoskeleton. Snails fossilized in different strata provide evidence of this stasis period.

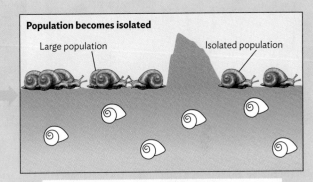

Population becomes isolated

Large population

Isolated population

Part of the snail population becomes isolated and can no longer interbreed with the rest of the population.

Reintroduction

The isolated population increases and expands into other areas, including its original territory.

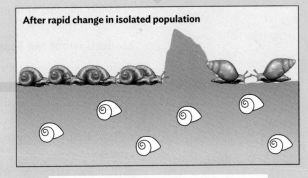

After rapid change in isolated population

Because this population is small, restricted to a single location, and undergoing very rapid change, it leaves behind no fossils of the intermittent forms.

Stasis

Over time, the new snail species outcompetes and replaces ancestral species. A static period follows, as a large population and a large territory make evolutionary changes less likely. Fossilized snails provide evidence of the new species.

(a)

(b)

FIGURE 8.6

Ancient Footprints at Laetoli **(a)** Fossilized footprints of our human ancestors in Laetoli, Tanzania, provide information about **(b)** bipedal locomotion in early hominins. What information about locomotion can anthropologists learn from footprints? (Figure 8.6b: "The Fossil Footprint Makers of Laetoli," © 1982 by Jay H. Matternes.)

from South Africa and Europe. Chemical analysis shows that early hominins ate a range of foods including meat and plants.

Limitations of the Fossil Record: Representation Is Important

To form a complete picture of life in the past, we need fossils that represent the full range of living things from the past to the present. Representation, then, is the crucial factor in creating a fossil record. The fuller and more representative the collection of fossils from specific animals and plants in any site or region, the richer will be our understanding of the various populations of these animals and plants within that site or region.

Some fossil species are remarkably well represented. Paleontologists have found thousands of fossils from some 55 mya, for example, representing many different kinds of early primates and animals of the period (see chapter 9). By contrast, many taxa are known from very limited fossil records, such as for the earliest apes of Africa (from around 20 mya). Key stages in the record of past life are missing because (1) paleontologists have searched for fossils in only some places—they simply have not discovered all the fossil-bearing rocks around the world; (2) fossils have been preserved in some places and not in others; and (3) rock sequences containing fossils are not complete in all places.

The Fayum Depression in Egypt helps illustrate these limitations. There, paleontologists have examined an unusually rich record of early primate evolution from about 37 mya to 29 mya (primate evolution is the subject of chapter 9). Hundreds of early primate fossils have been found in the Fayum geologic strata. The record ends at about 29 mya, however, when the rock stops bearing fossils. Did primates stop living there at 29 mya? Probably not. Rather, the geologic activity necessary for fossilization—the depositing of sediments—probably stopped after 29 mya. Without deposition and the burial of organisms, no new fossils were created.

Elsewhere in Africa, geologic strata dating to the same time period as the Fayum are exceedingly rare or they do not contain fossils. Primates might have lived in those areas, but sedimentation or fossilization or both simply did not occur.

Similarly, the record of early hominin evolution in Africa is mostly restricted to the eastern and southern portions of the continent. In all likelihood, early hominins inhabited all of Africa, certainly by 4 mya, but they were not preserved as fossils throughout the continent (early hominin evolution is the subject of chapter 10).

When fossil records are especially well represented over time, they help us discuss aspects of evolutionary theory, such as the timing and tempo of change. These records can indicate whether evolution is the gradual process that Charles Darwin wrote about in his *Origin of Species* (see chapter 2) or if its pace can speed up or slow down.

Fully interpreting the information in fossils means knowing both where the fossils were found and their ages. Without being able to place fossils in time, anthropologists cannot trace the evolution of past life (**Figure 8.7**).

8.2 Just How Old Is the Past?

Time in Perspective

Most of us have limited perspectives on time. We tend to think about yesterday, today, and tomorrow or perhaps next week. Long expanses of time might extend to our earliest memories. Because most of us were born after World War II, that conflict seems like part of the distant past. "Ancient" history might mean the beginning of the American Revolution in 1775 or Columbus's arrival at the Americas in 1492.

For scientists who deal with the distant past—such as geologists, paleontologists, physical anthropologists, and archaeologists—recent centuries constitute a tiny portion of time. Indeed, when put in the context of Earth's age (4.6 billion years) or the existence of life (at least 3.5 billion years), several centuries are not even an eyeblink in time. An appreciation of the history of life and (more immediately for this book) of primate and human evolution must be grounded in an understanding of the deep time involved. That is, to reconstruct and interpret evolutionary changes, it is crucial to place each fossil in time, answering the question *How old is it?* Without an answer to that question for each and every fossil, it is not possible to order the fossils in chronological sequence. Simply, without a chronological sequence, there is no fossil record.

Throughout Part II of this book, our normally narrow perspective on time broadens to include the vast record of natural history. The following discussion is a first step toward that broader sense of time.

Geologic Time: Earth History

The evolutionary history of life on Earth involves deep time, as represented by the geologic timescale (**Figure 8.8**). By placing all past life forms—as represented by fossils—on that scale, paleontologists record the major changes and events in the evolution of plants and of animals (**Figure 8.9**). Paleontologists order the evolution of major life-forms, as geologists order Earth history, in a series of three **eras**—the **Paleozoic,** the **Mesozoic,** and the **Cenozoic**—each subdivided by a series of **epochs.** Collectively,

Paleozoic The first major era of geologic time, 545–250 mya, during which fish, reptiles, and insects first appeared.

Mesozoic The second major era of geologic time, 230–66 mya, characterized by the emergence and extinction of dinosaurs.

Cenozoic The era lasting from 66 mya until the present, encompassing the radiation and proliferation of mammals such as humans and other primates.

epochs Divisions of periods (which are the major divisions of eras) in geologic time.

8.7

What Did They Look Like?

BRINGING FOSSILS TO LIFE THROUGH RECONSTRUCTION

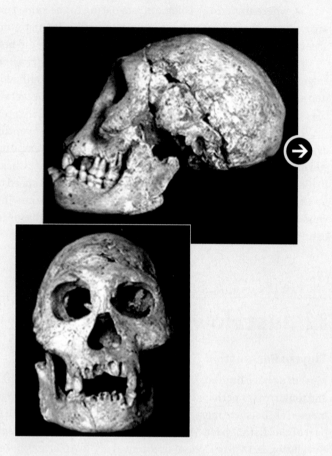

CONTEXT

Among the amazingly well-preserved fossil hominins discovered beneath the ruins of Dmanisi, a medieval town in the countryside of the Republic of Georgia, by David Lordkipanidze and his associates was the skull of a teenage boy, called D-2700. Dating to 1.7 mya, this skull is the first evidence of the genus *Homo* (*Homo erectus*) outside Africa. Soon after the fossil's discovery near the ruins of a medieval town, the eminent French paleoartist and sculptor Elisabeth Daynès was asked to reconstruct the teenager's physical appearance—what he might have looked like in life. Her reconstruction provides us with a picture of one of the earliest occupants of Eurasia.

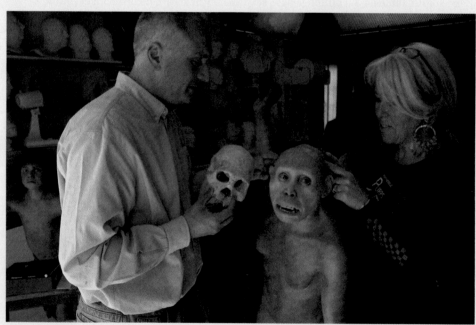

© 2007 Photographer P. Plailly/E. Daynès/Eurelios/LookatSciences Reconstruction Elisabeth Daynès Paris.

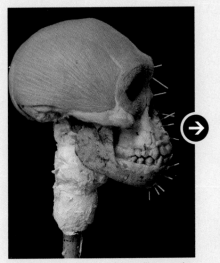

© 2007 Photographer
P. Plailly/E.Daynès/Eurelios/LookatSciences
Reconstruction Elisabeth Daynès Paris.

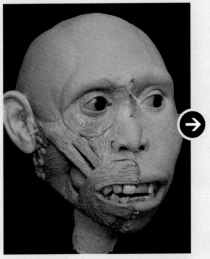

© 2007 Photographer
P. Plailly/E. Daynès/Eurelios/LookatSciences
Reconstruction Elisabeth Daynès Paris.

© 2007 Photographer
P. Plailly/E. Daynès/Eurelios/LookatSciences
Reconstruction Elisabeth Daynès Paris.

THE PROCESS: FROM DEATH TO LIFE

Producing a reconstruction of the living form for any fossil is difficult, and finishing just one can take up to four months. The process involves an interplay of art and science—for example, it requires an extensive knowledge of bones and of muscle and other soft tissue. Some of the process is guesswork, but most is based on knowledge of living forms and experience with creating reconstructions.

First, strips of clay are placed to mimic muscle size. The sticks mark approximations for the depth of the tissue over the bone. Second, tissue approximations are made, and then the tedious job begins of applying clay and molding the exterior surface. One of the huge challenges in producing a realistic reconstruction is the eyes. Without lifelike eyes, it is hard to make a model seem alive and compelling.

© 2006 Photographer
P. Plailly/E. Daynès/Eurelios
Reconstruction Elisabeth
Daynès Paris.

Finally, after the skin is placed over the muscles and other tissues, detailed painting creates skin texture, skin color, and facial expression. For this reconstruction, Daynès chose a whimsical smile, with the eyes focusing on something amusing. We can never know what the real hominin's facial expressions were like, but the individual had to be depicted as expressing emotion. While the Dmanisi boy does not look like anyone you would know, you undoubtedly recognize his humanness.

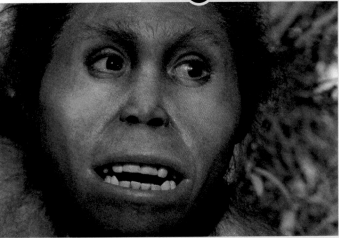

© 2007 Photographer P. Plailly/E. Daynès/Eurelios/LookatSciences
Reconstruction Elisabeth Daynès Paris.

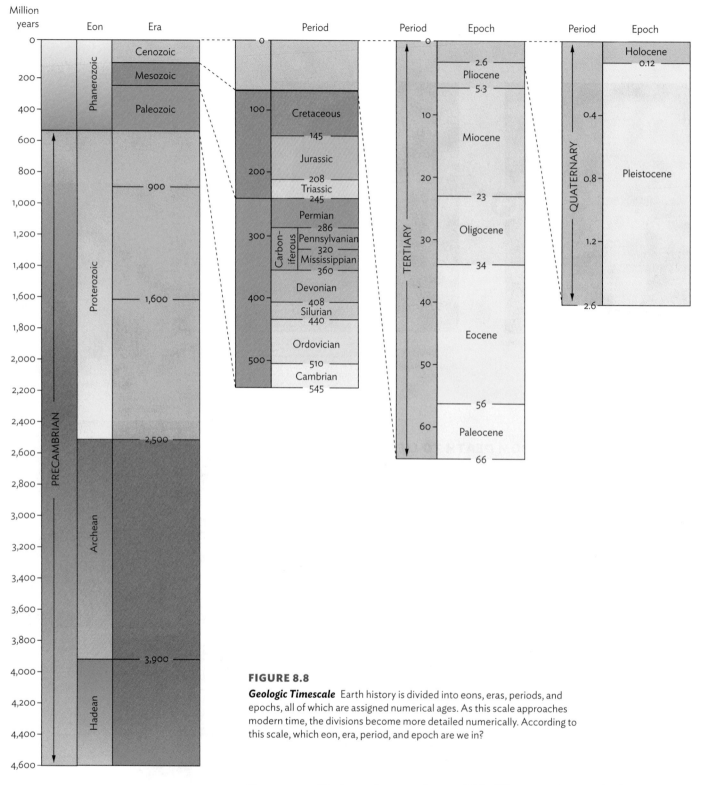

FIGURE 8.8

Geologic Timescale Earth history is divided into eons, eras, periods, and epochs, all of which are assigned numerical ages. As this scale approaches modern time, the divisions become more detailed numerically. According to this scale, which eon, era, period, and epoch are we in?

Pangaea A hypothetical landmass in which all the continents were joined, approximately 300–200 mya.

these eras and their epochs cover the past 545 million years. During this long expanse, an incredible amount of change—biological and geologic—has occurred.

In the upcoming chapters, we will look at some of the biological evolution during the current eon, especially in the Cenozoic era. Some of the most profound geologic changes have taken place within the Mesozoic and Cenozoic eras, or within the past 200 million years. At the beginning of this time frame, the supercontinent we call **Pangaea**—the

FIGURE 8.9

Evolution of Life Earth's geologic timescale demonstrates the evolution of major organisms. As shown in this chart, modern humans are one of the most recent organisms to have developed; our roots go much deeper, however, as our ancestors appeared millions of years ago.

original continent from which our continents derive—began a process of separation, which is still ongoing (**Figure 8.10**). By the time true primates appeared, 145 million years later, the Atlantic Ocean had formed, separating North America from Europe and South America from Africa. The gaps between North America and Europe and between South America and Africa continue to widen as the continental (**tectonic**) plates drift apart.

tectonic Refers to various structures on Earth's surface, such as the continental plates.

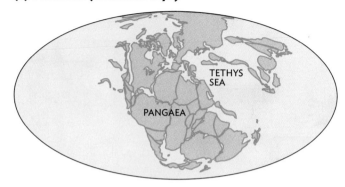

(a) Paleozoic (about 350 mya)

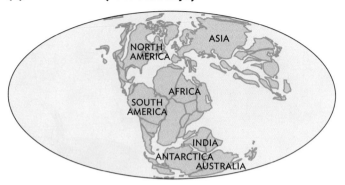

(b) Late Jurassic (about 150 mya)

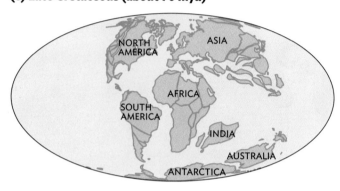

(c) Late Cretaceous (about 70 mya)

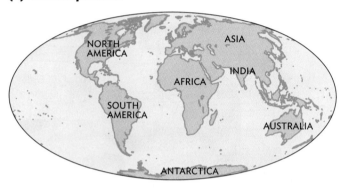

(d) Current position

FIGURE 8.10

Movement of Continents Earth's continents have been moving for hundreds of millions of years and continue to drift. In the Paleozoic (545–245 mya), all the land on Earth formed **(a)** a single mass, which we call *Pangaea*. Beginning in the Late Triassic (245–208 mya), this supercontinent began to break up into **(b)** separate continents. The initial split seems to have occurred in the northern part of Pangaea, creating the North Atlantic; the southern part, including South America, Africa, the Antarctic, and Australia, remained closed. In the Cretaceous (145–66 mya) **(c),** most of the continents were separate and the Atlantic Ocean was complete; however, the continents had yet to reach their **(d)** present-day positions.

Relative and Numerical Age

The events described above and the idea that Earth could be hundreds of millions of years old seemed preposterous to most scholars living even a few hundred years ago. Before the eighteenth century, not many people could fathom that time stretched more than several thousand years before the present, past what geologists call "historical" time, the time since written records began. In 1654, the archbishop of Armagh, Ireland, James Ussher (1581–1656), added up all the generations of religious patriarchs listed in the Old Testament of the Bible and reported that Earth was created at midday on Sunday, October 23, 4004 BC. Ussher's pronouncement became the definitive answer to the question raised by many—*How old is planet Earth?*

Other scholars turned to nonhistorical sources of information, determining that a geologic past began long before the historical past. Niels Stensen (also known by his Latinized name, Nicolaus Steno; 1638–1686), a Dane serving as the court physician to the grand duke of Tuscany, studied the geologic formations around Florence, Italy, and the fossils they contained. Hypothesizing that the fossilized shark teeth that he found far under the ground were prehistoric, Stensen concluded that in a series of geologic layers—the stratigraphic sequence—higher rocks are younger than lower rocks.

Steno's law of superposition laid the foundation for relative dating, which states

Steno's law of superposition The principle that the lower the stratum or layer, the older its age; the oldest layers are at the bottom, and the youngest are at the top.

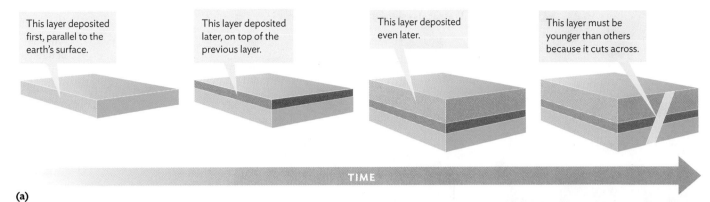

This layer deposited first, parallel to the earth's surface.

This layer deposited later, on top of the previous layer.

This layer deposited even later.

This layer must be younger than others because it cuts across.

TIME

(a)

the relative age of one event (such as the formation of a geologic stratum) or object (such as a fossil or an artifact) with respect to another (**Figure 8.11**). That is, the event recorded or object found on the bottom is the oldest, the event or object immediately above it is next oldest, and so forth. By contrast, the numerical age of an event or object is expressed in absolute years, such as 2,000 years ago, 1.3 billion years, 4004 BC, or AD 2014. Developed long before numerical dating, relative dating can be accomplished through several methods.

Relative Methods of Dating: Which Is Older, Younger, the Same Age?

STRATIGRAPHIC CORRELATION Geologic correlation of strata from multiple locations in a region—matching up strata based on physical features, chemical compositions, fossils, or other properties—helps place the passage of time in a larger context. This highly sophisticated method, first developed by William Smith, involves matching up physical and chemical characteristics of strata with the fossils found in those strata. Chemical characteristics make **stratigraphic correlation** possible across vast regions. For example, any volcanic eruption produces ash with an individual and highly specific chemical signature. The eruption's force, together with powerful winds, can spread the ash over hundreds or even thousands of kilometers, as when Krakatoa, an island volcano in Indonesia that erupted in 1883, sent ash as far as 3,700 miles (6,000 km) away (**Figure 8.12**). When an ash layer exists above or below a fossil, that fossil can be judged younger or older than the ash, depending on their relative positions. Such correlations, from various lines of evidence, involving millions of places around the world, have resulted in the geologic timescale.

CHEMICAL DATING Soils around the world have specific chemical compositions, reflecting their local geologic histories. For example, some soils contain fluorine. Once a bone is buried in fluorine-bearing soil, the bone begins to absorb the element. A bone that has been buried for a long time will have more fluorine in it than will a bone that has been buried for a short time.

Fluorine dating, one of the first **chemical dating** methods, was proposed by the English chemist James Middleton in 1844 (**Figure 8.13**). The Croatian paleontologist Dragutin Gorjanović-Kramberger applied fluorine dating to human and animal remains found in Krapina, Croatia, in the late 1890s and early 1900s (**Figure 8.14**). Hypothesizing that the bones buried in strata at the site had absorbed fluorine, he wanted to determine if the human bones, all representing humans called *Neandertals* (see chapter 10), were the same age as the animal bones. The animal bones were from long-extinct, Pleistocene forms of rhinoceroses, cave bears, and cattle. Some

NICOLAVS STENONIVS

(b)

FIGURE 8.11

Steno's Law of Superposition **(a)** This law, formulated by **(b)** Niels Stensen, states that the youngest strata are at the top and the oldest strata are on the bottom. In which situations would this law not apply?

stratigraphic correlation The process of matching up strata from several sites through the analysis of chemical, physical, and other properties.

fluorine dating A relative (chemical) dating method that compares the accumulation of fluorine in animal and human bones from the same site.

chemical dating Dating methods that use predictable chemical changes that occur over time.

FIGURE 8.12

Krakatoa The eruption of Krakatoa in 1883 was one of the most violent explosions in recorded history. The ash layer that resulted provided a frame of reference for dating materials found above and below. Anything found under the layer of ash existed before 1883; everything on top existed after 1883.

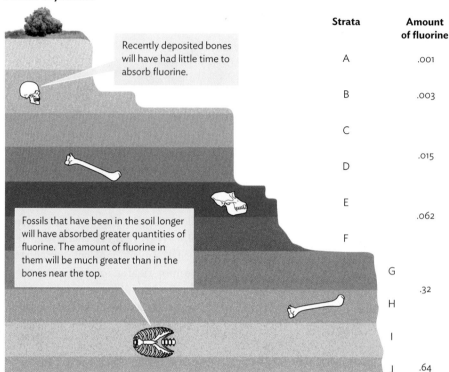

Present-day surface

Recently deposited bones will have had little time to absorb fluorine.

Fossils that have been in the soil longer will have absorbed greater quantities of fluorine. The amount of fluorine in them will be much greater than in the bones near the top.

Strata	Amount of fluorine
A	.001
B	.003
C	
D	.015
E	.062
F	
G	
H	.32
I	
J	.64

FIGURE 8.13

Fluorine Dating Bones absorb fluorine from surrounding soil.

Fluorine dating reveals the relative ages of fossil bones at the same site. It does not provide absolute dates, and it cannot be used to compare fossils from different sites because fluorine levels in soil vary from place to place.

biostratigraphic dating A relative dating method that uses the associations of fossils in strata to determine each layer's approximate age.

scientists believed that the Krapina Neandertals were not ancient, however, but had been living at the site in recent times only. They considered the Neandertals simply different from people living in Croatia in the late nineteenth and early twentieth centuries. If Gorjanović-Kramberger could show that the two sets of bones—human and animal—contained the same amount of fluorine, he could prove that the Neandertals were ancient and in fact had lived at the same time as the extinct animals. When the simple chemical analysis revealed that the Neandertal bones and the animal bones had very similar amounts of fluorine, this pioneering study demonstrated human beings' deep roots.

BIOSTRATIGRAPHIC (FAUNAL) DATING Gorjanović-Kramberger recognized that different strata include different kinds of fossils. He regarded these findings as chronologically significant. That is, the forms of specific animals and plants change over time, so the forms discovered within individual layers can help determine relative ages. **Biostratigraphic dating** draws on the first appearance of an organism in the fossil record, that organism's evolutionary development over time, and the organism's extinction. Pliocene and Pleistocene African rodents, pigs, and elephants and Eurasian mammals of all kinds have been especially useful for biostratigraphic dating because they show significant evolutionary change. By determining when certain animals lived, scientists have developed biostratigraphic markers, or **index fossils,** for assessing age. For example, giant deer—sometimes called Irish elk—provide useful information based on their extinction (**Figure 8.15**). That is, because the species appears to have died out in northern Europe around 10,600 yBP, the presence of Irish elk fossils in a northern European site indicates that the site predates 10,600 yBP.

Mammoths—relatives of modern elephants—first lived and evolved in Africa, then spread to Europe, Asia, and North America around 2.5 mya. Mammoths went extinct in Africa but continued to evolve elsewhere. After 2.5 mya, their molars became increasingly complex. Paleontologists have determined how these teeth changed from the species' emergence to its complete extinction. Therefore, when paleontologists discover fossilized mammoth teeth, they can determine the relative age of the site simply by looking at the molars. Likewise, changes in molar shape and size have helped paleontologists develop relative ages for Pliocene–Pleistocene pigs in East Africa and South Africa (**Figure 8.16**).

CULTURAL DATING Material culture can provide information for **cultural dating.** The first evidence of material culture—primitive stone tools called **pebble tools**—dates to about 2.6 mya. Although individually distinctive in appearance, pebble tools are not especially useful for bracketing small amounts of time, mainly because their forms changed so slowly. For example, a pebble tool from 2.5 mya is very much like one produced 1.8 mya. However, the presence of a certain kind of tool enables paleontologists to say that the site (and its hominin occupants) dates to a certain age (**Figure 8.17**).

Beginning in the later Pleistocene, stone tools and other components of material culture changed more rapidly. The various regional cultures in Europe collectively known as the *Upper Paleolithic* provide a number of "time-specific" artifacts, such as the small sculptures known as *Lion Men*. The first of these artifacts was found in a cave in Germany in 1939, neglected for 30 years in part because of World War II, and only recently restored (**Figure 8.18**).

FIGURE 8.14

Dragutin Gorjanović-Kramberger The Croatian paleontologist used fluorine dating at a site in Krapina, Croatia. The significance of this dating method was demonstrated by his results, which suggested that extinct animals and Neandertals had coexisted.

index fossils Fossils that are from specified time ranges, are found in multiple locations, and can be used to determine the age of associated strata.

(a)

(b)

FIGURE 8.15

Irish Elk **(a)** The skeleton of this giant deer shows how large the animal was; it stood more than 2.1 m (7 ft) tall at the shoulder. The man standing next to the skeleton was 1.85 m (6 ft, 1 in). **(b)** A reconstruction depicts the Irish elk.

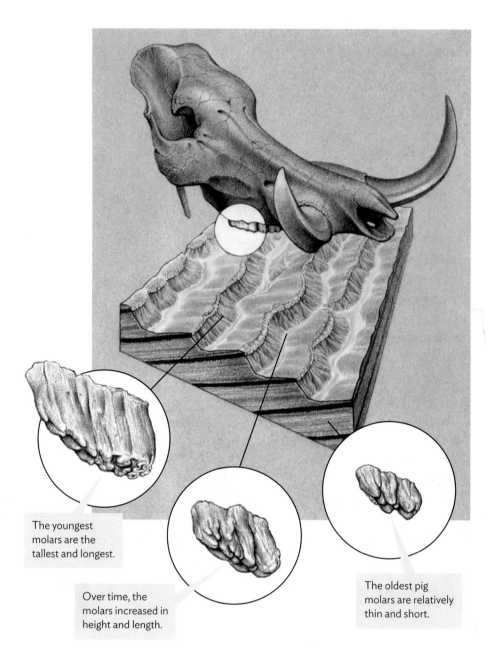

FIGURE 8.16

Fossil Pig Molars Changes in the size and shape of these teeth can be used for biostratigraphic dating in a method developed by the American paleontologists Jack Harris and Tim White. Over time, the molars became taller and longer.

In addition, fossil pig molars found in conjunction with layers of volcanic ash may be used for absolute dating, if paleontologists can determine the age of the ash. (On techniques for doing this, see "The Revolution Continues: Radiopotassium Dating" later in this chapter.) Because the teeth and the volcanic layer are associated chronologically, the teeth can then be used as time markers when found at other sites. ("Pig Dating: Stratigraphic Correlations," © 1985 by Jay H. Matternes.)

The youngest molars are the tallest and longest.

Over time, the molars increased in height and length.

The oldest pig molars are relatively thin and short.

In the Holocene, artifacts such as ceramics became even more time-specific. In fact, ceramics were invented during this period, and their forms changed rapidly (**Figure 8.19**).

Absolute Methods of Dating: What Is the Numerical Age?

THE RADIOMETRIC REVOLUTION AND THE DATING CLOCK When we say that the American Civil War took place after the American Revolution, we have provided relative ages for the two wars. That is, we have related the ages without specifying them. When we say that the American Civil War began in 1861 and the American Revolution began in 1775, we have provided numerical ages. That is, we have pinpointed the wars' beginnings in terms of years, a measure of scaled time. We know these dates thanks to written records, individuals having recorded all sorts of events associated with both

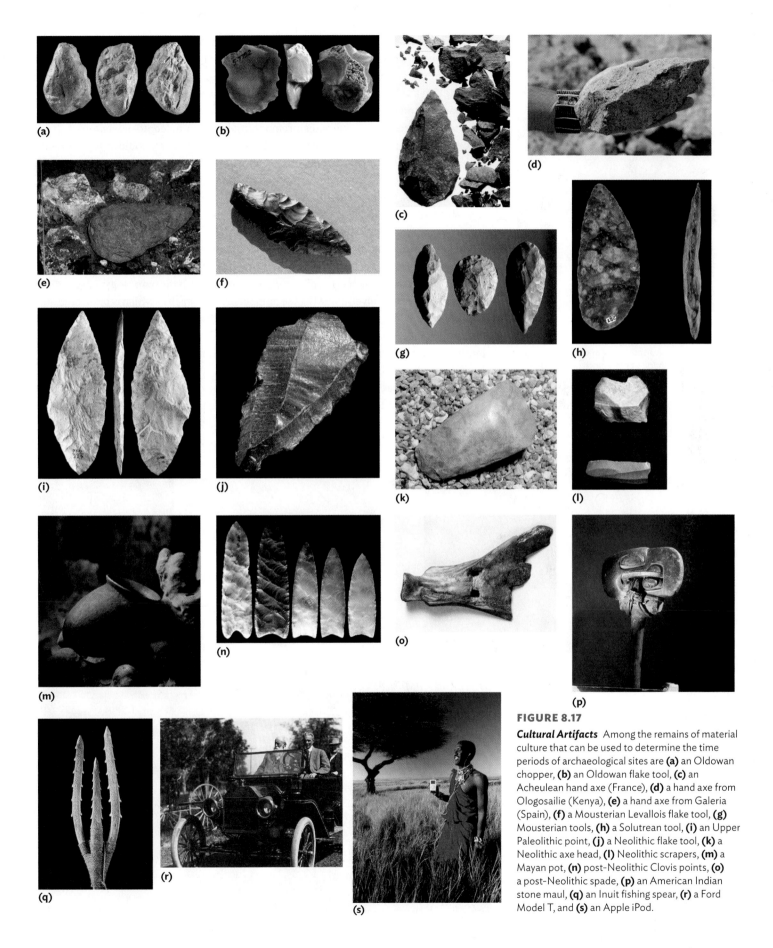

FIGURE 8.17

Cultural Artifacts Among the remains of material culture that can be used to determine the time periods of archaeological sites are **(a)** an Oldowan chopper, **(b)** an Oldowan flake tool, **(c)** an Acheulean hand axe (France), **(d)** a hand axe from Ologosailie (Kenya), **(e)** a hand axe from Galeria (Spain), **(f)** a Mousterian Levallois flake tool, **(g)** Mousterian tools, **(h)** a Solutrean tool, **(i)** an Upper Paleolithic point, **(j)** a Neolithic flake tool, **(k)** a Neolithic axe head, **(l)** Neolithic scrapers, **(m)** a Mayan pot, **(n)** post-Neolithic Clovis points, **(o)** a post-Neolithic spade, **(p)** an American Indian stone maul, **(q)** an Inuit fishing spear, **(r)** a Ford Model T, and **(s)** an Apple iPod.

FIGURE 8.18

Lion Man The discovery of another sculpture like this one, made of mammoth ivory and about 30 cm (11.8 in) high, would provide a relative date for the archaeological site. The site would be at least 30,000 years old.

wars (**Figure 8.20**). Since the time that Niels Stensen and his contemporaries began studying geologic features and fossils, scientists have been recording relative ages. By doing so, they have established the sequence of events in the geologic timescale—proving that the Eocene came before the Miocene, for example, and that ceramics were invented long after Neandertals lived in Europe. However, unlike historians, who often work with records containing dates, premodern geologists, paleontologists, and anthropologists had no means of providing numerical dates. Geologists could only group geologic events, paleontologists could only group species' lives, and anthropologists could only group peoples' lives and cultural events.

In the 1920s, the American astronomer A. E. Douglass (1867–1962) developed the first method for numerically dating objects and events, specifically ones including or involving wood. In studying sunspots and their impact on climate, Douglass noted that in temperate and very cold regions tree growth stopped in the winter and reactivated in the spring. This intermittence resulted in layers of growth, visible as a concentric ring pattern in the cross section of a tree. Douglass's **dendrochronology,** or tree-ring method of dating, involved counting the number of rings, each of which represented one year of growth (**Figure 8.21**). Tree-ring dating was first used on tree sections found in archaeological sites in the American Southwest. It works only when wood is as excellently preserved as it is in the Southwest, however, and thus can be applied in only a limited number of areas in the world.

Widely applicable numerical dating became possible in the nuclear age, after World War II (1939–45). In 1949, the American chemist Willard Libby (1908–1980)

(a)

(b)

(c)

FIGURE 8.19

Ceramics Like stone tools, sculptures, or other artifacts, ceramics can be used to provide relative dates for a site. Changes in size, material, shape, and decoration are well documented for series of ceramics in some locations. When a newly discovered ceramic piece belongs to a known temporal series, archaeologists determine where it falls in the chronology. Examples include **(a)** an Amratian vase, ca. 4000–3100 BC; **(b)** a vase created by Aristonothos from Greece, ca. 650 BC; **(c)** an Egyptian Ptolemaic alabaster jar, ca. 300 BC; **(d)** an Anasazi black-on-white jar, ca. 1000–1300; and **(e)** a water pitcher commemorating the 1796 US presidential election.

(d)

(e)

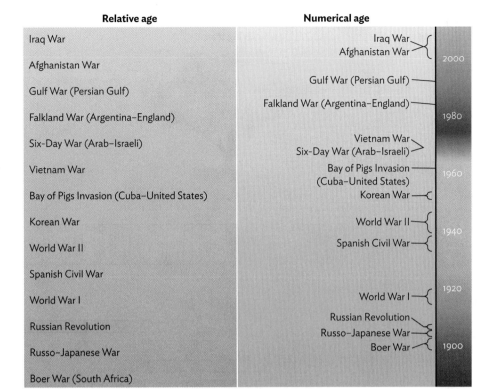

Relative age	Numerical age

Iraq War
Afghanistan War
Gulf War (Persian Gulf)
Falkland War (Argentina–England)
Six-Day War (Arab–Israeli)
Vietnam War
Bay of Pigs Invasion (Cuba–United States)
Korean War
World War II
Spanish Civil War
World War I
Russian Revolution
Russo–Japanese War
Boer War (South Africa)

Iraq War
Afghanistan War
Gulf War (Persian Gulf)
Falkland War (Argentina–England)
Vietnam War
Six-Day War (Arab–Israeli)
Bay of Pigs Invasion (Cuba–United States)
Korean War
World War II
Spanish Civil War
World War I
Russian Revolution
Russo–Japanese War
Boer War

2000
1980
1960
1940
1920
1900

FIGURE 8.20

Relative versus Numerical Wars of the twentieth and twenty-first centuries can be ordered relatively or numerically. The relative chart simply shows the order of events and does not specify when these events occurred or how long they lasted. The numerical chart provides dates and gives at least a rough sense of the wars' starting points and durations.

dendrochronology A chronometric dating method that uses a tree-ring count to determine numerical age.

radiocarbon dating The radiometric dating method in which the ratio of ^{14}C to ^{12}C is measured to provide an absolute date for a material younger than 50,000 years.

isotopes Two or more forms of a chemical element that have the same number of protons but vary in the number of neutrons.

discovered **radiocarbon dating,** an accomplishment for which he won a Nobel Prize. Scientists now had a means of determining the numerical age of past life-forms via the decay of radioactive elements.

The radiocarbon method, sometimes called the *carbon-14 method,* involves dating carbon **isotopes.** Isotopes are variants of an element based on the number of neutrons in the atom's nucleus. Some isotopes of an element are stable—in theory, they will last for an infinite amount of time, at least with respect to maintaining the same number of neutrons. Other isotopes are unstable—over time, they decay radioactively, transforming themselves into stable isotopes of either the same element or another element. Carbon has one radioisotope (unstable or radioactive isotope), identified as ^{14}C because it has an atomic mass of 14 (six protons and eight neutrons) in its nucleus. Carbon has two non-radioisotopes (stable isotopes), ^{12}C (carbon-12) and ^{13}C (carbon-13), which have an atomic mass of 12 (six protons and six neutrons) and 13 (six protons and seven neutrons), respectively. The radiocarbon method focuses on what happens to the radioisotope, ^{14}C. Over 5,730 years, half of the ^{14}C decays into ^{14}N. Over the next 5,730 years, another half of the ^{14}C decays again into ^{14}N, and so on, until eventually most of the radioisotope will have decayed. The number representing the time it takes for half of the radioisotope to decay is called the **half-life** (**Table 8.1**).

All living plants and animals (including you) absorb about the same amount of ^{14}C in their tissues, through the ingestion of very small amounts of atmospheric carbon dioxide (CO_2). During the life of a plant or animal, the ratio of ^{14}C to ^{12}C remains relatively constant. Once the organism dies, it stops absorbing ^{14}C and the ^{14}C begins to decay, but the ^{12}C does not decay. This means that the ratio of ^{14}C to ^{12}C changes over time—the longer since the death of the plant or animal, greater the amount of ^{12}C relative to ^{14}C. (**Figure 8.22**).

The great advantage of the radiocarbon method is that it has a precise baseline for the start of the clock—the death of the organism. The disadvantage for dating major

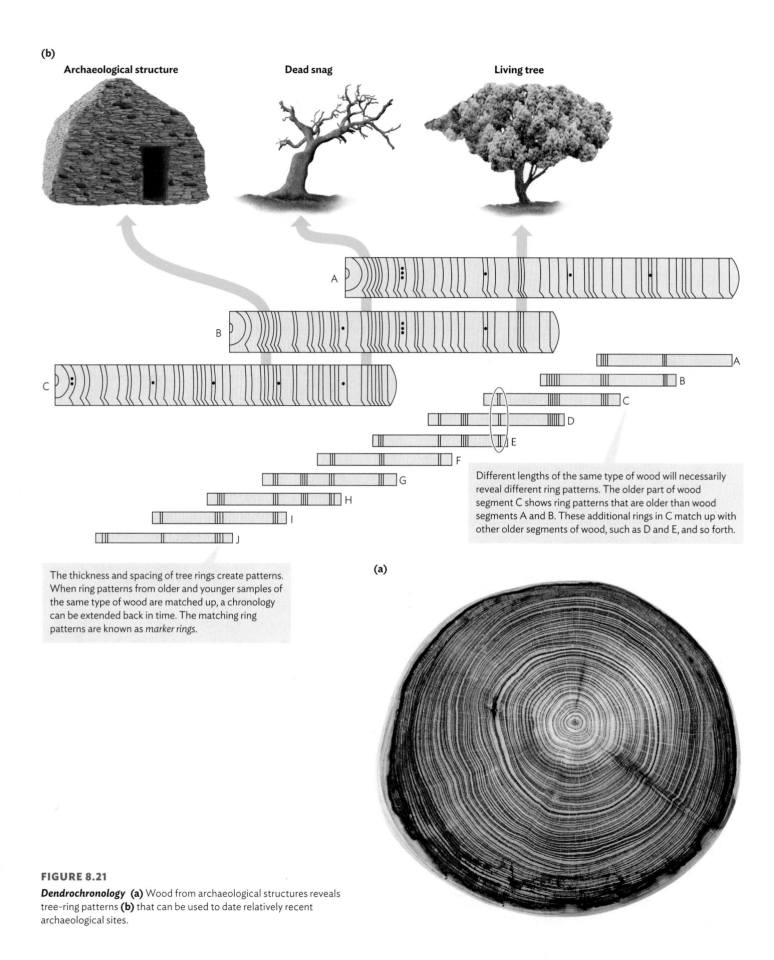

(b)

Archaeological structure

Dead snag

Living tree

A

B

C

A

B

C

D

E

F

G

H

I

J

Different lengths of the same type of wood will necessarily reveal different ring patterns. The older part of wood segment C shows ring patterns that are older than wood segments A and B. These additional rings in C match up with other older segments of wood, such as D and E, and so forth.

The thickness and spacing of tree rings create patterns. When ring patterns from older and younger samples of the same type of wood are matched up, a chronology can be extended back in time. The matching ring patterns are known as *marker rings*.

(a)

FIGURE 8.21

Dendrochronology (a) Wood from archaeological structures reveals tree-ring patterns (b) that can be used to date relatively recent archaeological sites.

Table 8.1 Isotopes Used in Radiometric Dating

Parent → Daughter	Half-Life (Years)	Material in Which the Isotopes Occur
$^{14}C \rightarrow {}^{14}N$	5,730	Anything organic (has carbon), such as wood, shell, bone
$^{238}U \rightarrow {}^{206}Pb$	4.5 billion	Uranium-bearing minerals (zircon, uraninite)
$^{40}K \rightarrow {}^{40}Ar$	1.3 billion	Potassium-bearing minerals (mica, feldspar, hornblende)
$^{40}Ar \rightarrow {}^{39}Ar$	1.3 billion	Potassium-bearing minerals (mica, feldspar, hornblende)
$^{235}U \rightarrow {}^{207}Pb$	713 million	Uranium-bearing minerals (zircon, uraninite)

events in primate and human evolution is that ^{14}C has a fairly short half-life, rendering its dates most accurate for only the past 50,000 yBP. Dates can be determined for another 25,000 years or so beyond that, but they are less precise owing to the very small amount of ^{14}C left.

THE REVOLUTION CONTINUES: RADIOPOTASSIUM DATING All organic materials contain carbon and thus can be dated through the radiocarbon method. By contrast,

FIGURE 8.22

Radiocarbon Dating This dating method was the first generation of radioisotope methods. Such dating methods remain among the most important for the determination of numerical dates.

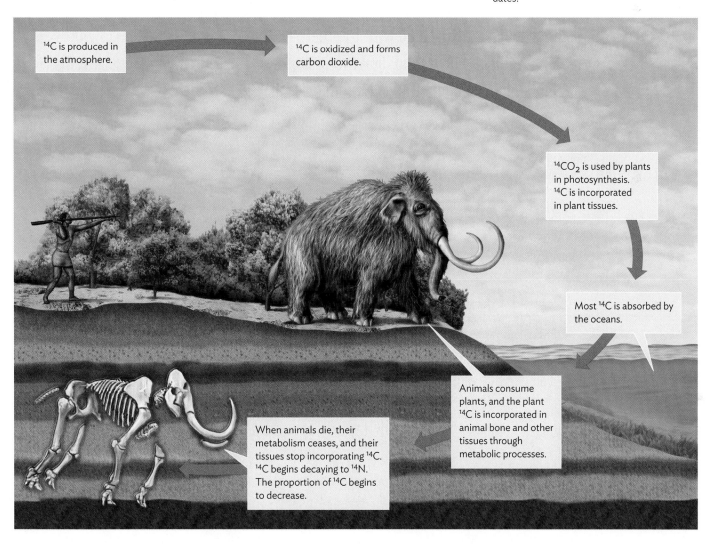

^{14}C is produced in the atmosphere.

^{14}C is oxidized and forms carbon dioxide.

$^{14}CO_2$ is used by plants in photosynthesis. ^{14}C is incorporated in plant tissues.

Most ^{14}C is absorbed by the oceans.

Animals consume plants, and the plant ^{14}C is incorporated in animal bone and other tissues through metabolic processes.

When animals die, their metabolism ceases, and their tissues stop incorporating ^{14}C. ^{14}C begins decaying to ^{14}N. The proportion of ^{14}C begins to decrease.

THE ATOMIC BOMB: RA

The Development of the Atomic Bomb Produces Insights Into the Past

We might think of absolute dating methods as related only to anthropology and geology, having little to do with the real world and the larger stage of world history. Radiocarbon dating, however, has its origins in a much bigger event: namely, the development of the atomic bomb.

By the 1930s, the basic chemistry of the radioactive isotopes of elements had been developed. By 1941, scientists were positioned to develop a bomb based on this chemistry. They knew that the rapid nuclear reaction needed to split the atoms of ^{235}U (uranium-235) would produce an explosion equivalent to that of many tons of TNT. This understanding laid the foundation for the Manhattan Project, a secret program in the United States to develop all the components and theory needed to create such a bomb. Begun in 1942, the project had constructed the first nuclear weapon by 1945. The atomic bomb was used by the United States on Hiroshima, and again on Nagasaki, both in Japan.

One crucial site for the bomb's development was Columbia University, where the physical chemist Harold Urey (1893–1981) and his team developed the method to separate ^{235}U from ^{238}U, which was needed for the nuclear reaction—the explosion of the bomb. Employed in Urey's lab was a young isotope chemist, Willard Libby, whose job was to figure out the separation. The knowledge that he gained about radioactive isotopes was instrumental in his next research project after the war, the development of a method to document the decay rates of the ^{14}C isotope to the ^{14}N isotope in organic remains. By precisely measuring this radiometric decay, Libby was able to determine the age of organic materials (wood, charcoal) containing carbon younger than 40,000 years.

Libby's method, the groundwork of which was done by isotope chemists working to develop the atomic bomb, revolutionized anthropologists' and geologists' ability to document the evolution of life in the late Pleistocene and the Holocene. The research on carbon set into motion the discovery of other isotopic transformations such as radioisotopes of uranium and of argon. These newer methods have provided the essential tools for dating significant parts of human evolution, including the earliest hominins. *Anthropology matters!*

DIOCARBON DATING

Atomic bombs (inset) had devastating effects when dropped on Hiroshima (August 6, 1945) and Nagasaki (three days later). In developing the scientific understanding to create such bombs, researchers gained an understanding of radioactive isotopes that is used today to date archaeological sites and their fossils.

igneous Rock formed from the crystallization of molten magma, which contains the radioisotope ⁴⁰K; used in potassium–argon dating.

radiopotassium dating The radiometric dating method in which the ratio of ⁴⁰K to ⁴⁰Ar is measured to provide an absolute date for a material older than 200,000 years.

fission track dating An absolute dating method based on the measurement of the number of tracks left by the decay of uranium-238.

amino acid dating An absolute dating method for organic remains such as bone or shell, in which the amount of change in the amino acid structure is measured.

nonorganic materials such as rocks contain other elements that can be dated radiometrically. Because the radioisotopes of these elements have very long half-lives, the radiometric clock is considerably longer for these nonorganic materials than for carbon-based materials. **Igneous** (volcanic) rock, for example, contains the radioisotope ⁴⁰K (potassium-40). ⁴⁰K decays very slowly from its unstable form to a stable gas, ⁴⁰Ar (argon-40)—its half-life is 1.3 *billion* years. It is usually not possible to date rocks much younger than 200,000 yBP, but ⁴⁰K's long half-life presents no limitation on the other end of the range. **Radiopotassium dating** certainly accommodates all of primate evolution.

The great strength of this method is the presence of volcanic rock in many places throughout the world. During a volcanic eruption, the heat is so extreme that it drives off all argon gas in the rock. The ⁴⁰K solid that is in the rock sealed by lava then begins to decay to ⁴⁰Ar gas, and the gas accumulates, trapped within the rock's crystalline structure. To date that rock—which could then be millions of years old—a scientist measures, with sophisticated instruments, the amount of gas (⁴⁰Ar) relative to the amount of nongas (⁴⁰K) in the rock. The more gas there is, the older the rock.

The radiopotassium method was first used to date the volcanic rock associated with an early hominin skull found by the British archaeologist Mary Leakey (1913–1996) in the lowest strata of Olduvai Gorge, in Tanzania, in 1959. At that time, scientists assumed that hominins had been around for perhaps a half-million years but not longer. When the associated volcanic rock at Olduvai proved to be 1.8 million years old, that dating nearly quadrupled the known time frame for human evolution. Since then, radiometric methods have helped paleontologists fine-tune the chronologies of primate evolution and human evolution.

In the 1990s, scientists developed an alternative method of radiopotassium dating, whereby they measure the ratio of ⁴⁰Ar gas to ³⁹Ar gas. In the argon–argon method, volcanic rock is bombarded with "fast" neutrons in a nuclear reactor. Like ⁴⁰K, ³⁹K is present in the volcanic rock, and the two isotopes, ⁴⁰K and ³⁹K, occur in the same amounts relative to one another, no matter how old the rock may be. The neutron bombardment converts the ³⁹K to ³⁹Ar. Because ³⁹Ar serves as a proxy for ⁴⁰K, the ratio of ⁴⁰Ar to ³⁹Ar reveals the rock's absolute age. This method's advantages over the potassium–argon method are that it requires less rock and the potassium does not have to be measured. Now routinely being used by paleontologists and geologists to date early hominins (see chapter 10), the method has made it possible to date hundreds of hominin (and other) fossils from 5 million yBP to *Homo sapiens'* origin, more than 100,000 yBP. Note, though, that radiopotassium can be used to date only igneous rock, not sedimentary rock.

Fission track dating is based on the radioactive decay of naturally occurring ²³⁸U (uranium-238; **Figure 8.23**). When the isotope decays, fragments produced in the decay, or fission, process leave a line, or track, measuring just a few atoms wide on the rock crystal. Thus, the greater the number of tracks, the older the material being dated. This method can date materials from the past several million years and has been used for dating volcanic ash and obsidian (volcanic glass).

NON-RADIOMETRIC ABSOLUTE DATING METHODS Several other, non-radiometric methods provide absolute dates. Among these methods, **amino acid dating** is the most useful in more recent settings (**Figure 8.24**). This method is based on the decay of protein molecules after an organism's death. Amino acids, the compounds that make up proteins (among the subjects of chapter 3),

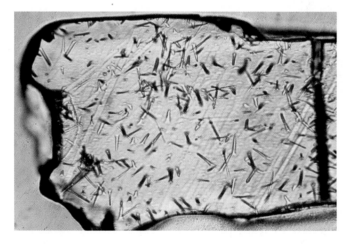

FIGURE 8.23

Fission Track Dating Fission track dating uses the number of tracks left behind by isotope decay.

come in two forms, l-isomers and d-isomers, respectively known as left-handed amino acids and right-handed amino acids. Basically, this distinction means that when a protein is viewed under high-power magnification with a specialized light called **polarized light,** the molecules bend light to the left (and are called l-isomers) or to the right (d-isomers). Most living organisms' tissues are composed of l-isomers. Once an organism dies, these l-isomers begin to transform to d-isomers. The longer the organism has been dead, the greater the number of ds, so the fossil's date is based on the ratio of l to d.

The limitation of amino acid dating is that the rate of the chemical decomposition resulting in the shift from l to d—a process called **racemization**—is largely determined by the temperature of the region. That is, a region with a higher average temperature will have a faster rate of chemical decomposition than will a region with a cooler average temperature. Therefore, the method is dependent on the local climate, and not broadly comparable across large regions. The age range for amino acid dating is generally 100,000–40,000 yBP but has been extended to 200,000 yBP in tropical settings and to nearly 3 mya in cooler settings. The method has provided useful dates for a variety of sites, but it is best known in human evolutionary studies for dating Border Cave in South Africa (145,000–70,000 yBP) and the human occupation during the Pleistocene in Britain.

Paleomagnetic dating is based on changes in Earth's magnetic field, which change the planet's polarity. In essence, movement of the planet's liquid (iron alloy) outer core creates an electric current that results in the magnetic field (**Figure 8.25**). When the magnetic field shifts, the magnetic north and south poles shift. The poles' shifts have been well documented. In the past 6 million years, for example, there have been four "epochs" of polar changes, or four different well-dated periods. Because certain metal grains align themselves with Earth's magnetic field as they settle and help form sedimentary rock, geologists can examine the orientation of these fragments to determine the planet's polarity at the time of the rock's formation. In addition, when molten igneous rock is produced, each new layer records the polarity, which can later be determined from the hard igneous rock.

Electron spin resonance dating relies on the measurement of radioisotope concentrations (for example, of uranium) that have accumulated in fossils over periods of time. Once buried, remains such as bones and teeth absorb radioisotopes and so record the radioactivity in the surrounding burial environment. The older the fossil, the greater the concentration, and this method can date material from a few thousand to more than a million years old.

Thermoluminescence dating is based on the amount of the sun's energy trapped in material such as sediment, stone, or ceramic (**Figure 8.26**). When such an object is heated—as in an early hominin's campfire—the energy it contains is released as light. The next time that same material is heated—as in the laboratory to derive a date—the amount of light released (measured as electrons that are from natural radiation, such as from uranium) reveals the amount of time since the material was first heated. This method can date materials back to about 800,000 yBP.

Scientists must consider various factors when choosing an absolute dating method, among them the material involved and the time range in which the fossilized organism likely lived. Some methods date the fossil, some date the *context* of the fossil, and others date either the fossil or the context. Radiocarbon, for example, can be used to date either the remains of the once-living organism or an associated organic substance, such as wood. To determine the age of a human skeleton, the bones can be dated directly. If, however, it can be proved that the deceased was buried at the same time a fire was lit nearby, the fire pit can be dated.

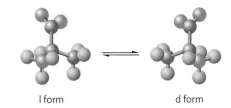

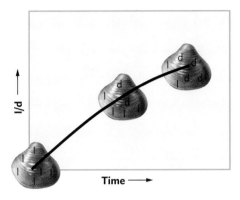

l form   d form

FIGURE 8.24
Amino Acid Dating Amino acid dating is based on changes in the form of amino acid molecules (from L to D) over time.

polarized light A kind of light used in amino acid dating because it allows amino acid changes to be observed and measured.

paleomagnetic dating An absolute dating method based on the reversals of Earth's magnetic field.

electron spin resonance dating An absolute dating method that uses microwave spectroscopy to measure electrons' spins in various materials.

thermoluminescence dating A dating method in which the energy trapped in a material is measured when the object is heated.

FIGURE 8.25

Paleomagnetic Dating Paleomagnetic dating derives from changes in Earth's polarity.

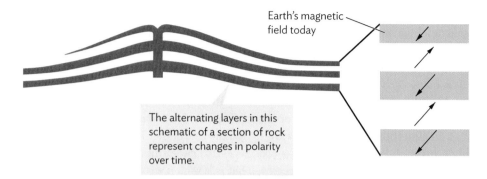

Earth's magnetic field today

The alternating layers in this schematic of a section of rock represent changes in polarity over time.

Mya	Era	Period	Epoch	Polarity

The black and white bars (N = normal, R = reversal) represent polarity changes, each of which is assigned beginning and ending dates. This chart shows the polarity changes over the past 25 million years.

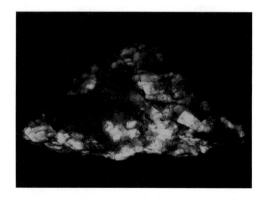

FIGURE 8.26

Thermoluminescence Dating
Thermoluminescence dating is related to the amount of light released when an object with stored energy is heated.

Genetic Dating: The Molecular Clock

The DNA in living organisms is an important source of information for retrospectively dating key events in their species' evolution, including divergence from closely related species and phylogenetic relationships with other organisms. In light of the well-founded assumption that a species accumulates genetic differences in general and mutations in particular over time at a more or less constant rate, it should be possible to develop a chronology showing the amount of time since two species diverged in their evolution. Simply, more closely related species should have more similar DNA than less closely related species have. In the 1960s, the American geneticist Morris Goodman and others developed the molecular clock for dating the divergences of the major primate taxa. This record indicates that Old World monkeys first diverged from all other primates at about 25 mya; gibbons diverged at about 18 mya, orangutans at about 14 mya, gorillas at about 12 mya; and the split occurred between chimpanzees and hominins about 9 mya (**Figure 8.27**). Molecular anthropologists and paleoanthropologists studying the respective genetic and fossil records find a general consistency in the dates for the origins of the major primate groups. As geneticists and anthropologists learn more about the primate genome, this method of retrospective dating is becoming

CONCEPT CHECK

How Old Is It?

Fossils are the primary source of information for documenting the evolution of past life. Paleontologists have developed various means for determining a fossil's age.

Method	Basis	Material	Date Range
Relative Age			
Law of superposition	Older is lower	Just about anything	Just about any time
Stratigraphic correlation	Like strata from different regions are related to the same event	Rocks and fossils	Just about any time
Biostratigraphic (faunal) dating	Evolution of animals	Bones and teeth	Just about any time
Chemical dating	Fossils absorb chemicals, such as fluorine, in soil	Bones	Less than 100,000 yBP
Cultural dating	Artifacts are time-specific	Technology generally	Up to about 2.5 mya
Numerical Age			
Dendrochronology	Tree growth	Specific tree types	Less than 12,000 yBP
Radiocarbon dating	Carbon-14	Anything organic	50,000 yBP to AD 1950
Radiopotassium dating	Potassium-40	Volcanic rocks	More than 200,000 yBP
Amino acid dating	Racemization	Bones, shells	Less than 3 mya
Fission track dating	Fission tracks on rock crystal	Volcanic rock	Up to 3 mya
Paleomagnetic dating	Shifts in Earth's magnetic field	Sedimentary and igneous rocks	Up to 5 mya
Electron spin resonance dating	Concentrations of radioisotopes	Bones, teeth	Several thousand years to more than 1 mya
Thermoluminescence dating	Trapped energy	Sediment, stone, ceramics	Up to 800,000 yBP

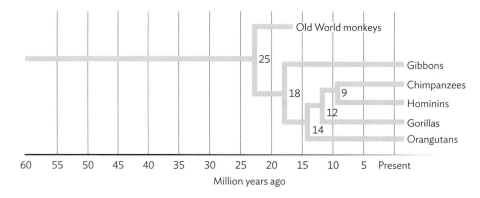

FIGURE 8.27

Genetic Dating: Divergence of Higher Primates Modern primates diverged from a common ancestor millions of years ago. A "molecular clock" helps determine the time since the divergence of monkey and ape species. This system assumes that species accumulate genetic differences over time at a regular rate.

increasingly refined. For example, studies of the human genome are revealing the rate of the appearance of mutations in newborn infants. These findings suggest a slower mutation rate than previously thought, making the split between chimpanzees and the first hominins 8–10 mya. This revision of the molecular clock is also more consistent with the dates for the earliest hominins, which exceed the divergence dates provided by Goodman many years ago (see chapter 10).

In summary: Anthropologists and other scientists who deal with deep time have various methods and research tools for answering questions about when past organisms were alive. Some of these methods and tools directly date fossils, and others date the fossils' geological contexts. Relative and absolute dating have brought about a far greater understanding of the evolutionary record than was imagined when fossils were first being discovered centuries ago. Placing fossils in order creates a detailed picture of the past, of the evolutionary sequence of events for specific organisms and for groups of organisms.

In addition to determining the ages of fossils, anthropologists seek to understand what the habitats were like in which past plants and past animals lived. This is a new area in the study of the past, and it is becoming increasingly clear that understanding environmental contexts—reconstructing past environments to shed light on the circumstances driving evolutionary change, such as major climate change—is crucial to understanding evolution in general and local adaptations in particular. In the next section, we will explore ways in which anthropologists reconstruct environments and landscapes.

8.3 Reconstruction of Ancient Environments and Landscapes

For much of the history of paleontology, the focus has been on evolutionary relationships (phylogeny). In studying the origins and morphological evolution of the various life-forms, paleontologists have asked questions such as *Which (now fossilized) species gave rise to primates? To the first apes? To the first hominins? To the first modern humans?* Phylogenetic questions remain central to the study of evolution, but the evolution of past organisms is not truly meaningful unless it is correlated with the circumstances under which the organisms lived and the processes that underlay their evolutionary changes. Scientists need to ask additional questions; for example, *Which conditions drove natural selection and other processes that account for the appearance, evolution, radiation, and extinction of past primates and humans?* This question pertains especially to the ecology of the setting the primates lived in—their habitat. Using models derived from the study of living animals, paleontologists can look at the bones of extinct animals and determine how they functioned during life and in what kinds of habitats they functioned. For example, as discussed in chapter 6, the long arms and short legs of apes are now well understood to be part of the species' adaptation to life in the trees—the apes are skilled at suspensory forms of locomotion. Therefore, when paleontologists find fossil apes with long arms, such as the Miocene ape *Oreopithecus,* they can infer that these primates lived in a habitat where trees were the dominant form of vegetation (**Figure 8.28**).

The Driving Force in Shaping Environment: Temperature

Temperature is perhaps the single most important feature of climate. Therefore, if scientists can reconstruct the temperature for a particular geologic stratum, they come very close to characterizing a past climate. Scientists cannot measure temperature in the past, but they can identify and study the effects of different temperatures on biology and geologic chemistry. Hot climates leave very different biological and chemical signals than those left by cold climates.

(a)   (b)

FIGURE 8.28

Life in the Trees **(a)** The skeleton and body reconstruction of *Oreopithecus* show that the ape's long arms were adapted to a suspensory form of locomotion. **(b)** Gibbons have a similar body style, adapted to life in the trees. What differences in skeletal anatomy would you expect in a primate that lived primarily on open grassland?

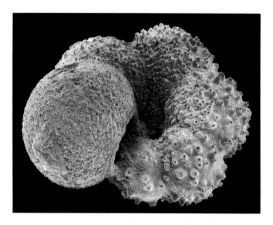

FIGURE 8.29

Foraminifera The chemical composition of these microorganisms found in sediments on the ocean floor provides information on past climates.

foraminifera Marine protozoans that have variably shaped shells with small holes.

Because of this close linkage of temperature with biology and chemistry, paleoclimatologists have reconstructed temperature changes for much of the Cenozoic (and before). Some of the best information on climate history—and especially temperature—is based on the study of **foraminifera** and other ocean-dwelling microorganisms (**Figure 8.29**). These microorganisms' tiny shells are preserved in sediments on the ocean floor worldwide, and their chemical compositions tell important stories about temperature change over time. While the microorganisms are alive, they ingest two of the three stable isotopes of oxygen, ^{18}O and ^{16}O, from the ocean water. Atmospheric temperature directly affects the water's temperature, which in turn affects the amount

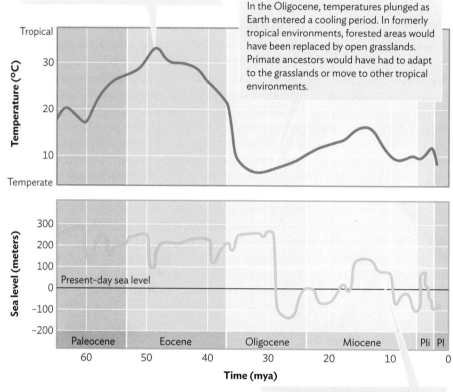

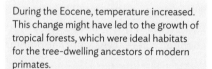

During the Eocene, temperature increased. This change might have led to the growth of tropical forests, which were ideal habitats for the tree-dwelling ancestors of modern primates.

In the Oligocene, temperatures plunged as Earth entered a cooling period. In formerly tropical environments, forested areas would have been replaced by open grasslands. Primate ancestors would have had to adapt to the grasslands or move to other tropical environments.

At the end of the Miocene, Earth entered another cooling period. Again, dramatic changes in habitat and climate occurred. The reduced forests and increased grasslands might have accounted, in part, for the evolution of bipedal locomotion.

FIGURE 8.30

Global Temperature and Climate Changes Changes in temperature during the Cenozoic have been documented by measuring ^{18}O in foraminifera shells. A decrease in ^{18}O indicates an increase in temperature; conversely, an increase in ^{18}O indicates a decrease in temperature. Note: "Pli" refers to Pliocene and "Pl" refers to Pleistocene.

of ^{18}O in the water. When temperature declines, the amount of ^{18}O in the water, and therefore in the microorganism, increases. When temperature increases, the amount of ^{18}O decreases. Geologists have taken core samples of sediments from the ocean floor and have tracked the ^{18}O content in the microorganisms within those sediments, producing a record of global temperature change (**Figure 8.30**).

Based on the isotope signatures of ancient sediments, we know that temperatures were high in the Paleocene, preceding the appearance of true primates, and that they peaked in the early Eocene. This warm period was followed by a gradual decline in temperature throughout the Eocene. At the boundary between the Eocene and Oligocene, about 34 mya, temperature sharply declined, then rose, then sharply declined again. Moderate ups and downs followed in the Oligocene and into the Middle Miocene. After a sharp decline about 17–15 mya, temperature leveled off for the remainder of the Miocene. Climate was drier and more seasonal about 10–5 mya, coinciding with the appearance of early hominins.

One of the most profound temperature changes, and thus dramatic alterations of climate and habitat, began at the end of the Miocene, about 6 mya (**Figure 8.31**). Sea levels are at their highest during warm periods; during cold periods, more water is tied up in ice and glaciers than during warm periods. This cold period likely added a permanent ice sheet on the continent of Antarctica; so much water was tied up in glacial ice that the Mediterranean Sea was nearly dry. During the Pleistocene (2.6 mya–12,000 yBP), periods of massive glaciation, or glacials, were followed by periods of relative warmth, or interglacials. Studies of such cold-and-warm patterns indicate that the time we live in, the Holocene, is not a separate epoch but simply another interglacial. More severely cold weather might be just around the corner!

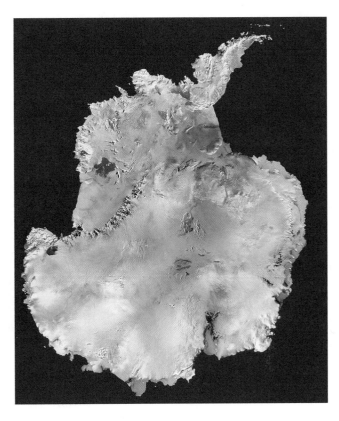

FIGURE 8.31

Antarctica During the latter part of the Miocene, glaciers advanced, tying up a great deal of water that once filled the Mediterranean Sea. Antarctica was covered by a massive ice sheet, as seen in this satellite image.

Chemistry of Animal Remains and Ancient Soils: Windows onto Diets and Habitats

Chemical analysis of the bones and teeth in fossils provides important information about past animals' diets and habitats. The reconstruction of diets and habitats is based on the plants those animals ate. Edible plants use either C_3 photosynthesis or C_4 photosynthesis. The type of photosynthesis determines how the plant extracts and uses carbon from atmospheric carbon dioxide (CO_2). In East Africa, to take one example, **C_3 plants** include trees, bushes, and shrubs associated with a relatively wet, wooded environment; **C_4 plants** are associated with open grasslands typical of tropical savannas. Because C_3 and C_4 plants extract and use carbon differently, the two stable isotopes of carbon in the plants (^{12}C and ^{13}C) have different ratios. C_3 plants have lower ratios of ^{13}C to ^{12}C than do C_4 plants (**Figure 8.32**). That is, the values for the stable isotope ratios are lower for C_3 plants than for C_4 plants.

When animals eat the plants, those ratios are transmitted to the body tissues (including bones and teeth) through digestion and metabolism. Thus, scientists can determine which kind of plant the animal ate based on the ratio of ^{13}C to ^{12}C in the animal's remains. The amounts of ^{13}C and ^{12}C are determined by placing a very tiny piece of bone or of tooth in an instrument called a *mass spectrometer.*

C_3 plants Plants that take in carbon through C_3 photosynthesis, which changes carbon dioxide into a compound having three carbon atoms; tending to be from more temperate regions, these plants include wheat, sugar beets, peas, and a range of hardwood trees.

C_4 plants Plants that take in carbon through C_4 photosynthesis, which changes carbon dioxide into a compound with four carbon atoms; these plants tend to be from warmer regions with low humidity and include corn, sugarcane, millet, and prickly pear.

(a)   (b)

FIGURE 8.32

C₃ and C₄ Plants C_3 and C_4 plants exhibit different ratios of ^{13}C to ^{12}C. **(a)** C_3 plants, such as wheat, and **(b)** C_4 plants, such as corn, have separate photosynthetic pathways that use CO_2 differently.

Similarly, the soils in which edible plants grow express different ratios of ^{13}C to ^{12}C. The plant's residue after decay preserves the stable carbon isotopes. Worldwide, the ratios in the soils, like those in the animals, tend to be lower in forested settings than in grasslands.

Numerous remains of Miocene apes and Pliocene and Pleistocene hominins and other animals have been found in Kenya (discussed further in chapters 9 and 10). The study of the isotopic compositions of these fossils has greatly informed scientists' environmental reconstructions. Today, the Serengeti grasslands of Kenya are dominated by C_4 grasses (**Figure 8.33**). It has long been assumed that the first hominins and their immediate apelike ancestors lived in such a setting. New evidence from the study of the ancient soils (paleosols) and animal bones in Kenya and elsewhere indicates an environment with relatively low ^{13}C to ^{12}C ratios (C_3 plant dominance). This means that if C_4 grasses typical of an open grassland were present, they were quite minimal. However, sometime after 6 mya, C_4 plants became dominant for a range of mammals, indicating a marked shift in ecology. Recent work at a site in Lemudong'o, Kenya, by the American anthropologist Stanley Ambrose and colleagues, shows that at about 6 mya the animals then living there, unlike the ones there today, lived among large trees and water. In particular, birds of prey that roost in large trees (such as the strigid owl) and the large number of colobine monkeys argue for a woodland habitat at 6 mya. Paleosols and fauna dating to about 5.6 mya at early hominin sites in the Middle Awash Valley of Ethiopia show a similar record of open woodland or wooded grasslands around lake margins. The combined evidence from the study of paleosols and animal fossils indicates that the earliest hominins lived in wooded settings, probably for some time after 5 mya (discussed further in chapter 10). This knowledge is crucial because it helps us

FIGURE 8.33

Serengeti Plain, Kenya These grasslands are mostly composed of C$_4$ grasses.

understand the environmental context in which our humanlike ancestors rose, and that rise is fundamental to who we are as biological organisms.

This chapter presented several key concepts for understanding the past, primarily the importance of fossils as windows onto the past. Once placed in time, fossils document and enable us to interpret change over time—they become the central record of evolution. In the upcoming chapters, we will apply this knowledge about fossils and how to evaluate them as we examine nonhuman and human primate evolution. We will look at the origin and evolution of primates, from their very beginning some 55 mya to the dawn of human evolution. Primates are part of a great adaptive radiation of mammals, a radiation that continues to the present day. Understanding primate evolution provides the context for understanding who we are as biological organisms.

CHAPTER 8 REVIEW

ANSWERING THE BIG QUESTIONS

1. **What are fossils?**
   - Fossils are the remains of once-living organisms, wholly or partially transformed into rock. The most common types of fossils are bones and teeth.

2. **What do fossils tell us about the past?**
   - Fossils provide an essential historical record for documenting and understanding the biological evolution of surviving and nonsurviving lineages.
   - Fossils provide information on chronology and geologic time.
   - Fossils and their geologic settings reveal past diets and environments, important contexts for understanding how past organisms evolved.

3. **What methods do anthropologists and other scientists use to study fossils?**

- Geologic time provides the grand scale of the evolution of life. Both relative and absolute (numerical) dates place fossils and past events in chronological sequence on that scale.
- Relative and absolute dates can be determined through various methods. Radioactive decay is central to some of the best methods of determining absolute dates.
- Past climates and habitat in general can be reconstructed via the stable isotopes of oxygen.
- Ancient animals' diets and their habitats can be reconstructed through the stable isotopes of carbon. This record reveals the increasing dominance of open grasslands in later Miocene and Pliocene times, the period when early hominins evolved.

KEY TERMS

amino acid dating
biostratigraphic dating
C_3 plants
C_4 plants
Cenozoic
chemical dating
cultural dating
dendrochronology
electron spin resonance dating
epochs
eras
fission track dating
fluorine dating
foraminifera
half-life
igneous
index fossils
isotopes
Mesozoic
paleomagnetic dating
Paleozoic
Pangaea
pebble tools
polarized light
racemization
radiocarbon dating
radiopotassium dating
sedimentary
Steno's law of superposition
strata
stratigraphic correlation
taphonomy
tectonic
thermoluminescence dating

STUDY QUIZ

1. **Which burial environments would best promote fossilization?**
   a. burial soon after death by sediments or volcanic ash
   b. burial after defleshing of bones by scavengers and insects
   c. burial in groundwater or acidic soils
   d. burial in a geologically active area with high ground pressure

2. **Relative methods of dating can tell us**
   a. the approximate numerical age of a fossil.
   b. the exact numerical age of a fossil.
   c. whether a fossil is older or younger than another fossil or artifact.
   d. the amount of organic material remaining in a fossil.

3. **Radiometric and non-radiometric absolute dating methods both**
   a. provide only a relative date.
   b. provide a numerical date.
   c. measure the radioactive decay of an unstable isotope.

   d. determine past climate history through stable isotope analysis.

4. **What must be considered when choosing a radiometric dating method?**
   a. The half-life of an isotope limits its usefullness to a certain date range.
   b. No radiometric dating methods can date organic materials.
   c. No radiometric dating methods can date inorganic materials.
   d. Fossils must be associated with another fossil to give a relative date.

5. **Stable isotope analysis of carbon in a fossilized tooth would be most useful for determining the**
   a. relative age of the tooth compared to another fossil.
   b. absolute age of the tooth.
   c. temperature of the animal's environment.
   d. types of plants consumed by the animal during life.

EVOLUTION REVIEW

THE FOSSIL RECORD

Synopsis The evolution of life on Earth has occurred on a geologic timescale that is almost unfathomable, with the first single-celled organisms appearing around 3.5 *billion* years ago and the first multicellular organisms appearing around 1.2 *billion* years ago. The evolution of the order Primates is more recent, occurring over the past 50 million years, and the evolution of our own branch (that is, hominins) more recent still, from approximately 7 mya to the present. The physical evidence, primarily bones and teeth, of these evolutionary processes constitutes the fossil record. Advances in scientific dating techniques and the ability to reconstruct ancient environments have greatly expanded paleontologists' and physical anthropologists' understanding of the timing of major evolutionary events, the tempo at which evolution occurs, and the environmental pressures operating on species in deep time. This knowledge sets the stage for the "big questions" regarding primate and hominin evolution that will be addressed in the subsequent chapters.

Q1. Identify the two main components around which paleontology, or the scientific study of the fossil record, is built. How does each of these components contribute to our understanding of biological evolution?

Q2. Identify the main difference between methods of relative dating and methods of absolute dating. Provide one example of the use of a relative dating technique and one example of the use of an absolute dating technique in addressing research questions about human evolution.

Q3. By definition, our knowledge of the fossil record will always be incomplete, but scientists are nonetheless able to test hypotheses regarding the evolution of our own and other species. Summarize the process by which an organism's remains become fossilized. What are some factors that can influence fossil discoveries and our knowledge of the fossil record?

Hint Think about events that can occur before, during, and after fossilization of an organism's remains.

Q4. Describe the process by which genetic dating can be accomplished via the molecular clock. How do physical anthropologists use both genetic dating and the fossil record to clarify evolutionary relationships and the timing of evolutionary events? How do the data sources for genetic dating and the fossil record differ from one another?

Hint Think about the kinds of organisms studied for genetic dating compared to those found in the fossil record.

Q5. Explain how gradualism and punctuated equilibrium differ with regard to the tempo, or rate, of evolutionary change. What types of environmental conditions may cause the tempo of evolution to speed up, resulting in the rapid change found in some areas of the fossil record?

ADDITIONAL READINGS

Klein, R. G. 1999. *The Human Career: Human Biological and Cultural Origins*, 2nd ed. Chicago: University of Chicago Press.

Lanham, U. 1973. *The Bone Hunters*. New York: Columbia University Press.

Lee-Thorp, J. A., M. Sponheimer, and N. J. van der Merwe. 2003. What do stable isotopes tell us about hominid dietary and ecological niches in the Pliocene? *International Journal of Osteoarchaeology* 13: 104–113.

Marshak, S. 2012. *Earth: Portrait of a Planet,* 4th ed. New York: Norton.

Mayor, A. 2001. *The First Fossil Hunters: Paleontology in Greek and Roman Times*. Princeton, NJ: Princeton University Press.

Taylor, R. E. 1995. Radiocarbon dating: the continuing revolution. *Evolutionary Anthropology* 4: 169–181.

Winchester, S. 2001. *The Map That Changed the World: William Smith and the Birth of Modern Geology.* New York: HarperCollins.

Wolpoff, M. H. 1999. *Paleoanthropology,* 2nd ed. New York: McGraw-Hill.

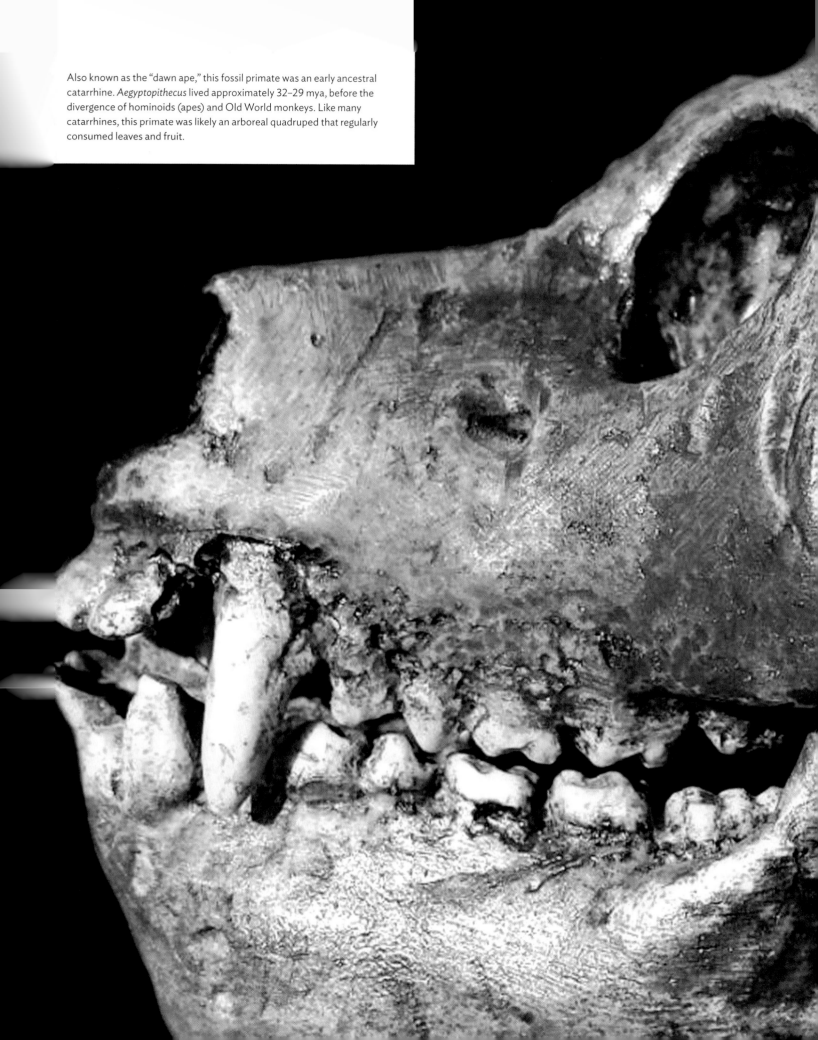

Also known as the "dawn ape," this fossil primate was an early ancestral catarrhine. *Aegyptopithecus* lived approximately 32–29 mya, before the divergence of hominoids (apes) and Old World monkeys. Like many catarrhines, this primate was likely an arboreal quadruped that regularly consumed leaves and fruit.

9

Primate Origins and Evolution

THE FIRST 50 MILLION YEARS

BIG QUESTIONS

1. **Why become a primate?**
2. **What were the first primates?**
3. **What were the first higher primates?**
4. **What evolutionary developments link past primate species and living ones?**

Remember Georges Cuvier, the Frenchman (introduced in chapter 2) who recognized that fossils are the remains of now-extinct animals and of plants? I bring him up again because of his central role in the study of primate evolution. The field would not have been the same had he not lived in the late eighteenth and early nineteenth centuries, when the scientific method, as we know it, began to take shape. As a child, Cuvier read the eighteenth-century biology luminaries Linnaeus and Buffon, and their works sparked in him a lifelong interest in natural history. He went on to attend college at the University of Stuttgart in Germany, and like many other bright college graduates at the time, he was recruited as a private tutor for a wealthy family, in his case in Normandy, France. While living with his host family, as luck would have it, he met France's leading naturalist and anatomist, Étienne Geoffroy Saint-Hilaire (1772–1844). Professor Geoffroy must have been impressed with young Cuvier because he hired Cuvier as his assistant in comparative anatomy at the new National Museum of Natural History in Paris. Cuvier became interested in the mammal

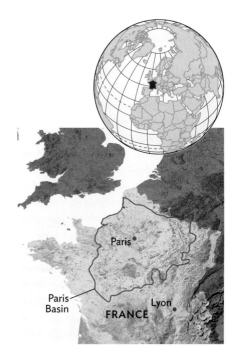

fossils around Paris, and his encyclopedic knowledge of anatomy enabled him to recognize similarities between animals represented by fossils and living animals.

Among the hundreds of fossil bones and fossil teeth that he studied was a tiny skull, which he found in a gypsum quarry at nearby Montmartre. Dating to the Eocene, this specimen was unlike any skull Cuvier had ever seen. Was the animal it had come from living or extinct? When he published his description of the fossil in 1822, he did not recognize the creature he called *Adapis parisiensis* as a primate (**Figure 9.1**).

By the late nineteenth century, other French paleontologists had realized that Cuvier's fossil was that of an early primate, a finding that has been substantiated time and time again during the twentieth century, making *Adapis* the first primate fossil described by a scientist. Cuvier, the founder of paleontology, had good reasons for not recognizing this animal as a primate. For one thing, *no* fossil record of primates existed then—just about everything discussed in this chapter was found long after Cuvier's time. For another, taxonomists had very little understanding of living primate variation, and they had not yet defined the order much beyond Linnaeus's classification scheme (discussed in chapter 2).

Although Cuvier's assessment was wrong, his meticulous description of the *Adapis* fossil was very important. Stories like this happen often in science: The original discoverer may not recognize the finding for what it is, mostly because there is no context or prior discovery. Nevertheless, the discovery provides later scientists with important evidence. In this case, Cuvier's pioneering detailed description began the long process of documenting primate evolution, a process that continues today. Moreover, Cuvier set the bar high for future paleontologists by demonstrating the value of thorough description. Most important, Cuvier's careful work planted the seeds for asking key questions about primate origins.

In the two centuries since Cuvier, many thousands of fossils of ancient primates have been discovered in Europe, Asia, Africa, North America, and South America (**Figure 9.2**), providing a record—relatively complete for some time periods, frustratingly incomplete for others—of the origins and evolution of the earliest primates and their descendants. In this chapter, we address the big questions by examining the fossil record for evidence of three key developments: the emergence of the first primates, the origins of higher primates (anthropoids), and the origins and evolution of the major anthropoid groups (monkeys, apes, and humans). The time frame for this chapter is expansive—more than 60 million years! We start in the early

FIGURE 9.1

***Cuvier and* Adapis** In describing the fossil remains of an animal he mistakenly thought was an ungulate or artiodactyl (hoofed mammal), Cuvier (here seated) named the specimen *Adapis,* Latin for "toward sacred bull." Later scholars realized that these remains were the first primate fossil ever recorded by a scientist.

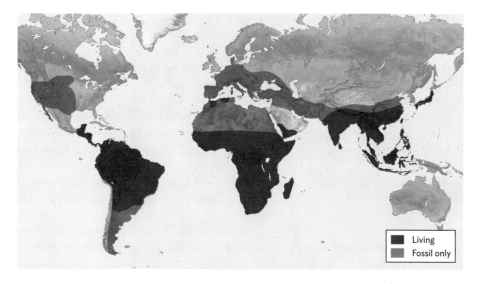

FIGURE 9.2

Living and Extinct Primates As this map indicates, fossils of extinct primate species have been found on every continent except Australia and Antarctica. Climate changes over millions of years probably explain why primates were once distributed more extensively throughout the world than are modern, living primates.

FIGURE 9.3

Primate Family Tree The variety of primates today is the result of millions of years of primate evolution. The different lineages represented by great apes, lesser apes, Old World monkeys, New World monkeys, and prosimians reflect divergences in primate evolution. For example, New World monkeys split off around 35 mya, and Old World monkeys diverged approximately 25 mya. The lineage leading to modern humans, however, diverged from the chimpanzee lineage much more recently, somewhere between 8 and 10 mya.

Paleocene, somewhere around 66 mya (about 10 million years or so before the emergence of the first true primate), and end in the late Miocene, around 5.3 mya, the dawn of human evolution. The record indicates that primates were highly successful and, like other mammals, underwent a cycle of adaptive radiations, followed by extinctions, and then new radiations of surviving lineages. These survivors are the primates occupying Earth today, including human beings (**Figure 9.3**).

9.1 **Why Did Primates Emerge?**

We know *what* primates are. For example, they are agile and adept at grasping, the claws of their ancestors have been replaced by nails, they have stereoscopic vision (the eyes are on the front of the head), they have a reduced sense of smell, and they have a big brain (**Figure 9.4**). *Why* they became what they are is far less clear. In the early 1900s, the British anatomists Sir Grafton Elliot Smith and Frederic Wood Jones proposed their **arboreal hypothesis** to explain primate origins. Smith and Jones hypothesized that primates' defining characteristics were adaptations to life in the trees: grasping

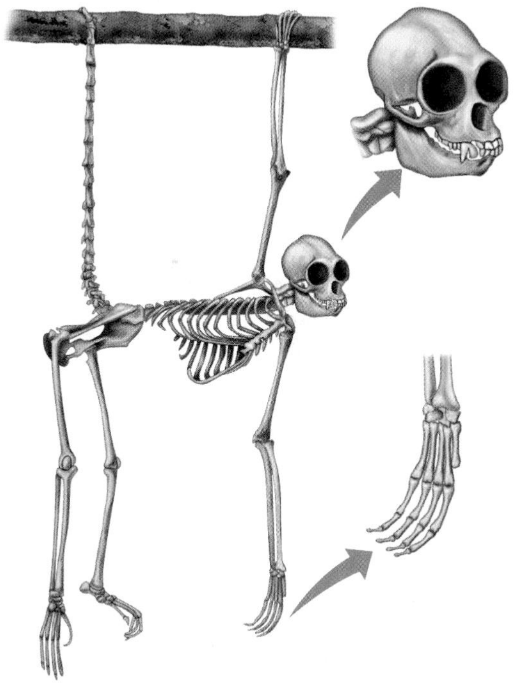

FIGURE 9.4

Primate Characteristics Primates differ from other mammals thanks to a unique combination of traits, such as forward-facing eyes, a postorbital bar or fully enclosed eye orbit, a large cranial vault, a reduced snout, and a versatile dentition. In the postcranial skeleton, primates usually have divergent big toes and divergent thumbs, grasping hands and grasping feet, and nails instead of claws on their fingers and their toes.

hands and grasping feet were crucial for holding on to tree branches, binocular vision allowed much greater depth perception for judging distance in the movement from place to place in the trees, smell was no longer necessary for finding food, and greater intelligence was important for understanding three-dimensional space in the trees. The movement from life on the ground to life in the trees, Smith and Jones surmised, put into motion a series of selective pressures that resulted in the ancestral primate.

The arboreal hypothesis continues to profoundly influence the way anthropologists think about primate origins and evolution. But in the early 1970s, the American anthropologist Matt Cartmill challenged the arboreal hypothesis. He pointed out that lots of mammals are arboreal (squirrels, for example), but except for primates none have evolved the entire set of characteristics that define the order Primates. (These characteristics include generalized structure, arboreal adaptation, and care of young; see chapters 6 and 7.) To account for primate origins, Cartmill proposed his **visual predation hypothesis.** He hypothesized that the first primate specialized in preying on insects and other small creatures, hunting them in tree branches or in forest undergrowth. Cartmill argued that the shift to life in the trees was not the most important factor in explaining primate origins. Rather, the catching of small prey—using both a highly specialized visual apparatus and the fine motor skills of grasping digits—set primate evolution in motion.

Although the visual predation hypothesis elegantly explains the visual adaptations, intelligence, and grasping abilities of primates, it leaves an important question unanswered: *What role do the primate characteristics play in the acquisition and consumption of fruit, which many primates eat?* The American anthropologist Robert Sussman has hypothesized that the visual acuity, grasping hands, and grasping feet of primates were mostly adaptations for eating fruit and other foods made available with the radiation of modern groups of flowering plants called *angiosperms.* In other words, the original primate adaptation was about getting fruit and not about preying on insects. Sussman reasoned that because there was little light in the forest, early primates required visual adaptations for seeing small objects. Moreover, their grasping toes helped the animals cling to tree branches while they picked and ate fruit, rather than having to go back to more secure and larger branches, as squirrels do when they eat nuts. Sussman's **angiosperm radiation hypothesis** is grounded in the acquisition of a new food source available in the early Cenozoic: fruit.

In reality, elements of all three hypotheses may have provided the evolutionary opportunities that resulted in primate origins. Indeed, primates' most special feature is their adaptive versatility, especially in an arboreal setting. Primates have evolved strategies and anatomical features that enhance their ability to adapt to new and novel circumstances. That evolution constitutes primates' story of origin.

visual predation hypothesis The proposition that unique primate traits arose as adaptations to preying on insects and on small animals.

angiosperm radiation hypothesis The proposition that certain primate traits, such as visual acuity, occurred in response to the availability of fruit and flowers after the spread of angiosperms.

9.2 The First True Primate: Visual, Tree-Dwelling, Agile, Smart

Primates in the Paleocene?

We know *generally when* the first primates appeared—almost certainly in the early Cenozoic era. But just how early in the Cenozoic is debated by the paleontologists who study early primate evolution. They have reached no consensus as to whether the first

(a)

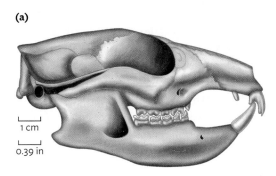

1 cm

0.39 in

(b)

FIGURE 9.5

Plesiadapis These primatelike mammals were likely an ancestral lineage leading to true primate ancestors. **(a)** As this *Plesiadapis* skull illustrates, plesiadapiforms did not possess primates' postorbital bar. And while primates have a versatile dentition, plesiadapiforms had very specialized anterior (front) teeth, which were separated from the posterior (rear) teeth by a large gap. In addition, *Plesiadapis* and other plesiadapiforms had much smaller brains than those of true primate ancestors. **(b)** This reconstruction of *Plesiadapis* reflects similarities to and differences from modern primates.

primates appeared in the Paleocene epoch, which began 66 mya, or in the following epoch, the Eocene, which began 56 mya. The Paleocene candidate for the first primates is a highly diverse, highly successful group of primitive mammals called the **plesiadapiforms,** which lived in western North America, western Europe, Asia, and possibly Africa. These animals represent an adaptive radiation that flourished over a 10-million-year period, beginning at the start of the Paleocene.

Despite their amazing diversity and geographic spread, by about 56 mya most of the plesiadapiforms had gone extinct. Were they primates? Probably not. The problem with attributing them to the Primate order is that they lack the key characteristics that define primates today. That is, in contrast to primates, the plesiadapiforms lacked a postorbital bar and convergent eye orbits, their digits were not especially well adapted for grasping tree branches (they lacked opposability), their digits lacked nails (they had claws), their teeth were highly specialized (some even had three cusps on their upper incisors, as opposed to the single cusp of most primates today), and their brain was tiny (**Figure 9.5**). Moreover, some plesiadapiforms lacked the auditory bulla, a part of the temporal bone that contains the middle-ear bones and is present in all primates. Because of their potential relationship with the first true primates, the American paleontologist Philip Gingerich has called them **Proprimates,** a separate order from Primates.

Eocene Euprimates: The First True Primates

Far better contenders for early primates are the **euprimates** (meaning "true primates"), which first appeared at the start of the Eocene, as early as 56 mya. Euprimates consisted of two closely related, highly successful groups: the **adapids** and the **omomyids.** Their fossils are found in the western United States, western Europe, Africa, and

plesiadapiforms Paleocene organisms that may have been the first primates, originating from an adaptive radiation of mammals.

Proprimates A separate order of early primate ancestors from the Paleocene, such as the plesiadapiforms.

euprimates The first true primates from the Eocene: the tarsierlike omomyids and the lemurlike adapids.

adapids Euprimates of the Eocene that were likely ancestral to modern lemurs and possibly ancestral to anthropoids.

omomyids Eocene euprimates that may be ancestral to tarsiers.

Asia and are the most common early primate fossils—accounting for about 40% of all species from the early Eocene, or about 200 species (**Figure 9.6**). Given the vast number of their fossils that have been collected—on the order of 100,000—anthropologists have an excellent picture of their physical description and their adaptive circumstances.

Were they primates? Almost certainly. Unlike the plesiadapiforms, adapids and omomyids had clear primate characteristics: the postorbital bar and convergent eye

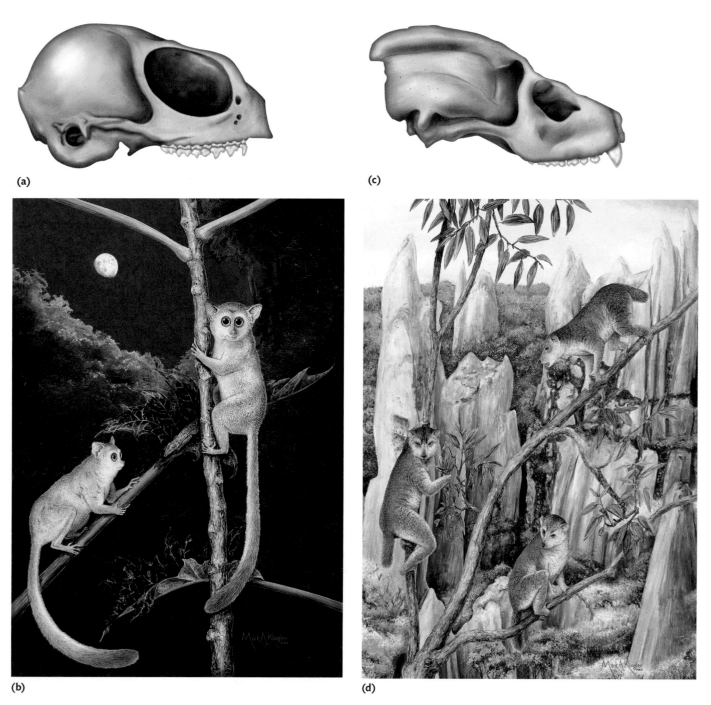

(a)

(c)

(b)

(d)

FIGURE 9.6

Omomyids and Adapids These two main groups of euprimates are likely related to tarsiers and lemurs, respectively. Unlike plesiadapiforms, omomyids and adapids are considered true primate ancestors because they possess many primate traits. **(a, b)** Omomyids, such as *Shoshonius* (shown here), had large eyes and large eye orbits on the front of the skull, grasping hands and grasping feet, and a reduced snout. Like tarsiers, these earliest primates were nocturnal. **(c, d)** Adapids, including Cuvier's *Adapis,* also had forward-facing eyes. However, adapids were diurnal and had longer snouts than omomyids.

orbits, long digits with opposability for grasping, digits with nails (not claws), nonspecialized teeth, and a large brain relative to body size. These features indicate that vision was essential to their adaptation, they were agile and tree-dwelling, their diet was not as specialized as that of the plesiadapiforms, and they were smarter than the earlier animals. Their body sizes were small but highly varied. Adapids were about the same size as some modern lemurs. One of the largest, **Notharctus,** weighed about 7 kg (15 lb). **Adapis,** known from many skulls and other parts of the skeleton, weighed a little more than 1 kg (2 lb). The adapids' incisors were flat and vertical, similar to those of many living anthropoids (**Figure 9.7**). In addition, like anthropoids, adapids had pronounced sexual dimorphism in body size and in canine size, some had lower jaws with two fused halves, and some had relatively short foot bones.

The omomyids differed from the adapids in having large and projecting central lower incisors, small canines, and wide variation in the other teeth. Unlike most adapids (and sometimes like living tarsiers), omomyids had a short skull, a short and narrow snout, and large eye orbits. Their large eye orbits held huge eyes adapted for night vision. Like the adapids, the omomyids consisted of widely diverse species and have left behind a great number of fossils, facts that speak to their high degree of success throughout the Eocene epoch.

From what primitive mammalian group did the adapids and omomyids evolve? Most of the plesiadapiforms are unlikely ancestors for the euprimates because they either went extinct before the Eocene or were too specialized to have given rise to Eocene primates. However, one plesiadapiform, *Carpolestes,* whose skeleton was found in

Notharctus A genus of one of the largest adapids from the Eocene.

Adapis A genus of adapids from the Eocene.

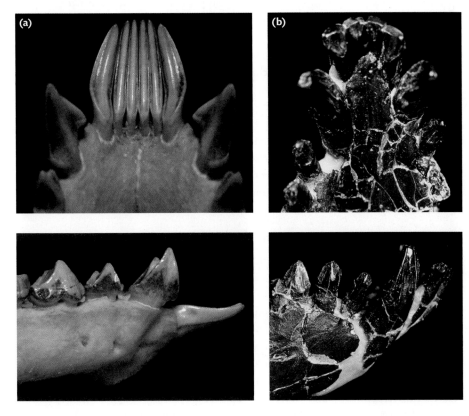

FIGURE 9.7

Incisor Variation **(a)** In modern lemur species, the lower incisors form a dental comb that projects horizontally from the mandible. **(b)** This feature was absent, however, in adapids, whose more vertical incisors resembled those of living monkeys and living apes.

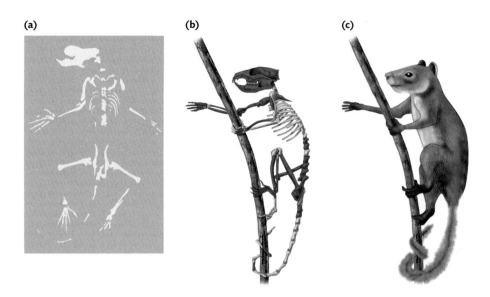

(a)   **(b)**   **(c)**

FIGURE 9.8

Carpolestes simpsoni **(a)** Fossilized remains such as these suggest that this species of plesiadapiforms is a link between primatelike mammalian ancestors and the earliest true primate ancestors. **(b)** In this reconstruction of the full skeleton, the fossilized remains are highlighted. **(c)** This reconstruction depicts what *Carpolestes* might have looked like in life.

Carpolestes A plesiadapiform genus from the Paleocene, probably ancestral to the Eocene euprimates.

Wyoming's Bighorn Basin, had a number of characteristics that would be expected in a transitional animal leading to what were clear primates later in time. **Carpolestes** had a grasping foot, made possible by an opposable big toe; it had long, grasping fingers; and it had a nail on the end of the first foot digit (**Figure 9.8**). This animal may be the link between proprimates of the Paleocene and euprimates of the Eocene.

The extinction of the plesiadapiforms, at the end of the Paleocene, and the appearance of the euprimates, at the beginning of the Eocene, coincided with a profound period of global warming. A rapid temperature increase around 55 mya created tropical conditions virtually everywhere around the world. The resulting creation of new habitats triggered an adaptive radiation of modern-appearing primates, the euprimates. In particular, the high global temperatures and high global humidity led to an expansion of evergreen tropical forest, the environment that made possible the growth of many mammalian groups, including the primates.

The Anthropoid Ancestor: Euprimate Contenders

Like the Paleocene proprimates preceding them, many of the euprimates went extinct, likely owing to a major change in climate involving a cooling trend, causing a change in habitat at the end of the Eocene. Some of them may have provided the ancestral base for strepsirhines and haplorhines. Based on the kind of skull and tooth evidence described above, Philip Gingerich has made the case that adapids represent the ancestral group for living lemurs and anthropoids, with lemurs evolving a tooth comb (missing in adapids) and anthropoids not evolving the tooth comb. Their flat incisors, general similarity with anthropoids, and great diversity suggest that adapids had an evolutionary relationship with anthropoids. However, some (or even all) of adapids' anthropoidlike features could simply be unevolved (primitive) traits of all primates. If that is the case, then an ancestral-descendant link between adapids and later primates would be difficult to prove.

The American anthropologist Frederick Szalay sees a strong resemblance between

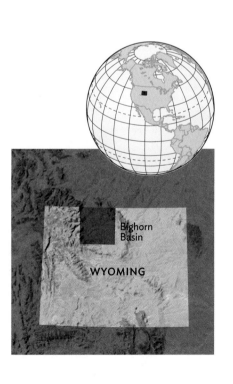

Bighorn Basin

WYOMING

omomyid fossils and living tarsiers, and a greater similarity between tarsiers and anthropoids than between lemurs and anthropoids. Therefore, he regards the omomyids as more likely candidates for the ancestry of anthropoids than are lemurs. However, the anatomical similarities between omomyids and tarsiers are more suggestive than definitive. No single characteristic links these Eocene primates with anthropoids. While the adapids or omomyids may be ancestral to anthropoids, the lack of clear transitional fossils between these archaic primates and later primates makes it unclear what the anthropoid ancestor was more than 40 million years ago.

Clues to the characteristics of the early haplorhines are seen in a remarkably well-preserved skeleton of an early primate, dating to 55 mya and known as *Archicebus* (**Figure 9.9**). Discovered in an ancient lake bed in the Jingzhou area of the Hubei Province, China, by a team led by the Chinese paleontologist Xijun Ni, this primate combines features of anthropoids and tarsiers. The presence of this primate in China at such an early date indicates that haplorhines originated in Asia. Although *Archicebus* may have not been the first haplorhine, it emerged very close to the split between haplorhines and strepsirhines. The bones of its heel and ankle resemble those of monkeys. Its skull resembles that of tarsiers, with small eye orbits and a short snout. In addition, the cusps on the molars are high and pointed, similar to what is seen in tarsiers. This mosaic of features suggests that haplorhines originated at 55 mya, on the boundary between the Paleocene and the Eocene. It also suggests that the first haplorhines were diurnal (and therefore had these small eye orbits), arboreal (and therefore had these foot, hand, and limb structures), and primarily insectivorous (as tarsiers are today). And in contrast to their great evolutionary significance, the earliest-known primates appear to have been tiny. *Archicebus* is estimated to have been even smaller than the mouse lemur (the smallest primate today), weighing only about 28 g (1 oz) and easily fitting into the palm of your hand.

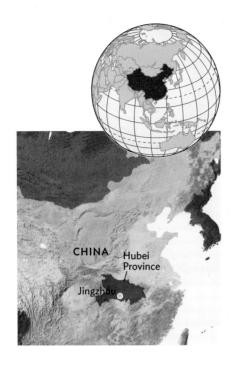

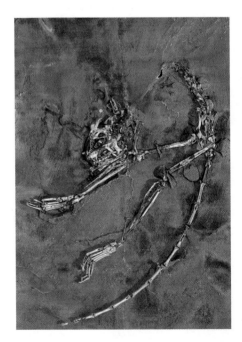

FIGURE 9.9

Archicebus This skeleton and reconstruction of *Archicebus* show its combination of anthropoid and tarsier features. Its heels and ankles resemble those of monkeys, whereas its small eyes and short snout resemble those of tarsiers.

THE FAYUM DE

HEARTLAND OF ANTHROPOID ANCESTORS

Apidium
A parapithecid genus from the Oligocene, possibly ancestral to anthropoids.

The Fayum Depression, the region located on the eastern edge of the Sahara Desert in North Africa, first came to paleontologists' attention in the late nineteenth and early twentieth centuries. Among the various fossils discovered at that time was a primate, the parapithecid *Apidium,* first recognized and reported on in 1908 by the eminent American paleontologist Henry Fairfield Osborne of New York's American Museum of Natural History. To Osborne and his contemporaries, it was clear that the Fayum was special—it held the record of the first anthropoids.

Unfortunately, owing to various events and circumstances, including the Fayum's remoteness and desolateness, no substantive work occurred there during the next five decades. While on a visit to the American Museum of Natural History in the 1950s, a young graduate student, Elwyn Simons, got a firsthand impression of the fossils collected 50 years before. He concluded that the Fayum deserved another look to address one of the most important questions in physical anthropology: *What were the first higher primates? Apidium* had all the makings of a higher primate, and where there was one fossil, Simons decided, there had to be more.

In 1961, Simons went to the Fayum for the first time to collect enough fossils to answer this question and to lay the groundwork for future work at what he hoped would prove an important site. During that trip and many more over the next four decades, Simons found more than 1,000 fossils of ancient primates, dating from the late Eocene and early Oligocene, in the area of the Fayum called the Qatrani Escarpment. By studying these fossils, he and his collaborators learned that the first higher primates had all the traits one would expect. In particular, the teeth morphology indicated that these primates ate fruit and seeds. That is, the low,

round cusps on the molars reflected the primates' ability to crush and pulp the fruit and seeds. (By contrast, the molars of primates that eat leaves tend to have

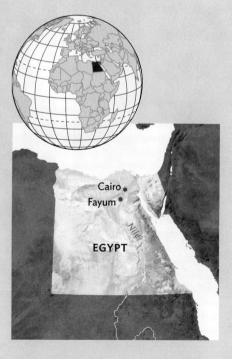

Situated in the Sahara Desert by the Nile River, Egypt's Fayum region has been a great source of paleoanthropological research, yielding numerous fossils, including those of primates.

tiny crests for shearing the leaves.) Simons and his collaborators hit the paleontological jackpot with their discoveries: the Oligocene Fayum primates proved to be the first irrefutable higher primates, with lots of anatomical details to reveal their adaptations.

Simons also wanted to better understand the ecological context for the higher primates' evolution. *What did the setting look like? What other kinds of animals were living at the same time and the same place?* These questions were tough to answer: they involved the collaboration of many other experts with varying interests, and they required the collection of many thousands of fossils representing both animals and plants. Through careful excavations, exact recording of fossils' locations, and precise dating of fossils' contexts through radioisotope methods (discussed in chapter 8), Simons and his colleagues constructed a highly detailed picture of the Oligocene landscapes in which the first apes lived. Painstaking research enabled these scientists to answer long-standing questions and to produce one of the most comprehensive pictures of past habitats for any time in any place in the world.

This section of the Fayum became a primary focus of research through Simons, who wished to find evidence of more fossil primates, such as *Apidium*. The exposure of geologic strata enabled researchers to access deposits from millions of years ago.

One way in which paleoanthropologists search for fossils in the Fayum is to sweep away layers of sand. Here, the American paleontologist Daniel Gebo exposes fossils of early primates.

The First Anthropoids

During the Eocene, a group of primates called **basal anthropoids,** whose fossils have been found in Asia and Africa, had the kinds of characteristics that would be expected in an anthropoid ancestor or even the earliest anthropoid. One of the most interesting basal anthropoids is the remarkably tiny ***Eosimias*** (meaning "dawn monkey"), found near the village of Shanghuang in Jiangsu Province, China, and dating to about 42 mya (**Figure 9.10**). It is one of a number of eosimiids found in southern and eastern Asia. Based on their observations of the teeth and the skeleton, especially of the foot bones, the American anthropologists Daniel Gebo and Christopher Beard regard *Eosimias* as the first true anthropoid. Especially convincing about their argument is the strong similarity between the shape and overall appearance of the tarsal (ankle) bones of *Eosimias* and the tarsal bones of fossil and living anthropoids. That is, *Eosimias*'s short calcaneus, or heel bone, was like that of an anthropoid (**Figure 9.11**). It was especially

Eosimias A genus of very small basal anthropoids from the Eocene.

FIGURE 9.10

Eosimias This basal anthropoid, first discovered in 1999, represents one of the earliest genera of catarrhines (Old World monkeys and apes). *Eosimias* is the smallest primate ancestor discovered to date. Its smallest species is about the size of a human thumb and about one-third the size of the smallest living primate, the mouse lemur of Madagascar, which weighs approximately 28 g (1 oz). The fossilized remains suggest they were arboreal insectivores and likely nocturnal.

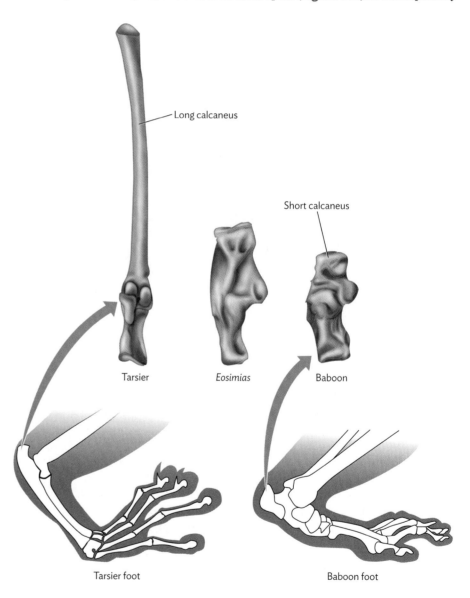

Tarsier   *Eosimias*   Baboon

Tarsier foot   Baboon foot

FIGURE 9.11

Calcaneal Variation Evidence for patterns of locomotion in *Eosimias* comes from some of the postcranial remains, especially bones of the ankle and foot. *Eosimias*'s calcaneus was more like that of an anthropoid (such as the baboon) than like that of a prosimian (such as the tarsier).

similar to the heel bones of South American monkeys, revealing that this primate moved in trees like a monkey. In addition, the upper canine and upper jaw would have given it a monkeylike face.

Another, somewhat later basal anthropoid is from the Fayum Depression in Egypt. Called **Biretia** by the American paleontologists Erik Seiffert and Elwyn Simons, it dates to the late Eocene, at about 37 mya. The presence of anthropoid characteristics in the teeth, such as the two-cusped (bicuspid) lower premolars, indicates that this animal, too, represents the beginnings of higher primates (**Figure 9.12**). If it is the first higher primate, then either anthropoid ancestry began in Africa or the earlier primates from Asia emigrated to Africa and evolved into the African anthropoids. Based on the limited evidence, it is not possible to say conclusively whether Asia or Africa is the ancestral home of the higher primates, the anthropoids. However, *Eosimias* and *Biretia* have the attributes that would be expected in an anthropoid ancestor. Given the earlier date for *Eosimias,* Asia could be the ancestral home for the higher primates. If so, then Asian basal anthropoids gave rise to all of the higher primates of Africa.

This discussion should make clear that the origin of anthropoids is murky. To understand the geographic (Asia versus Africa) and environmental contexts in which anthropoids arose, anthropologists are looking to the increasing fossil record of basal anthropoids and their remarkable diversity. Regardless of their geographic origins, the diversity of basal anthropoids found in both Asia and Africa suggests the beginnings of a tremendous radiation of a highly successful group of mammals.

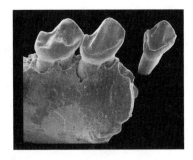

FIGURE 9.12

Biretia Its fossilized remains suggest that this animal was an anthropoid ancestor. For example, its lower premolars, with their two cusps, are structured like those of anthropoids.

Biretia A basal anthropoid genus found in the Fayum, Egypt, that may be ancestral to later anthropoids.

9.3 Early Anthropoids Evolve and Thrive

Beginning in the Oligocene epoch and coinciding with a period of widespread plant and animal extinctions, an episode of rapid global cooling occurred. With this shift in climate came new habitats and newly diverse primate taxa. The fossil record representing the evolution of these taxa is as remarkable in the Oligocene as the fossil record is in the Eocene. However, whereas Eocene primate fossils have been found in a wide variety of settings around the world, most of the Oligocene primate fossils have come from one primary region, the Fayum (see "How Do We Know: The Fayum Depression" earlier). Spanning about 8 million years of evolution, roughly 37–29 mya, the fossil record consists of a wide and abundant variety of plants and of animals. From these remains, scientists have constructed a detailed picture of the environment in northeast Africa (**Figure 9.13**). In sharp contrast to the desert landscape of the Fayum today—it is among the harshest and driest places in the world—the late Eocene–early Oligocene landscape was much like contemporary southeast Asia; namely, wet, warm, and tropical. The Fayum's major feature, Birket Qarun Lake, was long the focus for all organisms in the region. In addition to diverse primates, all sorts of animals lived there, including the ancestors of rodents (the earliest porcupines are from the Fayum), bats, hippopotamuses, elephants, crocodiles, and various birds. Plants are also represented by a diverse array of tropical taxa, such as mangroves, water lilies, climbing vines, figs, palms, and cinnamon. It must have been an amazing place.

The Fayum primates included various strepsirhines and at least three groups of primitive (but unmistakable) higher primates: **oligopithecids, parapithecids,** and **propliopithecids** (**Figure 9.14**). The oligopithecids were the earliest, dating to about 35 mya. The later parapithecids, such as their namesake genus, **Parapithecus,** are

oligopithecids The earliest anthropoid ancestors in the Oligocene, found in the Fayum, Egypt.

parapithecids Anthropoid ancestors from the Oligocene, found in the Fayum, Egypt.

propliopithecids Anthropoid ancestors from the Oligocene, found in Africa.

Parapithecus A genus of later parapithecids from the Oligocene, found in the Fayum, Egypt.

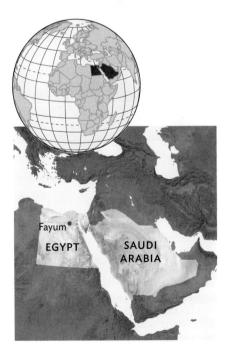

FIGURE 9.13

The Fayum Climatological and environmental reconstructions have provided a glimpse of what the Fayum was like when some of the earliest primates lived, at the end of the Eocene and the beginning of the Oligocene.

Propliopithecus Oligocene propliopithecid genus.

Aegyptopithecus A propliopithecid genus from the Oligocene, probably ancestral to catarrhines; the largest primate found in the Fayum, Egypt.

among these early anthropoids, and they retained some primitive characteristics. For example, parapithecids had three premolars. This condition may directly link parapithecids to platyrrhines (which also have three premolars), but having three premolars is more likely the ancestral condition that precedes the divergence of platyrrhines and catarrhines.

The propliopithecids consisted of several genera, but **Propliopithecus** and **Aegyptopithecus,** both dating to between 32 and 29 mya, are the most common of this group of primates. The propliopithecids had a more derived dental formula of 2/1/2/3, one fewer premolar than the parapithecids had. In this and other respects, they were more

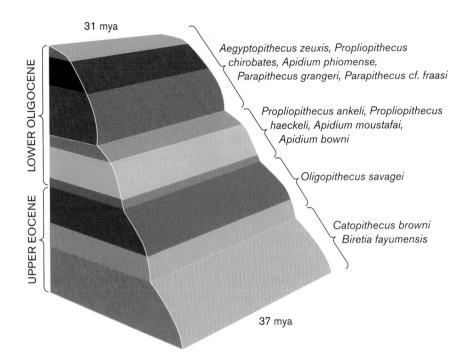

31 mya

LOWER OLIGOCENE

UPPER EOCENE

Aegyptopithecus zeuxis, Propliopithecus chirobates, Apidium phiomense, Parapithecus grangeri, Parapithecus cf. fraasi

Propliopithecus ankeli, Propliopithecus haeckeli, Apidium moustafai, Apidium bowni

Oligopithecus savagei

Catopithecus browni
Biretia fayumensis

37 mya

FIGURE 9.14

Primate Ancestors in the Fayum The earliest primate ancestor found in Fayum deposits is *Biretia fayumensis*. Various species of early prosimians and anthropoids have been recovered from Fayum deposits spanning the Oligocene.

catarrhinelike than the parapithecids. *Aegyptopithecus,* the largest of the Fayum primates (it weighed 6–8 kg [13–18 lb], or about the weight of a fox) is the best-known Fayum primate (**Figure 9.15**). *Aegyptopithecus* had a sagittal crest on the top of the skull where a large temporalis muscle was attached (see Figure 6.29 in chapter 6). Its brain was small compared to those of later catarrhines. The front and hind limbs were of relatively equal size, suggesting that the animal was a slow-moving, arboreal quadruped, similar to the modern howler monkey. Its overall appearance indicates that *Aegyptopithecus* was a primitive catarrhine—and a likely contender for the common ancestor of all later catarrhines.

FIGURE 9.15

Aegyptopithecus Shaded red in this reconstruction are the postcranial skeletal fossils of *Aegyptopithecus* that have been found in Fayum deposits. These recovered elements provide important information regarding the animal's mobility and form of locomotion: arboreal quadrupedalism.

When Were They Primates? Anatomy through Time

Primates have a number of anatomical characteristics that reflect both an adaptation to life in the trees and related behaviors. Contenders for primate status in the Paleocene generally lack these characteristics; two groups of closely related Eocene mammals—adapids and omomyids—have these characteristics.

Characteristic	Paleocene (66–56 mya)	Eocene (56–34 mya)	Present
Increased vision	No	Yes	Yes
Partially or fully enclosed eye orbits	No	Yes	Yes
Convergent eyes	No	Yes	Yes
Small incisors and large canines	No	Yes	Yes
Nails at ends of digits	No	Yes	Yes
Mobile, grasping digits	No	Yes	Yes
Short snout	No	Yes	Yes
Reduced smell	No	Yes	Yes
Increased brain size	No	Yes	Yes

Saadanius An early catarrhine Oligocene genus from a group of primates that gave rise to later catarrhines.

While the record of early catarrhines is best and mostly richly represented at the Fayum, at least one fossil representing an ancestor of monkeys, apes, and humans has been recovered from the modern country of Saudi Arabia (see locater map on p. 285). During the Oligocene, before the formation of the Red Sea, the continent of Africa and the Arabian Peninsula formed a single landmass. The remarkable radiation of primates in the Fayum suggests that similar habitats in Arabia supported similar kinds of primates. In their search for Oligocene fossils, the paleontologist Iyad Zalmout and colleagues found most of a skull of an early catarrhine, now known as **Saadanius.** Dating to about 28 mya and postdating *Aegyptopithecus,* this primate shared a number of features with the Fayum catarrhines, such as dental formula (2/1/2/3); upper molars with low, rounded cusps; and shape of the face. However, it differs from Fayum primates in having the bony auditory tube typical of later catarrhine primates.

According to the molecular evidence, the first anthropoids originated in the late Oligocene, likely between 30 and 25 mya (see chapter 8, "Genetic Dating: The Molecular Clock"). Two fossil primates found in Tanzania illustrate the split, by 25 mya, that led to the emergence of modern apes and modern monkeys. In the Rukwa Rift Basin of eastern Tanzania, the American paleoanthropologist Nancy Stevens and her team discovered the earliest ape and earliest Old World monkey, named *Rukwapithecus fleaglei* and *Nsungwepithecus gunnelli*, respectively. *Rukwapithecus* is represented by part of a mandible and teeth, and its second molar shares features with the second molars of later fossil apes. *Nsungwepithecus* is represented by part of a mandible and just one molar. While the bilophodont cusps of that molar are not fully modern, they are clearly cercopithecoid. As a representation of the split between apes and monkeys, this fossil record is modest; but it shows that ancestral apes and monkeys were present in East Africa at about the time most authorities expected.

The presence in the Arabian Peninsula and East Africa of the later Oligocene catarrhine underscores the strong likelihood that the ancestry of fossil and modern catarrhines is broadly based in the African–Arabian landmass during the later Oligocene.

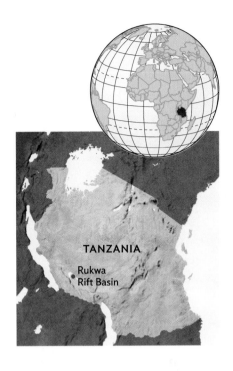

TANZANIA

Rukwa
Rift Basin

9.4 Coming to America: Origin of New World Higher Primates

Aegyptopithecus, the earliest definitive catarrhine, clearly evolved from some anthropoid in the Old World, almost certainly in Africa. But where did the other anthropoids, the platyrrhines, come from? The first South American primate is a primitive monkey called **Perupithecus,** represented by fossil molars from Santa Rosa, Peru, dating possibly as early as 36 mya. This primate is clearly more primitive than the next oldest platyrrhine fossil, **Branisella,** found near Salla, Bolivia, in geologic deposits dating to the very late Oligocene, about 26 mya. *Branisella*'s link with living species of platyrrhines is especially convincing owing to its having three premolars and, especially, three upper molars with a four-cusp chewing surface strongly similar to that of the upper molars in living New World monkeys, such as the owl monkey (**Figure 9.16**). The fossil record

Perupithecus The earliest genus of a platyrrhine, dating to the early Oligocene.

Branisella A South American genus from the Oligocene, ancestral to platyrrhines.

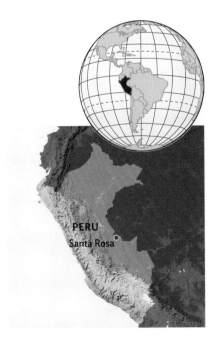

PERU
Santa Rosa

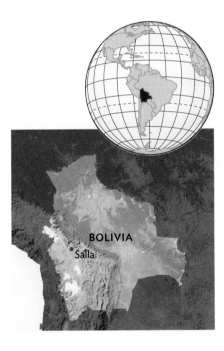

BOLIVIA
Salla

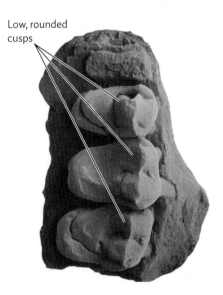

Low, rounded cusps

FIGURE 9.16

Branisella In the dental remains of this first definitive platyrrhine, the low, rounded cusps of its molars suggest that *Branisella* was frugivorous.

for South America is generally sparse after the late Oligocene, but it shows the general patterns of platyrrhine evolution. The fossil platyrrhines bear a striking resemblance to living platyrrhines, represented by cebids and atelids.

How Anthropoids Got to South America

One important question about the origins of platyrrhines is just how they got to South America. Four alternative hypotheses have emerged to explain primates' presence in South America (**Figure 9.17**). First, platyrrhines evolved from a North American anthropoid, then migrated to South America in the late Oligocene. Second, platyrrhines evolved from an African anthropoid and migrated across the Atlantic to South America. Third, platyrrhines evolved from an anthropoid in Africa that migrated south (mainly) on land to Antarctica and then to Patagonia, at the southern tip of South America. Fourth, Old World and New World anthropoids evolved independently from different lineages in Africa and South America, respectively.

One hypothesis suggests that the ancestors migrated south from North America, evolving into the platyrrhine species of the Oligocene.

A second hypothesis suggests that after originating in Africa, the ancestors migrated across the Atlantic Ocean to South America.

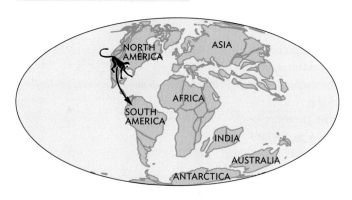

A third hypothesis suggests that the African ancestors reached South America not by water but by land; they migrated to the southern tip of Africa, crossed Antarctica, and eventually reached the southern tip of South America.

A fourth hypothesis suggests that platyrrhines and catarrhines originated independently.

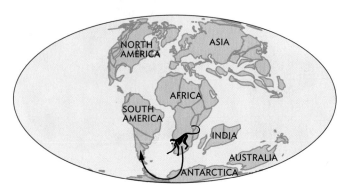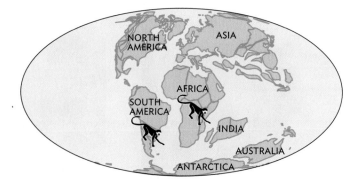

FIGURE 9.17

Platyrrhine Origins Many researchers believe the ancestors of New World monkeys originated in North America. Others believe they originated in Africa and then migrated to South America. As Africa and South America separated in the Mesozoic, how would ancestors in Africa have reached South America?

No evidence supports the first hypothesis—there were no anthropoids in North America during the Eocene or Oligocene. There were various euprimates, but none resembled the platyrrhines in South America during the late Oligocene.

Evidence supports the second hypothesis. There were early anthropoids in Africa (Fayum) beginning in the late Eocene, and they predated platyrrhines but looked remarkably similar to the earliest platyrrhines in South America (for example, they had three premolars). This resemblance indicates that platyrrhines originated in Africa *before* their appearance in South America. In addition, fossils indicate other similarities between animals in Africa and in South America.

The strong similarities between Old World and New World higher primates also support the third hypothesis. Migration across Antarctica would be impossible today, of course. However, migration over this major landmass would have been possible through much of the Eocene, when the climate there was much warmer and dryer.

Given the strong anatomical resemblance between African higher primates and South American higher primates, it is highly unlikely that anthropoids evolved independently in Africa and South America (**Figure 9.18**). DNA evidence that shows a strong relationship between Old World and New World higher primates is even stronger proof against the fourth hypothesis. In other words, these two groups did not evolve independently: they both originated in Africa.

On the face of it, it seems unlikely that primates migrated from Africa to South America via the Atlantic, especially in view of the wide and prohibitive expanse of open sea separating the west coast of Africa from the east coast of South America. At the time, however, areas of the ocean might have been shallow and dotted with series of islands. Moreover, primates might have crossed from Africa to South America via ocean currents, on natural rafts consisting of accumulated vegetation.

(a)　　　　　　　　　　　　　　　(b)

FIGURE 9.18

Old World and New World Monkeys The physical resemblance of **(a)** Old World monkeys and **(b)** New World monkeys suggests that platyrrhines originated in Africa, rather than North America. Their mode of reaching South America, however, is still highly debated.

9.5 Apes Begin in Africa and Dominate the Miocene Primate World

After the Oligocene, the strength and completeness of the higher primate fossil record derives from rich Miocene geologic deposits in East Africa, especially in the present-day countries of Kenya and Uganda (**Figure 9.19**). Just before this time, a warming trend in the late Oligocene provided the conditions for a shift in habitats and the appearance of a new and widespread radiation of a group of catarrhine primates called the **proconsulids,** mostly dating to roughly 22–17 mya (**Figure 9.20**). Recall that the last of the Oligocene primate fossils, in Egypt and Saudi Arabia, date to about 29–28 mya. This means that about a 6-million-year gap exists between the late Oligocene catarrhines (28 mya) and the first Miocene proconsulids (22 mya). As a consequence, the immediate ancestors of proconsulids are a mystery. However, the strong anatomical similarity in skulls and in teeth between Oligocene catarrhines from the Fayum and the Arabian Peninsula and the proconsulids of the Miocene indicates a likely ancestral-descendant relationship between the earlier and later groups. For example, all of these primates have a dental formula of 2/1/2/3, and their upper incisors are broad and flat.

The proconsulids are represented by a diversity of taxa—as many as 10 genera and 15 species—from the early and middle Miocene. In fact, the diversity of proconsulids is much greater than that of living apes today. For example, proconsulids ranged from the tiny ***Micropithecus,*** the size of a small New World monkey, to the namesake genus, ***Proconsul,*** a species of which, *Proconsul major,* was about the size of a modern male chimpanzee, weighing about 50 kg (110 lb). *Proconsul* is the best known of the early to middle Miocene apes from Africa, in part thanks to a nearly complete skeleton discovered on Rusinga Island, in western Kenya's Lake Victoria, in the late 1940s (**Figure 9.21**). Reflecting the proconsulids' biological diversity, their fossils have been found in a range of settings, representing different climates and environments, from open woodlands to tropics. Reflecting these different habitats, their diets varied considerably.

The skulls and teeth of the Miocene proconsulids were clearly like those of apes in overall appearance. The molars have the Y-5 pattern, and the cusps are wide and rounded for eating fruit. There are well-developed honing surfaces on the backs of the upper canines and the fronts of the lower third premolars. Comparisons of tooth wear in living apes and in extinct Miocene apes suggest that some of the extinct apes ate leaves and some ate nuts and fruit but that most of them routinely ate ripe fruit.

In contrast to the skulls and teeth, the rest of the skeleton of Miocene apes is generally like that of monkeys (**Figure 9.22**). Unlike the living apes, these primitive apes had front and hind limbs that were equally long and that lacked specializations for knuckle-walking or arm-swinging. Moreover, like Old World monkeys, *Proconsul* had wrist bones (carpals) that articulated directly with the ulna, one of the two forearm bones. This direct articulation, a primitive characteristic, indicates relatively limited wrist mobility, whereas living apes have highly mobile wrists for arm-swinging and arm-hanging. Proconsulids' elbows could straighten only so far, whereas living apes' elbows can extend completely. Proconsulids' feet combined primitive and derived features—some of the anklebones were slender, like monkeys', but the big toes were large, like apes'. The whole package suggests that *Proconsul,* unlike living apes, walked on the tops of tree branches on all fours. Because these creatures lacked a number of anatomical features that living hominoids share, they can be used as a model of the animals that gave rise to the last common ancestor of all later hominoids.

---

proconsulids Early Miocene apes found in East Africa.

Micropithecus A genus of very small proconsulids from the Miocene, found in Africa.

Proconsul A genus of early Miocene proconsulids from Africa, ancestral to catarrhines.

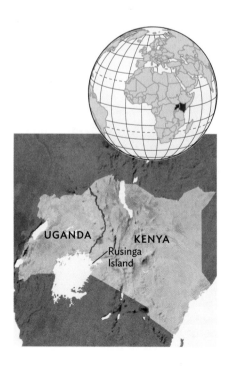

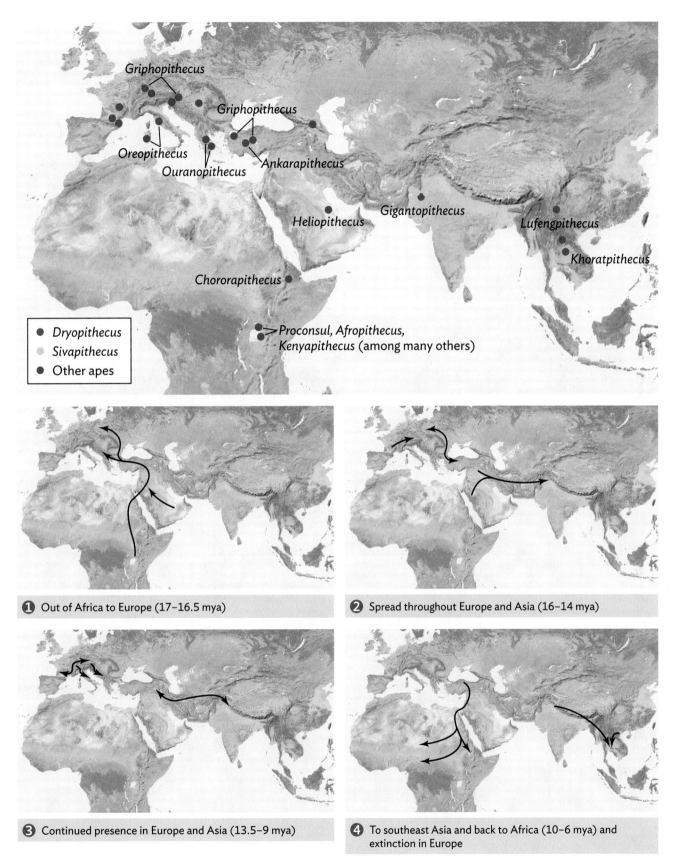

FIGURE 9.19

Miocene Ape Fossil Localities As the larger map illustrates, a variety of ape fossils have been found in Miocene deposits in Africa, Asia, and Europe. The first proconsulids, including *Proconsul, Afropithecus,* and *Kenyapithecus,* arose in East Africa. During the next 11 million years, they migrated from Africa to Europe and Asia, as shown in the four smaller maps. Numerous ape genera have been identified throughout these continents.

Primate evolution began with primitive primates in the Eocene, setting the stage for the origin of all hominoids. Euprimates of the Eocene had the basic characteristics of living primates, such as convergent eye orbits and grasping digits. In the past 20 million years, primates diversified in appearance and behavior. These changes included the shift, for some, from life in the trees to life on the ground, and eventually the beginning of bipedalism in the late Miocene. (Based on Fleagle, J. G. *Primate Adaptation and Evolution,* 2nd ed. 1999. Academic Press.)

Convergent eyes and grasping hands

Eocene 56–34 mya

Large eyes for nocturnal vision

Scenes from the late Eocene in the Paris Basin.
Top: The diurnal *Adapis* is feeding on leaves.
Bottom: Several taxa of omomyids (*Pseudoloris, Necrolemur, Microchoerus*). Note the large eyes, a nocturnal adaptation, typical of both ancient and modern prosimians who are active at night.

Oligocene 34–23 mya

Quadrupedal, monkeylike primate with superb arboreal skills

Scenes from the early Oligocene of the Fayum, Egypt. These anthropoid ancestors include *Aegyptopithecus*, *Propliopithecus*, and *Apidium*. These primates were adept arborealists, using their hands and feet for climbing and feeding.

Miocene 23–5.3 mya

Quadrupedal, apelike primate. Note the lack of a tail, an ape characteristic.

Scene from the early Miocene of Rusinga Island, Kenya. Apes first appeared during this period, and these are the first apes (two species of *Proconsul*, *Dendropithecus*, *Limnopithecus*). These and other taxa form the ancestry of all later apes and hominins. Note the range of habitats occupied by these primates within the forest, including some in the middle and lower canopies and some on the forest floor. These primates show a combination of monkeylike and apelike features, in the skeleton and skull, respectively.

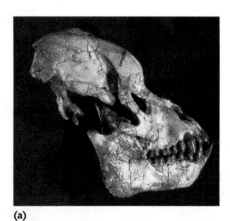

(a)

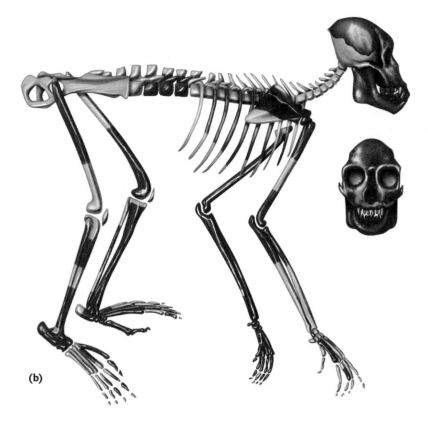

(b)

(c)

FIGURE 9.21

Proconsul This Miocene ape genus was first found in Kenya in 1909—it was the first fossil mammal ever discovered in that region of Africa. *Proconsul* literally means "before Consul"; *Consul* was the name given to chimpanzees that performed in European circuses. *Proconsul,* then, is considered an ancestor to apes, including chimpanzees. **(a)** The first skull of the genus was found in 1948 and was nearly complete. The cranial remains helped researchers determine that *Proconsul* was possibly an ancestor to apes. **(b)** Other fossil finds have helped researchers determine what *Proconsul's* full skeleton was like. Note that it lacked a tail, like all modern apes. Here, areas shaded red represent the parts of the skeleton that have been discovered. **(c)** An artist's reconstruction illustrates *Proconsul's* rainforest habitat and arboreal nature. (Figure 9.20c: "*Proconsul heseloni* Habitation," © 1992 by Jay H. Matternes.)

9.6 Apes Leave Africa: On to New Habitats and New Adaptations

The presence of ape fossils in Europe and Asia from about 17 mya (but not before) suggests that apes originated in Africa and then spread to Europe and Asia. The migration of primates (and other animals) from Africa to Europe and Asia was made possible by a land bridge created 23–18 mya by a drop in sea levels and the joining of the African–Arabian tectonic plate with Eurasia. After their dispersal into Europe and Asia, apes became more diverse than ever before, thus representing an extraordinary adaptive radiation, among the most successful among higher primates.

Apes in Europe: The Dryopithecids

By 13 mya, the early apes had successfully adapted to a wide range of new habitats. During this time, Europe was covered by a dense, subtropical forest that provided a rich

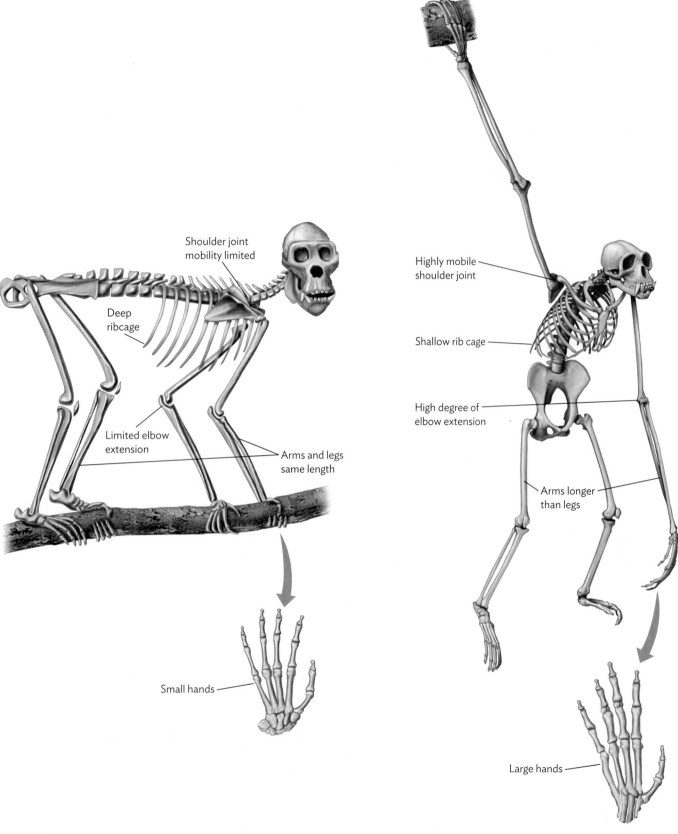

FIGURE 9.22

Proconsulid Body Plan The body plan of primitive, Miocene apes (left) differs from that of modern apes (right). The Miocene apes had a more monkeylike body, with smaller hands, a more restricted hip joint, and a more flexible spine. Modern apes have highly mobile shoulder joints and fully extendable elbow joints, enabling them to brachiate, or swing from branch to branch; the Miocene apes, by contrast, probably were arboreal quadrupeds, not needing the great mobility in their shoulders and their wrists. For the purposes of comparison, this Miocene ape, *Proconsul*, and this lesser ape, the modern gibbon, have been drawn the same size. In reality, *Proconsul* was about half the size of a gibbon.

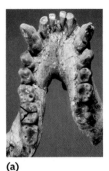 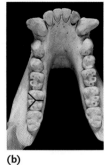

(a)   **(b)**

FIGURE 9.23

Dryopithecus **(a)** The mandible of *Dryopithecus*, a Miocene ape genus from Europe, like that of **(b)** a modern gorilla, includes the Y-5 molar pattern and low, rounded cusps. Both also have large canines, plus the diastema between the canine and the first premolar.

Dryopithecus A genus of dryopithecid apes found in southern France and northern Spain.

dryopithecids Early Miocene apes found in various locations in Europe.

sivapithecids Early Miocene apes found in Asia.

Sivapithecus A genus of Miocene sivapithecids, proposed as ancestral to orangutans.

Khoratpithecus A genus of Miocene apes from Asia, likely ancestral to orangutans.

Gigantopithecus A genus of Miocene pongids from Asia; the largest primate that ever lived.

variety of foods, especially fruit. **Dryopithecus,** the best-known genus within a group of great apes called **dryopithecids,** lived in the area of Europe that is now France and Spain. Larger than earlier apes—about the size of a chimpanzee—it was first discovered and described by the eminent French paleontologist Edward Lartet (1801–1871) in 1856 in St. Gaudens, southern France. *Dryopithecus* and its contemporary taxa are known from other European regions, such as Spain, Greece, and Hungary.

Dryopithecus resembled living apes in many ways: its canines were sharp and tusk-like; its cheek teeth were long and had very simple chewing surfaces, well-adapted for chewing fruit (**Figure 9.23**); and microscopic studies of cross sections of the teeth enamel indicate that these apes grew slowly. Their brains were larger than those of earlier primates, similar to those of modern chimpanzees. Their long forelimbs, grasping feet, and long, grasping hands were powerful and adapted for arm-hanging and arm-swinging, modern apes' main forms of locomotion.

Apes in Asia: The Sivapithecids

In Asia, the **sivapithecids** were the counterpart of Europe's dryopithecids. The best-known sivapithecid is **Sivapithecus,** an ape ancestor that thrived about 12–8 mya. Whereas chimpanzees and gorillas have thin-enameled teeth, *Sivapithecus* had thick-enameled teeth, adapted for eating hard, tough-textured foods such as seeds and nuts. Its robust jawbones were similarly adapted.

Because hominins also have thick-enameled teeth, primatologists once thought *Sivapithecus* was the ancestor of hominins. This hypothesis was rejected in 1979, when the anthropologists David Pilbeam and Ibrahim Shah discovered a partial *Sivapithecus* skull (**Figure 9.24**). *Sivapithecus* skulls are strikingly similar to those of living orangutans, with concave faces, narrow nasal bones, oval eye orbits from top to bottom, projecting premaxillas (the *premaxilla* is the area of the face below the nose), large upper central incisors, and tiny lateral incisors. Even more similar to living orangutans, however, is the newly discovered **Khoratpithecus**, a hominoid of the late Miocene (9–6 mya) in Thailand. Various features of this primate's teeth and lower jaw—for example, broad front teeth, and canines with a flat surface on the tongue side—indicate that this Miocene primate is living orangutans' most likely ancestor.

Closely related to *Sivapithecus, Khoratpithecus,* and other Asian Miocene apes is a very interesting pongid, **Gigantopithecus**, also from Asia, dating to about 8–0.5 mya (**Figure 9.25**). Appropriately named for its massive body, *Gigantopithecus* is the biggest primate that has ever lived, standing nearly 3 m (10 ft) tall and weighing as much as 300 kg (660 lb)! Its massiveness would have limited this fossil primate to the ground for all its activities. Like some of the other Miocene apes, it

FIGURE 9.24

Sivapithecus Originally found in the Siwalik Hills of modern-day India and Pakistan, this Miocene ape (center) has been proposed as ancestral to the orangutan (right). *Sivapithecus*'s facial features, for example, are far closer to the orangutan's than to those of other great apes, such as the chimpanzee (left). *Sivapithecus* has three species, any of which may be a direct ancestor to the orangutan; however, recent finds of another Miocene ape genus have called this ancestry into question.

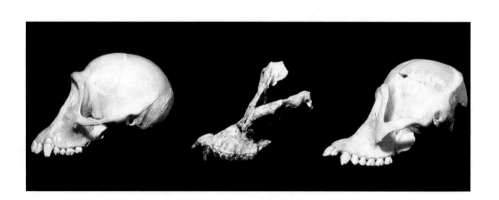

FIGURE 9.25

Gigantopithecus Bamboo was probably among the plant foods eaten by this enormous, herbivorous Miocene ape. Climate change and competition with other primate species likely brought about this ape's extinction.

had thick-enameled teeth and large, thick-boned jaws, adapted for eating very hard foods, likely nuts and seeds.

Dead End in Ape Evolution: The Oreopithecids

Around the same time *Gigantopithecus* emerged, a group of apes called **oreopithecids** lived in Europe. They appear in the fossil record around 8 mya and disappear around 7 mya. **Oreopithecus**, the best known of this group, has been found on the island of Sardinia and in coal mines in Tuscany, Italy. (Oreopithecids were also present in Africa at the same time as the proconsulids on that continent.) Its Miocene habitat was dense, tropical forests, and its teeth were highly specialized for eating leaves (**Figure 9.26**). Also known as the "Swamp Ape," *Oreopithecus* was a medium-size primate, weighing an estimated 30–35 kg (66–77 lb), but it had a tiny brain. Its relatively long arms indicate that it was adept at some form of suspensory locomotion, similar to that of a modern gibbon. Some of its hand adaptations foreshadow developments in hominin evolution.

Climate Shifts and Habitat Changes

During the period in which *Oreopithecus* and other later Miocene apes disappeared, Europe, Asia, and Africa experienced dramatic changes in climate and ecology. Several factors coincided to cause these changes: a shift in tectonic plates created the Alps, the Himalayas, and the East African mountain chains; ocean currents shifted; and the polar ice caps began to re-form. In Europe and then Africa, the once-lush tropical forests changed to cooler, dryer mixed woodlands and grasslands. As a result, tropical foods disappeared, including the apes' favored diet, fruit. In Asia, a decrease in rainfall, reduced forests, and decreased fruit availability likely contributed to the extinction of *Sivapithecus*.

oreopithecids Miocene apes that were found in Europe.

Oreopithecus A genus of oreopithecids found in Italy that was extinct within a million years of its appearance.

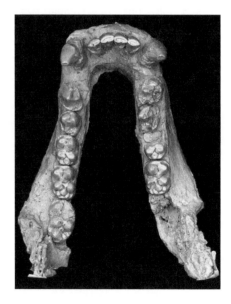

FIGURE 9.26

Oreopithecus The high, shearing crests on its molars suggest that this Miocene ape was folivorous. Like *Gigantopithecus,* this ancestral ape likely became extinct due to climate change.

The First Apes: A Remarkable Radiation

The apes' evolutionary glory days are in the Miocene epoch (23–5.3 mya), beginning in Africa and then spreading into Europe and Asia. Out of this remarkable adaptive radiation came the ancestors of living apes and of humans. All of these fossil primates had characteristics seen in living apes, especially in the teeth and the skull (Y-5 lower molars, 2/1/2/3 dental formula, broad incisors, large honing canines), but most were monkeylike in the postcranial skeleton (front and back limbs equally long).

Group	Characteristics	Age	Location
Proconsulids	Large range in size Tropics to open woodlands Thin enamel (e.g., *Proconsul*)	22–17 mya	Africa (Kenya, Uganda)
Dryopithecids	Some size range Tropics Thin enamel (e.g., *Dryopithecus*)	14–9 mya	Europe (France, Spain, Germany, Greece, elsewhere)
Sivapithecids	Some size range Tropics Thick enamel Skull like orangutan's (e.g., *Sivapithecus*)	14–8 mya	Asia (Pakistan, India, China, Thailand)
Oreopithecids	Large body Tiny brain Specialized molars for eating leaves Suspensory locomotion (e.g., *Oreopithecus*)	9–7 mya	Europe (Italy), earlier form in East Africa (Kenya)

Miocene Ape Survivors Give Rise to Modern Apes

A handful of ape taxa survived these dramatic disruptions in habitat. *Khoratpithecus*, for example, thrived for a time and gave rise to the orangutan of southeast Asia. The origins of the great apes of Africa and hominins are far less clear. In fact, only one small set of fossils—named *Chororapithecus* by their discoverer, the Japanese paleoanthropologist Gen Suwa—resembles similar parts of living great apes. These nine teeth from three individuals, found in Ethiopia and dating to about 10.5 mya, are remarkably similar to the modern gorilla's. Their existence suggests that late Miocene African pongids may have been the common ancestor of African apes and hominins. However, the fossil record in Africa between 13 mya and 5 mya is extremely sparse, leaving an 8-million-year gap until the first hominins' appearance, about 6 mya (discussed further in chapter 10). Therefore, the link between late Miocene African apes and later hominoids is unknown.

9.7 Apes Return to Africa?

Ape fossils from the late Miocene might be so scarce in East Africa because apes simply were not living there, at least not in great numbers, at that time. Unless the fossil record changes, somewhere other than Africa must be the source of living African apes' and humans' common ancestor. The Canadian primate paleontologist David Begun suggests that late Miocene Europe might yield that ancestor. He speculates that the similarities in dentition and skull between the Greek dryopithecid ***Ourano-pithecus,*** on the one hand, and African apes and early hominins, on the other, indicate an ancestral-descendant relationship between European great apes and African hominins. Begun argues that the climate changes in Europe prompted late Miocene apes to move from Europe back to Africa, essentially following the tropical forests, and the foods these forests provided, as forests and foods disappeared behind them. Some of the pongids adapted to forested settings, some lived in woodlands, and eventually one group, hominins, became committed to life on the ground. To date, the fossil record for the later Miocene is too incomplete to make clear whether early hominins descended from Miocene ancestry in Europe or in Africa.

Ouranopithecus A genus of Miocene dryopithecids found in Greece.

9.8 Monkeys on the Move

At the same time as the evolution and proliferation of ape taxa, an expansion and adaptive radiation of monkeys occurred, both in the New World (see "How Anthropoids Got to South America" earlier) and in the Old World. Primates recognizable as cercopithecoids—they have the distinctive bilophodont molars of Old World monkeys—first appeared during the early Miocene in North Africa and East Africa. These primitive primates are generally called **victoriapithecids.** *Victoriapithecus,* a prominent genus of the group, is just the kind of primate that would be expected for the ancestor of Old World monkeys.

victoriapithecids Miocene primates from Africa, possibly ancestral to Old World monkeys.

Beginning in the late Miocene, especially in the Pliocene and Pleistocene, and continuing to the present day, monkey taxa have proliferated enormously. While ape species were far more prevalent and diverse during the early and middle Miocene, far outnumbering the living groups, monkey species are far more diverse since the end of the Miocene. Today's monkey taxa are for the most part the descendants of the fossil species from the Pliocene and Pleistocene. By contrast, most of the ape and apelike taxa from the Miocene went extinct and left no descendants.

FINE MOTOR

Are They Uniquely Human?

Humans have a unique form of grip. Take a look at your own thumb—the right one if you are right-handed, the left one if you are left-handed. In its general form, your thumb is very similar to those of many other primates, except that the one you are looking at in your hand is proportionately longer in relation to the other four digits than is the case in other primates, both fossil and living species.

The relative length of your thumb makes possible the ability for you to touch and press the tip of your thumb against the tip of your index finger and other fingers. This special anatomy gives you a precision grip, allowing you to write with a pen or pencil. Moreover, at the base of the second through fifth digits—your index finger to your pinky finger—the articulation between the phalanges and the metacarpals has two surfaces, reducing the range of motion. At the base of the thumb,

however, the joint is more complex and allows a much greater range of motion and the ability to grasp using a power grip. The power grip is used, for example, for gripping a hammer and many other tools.

The hand bones of one Miocene ape, *Oreopithecus*, have received considerable attention. The Spanish paleontologist Salvador Moyà-Solà and his colleagues have argued that *Oreopithecus* had a relatively long thumb. If so, this primate, like humans (and hominin

Without opposable thumbs, humans would not be able to use the precision grip for finely manipulating small objects, as in holding a pencil, picking up a coin, or threading a needle (see "Arboreal Adaptation—Primates Live in Trees and Are Good at It" in chapter 6).

"What about your precious opposable thumbs now?"

SKILLS

ancestors), was able to touch the tip of its thumb to the tip of its index finger—it had the full opposability of the thumb that is uniquely human, allowing for precision and power gripping. The American paleoanthropologist Randall Susman has studied the hand bones of many primates, human and nonhuman, and found fundamental errors in Moyà-Solà's assessment of *Oreopithecus*'s hand. The bone that Moyà-Solà thought was the base of the thumb—the proximal phalanx—was actually a middle phalanx from another finger. Rather than being long like a hominin's, *Oreopithecus*'s thumb was short, just like any other ape's, past or present. *Oreopithecus* lacked the unique attributes of the hominin hand for either precision or power gripping.

The basic structure of the thumb is similar in all living primates, with two phalanges (the other four digits have three phalanges each) and one metacarpal making up the length of this digit; however, the thumb is substantially longer in humans.

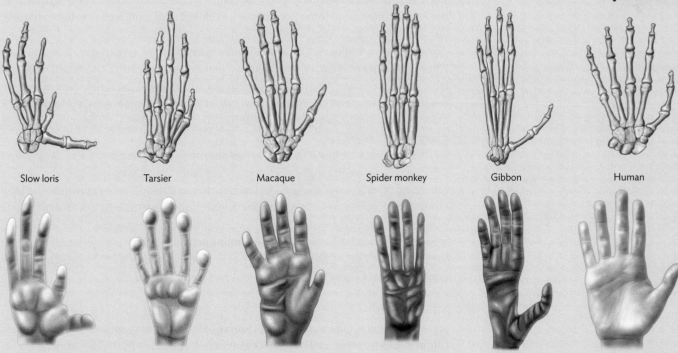

Slow loris   Tarsier   Macaque   Spider monkey   Gibbon   Human

(a)　　　　　　　　　　　　　　　　　　(b)

FIGURE 9.27

Theropithecus **(a)** Of the same genus as living gelada baboons, fossil *Theropithecus* species have been found in many areas of Africa. *Theropithecus* was folivorous, as reflected in the high, shearing crests of its molars, an unusual trait in cercopithecines. **(b)** Like their living counterparts, fossil *Theropithecus* species were likely terrestrial quadrupeds as their front and hind limbs were of similar length; however, the fossil species were substantially larger than the living gelada baboons.

Theropithecus A genus of fossil and living Old World monkeys found in Africa; it was more diverse in the past than it is today and was one of the first monkey genera to appear in the evolutionary record.

The rise in monkey species and the decline in ape species were not due to competition between the two groups. Rather, the origin and diversification of monkeys reflect habitat changes. The climates and environments of the early Miocene seem to have favored the adaptive radiation of apes, with most taxa then going extinct as climates and environments changed. The climates and environments of the late Miocene, and into the Pliocene and Pleistocene, seem to have favored the adaptive radiation of monkeys.

The Pliocene and Pleistocene fossil monkeys are divided into the same two subfamilies as Old World monkeys: cercopithecines and colobines. The cercopithecines are represented by three major groups: macaques; mangabeys, baboons, and geladas; and guenons. The fossil monkeys were widespread, as living species of monkeys are. The fossil monkeys and their living descendants are similar in many respects, such as skeletal and dental anatomy. For example, the fossil and living monkeys have virtually identical teeth (large, projecting canines) and cranial morphology.

Some of the Pliocene and Pleistocene monkeys were quite large. For example, **Theropithecus** *oswaldi,* one of the best-known fossil species of Old World monkeys from East, North, and South Africa in both the Pliocene and the Pleistocene, may have weighed as much as 80 kg (176 lb), the weight of a modern female gorilla (**Figure 9.27**). Males had enormous canines and would have been avoided by early hominins because they were so dangerous.

The colobines included three geographic groups of species: European, Asian, and African. These species differed in many ways from their living descendants, in part reflecting their greater geographic distribution and the diverse environments they occupied. One clear evolutionary trend in many monkey species is a decrease in body size. In other words, around the world during the later Pleistocene there were widespread extinctions of large animals, including primates. These extinctions might have been caused by human hunting, climate change, competition with other mammals, or a combination of these factors (discussed further in chapter 14).

All of primate evolution is a dynamic story, peaking at different times and different places with key events, such as the origins of all the major groups of higher primates (**Figure 9.28**). The record becomes even more fascinating in the late Miocene, with

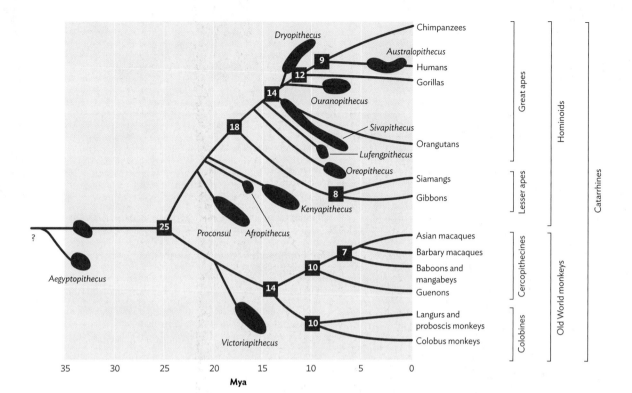

FIGURE 9.28

Catarrhine Origins This phylogeny represents catarrhine evolution. The numbers set in squares represent the estimated times of divergence. Balloons refer to approximate time ranges for fossil taxa. Old World monkeys and hominoids share a common ancestor; however, approximately 25 mya, Old World monkeys and hominoids split, each creating a separate evolutionary lineage. This last common ancestor, though, has not been discovered. Within the hominoid lineage, branching has occurred many times, including the branch leading to the lesser apes, around 18 mya, and most recently the branch leading to humans, approximately 9–8 mya. The Old World monkey lineage has also branched several times, most notably when colobines and cercopithecines split, approximately 14 mya.

the appearance of a new primate that is similar to but different from other primates. The first 50 million years of primate evolution, from the beginning of the Eocene to the past several million years of the Miocene, set the stage for the appearance of this new taxa—a primitive, humanlike primate. This ancestor's origin begins the 7-million-year history of the appearance, rise, and dominance of humans. That story begins in the next chapter.

CHAPTER 9 REVIEW

ANSWERING THE BIG QUESTIONS

1. **Why become a primate?**
   - According to the predominant theory, primate origins represent the radiation of a primitive mammalian ancestor that adapted to life in the trees. Other theories suggest that the origins may be more closely linked to preying on insects or eating fruit.

2. **What were the first primates?**
   - The first radiation of primates included the appearance of two primitive primate groups, adapids and omomyids, both at about 55 mya. These animals may have given rise to modern strepsirhines and modern haplorhines, but the exact phylogenetic relationship between the Eocene groups and later ones is unknown.

3. **What were the first higher primates?**
   - In the Eocene, primate taxa possessing a combination of strepsirhine and haplorhine characteristics appeared in Asia and Africa. These basal anthropoids may have been the first anthropoids.

   - Recognizable catarrhines (for example, *Aegyptopithecus*) were present 30 mya in Africa, and platyrrhines (for example, *Branisella*) were present 26 mya in South America. Platyrrhines likely descended from an early African anthropoid ancestor.

4. **What evolutionary developments link past primate species and living ones?**
   - The evolution of apes began in Africa and continued in Europe and Asia. Recognizable African apes first appeared about 22 mya (for example, *Proconsul*) and various Eurasian varieties (for example, *Sivapithecus*) somewhat later with the opening of a land bridge connecting these continents. Most apes went extinct in the later Miocene, although a few survived, giving rise to modern apes and humans.
   - Monkeys underwent a massive adaptive radiation in the Pliocene and Pleistocene, providing the foundation for the evolution of modern species.

KEY TERMS

adapids
Adapis
Aegyptopithecus
angiosperm radiation hypothesis
Apidium
arboreal hypothesis
basal anthropoids
Biretia
Branisella
Carpolestes
dryopithecids
Dryopithecus
Eosimias
euprimates
Gigantopithecus
Khoratpithecus
Micropithecus
Notharctus
oligopithecids
omomyids
oreopithecids
Oreopithecus
Ouranopithecus
parapithecids
Parapithecus
Perupithecus
plesiadapiforms
Proconsul
proconsulids
propliopithecids
Propliopithecus
Proprimates
Saadanius
sivapithecids
Sivapithecus
Theropithecus
victoriapithecids
visual predation hypothesis

STUDY QUIZ

1. **The _____ specifically links the evolution of primates to**
   a. arboreal hypothesis
   b. visual predation hypothesis
   c. angiosperm radiation hypothesis
   d. gymnosperm radiation hypothesis

2. **The earliest group with clear primate characteristics was**
   a. plesiadapiforms.
   b. euprimates.
   c. Fayum higher primates.
   d. strepsirhines.

3. **Platyrrhines ancestors most likely originated in**
   a. Africa.
   b. North America.
   c. South America.
   d. Madagascar.

4. **Which statement about ape evolution is *not* currently supported?**
   a. Apes and monkeys split in the early Miocene.
   b. The teeth of early apes are like those of living apes.
   c. Apes originated in Africa but later migrated to Europe and Asia.
   d. Miocene apes and living great apes have a continuous fossil record in Africa.

5. **Which statement about Old World monkey evolution is *not* currently supported?**
   a. Fully modern bilophodont molars first appear in the victoriapithecids.
   b. Many monkey species decreased in body size.
   c. Old World monkeys became more diverse than apes in the late Miocene.
   d. Ape diversity decreased due to direct competition with Old World monkeys.

EVOLUTION REVIEW

PRIMATE SOCIAL ORGANIZATION AND BEHAVIOR: THE DEEP ROOTS OF THE ORDER PRIMATES

Synopsis The origin of our own taxonomic order, the order Primates, extends more than 50 million years into the past. Various hypotheses—based on characteristics seen in both living and extinct primates, such as arboreal adaptations and visual acuity—have been proposed to explain why the first true primates arose deep in the past. The evolutionary history of the order Primates can be described as somewhat tumultuous. Fluctuations in climate and other environmental pressures during the Eocene, Oligocene, and Miocene epochs affected the survival and adaptive radiations of various fossil primate taxa to differing degrees. Fossils of primate ancestors are found across Africa, Asia, and Europe in the Old World as well as North and South America in the New World. The locations and characteristics of these fossils clarify the timeline of major evolutionary events that shaped the order Primates and illustrate that the geographic extent of primates in the past was much larger than the distribution of nonhuman primate species living today.

Q1. Describe the three hypotheses for explaining primate origins, discussed at the beginning of this chapter. Do you think the environmental pressures associated with each of these hypotheses are mutually exclusive or could all of these factors have influenced the origins and adaptability of the earliest primates?

Q2. Identify the four alternative hypotheses for explaining the presence of primates in South America. Summarize the evidence that supports each of these four hypotheses. Based on this evidence, assess how plausible each hypothesis is in explaining the origins of the New World primates.

Q3. Explain the role of climate fluctuations in the origins and evolution of the first true primates, the earliest anthropoids, the early Miocene "dental apes" (proconsulids), and the surviving ape species of the late Miocene.

Hint Focus on the ways that warming and cooling episodes affected habitable land areas, caused habitat changes, and affected availability of different food sources.

Q4. There is much less diversity among living ape species than among the many fossil ape taxa of the early Miocene and mid-Miocene. In contrast, there is much greater diversity among living monkey species than among the fossil monkey taxa of the late Miocene. Discuss the kinds of selective pressures operating in the late Miocene, Pliocene, and Pleistocene that favored an adaptive radiation of monkeys and contributed to decreased diversity among apes.

Q5. A bumper sticker reads, "If humans evolved from monkeys, then why are there still monkeys?" Using your knowledge of biological evolution in general, and the timeline of primate origins and evolution outlined in this chapter more specifically, counter the faulty logic behind this bumper sticker.

Hint See Figure 9.28 for a timeline of the key events in primate evolution.

ADDITIONAL READINGS

Beard, C. 2004. *The Hunt for the Dawn Monkey: Unearthing the Origins of Monkeys, Apes, and Humans.* Berkeley: University of California Press.

Begun, D. R. 2003. Planet of the apes. *Scientific American* 289(2): 74–83.

Fleagle, J. G. 2013. *Primate Adaptation and Evolution,* 3rd ed. San Diego: Academic Press.

Miller, E. R., G. F. Gunnell, and R. D. Martin. 2005. Deep time and the search for anthropoid origins. *Yearbook of Physical Anthropology* 48: 60–95.

Rose, K. D. 1994. The earliest primates. *Evolutionary Anthropology* 3: 159–173.

Ross, C. F. 2000. Into the light: the origin of Anthropoidea. *Annual Review of Anthropology* 29: 147–194.

Walker, A. and P. Shipman. 2005. *The Ape in the Tree: An Intellectual and Natural History of* Proconsul. Cambridge, MA: Belknap Press.

Often referred to as the "cradle of humankind," Olduvai Gorge is a ravine in East Africa's Great Rift Valley from which many hominin fossils have been recovered, providing insight into our evolutionary roots. Geologic activity and erosion have exposed some of the deepest and oldest layers of sediment, enabling paleoanthropologists to find fossils from strata that are nearly 2 million years old.

Olduvai
Gorge

TANZANIA

10

Early Hominin Origins and Evolution

THE ROOTS OF HUMANITY

BIG QUESTIONS

1. **What is a hominin?**
2. **Why did hominins evolve from an apelike primate?**
3. **What were the first hominins?**
4. **What was the evolutionary fate of the first hominins?**

Imagine yourself walking across the hot, desolate, and altogether inhospitable landscape of East Africa's Great Rift Valley. Imagine further that you have spent the better part of the past three decades—all your adult life—searching for early hominin fossils. Over those years, you have found evidence, such as stone tools, that early humans had lived in this place hundreds of thousands—even millions—of years ago. Still, no fossils—at least, none worth getting especially excited about. On this particular day, you see part of a bone sticking out of the ground, just like others you have seen over and over before. This one turns out to be different, though. Instead of being an animal of some sort, this fossil has *human* teeth—you have found a hominin, your first! In an instant, all your searching has been vindicated.

That scene describes exactly what happened to the English-born

FIGURE 10.1

Mary and Louis Leakey This husband-and-wife team conducted some of the earliest excavations in Olduvai Gorge.

anthropologist Mary Leakey (1913–1996) one sunny morning in July 1959 (**Figure 10.1**). She, along with her husband, the Kenyan anthropologist Louis Leakey (1903–1972), had searched high and low for early human bones in Olduvai Gorge, a side branch of the Great Rift Valley 50 km (31 mi) long. Since beginning their searches in the early 1930s, they had found ancient stone tools and ancient animal remains scattered about the landscape—lots of them. They wanted more, however. They wanted the remains of the people who had made the tools and had eaten the animals. Year after year, field season after field season, disappointment after disappointment, they searched for the bones and teeth that would represent our ancestors' roots.

What had motivated these two individuals to work so hard for so little payoff under such awful conditions? Simple. They were motivated by questions. In fact, the Leakeys were asking one of the fundamental questions of all time: *Who were the first humans?* The Leakeys demanded answers about human origins, and they were willing to do what had to be done to get those answers.

They started out with a pretty simple hunch about early hominins. Other scientists had found things in Olduvai Gorge—bones and tools, both in association with very old geologic strata—that strongly suggested the place would yield early hominin remains. Based on these findings, the Leakeys decided to investigate the gorge's geologic strata (**Figure 10.2**). Their work took a lot of time and resources, but it paid off well, laying the essential groundwork for our current understanding of the first humans and their place in evolution. In fact, the bits of bone and the teeth found in 1959 turned out to be a crucially important hominin skull (**Figure 10.3**). Not only did this discovery expand the territory in which early hominins were known to have lived—at that point, they were known just from South Africa—but it added a whole new dimension to their variability and geographic distribution. The Leakeys' pioneering work in East Africa was built around questions still central to paleoanthropology.

This chapter focuses on the fossil record of early human evolution. This record sheds light on the earliest humanlike ancestors. In order of origin and evolution, they are the pre-australopithecines (before the genus *Australopithecus*), which lived 7–4 mya, and the australopithecines, which lived 4–1 mya.

10.1 **What Is a Hominin?**

The morphological characteristics—and behaviors inferred from these characteristics—shared by living humans and their ancestors but not shared by apes reveal what is distinctive about hominins. For example, living humans speak, use language, depend fully on complex material culture, and have advanced cognition—living apes do not have these characteristics. Speech, advanced cognition, and complex material culture evolved in the human line long after the first hominins appeared in Africa, 7–6 mya, so these characteristics do not define a hominin (**Figure 10.4**). Speech likely developed only in the past 2 million years, and some authorities argue for its development late in that period. Evidence for material culture, in the form of primitive stone tools, dates to about 3.3 mya. As discussed in chapter 1, a hominin is much better understood as having two obligate behaviors—bipedal locomotion and nonhoning chewing—and the suite of associated physical characteristics that manifest these behaviors. The evidence is very clear: bipedal locomotion and nonhoning chewing preceded speech and material

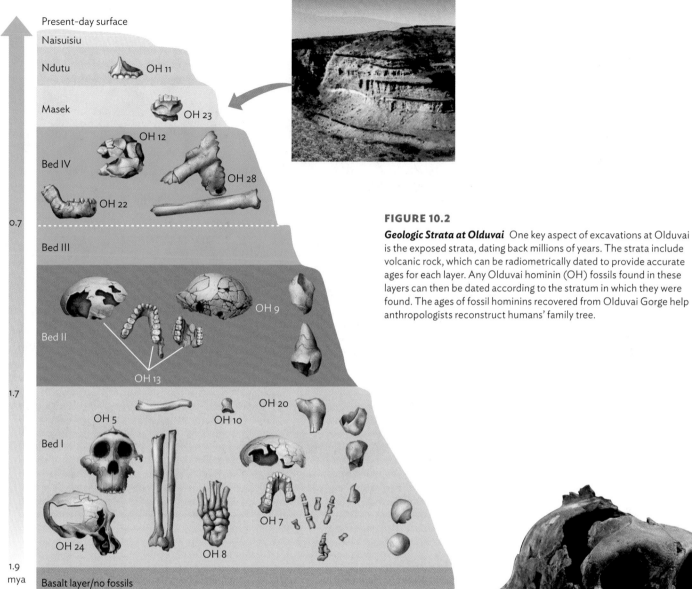

Present-day surface

Naisuisiu

Ndutu — OH 11

Masek — OH 23

Bed IV

OH 12

OH 28

OH 22

0.7

Bed III

Bed II

OH 9

OH 13

1.7

OH 20

OH 5

OH 10

Bed I

OH 7

OH 24

OH 8

1.9 mya

Basalt layer/no fossils

FIGURE 10.2

Geologic Strata at Olduvai One key aspect of excavations at Olduvai is the exposed strata, dating back millions of years. The strata include volcanic rock, which can be radiometrically dated to provide accurate ages for each layer. Any Olduvai hominin (OH) fossils found in these layers can then be dated according to the stratum in which they were found. The ages of fossil hominins recovered from Olduvai Gorge help anthropologists reconstruct humans' family tree.

FIGURE 10.3

Australopithecus boisei This fossil (OH 5) is one of the most famous ever recovered from Olduvai Gorge. The almost complete cranium is of an adult male. Its robust features and large molars caused anthropologists to classify it as a robust australopithecine. (Photo © David L. Brill, humanoriginsphotos.com)

culture by several million years. Like large brains, speech and material culture help define humans today but were not attributes of the earliest hominins.

Bipedal Locomotion: Getting Around on Two Feet

In the 1800s, when the entire human fossil record was a very small fraction of what it is today, numerous authorities believed that the beginning of bipedalism was not the hallmark event distinguishing humans from apes. Rather, these scientists believed that the most important initial evolutionary change was an increase in brain size, reflecting advanced (human) intelligence. They speculated that only with advanced intelligence would language, tool use, and the other behaviors that collectively define humanness have become possible. The focus on intelligence to the exclusion of other attributes helped bring about the rapid and uncritical acceptance of some purported early hominin ancestors that later turned out to be fake.

HUMAN–APE DIFFERENCES

HUMANS HAVE, APES LACK:

FIGURE 10.4

What Makes Us Human? Humans and apes differ in a number of key ways. For example, humans have and apes lack **(a)** bipedalism, **(b)** nonhoning chewing, **(c)** dependence on material culture, **(d)** speech, **(e)** hunting and cooperation, and **(f)** domestication of plants and animals. This suite of characteristics helps define what it means to be human.

Since then, the large early hominin fossil record has proved that bipedalism—and not human intelligence—was the foundational behavior of the Hominini (humans and human-like ancestors), preceding most attributes associated with humans and with human behavior by *millions* of years. More than any other characteristic, the shift from walking with and running with four limbs (arms and legs) to walking with and running with two limbs (legs) distinguishes hominins from the apes (and other non-human primates).

Seven distinguishing characteristics in the skeleton are associated with bipedalism (**Figure 10.5**; see also "What Is a Primate?" in chapter 6): the foramen magnum is positioned on the bottom of the skull, the spine is *S*-shaped, the ilium is short from front to back, the legs are long relative to the body trunk and arms, the knees are angled inward, the foot has a longitudinal arch, and the big toe (hallux) is not opposable. The

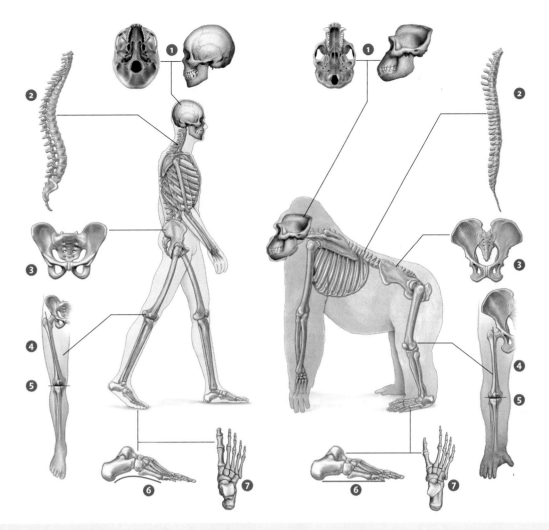

① **Position of the foramen magnum:** In humans, the foramen magnum is on the bottom of the skull, closer to the teeth. In apes, the foramen magnum is in a posterior position. This difference reflects the fact that the human head sits on top of the body trunk, whereas the ape head sits on the front of the trunk.

② **Shape of the spine:** In humans, the spine has an S-shape. In apes, it is straighter, almost C-shaped. The distinctive S-shape in humans is created by the concave curvature of the thoracic vertebrae, in front, and the concave curvature of the lumbar vertebrae, in the back. This arrangement, especially of the lumbar vertebrae, serves to position the body trunk's center of gravity above the pelvis, providing more stability during walking and running.

③ **Shape of the pelvis:** The human pelvis has a very different shape from the ape pelvis. Especially distinctive is the short ilium in the bipedal human. This morphology is an essential element of the stability of the pelvis during standing, walking, and running (discussed further in chapter 6).

④ **Length of the leg:** The relatively long leg of the bipedal human provides increased efficiency during stride. In hominins, the leg is generally longer relative to the arm than it is in apes. The long arm of the ape reflects its suspensory use in trees.

⑤ **Valgus knee:** The knees in the biped angle inward to give it a knock-kneed appearance. The angle formed by the long axis of the femur shaft and the horizontal at the knee—called the bicondylar angle—provides an angle greater than 90 degrees. This angle is significantly greater in humans than in most apes. The valgus knees place the feet together and beneath the center of gravity. By doing so, they provide stability in walking and running, especially when only one foot is on the ground during locomotion.

⑥ **Longitudinal foot arch:** The biped has a distinctive arch that runs from the front to the back of the bottom surface of the foot. This form gives increased leverage as the body pushes forward and serves as a shock absorber when the feet make contact with the ground during walking and running. Apes have flat feet, which reflect the adaptation of their feet for grasping.

⑦ **Opposable big toe:** The first digit of the foot—the big toe—is opposable in apes but not in humans. This difference reflects the function of the foot, which is solely (pun intended!) to support the body during walking and running in humans. The ape toe has a dual function, including terrestrial walking and grasping or manipulating objects. Humans have largely lost their ability to manipulate objects with their toes.

FIGURE 10.5

Seven Steps of Bipedalism This figure shows the seven key differences between a bipedal hominin and a quadrupedal pongid. The two skeletons are of a modern human and a modern gorilla. They are similar in overall form, reflecting their common ancestry. However, because the human is a biped and the gorilla is a quadruped, they have important anatomical differences. Anthropologists use these differences to identify patterns in fossils and to reconstruct their respective locomotor and related behavioral patterns.

Imagine yourself as a physical anthropologist who has just unearthed in East Africa a fossil skeleton of a hominoid dating to 4 or 5 mya. In examining your newly discovered skeleton, you would want to pay attention to these seven features. But you would need to be prepared for surprises, which you might encounter if your specimen is closer to or further away from the nearest ancestor of apes and humans.

FIGURE 10.6

Nonhoning versus Honing Chewing While humans have nonhoning chewing, primates such as gorillas (pictured here) have a honing complex, in which their very large canines cut food. The upper canines are sharpened against the lower third premolars.

position of the foramen magnum reflects the fact that the (bipedal) hominin carries its head atop its body, in contrast to the (quadrupedal) ape, which carries its head on the front of the body. The shortened ilium and pelvis generally reflect anatomical changes that coincided with the shift from quadrupedalism to bipedalism. Especially important is the reconfiguring of the gluteal muscles for stabilizing the hip in walking on two legs. Bipeds have distinctively long legs, which provide the ability to stride and to do so with minimal energy. The angling of the knees toward the midline of the body helps to place the feet below the body's center of gravity, thereby helping stabilize the biped when standing, walking, or running. The loss of opposability in the big toe reflects the use of this digit in helping propel the body forward during walking and running. The longitudinal arch acts as a kind of shock absorber, allowing the foot to sustain the demanding forces of body weight, especially during running and long-distance walking.

Nonhoning Chewing: No Slicing, Mainly Grinding

The second of the two major differences between living apes and humans (and human ancestors) is the way their dentitions process food (again, see "What Is a Primate?" in chapter 6). Apes and humans have evolved different dental characteristics, reflecting how each uses the canine and postcanine teeth (**Figure 10.6**). When apes grab on to food with their front teeth, the upper canines and lower third premolars cut and shred the food. Through evolution, apes' upper canines have become large, pointed, and projecting, with a sharp edge on the back (**Figure 10.7**). When the jaws are fully closed, each canine fits snugly in the diastema, the gap located between the canine and the third premolar on the lower jaw and the canine and the second incisor on the upper jaw. The sharp edge on the back of the upper canine hones, or rubs against, a sharp edge on the front of the lower third premolar, or sectorial premolar. This honing action helps maintain a sharp, shearing edge on both the canine and the premolar. The shearing edge

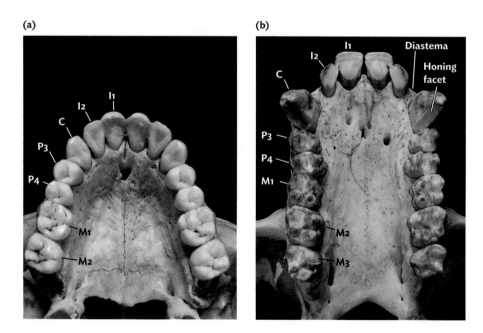

FIGURE 10.7

Human and Nonhuman Dentition **(a)** Humans' nonhoning chewing complex is characterized by canines that are much shorter than **(b)** those found in nonhuman primates' honing complex, such as this gorilla's. In addition, humans lack the diastema that nonhuman primates such as gorillas have. What other differences do you see?

is essential for slicing up leaves and fruit before they are chewed by the back teeth and swallowed. Apes' lower third premolar is also distinctive in having one large, dominant cusp on the cheek side of the tooth and a tiny cusp on the tongue side of the tooth.

In contrast, living and past hominins have small, blunt, and nonprojecting canines and no diastema. Hominin canines wear on the tips instead of the backs (**Figure 10.8**). The cusps on both sides of the lower third premolars are similar in size, or at least more similar in size than are apes' cusps. Unlike apes, hominins do not hone their canines as they chew.

Apes' and humans' postcanine teeth have many similar anatomical characteristics. The third and fourth premolars, upper and lower, have two cusps each. Apes' and hominins' upper molars have four cusps, and their lower molars have five cusps. Apes'

(a)

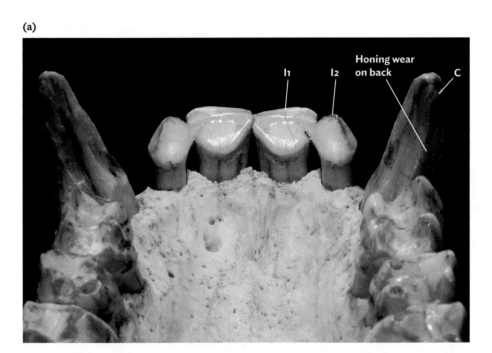

(b)

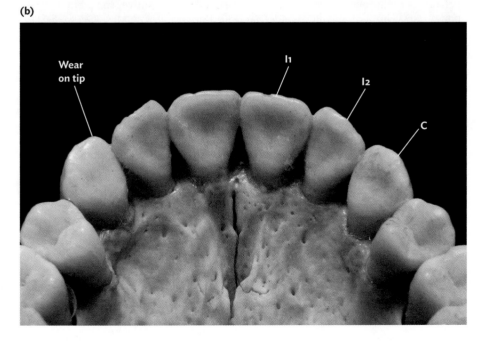

FIGURE 10.8

Canine Wear **(a)** This gorilla's dentition reveals honing wear on the back of the upper canine, caused by the tooth's rubbing against the lower third premolar. **(b)** This human's dentition reveals wear on the upper canine's tip, which is the point of contact between the upper canine and the lower teeth when the jaws are closed.

THE LESSON OF

SCIENCE AS A WAY OF KNOWING

Science is a powerful way of distinguishing between what is true and what is not true in the natural world.

In the nineteenth and early twentieth centuries, the leading hypothesis was that what makes us human is our very large brain, reflecting humankind's superior intelligence. Without a large brain, a creature simply was not human—a hominin—or a human ancestor, even if its skeleton resembled that of a human. Sir Arthur Keith, the influential anthropologist and anatomist, believed that humans had great antiquity. But the fossil record for early human evolution was not complete enough to support or refute his other hypotheses about human origins.

This story took a sudden turn, however, with the discovery between 1908 and 1916 of fossils in a gravel deposit in East Sussex, England, near Piltdown Common. The best-known Piltdown fossil was a skull unearthed by the amateur archaeologist Charles Dawson and the paleontologist Sir Arthur Smith Woodward. Meticulously reconstructed by Woodward and Keith, the skull was *modern* in appearance, having a large cranial capacity (1,400 cubic centimeters)—the predicted key physical attribute defining humanity—well within the range of fully modern *Homo sapiens*. However, the teeth (two molars) were quite like apes'. Woodward named the new fossil **Eoanthropus dawsoni** (meaning "Dawson's dawn man"). The news spread around the world: *the* human ancestor had been found, it was old (perhaps Pliocene), it had a big brain, and it was from England.

Not everyone accepted the new discovery as a legitimate fossil ancestor. One dissenter said that the jaw was so much like an ape's because it *was* an ape's, not a human's. This and other negative opinions went unheard. After all, the leading authorities of the time were staking their professional careers on the discovery.

A decade after the Piltdown discovery, with the fossil entrenched in anthropological lore, a new discovery was made thousands of miles away. In 1924, in the process of blasting limestone in a quarry near the village of Taung, South Africa, a quarry worker happened upon a fossil skull and associated fossilized impression of the brain. This fossil and its stone matrix were transported to Raymond Dart, a young anatomist at the medical school of the University of the Witwatersrand, Johannesburg. Although he thought this specimen might turn out to be another baboon fossil, Dart spent months removing the bones and teeth from the stone matrix. Two features revealed that this was no baboon: first, the position of the foramen magnum, beneath the skull, showed that it walked upright; second, its teeth were like a human's (the canines were tiny). However, it had a primitive, small brain like an ape's, only one-third the size of Piltdown's brain. This suggested that the creature was not a human but a human ancestor, key fossil evidence that proved Darwin right—the human ancestor was from Africa. Dart named it *Australopithecus africanus* (meaning "southern ape of Africa").

Had circumstances and timing been different, Dart's Taung child (about age four when it died, according to its dental development) would have been accepted by the scientific community as crucial evidence for early human origins and evolution. However, it was not accepted as anything other than just another ape—certainly not as a human ancestor—until nearly 30 years after its discovery. In the eyes of the scientific community, the hominin ancestor had already been found: Piltdown. The smallness of the Taung skull ran counter to consensus expectations; everything about Piltdown fit the picture developed by the scientific community for the roots of human ancestry.

PILTDOWN

Among the excavators at Piltdown Common were (second from left) Sir Arthur Smith Woodward and (third from left) Charles Dawson.

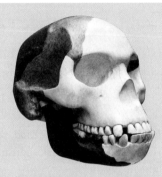

The Piltdown fossil was purported to be the "missing link" between apes and humans.

Long after the discovery of the Piltdown fossil, the earliest hominin fossil in South Africa, the Taung child, was discovered. (Photo © 1985 David L. Brill, humanoriginsphotos.com)

The story might have ended had the scientific process not continued. Beginning in the mid-1930s, Dart and his associates discovered other australopithecines in South Africa, first at Sterkfontein and soon after at Kromdraai, Swartkrans, and Makapansgat. By the late 1940s, a sizable sample of early hominins had been recovered, including, in 1947, a partial skeleton of *Au. africanus* from Sterkfontein showing incontrovertible evidence of bipedalism: a foramen magnum beneath the skull, and human-like leg bones. Moreover, no more fossils even remotely resembling *Eoanthropus dawsoni* were ever found. By the early 1950s, the evidence from South Africa had become so overwhelming that the British anatomist Sir Wilfrid Le Gros Clark weighed in to say that Dart was right—*Au. africanus,* not Piltdown, was the human ancestor.

If *Au. africanus* was the ancestor, who or what was Piltdown? Many scientific authorities began to question the validity of the Piltdown fossils, echoing what the dissenters had said 30 years before. New detailed studies of the Piltdown fossils resulted in some shocking news: the molars had been filed down, and the bones had been stained artificially to match the Piltdown skull; the fluorine tests of the skull and mandible indicated that the two had very different ages; and the canine had been filled with fine lead grains to make it feel like a fossil. All the evidence pointed to an enormous case of fakery, in which someone had placed these altered bones in the gravel pit at Piltdown.

After the Piltdown fossil had been exposed as a fraud, Dart was finally vindicated. So important was Dart's discovery that in 2000, *Science,* a leading scientific journal, proclaimed it one of the 20 scientific breakthroughs in the twentieth century that shaped the life of humankind.

No one has determined the perpetrator of the Piltdown hoax. The truth about human origins eventually emerged, however—a truth that could have come about only via the self-correcting process of scientific inquiry. That is the lesson of Piltdown.

ENGLAND

Piltdown Common, East Sussex

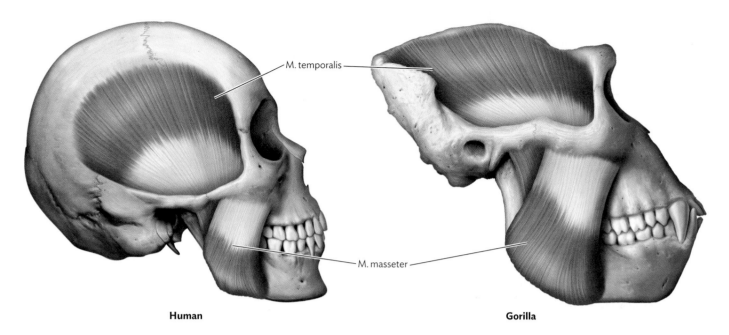

M. temporalis

M. masseter

Human

Gorilla

FIGURE 10.9

Masticatory Muscles Humans and other primates have powerful chewing muscles to process food. In humans, the temporalis muscle is vertically oriented, enabling a crushing ability. In nonhuman primates, this muscle is oriented horizontally, producing slicing motions.

and humans' back teeth crush and slice food, but with a different emphasis: humans crush food more than apes do. Apes use their molars more for slicing than crushing, reflecting their plant-heavy diet.

In apes and humans, grinding and slicing are facilitated by powerful chewing, or masticatory, muscles, especially the temporalis, masseter, and pterygoid muscles (**Figure 10.9**). Hominins place more emphasis on the front portion of these muscles, to provide greater vertical force in crushing food. Apes place more emphasis on the back portion of the masticatory muscles because slicing requires more horizontally oriented forces. As an additional aid in powerful crushing, hominins have evolved thick enamel on their teeth (**Figure 10.10**). Living apes have evolved thin enamel, reflecting diets dominated by plants and soft fruit. Among the hominoids, the only exception is the

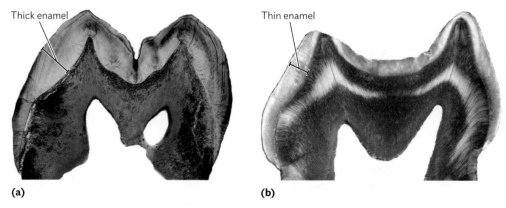

Thick enamel

Thin enamel

(a)

(b)

FIGURE 10.10

Enamel Thickness Enamel is the outermost layer of the exposed part of a tooth and is the hardest substance in the human body, enabling the tooth to grind and slice all types of food. Species with diets heavy in hard foods, such as seeds and nuts, have thicker enamel, allowing more of the enamel to be eroded or worn before the softer layers underneath are exposed. In these cross sections of **(a)** a human tooth and **(b)** a chimpanzee tooth, note how much thicker the human enamel is.

What Makes a Hominin a Hominin?

Hominins have a number of anatomical characteristics that reflect two fundamental behaviors: bipedal locomotion and nonhoning chewing.

Behavior	Anatomical Characteristics
Bipedalism	Foramen magnum on the bottom of the skull
	S-shaped spine
	Short pelvis from front to back
	Long legs
	Knees angled toward midline of the body
	Double-arched foot, including a well-developed longitudinal arch
	Nonopposable big toe
Nonhoning chewing	Blunt, nonprojecting canine
	Small canine relative to size of other teeth
	No diastema
	Wear on tips of canines and of third premolars
	Cusps on lower third premolar equal size

orangutan, which has evolved thick enamel—its diet includes tough foods that require heavy crushing.

Like bipedalism, hominins' nonhoning masticatory complex developed very early in the evolutionary record. Collectively, then, the distinguishing features of the Homininae are located in the anatomical complexes associated with acquiring and transporting food (locomotion) and chewing food (mastication).

10.2 Why Did Hominins Emerge?

The fossil record and genetic information continue to fill in the story of hominins' first appearance on the scene, in the late Miocene epoch, some 10–5.3 mya. But *why* did hominins evolve? Central to most arguments is bipedalism, the focal point in the study of human origins.

Charles Darwin's Hunting Hypothesis

Charles Darwin offered the first serious hypothesis about the first appearance of hominins. It was a simple but elegant adaptive model for explaining human origins.

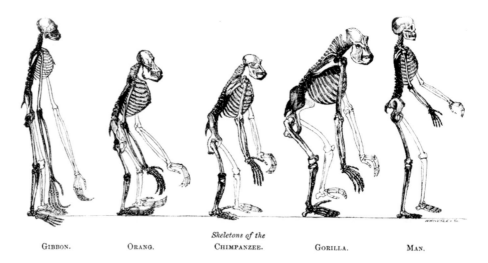

GIBBON.　　ORANG.　　*Skeletons of the*
CHIMPANZEE.　　GORILLA.　　MAN.

FIGURE 10.11

Ape and Human Skeletons Thomas Huxley studied apes' and humans' anatomies. This illustration, from the frontispiece of Huxley's *Evidence as to Man's Place in Nature* (1863), shows the overall similarity in the skeletons of assorted primates (note that the gibbon here is twice its actual size). The major differences between the apes' and humans' skeletons—limb proportions, pelvic shape, and spine curvature—are related to humans' bipedalism.

Drawing on the great British naturalist Thomas Huxley's anatomical research on the living apes of Africa (both Darwin and Huxley are discussed in chapter 2), Darwin concluded that because of the remarkable anatomical similarity between humans and African apes, Africa was hominins' likely place of origin (**Figure 10.11**). The characteristics that distinguish living humans from living apes, Darwin reasoned, derive from one key evolutionary event in their common ancestor: namely, the shift from life in the trees to life on the ground. He observed four characteristics that set living humans and living apes apart: (1) humans are bipedal, while apes are quadrupedal; (2) humans have tiny canines, while apes have large canines; (3) humans rely on tools in their adaptation, while apes do not; and (4) humans have big brains, while apes have small brains (**Figure 10.12**).

Building on these observations, Darwin asked what the advantages of bipedalism would be in a world where bipeds—early humans—ate mostly meat they acquired by killing animals with weapons. He concluded that bipedalism had freed the hands for carrying the weapons. To manufacture and use these tools, the early humans needed great intelligence. Once they had the tools, they did not need the big canines for hunting or for defense. Although he saw tool production and tool use as essential factors in the development of human intelligence, Darwin believed that humans' large brain resulted mainly from the presence of language in humans.

Scientists now know that tool use and the increase in brain size began well after the appearance of bipedalism and the reduction in canine size. The earliest known tools date to about 3.3 mya, and evidence of brain expansion dates to sometime after 2 mya. Therefore, it now seems doubtful that canine reduction began with tool use. Although Darwin's hypothesis was refuted, it provided an essential first step toward an understanding of hominin origins.

Since Darwin, other hypotheses have emerged to answer the question of why there are hominins. The starting point for these hypotheses is the knowledge that, after 17 mya, a massive adaptive diversification of apes occurred in Africa, resulting in many

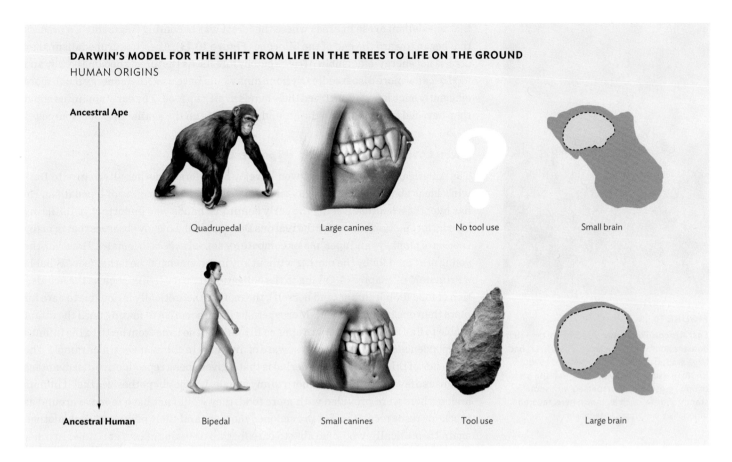

DARWIN'S MODEL FOR THE SHIFT FROM LIFE IN THE TREES TO LIFE ON THE GROUND
HUMAN ORIGINS

Ancestral Ape

Quadrupedal · Large canines · No tool use · Small brain

Ancestral Human

Bipedal · Small canines · Tool use · Large brain

FIGURE 10.12

Four Key Differences From Huxley's comparative studies of apes and humans, Darwin noted four differences between these two types of primates. In Darwin's time, there were no recorded instances of apes' making or using tools, so tools appeared a uniquely human phenomenon. Since then, however, apes have been seen making and using tools, such as when chimpanzees "fish" for termites with a rod and crack hard nuts with a "hammer and anvil" (see "Acquiring Resources and Transmitting Knowledge: Got Culture?" in chapter 7).

different taxa (see "Apes Begin in Africa and Dominate the Miocene Primate World" in chapter 9). At some point later, this diversity declined considerably, perhaps due in part to competition between apes and to the rising number of monkey species that were also evolving in the late Miocene epoch. Changes in climate and in habitat also likely influenced the decline in the number of ape taxa. Most important about the evolution of Miocene apes is that somewhere out of this ancestral group of ape species arose the animal that was more human than ape.

Darwin proposed that hunting was at the basis of the divergence. However, the archaeological record suggests that hunting began much later in human evolution. Hunting, at least in the sense of cooperation among individuals to kill an animal, likely did not begin until after 2 mya, at about the same time the brain began expanding. It now seems likely that hunting played an important role in later human evolution but not in hominin origins.

Peter Rodman and Henry McHenry's Patchy Forest Hypothesis

The American anthropologists Peter Rodman and Henry McHenry have proposed that human origins and bipedalism in particular may be related to the greater efficiency, in certain habitats, of walking on two feet rather than four feet. They suggest

FIGURE 10.13

East African Tree Cover Around the time that humans and bipedalism arose, East Africa had large amounts of discontinuous tree cover. Rodman and McHenry propose that the areas of open grassland, interspersed with some stands of trees, such as shown here, favored bipedalism over quadrupedalism.

that bipedalism arose in areas where the forest was becoming fragmented, a process that began toward the end of the Miocene (**Figure 10.13**). Apes' quadrupedalism, they note, is not energy-efficient in Africa's patchy forests. As the forests became patchy and food became more dispersed, early hominins would have used their energy much more efficiently once bipedalism freed their hands to pick up food. The early hominins could then have fed in trees and on the ground, depending on the availability of resources.

Owen Lovejoy's Provisioning Hypothesis

The American anthropologist Owen Lovejoy has offered another alternative to Darwin's ideas about the arboreal-to-terrestrial shift and the origins of bipedalism. He has hypothesized that freeing the early hominins' hands was important in initiating bipedal locomotion but not for the reasons Darwin cited. Lovejoy observes that in many species of monkeys and apes, males compete for sexual access to females. However, the young are cared for by the mother without any involvement of the father (see "What Is a Primate?" in chapter 6). Owing to the obligations of caregiving, such as the acquisition of food for her infant (and herself), the mother theoretically is not able to care for more than one infant at a time. Moreover, she is unreceptive to mating until the infant is able to find food on its own. In apes as in humans, the time from birth to the infant's independence can be rather long, upward of five years in chimpanzees, for example. The downside of this extended care period is that it gives apes a reproductive disadvantage because so few offspring can be born to any female. Lovejoy hypothesizes that if infants and mothers were provided with more food, they would not have to move around as much for resources. If males provisioned mothers and their offspring, each mother, again theoretically, would be able to care for two or more infants at a time. In other words, the mother could have more births—the time between births would be reduced.

Lovejoy makes the case that for early hominins, a monogamous father enhanced the survival of the mother and offspring by providing both food and protection from predators. This habitual provisioning required the male to have free hands for carrying food, so bipedalism arose. This model focuses on the selective and simultaneous advantages of monogamy and of pair-bonding, of food provisioning, of cooperation, and of bipedalism, all rolled into one distinctively human behavioral package.

Sexual Dimorphism and Human Behavior

Among all the hypotheses about hominin origins, Lovejoy's hypothesis had a unique focus on differences in female and male body sizes and on the implications of behavior with a decidedly human bent. Through field and laboratory studies, anthropologists have observed that in terms of body size, many living primate species are highly dimorphic sexually: males are considerably larger than females. This difference has come about because the larger the male, the more equipped it will be to outcompete other males for sexual access to females. Through natural selection, then, males in many primate species have maintained relatively large bodies. Some authorities argue that early hominins were highly dimorphic, in which case competing males were likely not involved in caring for their offspring. However, if early hominins were not especially dimorphic, then male competition for mates probably was not part of early hominin social behavior. The American anthropologist Philip Reno and his associates have studied early hominin bones to determine relative sizes of females and of males. Their analysis shows relatively little sexual dimorphism in body size, especially in comparison with apes. Such reduced sexual dimorphism suggests that males were cooperative, not competitive. This cooperative behavior could have included pair-bonding—one male paired with one female—a behavior pattern necessary for the kind of provisioning required in Lovejoy's hypothesis.

Bipedalism Had Its Benefits and Costs: An Evolutionary Trade-Off

All the hypotheses about human origins have suggested that an apelike primate evolved into an early hominin through completely positive adaptation. Bipedalism's advantages over quadrupedalism included an increased ability to see greater distances (thanks to an upright posture), greater ease of transporting both food and children, ability to run long distances, and the freeing of the hands for, eventually, such remarkable skills and activities as tool manufacture and tool use. However, the profound adaptive shift to bipedalism also had its costs. Standing upright yields a better view across the landscape, but it also brings exposure to predators. Standing or walking on two feet while simultaneously lifting or carrying heavy objects over long periods of time causes back injury, such as that associated with arthritis and with slipped intervertebral disks. Bipedalism also places an enormous burden on the circulatory system as it moves blood from the legs to the heart. The result of this burden is the development of varicose veins, a condition in which overwork causes the veins to bulge. Lastly, if one of a biped's two feet is injured, then that biped's ability to walk can be severely reduced. Unable to move about the landscape, an early hominin would have had limited chances of surviving and of reproducing. In short, bipedalism is a wonderful example of the trade-offs that occur in evolution. Only rarely do adaptive shifts, including one of the most fundamental human behaviors, come without some cost.

10.3 What Were the First Hominins?

Until the 1970s, the oldest hominin fossil dated to less than 4 mya. The earliest hominins were known from one genus, *Australopithecus,* found mostly in two key areas of Africa: in a series of limestone caves in South Africa and in sedimentary basins and associated river drainages in the Eastern Rift Valley (part of the Great Rift Valley) in Ethiopia, Kenya, and Tanzania (**Figure 10.14**). As we saw in the previous chapter, the latest African Miocene apes—the group of hominoids out of which the first hominins evolved—date to about 8 mya. Thus, the crucial time period during which hominins and the last common ancestor with apes (chimpanzees) split into separate lineages had been an unknown because of the 4-million-year gap in the fossil record (8–4 mya). Subsequently, however, hominins predating *Australopithecus* have been discovered in north-central and eastern Africa. These hominins have closed the gap between late Miocene ape evolution and the first hominins, the pre-australopithecines.

The Pre-Australopithecines

Pre-australopithecine fossils are few in number and quite fragmentary, but they have provided critically important information about the origins and earliest evolution of the Hominini. The pre-australopithecines had a number of primitive attributes, and in some respects they were more apelike than humanlike. They represent the first recognizable ancestors of the lineage leading to humans.

***SAHELANTHROPUS TCHADENSIS* (7–6 MYA)** The earliest pre-australopithecine is represented by most of a skull and other fossils found in central Africa, beginning in

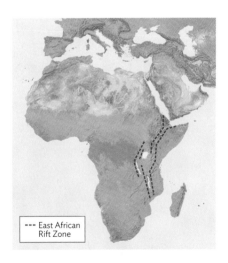

--- East African
Rift Zone

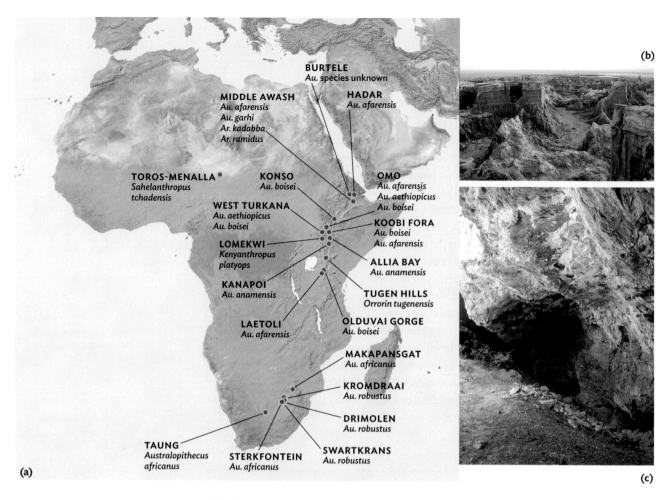

(a)

(b)

(c)

FIGURE 10.14

African Hominins **(a)** Many hominin fossils have been found in East Africa and South Africa. **(b)** In East Africa, layers of geologic strata have been exposed through erosion and geologic activities. The volcanic rock in these strata allows the layers to be dated directly, providing age estimates for the fossils found in them. **(c)** In South Africa, by contrast, many fossils have been found in limestone caves, which cannot be dated directly. Age estimates for fossils found there are made through other methods.

Sahelanthropus tchadensis The earliest pre-australopithecine species found in central Africa with possible evidence of bipedalism.

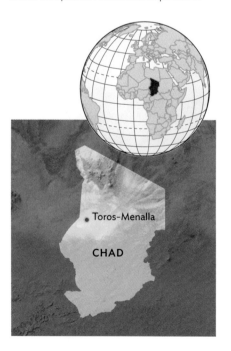

2001, by the French paleontologist Michel Brunet and his colleagues (**Figure 10.15**). Named ***Sahelanthropus tchadensis*** (meaning "genus named for the region of the southern Sahara Desert known as the Sahel") by its discoverers, this creature's fossils date to 7–6 mya. The finding's geographic location—the Toros-Menalla locality of the Djurab Desert in Chad—surprised many because it was 2,500 km (1,553 mi) from the Eastern Rift Valley, where all other early hominins in East Africa had been found for the past three-quarters of a century. The presence of early hominins in central Africa opens a third geographic "window" onto their evolution, the first two being later presences in East Africa and South Africa. In short, humans originated in Africa during the late Miocene and early Pliocene.

Cranial capacity, a rough measure of brain volume, is one important quantitative characteristic with which anthropologists determine the degree of humanness in individual fossil hominins. The fossil record of human evolution shows an increase in brain size, from the smallest in the oldest hominins (about 350 cubic centimeters, or cc) to the largest in *Homo sapiens* (about 1,450 cc). *Sahelanthropus* had a brain size of about 350 cc.

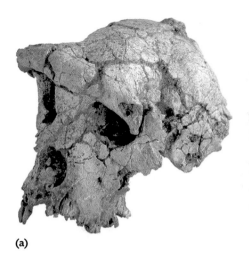

(a)

(b)

(c)

FIGURE 10.15

Sahelanthropus tchadensis **(a)** Among the first and few hominin fossils uncovered in central Africa, this skull belonged to a primate with a small and primitive brain like that of apes. Note the large browridge. **(b)** Left to right: Ahounta Djimdoumalbaye, Michel Brunet, and Mackaye Hassane Taisso examine the skull, which they found in Chad. **(c)** This artist's reconstruction depicts how *Sahelanthropus* might have appeared in life. Its many apelike features combined with bipedalism caused researchers to classify this creature as a pre-australopithecine, part of a group of very early hominin ancestors that bridge the gap between other hominin ancestors and apes.

Its brain was primitive and like that of apes. Moreover, this hominin had a massive browridge, larger than that of modern gorillas. However, the two critical attributes that define the Hominini are present in *Sahelanthropus*—the primate was likely bipedal (based on the position of the foramen magnum at the base of the skull), and the canine–premolar chewing complex was nonhoning. This combination of primitive (more apelike) and derived (more humanlike) features is to be expected in the oldest hominin, especially in apes' and humans' common ancestor. Its great age and primitive characteristics indicate that *Sahelanthropus* existed very close—the closest of any fossil known—to the divergence of their common ancestor into apes and hominins.

Also found at the same site were the bones and teeth of nonprimate animals, fossils that create a picture of *Sahelanthropus*'s habitat. These remains—of hugely diverse animal species, including fish, crocodiles, amphibious mammals associated with aquatic settings, bovids (hoofed mammals), horses, elephants, primates, and rodents associated with forests and grasslands—indicate that *Sahelanthropus* lived in a forest near a lake.

ORRORIN TUGENENSIS* (6 MYA)** Dating to around 6 mya, the fossils of at least five pre-australopithecines were found in the Tugen Hills, on the western side of Kenya's Lake Turkana. The discoverers, paleoanthropologists Brigitte Senut and Martin Pickford, named these hominins ***Orrorin tugenensis (the genus means "original man" in Tugen's local language). Among the 20 remains were several partial femurs, each missing the knee but indicating that these hominins were bipedal. For example, the femur's neck, the area that is at the top of the bone and articulates with the hip, was relatively long (**Figure 10.16**). A hand phalanx found at the site was curved like a living ape's, suggesting that *Orrorin* spent time in the trees. Like those of *Sahelanthropus*, the canines had wear on the tips and were nonhoning. The animal bones at the site indicated that *Orrorin* lived in a forest.

***ARDIPITHECUS KADABBA* AND *ARDIPITHECUS RAMIDUS* (5.8–4.4 MYA)** At Aramis, one of a number of important paleontological sites in the fossil-rich Middle Awash

Orrorin tugenensis A pre-australopithecine species found in East Africa that displayed some of the earliest evidence of bipedalism.

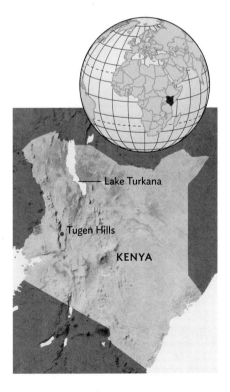

Modern human   *Orrorin*   Chimpanzee

Long neck   Short neck

No obturator externus groove

FIGURE 10.16

Orrorin tugenensis The most important skeletal remain of this pre-australopithecine is a proximal, or upper, portion of the femur, which has a long femoral neck and a groove for the obturator externus muscle. These characteristics are the same as in humans and hominin ancestors, suggesting *Orrorin* was bipedal. By contrast, apes (such as the chimpanzee) have a short femoral neck and no groove.

Location of obturator externus groove

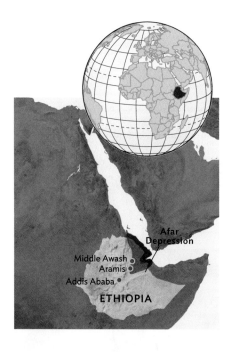

Afar Depression

Middle Awash
Aramis
Addis Ababa

ETHIOPIA

Ardipithecus kadabba An early pre-australopithecine species from the late Miocene to the early Pliocene; shows evidence of a perihoning complex, a primitive trait intermediate between apes and modern humans.

Ardipithecus ramidus A later pre-australopithecine species from the late Miocene to the early Pliocene; shows evidence of both bipedalism and arboreal activity but no indication of the primitive perihoning complex.

Valley of Ethiopia's expansive Afar Depression (**Figure 10.17**), the American physical anthropologist Tim White and his colleagues recovered the most spectacular of the pre-australopithecines (or, for that matter, any other early hominin assemblage). They began exploring the Middle Awash in the early 1980s as a potential place for finding fossils. At Aramis, beginning in the early 1990s and continuing for the next 15 years, they collected fossils intensively. Their team grew to include 70 scientists from 18 countries. What drew the team back to the site, field season after field season, interrupted for years by political unrest in the region, were the very strong signals for successful recovery of key fossils that would date from the period at or just after the origins of the human lineage. The team concluded that this would be the place to look for answers to questions about the transition from ape to hominin, from a primate that walked on all fours and used its arms to move in trees to a primate that walked on the ground. Eventually, the Middle Awash region yielded the longest continuous record of hominin evolution: more than 6 million years, dating from before the australopithecines through the appearance and evolution of early *Homo* to the first modern *H. sapiens* (discussed in chapters 11 and 12) and after.

The scientists of the Middle Awash project predicted that fossils they discovered from the Miocene and early Pliocene at Aramis would reveal hominin ancestors having a mosaic of apelike and humanlike characteristics. These ancestors would have set the stage for all of later human evolution. And indeed, among their findings were two species of a new genus of hominin, *Ardipithecus,* including the earlier **Ardipithecus kadabba** and the later **Ardipithecus ramidus** (in the local Afar language, *ardi* means "ground" or "floor" and *ramid* means "root"), dating to 5.8–5.5 mya and 4.4 mya, respectively. The earlier *Ar. kadabba* is known mainly from teeth, and these fossils show that hominins' canines wore from the tips (not the sides) but had some honing or polishing on the sides of the third lower premolar (**Figure 10.18**).

The later species of *Ardipithecus,* dubbed "Ardi" by its discoverers, is one of three or four fossil hominin discoveries of the many hundreds since the mid-nineteenth century that have transformed our understanding of the earliest period of human evolution. In

FIGURE 10.17

Middle Awash Valley, Ethiopia This hotbed of hominin fossil finds is located in the Afar Depression, an area of much geologic and tectonic activity. The Awash River flows through the depression, creating rich plant and animal life in the midst of an arid region. Because the Afar's floor consists of volcanic rock, radiometric dating methods can be used to provide age estimates for the fossils found in the geologic strata.

2009, _Science,_ the leading international journal for all scientific disciplines, devoted much of an issue to the description and interpretation of this hominin, calling the finding the "Breakthrough of the Year" (**Figure 10.19**). Anthropologists worldwide call it the breakthrough of the century.

Ardipithecus is remarkable, first of all, because it is represented by a huge assemblage of fossils. These fossils include the most complete early hominin skeleton found to date, along with bones and teeth of at least 35 other individuals, all bracketed to a depositional period of less than 10,000 years, an eyeblink in human evolution (**Figure 10.20**).

FIGURE 10.18

Ardipithecus kadabba The earlier form of this pre-australopithecine had an intermediate honing, or perihoning, complex in its dentition, while the later form lacked honing entirely. Shown here, the perihoning complex of an early form of _Ardipithecus_ (right) is similar to chimpanzees' honing complex (left). Together, these forms suggest that _Ardipithecus_ was an early hominin ancestor as its dental morphology was intermediate between apes' and humans'. (Photo © 2003 Tim D. White/David L. Brill, humanoriginsphotos.com)

FIGURE 10.19

Cover of Science Magazine The discovery of _Ardipithecus_ was such a fundamental development that _Science_ magazine called it the "Breakthrough of the Year."

10.20

From Discovery to Understanding
CONSTRUCTING A FUNDAMENTAL SCIENTIFIC THEORY

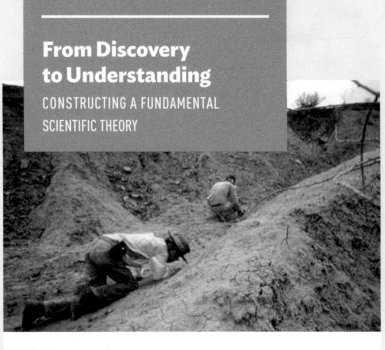

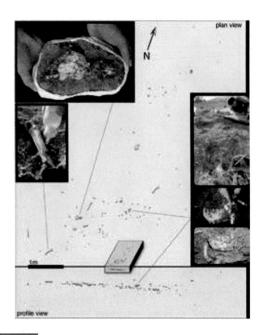

1 ◀ DISCOVERY

In the early 1980s, a multidisciplinary team of geologists, paleoanthropologists, and archaeologists first visited the region near the village of Aramis, in the Middle Awash Valley, identifying it as a place where Pliocene hominins could be found. Field teams collected intensively in the region from 1995 to 2005, in geological deposits dating to 4.4 mya. During the 10-year collection period, scientists and field workers literally crawled across the landscape on their hands and knees in search of hominins and other fossils. This herculean effort had an enormous payoff, producing one of the most important fossil records of early hominins ever found and an abundant record of plants and animals. The plant and animal fossils reveal that these early hominins inhabited a cool, wet forest.

2 ◀ RECOVERY

Once the fossils' locations had been recorded, it was important to remove the fossils as quickly as possible. The bones were soft and had to be treated with preservatives, and some had to be removed in plaster jackets. They were taken first to the field camp and eventually to the laboratory at the National Museum in Addis Ababa, Ethiopia, for detailed study. The 109 hominin fossils represented 36 individuals. Among them was a partial skeleton, field number ARA-VP-6/500. The oldest fossil hominin skeleton yet found, it predates Lucy's skeleton by more than a million years. The map plotting the fossils of this hominin shows that it was widely scattered and no bones were articulated. It took the researchers three years of hard work to recover the remains of this skeleton alone.

3 ◀ LAB WORK

Almost from the beginning of the discovery of fossils in this locality some years before, it was clear that they needed a new name. Tim White called it *Ardipithecus ramidus* (in the local Afar language, *ardi* means "ground" or "floor" and *ramid* means "root"). The partial skeleton, nicknamed "Ardi" by the field team, required years of cleaning, preparation, and reconstruction. For example, to assemble all the skull fragments into an accurate reconstruction, casts of each of the scores of pieces were made. The resulting images were combined with digital images to produce a composite picture (see the upper left corner of the facing page). Various indicators, including the size of the body, revealed that the hominin was a female adult, weighing 50 kg (110 lb) and standing 120 cm (4 ft) high.

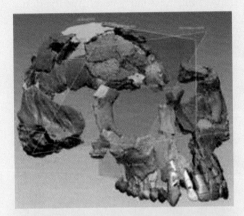

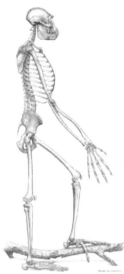

4 ▸ UNDERSTANDING ARDI: HEAD TO TOE

Skull and teeth The skull is very similar to those of other pre-australopithecines, such as *Sahelanthropus* (see p. 324), with its tiny brain (300–350 cc) and highly projecting face. It is probably like the skull of the nearest common ancestor of apes and humans. The teeth show none of the specializations seen in living apes, such as the big incisors and canines and sectorial complex of orangutans and chimpanzees. Wear on the teeth suggests that the hominin was omnivorous, eating nonabrasive foods and some hard foods. The canine shows no functional honing, and so these hominins processed their food like later hominins.

Upper limb and hand Especially striking about the upper limb and hand are their primitiveness. Compared with those of living humans, the forearm (radius and ulna) is extraordinarily long in relation to the upper arm. The elbow joint shows no evidence that these arms were used for suspension, however. The size and morphology of the hand indicate that the hominin did not knuckle-walk. Thus, knuckle-walking evolved in later apes. The fingers are quite long and had excellent grasping capability. Ardi walked on her palms when in the trees.

Pelvis The wide pelvis indicates full hominin status: Ardi walked bipedally when on the ground. In this respect, the pelvis is quite evolved, especially compared with the upper limb/hand and lower limb/feet. The lower part of the pelvis reveals evidence of muscles used in climbing.

Lower limb The lower limb and foot are adapted for bipedalism, but they also reveal characteristics that indicate significant time spent in the trees. For example, the foot has greatly elongated toes and a fully divergent big toe for grasping. No later hominin has this particular combination of features. While retaining its very primitive grasping capability, the foot also served in propelling the body forward when walking or running on the ground. Like the other parts of the skeleton, it is a mosaic of primitive and derived characteristics.

5 ▸ IMPLICATIONS FOR HUMAN EVOLUTION

This remarkable hominin skeleton, along with the other fossils found at Aramis, provides us with a new understanding of the origins and evolution of the human and ape lineages. This new understanding is made possible by this exceptionally complete fossil record and the unprecedented level and detail of multidisciplinary study, ranging from habitat reconstruction to the analysis of function and behavior of early hominins. The very primitive nature of this skeleton confirms that the divergence of the chimpanzee–human lineage was quite recent and provides insight into behavior and adaptation soon after the divergence. This fossil is the closest yet found to the common ancestor of chimpanzees and humans. Most important, all earlier models suggesting a chimpanzeelike ancestor for hominins are incorrect—the first hominin was not chimpanzeelike.

FIGURE 10.21

Origins of Bipedalism The earliest hominin ancestors, the pre-australopithecines, lived in a forested setting. Contrary to earlier hypotheses, bipedalism likely originated not in open grasslands, but an environment with trees. Shown here is a reconstruction of *Ardipithecus* in its East African late Miocene–early Pliocene habitat in East Africa.

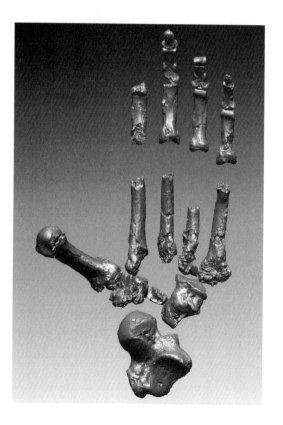

Second, the fossils provide us with a snapshot of the species: their behavior, their adaptation, and what life was like for them not long after the chimpanzee and human lineages had diverged from their common ancestor in the late Miocene. This picture includes unprecedented ecological detail derived from the study of thousands of fossilized plant and animal remains from the site in conjunction with the study of the fossil hominin remains. The ecological context shows that these early hominins lived in a forest. This discovery provides compelling evidence that—contrary to the hypotheses of Darwin and other authorities, and reaffirmed by most of the fossil record dating to the Pliocene and Pleistocene—the first hominins clearly did not evolve in the open grasslands (**Figure 10.21**). The forest context for pre-australopithecines had been suggested by paleoecological analyses of the settings for *Sahelanthropus* and *Orrorin,* but the ecological records from places where these pre-australopithecine fossils were found are not nearly as extensive as the ecological record for Aramis.

Like earlier species of *Ardipithecus,* the Aramis fossils have a primitive yet fully hominin masticatory complex, with short, nonprojecting canines and wear on the tips of the canines. The tooth enamel is not as thin as in extant apes, but it is thinner than in all later hominins. As noted by the physical anthropologist Owen Lovejoy and his colleagues, the lower limb and foot bones reveal that the big toe was opposable, more like that of an ape today and completely unlike a human's (**Figure 10.22**). Unlike an ape's foot, however, Ardi's foot lacked the flexibility required for grasping tree limbs and moving through trees. The musculature and construction of Ardi's foot were rigid, a hominin adaptation for using the foot to propel itself forward when walking bipedally. The phalanges of the feet and hands were curved, indicating grasping capabilities similar to apes'. In addition, Ardi's wrist lacked the articulations and specialized adaptations of today's suspensory, knuckle-walking great apes. These details show that Ardi was adapted to life in the trees *and* to life on the ground. It was a part-time biped and a part-time quadruped. It did not evolve from an ape that was suspensory in the trees and a knuckle-walker on the ground. Instead, as suggested by reconstruction of its skeleton, Ardi moved on its palms and feet along tree branches and walked upright on the ground.

Ardi's intermediate form of bipedalism is part of the ancestry of later hominins, which became fully committed to life on the ground. Ardi evolved from some apelike ancestor, but the great apes and hominins took two entirely different behavioral and associated anatomical pathways, the former evolving suspensory locomotion and knuckle-walking and the latter evolving efficient bipedalism and losing all arboreal behavior.

The extensive fossil record for *Ardipithecus* is beginning to be documented from other contexts in Ethiopia and extends the record possibly back further in time at the site of Gona, which like Aramis is located in the Afar Depression. There, a single tooth dates to 6.3 mya, whereas other teeth date to 5.5 mya. These fossils, discovered by American paleoanthropologist Scott Simpson and his field team, reveal an adaptive proliferation of hominin species in the late Miocene.

In summary, Ardi was clearly a primitive hominin, and its array of remarkable characteristics post-date the chimpanzee–human divergence. This record puts it on the evolutionary pathway to later hominins, the australopithecines, and us. Thus, *Ardipithecus* was a one of a few surviving hominoid lineages in the adaptive radiation of Miocene apes. It retained an arboreal adaptation but shares critically important anatomical characteristics with all later hominins.

FIGURE 10.22

Ardipithecus Foot There is evidence that *Ardipithecus* was bipedal. However, its big toe (hallux) is divergent like apes', indicating that this pre-australopithecine was arboreal at least some of the time. Like its dentition, this anatomical evidence suggests *Ardipithecus* was an intermediate genus. (Photo © 2003 Tim D. White/David L. Brill, humanoriginsphotos.com)

The Pre-Australopithecines

The first hominins spanned a 3-million-year period in Africa, about 7–4 mya. They had both apelike characteristics and the features that define hominins.

Hominin	Date(s)	Location
Sahelanthropus tchadensis	7–6 mya	Djurab Desert, Chad

Key features:

Skull and teeth found

Tiny brain (350 cc)

Skull like apes', with massive browridge

Hominin	Date(s)	Location
Ardipithecus kadabba	5.8–5.5 mya	Middle Awash Valley, Ethiopia

Key features:

Skull, teeth, postcranial bones found

Small brain

Some tooth wear on outside of third premolar (perihoning)

Thin enamel

Curved foot phalanges

Femur and pelvis indicate capable of bipedalism

Less than 1 m (3.3 ft) tall

Lived in wooded setting

Orrorin tugenensis	6 mya	Tugen Hills, Kenya

Key features:

Postcranial bones found

Femurs indicate likely bipedalism

Hand phalanx like apes' (curved)

Less than 1 m (3.3 ft) tall

Ardipithecus ramidus	4.4 mya	Middle Awash Valley, Ethiopia

Key features:

Skull, teeth, postcranial bones found

Small brain

No perihoning

Thin enamel (only hominin with thin enamel)

Curved foot phalanges

Femur and pelvis indicate capable of bipedalism

120 cm (3.9 ft) tall

Lived in wooded setting

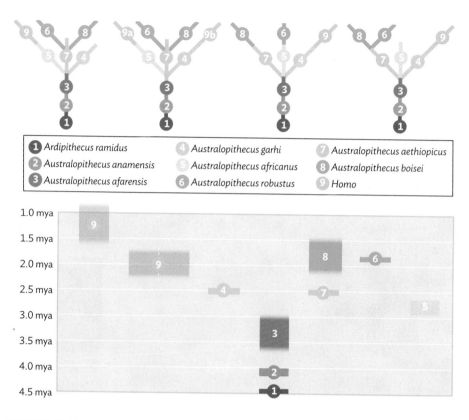

1 Ardipithecus ramidus	**4** Australopithecus garhi	**7** Australopithecus aethiopicus
2 Australopithecus anamensis	**5** Australopithecus africanus	**8** Australopithecus boisei
3 Australopithecus afarensis	**6** Australopithecus robustus	**9** Homo

FIGURE 10.23

Hominin Phylogenies These four alternative phylogenies depict the possible ancestor-descendant relationships among the many australopithecine species. In each tree, *Ardipithecus* is at the base, leading to its descendant *Australopithecus anamensis,* one of the earliest australopithecines. In the second tree, the 9a and 9b indicate that the *Homo* genus may have been the product of both ancestors. The bottom graph illustrates the general pattern of hominin evolution, showing the extinction of the australopithecines, with one lineage leading to the genus *Homo.*

Gona •

ETHIOPIA

The Australopithecines (4–1 mya)

The australopithecines are represented by hundreds of fossils, representing as many as 10 species. Some of the species represent members of ancestral-descendant lineages (**Figure 10.23**). That is, we can link an ancestral species with its descendant species. On the other hand, some species overlap in time, and some of the species and their evolutionary relationships remain unclear. Australopithecine variation is mostly in size and robusticity—ranging from relatively small and gracile to large and robust. As a group, the australopithecines had small brains, small canines, large premolars, and large molars (Table 10.1). The latest australopithecines' face, jaws, and teeth were very large.

Table 10.1 The Earliest Hominins Evolve

	Pre-Australopithecine	→	Australopithecine
Teeth	Wear on tip of canine, but with modified honing	→	Nonhoning
Bones	Vestiges of apelike arboreal traits	→	Loss of traits
Brain	Small	→	Slight increase

FIGURE 10.24

Alan Walker Walker (foreground) is seated in the bone bed at Allia Bay, where he was part of the team that recovered fragments of *Australopithecus anamensis*.

Australopithecus anamensis The oldest species of australopithecine from East Africa and a likely ancestor to *Au. afarensis*.

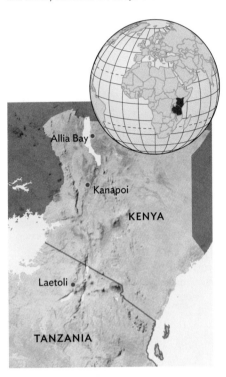

AUSTRALOPITHECUS ANAMENSIS (4 MYA) The oldest australopithecine species, ***Australopithecus anamensis*** (*anam* means "lake" in the Turkana language), was named and studied by the American paleoanthropological team of Meave Leakey, Carol Ward, and Alan Walker. *Au. anamensis* dates to about 4 mya and was found within Allia Bay and Kanapoi in the eastern side and to the south of Lake Turkana, Kenya (**Figure 10.24**). Other remains, found at Asa Issie, Ethiopia, have been studied by Tim White and his colleagues. This creature was broadly similar in physical appearance to *Ardipithecus*, enough to indicate a probable ancestral-descendant relationship between the two genera. Reflecting its relatively early place in australopithecine evolution, *Au. anamensis* has a number of primitive, apelike characteristics, including very large canines, parallel tooth rows in the upper jaw, and a lower third premolar with both a very large outer cusp and a very small inner cusp (**Figure 10.25**). The fossils were created in woodland environments.

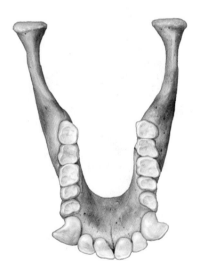

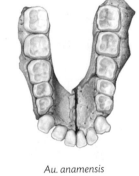

Au. anamensis

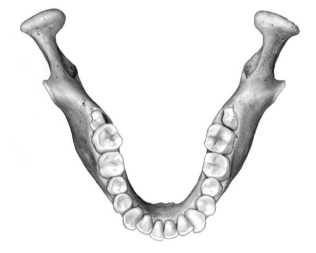

Modern human

Chimpanzee

FIGURE 10.25

Australopithecus anamensis Humans' mandible widens at the rear, causing the two rows of teeth to not be parallel to each other. By contrast, this australopithecine's mandible is like that of apes, *U*-shaped and with two parallel rows of teeth. Primitive features like this, combined with numerous hominin features, have led many researchers to conclude that *Au. anamensis* is the earliest australopithecine.

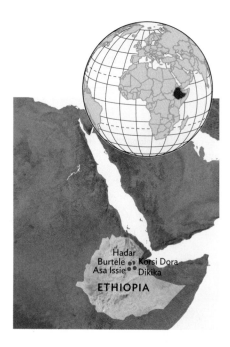

Australopithecus afarensis An early australopithecine from East Africa that had a brain size equivalent to a modern chimpanzee's and is thought to be a direct human ancestor.

Lucy One of the most significant fossils: the 40% complete skeleton of an adult female *Au. afarensis*, found in East Africa.

AUSTRALOPITHECUS AFARENSIS (3.6–3.0 MYA) Since the early 1970s, fossils representing ***Australopithecus afarensis*** have been found in four main sites: Laetoli, in Tanzania, and Hadar, Korsi Dora, and Dikika, all in Ethiopia (*Afar* is the name of the local tribe on whose land the fossils were found in Ethiopia). *Au. afarensis* is the best-known australopithecine and is represented by dozens of individuals from Laetoli and Hadar and single individuals from Korsi Dora and Dikika, collectively dating to 3.6–3.0 mya. The most spectacular of the *Au. afarensis* fossils are three partial skeletons from Hadar, Korsi Dora, and Dikika. They represent, respectively, an adult female—nicknamed "**Lucy**" after the Beatles' song "Lucy in the Sky with Diamonds"— an adult male, and a three-year-old child (**Figure 10.26**).

The completeness of these fossil remains gives us detailed insight into the biology of *Au. afarensis*. Lucy stood only a little more than 1 m (about 3.5 ft) and had somewhat short legs relative to the length of the arms and body trunk. Some authorities have argued that these short legs would have limited the stride in comparison with modern people. However, the male stood about 1.5–1.7 m (about 5–5.5 ft), and the features of the skeleton and limb bones indicate that the form of walking was likely quite similar to that of modern humans. This similarity suggests that Lucy's legs were not short because it had some form of limited bipedalism. Rather, Lucy simply was short. In addition to

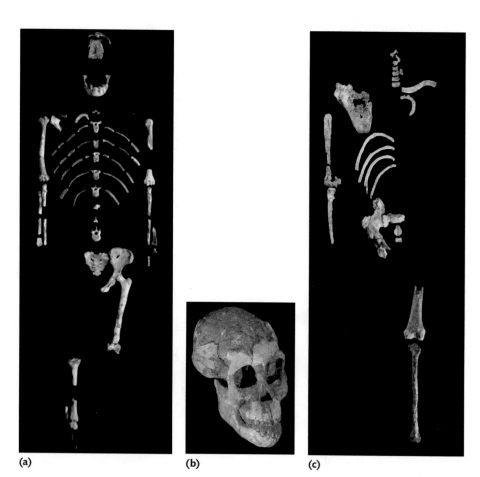

(a)   **(b)**   **(c)**

FIGURE 10.26

Australopithecus afarensis (a) As shown here, "Lucy" is a relatively complete skeleton, which helped researchers conclude that this species was bipedal. **(b)** Recently, the fossil remains of a three-year-old child were recovered and nicknamed "Lucy's baby." There are few children in the fossil record. **(c)** An adult male skeleton from Korsi Dora. (Photo [a] © 1985 David L. Brill, humanoriginsphotos.com; photo [c], Y. Haile-Selassie, Case Western Reserve University)

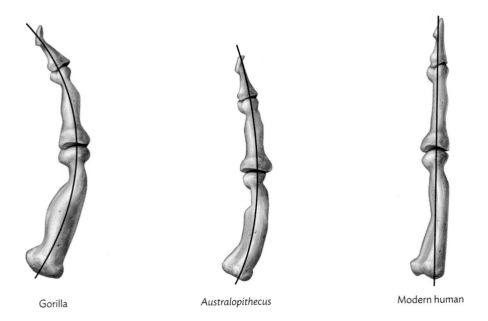

Gorilla   *Australopithecus*   Modern human

FIGURE 10.27

Finger and Toe Curvature Gorillas and other nonhuman primates have curved phalanges, which provide a better grip on tree branches and improve arboreal locomotion. In modern humans, this curvature has been lost in the hands and feet as humans are adapted to life on the ground. The phalanges of early hominins, including australopithecines, have an intermediate amount of curvature, which likely reflects an increasing adaptation to bipedalism but a retained ability to move through the trees.

limb bones, a partial pelvis, and ribs, a scapula has been preserved from the adult male. This bone shows that its shoulder was similar to that of a modern human. In other words, the adult skeleton has changed little in overall plan since the time when *Au. afarensis* lived on the African landscape. The phalanges from Lucy's skeleton are the same length as modern humans', but they are curved, like the pre-australopithecines'. The curvature suggests some potential arboreal locomotion using the hands (**Figure 10.27**). The capability for arboreal activity may also be expressed in the morphology of the scapulae (shoulder joints) of the Dikika juvenile, especially those traits indicating suspensory locomotion. That is, the shoulder joints in this child are angled more like an ape's than like a modern human's (**Figure 10.28**). Thus, *Au. afarensis* displays an

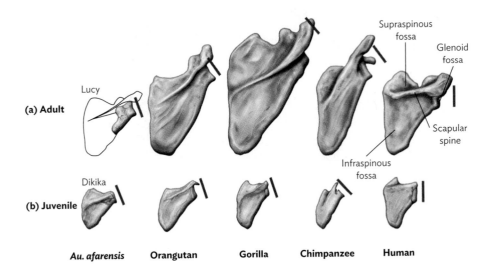

(a) Adult — Lucy

(b) Juvenile — Dikika

Au. afarensis   Orangutan   Gorilla   Chimpanzee   Human

Supraspinous fossa
Glenoid fossa
Scapular spine
Infraspinous fossa

FIGURE 10.28

***Shoulder joint of* Au. afarensis** The glenoid fossa of the shoulder joint of Lucy, an adult, and of the Dikika juvenile is oriented slightly upward, more like a modern ape than a modern human. The modern human's glenoid faces completely vertically. The angled glenoid fossa of *Au. afarensis* suggests climbing abilities.

FIGURE 10.29

Australopithecus afarensis *Cranium*
Although this species was bipedal, its brain size and canine size are more primitive and apelike. Other features of the dentition, however, are more homininlike, illustrating the creature's intermediate position between the pre-australopithecines and other, later australopithecines.

interesting mosaic of apelike and humanlike anatomical features. Regardless of how paleoanthropologists interpret the shoulder joint morphology, *Au. afarensis* clearly was an efficient, habitual biped that spent most of its time on the ground.

Au. afarensis's skull is known from many fragments and teeth, a child's skull, and a nearly complete cranium, the latter found by Donald Johanson in the early 1990s at Hadar (**Figure 10.29**). The cranial capacity of this creature and others from the taxon is about 430 cc, that of a small brain the size of an ape's. The hyoid bone of the child's neck is very much like an ape's. The apelike characteristics of the bone associated with speech indicates the strong likelihood that this hominin did not have speech. The canines are large in comparison with later hominins', the face below the nose projects like an ape's, and overall it looks primitive.

Its many similarities with *Au. anamensis* indicate an ancestral-descendant link between the two. *Au. afarensis* is not as primitive as the earlier hominin in that the two cusps of the lower third premolars are more equal in size. Moreover, *Au. afarensis*'s canines are smaller than those of the earlier species, and the upper tooth rows are parabolic and not parallel; in other words, more like humans' than like apes'. *Au. afarensis*'s mandibles are larger, perhaps reflecting an increased use of the jaws in chewing.

Of the three key *Au. afarensis* sites, Laetoli is especially extraordinary because of its assemblage of fossil hominins and because of its spectacular preservation of thousands of footprints left by numerous species of animals, ranging from tiny insects to giant elephants. Geologic evidence indicates the eruption of a nearby volcano, which spewed a thin layer of very fine ash across the landscape. Soon after the eruption, a light rain fell, causing the ash to turn into a thin, gooey layer of mud. Animals then traversed the landscape, among them three hominins that left tracks indicating they had simultaneously walked across the muddy terrain around 3.6 mya (**Figure 10.30**). The footprints are remarkable for having been preserved for millions of years and with such clarity, a

FIGURE 10.30

Laetoli Footprints These footprints, found in Tanzania, resolved any doubt as to whether *Au. afarensis* was bipedal. The tracks were made by three bipedal hominins, two adults and a child who walked in the footprints of one of the adults. In addition to the hominin footprints, many other prints were found at the site, including those of large animals, such as elephants and giraffes, and those of small animals, including rabbits and birds.

preservation made possible because the volcanic ash was wet carbonatite, which dries into a rock-hard substance. Physical anthropologists' study of these tracks reveals that the creatures were humanlike and had three key characteristics of bipedalism: round heels, double arches (front-to-back and side-to-side), and nondivergent big toes.

In contrast to earlier hominins, which were mostly associated with some type of forested environment, *Au. afarensis* lived in various habitats, including forests, woodlands, and open country. These diverse environments indicate that hominins became more successful at this time, especially after 4 mya, in adapting to and exploiting new habitats. That *Au. afarensis*'s tooth wear is more varied than that of earlier australopithecines indicates *Au. afarensis* probably had a more diverse diet than its predecessors did.

One of the most important characteristics of the Laetoli footprints is the nondivergent big toe. This feature indicates that the hominin had very minimal grasping ability in its toes. In this lack of ability, *Au. afarensis* resembles living humans and differs from living apes. The nondivergent big toe is clear evidence that *Au. afarensis* used its feet primarily in terrestrial locomotion, quite unlike the hominins living a million years earlier, *Ar. ramidus*. However, at least one other taxon of Pliocene hominin was walking around the East African landscape on considerably more primitive feet than *Au. afarensis*. At the Burtele site, in the Afar region of Ethiopia dating to 3.4 mya, the Ethiopian paleoanthropologist Yohannes Haile-Selassie and his team discovered the front half of a single right foot with a short but divergent opposable big toe. This foot belonged to a hominin that, at least in this one respect, was quite similar to *Ardipithecus*. Unlike the toe bones indicated in the Laetoli footprints, the second to fifth toe bones of the Burtele hominin are long and curved. This foot anatomy shows that the early hominin spent considerable time in the trees. The other characteristics of the foot bones indicate that this hominin walked bipedally. During this period of time, then, there were at least two contemporary hominins, one a climber and the other much more a biped, spending its time on the ground. Perhaps the foot bones from Burtele are from *Ardipithecus,* which would then have survived into the period of early *Australopithecus.* In any case, this fossil shows the presence of considerably more diversity in early hominin locomotion than the consensus had previously indicated.

AUSTRALOPITHECUS (KENYANTHROPUS) PLATYOPS (3.5 MYA) *Australopithecus* (or *Kenyanthropus*) *platyops* is a lesser-known hominin from about the same time as *Au. afarensis* (**Figure 10.31**). It was discovered by Meave Leakey and her colleagues at Lomekwi, on the western side of Kenya's Lake Turkana, in deposits that date to about 3.5 mya. Its habitat was mainly woodlands. Its face was unusually flat (*platyops,* from the Greek, means "flat face"), a derived feature in hominins, but retained some primitive characteristics.

AUSTRALOPITHECUS DEYIREMEDA (3.5-3.3 MYA) *Australopithecus deyiremeda* is the most recent fossil discovery of this genus. Found in deposits dating between 3.5 and 3.3 mya by Yohannes Haile-Selassie and his paleoanthropology field team in the Burtele area in the Afar region of Ethiopia, the fossils represented by jaws and teeth are distinctive, including having surprisingly small teeth. Not until later hominin evolution (e.g., with the appearance of *Homo*) are the teeth as small. Especially important about this discovery is the fact that it dates to the same time as *Au. afarensis* and *Au. (Kenyapithecus) platyops.* This record makes clear the presence of hominin diversity, more so than had previously been anticipated when the much better known and better represented *Au. afarensis* was first discovered more than four decades ago. That is, the presence of three species of contemporary australopithecines presents a record of considerable diversity in the genus *Australopithecus,* much more so than what was known

Australopithecus (or Kenyanthropus) platyops An australopithecine from East Africa that had a unique flat face and was contemporaneous with *Au. afarensis.*

Australopithecus deyiremeda An australopithecine, overlapping in time with *Au. afarensis* in East Africa.

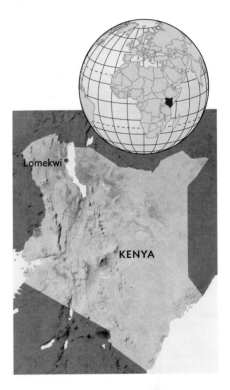

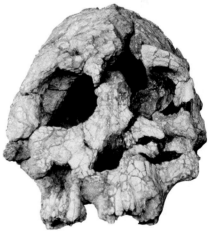

FIGURE 10.31

Australopithecus (Kenyanthropus) platyops A contemporary of *Au. afarensis*, this australopithecine was unique in having a flat face and small teeth. Its brain size, however, was similar to that of *Au. afarensis.*

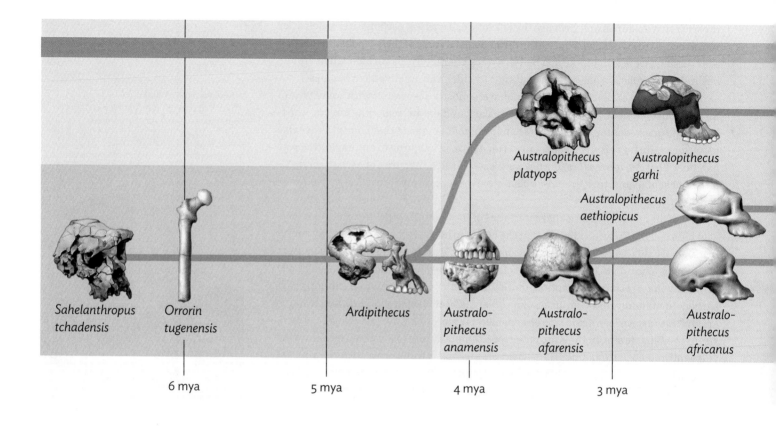

Australopithecus
platyops

Australopithecus
garhi

Australopithecus
aethiopicus

Sahelanthropus
tchadensis

Orrorin
tugenensis

Ardipithecus

Australo-
pithecus
anamensis

Australo-
pithecus
afarensis

Australo-
pithecus
africanus

6 mya   5 mya   4 mya   3 mya

Australopithecus garhi A late australopithecine from East Africa that was contemporaneous with *Au. africanus* and *Au. aethiopicus* and was the likely ancestor to the *Homo* lineage.

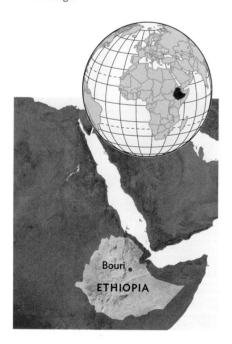

Bouri •
ETHIOPIA

just a few years ago. It also underscores the importance of fieldwork and discovery in order to develop an understanding of early hominin evolution.

Diversification of the Homininae: Emergence of Multiple Evolutionary Lineages from Australopithecus (3–1 mya)

The presence of variable hominin species of the genus **Australopithecus**, some of which were overlapping in time, indicates that the australopithecines were highly diverse, including in their locomotion, mastication, and other key aspects. About 3 mya the picture of diversity becomes even more complex with the appearance of new adaptive patterns associated with the origin and evolution of a new genus, the genus *Homo*. In addition to the anatomical differences, the key distinction between the lineages representing *Australopithecus* and *Homo* is that *Australopithecus* became extinct by about 1 mya (**Figure 10.32**), whereas the lineage represented by *Homo* survives to the present. Here, we look at the two emerging forms of early hominins, *Australopithecus* and *Homo*.

AUSTRALOPITHECUS GARHI (2.5 MYA) Soon after discovering *Au. afarensis* at Hadar, Johanson and White began to suspect that *Au. afarensis* was the most likely ancestor of the genus *Homo*. However, the ancestral-descendant linkage between the two taxa was difficult to identify, owing to the virtual lack of a hominin fossil record in East Africa dating to 3–2 mya, the time during which earliest *Homo* likely evolved (discussed further in chapter 11). In 1999, this picture changed dramatically when the Ethiopian paleoanthropologist Berhane Asfaw and his associates discovered a new *Australopithecus* species, which they named ***Australopithecus garhi*** (*garhi* means

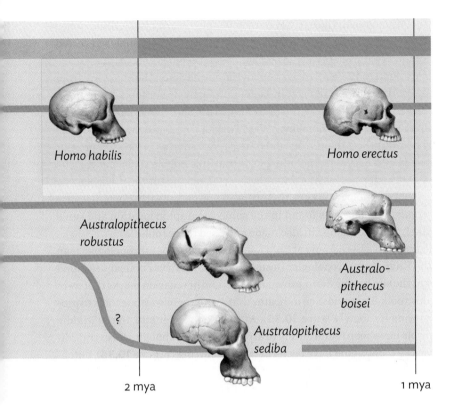

FIGURE 10.32

Hominin Lineages The evolutionary relationships among the various *Australopithecus* species suggest the appearance of two main lineages by 3 mya: one leading to modern *Homo sapiens* (top) and the other leading to a number of australopithecines (bottom). (This second lineage is shown here as separate lines in East Africa and South Africa.) The ancestor to australopithecine lineages is hypothesized to be *Au. afarensis*, which may be a descendant of *Ardipithecus* and *Au. anamensis*. Only the *Homo* lineage continued after 1 mya.

Within figure:

Homo habilis

Homo erectus

Australopithecus robustus

Australo-pithecus boisei

?

Australopithecus sediba

2 mya

1 mya

Oldowan Complex The stone tool culture associated with *H. habilis* and, possibly, *Au. garhi,* including primitive chopper tools.

Lower Paleolithic The oldest part of the period during which the first stone tools were created and used, beginning with the Oldowan Complex.

"surprise" in the Afar language). Found in Bouri, in Ethiopia's Middle Awash region, it dated to about 2.5 mya.

Au. garhi is represented by bones, teeth, a partial skeleton, and a skull (**Figure 10.33**). Its teeth were larger than the earlier australopithecines'. Its third premolar's two cusps were almost equal in size. As in *Au. afarensis,* beneath the nose the face had a primitive projection, and the brain was small (450 cc). For the first time in hominin evolution, the ratio of arm (humerus) length to leg (femur) length was much more humanlike than apelike, resulting from the femur's lengthening. This more humanlike ratio indicates a decreased commitment to the arborealism of earlier australopithecines. These features combined—especially the chronological position at 2.5 mya and the cranial, dental, and postcranial features—suggest that *Au. garhi* was ancestral to *Homo.* Environmental reconstructions based on animal remains and other evidence indicate that this hominin lived on a lakeshore, as was typical of later australopithecines and early *Homo.*

THE FIRST TOOLMAKERS AND USERS: *AUSTRALOPITHECUS* OR *HOMO*? Paleoanthropologists have found very primitive stone tools from a number of sites in East Africa dating mostly to the early Pleistocene, 2.6–1.6 mya. These stone tools are part of the **Oldowan Complex,** the first hominin culture and the earliest culture of the **Lower Paleolithic,** named by Louis and Mary Leakey from their work at Olduvai Gorge. The Leakeys concluded that these early stone tools must have been produced solely by the larger-brained early *Homo* found at the site, rather than by the contemporary smaller-brained australopithecines. Other evidence indicates, however, that at least some australopithecines made and used stone tools. Although much of the record

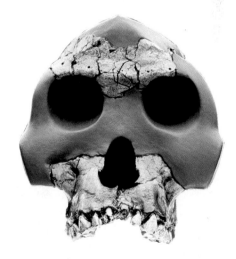

FIGURE 10.33

Australopithecus garhi This hominin may be the link between *Au. afarensis* and the *Homo* genus. That some of its traits are similar to those of *Au. afarensis* while others are similar to features of *Homo* suggests its intermediate status. (Photo © 1999 David L. Brill, humanoriginsphotos.com)

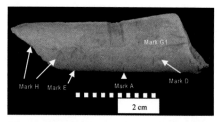

(a)

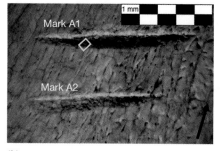

(b)

FIGURE 10.34

Cutmarks on Animal Bones Cutmarks on these animal bones from Dikika, Ethiopia, indicate stone tool use at 3.3 mya.

FIGURE 10.35

Oldest Stone Tools Stone tools found at Lomekwi, Kenya, date to 3.3 mya.

of early stone tool use dates to the early Pleistocene, the discovery of animal bones with cutmarks on them from Dikika, Ethiopia, dating to 3.3 mya, strongly suggested that the first toolmakers and users were in fact australopithecines and, in this setting, were *Au. afarensis* (**Figure 10.34a**). In particular, the cutmarks on the bones are from cutting meat and getting access to protein-rich marrow by use of tools. Even more convincing, however, is the discovery (first presented in 2015) of the actual presence of stone tools dating to 3.3 mya from Lomekwi, West Turkana, Kenya. Scores of artifacts where the early hominins left them, a circumstance referred to as *in situ*, are present at the site. These *in situ* artifacts, including Oldowan-like cobble tools and various other implements used for processing animals for food, document the presence of a well-established tool technology (**Figure 10.34b**), well pre-dating early *Homo*. Because *Au. (Kenyanthropus) platyops* was found in the same geographic location and same time, it seems likely that this hominin also made and used these tools.

Although no tools have been found at Bouri, the Belgian paleoanthropologist Jean de Heinzelin, the English anthropologist Desmond Clark, and their colleagues found mammal bones at the site having distinctive cutmarks and percussion marks that were produced by stone tools. This evidence indicates that *Au. garhi* used stone tools to process animal remains for food (**Figure 10.35**). At the Gona River site, in the Middle Awash region, tools have been found dating to around 2.6 mya. Though still extraordinarily primitive, the tools would have been effective at cutting (**Figure 10.36**), butchering, and other kinds of food processing.

The dominant tools, "chopper" tools and flakes (**Figure 10.37**), discovered in these early hominin sites were used to remove and process the meat from various animals, mostly herbivores. At least two activities were involved: use of flakes with sharp edges for cutting meat from bones, and use of choppers and cobbles to break and smash the bones to access the protein-rich marrow. One of the sites best known for such findings is the FLK 22 site at Olduvai Gorge, where the Leakeys found the famous *Australopithecus boisei* cranium in the late 1950s.

Archaeologists have long assumed that such primitive tools were used for cutting animal tissues to obtain the meat. In some South African caves, bone tools found by paleoanthropologists show distinctively polished patterns of microscopic wear. Through experiments, the South African paleoanthropologist Lucinda Backwell and the French paleoanthropologist Francesco d'Errico have shown this kind of wear to be produced by digging in the ground, especially digging in termite mounds. Their finding supports the idea that early hominins ate insects (in addition to meat). While the idea of eating insects is revolting to our Western tastes, insects would have provided

(a)

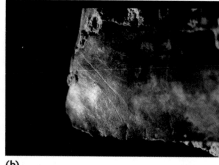

(b)

(c)

FIGURE 10.36

Tool Use and Au. garhi **(a)** A partial animal mandible with cutmarks, **(b)** a close-up of cutmarks, and **(c)** a scanning electron micrograph of cutmarks showing a clear signature of cuts created by stone tools held by a hominin, probably for butchering.

FIGURE 10.37
Oldowan Stone Tools at Gona A number of Oldowan tools were found at Gona, Ethiopia. Dating to 2.6 mya, these primitive tools were not found in association with hominin remains, so it is unclear which genera or species produced them. Among the remains were flaked pieces and "chopper" tools; these may have had various functions.

important proteins for our ancestors. Alternatively, the bone tools may have been used for digging up edible roots.

Evidence of earlier tool use pre-dating 3.3 mya might not have been found because tools may have been made—and probably were made—out of more ephemeral materials, such as wood and grass. In the kinds of environments in which the earliest hominins lived, these materials would not have survived. Other evidence suggests, though, that australopithecines used tools. For example, australopithecines' hand bones have anatomical features associated with finer manipulation than that used by living apes. The paleoanthropologist Randall Susman has found evidence of a flexor muscle in australopithecines' thumb, very similar to a muscle in living humans that is absent in apes. The flexor muscle makes possible the finer precision use of the thumb and other fingers for tool production and tool use. In addition, the internal structure of the hand bones in *Australopithecus* is similar to that of *H. sapiens*. In particular, the internal structure shows physical behavior involving forceful opposition of the thumb and fingers. This evidence, combined with presence of stone tools and/or cutmarks on animal remains in multiple settings, indicates that various species of *Australopithecus* incorporated material culture as a part of the behavioral repertoire for acquiring, processing, and consuming animal sources of protein.

Evolution and Extinction of the Australopithecines

In addition to *Au. garhi,* other australopithecine species lived in East Africa and South Africa. In East Africa, the species included earlier and later forms of robust australopithecines called ***Australopithecus aethiopicus*** (named for Ethiopia, the country where they were first found) and ***Australopithecus boisei*** (named for a benefactor who supported the discoverer's research), respectively. Some authorities refer to these hyper-robust australopithecines as the genus *Paranthropus*. The earlier hominin, *Au. aethiopicus,* from the west side of Lake Turkana, dates to about 2.5 mya and had a brain size of about 410 cc. The later hominin, *Au. boisei,* from Olduvai Gorge and around Lake

Australopithecus aethiopicus An early robust australopithecine from East Africa, with the hallmark physical traits of large teeth, large face, and massive muscle attachments on the cranium.

Australopithecus boisei Formerly known as *Zinjanthropus boisei;* a later robust australopithecine from East Africa that was contemporaneous with *Au. robustus* and *Au. africanus* and had the robust cranial traits, including large teeth, large face, and heavy muscle attachments.

FINDERS OF THE

It takes highly dedicated fossil hunters, committing their time, energy, and passion for scientific discovery.

The popular and the scientific accounts of a fossil discovery tend to make quite a splash about who made the discovery, which is almost always the paleontologist or anthropologist reporting the finding. What most who read the accounts do not know is that such discoveries are made by teams of highly trained, skilled individuals—who are often, unlike the famous scientists, native to the country in which the excavation occurred. Without the support of these individuals, many of the significant finds reported in the popular press and fundamental to science would not have happened.

Kenya, a hot spot for hominin fossil discoveries, is one place in which native people have played a major role in revealing the past. The best-known native Kenyan to have contributed in this way to the understanding of human origins is Kamoya Kimeu. Born ca. 1940 to a family of Ukambani, one of more than 70 ethnic groups in modern Kenya, Kimeu began work with Louis and Mary Leakey in the 1950s. In the early 1960s, he began his lifelong association with their son, Richard Leakey, looking for fossils in the Omo River Valley of Ethiopia, Lake Turkana, and elsewhere in Kenya. Kimeu and his team of a half-dozen highly skilled native Kenyans discovered a number of early hominin fossils, including the sole examples of some of the well-known australopithecines and the famous,

(*Left*) Paleontology field team headed by Komoya Kimeu (in white shirt), searching for hominin fossils in Kenya. (*Right*) Komoya Kimeu and Richard Leakey search the Kenyan landscape for potential hominin-bearing sites.

ANCESTORS

nearly complete skeleton of a *Homo erectus* adolescent (discussed further in chapter 11).

Hominin fossils are very rare, making up a tiny portion of the fossil record at most locations. Moreover, they are extremely hard to find and ridiculously fragile. At all stages, from first discovery to final recovery, these fossils require great attention. In all these areas, Kimeu personally trained his field team. Team members learned all the parts of bones and of teeth that are needed to recognize both hominins and all the other animals found in the region. Kimeu and his field group were also responsible for many of the logistics in running very difficult field projects, such as setting up camp upon arrival, breaking down camp before departure, supplying food and water, and even building airstrips in especially remote places.

While the benefits of Kimeu's work to field projects and to anthropology are obvious, the more important benefits were to him and to his team members, the families they supported, and Kenya's national heritage. Ultimately, humankind benefits from the hard work of Kimeu and his fellow Kenyans. For his efforts, Kimeu was awarded the National Geographic Society's LaGorce Medal, presented to him by President Ronald Reagan in a public ceremony at the White House.

Komoya Kimeu is awarded the National Geographic Society's John Oliver La Gorce Medal by former United States President Ronald Reagan, for contributions to science and public service to advance international understanding.

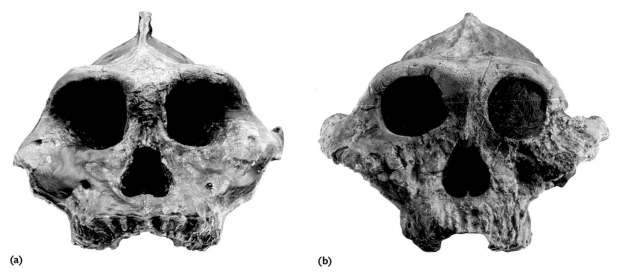

(a)   (b)

FIGURE 10.38

Robust Australopithecines **(a)** *Australopithecus aethiopicus* and **(b)** *Australopithecus boisei* had a large sagittal crest; large, flaring zygomatic, or cheek, bones; and large teeth. The description of these australopithecines as robust, however, applies only to their crania and is likely related to a diet rich in hard foods. Neither of these bipedal species had a robust postcranial skeleton. (Photo [a] © 1995 David L. Brill, humanoriginsphotos.com; photo [b] © 1985 David L. Brill, humanoriginsphotos.com)

Australopithecus africanus A gracile australopithecine from South Africa that was contemporaneous with *Au. aethiopicus, Au. garhi,* and *Au. boisei* and was likely ancestral to *Au. robustus.*

Australopithecus robustus A robust australopithecine from South Africa that may have descended from *Au. afarensis,* was contemporaneous with *Au. boisei,* and had the robust cranial traits of large teeth, large face, and heavy muscle attachments.

Australopithecus sediba A late species of australopithecine from South Africa that may have descended from *Au. africanus,* was a contemporary of *Au. robustus,* and expresses anatomical features found in *Australopithecus* and in *Homo.*

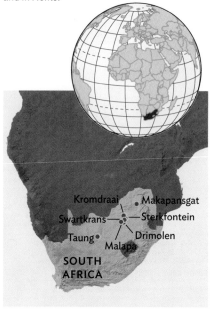

Turkana, dates to 2.3–1.2 mya and had a brain size of about 510 cc. Compared with earlier australopithecines, these remarkably robust australopithecines had smaller front teeth, larger back teeth, and larger faces. Their most visually striking characteristic was a massive attachment area, on the skull, for the temporalis muscle, resulting in a well-developed sagittal crest. Both their premolars and their molars were enormous. These big teeth with large chewing surfaces, combined with large chewing muscles, made robust australopithecines the ultimate grinders (**Figure 10.38**).

Australopithecines' greater cranial robusticity after about 2.5 mya indicates that they were increasingly focused on acquiring and eating foods that required more powerful chewing muscles than before. That is, they were eating harder foods. Robust australopithecines' presence in East Africa ended sometime before 1 mya, indicating that they became extinct at about that time.

The earliest evidence of hominins in South Africa was described by the paleoanthropologist and anatomist Raymond Dart. He named the species, initially found at the Taung site, ***Australopithecus africanus*** (**Figure 10.39**). Found also at Sterkfontein and Makapansgat, *Au. africanus* dates to about 3–2 mya and had larger teeth than those of *Au. afarensis* (**Figure 10.40**). After about 2 mya, there were at least two descendant species of australopithecines in South Africa, ***Australopithecus robustus*** (sometimes called *Parathropus robustus;* **Figure 10.41**) and ***Australopithecus sediba*** (**Figure 10.42**), dating to 2.0–1.5 mya and 2.0 mya, respectively. *Au. robustus* is represented by fossils from the cave sites in Swartkrans, Kromdraai, and Drimolen. *Au. sediba,* discovered in 2008, is from the Malapa cave.

Au. robustus, probably the longest-surviving species of the australopithecine lineage in South Africa, had large premolars, a big face, and a well-developed sagittal crest. These hominins were similar in many respects to their contemporary East African counterparts. Australopithecines' greater robusticity in South Africa and East Africa indicates a widespread adaptation involving an increased focus on foods that required heavy chewing. Anthropologists have long thought that this powerful masticatory complex—amply documented in later australopithecines—was well suited for chewing

FIGURE 10.39

Taung, South Africa Some of the earliest evidence of hominins in South Africa was discovered in a limestone quarry in Taung.

FIGURE 10.40

Australopithecus africanus This *Australopithecus africanus* cranium was discovered in a series of limestone caves known as Sterkfontein. Located in South Africa, this site has been declared a UNESCO World Heritage Site. Unlike the robust australopithecines also discovered in South Africa, this *Au. africanus* cranium is gracile.

FIGURE 10.41

Australopithecus robustus Also discovered in South Africa, this robust australopithecine shares many traits with East Africa's robust species. One of these traits, dietary specialization, might have led to the eventual extinction of both *Au. robustus* and the East African robust species as they were not able to adapt to vegetation changes caused by climate change. (Photo © David L. Brill, humanoriginsphotos.com)

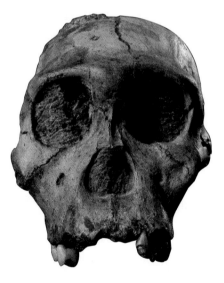

FIGURE 10.42

Australopithecus sediba Found in a cave in South Africa, this australopithecine is quite different from its contemporary, *Au. robustus*, in that its face and jaws are relatively gracile, at least as represented in the juvenile skull. The gracile nature of the skull may be due to the individual being a child; fully mature adult characteristics are not yet present. The very small brain is an australopithecine feature.

The Australopithecines

The australopithecines existed about 4–1 mya. Their fossils are from East Africa and South Africa. These creatures were still primitive in a number of ways, but they were more humanlike than apelike compared with the pre-australopithecines.

Hominin	Date(s)	Location
Australopithecus anamensis	4 mya	Lake Turkana, Kenya Awash River Valley, Ethiopia

Key features:

Skull fragments, teeth, postcrania found

Large outer cusp (like apes') on third premolar

Large canines

Parallel tooth rows in upper jaw (like apes')

Curved hand phalanx

Less than 1 m (3.3 ft) tall

Lived in wooded setting

Hominin	Date(s)	Location
Australopithecus afarensis	3.6–3.0 mya	Hadar, Ethiopia

Key features:

Skulls, teeth, postcrania (hundreds of pieces) found

Partial adult skeleton (Lucy)

Partial juvenile (three-year-old) skeleton

Small brain (430 cc)

Hyoid like apes'

Mandible larger in earlier Laetoli than in later Hadar

Smaller canines than in earlier species

Equal-size cusps on third premolar (like humans')

Parabolic tooth rows in upper jaw

Curved hand phalanges

Short legs

Footprints indicate bipedal foot pattern with no divergent big toe

Lived in wooded setting, but a more open one than associated with *Ardipithecus* or *Au. anamensis*

Hominin	Date(s)	Location
Australopithecus platyops	3.5 mya	Lomekwi, Kenya

Key features:

Skulls and teeth found

Flat face

Small brain (400–500 cc)

Contemporary with *Au. afarensis*, signaling split of australopithecine lineage into two

Lived in woodlands

Hominin	Date(s)	Location
Australopithecus deyiremeda	3.5–3.3 mya	Burtele, Ethiopia

Key features:

Mandibles, maxillae, teeth

Small teeth

Increased diversity of australopithecines—three contemporary species of *Australopithecus* in East Africa

Relatively small teeth

Hominin	Date(s)	Location
Australopithecus africanus	3.0–2.0 mya	Taung, South Africa Sterkfontein, South Africa Makapansgat, South Africa

Key features:
Skulls, teeth, endocast (impression of brain), postcrania, two partial adult skeletons found

Small brain (450 cc)

Moderate-size teeth

Equal-size cusps on third premolar

Phalanges not curved

Adult partial skeleton has apelike leg-to-arm ratio (short legs, long arms)

Lived in open grasslands

Hominin	Date(s)	Location
Australopithecus garhi	2.5 mya	Bouri, Ethiopia

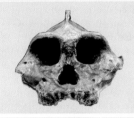

Key features:
Skulls, teeth, postcrania found

Small brain (450 cc)

Equal-size cusps on third premolar

Teeth larger than in earlier *Au. afarensis*

Ratio of upper arm length to upper leg length more humanlike than apelike

Curved foot phalanx (like *Au. afarensis*'s)

Lived in grasslands, on lakeshore

Tool maker/user (animal butchering)

Hominin	Date(s)	Location
Australopithecus boisei	2.3–1.2 mya	Olduvai, Tanzania Lake Turkana, Kenya

Key features:
Skulls and teeth found
Small brain (510 cc)
Massive posterior teeth
Robust skull with sagittal crest
Lived in open grasslands

Hominin	Date(s)	Location
Australopithecus aethiopicus	2.5 mya	Lake Turkana, Kenya

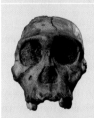

Key features:
Skull and teeth found
Small brain (410 cc)
Massive posterior teeth
Robust skull with sagittal crest
Lived in open grasslands

Hominin	Date(s)	Location
Australopithecus robustus	2.0–1.5 mya	Swartkrans, South Africa Kromdraai, South Africa Drimolen, South Africa

Key features:
Skulls and teeth found
Small brain (530 cc)
Massive posterior teeth
Robust skull with sagittal crest
Lived in open grasslands

Hominin	Date(s)	Location
Australopithecus sediba	2.0 mya	Malapa, South Africa

Key features:
Four partial skeletons (two adults, two juveniles)

Small brain (420 cc)

Relatively small teeth

Equal-size cusps on third premolars

Gracile face and jaws

Phalanges not curved

Short finger, long thumbs for precision grip

Long arms

Small, australopithecine-like skeleton

Homo-like pelvis

Lived in open grasslands

Table 10.2 Trends from Late Australopithecine to Early *Homo*

	Late Australopithecine	→	*Early* Homo
Brain		Increase in size	
Face		Reduction in size	
Teeth		Reduction in size	

small, hard food items, such as nuts and seeds. Studies of microwear on tooth surfaces and stable carbon isotopes from fossils suggest, however, that while robust australopithecines in South and East Africa chewed tough foods, they were eating significant amounts of low-quality vegetation. In East Africa in particular, the evidence from stable carbon isotope ratios indicates that *Au. boisei* mostly ate savanna (C_4) grasses. In this way, *Au. boisei* was like other contemporary grass-consuming mammals (such as horses, pigs, and hippopotamuses) but strikingly different from all other hominins. This reliance on grasses—perhaps as much as 80% of their diet was grass—would have required heavy grinding by the jaws and teeth.

The contemporary of *Au. robustus, Au. sediba,* is represented by the partial skeleton of a young male that was about 12 or 13 at the time of death, the partial skeleton of an adult female, and parts of at least two other individuals, including an infant. The cranial features are distinctively different from those of *Au. robustus.* The American paleoanthropologist Lee Berger, who lives and works in South Africa, and his collaborators found that the face, jaws, and teeth are relatively small. The cheekbones (zygomatics) do not flair outward, unlike those of *Au. robustus.* In addition, the broad pelvis and its overall shape are more *Homo*-like. The small body and relatively long arms, however, are more like those of australopithecines. Similarly, the hand has fingers with large, powerful muscles for grasping in arboreal settings, yet with a long thumb for precision gripping, perhaps for tool production and use. The brain was tiny, only about 420 cc, considerably smaller than the brains in any early *Homo*. The presence of features associated with *Homo* suggests that this australopithecine might have played a part in the ancestry of our genus. For example, genetic traits in the teeth of *Au. sediba* show strong affinities with other australopithecines in South Africa and with early and recent *Homo*. However, the presence of early *Homo* in East Africa well before *Au. sediba* indicates that the transition from *Australopithecus* to *Homo* first took place in East Africa. Nevertheless, this set of fossils from Malapa provides a record of complexity that challenges some of the earlier notions of the origins of *Homo*. Perhaps our genus originated at various times and places on the African continent.

As in East Africa, the australopithecines in South Africa went extinct by 1 mya. The reasons for this extinction are unclear. However, the lineage leading to *Homo* seems to have developed an increasingly flexible and generalized diet, whereas the later robust australopithecines' diets became less flexible and more specialized. This increasing focus on a narrower range of foods in the later robust australopithecines may have led to their extinction. Their brains show very little increase in size. The brains of South African *Au. africanus* and *Au. robustus* were only about 450 cc and 530 cc, respectively.

From the late Miocene through the Pliocene and into the Pleistocene—about 6–1 mya—the earliest hominins began to evolve. These diverse hominins had increasingly specialized diets, and their cranial morphology reflected this specialization. They experienced no appreciable change in brain size or body size, however. Thus, evolution focused on mastication. Eventually, however, a new genus and species of hominin, **_Homo habilis_**—having a larger brain and reduced chewing complex—made its appearance (**Table 10.2**). At that time, australopithecines were diverse, evolving, and a significant presence on the African landscape. This gracile hominin likely evolved from an australopithecine, and the ancestor may have been *Au. garhi*. This point in human evolution is critically important because it is the earliest record of a remarkable adaptive radiation, leading to the most prolific and widespread species of primate: us.

Homo habilis The earliest *Homo* species, a possible descendant of *Au. garhi* and an ancestor to *H. erectus;* showed the first substantial increase in brain size and was the first species definitively associated with the production and use of stone tools.

CHAPTER 10 REVIEW

ANSWERING THE BIG QUESTIONS

1. **What is a hominin?**
   - Hominins are defined by two obligate behaviors: bipedal locomotion and nonhoning chewing.

2. **Why did hominins evolve from an apelike primate?**
   - The origin of the Homininae is closely tied to the origins of bipedal locomotion. This form of movement may have provided early hominins with a more efficient means of exploiting patchy forests, freeing the hands for feeding in trees and on the ground.

3. **What were the first hominins?**
   - The pre-australopithecines were the earliest fossil hominins, dating to 7–4 mya. These hominins lived in forests.
   - The pre-australopithecines gave rise to the australopithecines, dating to 4–1 mya.
   - According to evidence from early stone tools of the Oldowan, stable isotopes, dental microwear, and craniofacial anatomy, early hominins underwent a wide range of diet-related adaptations. The record generally reflects increasing specialization, with preferred foods narrowing from meat to grasses.
   - The first hominins show considerable diversity in all anatomical characteristics, including both above and below the neck. Within the genus *Australopithecus,* some were highly terrestrial whereas others were strongly committed to an arboreal lifestyle.

4. **What was the evolutionary fate of the first hominins?**
   - The evolution of the australopithecine lineages resulted in generally increased robusticity of the chewing complex, no change in brain size, and eventual extinction. The change in the chewing complex reflected an increasing focus on eating hard or tough foods, especially plants.
   - By 2.5 mya, at least one australopithecine lineage gave rise to the genus *Homo.* At least two other distinct australopithecine lineages, one in East Africa and one in South Africa, went extinct around 1 mya.

KEY TERMS

Ardipithecus kadabba
Ardipithecus ramidus
Australopithecus aethiopicus
Australopithecus afarensis
Australopithecus africanus
Australopithecus anamensis
Australopithecus boisei
Australopithecus garhi
Australopithecus (or Kenyanthropus) platyops
Australopithecus robustus
Australopithecus sediba
Eoanthropus dawsoni
Homo habilis
Lower Paleolithic
Lucy
Oldowan Complex
Orrorin tugenensis
Sahelanthropus tchadensis

STUDY QUIZ

1. **Which characteristics were present in the earliest hominins?**
   a. communication through speech
   b. modification of stone to make tools
   c. bipedal locomotion
   d. increased brain size

2. **Which skeletal characteristic is *not* associated with the hominin evolution of bipedalism?**
   a. a foramen magnum on the bottom of the skull
   b. a shortened pelvis
   c. a varus knee
   d. an S-shaped spine

3. **Which dental characteristic is *not* a hominin adaptation?**
   a. nonhoning chewing
   b. small, blunt canines
   c. loss of the diastema
   d. thin tooth enamel

4. **Pre-australopithecines are distinguished from apes by both bipedalism and by**
   a. adaptation for a savanna or grassland environment.
   b. complete loss of adaptations for arboreal locomotion.
   c. an intermediate or complete loss of the honing complex.
   d. a significantly enlarged cranial capacity.

5. **How did the australopithecine lineage leading to *Homo* adapt its diet to prevent extinction?**
   a. consuming mostly low-quality vegetation
   b. relying on tough, hard foods
   c. focusing on a narrow range of foods
   d. developing a flexible and generalized diet

EVOLUTION REVIEW

THE FIRST HOMININS

Synopsis The earliest hominins arose during the transition from an arboreal lifestyle to a terrestrial lifestyle. For this reason, the fossils of these first hominin species (for example, *Ardipithecus ramidus*) have some anatomical features that reflect bipedalism and some features that reflect arborealism. Over the course of several million years, the arboreal traits, such as a grasping foot, disappear from the fossil record. Key anatomical changes that take place in later hominins include the remarkable increase in robusticity and size of the masticatory (chewing) apparatus. These changes disappear with the extinction of the hyper-robust australopithecines. Throughout the fossil record, especially after 2.6 mya, evidence of tool use is present. The use of tools may or may not have been fundamental to the success of the first hominins. Most authorities regard tool use and technology in general to be especially important for the appearance and evolution of the earliest members of our own genus, *Homo*.

Q1. Identify the two fundamental behaviors that first emerged in the pre-australopithecines and that reflected distinctive characteristics of the hominin evolutionary branch. Summarize the anatomical features present in early hominin species that are indicative of each of these behaviors.

Q2. Physical anthropologists often describe bipedalism as an adaptive trade-off, a characteristic with both benefits and costs associated with its evolution. Give two examples of the evolutionary benefits bipedalism provided to our early hominin ancestors. Also, give two examples of the evolutionary costs of bipedalism that are still encountered by humans today.

Q3. What factors explain the evolution of the robust faces and jaws of *Australopithecus*, especially in the early Pleistocene?

Hint Focus on the adaptive advantages of robust faces and jaws, and then consider the environmental factors that may have caused the conditions that *Australopithecus* was adapting to.

Q4. Discuss the major anatomical differences between some of the earliest hominins (for example, *Ardipithecus ramidus*) and some of the latest australopithecines (for example, *Australopithecus garhi* and *Australopithecus boisei*). Also, contrast the cranial and dental morphology of the gracile and robust australopithecines. Which of these two groups do you think is more likely to be directly ancestral to the first members of the genus *Homo*?

Q5. What role might climate fluctuations have played in the appearance and evolution of the first hominins?

Hint Climate change in the late Miocene caused tropical forests to shift to patchy forests and open grasslands and changed the kinds of foods that were available.

ADDITIONAL READINGS

Cartmill, M. and F. H. Smith. 2009. *The Human Lineage.* Hoboken, NJ: Wiley-Blackwell.

Conroy, G. C. and H. Pontzer. 2012. *Reconstructing Human Origins: A Modern Synthesis,* 3rd ed. New York: W. W. Norton.

Gibbons, A. 2006. *The First Human: The Race to Discover Our Earliest Ancestors.* New York: Doubleday.

Simpson, S. W. 2010. The earliest hominins. Pp. 314–340 in C. S. Larsen, ed. *A Companion to Biological Anthropology.* Chichester, UK: Wiley-Blackwell.

Spencer, F. 1990. *Piltdown: A Scientific Forgery.* London: Oxford University Press.

Walker, A. and P. Shipman. 1996. *The Wisdom of the Bones: In Search of Human Origins.* New York: Knopf.

White, T. D. 2002. Earliest hominids. Pp. 407–417 in W. C. Hartwig, ed. *The Primate Fossil Record.* Cambridge, UK: Cambridge University Press.

Located on the outer margins of the modem city of Johannesburg, South Africa, the Rising Star cave produced more than 1,500 fossils, far exceeding the number from any other site in the entire continent of Africa. The fossils found by excavators represent an early form of *Homo* combining both ancient and modem characteristics.

11

The Origins and Evolution of Early *Homo*

BIG QUESTIONS

1. **What characteristics define the genus *Homo*?**
2. **What were the earliest members of the genus *Homo*?**
3. **What are the key evolutionary trends and other developments in early *Homo*?**

Charles Darwin was struck by the great anatomical similarity of living humans and African apes. In 1871, writing about human origins without having seen a human fossil, he settled on Africa as the birthplace of the earliest hominins. But he was not the only leading scientist in the nineteenth century to think about human origins and where humans first evolved. Ernst Haeckel (1834–1919), Germany's preeminent anatomist and evolutionary biologist of the late nineteenth century, came up with an entirely different origins scenario. He reasoned that the Asian great ape, the orangutan, is more anatomically similar to humans than are the African great apes. Asia, not Africa, he concluded, must have been the hominins' ancestral homeland. In his extensive scholarly work about human origins and evolution, Haeckel went to great lengths to describe what the first hominin would have looked like. He even went so far as to propose a genus name for the ancestor: *Pithecanthropus,* meaning "ape-man."

Haeckel's books on early human evolution and its Asian origins profoundly inspired a precocious Dutch teenager, Eugène Dubois (1858–1940; **Figure 11.1**). Fascinated by Haeckel's ideas about

FIGURE 11.1

Eugène Dubois A Dutch anatomist and anthropologist, Dubois discovered the first early hominin remains found outside Europe.

evolution, Dubois devoured Darwin's *On the Origin of Species*. He enrolled in medical school at the University of Amsterdam at age 19 and received his medical degree at 26. In addition to being a well-trained physician, he was a superb scientist and was hired as a lecturer in the university's anatomy department. At the same time, his interests in evolution deepened. He became convinced that to truly *study* human origins, he had to *find* human fossils. Within a year of being promoted to lecturer he quit his job, gathered his resources, got hired as a physician for the Dutch colonial government, and moved with his wife and their baby to the Dutch East Indies (the modern country of Indonesia, which includes the islands of Sumatra and Borneo; **Figure 11.2**). His friends, neighbors, and associates thought he was reckless at best to risk his family's well-being as he looked for something that might never be found. Soon after landing in Sumatra in December 1887, Dubois assumed his new responsibilities as a physician at a military hospital, spending his money and free time in the pursuit of fossils. After trying to juggle medicine and fossil hunting, he talked the Dutch colonial government into letting him leave his day job to work for the Dutch as a full-time paleontologist. With the help of two civil engineers and a group of 50 convicts, he searched the island but found nothing. Meanwhile, he suffered from discomfort, fatigue, illness, and depression.

Desperate to avoid returning to Holland without having found fossils, Dubois pleaded with his superiors to let him shift his focus from Sumatra to nearby Java. The authorities accepted his assurances that Java would produce fossils. After his move to Java, Dubois heard about bones appearing out of the eroding banks of the Solo River, near the village of Trinil. Soon after commencing excavations in the late summer of 1891, he and his field crew discovered a human molar. Within a couple of months they found a partial skull, and later in the following year they found a complete femur (**Figure 11.3**). The skull was extraordinary. It was clearly not from *Homo sapiens*—it had a low and long braincase, no forehead to speak

FIGURE 11.2

Dutch East Indies On the island of Java, one of the southernmost islands of what is now Indonesia, Dubois discovered the hominin fossil later identified as *Homo erectus*.

of, and large browridges like apes'. Was it from an ape or a human or something between the two? By measuring the braincase's volume, he estimated that in life the brain had been about 1,000 cc, too big for a modern ape (a chimpanzee's brain is 400 cc) and too small for a modern human (the average human brain today is about 1,450 cc). He had found what he was looking for: the human ancestor. In fact, Dubois's anatomical study revealed that the femur was essentially identical to a modern human's—this primitive human ancestor was fully bipedal. Convinced that he had found what Haeckel had predicted, he called his fossil hominin **Pithecanthropus erectus,** meaning "upright-walking ape-man."

Dubois's ideas and the fossils he found met with mixed reactions, mostly negative. However, as the years went by, others found more hominin fossils in Java and elsewhere in Asia. It became clear to most anthropologists that Dubois's fossils from Java were early members of our genus but a different species, and these hominins are now called **Homo erectus.** Dubois's fossil turned out to be not from the earliest hominin or even from the earliest species of *Homo* (see chapter 10 and later in this chapter).

Dubois was wrong in thinking that evidence of the earliest human would be found in southeast Asia, but he was working in a scientific vacuum. Without today's fossil record to guide him, he drew the best possible conclusion from the evidence available and made crucially important discoveries about the genus *Homo*'s evolution. The only scientist of the time who set out a research plan to test a hypothesis about early human ancestors, he sought fossil evidence to establish evolutionary relationships. In contrast to the great evolutionists of the nineteenth century—Darwin, Haeckel, Huxley, and others—he endeavored to use fossils, not living animals' comparative anatomy, to test his hypothesis. This revolutionary development in anthropology set the stage for paleoanthropology, the study of early human evolution.

This chapter focuses on the earliest members of our genus: *Homo habilis* and *H. erectus.* These were the hominins that began to develop the characteristic behaviors that we see in living humans, that increasingly employed intelligence and displayed adaptive flexibility, and that first depended on material culture. During early *Homo*'s evolution, hominins began to colonize areas of the world outside Africa. The earliest fossil evidence, from around 2.5–1.0 mya, indicates that *H. habilis* and the earliest *H. erectus* lived at the same time as other hominins, the later australopithecines (discussed in chapter 10). Early *Homo*, however, adapted very differently from the australopithecines. These changes set the course for human evolution, the record of which is supported by abundant fossils.

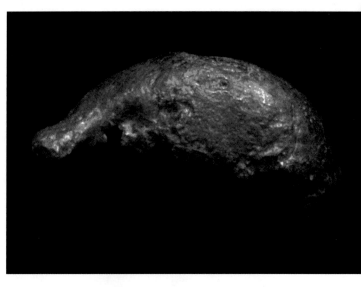

FIGURE 11.3

Java Man Dubois originally named this hominin fossil *Pithecanthropus erectus,* though it was nicknamed "Java Man" after the island on which it was found. Dubois recovered hominin remains, including this partial cranium.

Pithecanthropus erectus The name first proposed by Ernst Haeckel for the oldest hominin; Dubois later used this name for his first fossil discovery, which later became known as *Homo erectus.*

Homo erectus An early species of *Homo* and the likely descendant of *H. habilis;* the first hominin species to move out of Africa into Asia and Europe.

11.1 *Homo habilis*: The First Species of the Genus *Homo*

The Path to Humanness: Bigger Brains, Tool Use, and Adaptive Flexibility

Modern humans are distinctive in having large brains and in depending on material culture for survival. Rather than relying on their bodies for the collection, processing, and eating of food, modern humans rely on tools and technology as part of their adaptive strategy. These attributes are what scientists looked for in the fossil record when they sought the first species of our genus. Which of the multiple hominin species in the late Pliocene and early Pleistocene show brain size expansion? Which of the hominins with brain size expansion likely depended on tools and material culture for promoting adaptive success and behavioral flexibility?

Soon after the discovery of the massively robust australopithecine *Australopithecus*

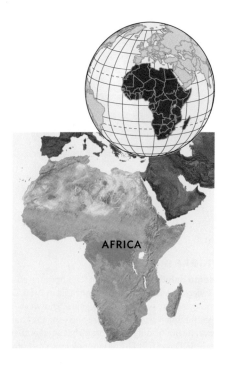

AFRICA

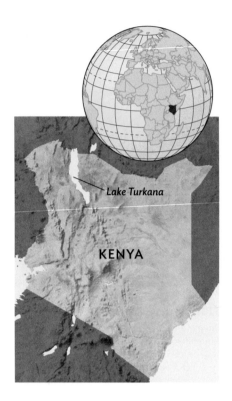

boisei ("OH 5" from Olduvai Gorge; see chapter 10), remains of a hominin having jaws, teeth, and a face that were relatively smaller and a brain that was relatively larger were found, also in Olduvai Gorge. Its describers—Louis Leakey, Philip Tobias, and John Napier—recognized the significance of this combination of characteristics and named the new hominin *Homo habilis* (meaning "handy man"). *H. habilis* is now known from Tanzania, Kenya, Ethiopia, Malawi, and South Africa—the same geographic distribution as that of the contemporary australopithecines (**Figure 11.4**). *H. habilis* found on the eastern side of Kenya's Lake Turkana is sometimes called *Homo rudolfensis* (**Figure 11.5**). The major difference is that *H. rudolfensis* is somewhat bigger than *H. habilis*. Because they have the same general body plan and overall morphology (bigger brains, smaller faces), here the two species are discussed as *H. habilis*.

As Leakey and his associates recognized, *H. habilis* differs in its anatomy from the robust australopithecines dating to about the same time in East Africa and South Africa. *Au. boisei* had an enormous chewing complex—its back teeth, jaws, and face were very large—but it had a small brain. In sharp contrast, *H. habilis* had a smaller chewing complex and a larger brain. Combined, the reduced chewing complex and increased brain size gave *H. habilis*'s skull a more rounded, or globular, appearance. Most anthropologists agree these attributes indicate that *H. habilis* began the lineage leading to modern humans.

Still unconfirmed is the identity of *H. habilis*'s immediate ancestor. The anthropologist Tim White's morphological comparisons between *H. habilis* and the earlier australopithecines suggest that the ancestor was *Australopithecus garhi* because its face, jaws, and teeth are most similar to *H. habilis*'s. White suggests that the evolutionary transition took place sometime around 3.0–2.5 mya. Consistent with this interpretation is the discovery of hominin fossils that combine australopithecine and *Homo* morphological characteristics. For example, from the site of Ledi-Geraru in the Afar region of Ethiopia, a partial mandible dating to 2.8 mya combines large teeth (*Australopithecus*) with *Homo*-like morphology. The discovery of a hominin with australopithecine

(a)   (b)   (c)

FIGURE 11.4

Homo habilis Many fossils of this hominin species have been recovered from East Africa and South Africa. **(a)** This specimen, known as "OH 24" or "Twiggy," was discovered in Tanzania in 1968. Dating to 1.8 mya, Twiggy had a larger brain and a less protruding face than australopithecines. **(b)** Slightly younger than Twiggy, this lower jaw, known as "OH 7," was found in Tanzania in 1960 and dates to 1.75 mya. Given its small dental size, researchers estimated that the brain size would have been smaller than in other *H. habilis* fossils. **(c)** This cranium, "KNM-ER 1813," was discovered in Kenya in 1973 and dates to 1.9 mya. Its brain capacity is somewhat smaller than that of other, later *H. habilis* specimens. (Photo [a] © 1997 David L. Brill, humanoriginsphotos.com; photo [c] © 1985 David L. Brill, humanoriginsphotos.com)

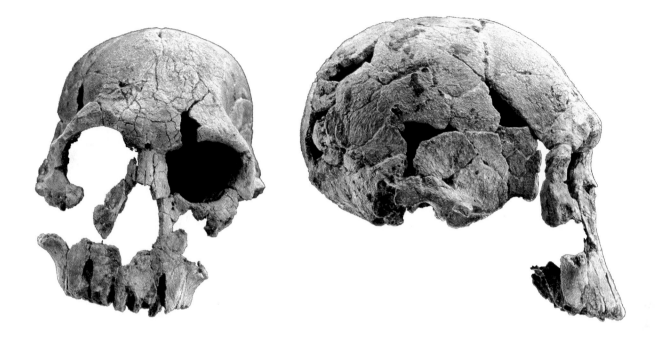

FIGURE 11.5

Homo habilis Owing to its larger size, this fossil hominin is believed by some researchers to be a separate species from *H. habilis,* called *Homo rudolfensis.* (Photos © 1995 David L. Brill, humanoriginsphotos.com)

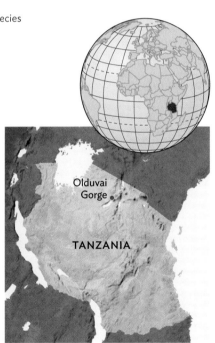

characteristics meets the expectation of early *Homo*; that is, the hominins represented by the Ledi-Geraru mandible have only minor differences with the ancestral hominins.

Homo habilis and *Australopithecus:* Similar in Body Plan

For many years, *H. habilis* was known from just skulls and teeth. Anthropologists had no idea what the rest of the skeleton looked like. Excavations at Olduvai Gorge in the 1980s by Donald Johanson and his associates led to the discovery of a very fragmentary but important skeleton of *H. habilis,* known as "OH 62." The skeleton is from an individual that was short—about 1.1 m (3.5 ft)—like the australopithecines. Also like the australopithecines, this individual had short legs in comparison with the arms. Although *H. habilis* walked bipedally, these short legs would not have been involved in the kind of efficient striding performed by living people. The gait would have been shorter.

Homo habilis's Adaptation: Intelligence and Tool Use Become Important

H. habilis's short legs indicate that the species retained a primitive form of bipedalism, more australopithecine than human. Much more telling about *H. habilis*'s adaptation and evolution are skull and teeth morphology and evidence of the making and use of stone tools. Fossil skulls and fossil teeth reveal that this hominin ancestor had a larger brain, smaller chewing muscles, and smaller teeth than did earlier and contemporary hominins, the australopithecines. Both the brain enlargement and the masticatory changes may be linked to the growing importance of tools. Anatomical evidence from the study of hand bones, such as the presence of muscles that would have provided the necessary precision grip, suggests that *H. habilis* and at least some of the australopithecines made and used tools. For several reasons, toolmaking and tool use were

Homo habilis: The First Member of Our Lineage

H. habilis was the first hominin to have anatomical and behavioral characteristics that foreshadowed the evolution of *Homo sapiens:* greater intelligence, reliance on tools, and dietary and behavioral flexibility.

(Photo © 1985 David L. Brill, humanoriginsphotos.com)

Location/Sites	Africa (Olduvai Gorge, Lake Turkana, Middle Awash, Omo, Uraha, Sterkfontein)
Chronology	2.5–1.8 mya

Biology and Culture (Compared with Australopithecines)

Feature	Evidence	Outcome
Tool use (Oldowan)	Skulls Teeth	Smaller face and smaller jaws Reduced size
Intelligence	Brain size	Increase (to 650 cc)
Diet (scavenging, plant collecting)	Plants available Body size	Perhaps more generalized No significant change
Locomotion	Leg length:arm length	No significant change

likely more important in *H. habilis*'s adaptation. First, stone tools are more common in *H. habilis* fossil sites than in *Australopithecus* fossil sites. Second, *H. habilis*'s expanding brain size indicates that it was smarter than *Australopithecus,* with a kind of cognitive advancement almost certainly linked to toolmaking and tool use. That is, *H. habilis* and the lineage it founded became reliant on intelligence, toolmaking, and tool use as central means of adaptation. In contrast, the australopithecines became increasingly specialized, focusing on a narrower range of foods that required heavy chewing. They may have made and used tools, but tools were not as fundamental to their survival and adaptation. *H. habilis*'s behavioral advances laid the foundation for later hominins' success, including their rapid spread out of Africa and to other areas of the globe.

Habitat Changes and Increasing Adaptive Flexibility

Environmental reconstruction of the East African and South African landscapes at 2.5 mya provides some insight into early *Homo*'s adaptive shifts. This reconstruction indicates a spread of warm-season (C_4) grasses, increasing habitat diversity, and increasing food resources for early hominins. Such information, along with skull and teeth morphology, suggests early *Homo*'s increasing dietary versatility. Tools may have played a central role in these early hominins' ability to exploit this increasingly diverse landscape. That is, stone tools were likely important for digging roots and tubers and for processing them for consumption. Such extremely primitive technology did not include the kinds of tools associated with later hominins that were clearly social, predatory hunters (discussed later; see "Evolution of *Homo erectus:* Biological Change, Adaptation, and Improved Nutrition"). Still, tools increased these early hominins' *capability* of eating a greater range of food, most of it plants or small animals, the latter acquired by luck and opportunity and perhaps scavenging. This dietary shift may be what spelled adaptive success for early *Homo* and extinction for late *Australopithecus.*

Early *Homo* in South Africa: *Homo naledi*

The record of human evolution is filled with unexpected discoveries, and more so perhaps for the African continent than for any other continent. At Rising Star Cave, located within a mile or so of the iconic Swartkrans, Sterkfontein, and Kromdraai australopithecine sites in the Blaaubank River valley in the Republic of South Africa (see chapter 10), spelunkers (or "cavers") recruited by paleoanthropologist Lee Berger discovered a remarkable cache of early hominin remains in 2013. The deep and torturous cave system made recovery of the fossils highly challenging (see "How Do We Know: Underground Astronauts," p. 360–361). To date, some 1,550 cranial, dental, and postcranial hominin fossils representing at least 15 individuals of various ages and both sexes have been found and described by Berger and his team (**Figure 11.6**). The sheer volume and number of fossils make this assemblage one of the largest collections of early hominins found at any one site in Africa or anywhere else in the world for that matter.

The general morphology of the series is representative of early *Homo,* and the skull is closest to *Homo erectus* in overall shape. However, Berger and his research team gave the fossils a new species name—*Homo naledi*—owing to the presence of distinctive characteristics. Like some of the record from South Africa, these fossils from Rising Star Cave are not dated owing to the fact that they are associated with sedimentary rock, which is not datable via the kinds of absolute methods used in other hominin

(a)   (b)

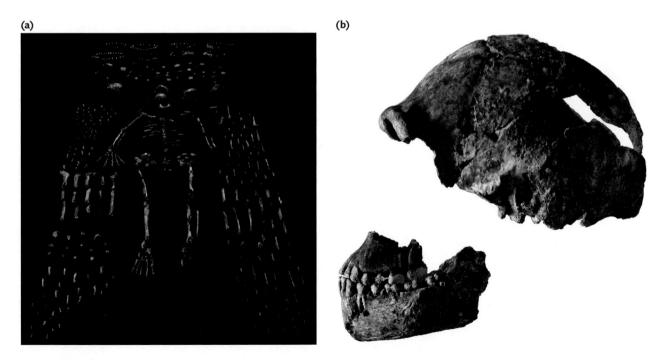

FIGURE 11.6

Homo naledi **(a)** The remarkable collection of *H. naledi* fossils representing at least 15 individuals reveals a hominin having a combination of primitive and derived characteristics. The hip region is australopithecine-like, but **(b)** the cranium is similar to *Homo erectus*'s protruding supraorbital torus and elongated cranial vault.

UNDERGROUND

FINDING EARLY *HOMO* IN SOUTH AFRICA

One of the central questions in human evolution is the timing and location of the origin of the early members of the genus *Homo*. The fossil record indicates that the earliest representative of *Homo* is from East Africa. Until recently, the record of early *Homo* in South Africa has been represented by very few fossils, with the most notable being a *Homo habilis* cranium from Swartkrans. That picture has dramatically changed with the 2013 discovery, and 2015 description, of an incredible cache of hominin fossils representing early *Homo* found in the Rising Star Cave in South Africa.

WATCH THE VIDEO

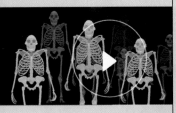

www.digital.
wwnorton.com/
ourorigins4

Paleoanthropologist Lee Berger, the discoverer of *Au. sediba* from nearby Malapa (see chapter 10), had long suspected that the old and complex cave systems in this region of the world held hidden fossils—a potentially richer trove than the iconic South African sites of Malapa, Swartkrans, Kromdraai, Sterkfontein, Makapansgat, and Taung worked by paleoanthropologists over the past century. Working on a hunch that fossils were waiting to be discovered, Berger recruited spelunkers ("cavers") to explore caverns and crevices in the Rising Star Cave. Within a remarkably short amount of time, their exploration of a previously unknown and deep chamber in the cave revealed a few bones. The pictures they took of the bones and subsequently showed to Berger sparked work at what turned out to be one of the most important hominin fossil sites in South Africa, Africa, and the world.

Soon after the initial discovery by the cavers, Berger enlisted a reconnaissance team to recover bones and teeth from the cave. All such field teams are special, but this one had to be particularly selective, as each of the crew members had to be able to fit into extraordinarily narrow cave shafts, just 7 inches wide in places. Berger recruited widely, noting he was looking for applicants that "…must be skinny and preferably small. They must not be claustrophobic, they must be fit, they should have some caving experience, climbing experience is

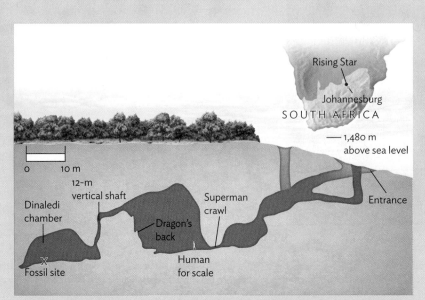

This diagram of Rising Star Cave illustrates the enormous physical difficulties confronting the excavation crew.

ASTRONAUTS

a bonus." Berger identified six persons, nicknamed the "Underground Astronauts," who fit this narrow description. Each of the team members selected for the field project—all skilled women scientists—knew from the outset of the expedition that they were in for the challenge of their lifetimes, but they had no idea the extent of the challenge. Within a day after getting started, the crew discovered that there were not just a few bones and teeth at the bottom of Rising Star Cave. Rather, by week's end, the field team found and collected 1,550 fossils representing nearly all bones of a skeleton and at least 15 different individuals representing both sexes across a range of ages. Berger and colleagues soon determined that these fossils represented a new hominin species, which they named *Homo naledi*.

As with all fossils, understanding the context in which the Rising Star Cave fossils were found is crucial in their interpretation. Therefore, all members of the team had to be well trained in excavation and documentation methods under very tough field conditions. No matter the location, every anthropologist who excavates skeletons knows that difficult conditions are associated with virtually every field site. The most common challenges include maintaining awkward body postures for long hours and being subjected to high heat, humidity, insects, and far worse. But the conditions in Rising Star Cave were especially demanding, including the long descent and difficult climb using safety ropes and harnesses; working in a dark, claustrophobic setting; and maintaining difficult postures for six-hour stretches of time. So, another key requirement for each member of the excavation team was the willingness to work in and ignore awful working conditions.

How did this elite team of field workers accomplish the recovery of bones and teeth under these kinds of abysmal circumstances? The answer is pretty simple: Their passion for discovery and for a greater understanding of the evolution of our early ancestors motivated them to persevere under grueling conditions. Clearly, their passion paid off. This remarkable team recovered more hominin fossils in about a week than had been recovered from any other single locality in Africa, amassing a sample of hominin remains that will generate questions about the origins and evolution of *Homo* for decades to come.

Just when we think we have all the answers, Rising Star and other remarkable discoveries emerge, giving us new perspectives on the past. For this site, a huge part of the discovery and the subsequent knowledge gained was made possible by the six talented and committed individuals who compose the Underground Astronauts.

The "Underground Astronauts," Rising Star Cave.

Recording the fossils deep inside Rising Star Cave.

sagittal keel A slight ridge of bone found along the midline sagittal suture of the cranium, which is typically found on *H. erectus* skulls.

localities associated with volcanic rock (see chapter 8). Despite this, and although the overall morphology of the *H. naledi* remains are distinctive, the combination of primitive, australopithecine morphology and derived characteristics suggests where *H. naledi* might fall in the broad hominin chronology. For example, there are some anatomical features that are not present in the australopithecines but are associated with *Homo erectus*, including, for example, a **sagittal keel**, a large browridge, thick cranial bones, and reduced tooth size. However, the estimated brain size for *H. naledi* is quite small—560 cc and 475 cc for males and females, respectively. The small brain, therefore, is more like the australopithecines discussed in the past chapter and the early *H. erectus* from Dmanisi, Georgia (discussed later in this chapter; see p. 370). The overall suite of cranial and postcranial features are thus consistent with the notion that *H. naledi* may be an earlier rather than later taxa of the genus *Homo*.

11.2 *Homo erectus:* Early *Homo* Goes Global

Beginning around 1.8 mya, a new hominin appeared, *H. erectus,* which had anatomical characteristics that distinguished it from *H. habilis.* As discussed earlier, it was the only descendant taxon of *H. habilis* and was among the earliest fossil hominins described, having been found by Eugène Dubois at Trinil in Java.

In the century since Dubois began his work in Java, many fossils with the same general attributes as the Trinil skull—large browridges, long and low skull, and bigger

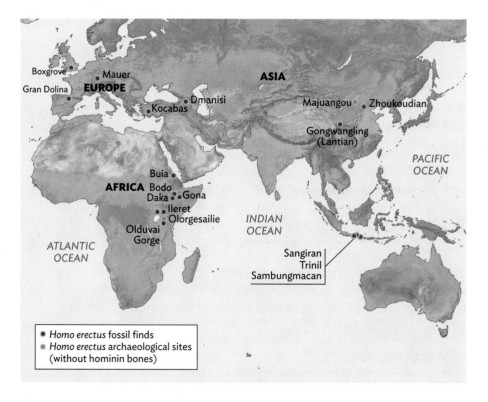

FIGURE 11.7

Homo erectus *Sites* Fossils of *H. erectus* have been discovered throughout Africa, Europe, and Asia.

brain—have been found in Europe, Asia, and Africa (**Figure 11.7**). These hominins collectively date to about 1.8 mya–300,000 yBP. During this fascinating and dynamic period of human evolution, hominins first left Africa, colonized vast areas of Asia and Europe, and underwent fundamental changes in culture and adaptation that shaped human biological variation.

Homo erectus in Africa (1.8–0.3 mya)

The earliest record of *H. erectus* comes from Africa, less than 2 mya. At that time, the last australopithecines were still around in East Africa and South Africa, and comparing the fossils of each reveals great differences in anatomy and adaptation between *H. erectus* and the last australopithecines (**Figure 11.8**). Among the earliest and the most spectacular of the *H. erectus* fossils is an 80% complete juvenile skeleton from Nariokotome, on the western side of Lake Turkana (**Figure 11.9**). This remarkably complete skeleton dates to about 1.6 mya. In contrast to *Australopithecus* and *H. habilis,* the Nariokotome hominin has several quintessentially modern anatomical features.

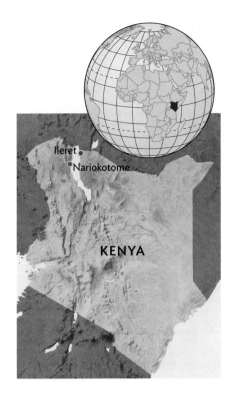

The presence of a sagittal crest to anchor large chewing muscles reflects this genus's hard diet of nuts and seeds.

The large premolars and molars enabled this genus to grind hard nuts and seeds.

Australopithecus boisei

The lack of a sagittal crest indicates this species had smaller chewing muscles, reflecting a much softer diet.

This genus had much smaller molars and thinner enamel, reflecting its softer diet.

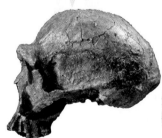 

Homo erectus

FIGURE 11.8

Australopithecus boisei *versus* Homo erectus While both of these genera were contemporaneous for a period of time in Africa, there are important differences in their cranial and dental morphologies.

One of the most striking modern characteristics is the combination of relatively short arms and long legs. That is, the *H. erectus* body plan is much more like that of a living human in its ratio of arm length to leg length. This change in limb proportions in *H. erectus* signals the beginning of a major alteration in the pattern of bipedal locomotion: *H. erectus* became completely committed to terrestrial life by adopting a fully modern stride. Life in the trees became a thing of the past.

Features of the pelvic bones and overall size indicate that the Nariokotome individual was likely a young adolescent male. He was quite tall, about 166 cm (66 in). Had he survived to adulthood, he would have grown to nearly 180 cm (71 in) in height. This change in height in comparison with *H. habilis* and the australopithecines indicates an enormous body size increase in this taxon. In addition, the Nariokotome boy's cranial capacity was about 900 cc (**Figure 11.10**). Even taking into account the body size increase (brain size and body size are roughly correlated), this expansion in brain size is large compared with similar changes in earlier hominins.

The Nariokotome skeleton is just one of many *H. erectus* fossils from East Africa.

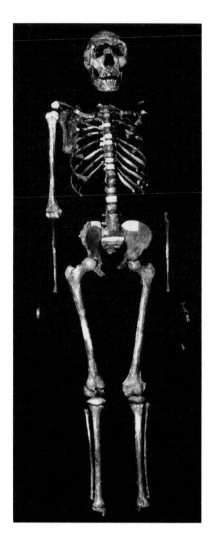

FIGURE 11.9

Nariokotome Researchers have debated the exact age of "Nariokotome Boy," also known as "Turkana Boy," but he was likely around 11 years old. Discovered in 1984, this *H. erectus* fossil is one of the most complete early hominin skeletons ever found.

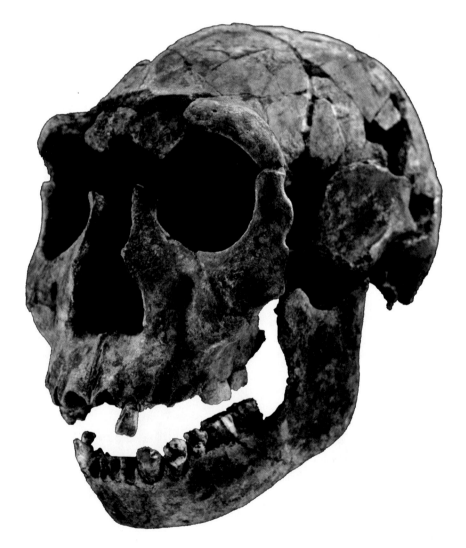

FIGURE 11.10

Nariokotome Skull The skull of the Nariokotome boy has been invaluable for relating brain size and overall body size in *H. erectus*. Why is that relationship important for us to know? (Photo © 1985 David L. Brill, humanoriginsphotos.com)

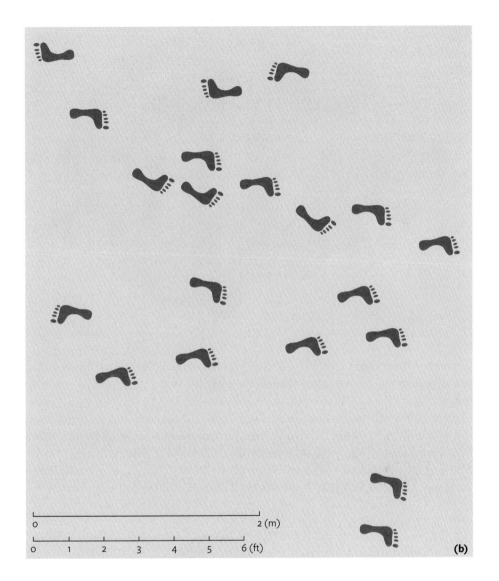

O

2 (m)

| O | 1 | 2 | 3 | 4 | 5 | 6 (ft) |

(b)

(a)

FIGURE 11.11

Footprints from Ileret, Kenya **(a)** Exposed surface showing numerous animal and hominin footprints. **(b)** Site drawing showing just the hominin footprints. Note the orientations of the tracks, showing different individuals walking at different times and in different directions. Can you figure out how many hominins made these tracks?

At Ileret, on the eastern side of Lake Turkana, the partial skull of a very small *H. erectus*—possibly a female—was found in geologic strata dating to about 1.6 mya. The skull's diminutive size and small browridges indicate the very high degree of variation in *H. erectus*. Some *H. erectus* individuals had very large and robust bones, whereas others—such as the hominin from Ileret—were quite gracile.

Just as significant as the Ileret fossil is the presence of multiple sets of footprints on an Ileret landscape dating to around 1.5 mya (**Figure 11.11**). Recall the footprints from Laetoli discussed in chapter 10, representing *Australopithecus afarensis* and dating to around 3.5 mya. These footprints provide a kind of fossilized picture of behavior: evidence of how early human ancestors walked. They reveal that the Ileret *H. erectus* walked just like a modern human. In fact, these prints provide the first solid evidence of fully modern walking. We know this because the footprints have all the fundamentals that we see in our feet, namely, the double arch (the long one extending from your heel to the base of your toes and the side-to-side one) and an adducted big toe (the big toe is close to the second toe), whereas in the Laetoli fossil the big toe and second toe are abducted (spread apart). Moreover, the prints are big, as would be expected given the great heights of *H. erectus* compared to earlier hominins. The pelvis and leg bones of *H. erectus* had strongly indicated the modern form of walking. The Ileret footprints

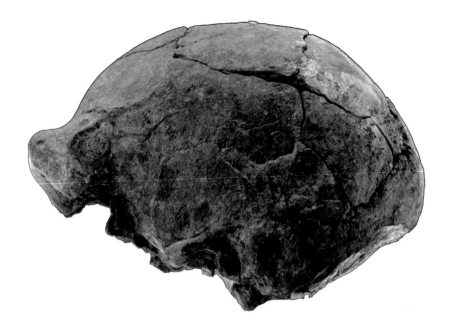

FIGURE 11.12

Daka Partial Cranium The Daka *H. erectus* fossil from the Middle Awash Valley, Ethiopia, has large browridges, a characteristic of many other *H. erectus* specimens in Africa and elsewhere. (Photo © 2001 David L. Brill, humanoriginsphotos.com)

provide further proof that this hominin had a foot adapted for activities requiring travel, such as hunting and long-distance walking, behaviors likely first seen with *H. erectus*.

Other key *H. erectus* fossils from Africa include a partial cranium found in Olduvai Gorge and dating to about 1.2 mya, a partial cranium and postcrania found at Daka and dating to 1 mya (**Figure 11.12**), a partial cranium found at Buia and dating to about 1 mya, a pelvis found at Gona and dating to 1.2 mya, and a cranium found at Bodo and dating to about 600,000 yBP (**Figure 11.13**). The Daka and Bodo crania are from the

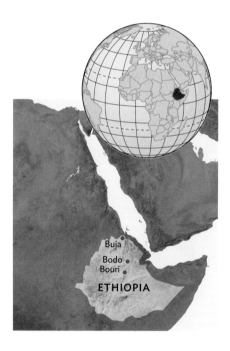

FIGURE 11.13

Bodo Cranium This *H. erectus* fossil has different cranial features from other specimens of this species. Note the large browridges and thick cranial bones.

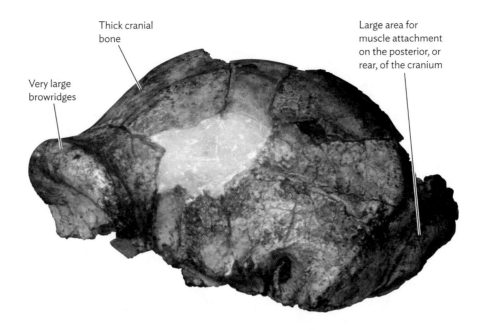

Very large browridges

Thick cranial bone

Large area for muscle attachment on the posterior, or rear, of the cranium

FIGURE 11.15
Olduvai Cranium This *H. erectus* fossil, known as "OH 9," has the largest browridges of any hominin species.

Middle Awash Valley (**Figure 11.14**, pp. 368–369), and the Buia cranium is from Eritrea. In contrast to the Nariokotome boy's skull and the skull from Ileret, the skulls from Olduvai Gorge, Daka, Buia, and Bodo are very robust, having thick cranial bones and very large browridges. The Olduvai cranium's browridges are the largest of any known hominin, before or since (**Figure 11.15**). Only some of this greater size can be accounted for by the Nariokotome boy's immaturity because the other three hominins were fully mature adult males.

During the process of cleaning the facial bones of the Bodo skull, Tim White found a series of barely visible linear marks on the left cheek, around the left eye orbit and the nose, and elsewhere on the cranium (**Figure 11.16**). Microscopic analysis of the marks

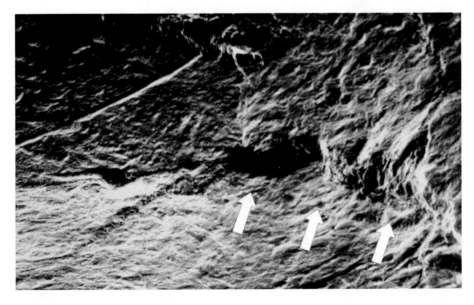

FIGURE 11.16
Ritual Defleshing? Viewed through a scanning electron microscope, cutmarks such as this one (arrows) indicate that stone tools were used to remove flesh from the Bodo skull. The arrows point to the groove left by the stone tool.

The source of a continuous fossil record from before 6 mya to about 50,000 yBP, the Middle Awash Valley is among the most fossil-rich regions in the world. The Daka Member (*Daka* being an abbreviation of the place-name Dakanihylo and *Member* meaning part) is among the most interesting areas of the Middle Awash. The area's rich fossil record of plants and animals dates to around 1 mya, the time of *Homo erectus*, and thus provides us access to the habitat there during this period of human evolution.

The American paleoanthropologist Henry Gilbert and his team have studied the thousands of fossils, ranging from the tiny ancestors of mice to the large animals. The record indicates a savanna/grasslands setting with wooded areas, ample water, and floodplains, unlike the dry desert of the region today.

This reconstruction shows what the Daka landscape might have looked like a million years ago, when *Homo erectus* hunted and gathered there. The following animal taxa are represented.

1   *Felids* (ancestors of lions and domestic cats) are exclusively carnivorous. Their abundance indicates that the area included plenty of animals that served as prey for them.

2   *Cercopithecids* ([2a] *Theropithecus oswaldi* and [2b] *Cercopithecoides alemayehui*) suggest the presence of forests and permanent rivers with associated wetlands.

3   *Equids* (ancestors of asses) indicate a broad range of habitats.

4   *Giraffids* (ancestors of giraffes) indicate the presence of large acacia trees.

5   *Hippopotamids* (ancestors of hippopotamuses) indicate the continuous availability of deep water and adjacent grasslands.

6   *Elephantids* (ancestors of elephants) are grazers and browsers and occupy a wide range of habitats.

7   *Rhinocerids* (at least two genera, ancestors of rhinoceroses) are typically associated with standing water (ponds) and grasslands.

8   *Suids* (ancestors of pigs) indicate the availability of water but with sometimes semiarid conditions.

9   *Murids* (ancestors of grass mice or rats) are especially common today in grasslands and savannas.

10   *Bovids* (ancestors of today's impalas, gazelles, sheep, ibex, oryx, kudu, and other bovines of the African landscape) are very numerous and indicate the presence of woodlands and brush thickets, large streams, and water supply continuous throughout the year. The fossil record indicates that the grasslands would have been full of herds of different bovid species.

11   *Hominins* (ancestors of *Homo sapiens*) at this point in evolution are adaptable to a wide range of habitats, but are exclusively terrestrial.

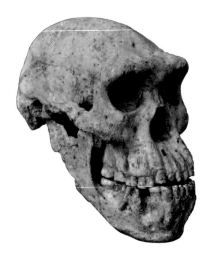

FIGURE 11.17

Dmanisi Extensive paleoanthropological investigations took place in the town of Dmanisi after early stone tools were discovered there in 1984. Since 1991, more than 20 hominin remains have been found, including skull 5 shown here. Discovered in 2005, the remarkable completeness of the skull—the most complete of early Pleistocene *Homo*—helps paleoanthropologists to understand the full morphology of the cranium, mandible, and teeth of some of the earliest members of our genus. Skull 5 has the combined features typical of *H. erectus* in having a long, low cranium and relatively large browridges. The individual combines a small braincase (brain size is 546 cc) with a large face. The high level of cranial robusticity compared to the other individuals at Dmanisi indicates that skull 5 is likely a male. This skull and other remains from Dmanisi provide evidence for a single evolving lineage of early *Homo* and for continuity of evolution from at least 1.8 mya across Africa, Europe, and Asia.

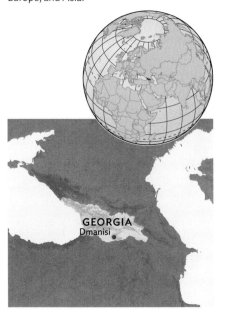

GEORGIA
Dmanisi

indicates that they were caused by a stone tool, perhaps as a contemporary hominin removed the soft tissue covering the facial bones. This activity may have been related to some ritual or to cannibalism. If so, it is the earliest evidence of body manipulation in human evolution.

Homo erectus in Asia (1.8–0.3 mya)

The earliest evidence of *H. erectus* in Asia consists of five skulls, other bones, and many stone tools found by the Georgian paleontologist David Lordkipanidze and his colleagues in Dmanisi, Republic of Georgia (**Figure 11.17**). The date for this important site, 1.8 mya, indicates that *H. erectus* colonized western Asia very soon after it began to evolve in Africa (**Figure 11.18**). Compared with some members of the African *H. erectus,* these hominins' faces and jaws were smaller and their browridges were less developed—all *habilis*-like facial characteristics. However, in overall shape the Dmanisi hominins' mandible and face strikingly resemble those of both the Nariokotome boy and the Ileret skull from East Africa. Also, like those of the Nariokotome skeleton, the leg bones are relatively long compared with the arm bones, at least as shown in the two partial skeletons—a child and an adult—found at the site. The oldest *H. erectus* from Dmanisi has a cranial capacity of only about 650 cc. The strong resemblance between the Dmanisi *H. erectus* and at least some of the East African *H. erectus* individuals indicates the relatedness of the Asian *H. erectus* and African *H. erectus.*

Workers discovered a partial *H. erectus* cranium—fragments of frontal and parietal

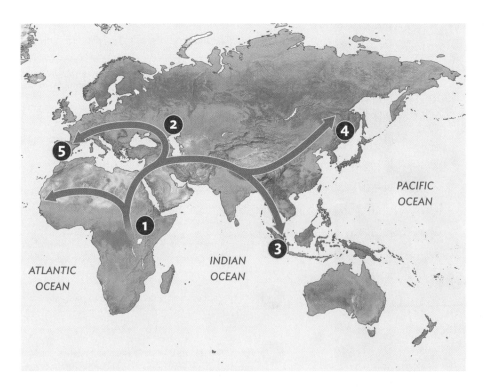

FIGURE 11.18

First Migration *Homo erectus* was the first hominin species to migrate out of Africa and expand into Europe and Asia. This map illustrates the movement: **(1)** earliest *H. erectus* in East Africa (Lake Turkana; ~1.8 mya); **(2)** early expansion of *H. erectus* into western Asia (Dmanisi, Georgia; ~1.7 mya); **(3)** rapid eastward expansion of *H. erectus* into southeast Asia (Sangiran, Indonesia; ~1.8–1.6 mya); **(4)** earliest butchered animal bones and stone tools attributed to *H. erectus* in northeast Asia (Majuangou, China; ~1.7 mya); **(5)** earliest fossil evidence of *H. erectus* in western Europe (Atapuerca, Spain; ~1.2 mya).

bones—of an adult male dating to much later (about 500,000 yBP) in a rock quarry near the village of Kocabaş, in the Büyük Menderes, a large valley system in western Turkey. Like many other *H. erectus* specimens from Africa and from Asia, the Kocabaş specimen has massive browridges and a **sagittal keel.** According to the American paleoanthropologist John Kappelman and his colleagues, the cranium's internal surface appears to have had a bone infection very similar to that caused by tuberculosis. This hominin is doubly significant, first in being the only one found in this vast region of western Asia, and second in being the first one showing signs of tuberculosis.

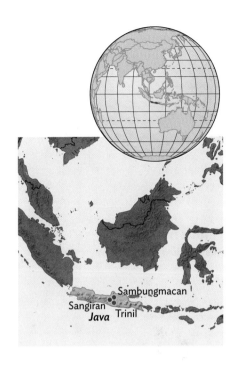

Since Dubois completed his fieldwork in the 1890s, *H. erectus* fossils have been found in a number of sites in Indonesia, especially in Java. Some of these remains are nearly as old as the Dmanisi remains. The earlier fossils, from the Sangiran site, date to as early as 1.8–1.6 mya. This early date shows that *H. erectus* rapidly spread eastward from western Asia. Thus, once the taxon had first evolved, it colonized areas outside Africa at a rapid pace, perhaps within less than a few hundred thousand years. The emerging picture is of *H. erectus*'s rapid, widespread movement throughout Asia. This rapid spread illustrates the hominin's high degree of adaptive success, a factor likely related to increasing intelligence, increasing reliance for survival on both material culture and tools, and overall greater ability at acquiring food and other resources.

Dating to 800,000 yBP, the most complete skull from eastern Asia is the Sangiran 17 cranium from Sangiran, Indonesia. Like the African fossils, it has thick cranial bones and large browridges. Its cranial capacity is about 1,000 cc (**Figure 11.19**). A slight ridge, or "keel," runs along the sagittal suture atop the skull, and this sagittal keel appears on *H. erectus* skulls from Asia, Africa, and Europe.

Later *H. erectus* fossils from Java, dating to between 1 mya and 500,000 yBP, include fossil remains from Sangiran and Sambungmacan, plus the original Trinil skull found by Dubois. These fossils show many of the same physical characteristics as the earlier ones but also some changes, such as larger brains and smaller teeth. Some of the best information about the first hominins outside Africa comes from China. The earliest hominin fossil is a partial skull from Gongwangling, near the village of Lantian, Shaanxi Province. The skull dates to about 1.2 mya. Like the fossils from Java, this specimen has large, well-developed browridges and thick cranial bones. Its cranial

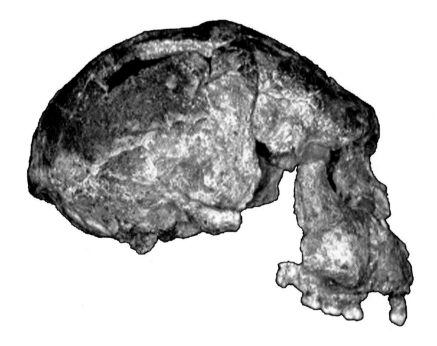

FIGURE 11.19

***Sangiran* Homo erectus** Excavations in Indonesia have uncovered many hominin fossils, including Dubois's Java Man and, shown here, the Sangiran 17 fossil. Note the long cranium, low forehead, and large browridges.

FIGURE 11.20

Zhoukoudian During excavations at this site in China between 1923 and 1927, *H. erectus* remains were discovered and called "Peking Man." Excavations continued until the early 1940s. Today, the place is a UNESCO World Heritage Site.

capacity is about 800 cc. The skull postdates the earliest evidence of hominins in north China, from Majuangou, by nearly 500,000 years. Both the animal bones with butchery marks and the stone artifacts found by the Chinese geologist R. X. Zhu and his collaborators date to nearly 1.7 mya, making them the earliest specimens from Asia.

The site yielding the most impressive *H. erectus* remains in eastern Asia is the cave in Zhoukoudian, on Dragon Bone Hill, near the modern city of Beijing. After being discovered in the 1920s, the cave was excavated into the early 1940s (**Figure 11.20**). Deposits dating to 780,000–400,000 yBP contained, in fragments, the bones and teeth of 40–50 individuals, as well as many stone tools and food remains (**Figure 11.21**). Tragically, the entire collection of priceless bones was lost during World War II, late in 1941. Fortunately, shortly before the loss, the eminent German anatomist and anthropologist

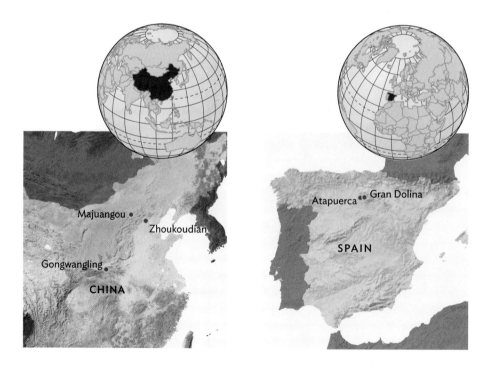

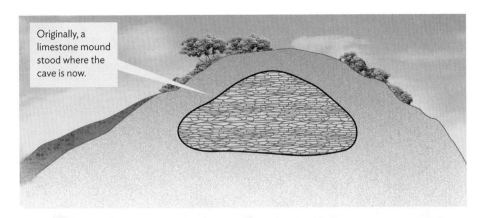

Originally, a limestone mound stood where the cave is now.

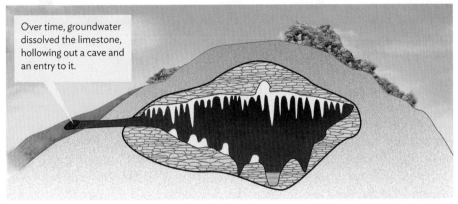

Over time, groundwater dissolved the limestone, hollowing out a cave and an entry to it.

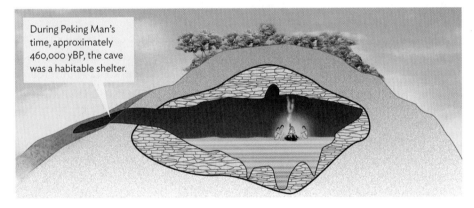

During Peking Man's time, approximately 460,000 yBP, the cave was a habitable shelter.

FIGURE 11.21

Cave at Zhoukoudian The cave in which Peking Man's remains were discovered took millions of years to form. In addition to the remains, stone tools were found there.

Franz Weidenreich (1873–1948) had thoroughly studied the bones and teeth, written detailed scientific reports, and made cast replicas, drawings, and photographs (**Figure 11.22**). This record has allowed scientists to continue studying the Zhoukoudian remains.

Homo erectus in Europe (1.2 Million–400,000 yBP)

The earliest presence and subsequent evolution of *H. erectus* were somewhat later in Europe than in Africa and Asia. The earliest fossil evidence of *H. erectus* in western Europe is from the Sierra de Atapuerca, northern Spain—at the cave sites of Sima del

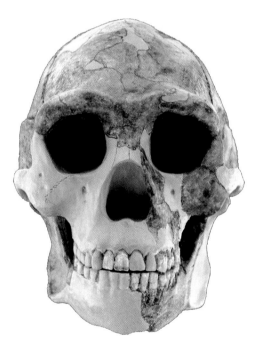

FIGURE 11.22

Peking Man Although the original remains of this *H. erectus* fossil are lost, excellent casts, such as this reconstructed skull, enable modern anthropologists to study this important hominin. (Photo © 1996 David L. Brill, humanoriginsphotos.com)

FIGURE 11.23

Gran Dolina In the mid-1990s, the excavation of this Spanish cave site uncovered fossil remains of at least six individual hominins along with hundreds of stone tools. In addition, ample evidence that both hominins and other animals were butchered there has led some researchers to suggest that these hominin ancestors practiced cannibalism. Like Zhoukoudian (see Figure 11.20), Gran Dolina is a UNESCO World Heritage Site.

Elefante, dating to about 1.2 mya, and of Gran Dolina, dating to about 900,000 yBP. The earlier site is represented by a partial mandible and some teeth, along with animal bones showing cutmarks from butchering. The later site, excavated by the Spanish paleontologist Juan Luis Arsuaga and his colleagues, is among the most important in Europe, owing to the discovery of fragmentary bones and teeth of a half-dozen hominins, along with many stone tools and animal bones (**Figure 11.23**). Animal bones and hominin bones had been cut with stone tools and purposely broken. This evidence indicates that hominins processed and consumed animals and other hominins (these practices are discussed further in chapter 10).

The most complete skull from Gran Dolina is Atapuerca 3, consisting of the left facial bones, upper jaw, and teeth of a child. This specimen provides a rare glimpse at what juveniles looked like at this point in human evolution (**Figure 11.24**). Juvenile or not, the cranium indicates that Atapuerca 3 appeared more modern than other members of *H. erectus* but was clearly ancestral to later hominins in the Atapuerca region and elsewhere in Europe. Indeed, its bones and teeth are similar in a number of ways to those of hominins that lived in Europe later in the Pleistocene: *H. sapiens.* For example, like the later hominins, the Gran Dolina adults have a wide nasal aperture (opening for the nose).

The only other *H. erectus* remains in Europe are a partial cranium from Ceprano, Italy, dating to 800,000 yBP; the Mauer jaw—a mandible and most of its teeth—from near Heidelberg, Germany, dating to 500,000 yBP; and a tibia from Boxgrove, England, also dating to 500,000 yBP.

Evolution of *Homo erectus:* Biological Change, Adaptation, and Improved Nutrition

How did *H. erectus* differ from earlier *Homo* species, such as *H. habilis?* One of the most obvious differences is *H. erectus*'s remarkable body size and height. Moreover, the increase in body size occurred rapidly, perhaps in less than a few hundred thousand years. That is, at 1.8 mya *H. habilis* was about the size of an australopithecine, but by 1.6 mya another hominin, *H. erectus,* was considerably taller and heavier. The American physical anthropologists Henry McHenry and Katherine Coffing estimate that from *H. habilis* to *H. erectus,* males' heights increased by 33% (to 1.8 m, or 5.9 ft) and females' heights by 37% (to 1.6 m, or 5.3 ft). In other words, *H. habilis*—like the australopithecines—was quite short (typically less than 1.2 m, or 4 ft), but *H. erectus*

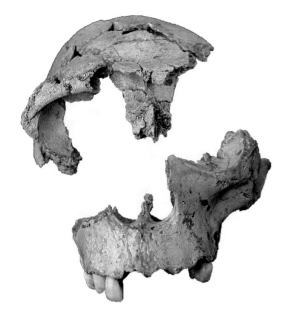

FIGURE 11.24

Atapuerca 3 These remains, from Gran Dolina, are the subject of debate as some researchers believe that the juvenile they came from belonged not to *H. erectus* but to a new species of hominin, *Homo antecessor.* Others believe that despite its more modern appearance, this hominin belonged to *H. erectus.*

was considerably taller (more than 1.5 m, or 5 ft). Most of this increase took place 2.0–1.7 mya (**Table 11.1**).

What caused the rapid increase in body size from *H. habilis* to *H. erectus?* Various factors were likely involved, such as climate change and its impact on food supply. But the fundamental reason was likely increased access to animal food sources—protein—acquired from hunting. That some primitive stone tools date to 3.3 mya indicates that early hominins were able to cut meat and process it.

Cutmarks made with stone tools have been found on bones of animal prey in Kenya and Ethiopia, at the Olduvai Gorge and Bouri sites, respectively. Indeed, the pattern of cutmarks found at Bouri indicates that even some late australopithecines, ones that preceded *Homo,* were skilled in animal butchery.

As the American anthropologist Pat Shipman's work has shown, at Olduvai Gorge, stone-tool cutmarks overlay animal tooth marks. This finding suggests that at least some of the behavior involving butchering was scavenging—eating animals killed by other animals—and not hunting (**Figure 11.25**). Other evidence of meat eating has been documented in the bone chemistry of early hominins and in wear on their teeth.

Meat eating likely started long before *H. erectus* appeared, but the technology available to earlier hominins and the minimal record of hunting prior to *H. erectus* suggest that meat was a minor part of this hominin's diet. Two things had to happen for early hominins to routinely acquire meat. First, to kill game, hominins had to become able to manufacture the right tools, especially stone tools that could be thrown or thrust accurately, such as spears. Second, hominins had to develop the social structure whereby a group of individuals—older adolescent and adult males, primarily—could efficiently track and kill game. Both developments were part of the increase in hominin intelligence at this time, as recorded by brain size expansion and more complex technology. Once hominins had developed the technological and social means of accessing animal food sources daily, they likely had increased access to high-quality protein. This increased access to protein would in turn have produced *H. erectus*'s bump in height—these hominins were taller than their ancestors due to

Table 11.1 Trends from *Homo habilis* to *Homo erectus*

	H. habilis	→	*H. erectus*
Teeth		Reduction in size	
Face and jaws		Reduction in size relative to size of braincase	
Brain		Increase in size	
Browridge		Increase in size	
Cranial bone		Increase in thickness	
Body		Increase in size	
Arms		Reduction in length	
Legs		Increase in length	

(a)

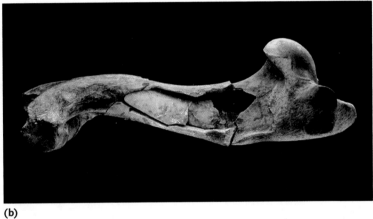

(b)

FIGURE 11.25

Hunters or Scavengers? **(a)** The cutmarks on this bone were made by stone tools, while **(b)** animal tooth marks and cutmarks are visible on the shaft of this antelope humerus. Cutmarks that occurred after animal tooth marks indicate that *H. erectus* scavenged for meat at least some of the time. (Photos © David L. Brill, humanoriginsphotos.com)

improved nutrition that came about by acquiring food (especially protein) through hunting.

Such increasingly sophisticated technology and increased dependence on culture were important in human evolution generally. The culture associated with this period of evolution, beginning around 1.8 mya, is called the **Acheulian Complex.** Acheulian stone tools are more sophisticated than Oldowan tools, were produced from a wider variety of raw materials, and were fashioned into a greater range of tool types, with a greater range of functions. This diversity suggests increased familiarity with the necessary resources and with their availability. Within this diversity, the dominant tool is the **handaxe (Figure 11.26)**. The handaxe's sharp edge was used in cutting, scraping, and other functions.

In addition, the tools became increasingly refined; better made than before, they clearly required a great deal of both learning and skill to produce. Acheulian tools are found in association with large animals, suggesting that these tools were used to kill large animals and butcher them. In Ethiopia's Middle Awash region, for example, tools are commonly associated with hippopotamus bones. In Olorgesailie, Kenya, the South African archaeologist Glynn Isaac recovered many baboon bones in addition to those

Acheulian Complex The culture associated with *H. erectus*, including handaxes and other types of stone tools; more refined than the earlier Oldowan tools.

handaxe The most dominant tool in the Acheulian Complex, characterized by a sharp edge for both cutting and scraping.

FIGURE 11.26

Olorgesailie **(a)** At this Acheulian site in Kenya, the remains of hundreds of butchered animals were found along with many handaxes and other tools. **(b)** This close-up shows the stone tools, with the handaxes in the middle.

(a)

(b)

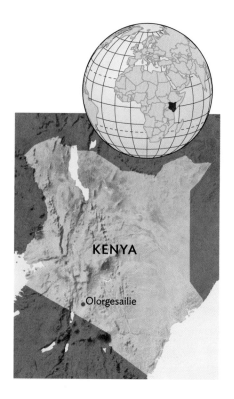

KENYA

Olorgesailie

of hippopotamuses, elephants, and other animals. All these bones have cutmarks from stone tools. In addition, the tools from this and other Acheulian sites display microscopic patterns of wear that are the same as those seen in experimental studies where anthropologists have butchered animals. Clearly, *H. erectus* had killed, processed, and eaten the animals at these sites, well before 1 mya (**Figure 11.27**). This record, from Olorgesailie and sites like it, indicates that hunting was well in place by the Middle Pleistocene. If body size increase was tied to acquisition of animal protein via hunting, it was well in place by somewhat greater than 1.5 mya.

In addition to the increase in body size, a key difference between *H. habilis* and *H. erectus* is the latter's much larger brain. From *H. habilis* to *H. erectus,* brain volume increased by 33% (from 650 cc to 950 cc). Some of the enlargement in brain size was due simply to the increase in body size generally. But even when accounting for the body size increase, there was still an increase in brain size. The increase in sophistication of technology and other cultural changes seen after 2 mya or so strongly suggests that this increase in brain size reflects an increase in intelligence and cognitive abilities generally. Simply, the adaptation of *H. erectus* placed an emphasis on intelligence, and there was likely a selective advantage for the cognitively advanced behaviors that characterized this hominin.

Anthropologists are keenly interested in the nature of the energy intake that would have been required to grow these very brainy ancestors. That is, the brain is an energetically "expensive" tissue. What did these hominins eat that "paid" the high energetic cost of a large brain? While a number of factors are likely to have operated, improved nutritional quality is central to understanding how the cost of increasing brain size was paid. Nutrition improved as a result of meat consumption and the rich source of protein that it provided. The British primatologist Richard Wrangham contends

FIGURE 11.27

Butchering This artist's reconstruction shows how early *Homo* likely processed animals in groups, using a variety of stone tools. (© 1995 by Jay H. Matternes.)

GIVING BIRTH TO BIG-

THE EVOLUTIONARY BENEFITS OF ROTATIONAL BIRTH

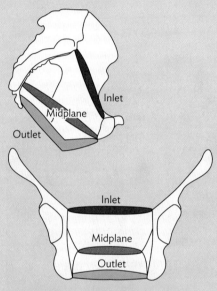

These side and frontal views of the human pelvis show the planes through which the infant passes.

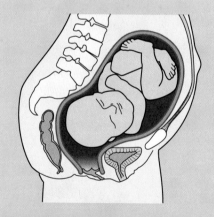

In human birth, assistance generally is needed to ease the infant's large head out of the birth canal.

obstetric dilemma Hypothesis pertaining to hominin mothers giving birth to a large-brained, large-bodied infant: Owing to the large brain, the birth process requires a wide pelvis, but efficient bipedalism requires a narrow pelvis.

One of the most fundamental trends in human evolution is the remarkable increase in the size of the brain. Recall that the earliest hominins—the pre-australopithecines and australopithecines—had an average brain size of just 500 cc, give or take, and sometimes considerably less. By the time *Homo erectus* evolved, average cranial capacity had more than doubled. Today, our brains are on average three times the size of the brains of the earliest hominins. That expansion represents unprecedented neurological evolution in mammals. It reflects the fact that in our lineage the evolutionary priority was on intelligence, cognition, and behaviors associated with them.

The significant increases in brain size began with *Homo habilis*, some 3–2 mya. This increase must have had important implications for the birth process. While the hominin needed to remain fully efficient in bipedalism, its pelvis needed to be restructured to allow for the birth of big-brained (that is, large-headed) babies. Simply, an **obstetric dilemma** emerged for the *Homo* lineage once the brain began to expand in size: how to integrate brain-size increase in the infant with a bipedal skeleton

of the mother that accommodated in the past a relatively small brain. Scientists have been investigating this important evolutionary issue by studying the living record of primate and human birth and relating it to the fossil record.

What does the living record reveal about the evolution of birth? Owing to humans' big brains, broad shoulders, and big bodies, human birth is a complex and risky process that requires assistance by others. Today, this assistance normally is provided by health professionals and trained midwives, almost always in controlled settings such as modern hospitals. Primates have smaller brains, so primate birth is simpler, shorter, far less dramatic, and far less painful than human birth. In addition, the living record shows that throughout the birth process, the orientation of the primate infant's head and the path the head follows through the birth canal are different from those of the human infant's head.

The American physical anthropologists Karen Rosenberg and Wenda Trevathan have documented the orientation of the heads of living primates and humans in the various stages of birth. Throughout, as the primate infant travels from the pelvic inlet to the midplane to the pelvic outlet, for most births the primate infant's head remains in its front-to-back orientation with the face forward. In living humans, by contrast, in the inlet stage the head is oriented facing transversely so that one side of the head is against the back of the mother's pelvis and the other side is against the front of her pelvis. In the midplane and outlet stages, the head and shoulders nearly always rotate 90 degrees so that the front of the head and the shoulders face the back of the pelvis. The head has to rotate because the long axis of the inlet is perpendicular to the axis of the outlet. Moreover, the longest axis of the head and the broadest axis of the shoulders are at a 90-degree angle to each other. The head rotates externally when the baby is delivered so that the shoulders can follow its path. The generally contrasting patterns

BRAINED BABIES

in primate and human birth reflect the differences in brain (and head) size and the constraints placed on the pelvis by bipedalism. Rotational birth appears to be the key evolutionary solution for accommodating the birth of large-brained babies and maintaining efficient bipedalism.

What does the fossil record show? The American physical anthropologists Robert Tague and Owen Lovejoy have reconstructed the pelvic inlet, midplane, and outlet of the early australopithecine Lucy (*Australopithecus afarensis*) and found that, in contrast to those of living humans, the inlet and outlet axes are parallel. Therefore, the head would likely not have rotated during birth. While mothers of *Au. afarensis* infants such as Lucy would have felt discomfort while giving birth, they would not have experienced the excruciating pain and difficulty associated with the complex rotation that occurs in living humans, nor would they have required assistance during the birth process.

At what point in human evolution did the pelvic modifications develop that led to rotational birth? Most fossil hominin pelvises are not well preserved, but the two *H. erectus* pelvises present some interesting evidence. One is from Gona, in the Middle Awash Valley of Ethiopia, and the other is from Nariokotome, on the western side of Lake Turkana, Kenya. Both are somewhat broad relative to the front-to-back dimension. In this respect, they are australopithecine-like. Based on this important record, Scott Simpson suggests that rotational birth was likely not present 2.0–1.5 mya. Therefore, at this time in human evolution, the pelvis retained some primitive traits, relative

breadth especially. Later in human evolution, brain size reached modern levels, and rotational birth and the complex social behavior associated with it appeared. Perhaps the first rotational births were in the early members of our own species, *Homo sapiens*. They might have occurred as late as 100,000 yBP, when the brain reached its current size. By that time, our ancestral mothers definitely would have benefited from assistance, as human mothers do today.

In *Australopithecus afarensis*, the long axis of the head is oriented transversely, aligned along the long axis of the pelvic inlet throughout the entire birth process. In living humans, the long axis of the head starts in transverse position (inlet stage), but then rotates 90 degrees (midplane stage). This rotation likely evolved relatively late in human evolution.

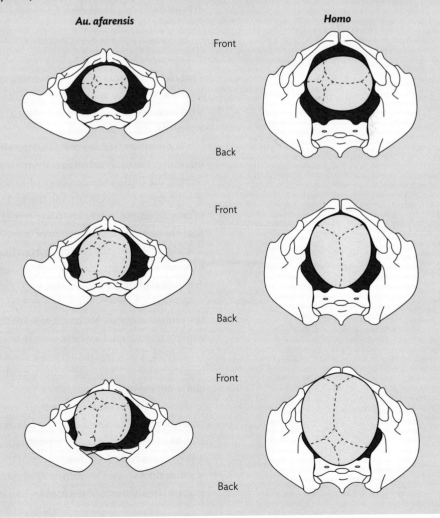

Au. afarensis
Homo
Front
Back
Front
Back
Front
Back

FIGURE 11.28

Wonderwerk Cave, South Africa This site may contain the earliest evidence for the controlled use of fire by early hominins.

that *H. erectus* was adapted to eating cooked meat and other cooked foods. These rich sources of energy would help explain the increases in brain size and body size. Cooking increases the digestibility of meat and other foods and improves the quality of the energy that it gives the eater.

Cooking would have required the ability to make and control fire. There are various claims for the early use of fire. By analyzing sediments from Wonderwerk Cave in South Africa, the Italian archaeologist Francesco Berna and his associates have determined that *H. erectus* made and used fire by 1 mya (**Figure 11.28**). The researchers' discovery of burned animal bones and plant remains in association with Acheulian tools indicates that these hominins used fire primarily for cooking. Fire may also have been used at Zhoukoudian, but the evidence from that locality is unclear and does not appear to have been made or controlled by human activity. That is, animal remains and stone tools are burned, but the type of burning is not associated with fire produced by hominins.

Fire also played a vital role in hominins' adaptation to regions of the globe where the temperature is cold much or all of the year. The controlled use of fire made possible a major expansion in where people could live and the manner in which they prepared their food. Thus, while there is not clear evidence for the use of fire at Zhoukoudian, hominins most likely had to have made and controlled fire in order to live there, especially during cold periods of the year.

Mostly important, however, *H. erectus* used fire to cook food. Before using fire, hominins ate plants and animals raw. But cooking these foods made them easier to chew and, as a result, made the very powerful jaws and large teeth of *H. erectus*'s predecessors less necessary. Indeed, the jaws and teeth of these Middle Pleistocene hominins were smaller than earlier hominins'. This size reduction was almost certainly related to the cultural innovations of the Middle Pleistocene, including both controlled use of fire and more advanced tool technology. These cultural developments were the harbingers of increasing environmental control and improved adaptive success, both of which form an ongoing theme of human evolution.

Another potential means of improving dietary quality and energy intake is food sharing. In this case, males would have hunted for meat and subsequently shared it with females and dependent children. Indeed, an extensive ethnographic record for living societies shows that food sharing happened in this manner universally. It is likely that this kind of provisioning was an essential element of increased access to high-quality nutrition. Thus, food sharing, meat eating, and cooking help explain the increase in brain size in human evolution, beginning especially with *H. erectus*.

CONCEPT CHECK

Homo erectus: **Beginning Globalization**

Homo erectus was the first hominin to inhabit territory all over the Old World. After first evolving in Africa, it spread rapidly to Asia and then to Europe. Increased intelligence, increased dependence on technology and on material culture, social hunting, and access to more protein and to better nutrition contributed to this early hominin's remarkable adaptive success.

(Photo © 1985 David L. Brill, humanoriginsphotos.com)

Location/Sites	Africa (Olduvai Gorge, Lake Turkana, Ileret, Bouri, Buia, Bodo, Olorgesailie); Asia (Dmanisi, Kocabaş, Trinil, Sangiran, Sambungmacan, Gongwangling, Majuangou, Zhoukoudian); Europe (Gran Dolina, Mauer, Boxgrove)
Chronology	1.8 mya–300,000 yBP in Africa 1.8 mya–300,000 yBP in Asia 1.2–0.4 mya in Europe

Biology and Culture (Compared with *Homo habilis*)

Feature	Evidence	Outcome
Tool use (Acheulian)	Skulls Teeth	Smaller face and smaller jaws Reduced size
Fire and cooking	Ash in habitation sites	Smaller face and smaller jaws
Intelligence	Brain size	Increase (average 950 cc)
Hunting and increased meat protein	Butchered large animals	Increased body size
Possible cannibalism	Cutmarks	New ritual or dietary innovation
Growth	Enamel perikymata	Slower growth, but not modern
Locomotion	Leg length:arm length	No significant change

TRACKING HUMAN

Fossils Are the Record of Transition and Process

Outside the academic setting, anthropologists are often challenged by people who question the theory of evolution. The challenges to evolution come in a number of forms. For example, opponents argue that because one cannot actually see evolution operating, it cannot exist.

Anthropologists point out that evolution is happening all around us. When new life is conceived, with half the chromosomes coming from the father and half from the mother, the fertilized egg contains a unique mix of genes, one that had never existed before. This process is evolution operating at its simplest level.

A much more common challenge to the theory of evolution, however, targets the validity and scope of the fossil record. Such statements are also based on misconceptions about the fossil record. For example, challengers say that the human fossil record lacks intermediate forms. One of the most commonly cited examples is the apparent gap in the past between apes and humans. Simply, how could living apes and living humans share a common ancestor if these species are not connected by transitional forms? As discussed in chapter 9, the earliest hominins, the pre-australopithecines and early australopithecines, had both apelike and humanlike attributes. Indeed, the earliest hominin was essentially an ape that walked bipedally. The pre-australopithecines are important transitional fossils. The few specimens conform to expectations about what the earliest hominin would have looked like—they have primitive apelike skulls, for example.

In fact, the record of biological change throughout much of human evolution is now well defined. The fossil record is sufficient to support a number of conclusions about the evolution of early *Homo*. For example, brain size increased gradually in early *Homo* and was likely associated with both increasing intelligence and tool use. Body length increased rapidly within the same period, the late Pliocene, as the short *Homo habilis* became the relatively tall *Homo erectus*. This transition may have taken place within less than a few hundred thousand years.

All fossils, like the genera and species they come from, represent transitions. Tens of thousands of hominin fossils now provide a remarkably diverse and comprehensive record of human transitions, or evolution. As the dating methods described in chapter 8 have shown, these fossils are anatomically and chronologically between modern humans and our earliest ancestors, who lived 6–5 mya. The record is compelling, and the unearthing of more and more fossils will help support the ideas behind evolution and more fully describe its processes.

In addition to the fundamental importance of fossils for documenting the phylogenetic record of human

EVOLUTION

ancestry, fossils tell us about specific adaptations over the last six million years of hominin evolution. As you have learned throughout this book, the history of humans—and all primates—is one of dynamic change. For example, there have been periods dominated by cold temperatures. Paleoanthropologists have documented patterns of morphology that may reflect adaptations to cold. For example, European Neandertals—a form of archaic *Homo sapiens* that you will read about in the next chapter—have remarkably wide openings for the nose (and see Figure 12.22, p. 408). These wide nasal apertures are suggestive of adaptation to cold environments. That is, a large, wide nose provides the hominin with greater interior surface area than a small, narrow nose. This is important because this larger surface area allows a more efficient means of warming and moistening the cold, dry air being inhaled. Some physical anthropologists suggest that this nasal morphology may have been important for maintaining relatively normal temperatures for the brain, a very temperature-sensitive element of the nervous system. However, other populations living in cold climates lack large, wide noses. This suggests that either the nasal morphology is not linked to environmental change, especially cold climates, or it may have been an adaptive solution for European Neandertals. Indeed, local adaptive solutions in some settings but not others are a record seen in many places and many times. Regardless of how this morphology is interpreted, it gives us a point of discussion of the remarkable amount of variation in our hominin ancestors and its importance for documenting our evolutionary past.

These and other hominin fossils have enabled researchers to draw conclusions about hominin evolution and human ancestry.

Patterns of Evolution in *Homo erectus*

Comparisons of all the *H. erectus* fossils from Africa, Asia, and Europe reveal important information about this early *Homo* species, both in general similarities across these continents and in the individual forms' evolution. *H. erectus* skulls are long, low, and wide at the base, and they have thick bone and large browridges. The African *H. erectus* tends to be the most robust, with the largest and thickest cranial bones. The Dmanisi and African forms are strongly similar—the sagittal keel, for example, is missing in Dmanisi and present only rarely in the African representatives. Morphological variations are likely related to differences in time and in geography, but the degree of variability is far smaller than that in other mammals.

Some authorities have interpreted the general similarity of *H. erectus* across Africa, Asia, and Europe and through time as representing evolutionary stasis. However, various morphological attributes show significant evolution in *H. erectus*, with earlier forms having considerably smaller brains than later forms. For example, the average Dmanisi skull is 650 cc, while the average Zhoukoudian skull is 1,200 cc. Overall, *H. erectus*'s brain size increased by some 30%. The American physical anthropologist Milford Wolpoff has also documented decreases in cranial bone thickness and browridge size. These characteristics indicate a decline in skull robusticity. Accompanying these changes is a reduction in tooth size, caused by the decreased demand on the face and jaws due to the increasing importance of technology and of cooking.

Hominins' increasing reliance on tools profoundly affected human biology. As tools began to perform the functions of the face and jaws in preparing food for consumption—that is, in cutting up, cooking, and processing meat and other food—there was a commensurate decline in the robusticity of these body parts, the anatomical area associated with mastication. In terms of both culture and biology, *H. erectus* evolved the contextual behavior—hunting, successful dispersal across large territory, adaptive success, and increasing dependence on and effective use of culture as a means of survival. The increased dependence on culture and the dominance of behaviors requiring technology in acquiring and processing food increased the diversity of environments occupied by *H. erectus*. The expansion of resources acquired and habitats occupied, coupled with the high degree of mobility, laid the basis for a high level of gene flow and the presence of a limited number of species—most likely, one species. The next chapter tracks and interprets the evolution of that species: *H. sapiens*.

After *Homo erectus*: Expect the Unexpected in Hominin Evolution

As we have seen in this chapter, the evolution of *H. erectus* is critically important, including adding to our understanding of biological variation, changing patterns of diet and adaptation, and identifying patterns of variation that characterize this taxon. In general, the emerging picture of human evolution from 1.5 mya to 0.5 mya ago or so shows the presence a hominin evolving over a period of a million years. The record shows generally increasing size of the body, brain, and masticatory complex. The patterns described in this chapter provide an essential adaptive platform for interpreting the process and outcome of the evolution of *H. erectus* and the origins and evolution of *H. sapiens* discussed in the upcoming chapters. But, there are lots of surprises in human evolution, one of which is *H. naledi*. The discovery of a hominin having a unique suite of anatomical characteristics found deep in a cave in South Africa demonstrates that paleoanthropologists have to be ready for the surprises that do not necessarily meet the consensus of the time. That is one of the exciting things about science—the twists, the turns, and the surprises of discovery.

Indeed, it is not just the early end of the evolution of the genus *Homo* that is turning

INDONESIA
Flores

up surprises, but also the later evolution. Simply, new discoveries in this discovery-rich discipline are revealing that there is a considerable amount of variation that does not fit the consensus. One of the most remarkable of these discoveries was made in 2014 on Flores Island, Indonesia, by paleontologists excavating deposits at the Mata Menge site, a site that dates to 700,000 yBP. Expecting to find the remains of *H. erectus*—at a time during which *H. erectus* was ubiquitous throughout Africa, Asia, and Europe—paleontologist Gerrit van den Bergh and fellow discoverers found something very new and very different. It was exciting enough to find hominin fossils—a partial adult mandible and six isolated teeth representing at least two children. But, quite unlike all hominins from Indonesia, and the rest of Asia and Africa and Europe dating to the Middle Pleistocene, the Mata Menge mandible (and, by inference, the rest of the skeleton) is *extraordinarily* small, perhaps representing an adult having half the body size of other contemporary hominins. The morphology of the teeth is similar in some respects to the much later, but also remarkably small, *Homo floresiensis* ("Hobbit"), also from Flores Island and dating between 100,000 yBP and 60,000 yBP (see chapter 12). The extremely small body size of the Mata Menge hominin and the much later *H. floresiensis* is unique in this region. The presence of an earlier and a later dwarf hominin suggests the presence of a dwarf lineage of hominins, specific to Flores Island.

The Mata Menge hominins are likely not *H. erectus*, but rather represent descendants of *H. erectus* that had settled on Flores Island in the Middle Pleistocene. At least for now, van den Bergh ascribes the Mata Menge fossils to *H. floresiensis*, owing to the resemblance in the teeth with the later hominin from Flores Island and its very small body size.

Importantly, the Mata Menge mandible and teeth add to the growing body of evidence showing considerable anatomical variation in the Middle Pleistocene, ranging from very small body size (Flores Island) to relatively large body size (just about everywhere else *except* Flores Island). Although the taxonomic identity of the Mata Menge hominin is preliminary, it nevertheless underscores the important point made earlier in this chapter and in this textbook in general regarding the remarkable adaptability of humans and their ancestors. For Mata Menge and the later hominin from Flores Island, the very small body size may have been due to their having lived on an island with limited food resources. We know that many species of animals living in island settings worldwide have reduced body size, owing to limited food resources. Simply, stunted size requires less caloric intake. Therefore, it would seem that small body size would have a selective advantage in these circumstances. But, this remains a point of speculation. What is not speculation, however, is that it is this remarkable variation that lays the groundwork for the evolution of modern people.

CHAPTER 11 REVIEW

ANSWERING THE BIG QUESTIONS

1. **What characteristics define the genus *Homo*?**

   • The genus *Homo* is defined by physical and behavioral attributes, including a relatively large brain, small face and jaws, and dependence on material culture for survival.

2. **What were the earliest members of the genus *Homo*?**

   • The earliest members of the genus *Homo* were *Homo habilis* and *Homo erectus*.

   • Fossils of *H. habilis* have been found in East Africa and South Africa and date to about 2.5–1.8 mya.

   • *H. erectus*, a geographically and morphologically diverse species, dates to about 1.8 mya–300,000 yBP. Its fossil record is represented in Africa, Asia, and Europe.

3. **What are the key evolutionary trends and other developments in early *Homo*?**

   • Compared to the australopithecines, early *H. habilis* experienced an enlargement of the brain and a general gracilization of the chewing complex (face, jaws, and teeth). These developments were linked with increases in tool production and use, dietary diversity, and intelligence.

   • Compared with *H. habilis*, *H. erectus* experienced a continued reduction in size of the chewing complex, increased brain and body size, and the first evidence of modern limb proportions.

   • *H. erectus* developed an increasingly innovative and complex technology, including more elaborate tools, organized social hunting, and controlled use of fire. These developments facilitated greater access to protein and improved nutrition, which likely explains the rapid increase in body and brain size around 2.0–1.7 mya. This increasing adaptive flexibility is a central theme of human evolution.

   • *Homo* increasingly became a predator genus in the early Pleistocene, and this change at least partly explains its remarkable and rapid geographic expansion. Successful predation was largely from hunting, but early *Homo* likely acquired food through hunting *and* scavenging.

   • The increased intelligence and full commitment to material culture as an adaptive strategy of *H. erectus* set the stage for the emergence and evolution of *Homo sapiens*.

   • Discoveries of dwarf hominins from Southeast Asia reveal new variation in Middle and Late Pleistocene hominins.

KEY TERMS

Acheulian Complex
handaxe
Homo erectus
obstetric dilemma
Pithecanthropus erectus
sagittal keel

STUDY QUIZ

1. **What anatomical feature did *Homo habilis* share with earlier australopithecine species?**

   a. a small brain
   b. a large chewing complex
   c. a large face and large jaws
   d. short legs relative to arms

2. **Where does *Homo naledi* most likely fit into the human lineage?**

   a. an early taxon of genus *Homo*
   b. a late taxon of genus *Homo*
   c. a descendant of *Homo erectus*
   d. actually an australopithecine

3. **Which of the following represents skeletal adaptation of *Homo erectus* contributed to its fully modern walking?**

   a. longer legs and shorter arms
   b. a more abducted big toe
   c. loss of arches of the foot
   d. decreased body height

4. **Which of the following is *not* a *H. erectus* behavioral innovation?**

   a. long-distance hunting and walking
   b. controlled use of fire for cooking
   c. production of symbolic material culture
   d. migration outside of Africa to Asia and Europe

5. **The rapid increases in *H. erectus* body and brain size are most likely linked to which diets?**

   a. a high-fiber diet of fruits and vegetables
   b. a high-fiber diet of grasses and seeds
   c. a high-protein diet of raw meat
   d. a high-protein diet of cooked meat

EVOLUTION REVIEW

THE ORIGINS OF *HOMO*

Synopsis The earliest members of our genus, *Homo,* arose nearly 2.5 mya and were characterized by an increase in brain size and a stronger reliance on material culture for survival. Key anatomical changes in *Homo habilis*—such as a larger brain, a less robust jaw, and smaller teeth—highlight the growing importance of tool use and dietary diversity as adaptations in the genus *Homo. Homo erectus* became the first hominin species to spread out of Africa to Europe and Asia, a global dispersal made possible by anatomical and cultural adaptations, including increased brain size, larger body size, more complex tool technology, use of fire for cooking, and emergence of hunting behaviors. The first members of *Homo* exhibited a series of evolutionary trends that set the stage for the ongoing evolution of the genus and the eventual emergence of our own species, *Homo sapiens.*

Q1. Name the three features outlined in this chapter that set the earliest member of our genus, *H. habilis,* apart from the australopithecines and that are defining characteristics of the genus *Homo.*

Q2. In some ways, the differences between *H. erectus* and *H. habilis* are more pronounced than those between *H. habilis* and the latest australopithecines. Provide three examples of anatomical characteristics in *H. erectus* that differ substantially from those observed in *H. habilis.* What are the evolutionary trends in these characteristics that are seen between these two species?

Q3. What are some of the roles that tool use and climate change may have played in shaping the adaptive flexibility (and evolutionary success) of *H. habilis* relative to the species of australopithecines living at the same time?

Hint Climate change in the early Pleistocene led to the spread of a grassland environment and increased habitat and resource diversity.

Q4. *H. erectus* is characterized by substantial changes in body size, brain size, material culture, and dietary and behavioral flexibility compared to earlier hominin species. Rather than being unidirectional (for example, increased brain size leads to complex material culture but not the other way around), how might all of these changes be part of an evolutionary feedback loop driven by biocultural adaptation?

Hint Consider the ways that certain behaviors emerging in *H. erectus* may have had anatomical, physiological, and nutritional effects, as well as the ways in which these effects may have further influenced behavioral flexibility.

Q5. *H. erectus* was the first hominin species to spread out of Africa to other areas of the globe. Use specific biological and cultural features and the concepts of survival, reproduction, and migration to explain why *H. erectus* was the first species capable of such a widespread existence.

ADDITIONAL READINGS

Antón, S. C. and C. C. Swisher III. 2004. Early dispersals of *Homo* from Africa. *Annual Review of Anthropology* 33: 271–296.

Begun, D. R. 2013. *A Companion to Paleoanthropology.* Chichester, UK: Wiley-Blackwell.

Culotta, E. 2016. Likely hobbit ancestors lived 600,000 years earlier. *Science* 352: 1260-1261.

Dunsworth, H. and A. Walker. 2002. Early genus *Homo.* Pp. 419–435 in W. C. Hartwig, ed. *The Primate Fossil Record.* Cambridge, UK: Cambridge University Press.

McHenry, H. M. and K. Coffing. 2000. *Australopithecus* to *Homo:* transformations in body and mind. *Annual Review of Anthropology* 29: 125–146.

Rightmire, G. P. 1990. *The Evolution of* Homo erectus. Cambridge, UK: Cambridge University Press.

Shapiro, H. L. 1974. *Peking Man: The Discovery, Disappearance and Mystery of a Priceless Scientific Treasure.* New York: Simon & Schuster.

Shipman, P. 2001. *The Man Who Found the Missing Link.* New York: Simon & Schuster.

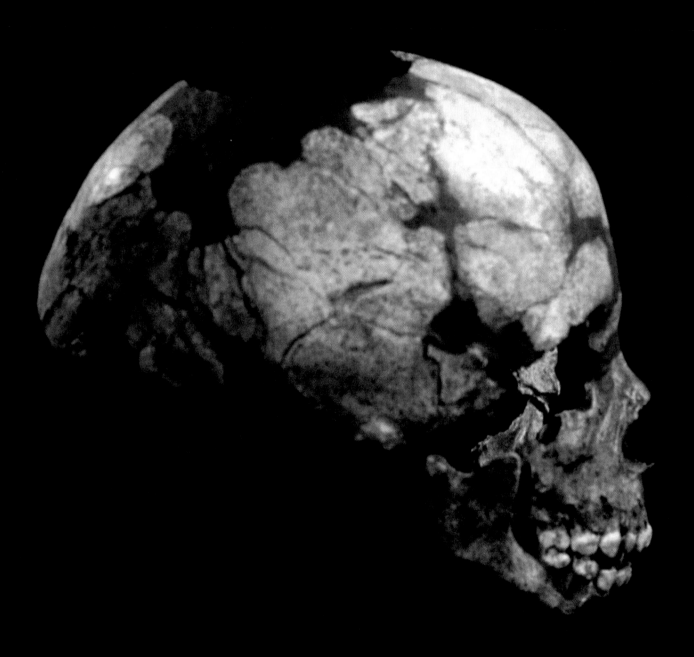

In this reconstruction, a Neandertal child from Roc-de-Marsal in Dordogne, France, shows a mix of modern and archaic features. Neandertals (a skull of which is also pictured here) are central to our understanding of the origins and evolution of modern humans, including key aspects of human growth and development. (© 2003 Photographer P. Plailly/E. Daynès/Eurelios—Reconstruction Elisabeth Daynès, Paris)

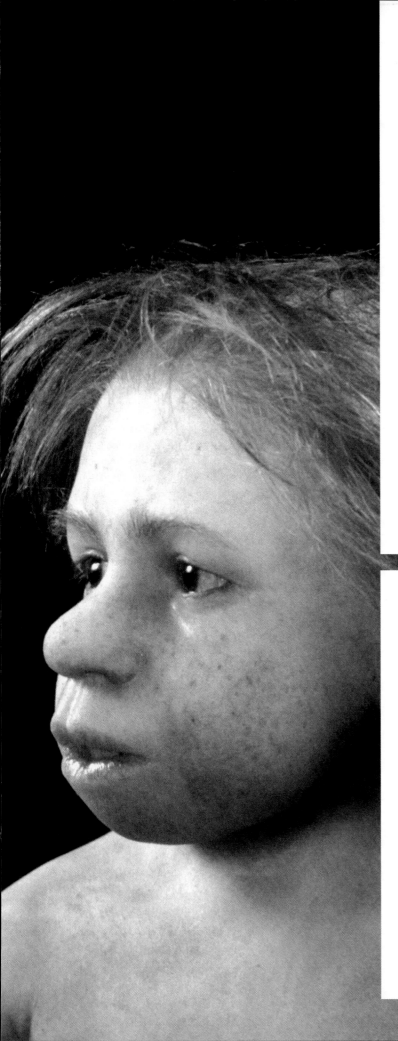

12

The Origins, Evolution, and Dispersal of Modern People

BIG QUESTIONS

1. **What is so modern about modern humans?**
2. **What do *Homo sapiens* fossils reveal about modern humans' origins?**
3. **How has variation in fossil *H. sapiens* been interpreted?**
4. **What other developments took place in *H. sapiens'* evolution?**

The Feldhofer Cave Neandertal was the first fossil hominin to receive serious attention from scientists. Prior to its (accidental) discovery in 1856, answers to questions about the physical characteristics and behaviors of human ancestors were highly speculative. The uncovering of this skeleton signaled a change for anthropology. Feldhofer Cave is located in Neander Valley (in German, *Neander Tal*), which is near Düsseldorf, Germany. Workers happened upon the skeleton while removing clay deposits from the cave as part of a limestone quarrying operation. Sometimes accidental discoveries like this are reported; often, they are not. The world of anthropology got very lucky because these workers picked up the skull and bones and took them to a local schoolteacher. As luck further had it, the teacher recognized these

GERMANY

Feldhofer
Cave

FIGURE 12.1

Feldhofer Neandertal This Neandertal's DNA has been used recently to test hypotheses concerning the genetic relationship between modern humans and Neandertals.

FIGURE 12.2

Rudolf Virchow Virchow made an influential but wrong pronouncement about the Feldhofer Neandertal skeleton. Among his many achievements was being the first researcher to recognize leukemia, a cancer of the blood and of bone marrow.

remains as human and passed them on to the anthropologist Hermann Schaafhausen at the University of Bonn. Schaafhausen studied the remains, quickly reported his findings to the German Natural History Society, and published a description in a leading German scientific journal. He described a skull having some archaic features, distinctive from modern humans'. In particular, the skull was long and low, different from modern people's but with some similarities, such as in brain size (**Figure 12.1**). Moreover, the skeletal remains of extinct Pleistocene animals also found in the cave indicated that this human had lived at the same time as these animals. At the time these breathtaking announcements were made, many authorities believed that humans had appeared very recently in the history of life, certainly postdating extinct animals associated with the great Pleistocene Ice Age.[1]

Schaafhausen and the Neandertal skeleton caught the attention of scientific leaders in Germany and around the world. One of these leaders was the top German anthropologist of the time, Rudolf Virchow (see chapter 1, "How Do We Know: Franz Boas Invents Anthropology, American Style"; **Figure 12.2**). In addition to being a leading authority on evolutionary theory, archaeology, and cultural anthropology, Virchow started the discipline of cell pathology (diseases of cells). He helped found several national scientific organizations and periodicals. He was a medical activist, a political leader known across Germany, and the teacher of others who would become leaders in science and medicine. In short, his pronouncements about the Feldhofer Cave skeleton would be taken very seriously by scientists. After looking carefully at the remains, he summarily dismissed any notion that they belonged to an ancestor of living humans. He argued that their characteristics—a long, low skull and bowed, thick limb bones—were those of some modern human afflicted with rickets and arthritis. Others disagreed. Thomas Henry Huxley (see Figure 2.19) argued that this was a primitive, potentially ancestral human. But Virchow's assessment was convincing to most, setting the course for years. Later, scores of remains showing the same morphology as the Feldhofer Cave skeleton and dating to the same period of the late Pleistocene were found. Eventually, Virchow's pathology hypothesis was rejected, and debate centered on the role of the Feldhofer Cave skeleton and others like it—a group of hominins we call *Neandertals*—in later human evolution.

In this chapter, we will look at *Homo sapiens'* evolution, from its origins in *Homo erectus*

---

[1] Excavations at the Feldhofer Cave in 1997 and 2000 produced more than 62 new bone fragments that are part of the original skeleton, part of at least one other adult, and part of a juvenile. Radiocarbon dates on these new bones indicate that this Neandertal site is about 40,000 years old.

to its development into modern humans. Neandertals play a central role in this discussion, which is also based on rich records—of fossils, genetic variation, culture, and behavior—from around the world. First, though, we will explore which aspects of the fossil record indicate the first appearance of modern people. Then, we will examine those aspects to understand just how anthropologists interpret the variation across the bones and teeth of *H. sapiens*.

12.1 What Is So Modern about Modern Humans?

What do physical anthropologists mean by *modern?* This question is very important because the answer to it provides us with the baseline from which to assess the origins, evolution, and geographic distribution of modern *Homo sapiens*. Physical anthropologists define *modern* on the basis of a series of distinctive anatomical characteristics that contrast with *archaic* characteristics found in earlier hominins (**Figure 12.3**). Modern people—people who essentially look like us—tend to have a high and vertical forehead, a round and tall skull, small browridges, a small face, small teeth, and a

(a)

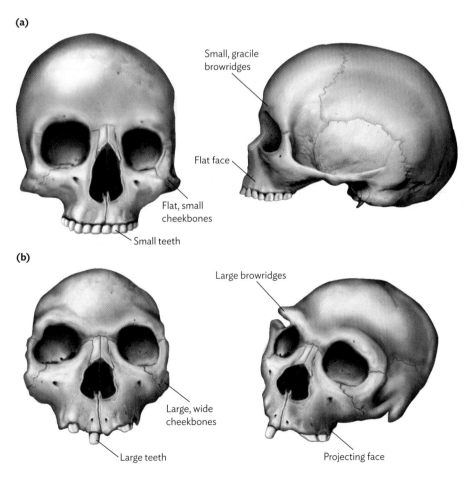

Small, gracile browridges

Flat face

Flat, small cheekbones

Small teeth

(b)

Large browridges

Large, wide cheekbones

Large teeth

Projecting face

FIGURE 12.3

Modern Human Features **(a)** Anatomically modern *Homo sapiens* possess a unique suite of traits that are absent in **(b)** archaic *H. sapiens*.

projecting chin (anthropologists call the latter a "mental eminence"). Below the neck, modern humans have relatively more gracile, narrower bones than their predecessors. Fossil humans having these cranial and postcranial characteristics are considered modern *H. sapiens*.

The immediate ancestors of modern people—archaic *H. sapiens*—differ from modern *H. sapiens*. Compared to modern *H. sapiens*, archaic *H. sapiens* have a longer and lower skull, a larger browridge, a bigger and more projecting face, a taller and wider nasal aperture (opening for the nose), a more projecting occipital bone (sometimes called an **occipital bun** when referring to Neandertals), larger teeth (especially the front teeth), and no chin. The postcranial bones of archaic *H. sapiens* are thicker than those of modern people.

Some hominin skeletons dating to the Upper Pleistocene have a mixture of archaic and modern features. The Skhul 5 skeleton from Israel, discussed later in this chapter, is an excellent example of a hominin with both archaic features, including a somewhat forward-projecting face and pronounced browridges, and modern features, such as a distinctive chin and no occipital bun (see Figure 12.38, p. 424). Similarly, the Herto skulls from Ethiopia have a combination of archaic and modern features, although the modern features dominate over the archaic ones (see Figure 12.34, pp. 420–21). The modern characteristics of their skulls indicate that the Skhul and Herto hominins were on the verge of modernity or were very early modern *H. sapiens,* perhaps the earliest in western Asia and Africa, respectively.

occipital bun A cranial feature of Neandertals in which the occipital bone projects substantially from the skull's posterior.

12.2 Modern *Homo sapiens:* Single Origin and Global Dispersal or Regional Continuity?

Homo sapiens' evolution begins with the emergence of archaic forms some 500,000–350,000 yBP. These early *H. sapiens* provide the context for modern *H. sapiens'* evolutionary development, which took place at different times in different places. The first modern *H. sapiens* appeared earliest in Africa, by 160,000 yBP, and latest in Europe, by about 35,000 yBP. The transition to fully modern *H. sapiens* was completed globally by about 25,000 yBP.

Two main hypotheses have emerged to explain modern people's origins (**Figure 12.4**). The *Out-of-Africa* hypothesis states that modern *H. sapiens* first evolved in Africa and then spread to Asia and Europe, replacing the indigenous archaic *H. sapiens* populations (Neandertals) living on these two continents. The *Multiregional Continuity* hypothesis regards the transition to modernity as having taken place regionally and without involving replacement. From this point of view, African archaic *H. sapiens* gave rise to African modern *H. sapiens,* Asian archaic *H. sapiens* gave rise to Asian modern *H. sapiens,* and European archaic *H. sapiens* gave rise to European modern *H. sapiens.* Both models seek to explain why today's human beings consist of just one genus and why that genus consists of just one species. The models differ, though, in accounting for that genus and species.

The Out-of-Africa model explains the single species of living humans by emphasizing a single origin of modern people and eventual replacement of archaic *H. sapiens* throughout Africa, Asia, and Europe. A simple story. The Multiregional Continuity model emphasizes the importance of gene flow across population boundaries—separate

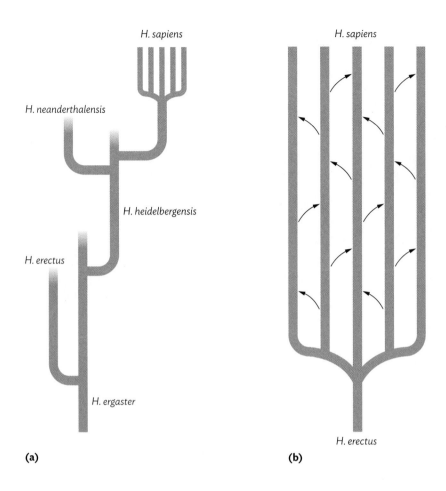

(a)

H. sapiens

H. neanderthalensis

H. heidelbergensis

H. erectus

H. ergaster

(b)

H. sapiens

H. erectus

FIGURE 12.4

Out-of-Africa versus Multiregional This important anthropological debate is about modern humans' origins. **(a)** This chart depicts one of the two hypotheses, Out-of-Africa, according to which modern humans originated in Africa and then migrated throughout the world. **(b)** This chart depicts the second hypothesis, Multiregional Continuity, according to which *Homo erectus* evolved into modern *Homo sapiens* in various geographic locations. The arrows represent continuous gene flow throughout human evolution. This hypothesis considers *H. ergaster* and *H. heidelbergensis* to be *H. erectus* and *H. neanderthalensis* to be *H. sapiens.*

species of humanity never arose owing to the constant interbreeding of human groups throughout human evolution. Not such a simple story.

Fossil and genetic records provide a wealth of information about modern human origins. We will now consider these records and draw some conclusions from them. We will then be ready to reassess the two hypotheses and to draw further conclusions about the origins of us—living people.

12.3 What Do *Homo sapiens* Fossils Tell Us about Modern Human Origins?

The fossil remains of archaic *H. sapiens* have been found throughout Africa, Asia, and Europe. In Africa, archaic *H. sapiens* evolved into modern *H. sapiens* at least by 160,000 yBP, perhaps as early as 200,000 yBP. In Asia and Europe, the archaics consisted of an early group and a late group, divided very roughly at about 130,000 yBP. To understand the biological changes involved in hominin groups' evolution, we need to compare some details of a number of key fossils.

Early Archaic *Homo sapiens*

The earliest forms of *H. sapiens* emerged around 350,000 yBP. They have been found in Africa, Asia, and Europe (**Figure 12.5**). Their evolution is clearly out of the earlier *H.*

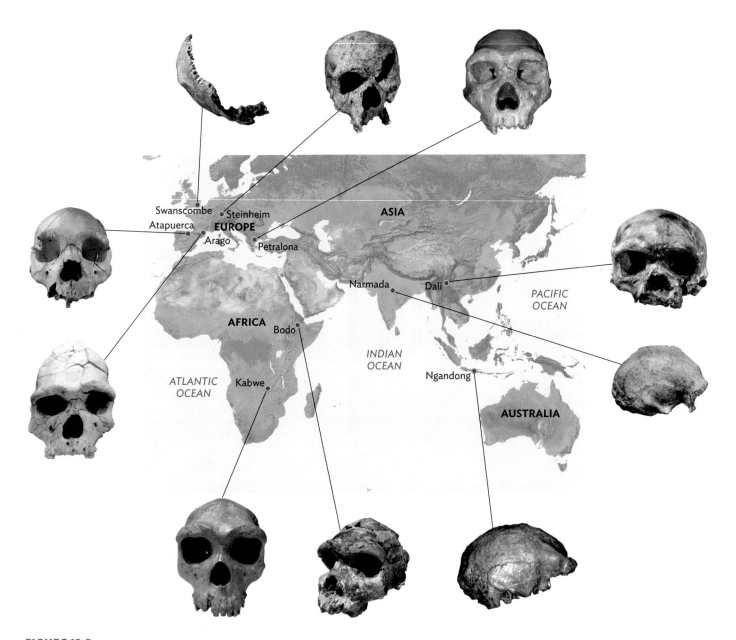

FIGURE 12.5

***Early Archaic* Homo sapiens** This map illustrates some of the sites in Africa, Asia, and Europe where the remains of early archaic *H. sapiens* have been found. (Arago skull photo © David L. Brill, humanoriginsphotos.com)

erectus populations. Anthropologists have documented this evolutionary transition in the three continental settings, noting, for example, the similarly massive browridges in archaic *H. sapiens* and in earlier *H. erectus*. Although quite primitive in key respects, all the fossils representing archaic *H. sapiens* and earlier *H. erectus* show continued reduction in skeletal robusticity, smaller tooth size, expansion in brain size, and increasing cultural complexity.

ARCHAIC *HOMO SAPIENS* IN AFRICA (350,000–200,000 YBP) One of several individuals found in the Kabwe (Broken Hill) lead mine in Zambia (formerly Northern Rhodesia) has enormous browridges, but the facial bones and the muscle attachment areas on the back of the skull for the neck muscles are quite small compared with those of *H. erectus* in Africa (**Figure 12.6**). The cranial capacity is about 1,300 cc. The skull is similar in appearance to those of early archaic hominins from Europe. Both the Zambian and the European skulls have *erectus*-like characteristics: a large face, large browridges, and

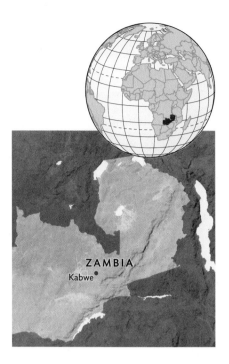

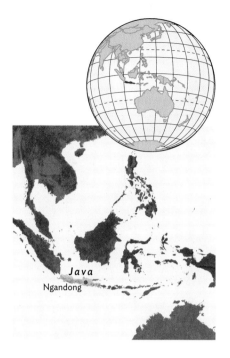

FIGURE 12.6

FIGURE 12.6

Kabwe This archaic *H. sapiens,* also known as "Broken Hill Man" or "Rhodesian Man," was among the first early human fossils discovered in Africa. Found by miners searching for metal deposits in caves, it was originally thought to be less than 40,000 years old.

thick cranial bones. However, archaic *H. sapiens* skulls, like their Asian counterparts, are higher than *H. erectus* skulls, reflecting a brain expansion in the later hominins.

EARLY ARCHAIC *HOMO SAPIENS* IN ASIA AND EUROPE (350,000–130,000 YBP) Some of the best-known fossils representing early archaic *H. sapiens* are from the Ngandong site on the island of Java (**Figure 12.7**). The skulls are represented by the braincases only—the faces are missing. Ngandong 11 has a brain size of about 1,100 cc, well within the range for early archaic *H. sapiens.* The skull is long and low, but compared with its *H. erectus* ancestor, the skull is somewhat higher, reflecting its larger brain. The brow-ridge is massive, certainly of the magnitude of many *H. erectus* examples.

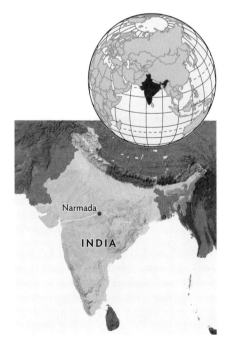

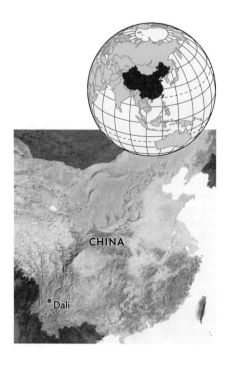

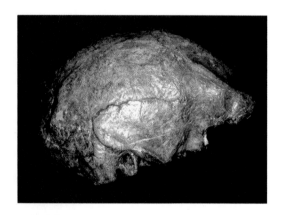

FIGURE 12.7

Ngandong Multiple skulls were found at this site in Java in the 1930s. The brain size of this early archaic *Homo sapiens* falls between that of *Homo erectus* and that of modern humans.

ATAPUERCA,

FOSSIL HOMININ BONANZA

One of the world's most spectacular fossil hominin sites is located in the hills of north-central Spain, about 15 km (9 mi) east of the town of Burgos.

Within a hill called *Sierra de Atapuerca,* a series of limestone caves has been studied for decades by speleologists (scientists who study caves), geologists, archaeologists, and paleontologists. In 1976, the paleontologist Trinidad Torres went into the cave known as *Sima de los Huesos* (meaning "Pit of Bones") in search of Pleistocene cave bear fossils for his doctoral dissertation research. Along with the cave bear bones, he collected a handful of hominin fossils—a mandible, mandible fragments, and teeth—all dating to the Middle Pleistocene. Even if no other fossils had been found at the site, this discovery would have been important, owing to the fact that only a few other hominin fossils from Europe are this old. Sima de los Huesos is among the half-dozen key sites at Atapuerca that have produced a fabulous wealth of fossils, tools, and other indications of human presence dating between 900,000 yBP and the recent past.

At Sima de los Huesos, in deposits dating to 430,000 yBP, excavators led by the paleontologist Juan Luis Arsuaga of Madrid's Complutense University recovered abundant fossils, but the most exciting of a series of spectacular discoveries was the nearly complete skeleton of an adult male, Atapuerca 5, excavated in 1992–94. Nicknamed "Miguelón" by its excavators, the skeleton provides a glimpse at the people of the Middle Pleistocene. In addition to the characteristics seen in the skull (see text and Figure 12.10), the limb bones are extraordinarily thick, indicating that this person led a highly demanding life, at least in terms of physical activity. Like the skull, the limb bones in many ways resemble those of Neandertals, who appeared later in time and in other parts of Europe. These similarities are consistent with the finding by the German paleogeneticist Matthias Meyer, whose analysis of nuclear DNA extracted from Sima de los Huesos bones and teeth shows that these Middle Pleistocene early archaic *Homo sapiens* are related to the Late Pleistocene Neandertals of Europe.

A number of the dentitions from Atapuerca display hypoplasias, or lines of arrested growth on the teeth. Generally, these lines result from periods of sickness, starvation, or both. The relatively low number—about one-third of the people had them—compared with that in other human populations suggests that these people were by and large healthy.

Hundreds of fossils, including hominin fossils, were discovered in caves located in these Spanish hills. This place is now a UNESCO World Heritage Site.

SPAIN

Of the hundreds of bones found in the sites at Atapuerca, some of the most fascinating are from the cave site of Gran Dolina. Dating to about 900,000 yBP, these fossils are evidence for the presence—the earliest—of *Homo erectus* in Europe. Paleoanthropologists found six individuals' remains at the cave's entrance, mixed with numerous stone tools and animal bones. As the paleoanthropologist Yolanda Fernández-Jalvo discovered, many of the hominin bones, like the animal bones, have cutmarks in areas of large muscle attachments. That is, a tool-wielding hominin took a stone knife and sliced flesh off the body. In the process of removing flesh, the stone tool left cutmarks on the bones. Bones with cutmarks include skulls, ribs, vertebrae, and clavicles. Some bones also have impact fractures and breakage, done to extract marrow. The reasons for this flesh removal are of course unknown, but the association with other animal bones indicates that the Gran Dolina people were eating each other. The similar modifications among human bones and animal bones at the cave provide the oldest evidence of cannibalism in human evolution.

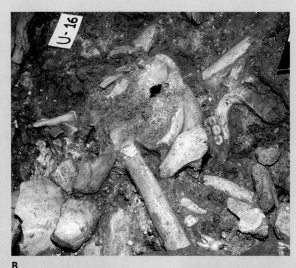

A

B

C

D

A

Beginning in the 1970s, excavations at several cave sites in Sierra de Atapuerca, including Sima de los Huesos and Galeria (shown here), yielded hundreds of bones.

B

Human remains, the remains of various animals, and numerous tools were recovered from many of these sites.

C

This skeleton is one of six discovered in the Gran Dolina cave.

D

Cutmarks on various bones, including the skull shown here, suggest the soft tissue was removed around the time of death; however, the reason for defleshing is unknown.

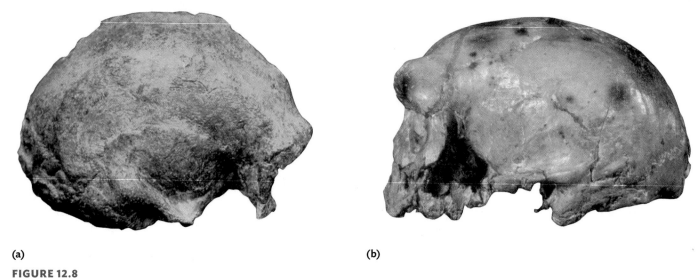

(a)   (b)

FIGURE 12.8

Asian Early Archaic **Homo sapiens** Like the Ngandong cranium, the crania of **(a)** Narmada and **(b)** Dali are robust, with thick cranial bones. The cranial capacity, however, indicates the brain size was much larger than in *Homo erectus* but somewhat smaller than in modern humans.

The Ngandong skulls share a number of features with other Asian early archaic *H. sapiens,* especially with Narmada (Madhya Pradesh, India) and Dali (Shaanxi Province, People's Republic of China) skulls (**Figure 12.8**). The crania are large and robust. The browridges are also quite large, although not as large as in *H. erectus.*

In Europe, well-known early archaic *H. sapiens* fossils include a skull and other remains from Arago, France; a skull from Petralona, Greece; a skull from Steinheim, Germany (**Figure 12.9**); and a partial skull from Swanscombe, England. Their average cranial capacity is 1,200 cc. These early archaic *H. sapiens* exhibit larger brains and rounder, more gracile skulls than *H. erectus.*

EARLY ARCHAIC *HOMO SAPIENS'* DIETARY ADAPTATIONS The earliest archaic *H. sapiens* had many of the same kinds of tools and material technology as the earlier

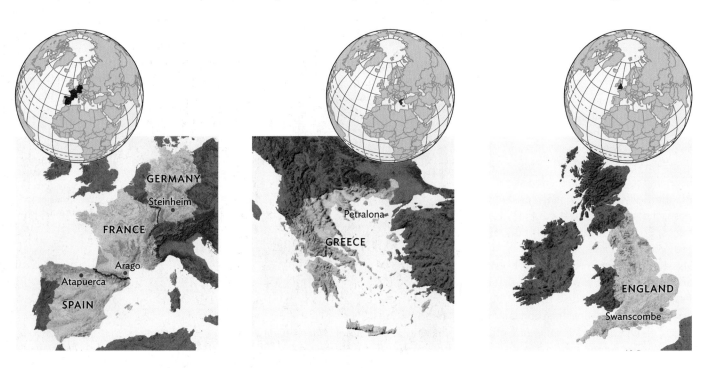

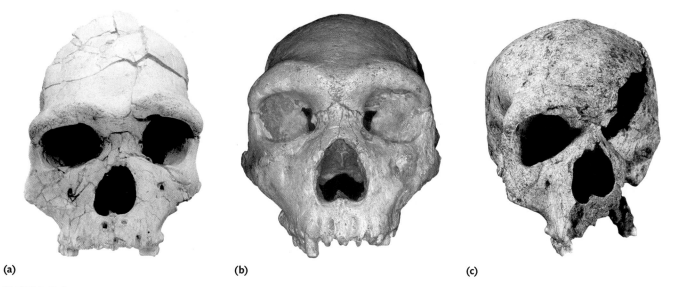

(a) **(b)** **(c)**

FIGURE 12.9

***European Early Archaic** Homo sapiens* Cranial remains from three prominent European sites—**(a)** Arago, **(b)** Petralona, and **(c)** Steinheim—have somewhat larger cranial capacities than other early archaic *H. sapiens*. Although these crania reflect a more modern appearance, they retain primitive features such as larger browridges. (Photo [a] © 1985 David L. Brill, humanoriginsphotos.com)

H. erectus, but *H. sapiens* used much more diverse tools to acquire and process food. Across the group, the face, jaws, and back teeth (premolars and molars) show a general reduction in size. The American physical anthropologist C. Loring Brace hypothesizes that selection for large back teeth lessened as tools became more important for processing food. Simply, with reduced selection, the teeth became smaller. Alternatively, as technological innovation changed the way teeth were used, the teeth may have been under *greater* selection for reduced size. Anthropologists have not reached a consensus on the mechanisms behind the reduction in tooth size except to say that cultural innovation and increased dependence on material culture likely played a role in this fundamental biological change.

At the same time that the importance of the back teeth diminished, the use of the front teeth increased. That is, during this period of human evolution, the incisors and canines underwent heavy wear. For example, in Atapuerca 5 from Spain, the front teeth are worn nearly to where the gums would have been in life (**Figure 12.10**). This evidence tells us that these hominins used their front teeth as a tool, perhaps as a kind of third hand for gripping materials. In European archaic *H. sapiens,* the front teeth show a size increase. The link between heavy use of the front teeth and increase in size of these teeth suggests the likelihood of selection for large front teeth.

Late Archaic *Homo sapiens*

The hominins from this period show a continuation of trends begun with early *Homo,* especially increased brain size, reduced tooth size, and decreased skeletal robusticity. However, in far western Asia (the Middle East) and Europe, a new pattern of morphology emerges, reflecting both regional variation and adaptation to cold. This new pattern defines the Neandertals. Neandertal features include wide and tall nasal apertures; a projecting face; an occipital bun; a long, low skull; large front teeth (some with heavy wear); a wide, stocky body; and short limbs.

The fossil record of the late archaic *H. sapiens* is fascinating. For the first time in human evolution, a number of fairly complete skeletons exist, allowing new insights

FIGURE 12.10

Atapuerca 5 One of many human skeletal remains found in Sima de los Huesos, Atapuerca 5 represents a nearly complete adult male skeleton. Its cranial capacity falls within the range of other Pleistocene humans, but its cranium is unusual in its degree of tooth wear. Notice that the front tooth is worn—that it has very little enamel left.

into the biology and behavior of these ancient humans. Moreover, the material culture includes new kinds of tools and reflects new behaviors that are modern in several important ways.

LATE ARCHAIC *HOMO SAPIENS* IN ASIA (60,000–40,000 YBP) For Asian late archaic *H. sapiens*, the record is fullest from sites at the far western end of the continent (**Figure 12.11**). Fossils from Israel form the core of discussions among anthropologists about modern people's emergence in western Asia. This record pertains to Neandertals from Amud, Kebara, and Tabun. The Amud Neandertals date to about 55,000–40,000 yBP and are best known from the complete skeleton of an adult male. He had an enormous brain, measuring some 1,740 cc, larger than earlier humans' and the largest for any fossil hominin (**Figure 12.12**). The Kebara Neandertals date to about 60,000 yBP and are represented by a complete mandible and body skeleton; the legs and cranium are

FIGURE 12.11

***West Asian Late Archaic* Homo sapiens** This map illustrates where late archaic *H. sapiens'* remains have been found in western Asia, along the eastern Mediterranean Sea.

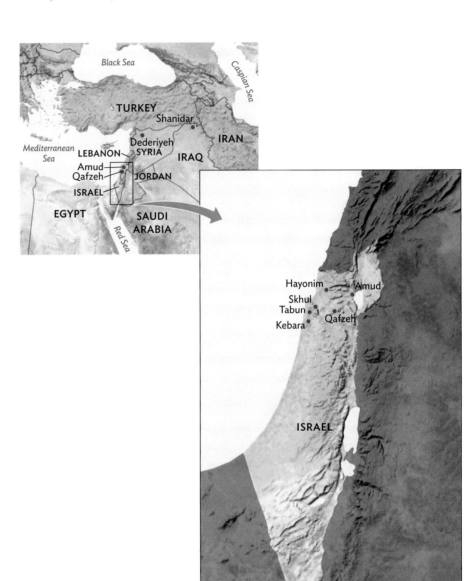

FIGURE 12.12

Amud Neandertal The exceptionally large cranial capacity of the Amud Neandertal indicates that this hominin's brain was at least as large as a modern human's.

missing (**Figure 12.13**). A nearly complete female Neandertal skeleton from Tabun was long thought to date to about the same time, but new thermoluminescence dating indicates that the skeleton may be as old as 170,000 yBP. Like the Amud male, she had a large brain.

The Amud and Tabun skulls have a number of anatomical characteristics that are strongly similar to those of contemporary populations of late archaic *H. sapiens* in Europe. For example, their eye orbits tend to be small and round, their nasal openings are tall and wide, and their faces project forward. These two skulls share a number of modern characteristics, however, such as the lack of the occipital bun and the presence of relatively small teeth.

Some of the most interesting Neandertals are from the Shanidar site in northern Iraq's Kurdistan region. These Neandertals—seven adults and three young children—have provided important insight into the lives, lifestyles, and cultural practices of late archaic *H. sapiens* (**Figure 12.14**). Shanidar 1, an older adult male dating to at least 45,000 yBP, is one of the most complete skeletons from the site (**Figure 12.15**). The face is that of a typical Neandertal, especially in its wide nasal aperture and forward projection. This individual's life history is written in his bones. A fracture on his upper face, well healed at the time of his death, may have been severe enough to cause blindness. Severe arthritis in his feet might have resulted from the constant stresses of traversing difficult, mountainous terrain.

Shanidar 1's upper incisors are severely worn, probably from his use of the front teeth as a tool for grasping and holding objects in the same or a similar way as the much earlier hominin from Atapuerca. This extramasticatory wear on the front teeth is determined by culture—Neandertals used their front teeth as a part of their "tool kit." Use of the front teeth as a tool has remained a hallmark of human behavior into

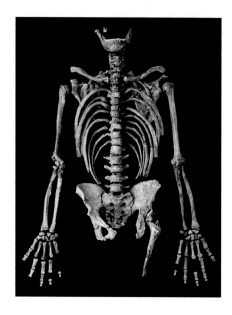

FIGURE 12.13

Kebara Neandertal The almost complete skeletal torso of this hominin was discovered in Kebara Cave, Israel. Even without a cranium and legs, this is one of the most complete Neandertal skeletons found to date. (Photo © 1985 David L. Brill, humanoriginsphotos.com)

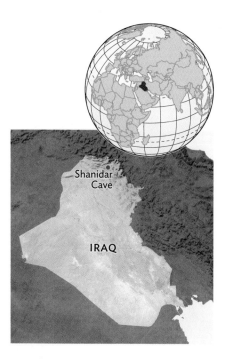

FIGURE 12.14

Shanidar This Iraqi cave site was excavated in the late 1950s by an American archaeological team. Evidence found with the Neandertal skeletons suggests that the Neandertals intentionally buried their dead and possibly performed some type of burial ceremony.

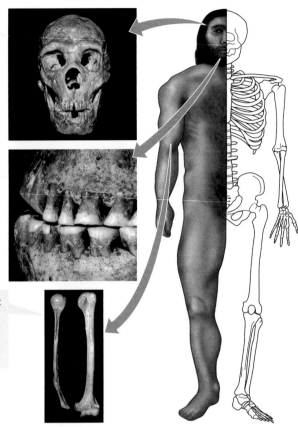

This individual has typical Neandertal characteristics, including large browridges and a large nasal aperture.

Anterior tooth wear indicates that the front teeth were being used as tools.

Atrophy of the right humerus (left humerus shown for comparison) may have resulted from an injury. The lower arm was likely amputated.

FIGURE 12.15

Shanidar 1 Neandertal The skeleton of this older adult Neandertal tells a life story of injury owing to accidents and violence. The majority of Neandertal skeletons have injuries.

recent times in a wide variety of cultures, including Native Americans who chew plant material to prepare it for basketry.

Shanidar 1 may have had personal reasons for using his front teeth as a tool. When he was excavated by the American archaeologist Ralph Solecki in the late 1950s, his lower right arm was missing. The American physical anthropologist T. Dale Stewart suggested that the lower arm may have been either amputated or accidentally severed right above the elbow. The humerus was severely atrophied, probably owing to disuse of the arm during life. The loss of the use of the arm meant that Shanidar 1 _had_ to use his teeth to perform some simple functions, such as eating or making tools. His survival likely depended on the use of his front teeth.

LATE ARCHAIC _HOMO SAPIENS_ IN EUROPE (130,000–30,000 YBP) The European late archaic _H. sapiens,_ Neandertals, are some of the best-known, most-studied fossil hominins in the world (**Figure 12.16**). Owing to the relative completeness of the fossil record, paleoanthropologists have been able to document and debate the meaning of their physical characteristics. The Neandertal record begins in eastern Europe, at the Krapina site in Croatia, which dates to 130,000 yBP (**Figure 12.17**). The record ends with fossils from Vindija, Croatia, dating to 32,000 yBP or somewhat later.

Like many Neandertal remains, the Krapina fossils were excavated more than a century ago. Not all such early excavations were carefully done. Fortunately, the excavator of the Krapina site—the Croatian paleontologist Dragutin Gorjanović-Kramberger (see Figure 8.14)—was extraordinarily meticulous in his recording of the excavation. During the period in which he excavated the site, 1899–1905, he kept detailed notes

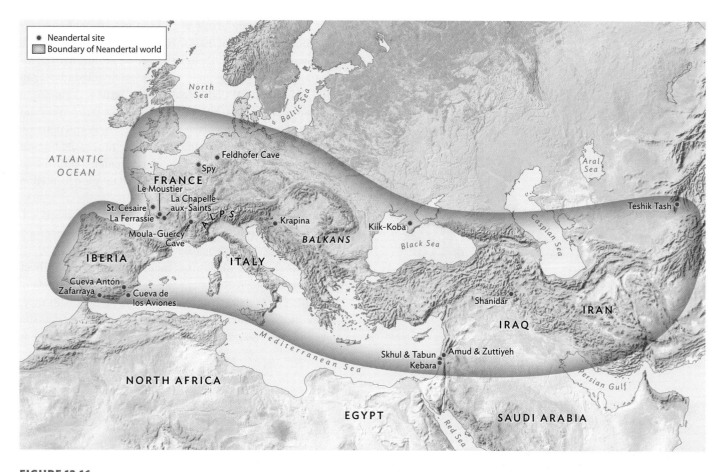

FIGURE 12.16

Neandertal Sites This map illustrates the various locations of Neandertal discoveries throughout southern and middle Europe and the Middle East as well as the suggested boundaries of the Neandertal range.

about where his workers found fossils and stone tools. He was especially careful in recording the stratigraphic locations of the several hundred bones and teeth found at the site.

The Krapina remains were recovered from a series of strata inside a rockshelter (not quite a cave—a rock overhang provides protection from the elements). The remains are highly fragmentary, making it difficult to identify key physical characteristics. The most complete cranium, Krapina 3, has the typical Neandertal features: round eye orbits, wide space between the eye orbits, wide nasal aperture, and protruding midfacial region (**Figure 12.18**). The Krapina front teeth are the largest of any known fossil hominin. In fact, tooth size comparisons with earlier and later humans in Europe indicate that in these Neandertals, the front teeth had increased and the back teeth had decreased. The front teeth are some of the biggest in human evolution.

The Krapina bones are mostly in fragments. The American anthropologist Tim White has found that some of these fragments display a series of distinctive cutmarks in places where ligaments (the tissue that connects muscle to bone) were severed with stone tools. The location and pattern of cutmarks on the Krapina Neandertal bones are identical to those on animal bones found at the site. That strategically placed cutmarks appear on human and animal bones indicates that these people ate animal *and* human tissue.

FIGURE 12.17

Krapina Croatian paleontologist Dragutin Gorjanovic-Kramberger and his team discovered more than 800 Neandertal fossils at this site. This image shows one of several monuments in present-day Krapina marking where the fossils were found.

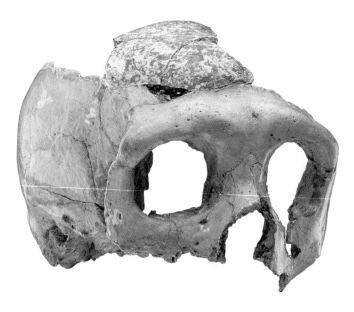

FIGURE 12.18

Krapina Neandertal This Krapina cranium has many features associated with Neandertals. Can you identify the key features that characterize it as Neandertal? (Photo © David L. Brill, humanoriginsphotos.com)

The Krapina Neandertals were not the only ones to practice cannibalism. From at least three other sites in Europe—the Moula-Guercy Cave in southeastern France, El Sidrón in northern Spain, and Goyet in Belgium—multiple individuals dating to 100,000 and 45,000 yBP display cutmark patterns very similar to those on animal remains (**Figure 12.19**). The cutmarks on cranial and postcranial bones involved removal of tissue and marrow extraction. Unlike other settings where the processed human and animal bones are mixed, the Neandertal remains at El Sidrón are not associated with animal remains, and they are located in a remote area of a complex system of caves.

Scientists cannot explain why cannibalism was practiced, but perhaps Neandertals ate human flesh to survive severe food shortages during their occupation of Ice Age Europe.

Many Neandertal skeletons, including some of the best known from western Europe, are relatively late, postdating 60,000 yBP. The skeleton from La Chapelle-aux-Saints, France, is especially well known because anthropologists used it as the prototype for all Neandertals in the early twentieth century. It

(a)

(b)

FIGURE 12.19

Moula-Guercy Neandertal fossils from this French cave site show evidence of butchery and, possibly, cannibalism. **(a)** The French archaeologist Alban Defleur examines the fragmentary remains of at least six cannibalized Neandertals. **(b)** Using a scanning electron microscope, researchers were able to closely examine cutmarks from a stone tool on a Neandertal cranial bone.

has the characteristic Neandertal cranial morphology, including a very wide and tall nasal aperture, a projecting midface, an occipital bun, and a low, long skull (**Figure 12.20**).

THE NEANDERTAL BODY PLAN: ABERRANT OR ADAPTED? The La Chapelle-aux-Saints skeleton is also one of the most complete Neandertals. The skeleton was first described in great detail by the eminent French paleoanthropologist Marcellin Boule (1861–1942) in the early 1900s. Professor Boule's scientific writings tremendously influenced contemporary and later scientists' interpretations of Neandertal phylogeny, behavior, and place in human evolution generally, basically continuing the earlier opinions expressed by Virchow (discussed at the start of this chapter). Boule argued that the Neandertal cranial and postcranial traits were simply too primitive and too different from modern people's to have provided the ancestral basis for later human evolution (**Figure 12.21**). He concluded that the La Chapelle individual must have walked with a bent-kneed gait—as in chimpanzees that walk bipedally—and could not have been able to speak. Simply, in his mind, Neandertals represented some side branch of human evolution—they were too primitive, too stupid, and too aberrant to have evolved into modern humans.

Boule's interpretations led to the prevailing view at the time (still held by some authorities) that Neandertals were evolutionary dead ends, replaced by the emerging modern humans and representing distant cousins of humanity that were not able to survive. In rejecting this view, we should take a closer look at some topics Boule addressed in his study of the La Chapelle skeleton.

One very distinctive feature of Neandertal faces is the *enormous* nasal aperture (**Figure 12.22**). The great size of the nasal aperture in many Neandertal fossils

FIGURE 12.20

La Chapelle-aux-Saints Neandertal Like Shanidar 1, this skull and the associated skeleton shows evidence of healed injuries and arthritis.

(a)

(b)

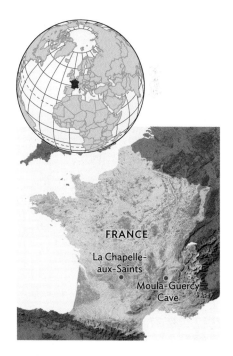

FIGURE 12.21

Neandertal Depictions **(a)** The La Chapelle-aux-Saints skeleton, here fleshed out by an illustrator in 1909, reinforced the notion that Neandertals were too stupid and too brutish to have evolved into modern humans. **(b)** More recent reconstructions show that Neandertals looked very similar to modern humans in many respects. In addition, estimates of brain size put them squarely within the modern human range.

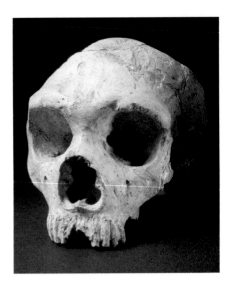

FIGURE 12.22

Nasal Aperture The large nasal aperture of Neandertal crania, such as this cranium from Gibraltar, may have been a cold adaptation.

indicates that these people had huge noses, in both width and projection. Such massive noses were one of the cranial characteristics that led Boule to believe that Neandertals were not related to later humans in an evolutionary sense. However, nasal features are more likely part of an adaptive complex reflecting life in cold climates during the Upper Pleistocene. The shape and size of any nose is an excellent example of the human face's highly adaptable nature, especially in relation to climate. One of the nose's important functions is to transform ambient air—the air breathed in from the atmosphere—into warm, humid air. Large noses have more internal surface area, thus providing an improved means of warming and moistening the cold, dry air that Neandertals breathed regularly. Moreover, the projecting nose typical of Neandertals placed more distance between the cold external environment and the brain, which is temperature-sensitive. Alternatively, the large noses of Neandertals may simply be due to the fact that their faces are so large. Regardless of the circumstances resulting in Neandertals' having large nasal apertures, many people and populations around the world today have wide, big noses, which are integral parts of their robust faces. These attributes are not uniquely Neandertal (**Figure 12.23**).

Other features of Neandertal skeletons are consistent with adaptation to cold. For example, the infraorbital foramina—the small holes in the facial bones located beneath the eye orbits—are larger in European Neandertals than in modern people (**Figure 12.24**). The foramina's increased size is due to the blood vessels that tracked through them having been quite large. The larger blood vessels may have allowed greater blood flow to the face, preventing exposed facial surfaces from freezing.

Most distinctive about the cold-adaptation complex in Neandertals are the shape of the body trunk and the length of the arms and legs. Compared with modern humans, European Neandertals were stocky—the body was short, wide, and deep (**Figure 12.25**). Neandertals' limbs were shorter than earlier or later humans'. This combination—stocky trunk and short limbs—is predicted by Bergmann's and Allen's rules (see "Climate Adaptation: Living on the Margins" in chapter 5). That is, animals that live in cold climates are larger than animals that live in hot climates (Bergmann's rule). The larger body trunk reduces the amount of surface area relative to the body size. This helps promote heat retention. Moreover, animals that live in cold climates have shorter limbs than animals that live in hot climates (Allen's rule). This, too, promotes heat retention in cold settings.

FIGURE 12.23

Modern Human Relatives? Some of the morphological traits associated with Neandertals can be found in modern humans, as illustrated by this photograph of the physical anthropologist Milford Wolpoff facing the reconstructed head of a European Neandertal. Might Neandertals have interbred with modern human ancestors, passing along some of these traits?

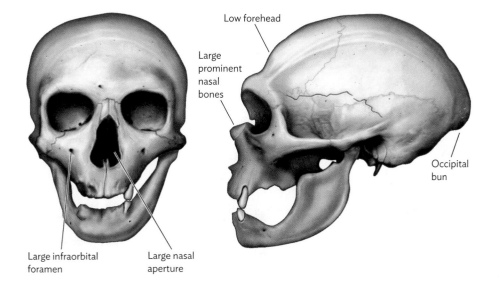

Low forehead

Large prominent nasal bones

Occipital bun

Large infraorbital foramen

Large nasal aperture

FIGURE 12.24
Cold-Adaptive Traits Large infraorbital foramina are among the Neandertal traits that likely were responses to a cold environment during the later Pleistocene. Note also the distinctive Neandertal traits—low forehead and projecting occipital bone (occipital bun).

Mousterian The stone tool culture in which Neandertals produced tools using the Levallois technique.

Middle Paleolithic The middle part of the Old Stone Age, associated with Mousterian tools, which Neandertals produced using the Levallois technique.

Levallois A distinctive method of stone tool production used during the Middle Paleolithic, in which the core was prepared and flakes removed from the surface before the final tool was detached from the core.

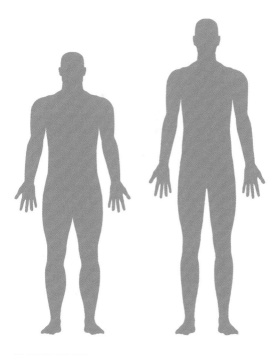

FIGURE 12.25
Neandertal Body Proportions A further adaptation to the cold appears in Neandertals' body proportions (left) compared with early modern humans' (right). Neandertals' much stockier body build reduced heat loss and increased heat retention. Early modern humans' narrower trunk, narrower hips, and longer legs reflected the warmer environment in which these people lived.

The American physical anthropologist Christopher Ruff has refined these concepts in interpreting human body shape morphology. He discovered that adaptation to heat or cold is not related to a person's height—some heat-adapted populations are quite tall, and some are quite short. Much more important is the width of the body trunk (usually measured at the hips), because the ratio of surface area to body mass is maintained regardless of height (**Figure 12.26**). This finding is borne out by a wide range of populations around the world today: populations living in the same climate all have body trunks of the same width, no matter how their heights vary. Populations living in cold climates always have wide bodies; populations living in warm climates always have narrow bodies. These dimensions are always constant in adaptation to heat or cold. In addition, the ratio of tibia (lower leg) length to femur (upper leg) length differs between people who live in hot climates and people who live in cold climates. Heat-adapted populations have long tibias relative to their femurs (their legs are long), but cold-adapted populations have short tibias relative to their femurs (their legs are short). Neandertals fit the predictions for cold adaptation: their body trunks are wide, and their tibias are short.

NEANDERTAL HUNTING: INEFFICIENT OR SUCCESSFUL? The French paleoanthropologists of the 1800s and early 1900s questioned Neandertals' humanness. They suggested that Neandertals were unintelligent, could not speak, and had a simplistic culture. Put in the vernacular expression, "Their lights were on, but nobody was home." Some paleoanthropologists continue to argue this point, viewing Neandertals as inefficient hunters and not especially well adapted to their environments. A growing body of archaeological and biological evidence, however, demonstrates that Neandertals were not clumsy mental deficients.

Neandertals were associated with the culture known as **Mousterian** or **Middle Paleolithic.** This culture's stone tool technology, lasting from about 300,000–30,000 yBP, includes a complex and distinctive type of flaking called the **Levallois** technique. This technique involves preparing a stone core and then flaking the raw materials for tools from this core (**Figure 12.27**). Contrary to the opinions of early anthropologists, this Neandertal technology was complex and required considerable hand–eye coordination. Moreover, anthropologists are learning that late Neandertals participated fully

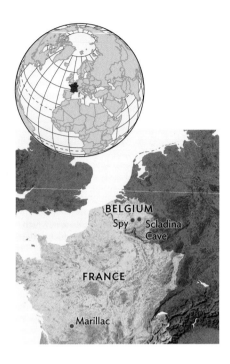

Modern Inuit
(260 cm²/kg)

Modern Nilotic
(301 cm²/kg)

Modern Pygmy
(314 cm²/kg)

FIGURE 12.26

Body Size and Body Shape The refinement of Bergmann's and Allen's rules regarding body size, body shape, and temperature adaptations is illustrated by these body types. The ratio of body surface area to body mass (square centimeters per kilogram) is given below each type. The greater the ratio, the more that body shape and that body size are adaptations to high temperatures. Individuals living in cold environments, such as the modern Inuit, have a lower ratio than individuals living in hot environments, such as the modern Nilotic. Because of their short stature, modern Pygmies appear to contradict Bergmann's and Allen's rules. However, body surface ratio reveals that Pygmies are well adapted to hot environments.

Upper Paleolithic Refers to the most recent part of the Old Stone Age, associated with early modern *Homo sapiens* and characterized by finely crafted stone and other types of tools with various functions.

in the **Upper Paleolithic,** the earliest cultures associated mostly with early modern *H. sapiens* in Europe, producing stone tools that were modern in many respects and certainly as complex as those produced by early modern humans. Moreover, the size, shape, and articulations of the Neandertal hand reflect the kind of precise manual dexterity crucial for the fine crafting of tools (**Figure 12.28**).

If Neandertals were not effective hunters, then they might have been less successful adaptively than modern people. One way to measure hunting success is to determine how much meat Neandertals ate. Butchered animals' bones are abundant in Neandertal habitation sites, indicating that Neandertals hunted the animals and processed the carcasses for food. Suggestive though this evidence is, the mere presence of animal remains does not reveal how *important* animals were in the people's diet. To find out how important meat was in Neandertals' diets, anthropologists have applied the powerful tools of bone chemistry and stable isotope analysis. Measurement of stable isotopes of both nitrogen and carbon in the bones of Neandertals—from Scladina Cave (Belgium), Vindija Cave (Croatia), and Marillac (France)—indicates that Neandertals ate lots of meat, at or nearly at the level of carnivores living at the same

A large stone of flint is chosen.

Small flakes are removed from the stone's perimeter using an antler or other tool.

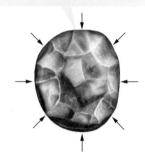

One side of the stone has flakes removed from the entire surface, giving it the appearance of a tortoise shell.

A heavy, specific blow is directed at one end of the stone, removing a large flake. This flake is convex on one side and flat on the other.

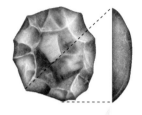

This flake can now be used for scraping or cutting. Further flake removal will produce a more specialized tool.

FIGURE 12.27

Levallois Technique To produce the Mousterian tools, Neandertals used a specific technique to remove flakes from flint cores. The use of such a technique indicates that Neandertals could visualize the shape and size of a tool from a stone core, an advanced cognitive ability.

time and place (**Figure 12.29**). The chemical signature of diet, then, is a powerful indicator of Neandertals' effectiveness in acquiring and consuming animal protein. That is, it shows that Neandertals were successful hunters. This is not to say that Neandertals depended wholly on animals as sources of food. Analysis of plant residues

FIGURE 12.28

Mousterian Tools Neandertals made these tools out of flint. The use of such tools would have replaced the use of front teeth as tools, reducing the amount of anterior tooth wear in some later Neandertals. (Photo © David L. Brill, humanoriginsphotos.com)

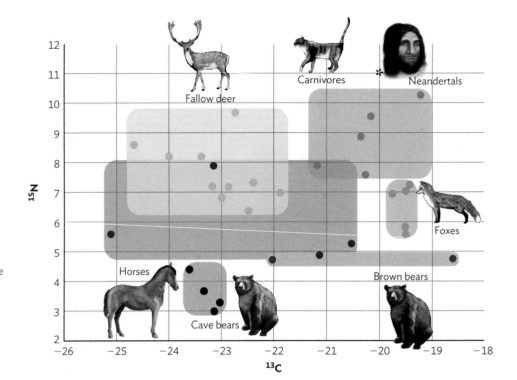

FIGURE 12.29

Neandertal Diet Measures of stable isotopes of both carbon and nitrogen, here labeled ¹³C and ¹⁵N, respectively, can be used to determine the relative amounts of different kinds of foods consumed. This graph shows the isotope values for a variety of herbivores and carnivores. Herbivores generally have lower isotope values than carnivores. Neandertals' isotope values (asterisk) are close to those of known carnivores, indicating that Neandertals ate plenty of meat.

calculus Refers to hardened plaque on teeth; the condition is caused by the minerals from saliva being continually deposited on tooth surfaces.

found in Neandertal tooth **calculus** shows that Neandertals ate a diversity of plants, some of which were cooked. Neandertals might have consumed some of these plants for medicinal purposes. The British archaeologist Karen Hardy and her associates have documented in calculus from El Sidrón the presence of bitter-tasting chemicals that are well-known appetite suppressants. The presence of residues of plants that lack nutritional value indicates that Neandertals might have self-medicated, but we cannot know for sure if they did.

Another indicator of their effective adaptation is the measurement of stress levels. The American physical anthropologist Debbie Guatelli-Steinberg and her associates found that hypoplasias, the stress markers in teeth that reflect growth disruption due to poor diets or poor health, are present in Neandertals but at a frequency no different from that of modern humans. This finding, too, suggests that Neandertals dealt successfully with their environments.

NEANDERTALS BURIED THEIR DEAD In many Neandertal sites, the remains have been found scattered about, commingled and concurrent with living areas. For example, the Krapina Neandertal fossils are fragmentary and were scattered throughout the site. That is, the deceased were treated no differently from food remains or anything else being discarded. In contrast, a significant number of skeletons have been found in pits. That is, excavation of some Neandertal sites in Europe and western Asia has shown that pits had been dug, corpses had been placed in the pits, and the pits had been filled in. For example, the Neandertal skeletons from Spy, Belgium; ones from various sites in France, such as La Chapelle-aux-Saints; several Shanidar individuals; and the Neandertals from Amud and Tabun, both in Israel, were found in burial pits (**Figure 12.30**).

Was burial of the dead a religious or ceremonial activity having significant symbolic meaning for the living? Or was burial simply a means of removing bodies from living spaces? Most of the intentionally buried skeletons were in flexed (fetal-oriented) postures. The hands and arms were carefully positioned, and the bodies were typically on their sides or backs. This vigilant treatment indicates that care was taken to place

FIGURE 12.30

Intentional Burial Like the Shanidar skeletons (among others), the La Chapelle-aux-Saints skeleton, shown here, provides evidence of intentional burial. When this individual was found in a pit, it was the first suggestion that Neandertals cared for their dead in a way similar to modern humans' methods.

the bodies in the prepared pits. The skeletons' postures suggest, therefore, that these burials were not just disposals. They represented purposeful symbolic behavior linking those who died and those who were living.

NEANDERTALS TALKED Fundamental to human behavior is the ability to speak as part of the repertoire of communication. Conversation is a key way that we present information and exchange ideas. Because early anthropologists believed that Neandertals lacked the ability to speak, they argued that Neandertals were not related to modern people in an evolutionary sense. This idea continues to the present. The American linguist Philip Lieberman and the American anatomist Edmund Crelin, for example, have reconstructed the Neandertal vocal tract. Because their reconstruction resembles a modern newborn infant's vocal tract, Lieberman and Crelin conclude that, like human babies, Neandertals could not express the full range of sounds necessary for articulate speech. Although interesting, their reconstruction of the Neandertal vocal tract is conjectural. Based on skulls alone, it necessarily lacks the anatomical parts (soft tissues) important for determining whether Neandertals had speech.

Indeed, one compelling line of evidence suggests that Neandertals were, in fact, able to speak. The Kebara Neandertal skeleton includes the hyoid bone, a part of the neck that can survive from ancient settings. Various muscles and ligaments attach it to the skull, mandible, tongue, larynx, and pharynx, collectively producing speech (**Figure 12.31**). The morphology of the Kebara Neandertal's hyoid is identical to that of a living human's. The Kebara people talked.

Even more convincing evidence that Neandertals spoke are findings from the study of microscopic wear patterns on the surfaces of incisors and canines, especially the study of the relationship with brain laterality. The human brain is distinctive in its laterality: the clearly defined left and right sides are an anatomical marker for the ability to speak. In right-handed humans, the left side of the brain is dominant. The left brain controls right-sided body movements, especially the use of the right hand and right arm. The left brain also controls speech and language production. In left-handed people, these connections are reversed. The right side of the brain is dominant, controls

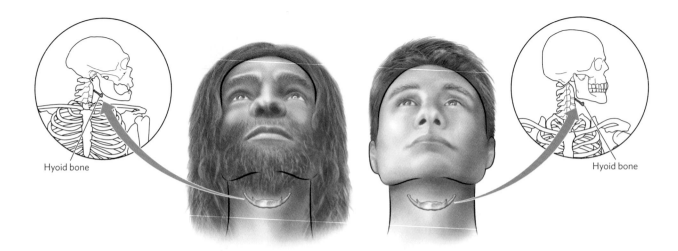

Hyoid bone

Hyoid bone

FIGURE 12.31

Did Neandertals Speak? The Kebara skeleton's hyoid is identical to a modern human hyoid, indicating that Neandertals could speak.

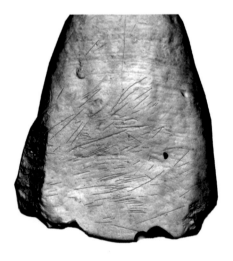

FIGURE 12.32

Handedness in Neandertals Shown here is an upper right first incisor of a Neandertal from the Vindija site in Croatia. The surface has more than 150 scratches (shown in red) produced by a stone tool rubbing against the tooth. Almost all the scratches are angled down toward the person's right. The red lines highlight the main scratches. This person had a left-dominant brain, was right-handed, and possessed the ability to speak.

left-side body movements, and controls areas critical for speech and language. Therefore, evidence of handedness (a preference for the right or left hand) is itself evidence for brain laterality. In fossil hominins, hand preference can be determined by looking at the scratches on the front teeth of fossil hominins.

The American physical anthropologist David Frayer and his associates have detected microscopic parallel scratches on the surfaces of upper incisors and canines of many fossil hominins, including Neandertals from Europe. It has long been thought that Neandertals (and lots of other hominins, including modern humans) used a "stuff-and-cut" method of meat processing before chewing the meat. This method consists of cutting a piece of meat by biting one end of it and holding the other end with the left hand, then holding a stone tool with the right hand to cut the meat. Often, cutting meat in this fashion inadvertently scratches the front teeth. When this happens, the scratches on the teeth have a highly distinctive pattern: they are parallel to each other, and they angle downward. When the stuff-and-cut method is performed experimentally, right-handed people end up with tooth scratches that angle downward to the right, and left-handed people end up with scratches that angle downward to the left.

Frayer and his research group examined the scratch patterns on the teeth of 17 Neandertals from different sites, finding that all but two of the Neandertals had scratch patterns consistent with right-handedness (**Figure 12.32**). The two exceptions had just the opposite, consistent with left-handedness. Similarly, in the early archaic *H. sapiens* from Sima de los Huesos dating to 500,000 yBP, all 12 individuals studied had the scratch pattern associated with handedness. The conclusion is simple: because Neandertals uniformly exhibited handedness, we know they had brain laterality. (As with modern humans today, most Neandertals and their predecessors had left-dominant brains and were right-handed.) And because they had brain laterality, we can conclude that Neandertals talked.

Genetic evidence also supports the notion that Neandertals spoke. The German geneticist Johannes Krause and his team successfully identified the *FOXP2* gene—a gene strongly implicated in the production of speech—from Neandertal bone samples from the El Sidrón site. Although it is not *the* gene for speech, it is part of a complex of genetic variation found in modern humans. Its presence in these late archaic *H. sapiens* indicates that Neandertals talked.

Archaic *Homo sapiens*

Archaic *H. sapiens* are the first of our species, beginning some 350,000 yBP globally and evolving locally from earlier *H. erectus* populations. After 150,000 yBP, regional patterns of diversity emerge, followed by simultaneous occupation of Europe by late archaic *H. sapiens* (Neandertals) and early modern *H. sapiens* by 40,000 yBP.

Locations (sites)*	Africa (Kabwe)
	Asia (Ngandong, Dali, Narmada, *Amud, Kebara, Tabun, Shanidar*)
	Europe (Sima de los Huesos, Swanscombe, Steinheim, Petralona, Arago, *Feldhofer Cave*, Atapuerca, *Spy, Krapina, Vindija, Moula-Guercy, La Chapelle-aux-Saints, Scladina Cave, Marillac, Les Rochers, Engis, El Sidrón, Monte Lessini, Teshik Tash*)
Chronology	350,000–30,000 yBP
Biology	Mixture of *H. erectus* and *H. sapiens* characteristics
	1,200 cc cranial capacity early
	1,500 cc cranial capacity late
	Both skulls and skeletons less robust than modern humans
	Reduced tooth size, but most of reduction in premolars and molars (front teeth increase in size)
	Appearance of Neandertal morphology after 130,000 yBP in Middle East and Europe (long, low skull; wide, large nose; large front teeth with common heavy wear; forward-projecting face; no chin; wide body trunk; short limbs)
	Distinctive mtDNA structure
	Distinctive nDNA structure but overlapping with living humans'
Culture and behavior	Some evidence of housing structures
	Large-game hunting
	Fishing and use of aquatic resources after 100,000 yBP
	More advanced form of Acheulian early
	Mousterian late (Europe)
	Increased use of various raw materials besides stone after 100,000 yBP
	Skilled tool production
	Burial of deceased after 100,000 yBP
	Symbolic behavior
	Social care of sick and injured
	Articulate speech likely

*Sites mentioned in text; italics denote sites where Neandertal (late archaic *H. sapiens*) remains have been found.

NEANDERTALS USED SYMBOLS Burial of the dead is only one of the countless contexts in which modern humans use symbolism. Think, for example, of all the signs, images, and codes you encounter every day, from the letters on this page to any jewelry you wear to your friend's tattoo. Decorative items such as perforated shells, some stained with pigments of various colors, have been well documented in the earlier Paleolithic in Africa and the Middle East, dating to 120,000—70,000 yBP. A number of anthropologists have suggested that Neandertals differed from modern *H. sapiens* in that they lacked symbolic behavior. This lack, in turn, is seen as a feature of Neandertals' purported cognitive inferiority to *H. sapiens*. However, the Spanish archaeologist João Zilhão and his colleagues have recently discovered clear evidence of symbolic behavior at two sites in Spain that date to 50,000 yBP. At Cueva de los Aviones and Cueva Antón, perforated marine shells similar to those in Africa and the Middle East had been painted with naturally occurring pigments, especially red, yellow, and orange. These shells were likely strung around an individual's neck. These body ornaments are evidence that Neandertals used symbolism at least 10,000 years before the appearance of modern *H. sapiens* in Europe. In addition, red ochre—a pigment derived from the mineral hematite—was used by hominins at least by 250,000 yBP in a range of European hominin contexts. Neandertals used symbols to communicate ideas and expressions.

The key point of this discussion of Neandertal characteristics—relating to climate adaptation, material culture, efficiency in hunting strategies, access to animal protein, treatment of the deceased, and the use of speech and symbolism—is that Neandertals likely were not weird humanlike primates, less adaptable and less intelligent than modern humans. The record shows that their behaviors, both in form and in symbol, were similar to modern humans'. The size and robusticity of their long bones show that Neandertals were highly physically active, more so than living humans. Such cultural and biological features reflect Neandertals' success in adapting to environmental circumstances of the Upper Pleistocene, not evolutionary failure. The empirical evidence disproves arguments that Neandertals were less than human.

Early Modern *Homo sapiens*

Modern *H. sapiens* from the Upper Pleistocene are represented in the fossil record throughout Africa, Asia, and Europe. During this time, hominins moved into other areas of the world. Later in this period, they spread into regions with extreme environments, such as the arctic tundra of Siberia in northern Asia. It was a time of significant increases in population size, increased ability through cultural means of adapting to

---

Table 12.1 Timeline for Major Upper Paleolithic Cultures of Europe

The Aurignacian (45,000–30,000 yBP)

- Associated with the first anatomically modern humans in Europe

The Gravettian (30,000–20,000 yBP)

- The Perigordian in France
- Earliest art, in the form of carved figurines
- Lagar Velho burial in Portugal

The Solutrean (21,000–17,000 yBP)

- France and Spain during the last glacial peak
- Made very fine stone points

The Magdalenian (17,000–12,000 yBP)

- Successful hunters of reindeer and horses
- Spread out across Europe as conditions improved at the end of the Ice Age
- Made many of the spectacular paintings and carvings

(a)

(b)

(c)

FIGURE 12.33

Chauvet Cave Art **(a)** Chauvet Cave is located a half-mile from the Pont d'Arc, a natural bridge in France's Ardèche River valley. The extensive cave system contains more than 400 images of late Pleistocene animals, especially lions, mammoths, and rhinoceroses. **(b)** Rhinos and lions are among the animals depicted in this Ardèche cave painting, which is about 30,000 years old. **(c)** Upper Paleolithic tools, such as these, include some of the forms seen in earlier periods of human evolution. However, new tools reflect the procurement of additional types of food, such as the barbed harpoon for catching fish. (Tool photos [c] © 1985 David L. Brill, humanoriginsphotos.com)

new and difficult landscapes, and the development of new technologies and subsistence strategies. (**Table 12.1** lists the four major Upper Paleolithic cultures of Europe and important events associated with each.) The cultures of the later Pleistocene, grouped in the Upper Paleolithic, are also known from their stunning imagery, including hundreds of artistic works in caves throughout Europe but concentrated especially in France and Spain (**Figure 12.33**). This period of human evolution also includes the universal appearance of the modern anatomical characteristics discussed at the beginning of this chapter. That is, in comparison with early archaic *H. sapiens*, there is a clear trend of increasing brain size and decreasing face, tooth, and jaw size and robusticity (**Table 12.2**). In addition, the postcranial bones become more gracile. Modern humans' evolution started much earlier in Africa than in Europe and Asia.

EARLY MODERN *HOMO SAPIENS* IN AFRICA (200,000–6,000 YBP) The African record for early *H. sapiens* is especially important because it includes the earliest evidence of modern people's anatomical characteristics. Crucially important fossil hominins from this time come from the Herto, Aduma, and Bouri sites in Ethiopia's Middle Awash Valley and from Omo in southern Ethiopia. The remains from Herto—partial skulls of two adults and of a child, dating to 160,000–154,000 yBP—show a

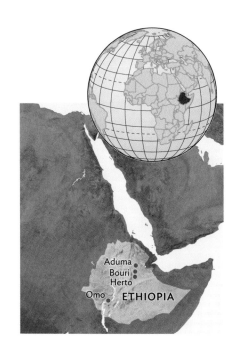

INJURY, OCCUPATION,

Learning about the Past from the Living

Humans' injury patterns tell quite a lot about particular societies' behavior, especially with regard to the risks of specific lifestyles or of specific occupations.

Some lifestyles and occupations are relatively risk-free. For example, office workers tend to suffer few injuries, aside from carpal tunnel syndrome, in which a nerve to the wrist is somehow squeezed and hampers hand function. Some lifestyles and occupations are prone to producing injuries, however. For example, construction workers, dancers, and professional football players are subject to fractures and joint injuries and are susceptible to arthritis.

Forensic anthropologists will examine a skeleton carefully to see what kinds of injuries the person sustained in life, assessing behavior patterns or a kind of occupation (or both) that may have caused the injuries. Specific bone injuries have been used to identify remains and to solve murders.

The American anthropologists Thomas Berger and Erik Trinkaus have noticed that Neandertal fossils tend to show lots of injuries. In fact, nearly every complete Neandertal skeleton displays some traumatic injury. For example, the Shanidar 1 skeleton (see "Late Archaic *Homo sapiens* in Asia (60,000–40,000 yBP)" earlier in the chapter) has numerous head injuries. Injuries around the left eye orbit may have been so severe that they affected this adult male's balance and even blinded that eye.

Most Neandertal injuries are in the upper body and the head. Given this very obvious pattern, Berger and Trinkaus compared the trauma in Neandertals with statistical data on injury patterns for various occupations, using workers' compensation and other records. They found a close match between the Neandertal injury pattern and an injury pattern associated with

cranial capacity of about 1,450 cc, close to the average for modern humans (**Figure 12.34**). In addition, many of the characteristics are essentially modern, including a relatively tall cranium, a vertical forehead, smaller browridges, and a nonprojecting face. Among the archaic features are significant browridges (though the trend is toward smaller) and a relatively long face. These remains may be from the earliest modern people in Africa or at least close to the earliest. German paleoanthropologist Günter Bräuer argues that modernization in Africa first took place in East Africa. The remains' overall appearance indicates that modern people emerged in Africa long before their arrival in Europe and western Asia. The remains from Omo may be as old as 195,000 yBP. If so, they are the oldest evidence of anatomically modern humans.

AND BEHAVIOR

a specific occupation in the United States. The Neandertal pattern resembles that of rodeo athletes, the people who ride angry broncos and bulls as a form of sport! Rodeo riders have lots of head and neck injuries resulting from the obvious—they get tossed off animals and sometimes land on their own heads and upper bodies. Does this similarity mean that Neandertals rode animals, either for sport or for transportation? Quite unlikely. Because Neandertals hunted with spears, Berger and Trinkaus suggest that they would have placed themselves in close proximity to the large animals they were hunting. Neandertal injuries, Berger and Trinkaus hypothesize, derived from contacts with enraged animals during hunts. Just like rodeo riding and other physically challenging pursuits, life for these Pleistocene hunters was tough! *Anthropology matters!*

The Neandertal injury pattern is similar to that of American rodeo riders, such as this tumbling bull rider. By comparing Neandertals and modern humans, anthropologists can gain insight into the physical risks Neandertals faced.

However, their dating is uncertain because the fossils were not positioned in the geologic context as clearly as the Herto fossils were.

Belonging to later contexts are the partial skulls from Aduma and Bouri, dating to about 105,000–80,000 yBP. Like the Herto skulls, these skulls have both premodern and modern characteristics. However, the most complete Aduma skull is modern in nearly every characteristic.

Skulls from two key locations in southern Africa provide important information about early modern *H. sapiens* that date to after 100,000 yBP. Among the fragmentary remains from Klasies River Mouth Cave, anthropologists have documented the presence of a chin, a distinctively modern characteristic, that dates to at least 90,000 yBP

12.34

The First Modern Humans:

BIOLOGY AND BEHAVIOR

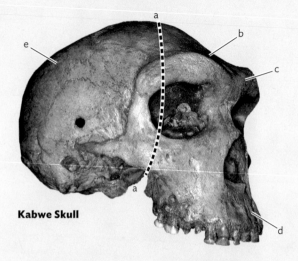

Kabwe Skull

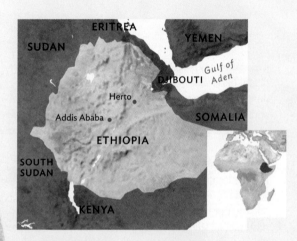

BEHAVIOR: HUNTING AND BUTCHERING

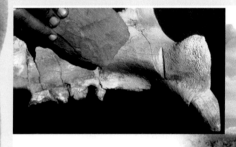

These early modern *Homo sapiens* were skilled hunters. They produced sophisticated stone tools (above) used for killing and butchering large game, such as hippopotamuses living along lake margins. At the Herto site, Tim White, Berhane Asfaw, Giday Wolde Gabriel, Yonas Beyene, and their team found more than 600 stone tools. These tools had multiple functions, mostly relating to the killing and butchering of animals for food.

Herto Reconstruction
© 2005 Jay H. Matternes

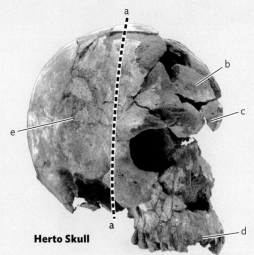

Herto Skull

© David L. Brill, humanoriginsphotos.com

	Skull characteristics	Kabwe 300,000 yBP	Herto 160,000 yBP
a	Braincase	Shorter	Taller
b	Forehead	Less vertical	More vertical
c	Browridge	Larger	Smaller
d	Face	Projecting	Retracted
e	Brain size	Smaller	Larger

Near the village of Herto, in the Middle Awash region of Ethiopia, the paleoanthropology team discovered hundreds of hominid skull fragments dating to about 160,000 yBP. When pieced together, the skull proved to be remarkably modern (see the drawing on the facing page). In contrast to earlier hominids, such as Kabwe (found in Zambia and dating to 300,000 yBP), Herto has a tall braincase, a vertical forehead, small browridges, a retracted face, and a large brain. In combination, these are definitive characteristics of modern people. White and his team had found the first modern human.

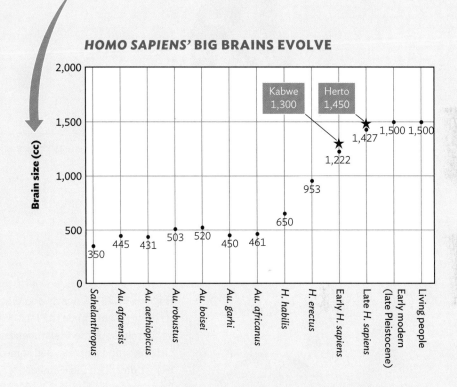

HOMO SAPIENS' BIG BRAINS EVOLVE

Brain size (cc)

Kabwe 1,300 — Herto 1,450

1,500 — 1,500

1,427

1,222

953

650

350 — 445 — 431 — 503 — 520 — 450 — 461

Sahelanthropus · *Au. afarensis* · *Au. aethiopicus* · *Au. robustus* · *Au. boisei* · *Au. garhi* · *Au. africanus* · *H. habilis* · *H. erectus* · Early *H. sapiens* · Late *H. sapiens* · Early modern (late Pleistocene) · Living people

Paleoanthropologists are learning that the stone tools used by the Herto people for butchering animals were also used for other purposes. The skull bones from a second adult display cutmarks made by stone tools on the face, front, side, and back, all created when flesh was removed from the skull (see the black-and-white photos at the right). This could have been done as part of some ancient ritual. The cutmarks are similar to ones found in skulls from New Guinea and from other places where the people were known to have practiced cannibalism.

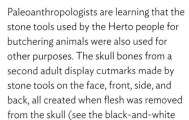

Table 12.2 Trends from Early Archaic *Homo sapiens* to Early Modern *Homo sapiens*

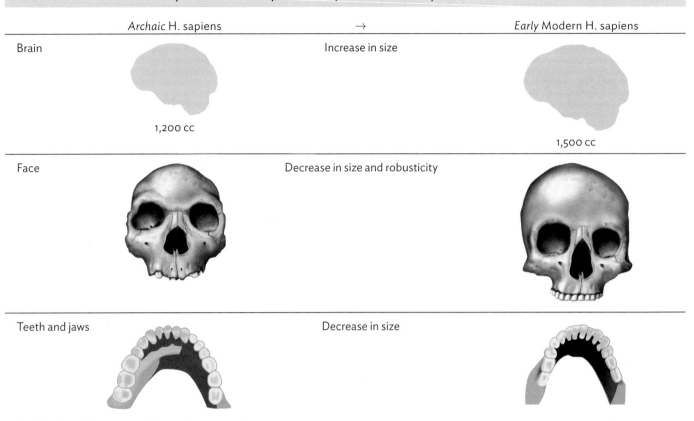

	Archaic H. sapiens	→	*Early* Modern H. sapiens
Brain	1,200 CC	Increase in size	1,500 CC
Face		Decrease in size and robusticity	
Teeth and jaws		Decrease in size	

(**Figure 12.35**). A nearly complete skull from Hofmeyr, dating to 36,000 yBP, bears a striking resemblance to Pleistocene modern Europeans.

Throughout the Pleistocene and well into the early Holocene, African hominins, although modern, retained some robusticity. For example, the skulls from Lothagam, Kenya, dating to the Holocene (ca. 9,000–6,000 yBP), are robust compared with living East Africans' (**Figure 12.36**). During this period, a number of characteristics seen in the region's living populations were present, such as wide noses. At Wadi Kubbaniya and Wadi Halfa, both in the Nile Valley, populations have some very robust characteristics, such as flaring cheekbones and well-developed browridges. These features contrast sharply with the gracile facial features seen later in the Holocene and in living people (these features are discussed further in chapter 13).

Similarly, the earlier Holocene skulls (ca. 9,500 yBP) found at Gobero, Niger, are long, low, and robust compared with later Holocene skulls from the same place (**Figure 12.37**). A later population of incipient pastoralists may have replaced the earlier hunter-gatherers. However, the reduction in robusticity more likely reflects evolution that occurred in this setting (see chapter 13).

EARLY MODERN *HOMO SAPIENS* IN ASIA (100,000–18,000 YBP) The earliest modern *H. sapiens* in Asia are best represented by fossils from western Asia, in fact from the same region as the Amud and Kebara Neandertals in Israel. The 90,000-year-old remains from Skhul have distinctively modern characteristics, suggesting that the people living there were modern *H. sapiens*. Among the most prominent remains from the site are several male skulls, of which Skhul 5 is the most complete. That the Skhul 5

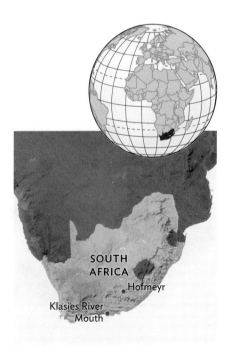

SOUTH
AFRICA
Hofmeyr
Klasies River
Mouth

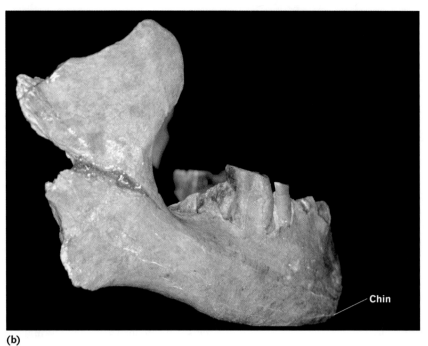

Chin

(a)

(b)

FIGURE 12.35

Klasies River Mouth Cave **(a)** Excavations at this site in southern Africa revealed evidence of early modern *Homo sapiens*. **(b)** One of the most important features found on these cranial remains is a chin on the mandible of this early modern *Homo sapiens* from South Africa.

cranium dates to before the Amud fossils indicates modern humans lived in the region before Neandertals (**Figure 12.38**).

Remains of the earliest modern people from eastern Asia are very scarce. Some of these remains are purported to be older than 60,000 yBP. At Zhiren Cave in south China, two molars and a partial mandible dating to at least 100,000 yBP show a combination of

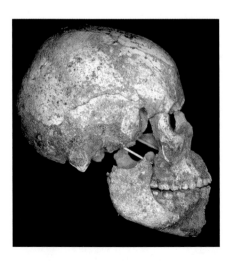

FIGURE 12.36

Lothagam Skull This Kenyan cranium illustrates early modern humans' rather robust nature. Note the projection both of the lower part of the front of the skull and of the mandible.

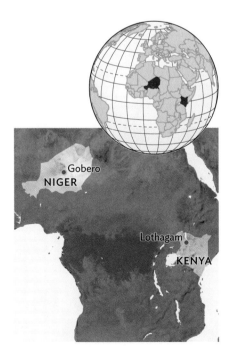

Gobero
NIGER

Lothagam
KENYA

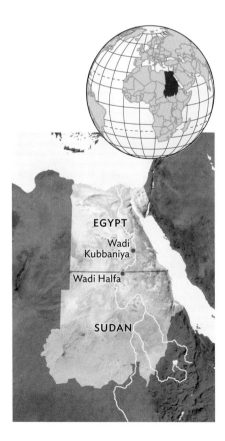

EGYPT

Wadi
Kubbaniya

Wadi Halfa

SUDAN

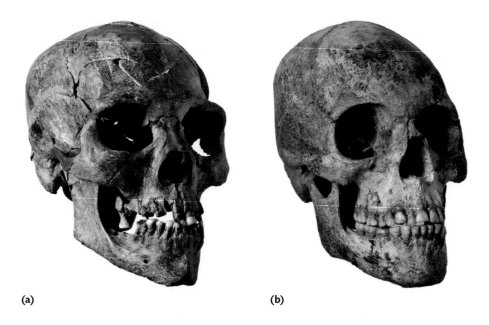

(a)   (b)

FIGURE 12.37

Gobero Crania **(a)** This adult male cranium from Gobero, dating to about 9,500 yBP, is long and low and has a wide, flat face. **(b)** In contrast, this adult male cranium, from the same site but dating to about 6,500 yBP (the middle Holocene), is high and has a narrow, gracile face. These differences could be due to local evolutionary change or the later arrival of a new population in the region having different craniofacial characteristics.

archaic and modern features. The mandible is relatively thick, like that of other archaic *H. sapiens*, but it has a chin like that of modern *H. sapiens*. Although not a fully modern *H. sapiens,* it is certainly a hominin that shows transitional characteristics leading to anatomical modernity. Other evidence for modern *H. sapiens* dates to 80,000 yBP from Fuyan Cave in south China. Although represented by just teeth, the morphology and relatively small size provides evidence for the presence of distinctively modern people in southern Asia, roughly contemporary with eastern Asia.

The earliest most complete fossil remains are a mandible and partial skeleton, dating to about 41,000 yBP, from Tianyuan Cave, China, and a skull dating to about 46,000 yBP from Tam Pa Ling Cave, Laos. Like the Zhiren Cave remains, these fossils have both archaic and modern features. For example, the Tam Pa Ling skull lacks a prominent

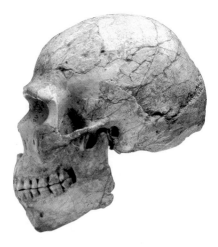

FIGURE 12.38

Skhul Cranium This skull possesses many characteristics associated with modern humans, including a chin, a less projecting face, small and gracile cheeks, and a high, vertical forehead. The browridges are still distinct but are much reduced compared with those of archaic *Homo sapiens*. (Photo © 1985 David L. Brill, humanoriginsphotos.com)

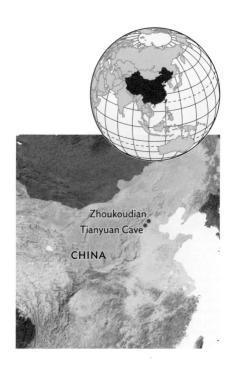

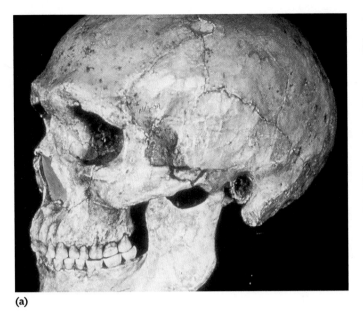 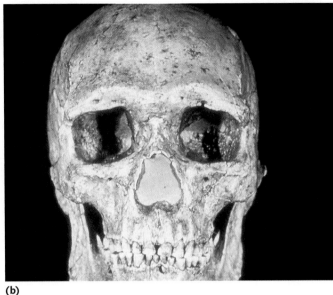

(a)　　　　　　　　　　　　　　　　　　　　(b)

FIGURE 12.39

Zhoukoudian Crania **(a, b)** One skull recovered from Zhoukoudian shows several modern human traits, but overall these crania are more robust than their modern Asian counterparts. In the older area of this site, the famous *Homo erectus* fossils were found prior to World War II.

supraorbital torus, a feature that is quite modern. Better known are three skulls from the Upper Cave at Zhoukoudian, China, dating to 29,000–24,000 yBP (**Figure 12.39**; this site is discussed further in chapter 11). The Upper Cave skulls are robust compared with living Asians', but the facial flatness is characteristic of native eastern Asians today. Similarly, the early modern people from Minatogawa (Okinawa), Japan, dating to about 18,000 yBP, are gracile but retain thick cranial bones and large browridges, especially compared with those of the later Holocene populations in eastern Asia.

ON THE MARGIN OF MODERNITY IN SOUTHEAST ASIA: *HOMO FLORESIENSIS* The discovery of skeletal remains dating to between 100,000 and 60,000 yBP from Liang Bua Cave on the island of Flores, Indonesia, may challenge long-standing conclusions about the evolution of modern people in far eastern Asia. In 2003, scientists found a skeleton with highly unusual characteristics (**Figure 12.40**). Dubbed the "Hobbit" by the popular press, this hominin had an extremely tiny brain (400 cc) and skull and stood only slightly above 1 m (3.3 ft). Anthropologists disagree on how to interpret these and other characteristics. The Australian anthropologists Peter Brown and Michael Morwood and colleagues regard the skeleton as evidence for the long-term presence of an archaic species of hominin, distinctive from modern people. In fact, they consider it a newfound species of *Homo,* which they call ***Homo floresiensis.*** In their interpretation of this dwarf species' existence, a group of primitive humans became isolated earlier in human evolution, and their isolation led to a unique pattern of biological variation.

Alternatively, the Indonesian paleoanthropologist Teuku Jacob and colleagues argue that this hominin was not part of a different species but a modern human who suffered from **microcephaly** or some other genetic or developmental abnormality. They point out that some cranial features of *H. floresiensis* are within the modern range of variation seen in living populations from the larger region. In addition, some of the creature's anatomical characteristics (such as a small or absent chin and rotated premolars) resemble those of populations now living in the immediate region.

There are strengths to both arguments for interpreting the remains of the hominin

Homo floresiensis Dubbed the "Hobbit" for its diminutive size, a possible new species of *Homo* found in Liang Bua Cave on the Indonesian island of Flores.

microcephaly A condition in which the cranium is abnormally small and the brain is underdeveloped.

FIGURE 12.40

Flores Woman A recent discovery on Flores Island, Indonesia, has become the source of much debate in anthropology. Some researchers believe this "Hobbit" represents a group of early hominins that evolved in isolation in the far western Pacific region. Others believe this skeleton belonged to a modern human who had some developmental or genetic abnormality. (Reconstruction photo [left] © 2007 Photographer P. Plailly/E. Daynès/Eurelios/Look at Sciences—Reconstruction Elisabeth Daynès, Paris)

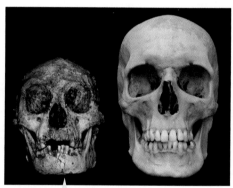

The cranium is very small, especially compared with that of a modern human.

This artist's reconstruction shows what Flores Woman may have looked like in life.

Based on measurements of the long bones, the Flores individual would have been approximately 1.0 m (slightly more than 3 ft) tall, considerably shorter than the average modern human.

from Liang Bua. However, the discovery of an earlier dwarf hominin from Mata Menge, also from Flores and dating to 700,000 years ago (see Chapter 11, pp. 386–87), suggests both the validity of a new species having deep temporal roots in the region and the strong possibility for an earlier ancestor of this hominin. Moreover, the similarities in tooth and body size of the Liang Bua and Mata Menge hominins argue for an ancestral-descendant relationship. Regardless of their interpretation, the hominin from Liang Bua and its predecessor dwarf hominin from Mata Menge represent a highly unusual morphology at the extremes of hominin variation in the middle to late Pleistocene.

EARLY MODERN *HOMO SAPIENS* IN EUROPE (35,000–15,000 YBP) Early modern people are known from various places throughout Europe. The earliest modern *H. sapiens* in Europe is from Peştera cu Oase, Romania, and dates to 35,000 yBP. The Oase 2 skull from that site is distinctively modern, contrasting with Neandertals that lived during the same time. For example, Oase 2 has very reduced browridges and a generally gracile appearance. Almost as old are remains from Mladeč, Předmostí, and Dolni Vestonice, all in the Czech Republic, dating to 35,000–26,000 yBP. The half-dozen Mladeč skulls (35,000 yBP) show remarkable variability, including a mix of Neandertal characteristics in some (occipital bun, low skull, large browridges, large front teeth, and thick bone) and modern characteristics in others (nonprojecting face, narrow nasal opening). The Předmostí and Dolni Vestonice skulls retain a few Neandertal characteristics, but they are clearly more modern in appearance than the Mladeč people (**Figure 12.41**). Some Neandertal features persist well into recent times in eastern Europe, especially in the facial region (**Figure 12.42**).

Western Europe has virtually no fossil record for the earliest modern people, those contemporary with the populations represented by the Mladeč and Předmostí fossils. The skeleton of a five-year-old child from Lagar Velho, Portugal, dating to 24,000 yBP,

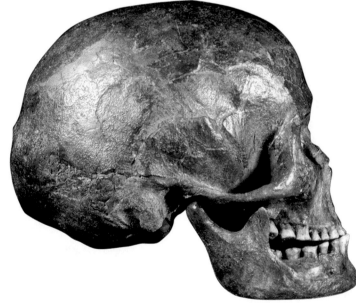

(a)

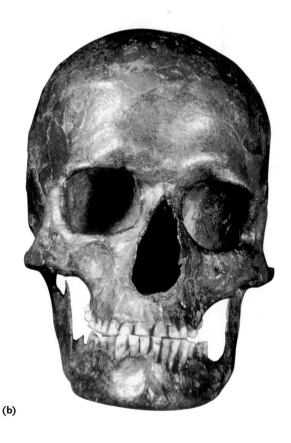

(b)

FIGURE 12.41

Dolni Vestonice Skull **(a, b)** This cranium, from Dolni Vestonice, combines modern human and Neandertal characteristics.

FIGURE 12.42

Neandertal Traits in Modern Humans The La Chapelle-aux-Saints cranium (bottom; see also Figure 12.20) and a modern Croatian cranium (top) share four major facial similarities.

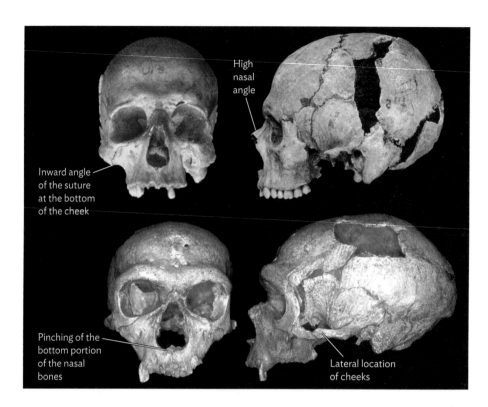

High nasal angle

Inward angle of the suture at the bottom of the cheek

Pinching of the bottom portion of the nasal bones

Lateral location of cheeks

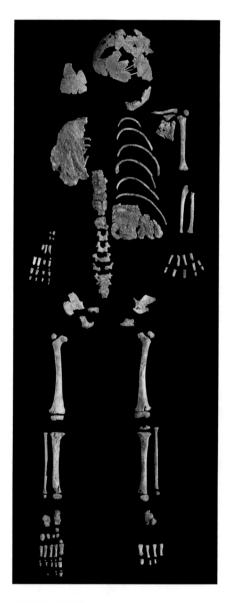

FIGURE 12.43

Lagar Velho This skeleton of a child was discovered at a rockshelter site in Portugal's Lapedo Valley.

has a number of archaic, Neandertal-like cranial and postcranial features, such as its limb proportions and robusticity (**Figure 12.43**).

The best-known western European representatives of early modern people are the remains of a half-dozen individuals from Cro-Magnon, in Dordogne, France, and remains from the Grimaldi Caves, in the Italian Riviera region, all of these dating to about 30,000–25,000 yBP. The Cro-Magnon remains are often presented as the archetypical example of the earliest modern people, but in fact people varied considerably

CZECH REPUBLIC
Mladeč
Předmostí
Dolní Věstonice
ROMANIA
Peștera cu Oase

Lagar Velho
PORTUGAL

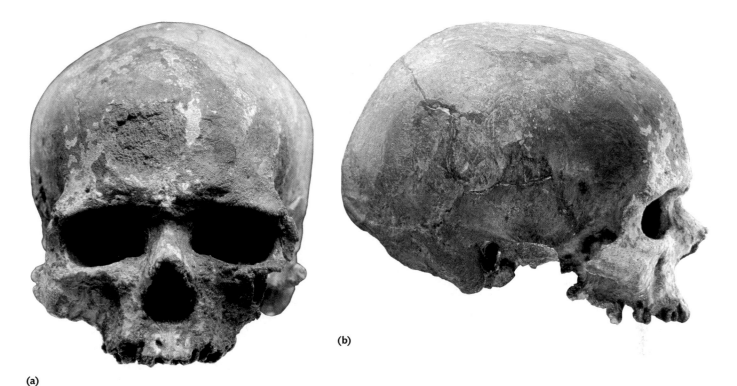

(b)

(a)

FIGURE 12.44

***Cro-Magnon* (a, b)** In 1868, a geologist discovered skeletons in a rockshelter in Cro-Magnon, France. These remains are anatomically modern, with a number of features distinct from Neandertals', including a high and vertical forehead, flat browridges, a much narrower nasal aperture, and an overall gracile skull. (Photos © David L. Brill, humanoriginsphotos.com)

during this time. Collectively, though, both ensembles of skeletons from western Europe have distinctively modern features: vertical forehead, narrow nasal aperture, and small browridges (**Figure 12.44**). In addition, unlike Neandertals, their tibias are long and their body trunks are narrow. Like Neandertals, these people lived in cold climates of the late Pleistocene, but their very different body morphology suggests adaptation to warmer climates. (The implications of these skeletal features for the origins of modern *H. sapiens* are discussed later in this chapter.)

Overall, comparisons of earlier with later early modern *H. sapiens* in Europe indicate a trend toward gracilization—the faces, jaws, and teeth became smaller and the faces became less projecting. In addition, comparison of early and late Upper Paleolithic heights reconstructed from the long bones shows that the later early modern people were shorter. The decrease in the height of early modern people may have been caused, at the very end of the Pleistocene, by both a decrease in the quality of nutrition and resource stress. That is, during the last 20,000 years of the Pleistocene, food procurement intensified—more effort was put into acquiring and processing food for the same amount of caloric intake as before. This change may have occurred because human population size was increasing, placing increased pressure on food resources. An outcome of this change was a global increase in the range of foods eaten. Archaeological evidence shows that the later early modern humans hunted and collected smaller and less desirable (because not as protein-rich) foods, such as small vertebrates, fish, shellfish, and plants. As the American anthropologist Trent Holiday has also shown, the late Upper Paleolithic people had wider body trunks and shorter legs than the early Upper Paleolithic people. The morphological shift indicates an adaptation to cold during the late Upper Paleolithic, a highly dynamic period of human adaptation and evolution.

FRANCE
Cro-Magnon

Grimaldi Caves
ITALY

Early Modern *Homo Sapiens*

Early modern *H. sapiens* occurred first in Africa, and later in Asia and Europe. The peopling of Europe, Asia, and Africa by only modern *H. sapiens* was complete by 25,000 yBP.

Locations (sites)*	Africa (Herto, Aduma, Bouri, Omo, Klasies River Mouth Cave, Lothagam, Wadi Kubbaniya, Wadi Halfa)
	Asia (Skhul 5, Tianyuan, Minatogawa)
	Europe (Peștera cu Oase, Mladeč, Předmostí, Dolni Vestonice, Cro-Magnon, Grimaldi)
Chronology	160,000 yBP in Africa
	90,000 yBP in western Asia
	35,000 yBP in eastern Asia
	32,000 yBP in Europe
Biology	Vertical forehead, high skull, rounder skull, reduced facial robusticity, smaller teeth, reduced midfacial prognathism, 1,500 cc cranial capacity
	Heat-adapted body morphology (small trunk, long limbs)
Culture and behavior	Upper Paleolithic
	Increased visible symbolic behavior (cave art)
	Burial of deceased with grave goods
	Decreased hunting, increased fishing, aquatic foods, likely more plants, and reduced focus on big-game animals
	Technology changes reflect increased focus on fishing (e.g., bone harpoons)

*Sites mentioned in text.

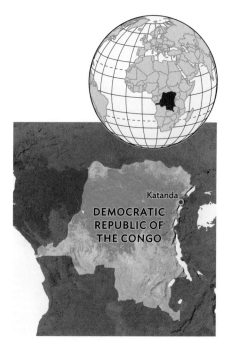

Katanda

DEMOCRATIC REPUBLIC OF THE CONGO

Modern Behavioral and Cultural Transitions

Anthropologists are learning that various behavioral and cultural practices developed at different places and different times in the later Pleistocene, culminating in full modernity in *H. sapiens* globally. In many respects, the fossil record and the cultural record show that modern behaviors and practices began, biologically and culturally, in Africa. For example, fishing and the use of aquatic resources as an important part of diet are first documented at Katanda, in the Democratic Republic of Congo, where early modern *H. sapiens* were exploiting huge catfish by at least 75,000 yBP. This development is part of a larger package of behaviors associated with modern humans, including more specialized kinds of hunting, wider employment of raw materials (such as bone) for producing tools, advanced blade technology, and trade (**Figure 12.45**). However, as

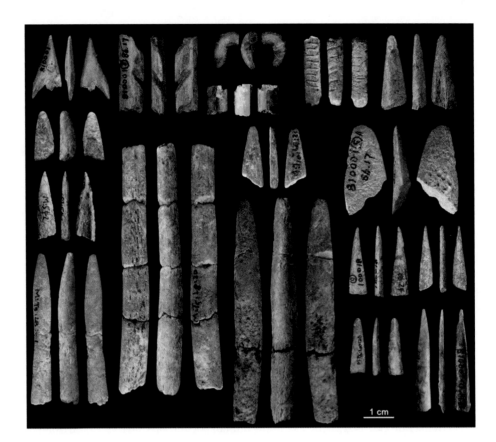

FIGURE 12.45
Modern Human Tools Early modern humans used a variety of specialized tools, including bone tools shaped for specific purposes. Dating between 35,000 and 18,000 yBP, tools made from bone from Ma'anshan Cave are the oldest in China.

discussed earlier (see "Neandertals Used Symbols"), symbolic behavior and cognitive advancement were also present in Europe, albeit later than in Africa. The successful adaptation of symbolically advanced late archaic *H. sapiens*—the Neandertals—in Europe shows that the story of later evolving humans is complex. Neandertals were fundamentally no different from modern *H. sapiens,* especially in regard to a number of behaviors—burial of the dead, speech, and symbolism—that remain with us today.

12.4 How Has the Biological Variation in Fossil *Homo sapiens* Been Interpreted?

At the beginning of this chapter, you read about the two key models that anthropologists use to explain modern *H. sapiens'* origins: the Out-of-Africa model and the Multiregional Continuity model. After having learned what the fossil record reveals about the variation in late archaic *H. sapiens,* you should be starting to see what this record reveals about modern humans' origins. Now remember the question posed at the beginning of this chapter: *Which of the two models best explains modern* H. sapiens' *origins?*

The European fossil record from 40,000–30,000 yBP provides clues about modern *H. sapiens'* origins in Europe. The earliest modern *H. sapiens* were present as early as 35,000 yBP at Mladeč (Czech Republic) and at Peştera cu Oase (Romania). The latest archaic *H. sapiens,* the Neandertals, survived until at least 32,000 yBP or so at Vindija

(Croatia). The overlap in dates between Neandertals and early modern humans indicates that the two groups coexisted in eastern Europe for at least several thousand years. This finding argues against the Multiregional Continuity model, which sees archaic *H. sapiens* as having evolved locally into modern *H. sapiens.* That the earliest modern *H. sapiens* had clear Neandertal features (such as the occipital bun) indicates interbreeding between Neandertals and early modern people. This finding argues against the Out-of-Africa model, which sees no gene flow between Neandertals and early modern humans. We will now see if the genetic record provides additional insight into modern *H. sapiens'* origins in Europe.

Ancient DNA: Interbreeding between Neandertals and Early Modern People?

Analysis of mitochondrial DNA (mtDNA), the DNA inherited only via the mother, offers potential clues about modern people's origins (mtDNA is among the topics of chapter 3). Comparisons of mtDNA from more than a dozen Neandertal skeletons—from Engis and Scladina in Belgium, Les Rochers de Villeneuve and La Chapelle-aux-Saints in France, Monte Lessini in Italy, El Sidrón in Spain, Feldhofer Cave in Germany, Mezmaiskaya in Russia, Teshik Tash in Uzbekistan, and Vindija Cave in Croatia—with that of early modern humans and living humans shows *similarity* among Neandertals and *dissimilarity* between Neandertals and modern humans. The German molecular geneticist Matthias Krings and his associates found, for example, that 27 mtDNA base pairs of a sequence of 378 base pairs from the Feldhofer Cave Neandertal differ completely from living Europeans'. In contrast, living human populations have an average of just eight differences among them. These genetic differences seem to support the hypothesis that no gene flow occurred between Neandertals and modern humans during the later Pleistocene and, importantly, that Neandertals contributed none of their genetic material to the modern human gene pool. Neandertals underwent extinction, pure and simple. However, the extinction hypothesis may not be the best one. That is, mtDNA is just a tiny part of the human genome and reflects only a small fraction of the genetic code. The failure of one part of the genome to survive to the present does not mean that the entire genome became extinct. Moreover, it is possible that mtDNA lineages have been lost owing to genetic drift. Simply, much more of the genome is needed to have a more complete picture.

Only recently has the remarkable scientific technology been available to analyze nuclear DNA to reconstruct the Neandertal genome. Such a reconstruction would make it possible to address the important question of the Neandertal contribution (if any) to the modern human genome. In a breakthrough study led by Swedish geneticist Svante Pääbo, a new technology applied to the analysis of three female Neandertal bones from Vindija Cave at last has provided the sequence of 4 billion base pairs representing the Neandertal genome. Pääbo and his team used *high-throughput DNA sequencing,* a technology through which much of a genome can be sequenced from a compilation of various genome fragments recovered from fossil bones. The results are breathtaking: Eurasians and Neandertals share between 1% and 4% of their nuclear DNA, an indication of a small but significant admixture. Given that Africans share no nuclear DNA with Neandertals, the admixture occurred between early modern Europeans and Neandertals after early modern people left Africa. People living today outside of Africa have DNA that likely originated from Neandertals. In that sense, the Neandertals are still with us! In fact, new studies of nuclear DNA in Neandertals shows the presence of alleles indicating risk for disease. In this way, Neandertal biology has contributed to shaping the biology of modern *H.sapiens.*

But early modern *H. sapiens* may not have interbred with just Neandertals. Beginning in 2010, analysis of mitochondrial and nuclear DNA recovered from a hominin hand bone, foot bone, and a few teeth dating to 40,000 yBP from Denisova Cave, in southern Siberia, revealed a hominin genome that is neither Neandertal nor modern human. Svante Pääbo and his team, who reconstructed the Denisovan genome, expected to find a genome that was either Neandertal or modern human, but they came up with something very different from both. The only similarity they could find with living people is from populations living in Melanesia (New Guinea and Bougainville Islands) and China. These findings suggest that genetic diversity in late Pleistocene Europe is more complex than previously thought. Namely, the genome came to include contributions from some widespread populations that modern humans encountered as they migrated throughout Europe (the Neandertals) and from some very isolated people (the Denisovans). The Denisovans are likely archaic *H. sapiens* sharing a common origin with Neandertals. However, because paleoanthropologists have found only a few bones and teeth, we do not know what the Denisovans looked like. The genetic evidence strongly suggests that modern humans migrated from Africa and interbred with hominin species beyond just Neandertals. In fact, the European continent appears to have been inhabited by various isolated peoples. As research continues, the picture of genetic variation in humans on the evolutionary pathway toward modernity becomes increasingly complex.

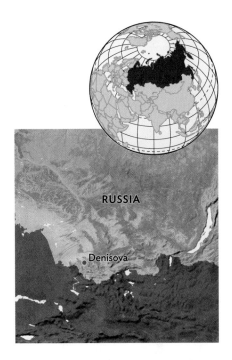

Living People's Genetic Record: Settling the Debate on Modern Human Origins

Living people's genetic record helps settle the question about whether the Out-of-Africa model or the Multiregional Continuity model explains modern *H. sapiens'* origins. The American geneticist and molecular biologist Rebecca Cann and her collaborators have found that sub-Saharan African populations are more genetically diverse than populations from any other region of the world. That is, genes of people living south of the Sahara Desert today are more variable in frequency than are genes of people living in Europe, Asia, the Americas, and Australia (**Figure 12.46**). This pattern is also present in the phenotypic variation of anatomical characteristics (for example, cranial measurements).

Two explanations exist for Africa's greater genetic diversity. First, a population or group of populations that has been around a long time will have accumulated more mutations—hence, greater genetic variation—than a population or group of populations that has been around a short time. Therefore, Africa's greater genetic diversity may mean that modern people have existed longer there than in Asia or Europe.

On the basis of their assessment of mutation rates, Cann's group came up with a figure of 200,000 yBP for the first early modern *H. sapiens'* appearance, and this date is consistent with the earliest record of modern *H. sapiens* in Africa. Calculations based on other sources of genetic material, such as from the Y chromosome, provide broadly similar results.

The alternative explanation for Africa's greater genetic diversity lies in its population structure compared with that of other continents. The American anthropological geneticist John Relethford observes that population size tremendously influences genetic diversity. As discussed in chapter 3, if the breeding population is small, genetic drift is a potentially powerful force for altering gene frequencies. Over time, genetic drift reduces genetic diversity in a small population (such as might have been the case in Europe and Asia). For example, if a group of 10 people splits off from a group of 1,000 people, the two resulting groups will show very different patterns of gene frequency change. The smaller population will be less variable, whereas its parent population

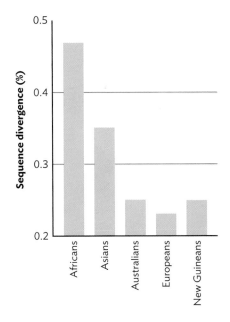

FIGURE 12.46

Genetic Diversity Patterns of genetic diversity have been used to assess the Out-of-Africa and Multiregional Continuity models of modern humans' origins. This graph shows genetic diversity within several major geographic groups, expressed as the average amount of genetic sequence divergence in percent. Note the much greater genetic diversity in Africans compared with other groups. (Source: Cann, R. L., M. Stoneking, and A. Wilson. 1987. Mitochondrial DNA and human evolution. *Nature* 325: 31–36.)

will be more variable. Relethford argues that because in the remote past Africa had a significantly larger breeding population size than other continents did, Africa now has greater genetic diversity.

12.5 Assimilation Model for Modern Human Variation: Neandertals Are Still with Us

The more modern characteristics of East African skeletons from the Upper Pleistocene (for example, Herto) provide compelling evidence that modern variation originated in Africa. The fossil record and the genetic record indicate, however, that neither

Models for Explaining Modern *Homo sapiens'* Origins

With more complete and growing fossil and genetic records of human evolution, it is now possible to weigh the strengths and weaknesses of hypotheses that best explain the origins of modern *Homo sapiens*.

Model	Features	Proponent
Out-of-Africa	Modern biology, behavior, and culture originated in Africa. Modern humans spread from Africa to Europe after 50,000 yBP. Modern humans replaced all populations once arriving in Europe, with no gene flow.	Christopher Stringer
Multiregional Continuity	Modern humans evolved from earlier archaic populations in their respective regions (Africa, Europe, Asia). Throughout evolution, there is always significant gene flow on the borders of populations. There is continuity of morphology in all regions of the globe.	Milford Wolpoff
Assimilation	Modern humans first evolved in Africa, then spread to Europe and Asia. Once they arrived in Europe and Asia, modern humans underwent gene flow with Neandertals.	Fred Smith, Erik Trinkaus

the Out-of-Africa model nor the Multiregional Continuity model adequately explains modern humans' origins. The Out-of-Africa model correctly accounts for the origin of modern human variation, but it incorrectly asserts that no gene flow occurred between Neandertals and modern *H. sapiens*. The Multiregional Continuity model is not correct about modern *H. sapiens'* regional development. However, it is correct about gene flow and the notion that Neandertals have contributed to modern *H. sapiens'* gene pool.

In other words, elements of both models explain the emergence and evolution of fully modern people worldwide in the Upper Pleistocene. That is, sometime within 200,000–100,000 yBP, a population of modern heat-adapted *H. sapiens* migrated from Africa to Europe and Asia. Once arriving in Europe, this population encountered members of their species—the Neandertals—who were as behaviorally and technologically complex as they. Neandertals, cold-adapted people, had evolved from earlier *H. sapiens* populations in Europe—the early archaic *H. sapiens*—and they interbred with the newly arrived modern *H. sapiens*. Therefore, Neandertals' disappearance after 30,000 yBP or so likely resulted not from their extinction but from their *assimilation* by much larger, more genetically diverse populations of modern humans migrating into Europe from Africa during the late Pleistocene (**Figure 12.47**). Neandertals contributed to the gene pool of today's European and European-descended populations, leaving their genetic, behavioral, and adaptive legacy with modern humans in Europe and in Asia.

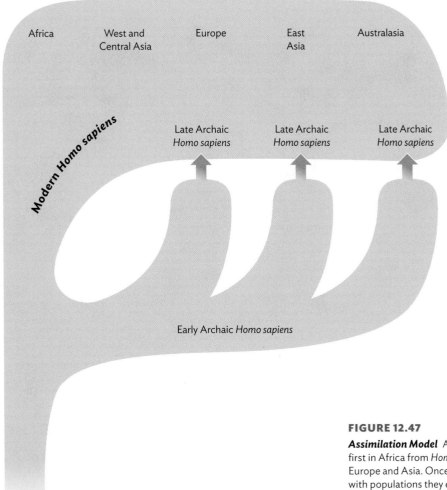

FIGURE 12.47

Assimilation Model According to this model, modern *Homo sapiens* evolved first in Africa from *Homo erectus*. Groups of *Homo sapiens* then spread to Europe and Asia. Once in Europe and Asia, these modern *H. sapiens* interbred with populations they encountered, the late archaic *H. sapiens* (Neandertals). This admixture is the biological foundation for modern *H. sapiens* living outside of Africa today.

12.6 Modern Humans' Other Migrations: Colonization of Australia, the Pacific, and the Americas

This chapter and the preceding one have emphasized migration's critical importance in human evolution. In the first wave out of Africa, *H. erectus* spread rapidly throughout Asia and Europe. In the second wave out of Africa, early modern *H. sapiens* assimilated and eventually replaced the descendants of *H. erectus* in Asia and Europe. The last 50,000 years of the Pleistocene saw fully modern people spread not only into Asia and Europe but also to continents that had previously not been occupied by people. Prior to 50,000 yBP, humans occupied only three of the six inhabitable continents: Africa, Asia, and Europe. After 50,000 yBP, populations migrated from the southeastern fringes of Asia to Australia, eventually fanning out from west to east across the hundreds of islands that dot the Pacific Ocean. In the last few millennia of the Pleistocene, humans spread to the Americas (**Figure 12.48**). These movements, and their accompanying adaptations to unfamiliar environments, are no less a part of human evolution than are bipedalism, language use, and all the other key developments discussed in this chapter and chapter 11.

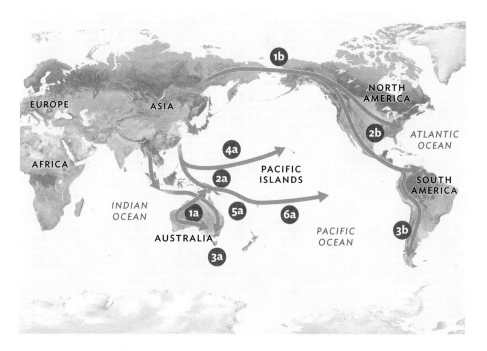

FIGURE 12.48

Modern Humans' Migrations Another major research question in physical anthropology focuses on modern humans' spread from Asia to Australia, the Pacific, North America, and South America. This map shows modern humans' migration patterns from southern Asia **(1a–6a)** and eastern Asia **(1b–3b)** beginning in the late Pleistocene: **(1a)** earliest migration of modern *Homo sapiens* into Australia (Lake Mungo; ~50,000–40,000 yBP); **(2a)** earliest evidence of modern human occupation of New Guinea and adjacent islands (Bobongara; ~35,000 yBP); **(3a)** earliest evidence of modern human occupation of Tasmania (Warreen Cave; ~33,000 yBP); **(4a)** early expansion into Oceania (Mariana Islands; ~1500 BC); **(5a)** oceanic expansion into western Polynesia (Tonga and Samoa; ~1000 BC); **(6a)** expansion into eastern Polynesia (Cook Islands; ~AD 700); **(1b)** earliest evidence for expansion from northeast Asia into North America (Beringia; ~15,500 yBP—or Clovis, New Mexico; ~12,000 yBP); **(3b)** proposed coastal route for colonization of the New World and South America (Monte Verde, Chile; ~14,500 yBP).

What motivated these early modern people to move? Among the multiple reasons, four are most important: population increase, disappearance of food resources, increased competition with neighbors for remaining resources, and climate deterioration. That is, a population's resources—food especially—are available in finite quantities. As Relethford has shown through genetic studies, African populations expanded rapidly during the late Pleistocene. These increases, as populations outgrew their carrying capacities, were the prime force stimulating anatomically modern people to move into Asia and Europe. Similarly, as population size expanded in Asia and Europe, humans continued to move and began to occupy vast regions of the globe.

Beginning in the very late Pleistocene, eastern Asia became the stepping-off point for migrations to previously unoccupied continents. Southeast Asia served as the stepping-off point for the movements to Australia and across the Pacific as people eventually occupied most of the 20,000–30,000 islands between Australia and the Americas. Northeast Asia served as the stepping-off point for the spread to North America and South America.

Down Under and Beyond: The Australian and Pacific Migrations

In the late Pleistocene, sea levels were considerably lower than they are today, by as much as 90 m (300 ft), exposing land surfaces now submerged by water and making them available for human occupation and movement between landmasses. Australia, New Guinea, and Tasmania constituted a single landmass, which we call *Greater Australia* (**Figure 12.49**). The islands of Sulawesi, Borneo, and Java were connected

FIGURE 12.49

Land Bridge During the late Pleistocene, temperatures were much cooler and a great amount of seawater was locked in glaciers. As a result, sea levels were at their lowest, exposing shallow land, such as the Sunda shelf in southeast Asia. On this map, the exposed land is white. Some of it connected the islands of southeast Asia (Borneo, Java, and Sumatra) with the Asian mainland, and some of it connected Australia with New Guinea and Tasmania. Despite the increased land area, traveling to Australia would have still required a sea voyage; however, there was much less distance between southeast Asia and Australia. Modern researchers are unable to investigate evidence of the people who once inhabited the areas that are now underwater.

FIGURE 12.50

Lake Mungo This Australian site has yielded the oldest human skeleton in Australia.

shovel-shaped incisors A dental trait, commonly found among Native Americans and Asians, in which the incisors' posterior aspect has varying degrees of concavity.

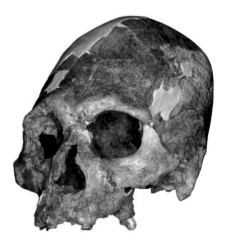

FIGURE 12.51

Kow Swamp This Australian site has yielded skeletons much more robust than those discovered at Lake Mungo. In fact, Alan Thorne, who excavated the skull, originally believed the remains to be a *Homo erectus* skeleton rather than a modern human skeleton.

to mainland Asia. Even at the peak of the late Pleistocene's coldest period, when sea levels were at their lowest, a considerable distance of open water separated Greater Australia from Asia. At least 70 km (43.5 mi) of open water separated Sulawesi and Borneo from Australia. To traverse open water from southeastern Asia to Australia, late Pleistocene humans would have needed sophisticated boating technology and equally sophisticated navigational skills. No evidence of such technology and skills has been found. Modern humans seem to have had simply enough know-how to reach Australia, which they ultimately colonized.

The earliest archaeological evidence of humans in Australia is from Lake Mungo, in western New South Wales, dating to about 42,000 yBP (**Figure 12.50**). The two skulls from Lake Mungo, from an adult male and an adult female, have modern characteristics: the skulls are high and have rounded foreheads with small browridges. In overall appearance, the skulls resemble ones from Kow Swamp in Victoria's Murray River valley, which date to 13,000–9,000 yBP (**Figure 12.51**). However, the Kow Swamp skulls are more robust, with larger browridges, larger and more robust faces, and lower foreheads than the Lake Mungo skulls. These early Australians share features with *H. erectus* and later Indonesian hominins, especially in the facial skeleton, such as in the shape of the eye orbits. These anatomical similarities suggest a common genetic origin, thereby indicating regional continuity of human populations and their biological evolution.

These early Australians also bear a strong similarity to native people who inhabit the continent today; the anatomical evidence indicates an ancestral-descendant relationship. However, mtDNA from the Lake Mungo and Kow Swamp skeletons differs substantially from that of living native Australians. Based on the mtDNA evidence alone, one might conclude that the ancient populations represented by the Lake Mungo and Kow Swamp skeletons were not ancestral to living native Australians, but this conclusion runs counter to a range of cultural and archaeological evidence. As with the Neandertal mtDNA lineages discussed earlier, a more likely explanation for the disparity between ancient and modern genes in Australia is that the mtDNA sequence in ancient anatomically modern people has not survived to the present. This Australian evidence is an important example of the very different evolutionary pathways that mtDNA and anatomical evolution can take. The fossil remains show continuity with modern native people of Australia, but the mtDNA lineage went extinct at some point after 40,000 yBP.

Southeast Asia is also the point of origin for populations that eventually dispersed throughout the Pacific Ocean. Unlike Australia, which was settled by 40,000 yBP, most of the Pacific islands extending from east of New Guinea to Easter Island were not settled until well after 5,000 yBP. In fact, east of the Solomon Islands, settlement across the vast Pacific did not begin until after about 1500 BC, ending with humans' arrival on Easter Island around AD 600.

Arrival in the Western Hemisphere: The First Americans

The American physical anthropologist Aleš Hrdlička first noted the remarkable similarity in the shapes of the upper incisors of eastern Asian and Native American peoples, past and present. He observed that Asians and Native Americans have **shovel-shaped incisors** (**Figure 12.52**). In these incisors and many other dental features, the American anthropologists Albert Dahlberg and Christy Turner have identified a common ancestry for eastern Asians and Native Americans. Common ancestry is supported by the fact that most Native Americans today have exclusively blood type O. Moreover, the alleles for this blood type are present with only limited variation. It is highly likely, therefore, that the founding population had these characteristics.

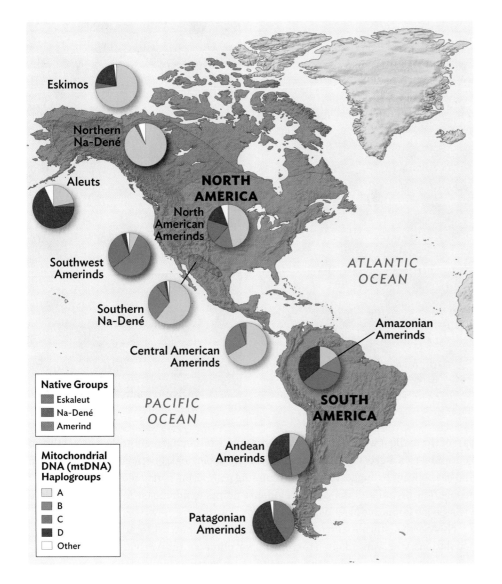

Native Groups
- ▨ Eskaleut
- ▨ Na-Dené
- ▨ Amerind

Mitochondrial
DNA (mtDNA)
Haplogroups
- ▨ A
- ▨ B
- ▨ C
- ▨ D
- ☐ Other

FIGURE 12.52

Shovel-Shaped Incisors A dental characteristic often found in East Asians is the shoveled appearance of the back, or lingual side, of the incisors. That this trait has also been found in Native Americans likely reflects their descent from East Asians.

FIGURE 12.53

Native American Mitochondrial DNA (mtDNA) Studies of mtDNA haplogroups in Native Americans have yielded information about human migrations from Asia to the Americas. This map shows the relative amount of each haplogroup in various native groups (the Eskaleut, the Na-Dené, and the Amerind).

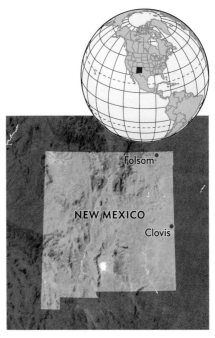

Additional clues about the peopling of the Americas appear in modern and ancient Native Americans' mtDNA. For 95% of living Native Americans throughout North America and South America, mtDNA falls into any one of four haplogroups—A, B, C, or D. (As discussed in chapter 3, mtDNA is inherited just from the mother, so the haplogroup unit reflects the maternal line of inheritance.) Notably, the same pattern of four main haplogroups has been found in mtDNA recovered from ancient Native American skeletons. This sharing of haplogroups by modern people and ancient skeletons indicates a common founding ancestry for present and past Native Americans. Moreover, Native Americans share haplogroups with northeastern Asians. The evidence indicates that the haplogroups were present in Asians who migrated to the Americas (**Figure 12.53**). The presence of all four groups throughout the Americas and the great similarity of the nucleotide sequences suggest that they share a common ancestry in a single founding population that arrived in the Americas from Asia via one migration. Consistent with the mtDNA evidence from skeletal remains is the emerging record provided by the sequencing of the nuclear DNA from a Paleoindian young boy's skeleton from Anzick, Montana, dating to the late Pleistocene (ca. 12,700 yBP). The strong similarity of the genome with that of native people today indicates that the person was

(a)

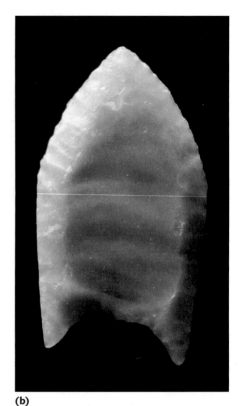

(b)

FIGURE 12.54

Paleoindians **(a)** This first group of inhabitants in the Americas likely hunted a variety of megafauna, such as the mammoth shown here and a wide range of other animals. **(b)** The tools the Paleoindians hunted with included a specialized, fluted projectile point, which we call a *Folsom point*. An extraordinary amount of skill was required to make this tool.

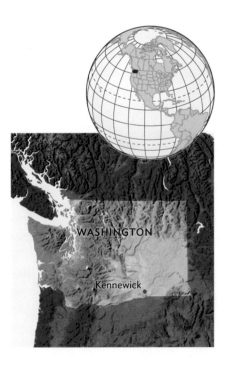

part of the earliest wave of migration giving rise to all indigenous groups in North and South America. Research by the American anthropological geneticist Connie Mulligan and her colleagues suggests that the founding population consisted of only about 800 people. The dental and the genetic evidence points to northeast Asia during the late Pleistocene for native New World people's origin.

This northeastern Asian origin indicates that in contrast to Australia's founding populations, who were adapted to tropical, wet climates, the Americas' founding populations were adapted to cold, dry climates. Both migrations indicate that these founding humans were adapted to extreme environments at the margins of human capabilities.

In contrast to the migrations to Australia and the Pacific, where the founders traveled across open seas, migrations to the Americas occurred via a land route or along the deglaciated Pacific coastline. If it was a land route, it was likely across the Bering land bridge (which we call *Beringea*), connecting Siberia and Alaska. Like those in the western Pacific Ocean, this land route was created when sea levels reached a low point during the later Pleistocene, exposing areas of land that are now submerged.

Genetic dating based on mutation rates of mtDNA and Y chromosomes, as well as single nucleotide polymorphisms (SNPs; see chapter 4), indicates that the migration from Asia to the Americas likely took place by 15,000 yBP. The genetic dating is consistent with the dates on the earliest archaeological sites in the Americas, such as from the Page-Ladson site in Florida, dating to 14,550 yBP. The genetic findings indicate that one early migration resulted in the ancestral population for most Native Americans of North America and South America today. The uniform distribution of haplotypes across the Americas indicates that the migration was a rapid process and not a slow diffusion. Two other smaller and much later migrations from Asia yielded the founding populations of (1) Na-Dené speakers of northwestern North America and the Navajo and Apache of the southwestern United States and (2) the speakers of Eskimo-Aleut languages, respectively. In North America, the earliest well-documented archaeological record of habitation and material culture (especially stone artifacts) dates to around 11,500 yBP. The earliest people associated with this and other early cultures are called **Paleoindians.** They are well known from stone artifacts, especially large spear points associated with pre-Clovis, **Clovis,** and later **Folsom** cultures. The Paleoindians hunted various animals, but they are best known for hunting **megafauna,** the large Pleistocene game such as the mammoth, steppe bison, and reindeer/caribou, and processing the meat from these animals for food (**Figure 12.54**).

Pleistocene megafauna became extinct by the early Holocene, and some evidence suggests that in the Americas and Australia, humans hunted these large animals to extinction. It seems unlikely, however, that small numbers of humans could have killed so many animals in such a short time. These extinctions were more likely due to climate change at the end of the Pleistocene and the changes in habitats frequented by large mammals. If humans' hunting during the late Pleistocene and early Holocene was involved, it played a very minor part.

The Paleoindians differed anatomically from recent Native Americans. The Paleoindians' skulls were relatively long and narrow, and their faces were robust, with large attachment areas for the masticatory muscles. In contrast, many late prehistoric and living Native Americans have short, round skulls with gracile faces. For example, the Paleoindian skull from Kennewick, Washington, dating to 8,400 yBP, is long and narrow; the face and jaws are robust (**Figure 12.55**). These differences between the Paleoindians and modern Native Americans have been interpreted to mean either that the Paleoindians are not the living Native Americans' ancestors or, alternatively, that the Paleoindians are the living Native Americans' ancestors but cranial morphology has changed due to evolutionary forces and other processes over the past 10,000 years in the Americas (discussed further in chapter 13).

In 2015, Danish paleogeneticist Eske Willerslev and his team at the Natural History Museum of Denmark discovered that the genetic variation—autosomal, mtDNA, and Y-chromosomal—is strongly similar between Kennewick Man and recent Native Americans, which makes it unlikely that Paleoindians are not the ancestors of modern Native Americans. That is, the ancestral-descendant genetic relationship supports the hypothesis that the cranial morphology evolved *in situ* and was shaped by later processes, such as those involving use of the face and jaws in mastication. This record is consistent with study of Paleoindians from the Yucatán Peninsula in Mexico showing different morphology in Paleoindians than in later populations, yet with clear genetic links between the earlier and later populations. Overall, this important record—fossil and genetic—shows that Paleoindians have a different cranial morphology than modern Native Americans, but with clear genetic ties between the two. In summary: Like all other populations you have read about in this book, populations native to the Americas have evolved.

Modern humans' emergence and subsequent dispersal around the globe marks a remarkable period of population expansion and behavioral and biological diversification. The geographic biological diversity in the world today was likely well in place by the end of the Pleistocene. The rapid expansion of human population size resulted in increased types of foods eaten. The adoption and increased use of fish and aquatic life in general during the late Pleistocene likely reflects humans' need for alternative foods as population size expanded. Such dietary expansion set the stage for one of the most dramatic adaptive shifts in human evolution, the shift from eating plants that were gathered and animals that were hunted to eating plants and animals that were both domesticated. In the next chapter, we will look at this important transition's biological implications for humans over the past 10,000 years of our evolution.

Paleoindians The earliest hominin inhabitants of the Americas; they likely migrated from Asia and are associated with the Clovis and Folsom stone tool cultures in North America and comparable stone tool cultures in South America.

Clovis Earliest Native American ("Paleoindian") culture of North America; technology known for large, fluted, bifacial stone projectile points used as spear points for big-game hunting.

Folsom Early Native American (immediately following Clovis) culture of North America; technology known for large, fluted, bifacial projectile points used as spear points for big-game hunting.

megafauna General term for the large game animals hunted by pre-Holocene and early Holocene humans.

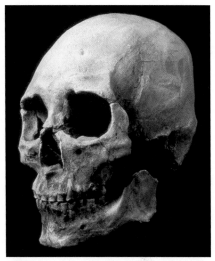

(a)

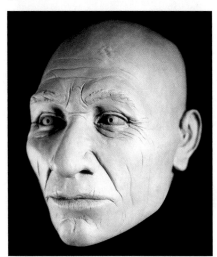

(b)

FIGURE 12.55

Kennewick Man **(a)** Discovered on the banks of the Columbia River, Kennewick Man represents the Paleoindians. **(b)** This artist's reconstruction shows the Paleoindians' likely facial appearance.

CHAPTER 12 REVIEW

ANSWERING THE BIG QUESTIONS

1. **What is so modern about modern humans?**
   - Distinguishing characteristics of modern humans include small faces, jaws, and teeth; a vertical and high forehead; narrow nasal apertures and body trunks; and long legs.

2. **What do *Homo sapiens* fossils reveal about modern humans' origins?**
   - Early archaic *H. sapiens* evolved from *Homo erectus*.
   - In Africa, nearly modern people evolved 200,000–150,000 yBP. After 130,000 yBP, an archaic form of *H. sapiens* called Neandertals occupied western Asia and then Europe.
   - From about 40,000–30,000 yBP, multiple hominin groups occupied Europe: Neandertals, modern *H. sapiens*, and Denisovans.

3. **How has variation in fossil *H. sapiens* been interpreted?**
   - The Out-of-Africa model argues that modern *H. sapiens* migrated from Africa to Asia and Europe, replacing native late archaic *H. sapiens*, including Neandertals.

   - The Multiregional Continuity model argues that modern *H. sapiens* arose regionally in each of the three inhabited continents: Africa, Asia, and Europe.
   - Physical characteristics and DNA in fossils Neandertals were assimilated through admixture with early modern *H. sapiens* and did not go extinct.

4. **What other developments took place in *H. sapiens'* evolution?**
   - More advanced tools, diet diversification, and symbolism appeared first in Africa and later in Europe and Asia.
   - Neandertals were likely capable of articulate speech.
   - Neandertals and contemporary humans were the first species to intentionally bury their dead.
   - Fully modern humans migrated to Australia by 40,000 yBP and to North and South America by 15,000 yBP.
   - Modern human populations globally have evolved in significant ways morphologically since the late Pleistocene, as established by the ancient DNA record.

KEY TERMS

calculus
Clovis
Folsom
Homo floresiensis
Levallois
megafauna
microcephaly
Middle Paleolithic
Mousterian
occipital bun
Paleoindians
shovel-shaped
   incisors
Upper Paleolithic

STUDY QUIZ

1. **What distinguishes early archaic *Homo sapiens* from *H. erectus*?**
   a. presence in Asia and Europe
   b. loss of large browridges
   c. development of a projecting chin
   d. reduction in skeletal robusticity

2. **What aspect of Neandertal culture supports their intelligence?**
   a. their simpler Mousterian stone.
   b. inefficient hunting techniques.
   c. no communicating by speech.
   d. symbolic burial rituals.

3. **Modern *H. sapiens* most likely evolved**
   a. from archaic *H. sapiens* already living in Africa, Asia, and Europe.
   b. in Africa and replaced archaic *H. sapiens* in Asia and Europe.
   c. in Asia and Europe and replaced archaic *H. sapiens* in Africa.

   d. in Africa and assimilated archaic *H. sapiens* in Asia and Europe.

4. **How did modern *H. sapiens* reach North and South America?**
   a. They crossed the Pacific Ocean from Australia.
   b. They migrated from southeast Asia via the Pacific islands.
   c. They migrated from northeastern Asia along the Bering land bridge.
   d. They traveled from southern Africa through Antarctica.

5. ***Homo floresiensis* has NOT been proposed to be**
   a. a modern human with a developmental abnormality.
   b. within the range of variation of local human populations.
   c. an isolated descendant of an earlier hominin species.
   d. a descendant of modern humans.

EVOLUTION REVIEW

THE ORIGINS OF MODERN PEOPLE

Synopsis Since some of the earliest discoveries of hominin fossils, such as that of the Neandertal skull found in Germany in 1856, physical anthropologists have uncovered an amazing amount of information about our evolutionary past. Fossil discoveries, as well as the application of new technologies in genetic research, have helped clarify the relationship between anatomically modern humans and our evolutionary cousins, the Neandertals. These results have also helped determine the most likely scenario for the origin and subsequent global dispersal of our own species, *Homo sapiens,* from approximately 200,000 yBP to the present. The remarkable discoveries made and rigorous scientific study performed by paleoanthropologists continue to inform our understanding of what it means to be human.

Q1. Provide two examples of anatomical features that physical anthropologists consider to be "modern" when defining modern humans as a species (*H. sapiens*). Also, identify two ways in which these "modern" features contrast with the morphological characteristics present in earlier members of the genus *Homo.*

Q2. As discussed in chapter 5, modern human variation is highly influenced by environmental factors. Describe three cranial and postcranial features of Neandertal skeletons that are likely adaptations to the cold climates of Upper Pleistocene Europe.

Q3. Many early descriptions and modern popular depictions portray Neandertals as particularly primitive in comparison to modern humans. Summarize the aspects of Neandertal behavior and culture that strongly counter the assumption that they were simplistic, cognitively deficient evolutionary failures.

Q4. Contrast the Out-of-Africa and Multiregional Continuity models for explaining the origins of anatomically modern *H. sapiens.* Using both fossil and genetic evidence, outline how neither model by itself adequately explains modern human origins but how elements of both contribute to the Assimilation model.

Hint Consider the genetic evidence from both fossil specimens and living human populations.

Q5. More than 1.5 million years after *Homo erectus* became the first hominin species to migrate out of Africa, modern *H. sapiens* also spread from Africa to Europe and Asia and from there to Australia and the Americas. What kinds of environmental pressures contributed to the dispersal of modern *H. sapiens* across all regions of the globe? What do the migrations of modern humans into Australia (at least 40,000 yBP) and the Americas (at least 15,000 yBP) tell us about the range of human variation and adaptability in the past? How does this compare to the diversity we see in human populations today?

ADDITIONAL READINGS

Bräuer, G. 2008. The origin of modern anatomy: by speciation or intraspecific evolution. *Evolutionary Anthropology* 17: 22–37.

Disotell, T. R. 2012. Archaic human genomics. *Yearbook of Physical Anthropology* 55: 24–39.

Hodges, G. 2015. First Americans. *National Geographic* 2217(1): 124–137.

Meltzer, D. J. 2009. *First Peoples in a New World: Colonizing Ice Age America.* Berkeley: University of California Press.

Nowell, A. 2010. Defining behavioral modernity in the context of Neandertal and anatomically modern human populations. *Annual Review of Anthropology* 39: 437–452.

O'Rourke, D. H., M. G. Hayes, and S. W. Carlyle. 2000. Ancient DNA studies in physical anthropology. *Annual Review of Anthropology* 29: 217–242.

Relethford, J. H. 2001. *Genetics and the Search for Modern Human Origins.* New York: Wiley-Liss.

Ruff, C. B. 1993. Climatic adaptation and hominid evolution: the thermoregulatory imperative. *Evolutionary Anthropology* 2: 53–60.

Weaver, T. D. 2009. The meaning of Neandertal skeletal morphology. *Proceedings of the National Academy of Sciences* 106: 16028-16033.

Wolpoff, M. H. and R. Caspari. 1997. *Race and Human Evolution: A Fatal Attraction.* New York: Simon & Schuster.

Once humans began practicing agriculture, corn, wheat, and rice became three of the main crops they cultivated. The movement from procuring wild food to producing food has had many varied outcomes for modern *Homo sapiens*, including changes in health, well-being, and lifestyle.

13

The Past 10,000 Years

AGRICULTURE, POPULATION, BIOLOGY

BIG QUESTIONS

1. **When, where, and why did agriculture first develop?**

2. **How did agriculture affect human living circumstances?**

3. **How did agriculture affect human biological change?**

One of my greatest disappointments as a child was when my dentist told me my teeth were crooked and had to be straightened. My dentist was able to fix the problem by removing a lower third premolar on each side of my mandible, making room for other teeth to grow without crowding taking place. Most of my friends were not so lucky: the problems with their teeth required years of treatment, which involved painful throbbing after each orthodontic visit (in which the braces were tightened as in some kind of medieval torture); a tinny flavor no matter what was eaten; food stuck in the wiring; and, perhaps worst of all, dietary restrictions (no popcorn, no gum, no caramel, nothing sweet and sticky)—in short, none of the wonderful comforts of "civilization" (**Figure 13.1**).

Tooth crowding and malocclusion—improper fit of the upper and lower teeth, sometimes called *underbite* or *overbite*—are commonplace around much of the world today. Millions of people have crowded, misaligned teeth. This phenomenon has not always been

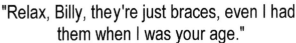

"Relax, Billy, they're just braces, even I had them when I was your age."

(a)

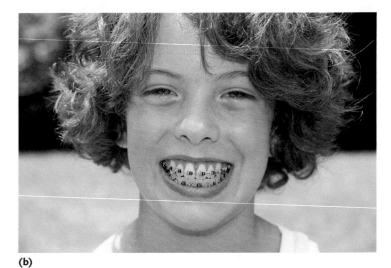

(b)

FIGURE 13.1

Braces **(a)** Straightening teeth has become so common that orthodontics in the United States is a multibillion-dollar industry. Among the braces used are **(b)** the standard wires and apparatus, both stainless steel. ([a] www. CartoonStock.com)

the case, however. It has occurred mostly within the past 10,000 years—the Holocene. What happened?

This development, not present for most of human evolution, came about because of changes in *what* humans ate and *how* they prepared food for consumption. Namely, they switched from a diet of wild plants and wild animals to a diet partly based on domesticated plants and domesticated animals. In other words, in many areas of the world humans gave up hunting and gathering for agriculture (farming). Simply, they shifted from *foraging* for their food to *producing* their food. Moreover, they invented pottery, which was used for, among other functions, boiling food into soft mushes. As a result of this new technology, foods became much softer than ever before. These changes in what was eaten and how it was prepared reduced the stresses on humans' chewing muscles. This reduced stress, like that on any muscle, also reduced the underlying bone. Basically, we have smaller jaws because our ancestors began eating softer foods. (Remember Wolff's Law, discussed in chapter 5: bone develops where it is needed and recedes where it is unnecessary.)

Tooth size is under stronger genetic control than is bone size, and as a result, tooth size is less affected by the environment. And as a consequence, humans' teeth had much less room to grow, resulting in the remarkable increase in crowded and poorly occluded teeth (**Figure 13.2**). The malocclusion epidemic, part of recent human evolution, is one of many consequences of our species' dietary change and but one example of our very dynamic biology.

13.1 The Agricultural Revolution: New Foods and New Adaptations

Up until this point—to around 10,000 yBP or so—humans had acquired *all* their food through hunting and gathering. They hunted, trapped, fished, and otherwise collected animals big and small, terrestrial and aquatic, and they collected a huge variety of plants. During the later Pleistocene, they began to intensively exploit fish and shellfish in oceans, lakes, and streams. In the final centuries of that epoch, at the key environmental transition from the Pleistocene's cold and dry climate to the Holocene's warm and wet climate, people began to control animals' and plants' growth cycles through a

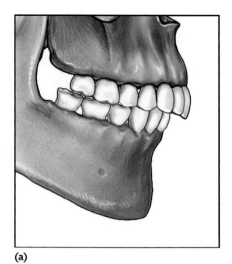
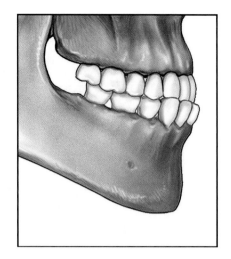

(a)   (b)

FIGURE 13.2

Malocclusion Two major forms of malocclusion can be corrected with orthodontic treatments, including braces. **(a)** An overbite occurs when the maxillary teeth extend farther forward than the mandibular teeth. An underbite occurs when the mandibular teeth extend farther forward than the maxillary teeth. **(b)** This maxilla, from a prehistoric site in Windover, Florida, shows substantial crowding of the teeth. While dental crowding and malocclusion appear in some archaeological skeletal remains, both conditions became common only after humans adopted agriculture.

process anthropologists call **domestication.** Eventually, humans replaced nearly all the wild animals and wild plants in their diets with domesticated animals and domesticated plants. This dramatic change in lifeway—where people at the end of the Pleistocene and in the early Holocene raised the animals and grew the plants they ate—is associated with the period called the **Neolithic.**

By any measure, agriculture ranks as one of the most transformative developments in the record of hominin evolution. It was the foundation for the profoundly important adaptive transition from foraging to farming. I rank agriculture up there with bipedalism and speech as being fundamental to who humans are as an organism. As will be discussed in this chapter, this shift had important and long-lasting implications for *Homo* as an evolving species. For example, many diseases we have today are linked in one way or another to this remarkable change in lifeway.

For 99.8% of the 7 million years of human evolution, hominins had eaten plants of all kinds, but not until very recently had they *grown* them. Domesticated plants quickly became an integral part of food production across much of the globe, but that quickness is relative to the geologic timescale. Rather than happening overnight, in other words, the shift from foraging to farming took place over centuries and likely involved many successes and failures as the process unfolded for different human populations around the world (**Figure 13.3**). But compared with evolutionary changes that took place over thousands or hundreds of thousands of years, the transitional process of domestication—the dietary changes, biological adaptations, and resulting health changes—was quite rapid.

Authorities agree on where and when domestication took place, based on the study of plant and animal remains found in archaeological sites. In addition, breakthroughs in plant and animal genetics provide new windows on the origins of domesticated species. That is, the domesticated descendants of formerly wild plants and formerly wild animals have undergone genetic changes compared with the ancestral forms. These genetic changes have been documented via breeding experiments and by the extraction and study of DNA. The changes were brought about by humans' selecting food products that were beneficial to them. For example, they probably selected many plants

domestication The process of converting wild animals or wild plants into forms that humans can care for and cultivate.

Neolithic The late Pleistocene–early Holocene culture, during which humans domesticated plants and animals.

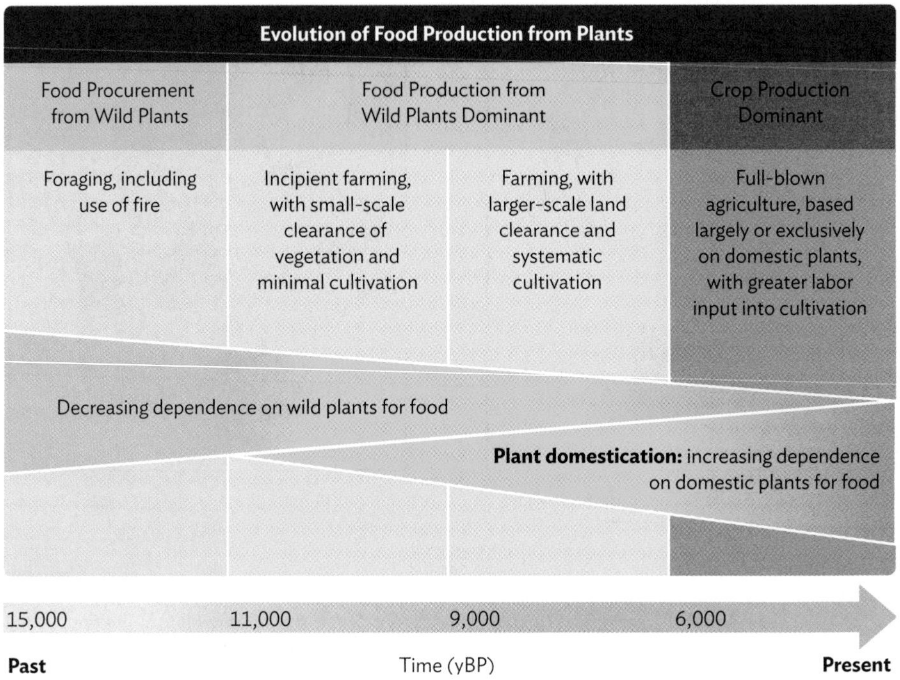

Evolution of Food Production from Plants

Food Procurement from Wild Plants	Food Production from Wild Plants Dominant		Crop Production Dominant
Foraging, including use of fire	Incipient farming, with small-scale clearance of vegetation and minimal cultivation	Farming, with larger-scale land clearance and systematic cultivation	Full-blown agriculture, based largely or exclusively on domestic plants, with greater labor input into cultivation

Decreasing dependence on wild plants for food

Plant domestication: increasing dependence on domestic plants for food

15,000   11,000   9,000   6,000

Past   Time (yBP)   **Present**

FIGURE 13.3

Adoption of Agriculture As this chart illustrates, humans did not simply abandon foraging and adopt agriculture. Initially, they foraged for wild plants to supplement their farming of cultivated plants. Over time, they depended less on wild plants and more on domesticated plants.

with soft outer coatings and large seed yields. In a very real sense, humans practiced artificial selection, as opposed to natural selection. The resulting changes proved very deleterious for some of the species being domesticated. In wheat, the part holding all the edible sections is called the *rachis*, and at some point humans selected wheat with a hard rachis for storage and later consumption. This selection, in turn, selected for plants with a hard rachis. After many generations, the wheat was unable to reproduce itself because humans had selected for plants that could not do so without human intervention (annual planting manually).

The American archaeologist Melinda Zeder regards one important outcome for humans to be the increased security and predictability of food access. This was a mutualistic relationship with their plant and animal "partners" in that plants and animals experienced increased reproductive fitness and range expansion.

Authorities disagree on the *cause* for this dramatic, worldwide change in food acquisition. They are learning, however, that the change likely did not have only one cause. At least two factors probably brought about this agricultural revolution. First, the environment changed radically, going from cooler, drier, and highly variable during the later Pleistocene to warmer, wetter, and more stable during the Holocene (**Figure 13.4**). This abrupt environmental change brought about new conditions—local climates and local ecologies—suited to the domestication of plants and of animals. Second, almost everywhere agriculture developed, human population increased at the same time.

Population Pressure

Changes in climate and in ecology would not have resulted in plant and animal domestication, of course, without people. Almost everywhere agriculture developed, strong archaeological evidence indicates that the number and size of living sites had increased. For example, on the Georgia coast of eastern North America (see the opening discussion in chapter 1), the beginning of agriculture coincided with an increase in the number and especially the sizes of villages. As human population sizes grew all over the world, people likely needed more food than hunting and gathering could provide. This population

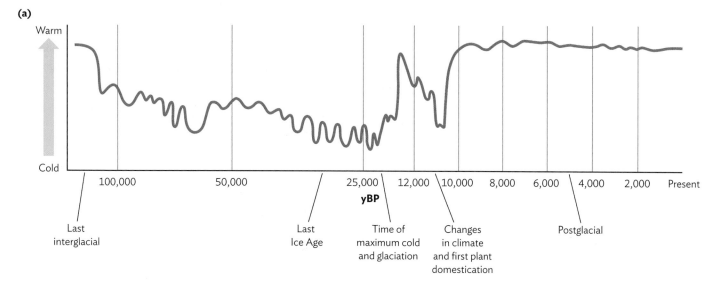

(a)

Warm

Cold

100,000   50,000   25,000 12,000 10,000 8,000 6,000 4,000 2,000 Present

yBP

Last
interglacial

Last
Ice Age

Time of
maximum cold
and glaciation

Changes
in climate
and first plant
domestication

Postglacial

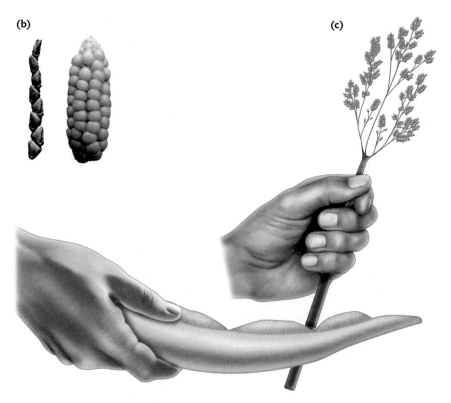

(b)

(c)

FIGURE 13.4

Temperature Changes and Plant Domestication **(a)** Over the past 120,000 years, as this timeline shows, Earth's temperature has fluctuated substantially. Around 11,000 yBP, a rapid warming trend created new habitats favorable for plant domestication. **(b)** The first grains were the wild ancestors of the domesticated varieties we know today. The wild ancestor of maize (right) is teosinte (left). **(c)** Domestication began with humans' harvesting of wild plants using late Paleolithic technology, such as this tool, an antler handle with stone microblades inserted into it.

pressure model suggests that humans *had* to develop a new strategy for feeding the ever-growing world population, and thus agriculture came into being. Domestication, especially of plants, produced more food per unit area of land than had hunting and gathering—more people could be fed from the same amount of land. In addition, agriculture provided food that could be stored for long periods. As an adaptive solution to population increase, domestication once again shows humans' remarkable flexibility in new and challenging circumstances.

Regional Variation

Plant and animal domestication was not just a one-time event, first occurring in one place and then spreading globally. Rather, domestication—in particular, plant domestication—started in at least 11 independent regions around the world (**Figure 13.5**). Out of these primary centers, the idea spread through a process of diffusion in some areas and through the movement of agricultural people in others. The process evolved slowly in some areas and quickly in others. Eventually, every inhabitable

(a)

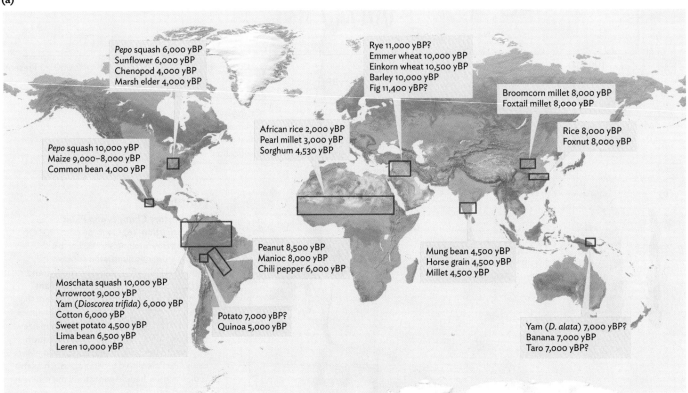

(b)

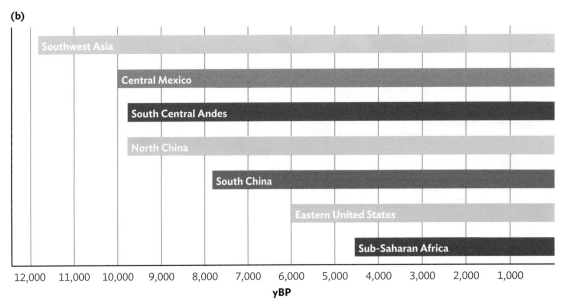

FIGURE 13.5

Worldwide Plant Domestication **(a)** This map shows the 11 separate centers of plant domestication. At each location, different types of domesticated plants were cultivated, including maize in Central America, sunflowers in eastern North America, cotton in South America, millet and sorghum in Africa, wheat in the Middle East, and banana trees in New Guinea. **(b)** This chart illustrates the approximate times of plant and animal domestication in the major regions of the world.

continent except Australia saw the change. In some regions, newly domesticated plants replaced earlier ones. For example, in the American Midwest, native seed crops—goosefoot, sumpweed, and sunflowers—were farmed about 6,000–1,000 yBP. Later, corn replaced these crops, probably owing to its greater productivity and potential for feeding more people than before.

Archaeological evidence and genetic studies of domesticated plants indicate that prior to becoming agricultural at the end of the Pleistocene, people living in southwestern Asia began to intensively harvest the grains of wheat's and barley's wild ancestors. These grains provided food for the growing populations that were beginning to live in small, settled communities for at least part of the year. For the other part of the year, people were likely out and about, hunting and gathering. Within 1,000 or so years after this combined practice of exploiting wild grains and foraging, sometime around 11,500 yBP, people began to manipulate the growth cycles of plants. This manipulation was probably based on the simple observation that some seeds falling to the ground grew into new plants. People figured out what circumstances were conducive to the plants' growth, such as adequate water and protection from animals that might eat the plants. It would have been important for the people harvesting these plants to realize that if the seeds were placed in the ground, they would sprout new plants that could grow to full maturity. These mature plants could then be harvested, just as the plants' wild ancestors were harvested generations before.

The archaeological record suggests that farming began in southeastern Turkey by 10,500 yBP or so. By 8,000 yBP, early agricultural communities had sprung up across a vast swath extending from the eastern side of the Mediterranean across an arch-shaped zone of grasslands and open woodlands known as the *Fertile Crescent* (**Figure 13.6**). Once domestication developed, within a short time villages sprang up; some of these villages developed into cities. For example, the early agriculture-based settlements of Jericho and Çatalhöyük, in Israel and Turkey, respectively, grew from tiny villages consisting of a few huts to the first cities, containing several or more thousands of people living in close, cramped settings (**Figure 13.7**).

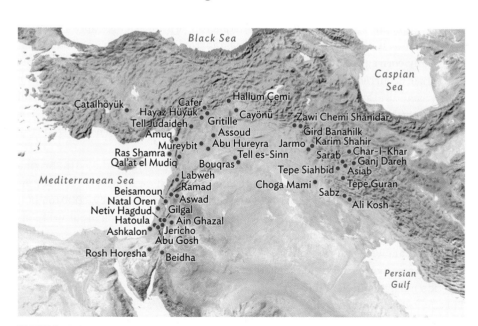

FIGURE 13.6

Southwestern Asia and the Fertile Crescent Southwestern Asia, especially the region known by anthropologists as the Fertile Crescent, has numerous archaeological sites that date between 11,500 and 8,000 yBP and contain evidence of early agriculture.

(a)

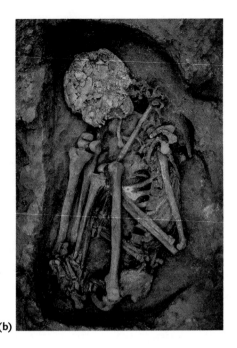

(b)

FIGURE 13.7

Çatalhöyük One of the earliest agricultural communities in southwest Asia, Çatalhöyük eventually grew into a city with a large sedentary population. **(a)** This reconstruction shows how closely spaced the houses and other buildings were in the burgeoning city. **(b)** Skeletal remains have been discovered at the Çatalhöyük site, such as this Neolithic adult male. An obsidian knife can be seen on his left shoulder. (Photo courtesy of Scott Haddow.) Skeletons such as these provide an immense amount of information about life in this early city.

Plant domestication was nearly as early in China (millet at 10,000 yBP and rice at 8,000 yBP) as in southwestern Asia (**Figure 13.8**). By this time, the form of agriculture identified by archaeologists was well along in its development, so agriculture likely developed in China earlier than that, perhaps by several thousand years. Other early domesticated plants are from Mexico (bottle gourds, 10,000 yBP; corn, 9,000 yBP), New Guinea (taro and banana trees, 7,000 yBP), eastern North America (squash, sunflowers, and goosefoot, 6,000 yBP), South America (potatoes, sweet potatoes, and manioc, 5,250 yBP), and Africa south of the Sahara Desert (sorghum and yams, 4,500 yBP).

Like most other technological innovations, agriculture spread by diffusion out of the primary centers, usually for very long distances. Corn, for example, spread from its primary center in Mexico (probably in the lowland tropics) to the American Southwest. Eventually, corn agriculture reached North America's Atlantic coast about 1,000 yBP. The spread occurred not through people carrying corn but through people describing their agricultural successes to neighbors, those neighbors telling their neighbors, and so forth, until the idea spread for thousands of miles over a series of generations. For some areas of North America, the adoption and intensive use of corn occurred very rapidly, perhaps within a few generations.

Another important area of the world where anthropologists have studied the origins and diffusion of agriculture consists of both far western Asia and Europe. From southwestern Asia, the domestication of wheat and barley spread to Greece by 8,000 to 7,000 yBP, and then throughout Europe. The idea of agriculture spread through cultural contact and the exchange of knowledge. New analysis by Ayça Omrak and her paleogenetics team of the ancient DNA of Neolithic skeletons in western Anatolia (modern Turkey) and in Europe, however, reveals sharing of significant elements of the genome. These genetic similarities in Neolithic Anatolians and Europeans signal significant gene flow. This indicates that the movement of early farmers from western Asia to Europe was widespread enough to result in the patterns of genetic diversity seen today in Europe and European-descent populations.

Animals were also domesticated around the world, beginning with dogs between

FIGURE 13.8

Rice There are more than 20 varieties of wild rice and two types of domesticated rice, the first of which was domesticated in southern Asia approximately 8,000 yBP. The second variety of domesticated rice was established in western Africa between 1500 BC and 800 BC.

30,000 and 15,000 or so years ago. By 8,000 yBP, goats, sheep, cattle, and pigs were domesticated. These animals were important in Asia and later Europe, but domesticated plants were far more fundamental to the growing human populations' survival at the global scale.

Survival and Growth

The importance of domestication for human evolutionary history cannot be overestimated. Domestication fueled humans' remarkable population growth in the Holocene, and it formed the foundation for the rise of complex societies, cities, and increasingly sophisticated technology. Archaeologists are learning that domesticated plants served as both a food staple and a source of drink, especially alcoholic drink. In China, for example, chemical analysis of residue inside ceramic vessels shows that perhaps as early as 8,000 yBP grapes and rice were fermented for wine.

The arrival of European explorers and colonists in the Americas had an enormous impact on the kinds of domesticated plants consumed by world populations. That is, beginning with Columbus's voyages, different plants were transported and grown throughout the world. Corn, for example, was taken back to Europe by early explorers. By the middle of the 1500s, its use as a food had spread widely, and it had become an important part of diets, especially in Africa.

Today, domesticated plants are crucial for sustaining human populations. Two-thirds of calorie and protein intake comes from the key cereal grains domesticated in the earlier Holocene, especially wheat, barley, corn, and rice. Rice has fed more people since its domestication than any other plant. It now accounts for *half* the food consumed by the 1.7 billion people in the world whose diets include rice and for more than 20% of all calories consumed by humans today. Rice and these other cereal grains are now aptly called **superfoods.**

superfoods Cereal grains, such as rice, corn, and wheat, that make up a substantial portion of the human population's diet today.

BIOARCHAEO

RECONSTRUCTING PAST DIETS AND INFERRING NUTRITION

The foods we eat say a lot about who we are. Perhaps of most importance, our foods determine our nutrition and therefore influence our health and well-being. Nutrition also affects our ability to be productive, to undergo normal growth and development, to survive to adulthood, and to produce healthy offspring.

It comes as no surprise, then, that physical anthropologists are so interested in diet in both past and living populations. An understanding of diet is at the top of the list for knowing why some human populations are successful and others are not. For much of the history of anthropology, the diets of past populations were reconstructed solely by identifying the remains of plants and animals that discovered in places where people once lived. Unfortunately, in many instances, plant and animal remains either do not preserve well or do not preserve at all. Even under the best of circumstances when these remains are preserved, their identification really only tells us *what* the human groups were eating. They often do not provide a picture of what foods were particularly important or the quantity eaten. We need to know how important specific foods were in the diets of past people in order to infer the nutrition that these foods provided.

In the late 1970s, two scientists—J. C. Vogel, a geochemist, and Nikolaas van der Merwe, an archaeologist—applied a new method of reconstructing diet by measuring the relative amounts of the two stable isotopes of carbon, ^{13}C and ^{12}C, in human bones from archaeological contexts. Because corn has a higher ratio of ^{13}C to ^{12}C (called the $\delta^{13}C$ ratio), they hypothesized that the bones of humans who ate corn during their lifetimes should also show a higher $\delta^{13}C$ ratio than the bones of humans who ate no corn. This is simply because the human body and all of its tissues

metabolize the elements provided by food, such as corn, including carbon.

Indeed, Vogel and van der Merwe's preliminary study showed a marked difference in the bones of pre-corn hunter-gatherers compared to corn farmers in New York State, with the former (predictably) having lower $\delta^{13}C$ ratios than the latter. This preliminary but prescient study revolutionized how we document dietary patterns for many past populations globally.

Building on their work, in collaboration with American physical anthropologist Margaret Schoeninger, I undertook a comprehensive regional study of the Georgia coast and the coast and inland of northern Florida—the region of eastern North America colonized by Spain in the sixteenth and seventeenth centuries (see chapter 1, pp. 3–4). In this setting, archaeological evidence (plant remains) and historical documents (diaries, travel accounts, and early descriptions of native activities) are contradictory about what people did or did not eat in the region. The archaeological record suggested little or no consumption of corn prior to arrival of the Spaniards. After their arrival, however, native peoples adopted and depended to a strong degree on corn. Schoeninger and I believed that a more compelling record of diet could be constructed via the analysis of stable isotope ratios. As discussed in this chapter, a dominance of domesticated plants in the diet, especially corn, signals relatively poor-quality nutrition owing to the fact that they are protein-poor foods (see pp. 472–475). Overly narrow diets based on corn should predict negative impact on health, including relatively poor growth and higher prevalence of dental caries, infection, and iron deficiency.

We took bone samples from several hundred skeletons from the region and measured their ratios of

CHEMISTRY

stable isotopes of carbon and other elements. Our results were clear: We found a very pronounced near-continuous increase in the $\delta^{13}C$ ratio with time, reflecting the adoption of a corn-based diet in the last several centuries of prehistory before the arrival of Europeans, followed by a highly significant increase in corn consumption during the Spanish colonial period.

There is a caveat, however. We also knew that these coastal populations ate various seafoods based on the abundant shellfish and fish remains found where these populations were living. It turns out that marine foods can mimic the $\delta^{13}C$ ratios of corn due to the manner in which marine foods metabolize carbon. So, we used yet another set of stable isotopes—^{15}N and ^{14}N—and their ratios ($\delta^{15}N$) in order to distinguish marine foods (fish and shellfish) from corn in the diet. Populations eating a lot of seafood tend to have higher $\delta^{15}N$ values than populations not eating seafood. By plotting the values for each individual using both $\delta^{15}N$ and $\delta^{13}C$ values in a bivariate graph, this distinguishes the relative contributions of seafood and corn in diet over time.

Our analysis revealed a dramatic change in diet for the inhabitants of the region. Using St. Catherines Island, Georgia, as a microcosm of dietary change, we compared the stable isotope ratios for the Early Prehistoric, Late Prehistoric, and Santa Catalina de Guale colonial mission. This record shows a clear shift in diet from high seafood consumption and no corn in the Early Prehistoric, to still high seafood consumption but with corn in the Late Prehistoric, to limited seafood consumption and more corn in the Mission people. From this record, we can infer an increasingly lower access to

iron and increasing focus on a food that causes dental caries. Moreover, the region as a whole shows the same trend of reduced access to protein and increased focus on iron-poor, cariogenic corn.

Our earlier research on St. Catherines Island and the region generally showed an increase in dental caries and other indicators of increasingly poor health, especially during the contact period after arrival of the Spaniards and the establishment of missions in the region. Our application of chemistry to bones of the long-deceased helped us to understand why—it is explained at least in part by poor nutrition and increasing focus on carbohydrates. Increased accuracy in dietary reconstruction from the study of bone chemistry helped us to know with more certainty the diets of past people.

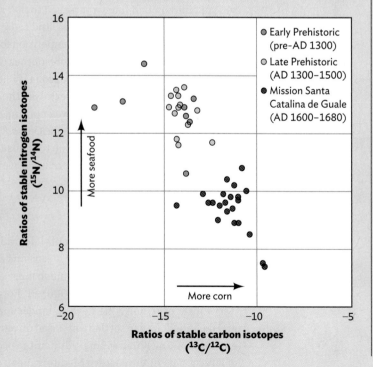

This graph shows the temporal change in stable carbon and stable nitrogen isotope ratios in bone samples from St. Catherines Island, Georgia, including the Early Prehistoric hunter-gatherers. The Late Prehistoric farmers, and the Mission farmers from Santa Catalina de Guale. Each dot represents a person. These ratios measure the relative reliance on corn and seafood, respectively. Notice the dramatic drop in seafood consumption and increase in corn consumption peaking during the Mission period.

13.2 Agriculture: An Adaptive Trade-Off

Most people assume that the adoption of agriculture was a highly positive development in human history. Indeed, agriculture's potential for supporting large numbers of people living in a concentrated setting and for creating surplus and, thus, wealth for some laid the foundation for the great civilizations of the past—such as in China, South America, and Mexico—and those of today. Beginning with the earliest cities in the early Holocene, no complex society, anywhere in the world, would have been possible without an agricultural economic base. Writing, art, business, technology, and just about every other feature of modern life came about because of agriculture. However, the rise of complex societies, of civilizations, and of technologically sophisticated ways to acquire both food and other resources also brought about a number of profound, and largely negative, consequences for humankind.

Population Growth

Probably the single most visible characteristic associated with the shift from foraging to farming is the increase in population size. Called the *Neolithic demographic transition*, this shift from low birthrate to high birthrate resulted in a rapid increase in the world's population. The greater number of births was brought about by a reduced period of weaning. The availability of grains cooked into soft mushes and fed to infants made it possible to wean infants earlier in their lives. With earlier weaning, spacing between births was reduced, and mothers were able to produce more offspring.

The first major demographic transition in human evolution spurred a remarkable increase in human population around the globe. This pattern continues to the present day and continues to place increased demands on the environment. (This development is discussed further in chapter 14.)

The growth of human population in the past 10,000 years is staggering. The world population around 10,000 yBP was probably no more than 10 million people. By 2,000 yBP, population had likely increased to 250 million or 300 million. By AD 1850, population had increased to 1 billion, and today it is more than 7 billion (**Figure 13.9**). Increasing population leads to competition for resources. As towns and cities began to compete for increasingly limited resources (for example, arable land for crops), organized warfare developed. Interpersonal violence has a long history in human evolution, going back at least to Neandertals in the late Pleistocene. But the level of violence among pre-Holocene hominins was nothing compared with the organized warfare of early civilizations in southwest Asia, Central America, and South America or with the medieval wars in Europe, where up to thousands of people were killed (**Figure 13.10**). As the study of human remains shows, organized violence has likely been present in small societies as well.

Environmental Degradation

The consequences of environmental degradation, like those of extreme population growth, are well documented by historians and ecologists for recent human history. This degradation actually has a much more ancient origin, beginning with plant and animal domestication around 10,000 yBP. For much of the region surrounding the Mediterranean, especially the Levant, landscapes have been substantially transformed and degraded. Dense settlement based on agrarian economies has contributed to soil erosion, making it increasingly difficult to produce food. Around 8,000 yBP, a number of large towns in the eastern Mediterranean were abandoned, probably due mostly to

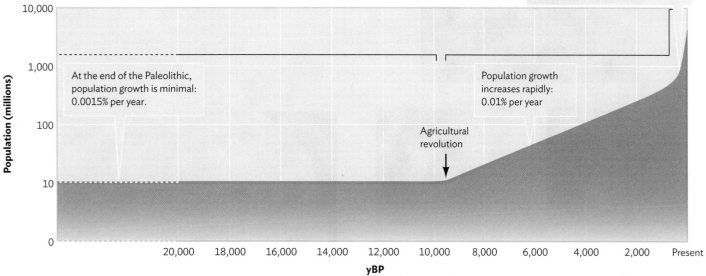

At the end of the Paleolithic, population growth is minimal: 0.0015% per year.

Population growth increases rapidly: 0.01% per year

Agricultural revolution

FIGURE 13.9

World Population Size This graph shows the trend in population size on a global scale. Until 10,000 yBP and the advent of agriculture, population remained constant, numbering less than 10 million people. After the agricultural revolution, however, population skyrocketed.

a period of climate drying. Contributing to the abandonment, however, was human activity, such as overgrazing with goats, which resulted in damaging erosion. Moreover, the amount of fuel, especially wood, needed to support the community resulted in the destruction of native vegetation and the desiccation of landscapes (**Figure 13.11**).

CONCEPT CHECK

The Good and Bad of Agriculture

Agriculture had many advantages for human adaptation. But it also had trade-offs, with both advantages and disadvantages.

Advantages

Support for larger numbers of people

Creation of surplus food

Long-term food storage, especially of grains

Disadvantages

Increased demands on the environment (land degradation)

Pollution

Conflict between populations competing for the same lands

Loss of wild species through overhunting

Decline of biodiversity

Health costs and quality-of-life implications

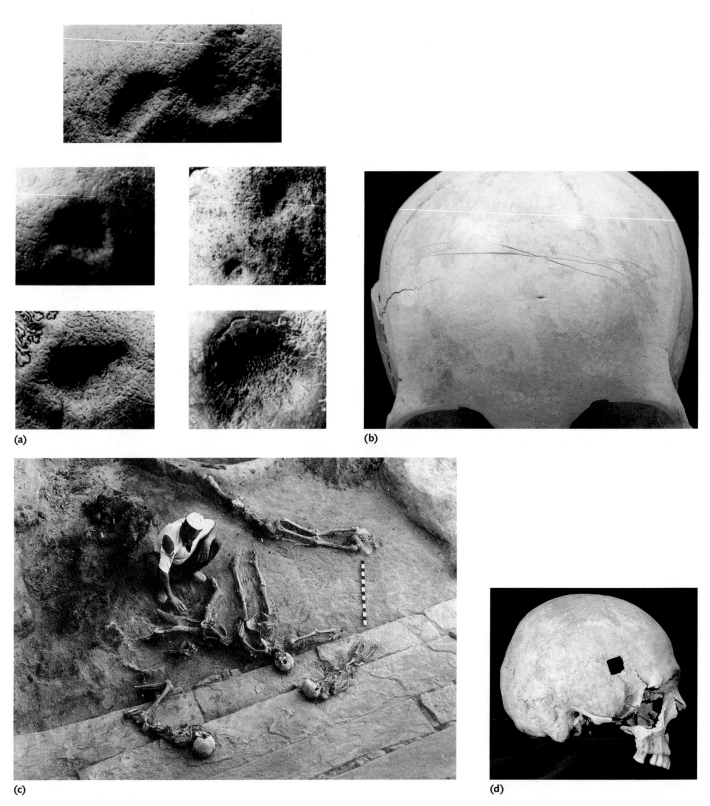

(a)

(b)

(c)

(d)

FIGURE 13.10

Interpersonal Conflict Skeletons from all regions of the world provide evidence of warfare and of organized violence, especially after the adoption of agriculture and the creation of towns and then cities. **(a)** Cranial depression fractures, such as these on prehistoric Native American remains from southern California, are the result of blunt-force trauma. **(b)** Cutmarks on this cranium—of a late prehistoric Native American from Norris Farms, Illinois—indicate that the individual was scalped. **(c)** These skeletons are the remains of victims of battle in ninth-century-BC Iran. They were discovered on the floors of buildings that had been burned during the conflict. (Photo: Penn Museum image no. 78138.) **(d)** This cranium received its puncture wound (square hole) during a late medieval massacre, the Battle of Towton, in England.

FIGURE 13.11

Human Impact With the domestication of plants and of animals, humans began having a greater impact on the world. Soil erosion, deforestation, and overgrazing have contributed to many environmental problems. Excessive tree-cutting, such as shown here in China, can lead to greater soil erosion and to desertification.

Likewise, the recent collapse of coastal ecosystems worldwide clearly had its start in overfishing—especially of large vertebrates (for example, whales) and shellfish—beginning thousands of years ago. Simply, the dramatically altered ecosystems worldwide have caused biodiversity to crash, a development that appears to be accelerating. The American anthropologist Jeffrey McKee argues that one primary force behind the reduction in biodiversity is expanding human population size. He predicts that if left unchecked, the population will outstrip the arable land available to produce the plants and animals consumed by humans. Thus, the increased food supply that resulted from the agricultural revolution in the Holocene could, in the not-too-distant future, lead to a food crisis (discussed further in chapter 14).

13.3 How Did Agriculture Affect Human Biology?

A misperception shared by the public and anthropologists is that with the appearance of essentially modern *Homo sapiens* in the late Pleistocene, human biological evolution ground to a halt. That is, many think that humans stopped evolving biologically once they became modern, in the Upper Paleolithic. Unlike recent humans' cultural evolution (for example, increasing use of technology and development of the arts), humans' biological evolution since the closing days of the Pleistocene has gone largely unrecognized.

In the remainder of this chapter, we will examine the human biological changes that accompanied the agricultural revolution—changes linked directly or indirectly to the fundamental change, discussed earlier, in how humans have acquired resources, especially food. At the end of the chapter, we will revisit the question of why humans made this remarkable transition. Some very compelling reasons exist to believe that agriculture has contributed to *H. sapiens'* evolutionary success, at least as measured by humankind's remarkable population increase since then.

FIRST WAR

The Massacre at Kilianstädten

Violence and interpersonal conflict have long been a part of the fabric of human behavior.

WATCH
THE VIDEO

www.digital.
wwnorton.com/
ourorigins4

The Neolithic mass grave at Kilianstädten, Germany. After the massacre, the remains of the dead were collected and thrown haphazardly into a trench. These remains represent some of the earliest evidence of warfare.

The record of violence—where one individual does bodily harm to another—extends back before the appearance of modern *Homo sapiens*. For example, several of the Krapina Neandertals (see chapter 12) display cranial injuries caused by blows to their heads. However, these injuries were likely isolated occurrences involving no more than two individuals and certainly do not qualify as what we consider to be warfare. The record of systematic, planned aggression involving multiple attackers and multiple victims—that is, warfare—is not present until quite recently in human evolution. In fact, the record of systematic violence does not become visible until the first appearance of farming, beginning in the Neolithic.

The Neolithic involved profound changes in foods eaten, settlement location and size, and living conditions in general. It is a time during which people settled in permanent communities where considerable economic investment in crops and livestock was made within a relatively restricted region. It is likely that these circumstances are related to the origins of organized conflict, especially warfare. Essentially,

population size increase and competition for land set the stage for one group fighting with another, usually with deadly outcomes for entire groups of individuals.

The first instances of warfare are well documented from the study of massacre victims from Neolithic farming settlements in central Europe, dating to circa 7,600–6,900 yBP. These massacres provide evidence of conflict involving multiple deaths occurring in one catastrophic event. The Kilianstädten site in Germany contains an especially well-preserved record of massacre. A burial pit at this locality contained the disarticulated and jumbled skeletal remains of 26 individuals who died under violent attack by a foreign group. Study of the victims' remains led by German physical anthropologist Christian Meyer revealed that the remains are equally represented by children and adults. Some of the children were less than six years old when they died violently, including one six-month-old infant. Most of the adults were younger adult males, and only two were older than 40. Like other early farming populations, the victims have an elevated frequency of disease, including tuberculosis and various infections often

FARE

associated with living in close, crowded conditions (see Figure 13.26).

Most striking about the record of violence at Kilianstädten is the elevated frequency of blunt-force cranial trauma and fractures of the limb bones. The blunt-force cranial injuries were caused by an attacker hitting the victim's head with a stone implement. Most of the cranial injuries are to the left parietal bone, indicating that the victim was facing a right-handed attacker. The limb-bone fractures are especially prevalent in the distal tibias. More than half of the tibias had fractures that occurred at the time of death. In combination, the very consistent pattern of trauma reveals that the heads and lower legs were targeted during the attack. At some point after the attack, a large, linear pit was dug. The remains of the deceased were haphazardly deposited in the pit, and the pit was refilled with dirt. The random positioning of the bones and bodies suggest that the burial was rapid.

The Kilianstädten massacre was not an isolated occurrence. Rather, a number of Neolithic localities in Germany and elsewhere show remains with the same kinds of injuries and haphazard disposal of the deceased. Collectively, the record indicates that specific communities were singled out; men, women, and children were beaten, tortured, and killed in violent, painful ways; and the bodies were disposed of in a highly careless fashion. The reasons for the extreme violence and why these particular groups bore the brunt of attack will never be known, but they were likely close neighbors and in competition for land. Perhaps climatic changes taking place during this time made agriculture less predictable, resulting in a reduced availability of foods derived from crops. As shown by numerous studies, there are clear

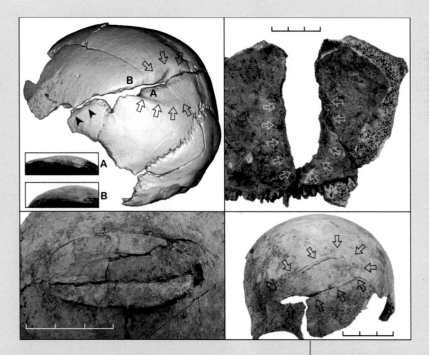

Cranial trauma of victims of the massacre was intentional and deadly. The arrows in the examples of victims point to massive fractures caused by sharp stone weapons.

associations between uncertainty of food production and elevated violence. Regardless of the causes or circumstances, the Kilianstädten and contemporary massacre sites in Neolithic Central Europe exemplify a new kind of violence involving careful planning with lethal intent. The study of these massacre skeletons provides an important window onto the people that lived and died in Neolithic Central Europe and vital insights into the beginning of warfare.

The study of conflict in past populations when viewed in the context of a setting involving competition for resources by two or more groups of people provides a basis for understanding warfare and conflict today. Namely, there are various outcomes of competition between social groups, including conflict, resulting in injury and death. Indeed, anthropology matters.

The Changing Face of Humanity

As discussed at the beginning of this chapter, the foods we eat and the manner in which they are prepared tremendously influence our physical appearance. The relationship between food and morphology is well illustrated by the major anatomical changes throughout human evolution. As discussed in chapter 10, the massiveness of the late australopithecines' face and jaws was clearly linked to the hard foods those hominins ate, such as seeds. Generating the power to chew hard foods required large masticatory muscles (and their bony support). Thus, the well-developed sagittal crests of some later australopithecines—such as *Australopithecus aethiopicus*—are adaptations related to chewing. Over the course of human evolution after the australopithecines, the face and jaws have continually reduced in size and robusticity, reflecting a general decrease in the demand placed on the jaws and teeth as culture became increasingly complex and foodstuffs changed.

The reduction in size of the face and jaws is a general theme throughout human evolution, including during the Holocene and with the dietary adoption of domesticated plants. For example, in studying skulls from England that dated to the past couple of thousand years, Sir Arthur Keith documented a clear reduction in the size of the face and jaws. He believed that this reduction came about from eating soft foods, such as cooked cereal grains. Other physical anthropologists have noted similar changes in many other places of the world. In Sudan's Nile Valley—the region known as Nubia—hunter-gatherers living during the time immediately preceding agriculture had long and narrow skulls, whereas their descendants had short and wide skulls. My own work on the Atlantic coast of the southeastern United States shows similar trends.

TWO HYPOTHESES To explain why the human skull changed shape in Nubia during the past 10,000 years, anthropologists in the 1800s and most of the 1900s offered an explanation based on old concepts of race (see chapter 5 for discussion of race). In Nubia, for example, they believed that the change occurred because short-headed people invaded territory occupied by long-headed people. These earlier anthropologists viewed head shape as unchanging and essentially a diagnostic racial marker. They were correct that humans living in specific areas of the globe have physical characteristics in common. However, since then, anthropologists have learned that human facial and skull forms are highly plastic, as are other parts of the skeleton.

The American physical anthropologists David Carlson and Dennis Van Gerven have offered an alternative hypothesis, which explains differences in head shape in Nubia but can be applied globally. Their **masticatory-functional hypothesis** states that change in skull form represents a response to decreased demands on the chewing muscles—temporalis and masseter—as people shifted from eating hard-textured wild foods to eating soft-textured agricultural foods, such as millet. (**Figure 13.12** lays out the hypothetical steps of this process.) To be sure, the millet grains eaten by ancient Nubians were not especially soft in their uncooked form. However, early in the Holocene, a critical change occurred in human technological evolution: the invention of pottery for storing food or cooking it (**Figure 13.13**). By *cooking,* I mean not a simple warm-up but cooking for hours until foods become soft mushes, rather easily chewed. The chewing of these mushes would have required far less powerful muscles. Because light use of muscle produces limited bone growth, the later Nubians, eating soft foods, had reduced faces.

Carlson and Van Gerven's explanation for much of the change in human head shape during the Holocene is strongly supported by evidence from living species, including humans. For example, experimental research shows that primates fed soft foods have a relatively shorter skull with a smaller face and jaws than those of primates fed hard foods.

masticatory-functional hypothesis The hypothesis that craniofacial shape change during the Holocene was related to the consumption of softer foods.

IMPLICATIONS FOR TEETH These changes in skull size and skull shape had enormous implications for our teeth. Today, the high numbers of people with orthodontic problems—malocclusions ranging from simple overbite to very poorly aligned teeth—contrast sharply with the few such problems found in ancient hominins and throughout much of prehistory. The American physical anthropologist James Calcagno has noted a number of exceptions, which may have influenced the size of our teeth, but malocclusions are rare prior to the modern era.

Why, then, do so many people around the globe have dental malocclusions? As with general skull shape, food plays an especially important role. Animals fed soft-textured foods develop far more occlusal abnormalities, such as crooked teeth, misaligned jaws, and chewing problems, than do animals fed hard-textured foods. The study of many thousands of skulls has shown that tooth size and jaw size have reduced in the past 10,000 years but at different paces. Bone is greatly subject to environmental factors, so a child fed softer foods than his or her parents ate will have appreciably reduced jaws. By contrast, teeth are controlled much more by genes, so over the course of evolution teeth have reduced far less than jaws have. Simply, the greater reduction of the bones supporting the teeth has led to greater crowding of

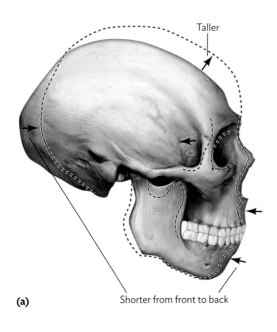

(a)

Taller

Shorter from front to back

FIGURE 13.12

Craniofacial Changes (a) The overall reduction in cranial size over the course of human evolution can be seen in Nubians' skeletal remains. Here, the dashed line indicates the craniofacial changes that have occurred between the Mesolithic foragers and the later agriculturalists. The skull has become shorter from front to back and, simultaneously, has gotten taller. (b) As presented in this flowchart, the Nubians' craniofacial changes resulted from alteration in diet associated with eating softer foods. In changing their diet, the Nubians were placing less demand on their chewing muscles. As a result, the associated bones changed; facial bones and jaws became smaller, and the cranial vault became rounder. The reduction in jaw size left less room for teeth, and the increased crowding resulted in malocclusion.

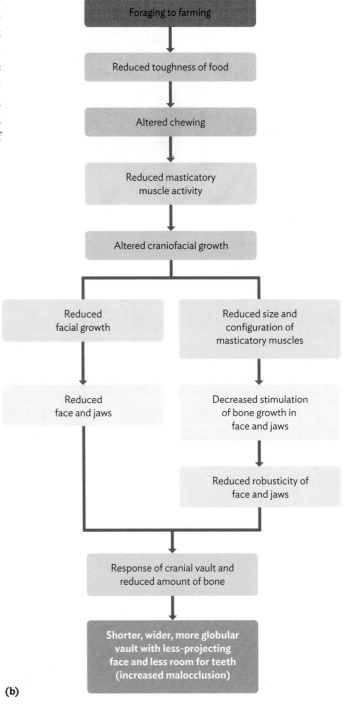

(b)

FIGURE 13.13

Pottery Vessels, such as this terra-cotta pot, were an important invention. Such containers made possible both the storage of food for periods of time and the cooking of food into softer forms.

teeth. This disharmony underscores the complex nature of our biology, which involves an interplay between intrinsic (genetic) factors and extrinsic (environmental) factors.

Malocclusion is a clearly negative result of humans' eating soft foods. A positive result is that our teeth have very little wear because eating soft foods places less stress on the chewing surfaces.

Building a New Physique: Agriculture's Changes to Workload and Activity

One major debate in anthropology concerns the extent to which the agricultural revolution improved the quality of human life, including workload. Did people have to work more or work less to acquire food through agriculture rather than through hunting and gathering? The eminent American archaeologist Robert Braidwood characterized the lifestyle of a typical hunter-gatherer as "a savage's existence, and a very tough one ... following animals just to kill them to eat, or moving from one berry patch to another." About the time Braidwood was writing this in the 1960s, the Canadian cultural anthropologist Richard Lee and the American physical anthropologist Irven DeVore organized what turned out to be one of the most important conferences in the modern era of anthropology. They invited experts in different areas of anthropology from around the globe to determine the quality of life of hunter-gatherers, ancient and modern. A key component in assessing the quality of life was workload. If Braidwood was correct, hunter-gatherers had to work very hard, basically spending all waking hours in the food quest, getting food wherever and whenever possible. However, Lee and others reported that hunter-gatherers might not have had it all that bad when it came to workload. In fact, in his research on the Ju/'hoansi (!Kung) of southern Africa, Lee found that these hunter-gatherers had a great deal of leisure time (**Figure 13.14**).

Lee's work in the 1960s set in motion the work of a whole generation of anthropologists, who addressed both his observations and his hypotheses. Science works this way, of course—old hypotheses are often rejected as new observations are made, and new observations generate new hypotheses. Indeed, the subsequent work showed that hunter-gatherers have quite diverse workloads. Anthropologists realized that workload depended highly on the local ecology and the kinds of foods being eaten. For example, in how they acquire plants and animals, people living in the tropics differ greatly from people living in the Arctic.

How do scientists know how hard or how easy a lifestyle was? Obviously, they cannot observe the behavior of dead people. But physical anthropology offers a way to reconstruct past behavior. Biomechanics, an area of great interest to physical anthropologists, provides enormous insight into the evolution of the body below the neck in relation to workload and to other activity. As with the bones of the face and of the jaws, the bones of the postcranial skeleton are highly plastic during the years of growth and of development, all the way through adulthood. The general shape and size of bones—the femur, in the leg, for example, or the humerus, in the arm—are determined by a person's genes. However, the finer details are subject to work and activity. Highly physically active people's bones tend to be larger and more developed than those of not so physically active people.

Borrowing from how engineers measure the strength of building materials—such as the I-beam used in the construction of a bridge or of a building—physical anthropologists have developed a means for assessing the robusticity of bone cross sections. Based on the simple premise that material placed farther away from an axis running down the center of the bone is stronger than material placed closest to the axis (**Figure 13.15**), it has become possible to look at the degree of bone development and determine by empirical means how bone strength has changed over the course of human evolution to the present. Bone comparisons—from hunter-gatherers' to later agriculturalists' to modern peoples'—show a remarkable decline in size.

FIGURE 13.14

Leisure Time While foragers, such as this band of !Kung, must spend many hours searching for and hunting for food, their work does not preclude them from relaxing for periods of time. However, studies of numerous foraging groups have shown a great deal of variation in the workloads and amounts of leisure time of hunter-gatherers.

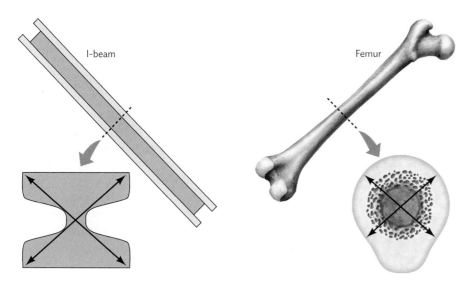

FIGURE 13.15

Cross-Sectional Geometry Using engineering principles, physical anthropologists can gain insight into activity patterns by examining the cross sections of long bones, such as the femur and the humerus. The shapes of long bones, like those of I-beams (building materials used for structural support), maximize both strength and ability to resist bending by distributing mass away from the center of the section.

BONES AND

The shapes and sizes of bones are determined largely by each species' genetic plan. However, because individual bones have a significant amount of plasticity, their shapes can be reconfigured, especially those of arm and leg bones.

These reconfigurations are determined by environmental factors, in particular the stresses from muscles and from body weight. By studying these reconfigurations in skeletons, physical anthropologists learn a great deal about past peoples' lifestyles.

One breakthrough in physical anthropologists' understanding of earlier humans' physical activity has

A

Bending a ruler helps illustrate the principles of biomechanics.

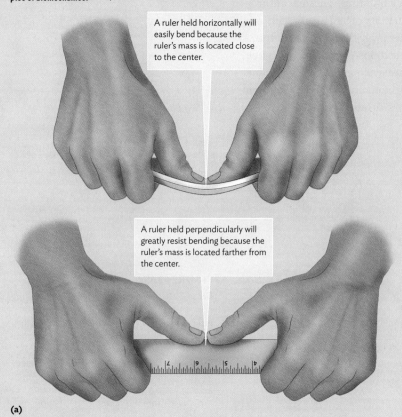

A ruler held horizontally will easily bend because the ruler's mass is located close to the center.

A ruler held perpendicularly will greatly resist bending because the ruler's mass is located farther from the center.

(a)

been the application of biomechanics to bones. (See the text and Figures 13.15 and 13.16.) To visualize these biomechanical principles, hold a plastic ruler flat, with one hand at each end, and bend it. Now rotate the ruler 90 degrees to the perpendicular, again with one hand at each end, and try to bend it. On the flat plane, the ruler bends easily because its mass is distributed close to the central axis, so its bending "strength"—actually, resistance to bending—is low. On the perpendicular plane, the ruler is almost impossible to bend because its mass is distributed farther from the central axis, so its bending strength is high. In this plane, it resists bending forces you have applied to the ruler with your hands.

Now imagine a perfectly circular hollow tube, seen in cross section. In the different planes across the section, the bending strength is equal. However, if the tube is a little flattened, the elongated section has greater resistance to bending because the tube's mass is placed farther from the central axis than it is in the narrow section. Now replace that hollow tube with a femur or humerus.

To assess the bending and torsional (or twisting) strength of that limb bone, physical anthropologists measure biomechanical properties called *second moments of area*. Engineers call these properties I, which denotes bending strength, and J, which denotes twisting strength. Physical anthropologists measure these properties in relation to two primary axes in a bone cross section, the x-axis and the y-axis, or I_x and I_y. The I_x values measure the front-to-back bending, and the I_y values measure the side-to-side bending. J is the sum of these two values. The larger the I or J values, the greater the bone's ability to resist breaking

BEHAVIOR

C

This cross section illustrates two second moments of area: *I*, which reflects bending strength in one of two dimensions, and *J*, which reflects torsional strength. The relative strength of any second moment of area (SMA) reflects the individual's activity patterns.

B

Because it is perfectly round, the cross section on the left has equal strength, or equal resistance to bending, in all directions. The slightly flattened cross section on the right, however, has greater strength in the *y*-axis than in the *x*-axis because the material is distributed farther from the central point.

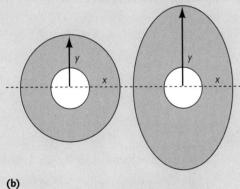

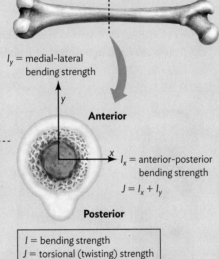

I_y = medial-lateral bending strength

I_x = anterior-posterior bending strength

$J = I_x + I_y$

Anterior

Posterior

(b)

| I = bending strength |
| J = torsional (twisting) strength |

(c)

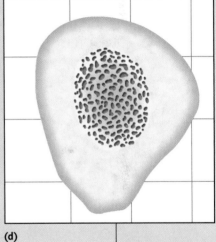

(d)

D

This cross section is taken at the midpoint of an adult femur diaphysis from a prehistoric site in Nevada. That this cross section is especially elongated from top to bottom (front and back of the bone) indicates high bending strength in that direction. The bone came from a population that was likely both physically active and engaged in long-distance movement.

from the forces of walking, of running, or of lifting heavy objects.

Measurement involves first getting a good image of the bone's cross section. Doing so might mean cutting the bone to physically expose the cross section, usually in the mid-diaphysis. If cutting is impossible, a cross section can be created by taking a CAT (computed axial tomography) scan of the bone, just as a radiologist would as part of a medical examination. On the section, the physical anthropologist traces the bone's outer perimeter, or periosteal surface, and inner perimeter, or endosteal surface, with an electronic stylus hooked up to a computer loaded with engineering software that automatically calculates the second moments of area.

American physical anthropologist Christopher

Ruff has pioneered this method of assessing bone strength to document and interpret major (and very minor) trends in populations' physical activity and in adaptions to that activity. He has found one very clear trend in human evolution: bone strength in *Homo* has declined dramatically, but especially in the past 10,000 years. However, comparisons between earlier North American hunter-gatherers and the prehistoric farmers who descended from them reveal that bone strength has increased in some settings and decreased in others. This variation pattern reflects the highly localized nature of the shift from foraging to farming. The study of bone biomechanics reveals that, whatever the change may have been for a particular region, the transition had a major impact on physical activity and lifestyle generally.

Physical anthropologists' studies have shown that populations respond differently to the adoption of an agricultural lifestyle. For example, in our research on skeletons from the Atlantic coasts of Georgia and Florida, Christopher Ruff and I have found that agricultural populations' bones became smaller, which we interpret to mean that those populations worked less hard than their hunter-gatherer ancestors (**Figure 13.16**). We have also found a decrease in **osteoarthritis,** a disorder of the skeletal joints that results from excessive stresses on places where the bones articulate (**Figure 13.17**). In contrast, the American physical anthropologist Patricia Bridges has discovered a clear increase in bone size in Alabama populations. Which is correct? Did workload increase or decrease? Actually, both are correct. Coastal settings involved very different means of food production compared to noncoastal settings, reflecting the regions' differences in terrain and in other kinds of nonagricultural foods. On the Georgia coast, people collected seafood in addition to practicing agriculture. In noncoastal Alabama, people supplemented agriculture with terrestrial foods, such as deer.

In general, the reduction in human bone size represents an overall evolutionary trend in the past 20,000 years. Thanks to the increasing tool complexity and greater cultural sophistication, the biological changes came about as physical strength was replaced with technology. Ruff's studies of human remains from around the world indicate that the reduced bone mass reflects about a 10% decrease in body weight during this period. Simply, a decrease in mechanical demand on the body and its skeletal elements has resulted in increasing gracility, especially in modern humans.

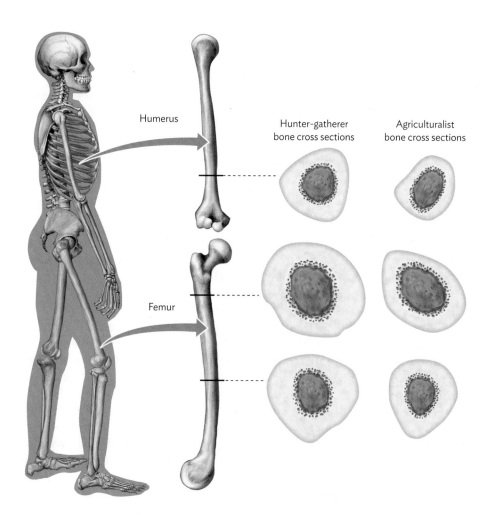

Hunter-gatherer bone cross sections

Agriculturalist bone cross sections

Humerus

Femur

FIGURE 13.16

Activity Pattern Comparison Physical anthropologists compared cross sections of the femurs and humeri from prehistoric hunter-gatherers and agriculturalists living on the southeastern US Atlantic coast (modern states of Georgia and Florida; see the opening paragraphs of chapter 1) to determine whether significant changes in the native populations' activity patterns had occurred with the shift to farming. The larger sections in the hunter-gatherers indicate greater bone strength than in their agricultural descendants. The reduced bone strength in the Mission-era Indians reflects less mechanical stress in the prehistoric farmers in this setting.

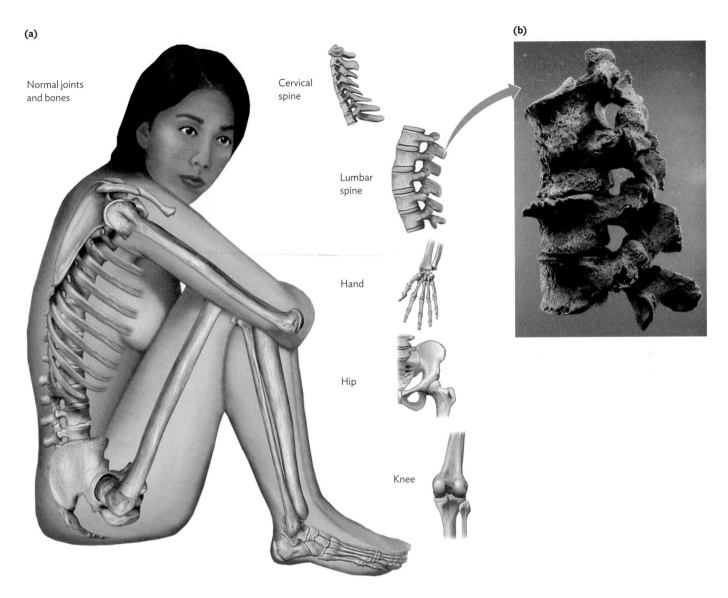

(a) Normal joints and bones

Cervical spine

Lumbar spine

Hand

Hip

Knee

FIGURE 13.17

Osteoarthritis **(a)** Degenerative joint disease, or osteoarthritis, can occur in a variety of sites throughout the body, commonly in the vertebrae, hips, knees, and hands. **(b)** The lumbar vertebrae, toward the base of the spine, are often among the first bones affected by osteoarthritis. This condition results from stress on the back due to lifting and carrying, and its presence on a skeleton indicates the repetition of physically demanding activity.

Health and the Agricultural Revolution

POPULATION CROWDING AND INFECTIOUS DISEASE The population increase during the Holocene, discussed extensively earlier in the chapter, was linked with agriculture and increased food production. As the population increased, communities grew more committed to raising crops and became more sedentary, living in one place the entire year. Before then, the smaller number of people had moved around at least on a seasonal basis. The increase in size and density of the population, especially when the population remained in place, had enormous, negative effects on people's health. In short, humans began to live in conditions crowded and unsanitary enough to support pathogens.

Consider the overcrowded cities around the globe today. In the urban slums of Bombay, India, or Rio de Janeiro, Brazil, or La Paz, Bolivia, or even within developed nations where sanitation is carefully regulated and monitored, the crowding sets up conditions

Labor, Lifestyle, and Adaptation in the Skeleton

The human skeleton responds to activity, reflecting the person's lifestyle. Hunter-gatherers' skeletons and agriculturalists' skeletons vary in patterns that reveal different levels of activity, including that of workload; but hunter-gatherers' skeletons tend to show higher levels of responses resulting from higher or more strenuous activity.

Hunter-Gatherers	Agriculturalists
Bones with higher second moments of area	Bones with lower second moments of area
Larger, more robust bones	Smaller, less robust bones
Much tooth wear	Little tooth wear

periosteal reaction Inflammatory response of a bone's outer covering due to bacterial infection or to trauma.

for increased interpersonal contact and the spread of infectious microorganisms and viruses (**Figure 13.18**).

During the Holocene, especially in agricultural settings, crowding seems to have produced illnesses and injuries. Any kind of injury to the outer surface of bone can cause a **periosteal reaction,** or bone buildup, which is sometimes combined with an abnormal expansion of a bone's diameter. The reaction is caused by localized infection, such as from the so-called staph bacteria, *Staphylococcus aureus*. The infection essentially stimulates new bone growth, hence the swollen appearance (**Figure 13.19**).

FIGURE 13.18

Overcrowding One negative effect of agriculture and the resulting increase in sedentism is overcrowding. In overcrowded slums, such as this one in Bombay, India, unsanitary conditions help increase the levels of infectious microorganisms and thus lead to disease outbreaks.

Most periosteal reactions are nonspecific, so anthropologists cannot tell exactly what caused them. Anthropologists find, however, a general increase in periosteal reactions on the limb bones of skeletons from crowded settings in the Holocene. Such reactions are practically nonexistent in human groups predating that time.

Some infections identified on bones from Holocene populations have a specific pattern that suggests the diseases that caused them. In the American Midwest and Southeast, for example, tibias are swollen and bowed, while crania have distinctive uneven, pitted texture (**Figure 13.20**). Both kinds of bone deformation are caused by a group of diseases called **treponematoses,** which include venereal syphilis, nonvenereal (also called *endemic*) syphilis, and yaws. Anthropologists, historians, and others debate the origin of venereal syphilis, some blaming native populations, some blaming Christopher Columbus and his ship crews, and some arguing for the appearance of a wholly new disease sometime after the initial European explorations of the New World. However, the pattern of bone changes in the New World prior to the late 1400s suggests a nonvenereal syphilis, one passed not by sexual contact but by casual contact, such as by a mother holding her child.

Many other infectious diseases likely affected Holocene populations worldwide. The skeletal indicators of tuberculosis, for example, are widespread in parts of the New World, of the Old World, and of Australia, well before the time of European exploration. For much of the mid-twentieth century, many medical practitioners thought this microbial infection had been conquered; but today, 2–3 million people die annually from the disease. Other modern diseases made possible by overcrowding include, but are not limited to, measles, mumps, cholera, smallpox, and influenza. Some of these diseases have an Old World origin, but the New World was hardly a disease-free paradise before their introduction. Bioarchaeologists have documented many poor health conditions and evidence of physiological stress before the Europeans' arrival in North and South America.

FIGURE 13.19

Periosteal Reaction The tibia is a common site of periosteal reactions. Here, a pathological tibia from St. Catherines Island, Georgia, on the left, has an irregular surface because new bone has been deposited unevenly. A normal tibia, on the right, has a smooth surface, free of any reactive bone.

treponematoses A group of related diseases (venereal syphilis, yaws, endemic syphilis) caused by the bacteria *Treponema*, which causes pathological changes most often to the cranium and tibiae.

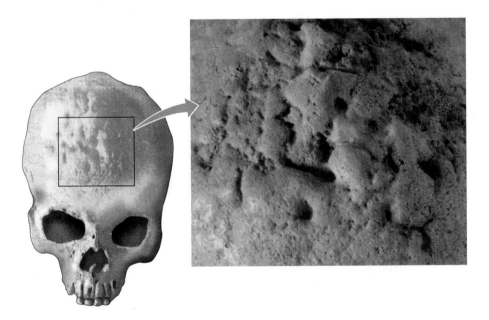

FIGURE 13.20

Treponematosis The lesions on this cranium indicate that this individual from the prehistoric southeastern United States suffered from treponematosis. The undulating surface of the skull shows active and healed lesions caused by the disease's long, slow progression.

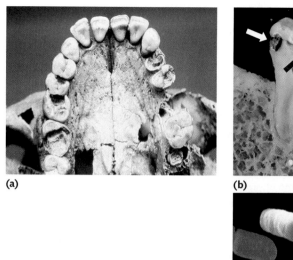

(a)

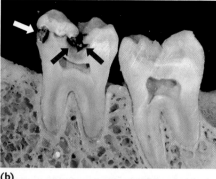

(b)

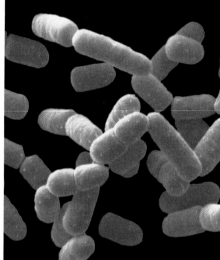

(c)

FIGURE 13.21

Dental Caries (a) Cavities are more common in individuals with carbohydrate-rich diets. As a result of the digestion of carbohydrates, carious lesions form as the enamel of the teeth deteriorates. In extreme cases, the pulp of the teeth can be affected. **(b)** This cross section of a tooth affected by dental caries shows two common locations of cavities: the occlusal, or chewing, surface (black arrows) and between successive teeth (white arrow). **(c)** *Lactobacillus* is one of the two main bacteria that cause dental caries.

dental caries A disease process that creates demineralized areas in dental tissues, leading to cavities; demineralization is caused by acids produced by bacteria that metabolize carbohydrates in dental plaque.

THE CONSEQUENCES OF DECLINING NUTRITION: TOOTH DECAY All domesticated plants have nutritional drawbacks. Because they are carbohydrates, they promote **dental caries,** commonly known as tooth decay or "cavities" (**Figure 13.21**). Caries is a process in which the natural bacteria in your mouth—common culprits are *Streptococcus mutans* and *Lactobacillus acidophilus*—digest the carbohydrates there. One end product of this digestive process is lactic acid, which literally dissolves tooth enamel. In industrial societies today, dentists stabilize caries by removing diseased parts of teeth and filling the cavities with composite material to stop the spread of decay. In the ancient world, dentistry was mostly nonexistent, and cavities grew until the teeth fell out or, in some instances, people with cavities died from secondary infections.

Different domesticated plants promote tooth decay at varying rates. Rice does not seem to cause it to the same extent as other domesticated plants. Corn causes it considerably. Once post–AD 800 populations in eastern North America had adopted corn agriculture, the frequency of their dental caries rose dramatically (**Figure 13.22**).

NUTRITIONAL CONSEQUENCES DUE TO MISSING NUTRIENTS: REDUCED GROWTH AND ABNORMAL DEVELOPMENT The popular and the academic literatures suggest that agriculture has improved humans' nutrition. This conclusion makes sense given the huge worldwide investment in agriculture, even today. However, the assessment of superfoods' nutritional content argues otherwise.

In most places where early populations relied on agriculture, there existed the potential for abnormal growth and development because of the nutritional limitations of domesticated plants. Dietary reconstructions of past societies by archaeologists and studies of living agrarian populations in different settings indicate that agriculturalists' diets tend to overemphasize one plant or a couple of them, such as rice in Asia, wheat in Europe and temperate Asia, corn in the Americas, and millet or sorghum in Africa. Thus, many groups, especially in the later Holocene, received poor nutrition from an increasingly narrow range of foods. A well-balanced diet, as your parents and teachers have told you time and again, involves variety from all the food groups.

Domesticated plants have nutritional value, of course, but they also present a range of negative nutritional consequences. For example, corn is deficient in the amino acids lysine, isoleucine, and tryptophan, and a person who does not receive the right amount of even one amino acid will neither grow normally nor develop properly. In addition, vitamin B_3 (niacin) in corn is bound chemically, and corn also contains phytate, a chemical that binds with iron and hampers the body's iron absorption. Also, grains such as millet and wheat contain very little iron. Rice is deficient in protein and thus inhibits vitamin A activity.

Numerous societies worldwide have developed strategies for improving these foods' nutritional content. For example, corn-dependent populations commonly treat corn with alkali, a weak solution of lye. This treatment increases availability of niacin and improves the quality of the protein. Such treatments cannot, however, entirely make up for the negative consequences of dietary overreliance on these plants.

One of the most obvious ways of assessing the impact of nutritional change in the Holocene is by looking at the growth of bones and of teeth. Like any other body tissues, bones and teeth grow to their full genetic potential only if they receive proper nutrition. Anthropologists are able to identify a few indicators of growth stress in skeletal and dental records from fossils, but these indicators are generally nonspecific; that is, they are not linked to a precise cause (for example, a particular vitamin that the person

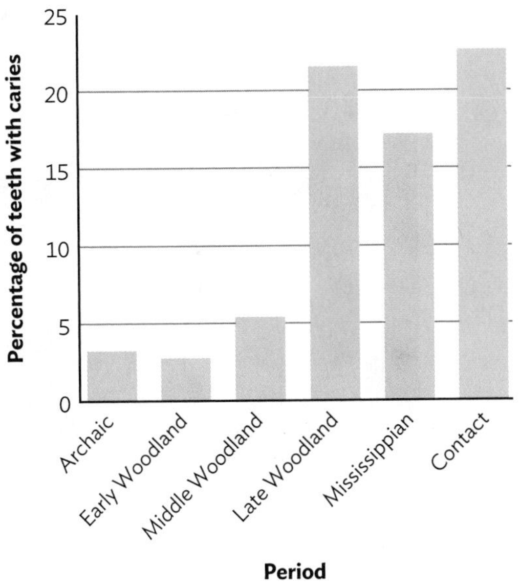

FIGURE 13.22

Changes in Oral Health This chart shows temporal changes in dental caries in eastern North America. During the Archaic, Early Woodland, and Middle Woodland periods, which predate AD 800, the region's native inhabitants were hunter-gatherers. During the Late Woodland, Mississippian, and Contact periods, which postdate AD 1000, the adoption of agriculture caused a large increase in dental caries.

CONCEPT CHECK

Health Costs of Agriculture

Because of population increase, crowding, and poor nutrition, human populations' health declined in many settings globally.

Health Indicator	Hunter-Gatherers	Agriculturalists
Infection (periosteal reactions)	Low	High
Dental caries	Low	High
Child growth and development	Normal	Reduced
Enamel defects (hypoplasias, microdefects)	Low	High
Iron deficiency (porotic hyperostosis, cribra orbitalia)	Low	High
Adult height	Normal	Reduced

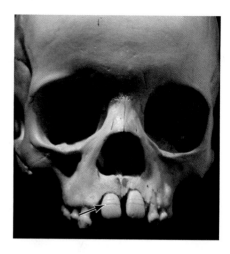

FIGURE 13.23

Enamel Hypoplasias These defects reflect stress episodes that occurred during tooth development. Individuals with multiple hypoplasias on each tooth underwent several stress episodes.

iron deficiency anemia A condition in which the blood has insufficient iron; may be caused by diet, poor iron absorption, parasitic infection, and severe blood loss.

heme iron Iron—found in red meat, fish, and poultry—that the body absorbs efficiently.

nonheme iron Iron—found in lentils and beans—that is less efficiently absorbed by the body than is heme iron.

porotic hyperostosis Expansion and porosity of cranial bones due to anemia caused by an iron-deficient diet, parasitic infection, or genetic disease.

cribra orbitalia Porosity in the eye orbits due to anemia caused by an iron-deficient diet, parasitic infection, or genetic disease.

was deficient in). These stress indicators are also related to multiple factors that may or may not include nutrition. Nonnutritional factors often include infection or infectious disease. Yet, as studies of living populations have shown, nutrition and infection have a synergistic relationship: poor nutrition worsens the infection, and vice versa; essential nutrition is used to fight the infection and is taken away from the growth process. Despite such complications, anthropologists have found these indicators to be very informative about the history of stress both in individuals and in populations.

Deficiencies in dental enamel are one of the most important nonspecific stress indicators. Typically, the deficiencies appear as lines, pits, or grooves, any of which occur when the cells responsible for enamel production (called **ameloblasts**) are disrupted. Consequently, when the disturbance ends (the illness or the infection is over) a defect, or hypoplasia, is left (**Figure 13.23**). Defects of this kind are commonplace in earlier humans' teeth—indeed, researchers have found them in australopithecines—but they are rare through most of human evolution. Some hunter-gatherer populations have high frequencies, but hypoplasias became relatively common in Holocene populations. The high frequency in agriculturalists around the world was caused by two factors: decline in nutritional quality and increase in infectious disease. (Other dental defects, visible in teeth only with a microscope, reflect very short-term stress episodes, lasting several hours to several days. Virtually everyone has microscopic defects in the deciduous teeth, created as a result of birth stress.)

NUTRITIONAL CONSEQUENCES OF IRON DEFICIENCY Other markers of stress and of deprivation in agricultural populations can be linked to specific causes. **Iron deficiency anemia,** a problem that plagues many millions of people around the globe, results when the body receives limited iron. Iron is necessary for many body functions and is an essential element in hemoglobin, serving in the transport of oxygen to the body tissues. Iron—specifically, **heme iron**—enters the body easily through meat eating because the amino acids from the digestion of meat promote iron absorption. Iron from plants—**nonheme iron**—is not as readily available because various substances in plants inhibit iron absorption (see the earlier discussion on corn). Citric acid found in various fruits, however, may promote iron absorption.

Some authorities believe that iron deficiency is rarely caused by dietary stress and is more often related to nondietary factors. Parasitic infections, for example, are a primary cause of iron deficiency anemia in many regions of the globe. One such infection, hookworm disease, is caused when someone inhales or ingests hookworm larvae. The worm (*Ancylostoma duodenale, Necator americanus*) extracts blood from its human host by using the sharp teethlike structures in its head to latch itself to the intestinal wall (**Figure 13.24**). When several hundred or more of these worms are present, severe blood loss—and therefore anemia—can result.

Abundant evidence of anemia exists among skeletons in numerous settings worldwide. In response to anemia, red blood cells increase in production, potentially leading to **porotic hyperostosis** in skulls and **cribra orbitalia** in eye orbits (**Figure 13.25**). These abnormalities were quite rare before the Holocene but then suddenly appeared, especially in agricultural groups.

NUTRITIONAL CONSEQUENCES: HEIGHTS ON THE DECLINE In many regions where farming was adopted, adult heights declined appreciably. That people simply stopped growing as tall has been documented in western Europe, the eastern Mediterranean, Nubia, southern Asia, the Ohio River valley, and central Illinois. The Peruvian physical anthropologist Lourdes Márquez and Mexican physical anthropologist Andrés del Ángel have found a general decline in height among the Maya of the first millennium AD, a time in which this ancient civilization experienced a deterioration in environment and in living circumstances. Thus, for some groups shorter height might have been the biological result of adopting agriculture, but for other groups it might have been an adaptation to reduced resources, as smaller bodies require less food. However, all the human populations whose height decreased because of stress also experienced elevated infectious disease loads, anemia, malnutrition, and other factors indicating that a smaller body does not confer an adaptive advantage. These people were smaller but not healthier (**Figure 13.26**).

13.4 If It Is So Bad for You, Why Farm?

This question brings us back to some points about evolution raised in earlier chapters. Namely, the key components of evolution are survival to the reproductive years and production of offspring. One documented fact about the Holocene is that human fertility greatly increased during this time. That women gave birth to more babies was likely made possible by the reduced spacing between births in agricultural groups. Simply, because women were settled and not spending time moving about the landscape, they could bear children more frequently. Therefore, a population with a reduced quality of life might still have very high fertility. This combination, of course, is present through much of the developing world, such as in Peru, Bangladesh, Mexico, Thailand, and many African countries.

We have seen the evidence—a huge record—showing that the adoption of agriculture resulted in the development and spread of infectious disease and a reduction in health generally (**Figure 13.27**). Agriculture's positive side is that it provides both more calories per unit of land and the resources for population increase. And evolution dictates that organisms, including humans, engage in behaviors that increase the potential for and outcome of reproduction. Human health might have been adversely affected by the adoption of agriculture, but more and more individuals survive to reproductive age and reproduce: that is the central element of success in an evolutionary framework. Agriculture is one of a number of adaptive trade-offs in human evolution. Many of you

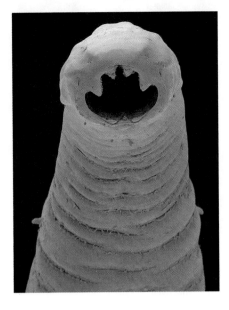

FIGURE 13.24

Hookworm Parasites, such as this hookworm, can cause iron deficiency. Today, hookworms are commonly found in subtropical regions of North Africa, India, and elsewhere.

(a)

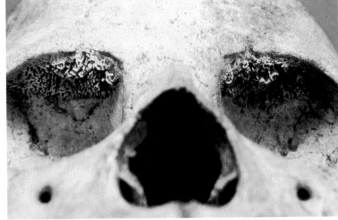
(b)

FIGURE 13.25

Porotic Hyperostosis and Cribra Orbitalia **(a)** In porotic hyperostosis, which results from anemia, the cranial bones become porous as the marrow cavities expand from the increased production of red blood cells. **(b)** Anemia can also give the eye orbits a porous appearance, called cribra orbitalia.

13.26

Biological Consequences of the Agricultural Revolution

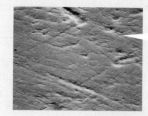

Dental microwear—
Note the striations and pits.

LIFESTYLE

Agriculture has long been considered an improvement in the human condition. Pathology and other evidence from human remains reveals, however, that the shift from foraging to farming had generally negative consequences for lifestyle and health. Changes in food composition and food preparation technology resulted in alterations to the skull and teeth. Workload in particular and activity in general were altered as populations around the world began to produce their food by farming and herding.

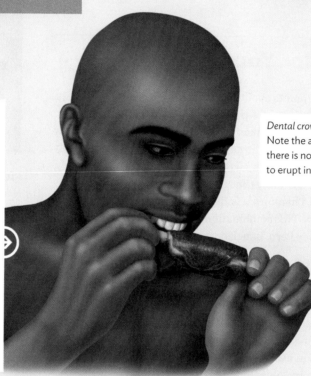

Some of the skeletal signatures of chewing and activity in general include malocclusion and tooth crowding, wear on teeth, more rounded skull, and smaller teeth. In some areas of the world, there was an increase in degenerative conditions affecting the major articular joints of the skeleton, such as the shoulder, the spine, and knee joints. Trauma patterns, such as limb fractures, also changed as human populations became exposed to new risks.

Dental crowding—
Note the angle of the third molar, as there is not enough room for this tooth to erupt in the proper position.

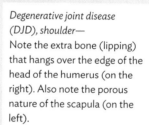

Lipping

Degenerative joint disease (DJD), shoulder—
Note the extra bone (lipping) that hangs over the edge of the head of the humerus (on the right). Also note the porous nature of the scapula (on the left).

Tuberculosis—
Note the way in which the vertebrae tip forward at the point where two vertebral bodies have collapsed.

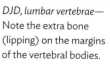

DJD, lumbar vertebrae—
Note the extra bone (lipping) on the margins of the vertebral bodies.

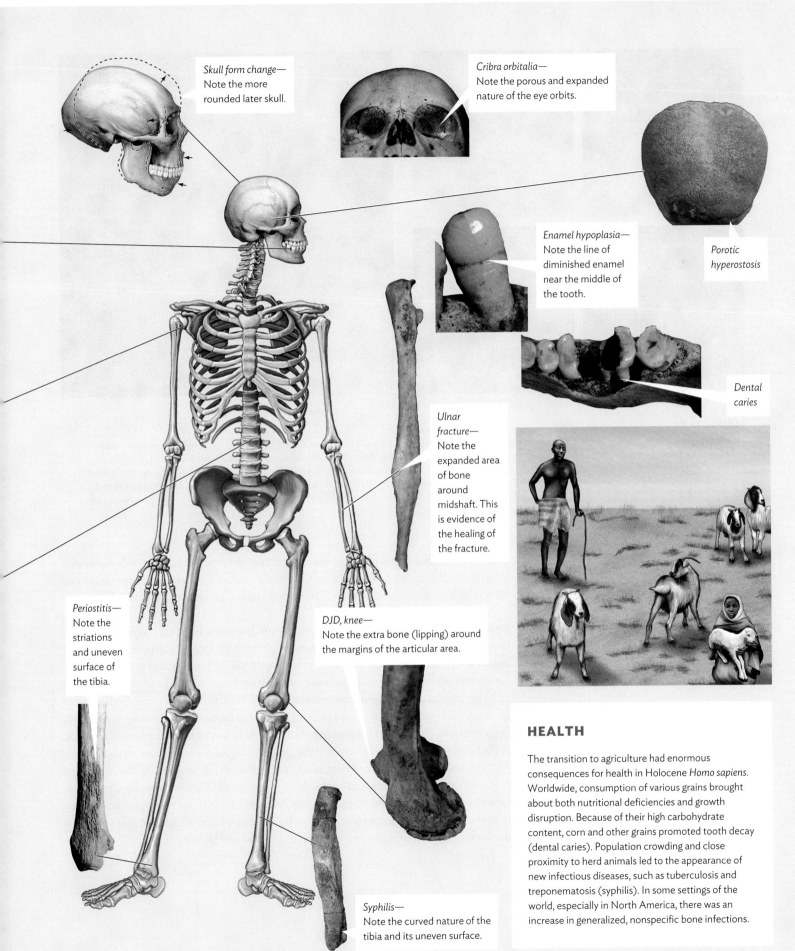

Skull form change— Note the more rounded later skull.

Cribra orbitalia— Note the porous and expanded nature of the eye orbits.

Porotic hyperostosis

Enamel hypoplasia— Note the line of diminished enamel near the middle of the tooth.

Dental caries

Ulnar fracture— Note the expanded area of bone around midshaft. This is evidence of the healing of the fracture.

Periostitis— Note the striations and uneven surface of the tibia.

DJD, knee— Note the extra bone (lipping) around the margins of the articular area.

Syphilis— Note the curved nature of the tibia and its uneven surface.

HEALTH

The transition to agriculture had enormous consequences for health in Holocene *Homo sapiens*. Worldwide, consumption of various grains brought about both nutritional deficiencies and growth disruption. Because of their high carbohydrate content, corn and other grains promoted tooth decay (dental caries). Population crowding and close proximity to herd animals led to the appearance of new infectious diseases, such as tuberculosis and treponematosis (syphilis). In some settings of the world, especially in North America, there was an increase in generalized, nonspecific bone infections.

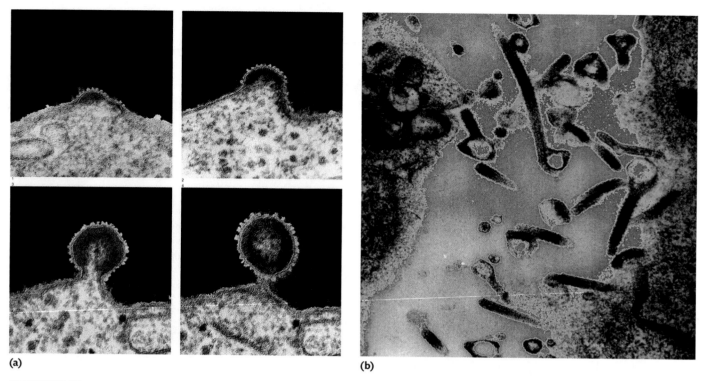

(a)   (b)

FIGURE 13.27

New Pathogens The pattern of population concentration and increase that started in the Holocene, during the agricultural revolution, established the conditions for the appearance and evolution of old and new infectious diseases. In addition, the conditions have become ripe for the evolution of new pathogens, such as the viruses that cause Ebola and acquired immune deficiency syndrome (AIDS), and prions that cause mad cow disease. **(a)** The AIDS virus, known as *human immunodeficiency virus* (*HIV*), infiltrates human white blood cells, an essential part of the immune system. The virus forces the white blood cells to produce more virus particles (red). **(b)** The Ebola virus causes a hemorrhagic fever that can be life-threatening. The virus has a long, filamentous appearance, as shown in this electron micrograph.

likely regard production of crops, and agriculture generally, as an entirely beneficial experience. But, as an adaptation, agriculture is part of a culture that represents our unique human adaptation to our environment and is a product of natural selection.

The challenges facing humans beginning in the Holocene had their roots long before the agricultural revolution. As discussed in chapter 12, later Pleistocene people had begun to exploit less desirable foods, such as wild plants and aquatic foods. Domestication and especially agriculture were an adaptive response to these challenges and laid the foundation for rapid population expansion and the rise of cities and complex societies. The resulting focus on a limited number of foods in turn created new health and growth challenges that placed populations at risk. In the next chapter, we will look at the further ramifications of these developments—at the current status of health, biology, and adaptation in light of continued environmental deterioration, the increased focus on poor-quality foods, and unabated human population growth. Although agriculture's health consequences began long ago, we suffer from these same problems today in somewhat different forms (such as obesity and other human-induced diseases). The past creates the circumstances for both the present and the future.

CHAPTER 13 REVIEW

ANSWERING THE BIG QUESTIONS

1. When, where, and why did agriculture first develop?

- During the Holocene epoch (the most recent 10,000 years, *Homo sapiens* included domesticated plants and animals in their diets for the first time.
- The earliest agriculture occurred in the eastern Mediterranean (the Levant). It arose in 11 other centers independently around the world.
- Plant and animal domestication may have arisen to feed the ever-increasing human population.

2. How did agriculture affect human living circumstances?

- Agriculture (and associated population increase) resulted in population sedentism and crowding. This provided the conditions conducive to the spread and maintenance of infectious disease.
- Nutrition shifted from a generalized diet to one focused on carbohydrates and poorer-quality protein.
- In most settings, agriculture caused a decline in workload and activity.

3. How did agriculture affect human biological change?

- Poorer-quality diets led to a decline in health as foragers became farmers.
- The shift from hard foods to soft ones resulted in facial bones reducing in size faster than the teeth. As a result, humans now have many more orthodontic issues requiring the artificial straightening of teeth.
- Decreased workload and activity resulted in a general tendency toward increased gracilization of the skeleton.
- The decline in health did not affect human reproductive performance. Human population grew from well under 1 million to perhaps several million by the close of the Pleistocene. Today, the human population exceeds *7 billion*.
- The adoption of agriculture was an evolutionary trade-off: human health was adversely affected, but more individuals survived to reproductive age and produced offspring. The population explosion that resulted from the increased food supply represents the core of adaptive success.

KEY TERMS

ameloblasts
cribra orbitalia
dental caries
domestication
heme iron
iron deficiency
  anemia
masticatory-
  functional
  hypothesis
Neolithic
nonheme iron
osteoarthritis
periosteal reaction
porotic
  hyperostosis
superfoods
treponematoses

STUDY QUIZ

1. Why did domestication of plants and animals occur in the Holocene?

a. The warmer, wetter environment supported agriculture.
b. The cooler, drier environment supported agriculture.
c. Wild populations of plants decreased.
d. Wild populations of animals decreased.

2. Plant domestication began in _____ and spread through _____

a. a single location; conquest
b. a single location; diffusion and migration
c. multiple locations; conquest
d. multiple locations; diffusion and migration

3. During the agricultural revolution, the overuse of scant resources led to

a. environmental degradation and organized warfare.

b. cooperation and fair distribution of resources between settlements.
c. a return of most human populations to hunting and gathering.
d. a return of most domesticated plants and animals to the wild.

4. The masticatory-functional hypothesis states that with a diet of cooked, soft-textured foods, face and jaw size

a. increases, so teeth cannot fill the mouth.
b. decreases, so teeth become crowded.
c. decreases, so teeth develop caries.
d. do not change enough to affect tooth function.

5. Iron deficiency appears in the skeleton as

a. periosteal reaction.
b. porotic hyperostosis.
c. enamel defects.
d. tooth crowding (malocclusion).

EVOLUTION REVIEW

THE ORIGINS AND BIOCULTURAL CONSEQUENCES OF FARMING

Synopsis One of the most fundamental transitions in recent human evolution is the shift from hunting and gathering to agriculture. For 99.8% of the 7 million years of our evolutionary past, humans and our hominin ancestors were foragers. Only within the past 10,000 years or so have humans undertaken the process of plant and animal domestication and become farmers the world over. In fact, many of the issues we face and will encounter in the future—such as environmental degradation, population growth, nutritional stress, and infectious disease—can be traced, in part, to agriculture and its influence on human biocultural evolution.

The story of what it means to be human is one of adaptation, both biological and cultural. The ongoing evolution of our species will be shaped by newly emerging environmental and ecological pressures that will continue to test human adaptability and resilience.

Q1. Provide four examples of characteristics that indicate a decline in health among agriculturalists compared to their hunter-gatherer counterparts.

Q2. Explain how a combination of evolutionary and nonevolutionary factors has influenced the changes in cranial and facial form that accompanied the transition to agriculture. What kinds of complications have resulted from these changes? How do humans intervene to respond to these complications?

Q3. After the agricultural transition and subsequent increase in population size, what were the consequences, especially with regard to prevalence of infectious disease?

ADDITIONAL READINGS

Bridges, P. S. 1996. Skeletal biology and behavior in ancient humans. *Evolutionary Anthropology* 4: 112–120.

Gasperetti, M. A. and S. G. Sheridan. 2013. Cry havoc: interpersonal violence at Early Bronze Age Bab edh-Dhra'. *American Anthropologist* 115: 388–410.

Katzenberg, M. A. 2008. Stable isotope analysis: a tool for studying past diet, demography, and life history. Pp. 413–441 in M. A. Katzenberg and S. R. Saunders, eds. *Biological Anthropology of the Human Skeleton,* 2nd ed. New York: Wiley-Liss.

Larsen, C. S. 1995. Biological changes in human populations with agriculture. *Annual Review of Anthropology* 24: 185–213.

Ruff, C. B. 2008. Biomechanical analyses of archaeological human skeletons. Pp. 183–206 in M. A. Katzenberg and S. R. Saunders, eds. *Biological Anthropology of the Human Skeleton,* 2nd ed. New York: Wiley-Liss.

Smith, B. D. 1995. *The Emergence of Agriculture.* New York: Scientific American Library.

Walker, P. L. 2001. A bioarchaeological perspective on the history of violence. *Annual Review of Anthropology* 30: 573–596.

White, T. D. 2001. Once were cannibals. *Scientific American* 265(2): 58–65.

PART III

THE FUTURE

The Shape of Things to Come

Physical anthropology is a broad field of scientific inquiry, covering the present and the past. Much of this book has been about the past, beginning with the earliest primates and their immediate ancestors. The book will now conclude by looking at the world we live in—the natural world of the early twenty-first century—and predicting what is in store for us in the future. This future depends in large part on what you and I and our fellow humans decide, mainly because for the first time in our evolution, we as a species are profoundly affecting our natural world. As discussed in the chapter that follows, our population growth and our technology have in relatively recent history changed the environment and the climate. Ultimately, these changes could affect food production, where we can live, and our future well-being. In the near future, the next several centuries, Earth will likely be somewhat warmer, a change that will alter the environmental context for our future evolution. What form or forms will that evolution take? *Homo sapiens* could experience a period of relative stasis. However, the lessons of the past—the biological changes we have seen in the recent past and that are ongoing today—suggest otherwise. Rather, millennia from now we may evolve into a new species or cease to exist altogether. Our remarkable intelligence and dependence on culture will determine the story.

Planet Earth and all of its occupants, including its diverse array of nonhuman and human primates, have never before lived in a more precarious setting. Although our challenges are largely human-caused, we nevertheless have an opportunity to address them, building a more sustainable world.

Air pollution brought on by automobile exhaust and by coal burning for energy production has caused global warming. This image from Beijing, China, tells part of the story of the biological effects on humans and other organisms in the near and distant future.

14

Evolution

TODAY AND TOMORROW

BIG QUESTIONS

1. **What are the most important forces shaping human biology today?**
2. **What are the biological consequences of global climate change, population increase, and technology?**
3. **Are we still evolving, and if so, what will human biology look like in the future?**

Geologists have long known about the stuff, a black, dense material buried below Earth's surface. Early paleontologists recognized it as the fossilized remains of plants and of animals, millions of organisms that lived eons ago and have been compressed over time into this rock-hard mass. Early physicists studied its remarkable burning properties, concluding that as a fuel it was far more efficient than wood.

Coal burns so efficiently and with such intensity that in the late eighteenth century many recognized it as just the right fuel for factories, which were beginning to sprout up around Britain and would soon appear in continental Europe and the United States. In the early to mid-nineteenth century, as the railroad industry developed, coal became the perfect fuel for the powerful engines that pulled trains long distances. It proved ideal for heating homes, too. Owing to the cumulative effects of all this coal burning and other human impacts, planet Earth is experiencing profound and long-lasting environmental change; thus many scientists argue that we're in a new geologic epoch called the **Anthropocene.** Whether or not a new epoch has emerged, it is clear that humans have affected the environment on a global scale.

Anthropocene Proposed new geologic epoch characterized by the profound role of humans in changing the land surface and the composition of the atmosphere in significant ways.

Humans had long been altering the environment, such as by clearing forests for cultivation. But a new chapter in human evolution began with the large-scale atmospheric changes brought about by coal burning. Although just a few hundred years old, this episode in our species' history is having, and will have for the foreseeable future, important implications for biology and evolution, not just of humans but of all living organisms. Charles Darwin and his contemporaries would never have predicted humans' singular impact on the world.

In this final chapter, we will look at our rapidly changing world and speculate about its future, especially about how the changing environment will relate to human biology and evolution. Climate change, population growth, and technology have shaped the current environment; and they will profoundly affect environments to come. And as the world changes, you, your generation, and future generations will change.

14.1 The Forces of Change: A Warming Planet, Increasing Population, and Shifting Technology

Global Warming

global warming The increase in the average temperature of Earth's atmosphere in response to the greenhouse effect; a cause of climate change.

You have no doubt heard about **global warming.** The discussion of global warming and ecosystem changes is everywhere in the popular press and is hotly debated among scientists and the public alike. The phrase refers to the increase in the average temperature of Earth's atmosphere and sea that has come about within the most recent period of human history, especially in the past few decades. Abundant scientific evidence proves that global warming is real. Analysis of ice cores from the Arctic, Antarctica, glaciers, and other ice masses around the world reveals a stratigraphic record of climate change. One very obvious spike in Earth's temperature—about 0.8 °C (1.3 °F)—occurred within the past century (**Figure 14.1**). That might not sound like much of a temperature increase—can you tell the difference if the temperature rises from 67 °F on Monday to 68.3 °F on Tuesday?—but even this modest boost can visibly affect Earth's ecosystems. Since records first started to be kept in the nineteenth century, the warmest years on record were 2012, 2013, and 2015. When did this trend start, leading to the conditions

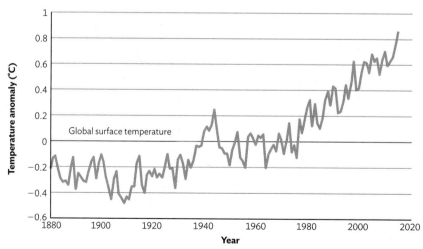

FIGURE 14.1

Temperature Change For nearly 140 years, as this chart shows, global surface temperature (land and ocean) has increased.

FIGURE 14.2

Mount Kilimanjaro Among the many glaciers around the world that have begun to melt is the glacier atop Mount Kilimanjaro, which likely will disappear within the next several decades if global warming is not reduced.

today? That remains unclear, but almost certainly human effects on the environment commenced with the use of fire beginning in the Pleistocene (see chapter 11). Some authorities point to the advent of farming at the beginning of the Holocene, which resulted in anthropogenic effects such as the clearing of natural vegetation in favor of domesticated plants (see chapter 13). These changes may well define the beginning point for human effects on the environment, but geographers Simon Lewis and Mark Maslin argue that the tipping point likely began much more recently, perhaps with the Industrial Revolution in the eighteenth and nineteenth centuries.

One critical signal of change is the melting of glaciers and of other ice masses around the world. For example, during the past century the magnificent glacier atop Tanzania's Mount Kilimanjaro has shrunk by 85% (**Figure 14.2**). The large ice masses in the Arctic and in Antarctica are also diminishing in size or disappearing. Such melting has increased sea levels by about 12 cm (5 in) within the past 100 years. The polar ice masses along with glaciers around the world are melting at an alarming and increasing rate. This melting is best explained by global warming.

Warming has occurred during other periods in the planet's history. As discussed in chapter 9, for example, a global warming and the widespread appearance of tropical forests at the beginning of the Eocene laid the foundation for the rise of primates. Even within the past 10,000 years, warming periods have created droughts and other dramatic environmental shifts. Critics of the idea of global warming point out this fact and suggest that the current warming is nothing new. There is something new about the warming trend today, however. For the first time in Earth's history, humans have—at least in part—caused the change. That is, global warming is **anthropogenic.**

Like other developments in human history, this dramatic influence on the environment began with technology. In this instance, the technology involved innovations in energy consumption and the burning of coal, a **fossil fuel** (**Figure 14.3**). During the Industrial Revolution, in the late eighteenth and the nineteenth centuries, coal became the fuel of choice for powering factories. Recall the peppered moths in nineteenth-century Great Britain (see "Natural Selection in Animals: The Case of the Peppered Moth and Industrial Melanism" in chapter 4). Their evolution—into a dark version, owing to the covering of the landscape with black residue from coal burning in factories and in homes—was a harbinger of changes to come. In addition to coal particles, carbon dioxide (CO_2), other gases (such as methane and nitrous oxide), and water

anthropogenic Refers to any effect caused by humans.

fossil fuel Combustible material, such as oil, coal, or natural gas, composed of organisms' remains preserved in rocks.

GLOBAL CLIMATES ARE

One way to see how we affect the world is to look at the world before humans arrived.

Reliable information about past climates provides fundamental insights about evolution, thanks to the inextricable links between evolution (including the biological variation within it) and the environment (including resources such as food). Scientists reconstruct past climates in various ways, but among the best sources of information are the ice masses that have accumulated around the world, such as the polar ice sheets in Greenland and Antarctica; smaller glaciers in the high Arctic; and the glaciers in high-altitude regions such as the Andes in Peru and Bolivia and the Himalayas in Asia. What is so special about ice? Specifically, how do scientists extract information about temperature and about climate from it?

Ellen Mosley-Thompson and Lonnie Thompson hold an ice core, analysis of which can yield information about past global climate changes over many centuries.

RAPIDLY CHANGING

Recognizing ice's potential for tracking climate history, the American paleoclimatologists Lonnie Thompson and Ellen Mosley-Thompson have spent the past 30 years collecting ice cores from all over the world. These cores are 10 cm (4 in) in diameter and can be hundreds of meters (hundreds of feet) long. They can be hundreds of thousands of years old. The oldest ice core on record, from Antarctica, reaches back 800,000 years.

Like many other scientists you have read about in this book, Thompson and Mosley-Thompson and their field teams have gone to great lengths to collect their data. Through deep snow, often in subzero weather, they have hauled an average of 6 tons of equipment to places that are very difficult to reach, such as very high mountaintops, many exceeding 5 km (16,000 ft) above sea level. While they sometimes use draft animals such as horses or yaks, the researchers and locally hired people often carry the coring equipment, which is specially designed for its purpose.

Seeking physical and chemical properties that are preserved within the ice and that allow climate changes to be tracked, they read the cores much the way dendrochronologists read tree rings (see "Absolute Methods of Dating: What Is the Numerical Age?" in chapter 8). The cores contain much more information than tree rings, however. Because the ice derives from snowfall, it contains whatever the snow captured as it fell—materials such as dust, pollen, and particles from volcanic eruptions. An important component of this record consists of the stable isotopes of oxygen, ^{18}O and ^{16}O, whose relative abundance (or ratio) reveals details about temperature changes. Snow forming at warmer temperatures generally contains higher levels of ^{18}O relative to ^{16}O, while snow forming at cooler temperatures will contain less ^{18}O relative to ^{16}O. Thus, an ice core section enriched in ^{18}O relative to

Researchers travel to remote locations to drill through the snow to obtain ice cores.

^{16}O generally indicates the climate was warmer when that ice formed.

For the Holocene, the picture is very clear. Elevated levels of ^{18}O relative to ^{16}O in most ice cores indicate that the past 50 years were the warmest 50-year period in the past *2,000* years and, in some places, for the entire Holocene! Our climate is clearly going to grow even warmer and less hospitable.

(a)

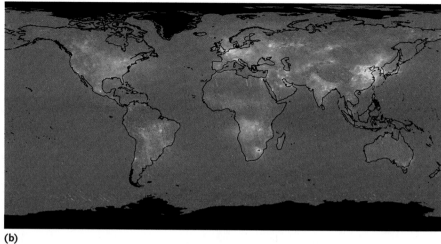

(b)

FIGURE 14.3

Coal Burning One of the main contributing factors to global warming is the burning of fossil fuels, especially coal. **(a)** As coal is burned, large amounts of both carbon dioxide and nitrogen dioxide are released into the atmosphere, contributing to the "greenhouse effect" associated with global warming. **(b)** This map shows nitrogen dioxide concentrations in the lower part of Earth's atmosphere. The yellow and red areas reflect the highest concentrations, generally located near highly industrialized areas. The blue and black areas represent lower concentrations.

vapor—collectively known as "greenhouse gases"—have been building in Earth's atmosphere. These gases are literally trapped between the planet's surface and the outer atmosphere. Because of the accumulation of greenhouse gases from factory emissions and from the burning of fossil fuels in industry and in transportation, Earth's surface has been warming. Other factors that have contributed to global warming include deforestation and farming, events that began in the early Neolithic. Therefore, while global warming is quite recent, the "seeds" for it were sown with the agricultural revolution, perhaps as long ago as the early Holocene. Another growing contributor to the rise in greenhouse gases is the remarkable increase in meat production worldwide. Deforestation and other processes are resulting in increased atmospheric CO_2 at an alarming rate. The bulk of global warming is due to the recent trapping of CO_2 in Earth's atmosphere. Throughout the history of our planet, when CO_2 has increased in the atmosphere, temperature has risen.

Why should we be concerned about global warming? (I would not mind warmer winters in my home state, Ohio!) As you know from previous chapters in this book, temperature fluctuations heavily influence biology and evolution. They are a key component of climate changes, and climate changes—by altering food sources, for example—are an important engine of evolutionary change. Should global warming continue at the present rate, it will profoundly influence biological systems, including our own. For example, climate scientists anticipate wildly fluctuating weather patterns, including heat waves, which will be potentially lethal for many around the globe.

Climate scientists also predict a shifting pattern of precipitation, with increasing dryness in regions such as the American Southwest and Midwest, northern Mexico, and the Caribbean, and in areas around the Mediterranean Sea. The American climatologist Richard Seager believes that by the mid-twenty-first century, the American Southwest will have permanently returned to its Dust Bowl days (**Figure 14.4**). This dryness will result in the loss of some species and the rise of others, depending on what kinds of plants and animals thrive (or decline) in particular habitats. For humans, agriculturally rich areas and other food sources will likely be threatened. The great agricultural regions of China, the American Midwest, and India will be jeopardized.

FIGURE 14.4

Dust Bowl Humans have caused several environmental catastrophes. The Dust Bowl of the 1930s, for example, resulted from soil overuse, leading to severe erosion. During a substantial drought, the damaged soil blew away in large clouds or dust storms. Hundreds of thousands of Americans were left homeless, and many died from malnutrition and dust pneumonia.

Even a slight rise in temperature could reduce agricultural production. High-latitude regions such as the northern United States and Europe will likely receive increased precipitation, resulting in greater crop production, but on balance, climatologists and others foresee a reduced food supply.

As glaciers and polar ice masses melt, sea levels are rising and will continue to do so. The resulting flooding of low-lying areas—for example, in the large delta regions in Africa and Asia, such as those associated with the Nile and Brahmaputra Rivers—will threaten the lives and livelihoods of millions of people. Since 1901, sea levels have risen by 15–19 cm (7–7.5 in). By the end of the twenty-first century, sea levels are expected to rise another 26–82 cm (10–32 in). This increase would inundate low-lying areas, including much of peninsular Florida, Bangladesh, and most major coastal cities. For those dry areas of the world that depend on melting glacial ice and melting snowfall to maintain streams and wells, these important sources of water will disappear, making millions of acres of land uninhabitable.

You can probably guess the impact of these environmental changes on organisms and biological systems. As evolution always dictates, organisms and biological systems that can adapt to the changes via natural selection will succeed. Those that cannot adapt will go extinct. For human beings around the globe, the changes anticipated will be the greatest challenge to health ever.

Human Population Growth

Of the 7.4 billion people in the world today, nearly 1 billion suffer from malnutrition, and this health crisis is fueled by climate extremes (**Figure 14.5**). Jonathan Patz, an American scientist who studies the relationship between health and climate, predicts that global changes are having, and will continue to have, a marked impact on human health (**Figure 14.6**). Climate changes are bringing about illness and death owing to extreme heat, extreme cold, storms, droughts, declines in air and water quality, and the evolution of disease-causing microorganisms.

The World Health Organization predicts that the global risk of negative health outcomes—disease, infection, and death—for humans will *double* by 2030. That estimate is based mainly on climate change projections, but human population growth, especially in Africa and in parts of Asia, is and will continue to be the greatest

BIODIVERSITY

The Human Role

One way in which humans are most dramatically affecting the environment is through overpopulation. The large increase in population size has led to the loss of many animals' natural environments. Rio de Janeiro, Brazil, is a prime example of this problem. This city has undergone substantial population increase as people have migrated there from rural areas. Within the city, large forests have been clear-cut to make room for the ever-growing population and its housing.

Scientists have long known that biodiversity is an indicator of the health of ecological systems across the globe. Variation in kinds of taxonomic forms is important for the future of humankind and of other organisms.

Among biodiversity's many functions are helping provide soil suitable for agriculture and regulating the atmosphere's chemistry. Many scientists have come to recognize the human population's influence on biodiversity reduction. This anthropogenic history extends perhaps at least back into the Pliocene but is clearly visible in the Holocene. Physical anthropologist Jeffrey McKee and collaborators Paul Sciulli, David Fooce, and Thomas Waite identified two issues about human population that have never been sorted out; namely, population growth rates and population

density. Many authorities assume that biodiversity decline is driven by human population growth. Few have suggested that biodiversity reduction is density-driven. That is, the greater a population's density—the more people per geographic region—the greater the threat to biodiversity.

To test that hypothesis, McKee and his collaborators studied the taxonomic diversity of mammal and bird species, the most diverse organisms in a wide range of countries. They listed all the threatened mammal and bird species from a 114-country species database compiled by the International Union for Conservation of Nature. Their statistical analysis of this list and population information produced two clear results. First, human population growth rates were not correlated with threats to these species. Second, human population density was strongly correlated with numbers of threatened species throughout the world. In other words, as population density has increased in a geographic area, the species richness there has declined.

The numbers are frightening. With unabated population density increase, by 2020 most nations will see a 7% reduction in species diversity and by 2050 another 14% reduction. These reductions are an important signal for extinction in the not-so-distant future, perhaps not in your lifetime but certainly within the lifetimes of your children and grandchildren. While extinction is hardly new on Earth, the alarming increase in extinctions brought about by human population density

DOWNTURN

A

B

A

Rio de Janeiro's loss of forest has caused several primate species, such as the golden lion tamarin, to become endangered. If measures are not taken to ensure its survival, this species may soon become extinct.

B

Cocoa beans drying at a farm in Ivory Coast. Cocoa farms have completely replaced the forest in some regions, destroying the habitat of primates.

is unprecedented. In the larger picture, entire ecosystems are threatened, reducing humans' and other organisms' ability to produce food. Given the projected global climate changes, the threats to biodiversity may be more dire than predicted by human population density increases alone. McKee and his collaborators make the strong case that a slowdown in human population density will be key to maintaining not only Earth's biodiversity but Earth itself.

In addition to threatening the health of ecological systems, decrease in biodiversity threatens human health. The US Intergovernmental Panel on Climate Change has investigated how decreased plant and animal diversity will affect human health, and its findings reveal clearly that such losses will have highly negative effects on health, primarily because decreased biodiversity often increases transmission of infectious disease. For example, the cutting down or fragmentation of forests results in the loss of trees and thus the loss of habitat for the plants and animals that are adapted to a forest landscape. The loss of species of primates is occurring worldwide owing to economic-driven deforestation. For many settings, the loss of natural habitats is linked to aggressive agribusiness, such as cocoa farming in Ivory Coast of West Africa. In this

setting (and see Figure 6.2 in chapter 6), primatologist Anderson Bitty and his team report a complete loss of species of colobus monkeys, even in protected areas. While the economic gains for the country are significant, the loss of primate species is dramatic and will become irreversible without immediate and aggressive conservation efforts.

Plants and animals and their diversity serve a protective role for humans. In fact, many contemporary deadly viruses, while actually quite old, have only recently emerged owing to disruptions of species diversity and habitat losses. One key example is the spread of the West Nile virus. The virus is transmitted by mosquitoes, for which several species of birds serve as hosts. New studies show that in regions of the United States where there is low bird diversity, there is increased risk or prevalence of the disease caused by the virus—West Nile encephalitis. In those regions with low bird diversity, the species that tend to remain are ones that promote the amplification of the virus, causing high infection rates in both the mosquitoes and people. Other infectious diseases on the "watch list" for being promoted by low biodiversity include Lyme disease, malaria, schistosomiasis, and hantavirus disease. *Anthropology matters!*

FIGURE 14.5

Drought and Malnutrition Sudan's drought in 1984–85 led to severe malnutrition for thousands of Sudanese, especially children, like the brother and sister seen here in a refugee camp in the Darfur region. After the drought decimated livestock and crops, many people migrated from the country, and those who remained were in conflict over food and water. Additional droughts occurred there in 1989, 1990, 1997, and 2000.

contributing factor. While health and quality of life might decline globally, the greatest burden will fall in regions where a lack of resources leaves people least able to adapt to the new risks.

Today, more than 50% of the world's population lives in cities, and these people are

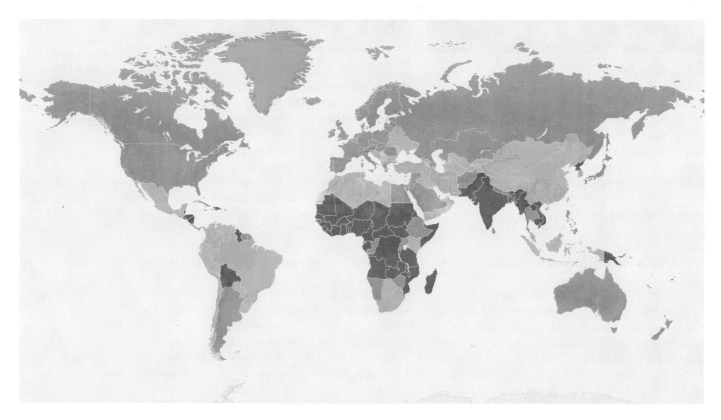

FIGURE 14.6

Climate Change and Mortality Based on data from the Climate Vulnerability Monitor by DARA International, this map shows the levels of human mortality due to climate change, predicted to be approximately 100 million people by the year 2030. The study suggests that the increases in mortality will be due to climate-sensitive health issues, such as from malnutrition, communicable diseases, and cardiovascular disease.

especially vulnerable to the effects of a warming climate. In cities, the relative lack of vegetation and of other natural land cover exacerbates greenhouse-gas warming. Concentrations of elevated heat, produced from roads and rooftops and other heat-storing materials, result in temperatures far higher than normal. More than 25% of the urban populations worldwide are packed into slums lacking sanitation, including the disposal of human and other wastes.

These circumstances, coupled with human population growth, have yielded what the United Nations calls a global "silent tsunami" killing many thousands from infections and disease. Population increase creates many new hosts for new and newly emerging infectious diseases, and "more hosts" translates into more organisms (**Figure 14.7**). Some of the new infectious diseases are making a rapid appearance and having a profound impact. In 2013, there was only one case of introduction of the Zika virus into the Americas. Within just two years, some 30,000 cases of infection from the virus were reported in Brazil, spreading from there throughout northern South America and Central America. The virus was first identified in a rhesus monkey in Uganda, but like

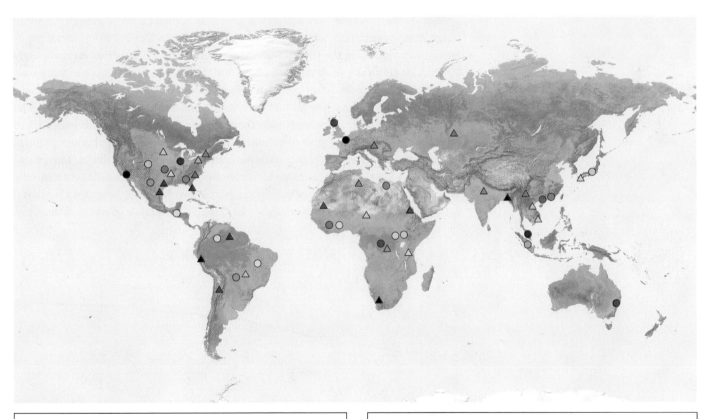

New Infectious Diseases

- Creutzfeldt-Jakob diseases
- Cryptosporidiosis
- Cyclosporiasis
- E. coli O157:H7
- Ebola hemorrhagic fever
- Enterovirus 71
- H5N1 influenza
- Hantavirus pulmonary syndrome
- Hendra virus
- Hepatitis C
- HIV
- Lassa fever
- Marburg hemorrhagic fever
- Nipah virus
- SARS
- Whitewater arroyo virus
- Zika virus

Reemerging Infectious Diseases

- ▲ Cholera
- ▲ Dengue
- ▲ Diphtheria
- △ Drug-resistant malaria
- △ Human monkeypox
- △ Lyme disease
- ▲ Multidrug-resistant tuberculosis
- ▲ Plague
- ▲ Rift Valley fever
- ▲ Typhoid fever
- △ Vancomycin-resistant *S. aureus*
- ▲ West Nile virus
- ▲ Yellow fever

FIGURE 14.7

Emerging and Reemerging Diseases This map shows the many new (●) and reemerging (▲) infectious diseases throughout the world. Some of the reemerging diseases, such as tuberculosis and malaria, are becoming increasingly drug-resistant.

other infectious viruses it mutated and spread to regions of the world that provided conditions for remarkably rapid transmission to and among humans. Transmitted by various mosquito species, the resulting infection is usually mild. However, there is an apparent association between mothers infected during pregnancy and their having offspring born with microcephaly. And, in 2015, the U.S. Centers for Disease Control and Prevention announced that this brain defect is caused by the virus. To make matters worse, it also appears that the effects can also include problems in ears, eyes, and possible other organs.

As discussed in chapter 11, humans' use of land—particularly the shift from farmland to urban and suburban sprawl—affects health and can affect disease transmission. For example, alterations in land cover, such as the loss of trees, together with increases in temperature and humidity, can encourage mosquitoes to breed, and mosquitoes help spread pathogens such as those associated with malaria (caused by a parasite; see chapter 5). In highland Uganda, to cite just one place afflicted by malaria-carrying mosquitoes (90% of malaria occurs in Africa), temperatures are much higher in villages associated with cultivated swamps.

Worldwide, however, technology has generally helped increase human longevity by improving sanitation, medical care, and quality of life. The growing human population is also aging. In the United States, for example, people now live approximately 30 years longer than people who were born in 1900 (**Figure 14.8**). This positive development comes at a cost. After age 40, for example, all adults experience osteoporosis, or age-related bone loss (see "Adult Stage: Aging and Senescence" in chapter 5). The longer people live, the more bone mass they lose and the more susceptible they are to bone fractures. In addition, as discussed in chapter 5, bone growth depends on physical activity. Relatively sedentary children develop less bone mass during the critical growth-and-development years, and inactive adults lose more bone mass in later life. With industrialization and mechanization, people have become less active. Compared with 100 years ago, today more people work sitting down (often at computers) than, say,

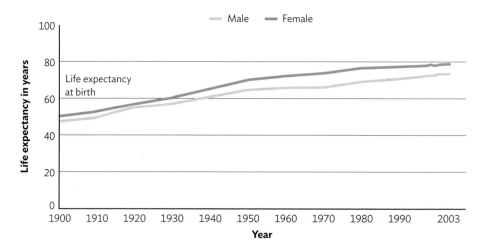

FIGURE 14.8

Life Expectancy This chart shows the increase in US life expectancy since 1900. Regardless of decade, females continuously have a greater life expectancy than males. But whereas Americans born in 1900 could expect to live into their late 40s, today's life expectancy at birth has risen to 78 years. Note that this figure compares favorably with those in other industrialized countries, is higher than in developing countries, and is considerably higher than in Third World nations. Life expectancy has taken a downturn in the former republics of the Soviet Union, for example, because of increased disease, alcoholism, and declining nutrition. Life expectancy has declined in Africa because of the AIDS epidemic.

plowing fields or using heavy machinery in a factory. In the 1960s, the Scottish nutrition scientist John Chalmers and the Chinese nutrition scientist K. C. Ho predicted a trend of increased osteoporotic fracture for older adults, and their prediction has come true. For example, in Hong Kong, hip fractures among women increased at alarming rates during 1966–85 (**Figure 14.9**). In Beijing, just between the years 2002 and 2007, hip fractures in men and women over age 50 tripled! Hip fractures occurred rarely in hominins, so this trend is a very recent one in human evolution and is caused by increased longevity and changing lifestyle. Other debilitating conditions and illnesses that will affect aging societies around the world include heart disease, osteoarthritis and immobility, and various cancers.

In addition to affecting human health, the human population explosion is affecting Earth's biodiversity in strongly negative ways. Humans have long displaced other species, but only recently have humans decimated so many of the world's plants and animals (for more on this topic, see "Anthropology Matters: Mitigating Primate Endangerment: Conservation of the Northern Muriquis of Brazil" in chapter 6).

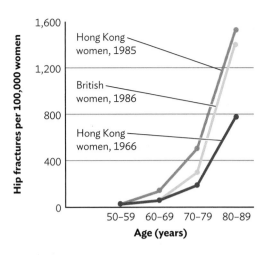

FIGURE 14.9

Hip Fractures As this chart shows, rates of hip fractures among Hong Kong women were much higher in 1985 than in 1966. Hong Kong citizens' traditionally low calcium intakes were partly responsible, as was increased inactivity brought about by technology.

CONCEPT CHECK

Forces Shaping Our World: Climate, Population, and Technology

The world is different from what it was just a century ago. The combined effects of climate change, population increase, and technology are affecting health and laying the groundwork for future evolution.

Force	Effect
Global warming (from greenhouse gases)	Rapid climate change, especially warming of Earth's atmosphere (resulting in melting of ice masses, coastal flooding, drying in some areas)
	Potential negative impact on food production
	Promotion of disease vectors (e.g., mosquitoes, rodents, ticks, and the pathogens such organisms carry)
Population increase (from increased food availability, cultural and social factors, natural fertility)	Increased demands on food production
	Declines in biodiversity
	Appearance of new, population-dependent pathogens and associated diseases (made worse by global warming)
Technology	Increasingly gracile skeleton
	Alteration in cranial form
	Increased malocclusions, more osteoporosis, and other morbid conditions associated with aging (e.g., osteoarthritis, cancers, heart disease)

The Nutrition Transition

If you were to travel back in time, even to a period as recent as that of the American Civil War (1861–65), and compare people living today with those of the past, you would likely observe some major differences in body morphology. As discussed in chapter 13, people are taller than they were two centuries ago. In part because of that height increase, they are also heavier. But a big part of the weight increase is greater percentage of fat relative to other body tissues—Americans are fatter now than were their ancestors in the nineteenth and twentieth centuries (**Figure 14.10**). In fact, about two-thirds of adults and about one-fifth of children are overweight or obese.

Much of the trend for increased body weight is best explained by shifts in the types of foods eaten. Americans' body weights vary according to socioeconomic status: because lower-income families tend to consume less protein and fiber and more saturated fat and sugar, they tend to be heavier and to have a higher incidence of obesity than higher-income families. Overall, however, the "Western diet" is now high in saturated fat, sugar, and refined foods that are low in fiber. The **nutrition transition**—the term scientists use to describe the shift from a relatively low-fat diet to a high-fat, high-carbohydrate diet—and the resulting spread of obesity have recently become a worldwide epidemic. Since the year 2000, the American nutritionist Barry Popkin has

nutrition transition The shift in diet to one that is high in saturated fat and sugar; a cause of the global obesity epidemic.

1850
5 ft 7.4 in
and 146 lb

2000
5 ft 9.5 in
and 191 lb

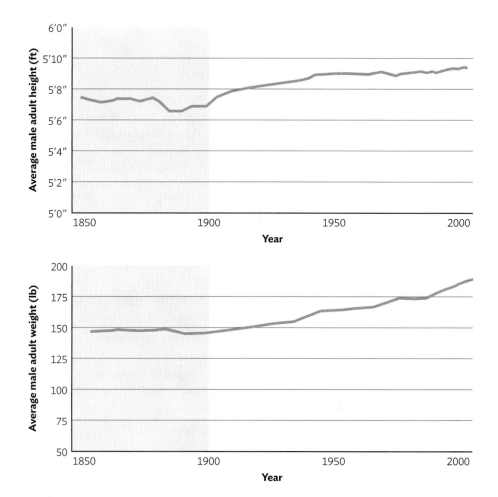

FIGURE 14.10

Body Changes Since 1850, Americans have, on average, become taller and heavier. As these charts show, adult male height has increased by approximately 5 cm (2 in), and adult male weight has increased by more than 18 kg (40 lb). Both changes seem related to cultural changes in modernity: the height increase is likely due to better nutrition, while the large weight increase is probably due to overnourishment.

(a)

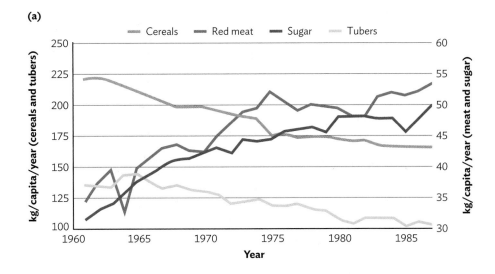

(b)

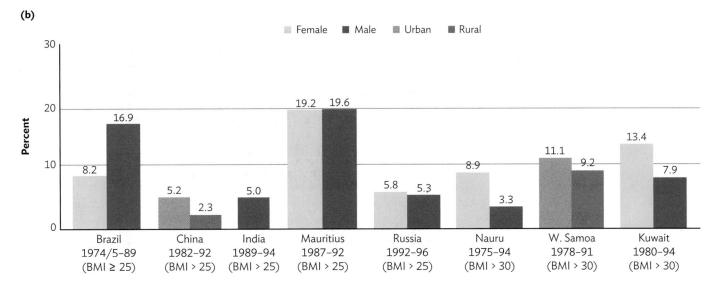

FIGURE 14.11

Food Consumption Changes Countries throughout the world are "Westernizing" their diets. **(a)** As this chart shows, between 1961 and 1987 consumption of both cereals and tubers decreased in the Soviet Union, while consumption of both sugar and red meat increased there. At the same time, the Soviet Union experienced an increase in chronic diseases such as cardiovascular disease and diabetes, both of which are linked to high consumption of sugar and of red meat. **(b)** This chart shows the obesity increases in various lower-income countries affected by the nutrition transition (BMI = body mass index).

documented the effects of the rapid, worldwide adoption of Westernized economies. He notes that, owing to dietary change and reduced physical activity, obesity levels in many parts of the developing world now match those in developed countries such as the United States (**Figure 14.11**).

Brazil provides perfect examples of the nutrition transition's effects on populations. Just a generation ago, the rural Ribeirinhos people, who live in Brazil's Amazon River valley, were essentially isolated from the rest of the world and depended mostly on a subsistence economy; that is, on producing what they needed to survive (see "Postnatal Stage: The Maturing Brain, Preparing for Adulthood" in chapter 5). In studying Ribeirinhos communities, the American physical anthropologist Barbara Piperata has asked at what point biological changes occur as a result of lifestyle changes due to involvement in a market economy; that is, one based on buying and selling. As Piperata explains, these societies are shifting from acquiring food and other resources locally—raising crops, acquiring other food by fishing and by collecting—to depending on wage labor and using earnings to purchase food. She has found that as the societies gain access to Western diets, their proportions of overweight and obese members rise. Their adult males are disproportionately heavier and more obese than their adult females, mainly because the males become involved in wage labor whereas the females continue to work in the traditional, household-based subsistence economy.

What is so bad about being overweight or obese? Simply, these conditions are precursors for multiple health problems. For example, being obese predisposes a person to cardiovascular disease, diabetes, respiratory disease, psychological disorders, depression, and sleep disorders. The incidence of diabetes alone has increased in adults by some 90% in the past decade. (For more on the effects of overweightness and obesity, see "Nutritional Adaptation: Energy, Nutrients, and Function" in chapter 5.)

Hypersanitation, Health, and the Hygiene Hypothesis

As a child, I was continually reminded by my mother to keep clean, stay out of the dirt, and wash my hands. I no doubt skipped the hand-washing many times, and I almost certainly got sick as a result. Depending on their kind, microbes on the hands are a leading cause of illness, such as through food contamination. It turns out, however, that overdoing cleanliness also has negative health consequences. And events in childhood may have consequences for health in adulthood (for another perspective, see "Anthropology Matters: Coronary Heart Disease Starts Early: Prenatal Origins of a Common Killer" in chapter 5).

A new body of research by anthropologists and others is showing that exposure to microbes early in life stimulates the immune system. The American physical anthropologist Thomas McDade and his colleagues argue that exposure to everyday germs plays a key part in prompting the immune system to perform the functions it should in later life. Usually, these kinds of exposures—such as playing in dirt—do not cause infection. McDade and his colleagues tracked Filipinos from birth until early adulthood and found that those who had been exposed to more bacteria had lower levels of C-reactive protein, a marker of inflammation. When the body is fighting an infection, for example, it produces a higher level of this protein.

hygiene hypothesis The proposition that increasing allergies among children are the result of decreased exposure to microbes, such as those found in dirt.

These findings are consistent with the **hygiene hypothesis** proposed by the British epidemiologist David Strachan, who has been studying a growing epidemic of allergies worldwide. Strachan and others have documented a rapid growth in negative reactions to a wide range of foods and other aspects of daily living. Some 50 million people in the United States alone have allergies. Manifestations of allergies—sneezing, itching, rashes, breathing difficulties, sore throats—are becoming more and more widespread. The American immunologist Scott Sicherer has found that allergies to peanut butter doubled between 1997 and 2002. Like infection, these reactions are signs that the immune system is responding to what it perceives as foreign antigens. The body is basically attempting to produce antibodies for something that is not a danger under normal circumstances. (Dust particles in the atmosphere are not life-threatening!) However, like some infections, allergic reactions can be dangerous, even life-threatening.

What is causing this remarkable rise in allergic conditions? There is a genetic component because parents with allergies or precursor conditions (such as asthma) are far more likely to have children with allergies. However, while genetic evolution can occur quickly, it cannot occur fast enough to explain the current allergy epidemic. Rather, the generally deteriorating environmental conditions are also at work—at least those conditions that elicit immune responses associated with allergies. Health scientists regard the changes as resulting from a combination of factors, including diet (such as the reduced intake of fresh fruits and fresh vegetables, more intake of processed and refined foods, and lower intake of minerals), overuse of antibiotics, and a range of environment pollutants (**Figure 14.12**). For example, children who grow up near major roads and highways have more allergies, perhaps due to exposure to automobile exhaust. Exposure to allergens can cause allergies.

Like obesity, infections and allergies are a growing epidemic associated with our rapidly changing world. Wherever industrialization is occurring, infections and allergies are on the rise. Where no industrialization is present, such as in remote areas of Africa and of Latin America, infections and allergies are considerably less frequent than in the developed world. Strachan, like McDade, makes the case that the allergy epidemic has been brought about by overcleanliness. Modern culture has reduced the need for some normal biological processes. Just as early exposures to microbes can stimulate the immune system, early exposure to allergens can protect against the development

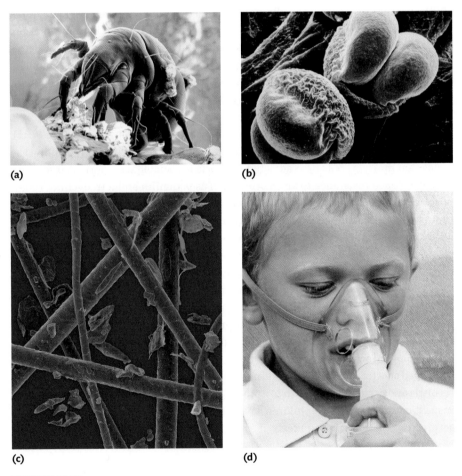

(a)

(b)

(c)

(d)

FIGURE 14.12

Allergens Numerous allergens are constantly present in our environment; however, not all people have a reaction to them. **(a)** Dust mites—such as the one here magnified considerably—feed on organic waste, such as shed human skin cells, and are considered one of the leading causes of asthma. **(b)** Pollen, such as these spores from a pine tree, produce a plant's male gametes and are dispersed by the wind. As wind dispersal is random, plants produce large quantities of these lightweight grains to ensure that pollination occurs, but the grains can cause an allergic reaction known as *hay fever*. **(c)** Dander, or skin flakes, from animals are known to cause allergies in approximately 10% of the population. **(d)** In some cases, allergies can become serious, leading to asthma attacks. Although rare, the most severe reactions, called *anaphylaxis,* can be life-threatening.

endotoxins Toxins released by bacteria when they break down or die.

of allergies. Strachan has found that the allergic diseases hay fever and eczema, for example, were less frequent in families with more children than in those with fewer children. Children with lots of siblings are exposed to more infectious agents that cause allergies than are children with no or few siblings. Strachan argues that specific components called **endotoxins** play an important role in the body's natural development of its immune system. Hygiene and protection against allergens are important, of course. But these practices and their unintended results tell a story about adaptation. The human body has evolved biological mechanisms that require specific conditions to function normally. When the environmental conditions change, the body's mechanisms function abnormally.

14.2 Our Ongoing Evolution

Huge changes are occurring on our planet and in the human (and other) populations occupying it. These changes have real meaning for our future, including our evolution. But is there evidence of ongoing biological change in general and evolution in particular? In a word, plenty. Owing to technological innovations and their effects, humans are the most dominant evolutionary force on all the other living organisms. Abundant examples exist of humankind's role in other species' evolution. Even before the Swiss chemist Paul Müller could receive the Nobel Prize in 1948 for his discovery that DDT killed insects, houseflies' resistance to this chemical was being reported (**Figure 14.13**). By 1990, some 500 mosquito species had developed resistance to DDT, dashing the hopes that malaria could be eradicated. Bacteria associated with horrific infections have developed resistance to antibiotics, such as penicillin and tetracycline. Today, hospitals report that bacteria such as *Staphylococcus aureus* are almost always resistant to penicillin, and the list of resistant bacteria is growing. The evolution of new, antibiotic-resistant strains of *Mycobacterium tuberculosis* is a big part of the dramatic rise in human deaths due to this bacterium—more than 1 million people die from tuberculosis each year. Meanwhile, fish are evolving slower growth and thinner bodies owing to overfishing. Salmon males, for example, are under strong selection for smaller size, and they are returning to the sea earlier to increase their survival.

As discussed in chapter 13, all accounts indicate that the human biological changes that began largely with the transition from foraging to farming are continuing today. For example, since the late 1960s, children in rural Oaxaca, southern Mexico, have developed shorter, rounder heads and narrower faces. The American pediatrician Bertis Little and her collaborators suggest that these changes have resulted from a decline in masticatory stress as the children have eaten softer, more processed corn and other soft foods. (For more on the effects of eating softer foods, see "The Changing Face of Humanity" in chapter 13.) As the nutrition transition spreads worldwide, occlusal abnormalities will no doubt increase.

These changes—to the human head and dental appearance—are likely due to differences in humans' use of their jaws and teeth rather than to genetic evolution. Still, they are important biological alterations because they are literally changing humanity's face, and in a relatively short time. Growing evidence also suggests that natural selection continues to play an important role in our biology. Geneticists have identified a couple dozen genes that appear to confer selective advantages. The classic example, discussed in "Natural Selection in Humans: Abnormal Hemoglobins and Resistance to

FIGURE 14.13

DDT Resistance Many countries have used DDT, the first modern pesticide, for decades. As a result, numerous insects, such as the fruit fly (shown here), have developed a resistance to it. In 1972, the United States banned DDT because its use caused a serious decline in birds, such as the bald eagle.

Malaria" in chapter 4, is the sickle gene. Human populations living in areas of endemic malaria have a selective advantage if they carry the allele for sickle-cell anemia. Similarly, *G6pd* alleles offer selective advantages in these same regions.

In the late 1990s, Iceland began an aggressive campaign to gather genetic information on its nearly 300,000 inhabitants to identify and isolate specific genetic diseases. In this effort, geneticists found a 900,000-nucleotide-base-pair stretch of DNA with a very noticeable inversion, the H2 haplotype, on chromosome 17. The trait is widely diverse in human populations, present in about 18% of Icelanders, 21% of Europeans, 6% of Africans, and 1% of Asians. This diversity could be due to genetic drift or perhaps to natural selection. Natural selection as a force of evolution is strongly implicated because in Icelandic populations, H2 women have 3.5% more children than do non-H2 women. Although this sounds like a low fertility difference, even such a small discrepancy can have a big influence on evolution when played out over multiple generations. That is, if in every generation the difference in fertility between H2 and non-H2 women is 3.5%, over time the frequency of H2 individuals will be far greater than that of non-H2 individuals. Anthropological geneticists hope to figure out the functions or advantages of the H2 haplotype.

An exciting recent breakthrough in the search for a way to prevent human immunodeficiency virus (HIV) and the disease it causes, acquired immunodeficiency syndrome (AIDS), is the discovery of the link with the D32 mutation at the CCR5 locus. CCR5 is a key protein that facilitates HIV's entry into target cells in the human body. Heterozygous carriers of the mutation have a reduced susceptibility to HIV infection, and homozygous carriers are resistant to HIV infection. The mutation is present mostly in European and western Asian populations, with an average frequency of 10%. It is absent in other populations. Geneticists have determined that it is relatively recent, less than 5,000 years old. The leading hypothesis is that it conferred a resistance to smallpox and plague, and individuals with the mutation benefited when HIV/AIDS emerged. Regardless of the origin, those with the variant have an adaptive advantage.

Pale skin and other obvious phenotypes are likely still evolving. While much of this record and discussion focuses on the genotype, natural selection is operating on the phenotype. That is, the earliest immigrants to Europe were probably dark-skinned. It has long been thought that when earlier hominins migrated to Europe and northern latitudes in general, they immediately developed lighter skin. As discussed in "Climate Adaptation: Living on the Margins" in chapter 5, these early Europeans would have become less pigmented, thereby absorbing ultraviolet rays and producing more vitamin D for bone development and calcium availability. Recent genetic analysis reveals that the gene for pale skin (less melanin), the *SLC24A5* gene, is present in many Europeans but not in Asians or Africans. Moreover, the mutation and selection for it likely occurred just in the past 10,000 years, certainly long after humans first migrated to Europe hundreds of thousands of years ago. The Italian geneticist Luca Cavalli-Sforza hypothesizes that the skin-color change came late because earlier populations had ready access to vitamin D from the foods they ate. However, once they began farming, the key sources of the vitamin—from fishing, herding, and hunting and gathering—became less available, creating a greater advantage for having light skin. This very recent skin-color change indicates that evolution is ongoing.

Another recent development in human evolution is adaptation to hypoxia at high altitudes. Anthropologists have long known that humans living at high altitudes have adapted to the low levels of oxygen in those settings (see "Climate Adaptation: Living on the Margins" in chapter 5). Until recently, however, it was unclear whether this change was genetic (and therefore favored by natural selection) or simply physiological (and therefore having little to do with evolution). In just a matter of weeks in 2010, three teams working independently—one led by the American physical anthropologist Cynthia Beall, one led by the Chinese geneticist Xin Yi, and one led by the American geneticist Tatum Simonson—reported on specific sets of genes found in Tibetan populations living at high altitudes. By studying the Tibetans' genomes, the research teams found strong evidence that the gene *HIF2a* is present at higher frequencies in these groups than among those living at lower altitudes. They also found an association between this gene and a low concentration of hemoglobin in the blood.

When people who live at low altitudes travel to high altitudes, their bodies respond to the lower levels of oxygen by increasing their number of red blood cells to in turn increase their hemoglobin. The Tibetan people studied, however, have the same level of hemoglobin as those living at sea level or low altitudes. How could populations living at high altitudes maintain such low levels of hemoglobin? Why would they maintain such levels?

For people who travel from low to high altitudes, higher levels of red blood cells and hemoglobin result in thicker, more viscous blood. At first, this change solves the problem of reduced oxygen. Over the long run, the thicker blood becomes a detriment because it is less able to provide oxygen to the body tissues. In addition, the change in elevation has a profoundly negative effect on fetal growth and the maternal environment: more red blood cells and hemoglobin in the mother reduce the growth of her fetus and increase its risk of mortality. For these reasons, there is strong natural selection in high-altitude populations to maintain ideal levels of red blood cells and hemoglobin. In the Tibetan populations studied, that evolutionary force has yielded the *HIF2a* gene—a shift in the genome brought about by the reduced level of oxygen.

Other phenotypes also appear to be under selection. For example, in the phenotypes of numerous populations, the American evolutionary biologist Stephen Stearns and his associates have found strong evidence of selection for height, age at first birth, and age at last birth. Much of this record appears to reflect stabilizing selection, whereby a population is maintaining certain biological parameters (see "Patterns of Natural Selection" in chapter 4). However, unlike the phenotypes discussed here that have few genes, these phenotypes are polygenic, rendering an understanding of their genotypes far less clear.

As discussed in chapter 8, evolution can be fast or slow, depending on external circumstances, such as sudden change in habitat or food source (see "How Do We Know: The Fossil Record: The Timing and Tempo of Evolution"). Some anthropologists have hypothesized that increased human population, especially in the past 40,000–50,000 years, has affected the speed of evolutionary change. The American physical anthropologist John Hawks and his colleagues have documented a close relationship between population size and having selective advantages. They make the case that population growth causes an acceleration of adaptive evolution because the more individuals, the higher the number of mutations. Therefore, population growth predicts an increase in the likelihood of new adaptive mutations. In the past 10,000 years or so, especially with the advent of agriculture and the remarkable population increase, the species *Homo sapiens* has experienced rapid skeletal evolution (see "Health and the Agricultural Revolution" in chapter 13). In addition, a host of dietary changes have led to strong selection (for a discussion of one such change, lactase, see "Anthropology Matters: Got Milk? The LCT Phenotype: Lactose Tolerance and Lactase Persistence" in chapter 4). It has long been thought that cultural adaptations would slow or stop evolution altogether. Indeed, scientists and laypersons share the impression that human evolution ended in the Upper Paleolithic. Hawks and colleagues' research suggests the opposite: evolution is likely speeding up as population size continues to mushroom and new mutations are introduced. If they are right, then human evolution has accelerated in the past 10,000 years, and it should continue to accelerate as the world population increases and as contacts and social interactions increase.

14.3 Who Will We Be Tomorrow?

Evolution began in the remote past, but it remains ongoing in humans and all other organisms. Few evolutionary biologists are comfortable with predicting future evolution, mainly because evolution is nonlinear and its course depends on current—that is, ever-changing—circumstances. The eighteenth-century pioneers of evolutionary biology could not have predicted the dramatic changes the peppered moth underwent in the nineteenth and twentieth centuries, for example. Today, the evolutionary record makes clear that evolution, whatever its forms, *will* continue.

Other inarguable predictions about the future are that humans will continue to consume energy, human population size will continue to increase, and the global climate will continue to change. If we are not successful at mitigating the negative outcomes of these changes, then these factors will present organisms with increasing challenges and likely new selective pressures. This chapter has painted a rather dark picture of our changing world—as we have more and more impact on the planet and its environment, we seem to be on a collision course with disaster. Just as humans have helped create these environmental changes, they will need to develop means of slowing global warming, most likely by modifying technologies and lifestyles to limit the production of greenhouse gases.

This field (and this book) is about the circumstances that create the basis for evolutionary changes, such as the dramatic shifts in climate predicted in the near and distant future. The warming trends have begun to melt massive ice sheets, resulting in rising sea levels and alteration of weather patterns in major ways. These changes will create circumstances that are positive for some organisms (for example, pathogens in the Arctic) and negative for others (for example, agricultural crops, the growth of which will be adversely affected). We live in a dynamic world, resulting in nonstop biological adjustments, adaptations, and declines.

One key theme in this book is that humans adapt remarkably well to novel circumstances, and an enormous component of this resilience is culture, especially technology and material culture in general. Some technology has negatively influenced the world, including the technology associated with industrialization and the burning of fossil fuels. At the same time, human technology has produced a growing global economy and ways of producing more food, increasing the population, which is living longer.

Scientists expect some regions of the world to be hit hard by temperature change, environmental disruption, food shortages, increased infectious disease, and other challenges. Still, the record of human evolution over the past 5 million years suggests that humans will develop means for dealing with such problems. Time will tell if humans are able to use culture, intelligence, and innovation to thrive in this changing world. That has been the story so far, and I believe it will continue.

CHAPTER 14 REVIEW

ANSWERING THE BIG QUESTIONS

1. **What are the most important forces shaping human biology today?**

   - Global warming is altering the environment. Left unchecked, it potentially will threaten food production and continue to negatively affect health.
   - Population increase is burdening resources and reducing well-being.
   - Technology is creating new opportunities for human life but also new threats to it.

2. **What are the biological consequences of global climate change, population increase, and technology?**

   - Global warming potentially threatens future food supplies for the growing world population, especially in poorer regions.
   - Population increase places stress on resources, including food supplies.
   - Population increase and associated crowding lead to poor sanitation and enhance the spread of existing and newly emerging infectious diseases.
   - Population increase contributes to a decline in Earth's biodiversity.
   - Technological change in food production allows access to cheaper, less nutritional food for a growing proportion of the world population. Labor-saving technology and transportation result in reduced physical activity. All of these technological changes promote obesity and poor health generally.

3. **Are we still evolving, and if so, what will human biology look like in the future?**

   - Abundant evidence indicates continued evolution in humans and in other organisms.
   - Little can be said about future evolution. If environmental circumstances (global warming, for example) continue in their predicted direction, almost certainly conditions eliciting evolutionary change will occur.

KEY TERMS

Anthropocene
anthropogenic
endotoxins
fossil fuel
global warming
hygiene hypothesis
nutrition transition

STUDY QUIZ

1. **The Anthropocene is defined by**
   a. the industrialization of agriculture.
   b. humanity's role in changing the land and air of the planet.
   c. a natural warming of Earth's atmosphere unrelated to human activity.
   d. an end to the continued biological evolution of humans.

2. **Which effect of global warming will impact coastal regions the most?**
   a. melting of polar and glacial ice masses
   b. shifting precipitation patterns altering agricultural potential
   c. increased frequency of extreme weather events
   d. uniform temperature increases across the globe

3. **In developed countries, technology has worsened**
   a. activity levels.
   b. sanitation.
   c. medical care.
   d. life expectancy.

4. **The hygiene hypothesis states that allergies are rapidly increasing worldwide because of**
   a. overcrowding of growing populations in unsanitary conditions.
   b. hypersanitation preventing early exposure to allergens.
   c. more individuals with allergies surviving to reproduce.
   d. humans evolving to become more vulnerable to allergens.

5. **Given our advanced technologies, are humans still evolving today?**
   a. No, because they can culturally adapt to any problem.
   b. Yes, but technological adaptation has slowed the pace.
   c. Yes, but the pace has slowed because of increased population.
   d. Yes, but the pace has increased because of increased population.

EVOLUTION REVIEW

THE FUTURE OF THE HUMAN CONDITION

Synopsis As you have learned throughout this textbook, much of what physical anthropologists study focuses on the evolutionary processes operating on primates and hominins in the past and the variation observed among living nonhuman primates and humans today. Our understanding of these key research areas, however, also sets the stage for physical anthropologists to make practical contributions to contemporary issues facing our population and to answer questions about the forces that will affect the future of humanity. The story of what it means to be human is one of adaptation—both biological and cultural—and the holistic and biocultural approaches characteristic of physical anthropology allow this story to be told in grand detail. As this story continues, the ongoing evolution of our species will be shaped by newly emerging environmental and ecological pressures. In a changing world, human adaptability and resilience will continue to face challenges.

Q1. How is the current episode of global warming distinct from other fluctuations in climate that influenced the origins and evolution of nonhuman primates (see chapter 9) and fossil hominins (see chapters 10–12) over the course of the past 50 million years? How might global warming act as an environmental pressure to shape the evolution of living organisms, including humans? How might humans adapt, both biologically and culturally, to these changing conditions?

Q2. We might consider the origin, dispersal, and growth of *Homo sapiens* populations—such that our own species now occupies virtually all regions of Earth—to be the earliest form of globalization. Today, globalization is characterized by the movement of ideas and products between the individuals and societies that make up our worldwide population. How does the process of globalization affect human biocultural variation and evolution?

Hint Think about the ways in which changes in nutrition and technology affect health and lifestyle across a wide range of population settings.

Q3. Are humans still evolving? What selective pressures will likely play the largest role in shaping what the future of the human condition will be 10 years, 50 years, and even 500 years from now?

ADDITIONAL READINGS

Caballero, B. C. and B. M. Popkin. 2002. *The Nutrition Transition: Diet and Disease in the Developing World.* London: Academic Press.

Colbert, E. 2007. *Field Notes from a Catastrophe: A Frontline Report on Climate Change.* London: Bloomsbury.

Epstein, P. R. and D. Ferber. 2011. *Changing Planet, Changing Health: How the Climate Crisis Threatens Our Health and What We Can Do about It.* Berkeley: University of California Press.

Garrett, L. 1994. *The Coming Plague: Newly Emerging Diseases in a World Out of Balance.* New York: Farrar, Straus, and Giroux.

Gore, A. 2006. *An Inconvenient Truth: The Planetary Emergency of Global Warming and What We Can Do about It.* New York: Rodale Press.

McKee, J. K. 2003. *Sparing Nature: The Conflict between Human Population Growth and Earth's Biodiversity.* New Brunswick, NJ: Rutgers University Press.

Myers, S. S. and J. A. Patz. 2009. Emerging threats to human health from global environmental change. *Annual Review of Environmental Resources* 34: 223–252.

Palumbi, S. R. 2001. Humans as the world's greatest evolutionary force. *Science* 293: 1786–1790.

Taubes G. 2008. The bacteria fight back. *Science* 321: 356–361.

STUDY QUIZ ANSWERS

CHAPTER 1
1. c; 2. b; 3. a; 4. d; 5. a

CHAPTER 2
1. d; 2. d; 3. a; 4. b; 5. a

CHAPTER 3
1. c; 2. a; 3. d; 4. a; 5. c

CHAPTER 4
1. c; 2. b; 3. d; 4. b; 5. b

CHAPTER 5
1. c; 2. c; 3. d; 4. b; 5. d

CHAPTER 6
1. d; 2. a; 3. a; 4. b; 5. c

CHAPTER 7
1. a; 2. b; 3. d; 4. d; 5. d

CHAPTER 8
1. a; 2. c; 3. b; 4. a; 5. d

CHAPTER 9
1. c; 2. b; 3. a; 4. d; 5. d

CHAPTER 10
1. c; 2. c; 3. d; 4. c; 5. d

CHAPTER 11
1. d; 2. a; 3. a; 4. c; 5. d

CHAPTER 12
1. d; 2. d; 3. d; 4. c; 5. d

CHAPTER 13
1. a; 2. d; 3. a; 4. b; 5. b

CHAPTER 14
1. b; 2. a; 3. a; 4. b; 5. d

APPENDIX: THE SKELETON

The skeleton is an essential part of the biology of living primates, human and nonhuman alike, and is discussed to one extent or another in many chapters of this book. Very likely, your instructor will want you to learn the essentials of primate osteology (that is, skeletal anatomy), including the names and parts of bones. This appendix provides a brief guide to that osteology, including the major bones and their parts. It presents a human skeleton, an ape (chimpanzee) skeleton, a monkey skeleton, a human skull, and close-ups of the foot bones, hand bones, and pelvic bones of the human and the ape to illustrate important differences between the bipedal and quadrupedal primates.

For more details on osteology and anatomy, see Tim White and Pieter Folkens's *The Human Bone Manual* (Burlington, MA: Elsevier Academic Press, 2005) and Daris Swindler and Charles Wood's *An Atlas of Primate Gross Anatomy* (Seattle: University of Washington Press, 1973).

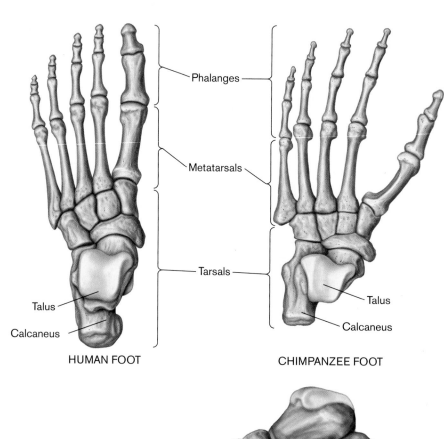

Phalanges

Metatarsals

Tarsals

Talus

Calcaneus

HUMAN FOOT

Talus

Calcaneus

CHIMPANZEE FOOT

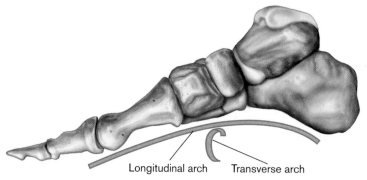

Longitudinal arch   Transverse arch

HUMAN FOOT (MEDIAL VIEW)

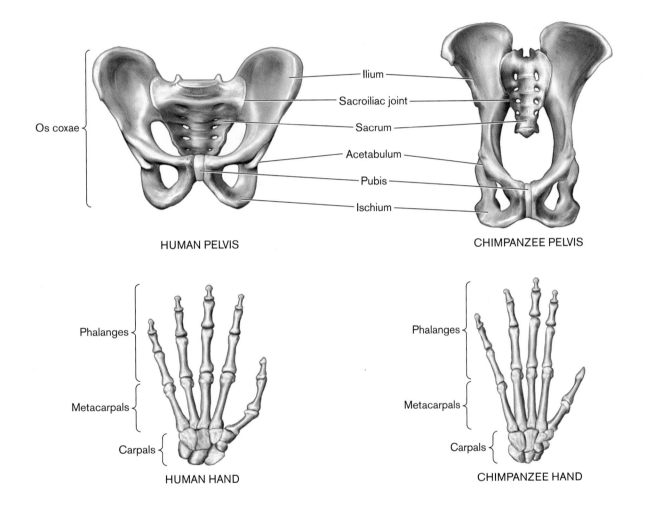

Ilium

Sacroiliac joint

Sacrum

Acetabulum

Pubis

Ischium

Os coxae

HUMAN PELVIS

CHIMPANZEE PELVIS

Phalanges

Metacarpals

Carpals

HUMAN HAND

Phalanges

Metacarpals

Carpals

CHIMPANZEE HAND

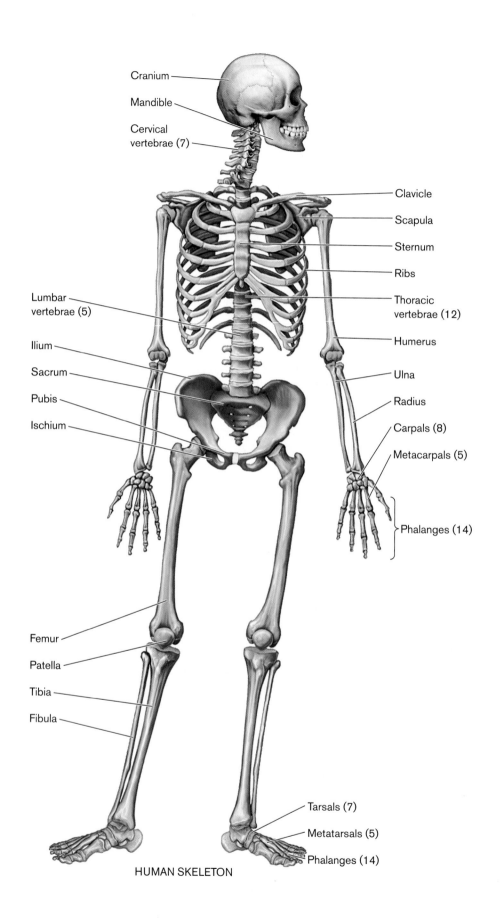

Cranium

Mandible

Cervical
vertebrae (7)

Clavicle

Scapula

Sternum

Ribs

Thoracic
vertebrae (12)

Lumbar
vertebrae (5)

Ilium

Sacrum

Pubis

Ischium

Humerus

Ulna

Radius

Carpals (8)

Metacarpals (5)

Phalanges (14)

Femur

Patella

Tibia

Fibula

Tarsals (7)

Metatarsals (5)

Phalanges (14)

HUMAN SKELETON

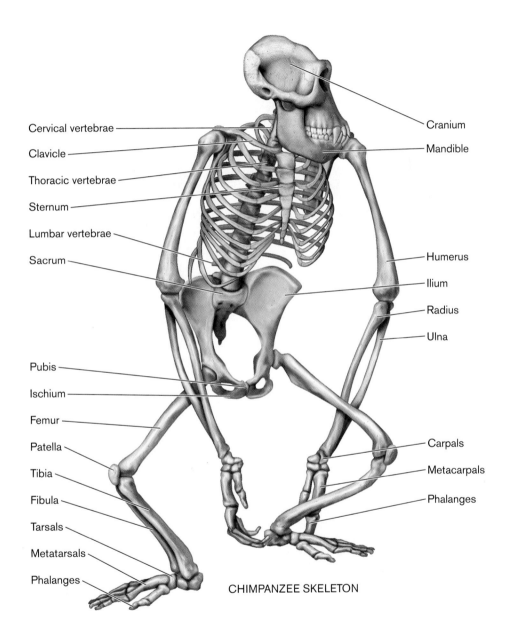

Cervical vertebrae

Clavicle

Thoracic vertebrae

Sternum

Lumbar vertebrae

Sacrum

Pubis

Ischium

Femur

Patella

Tibia

Fibula

Tarsals

Metatarsals

Phalanges

Cranium

Mandible

Humerus

Ilium

Radius

Ulna

Carpals

Metacarpals

Phalanges

CHIMPANZEE SKELETON

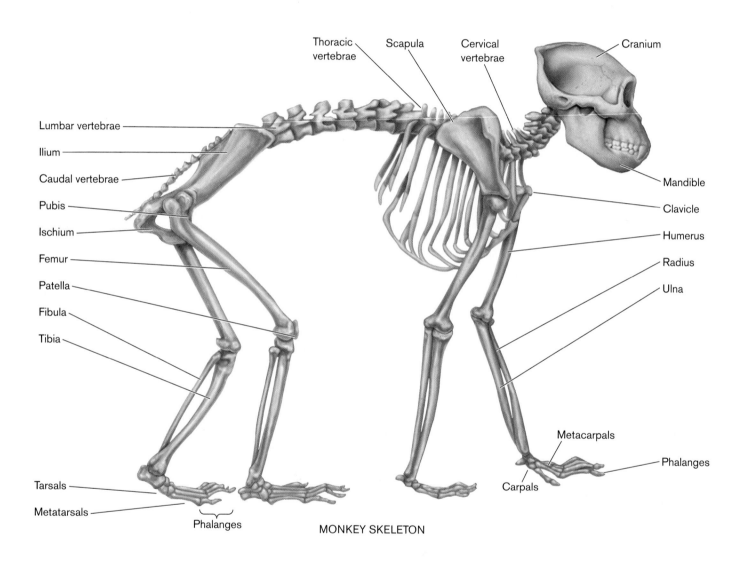

Thoracic vertebrae

Scapula

Cervical vertebrae

Cranium

Lumbar vertebrae

Ilium

Caudal vertebrae

Pubis

Ischium

Femur

Patella

Fibula

Tibia

Tarsals

Metatarsals

Phalanges

Mandible

Clavicle

Humerus

Radius

Ulna

Metacarpals

Phalanges

Carpals

MONKEY SKELETON

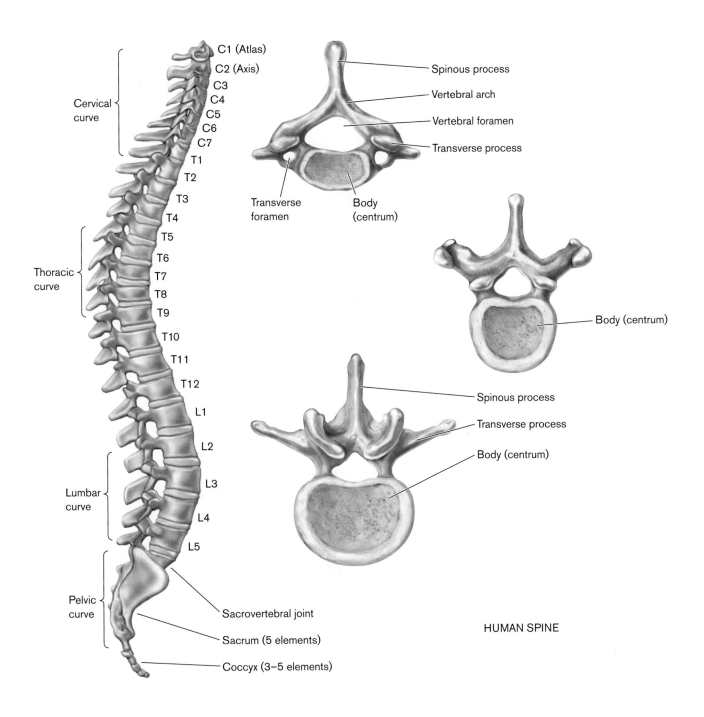

C1 (Atlas)
C2 (Axis)
C3
C4
C5
C6
C7
T1
T2
T3
T4
T5
T6
T7
T8
T9
T10
T11
T12
L1
L2
L3
L4
L5

Cervical
curve

Thoracic
curve

Lumbar
curve

Pelvic
curve

Spinous process
Vertebral arch
Vertebral foramen
Transverse process

Transverse
foramen

Body
(centrum)

Body (centrum)

Spinous process
Transverse process
Body (centrum)

Sacrovertebral joint
Sacrum (5 elements)
Coccyx (3–5 elements)

HUMAN SPINE

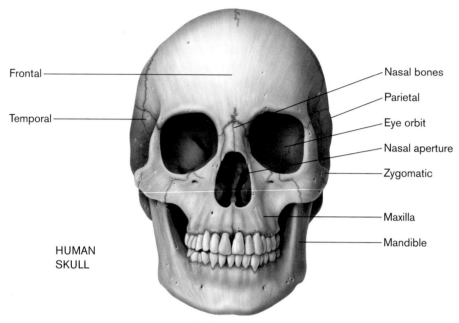

Frontal

Temporal

Nasal bones

Parietal

Eye orbit

Nasal aperture

Zygomatic

Maxilla

Mandible

HUMAN
SKULL

FRONTAL VIEW

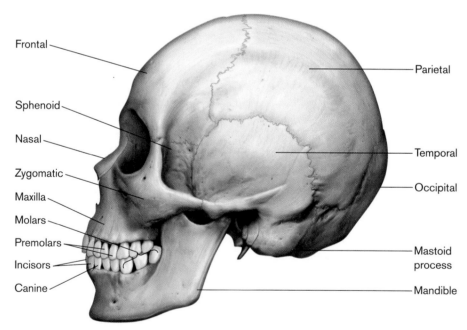

Frontal

Sphenoid

Nasal

Zygomatic

Maxilla

Molars

Premolars

Incisors

Canine

Parietal

Temporal

Occipital

Mastoid
process

Mandible

LATERAL VIEW

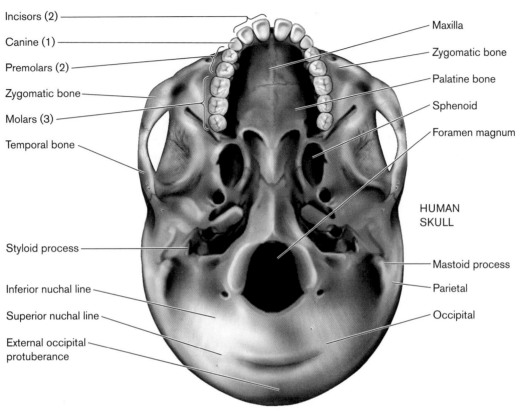

Incisors (2) — Maxilla

Canine (1) — Zygomatic bone

Premolars (2) — Palatine bone

Zygomatic bone — Sphenoid

Molars (3) — Foramen magnum

Temporal bone —

HUMAN
SKULL

Styloid process —

Mastoid process

Inferior nuchal line — Parietal

Superior nuchal line —

External occipital
protuberance — Occipital

BASILAR VIEW

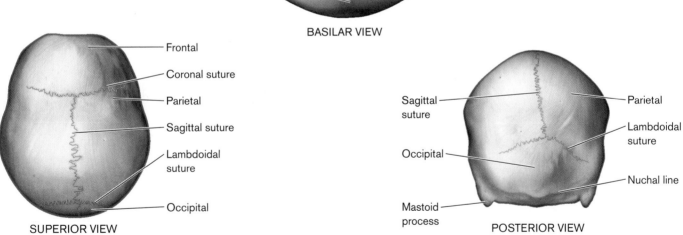

Frontal

Coronal suture

Parietal

Sagittal suture

Lambdoidal
suture

Occipital

SUPERIOR VIEW

Sagittal
suture — Parietal

Lambdoidal
suture

Occipital —

Nuchal line

Mastoid
process — POSTERIOR VIEW

FEMUR

TIBIA

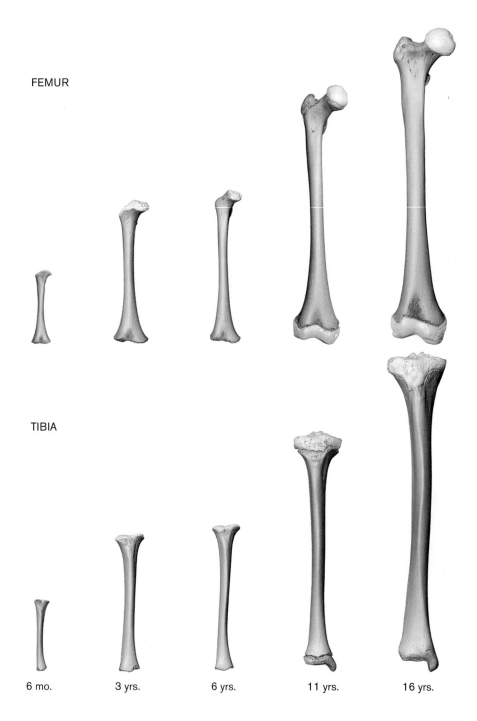

6 mo.   3 yrs.   6 yrs.   11 yrs.   16 yrs.

GLOSSARY

abnormal hemoglobin Hemoglobin altered so that it is less efficient in binding to and carrying oxygen.

Acheulian Complex The culture associated with *H. erectus,* including handaxes and other types of stone tools; more refined than the earlier Oldowan tools.

adapids Euprimates of the Eocene that were likely ancestral to modern lemurs and possibly ancestral to anthropoids.

Adapis A genus of adapids from the Eocene.

adaptations Changes in physical structure, function, or behavior that allow an organism or species to survive and reproduce in a given environment.

adaptive radiation The diversification of an ancestral group of organisms into new forms that are adapted to specific environmental niches.

adenine One of the nitrogen bases that make up DNA and RNA; it pairs with thymine in DNA molecules and uracil in RNA molecules.

adenosine triphosphate (ATP) An important cellular molecule, created by the mitochondria and carrying the energy necessary for cellular functions.

admixture The exchange of genetic material between two or more populations.

adult stage The third stage of life, involving the reproductive years and senescence.

Aegyptopithecus A propliopithecid genus from the Oligocene, probably ancestral to catarrhines; the largest primate found in the Fayum, Egypt.

aging The process of maturation.

allele One or more alternative forms of a gene.

Allen's rule The principle that an animal's limb lengths are heat-related; limbs are longer in hot environments and shorter in cold environments.

altruistic Refers to a behavior that benefits others while being a disadvantage to the individual.

ameloblasts Cells that make tooth enamel.

amino acid dating An absolute dating method for organic remains such as bone or shell, in which the amount of change in the amino acid structure is measured.

amino acids Organic molecules combined in a specific sequence by the ribosomes to form a protein.

anatomical Pertaining to an organism's physical structure.

angiosperm radiation hypothesis The proposition that certain primate traits, such as visual acuity, occurred in response to the availability of fruit and flowers after the spread of angiosperms.

Anthropoecene Proposed new geologic epoch characterized by the profound role of humans in changing the land surface and the composition of the atmospheree in signficant ways.

anthropogenic Refers to any effect caused by humans.

anthropology The study of humankind, viewed from the perspective of all people and all times.

anthropometry Measurement of the human body.

antibodies Molecules that form as part of the primary immune response to the presence of foreign substances; they attach to the foreign antigens.

anticodons Sequences of three nitrogen bases carried by tRNA; they match up with the complementary mRNA codons, and each designates a specific amino acid during protein synthesis.

antigens Specific proteins, on the surface of

cells, that stimulate the immune system's antibody production.

Apidium A parapithecid genus from the Oligocene, possibly ancestral to anthropoids.

arboreal Tree-dwelling, adapted to living in the trees.

arboreal adaptation A suite of physical traits that enable an organism to live in trees.

arboreal hypothesis The proposition that primates' unique suite of traits is an adaptation to living in trees.

archaeology The study of historic or prehistoric human populations through the analysis of material remains.

Ardipithecus kadabba An early pre-australopithecine species from the late Miocene to the early Pliocene; shows evidence of a perihoning complex, a primitive trait intermediate between apes and modern humans.

Ardipithecus ramidus A later pre-australopithecine species from the late Miocene to the early Pliocene; shows evidence of both bipedalism and arboreal activity but no indication of the primitive perihoning complex.

artifacts Material objects from past cultures.

Australopithecus An early hominin genus, representing as many as 10 species, found in East and South Africa from 4–1 mya.

Australopithecus aethiopicus An early robust australopithecine from East Africa, with the hallmark physical traits of large teeth, large face, and massive muscle attachments on the cranium.

Australopithecus afarensis An early australopithecine from East Africa that had a brain size equivalent to a modern chimpanzee's and is thought to be a direct human ancestor.

Australopithecus africanus A gracile australopithecine from South Africa that was contemporaneous with *Au. aethiopicus, Au.*

garhi, and *Au. boisei* and was likely ancestral to *Au. robustus.*

Australopithecus anamensis The oldest species of australopithecine from East Africa and a likely ancestor to *Au. afarensis.*

Australopithecus boisei Formerly known as *Zinjanthropus boisei;* a later robust australopithecine from East Africa that was contemporaneous with *Au. robustus* and *Au. africanus* and had robust cranial traits, including large teeth, large face, and heavy muscle attachments.

Australopithecus garhi A late australopithecine from East Africa that was contemporaneous with *Au. africanus* and *Au. aethiopicus* and was the likely ancestor to the *Homo* lineage.

Australopithecus (or Kenyanthropus) platyops An australopithecine from East Africa that had a unique flat face and was contemporaneous with *Au. afarensis.*

Australopithecus robustus A robust australopithecine from South Africa that may have descended from *Au. afarensis,* was contemporaneous with *Au. boisei,* and had the robust cranial traits of large teeth, large face, and heavy muscle attachments.

Australopithecus sediba A late species of australopithecine from South Africa that may have descended from *Au. africanus,* was a contemporary of *Au. robustus,* and expresses anatomical features found in *Australopithecus* and in *Homo.*

autolysis A process of "self-digestion" in which the high-carbon-dioxide environment within a decomposing body results in breakdown of the cells of the body.

autosomes All chromosomes, except the sex chromosomes, that occur in pairs in all somatic cells (not the gametes).

balanced polymorphism Situation in which selection maintains two or more phenotypes for a specific gene in a population.

basal anthropoids Eocene primates that are the earliest anthropoids.

basal metabolic rate (BMR) The rate at which an organism's body, while at rest, expends energy to maintain basic bodily functions; measured by the amount of heat given off per kilogram of body weight.

basal metabolic requirement The minimum amount of energy needed to keep an organism alive.

Bergmann's rule The principle that an animal's size is heat-related; smaller bodies are adapted to hot environments, and larger bodies are adapted to cold environments.

bilophodont Refers to lower molars, in Old World monkeys, that have two ridges.

bioarchaeology The study of human skeletal remains from archaeological sites.

biocultural approach The scientific study of the interrelationship between what humans have inherited genetically and culture.

biological (physical) anthropology The study of the evolution, variation, and adaptation of humans and their past and present relatives.

biostratigraphic dating A relative dating method that uses the associations of fossils in strata to determine each layer's approximate age.

bipedalism Walking on two feet.

Biretia A later basal anthropoid genus found in the Fayum, Egypt, that may be ancestral to anthropoids.

blending inheritance An outdated, disreputed theory that the phenotype of an offspring was a uniform blend of the parents' phenotypes.

bone mass The density of bone per unit of measure.

brachiators Organisms that move by brachiation, or arm-swinging.

Branisella A South American genus from the Oligocene, ancestral to platyrrhines.

C_3 plants Plants that take in carbon through C_3 photosynthesis, which changes carbon dioxide into a compound having three carbon atoms; tending to be from more temperate regions, these plants include wheat, sugar beets, peas, and a range of hardwood trees.

C_4 plants Plants that take in carbon through C_4 photosynthesis, which changes carbon dioxide into a compound with four carbon atoms; these plants tend to be from warmer regions with low humidity and include corn, sugarcane, millet, and prickly pear.

calculus Refers to hardened plaque on teeth; the condition is caused by the minerals from saliva being continually deposited on tooth surfaces.

canine–premolar honing complex The dental form in which the upper canines are sharpened against the lower third premolars when the jaws are opened and closed.

capillaries Small blood vessels between the terminal ends of arteries and the veins.

Carpolestes A plesiadapiform genus from the Paleocene, probably ancestral to the Eocene euprimates.

catastrophism The doctrine asserting that cataclysmic events (such as volcanoes, earthquakes, and floods), rather than evolutionary processes, are responsible for geologic changes throughout Earth's history.

Cenozoic The era lasting from 66 mya until the present, encompassing the radiation and proliferation of mammals such as humans and other primates.

chemical dating Dating methods that use predictable chemical changes that occur over time.

chromosomes The strand of DNA found in the nucleus of eukaryotes that contains hundreds or thousands of genes.

clade Group of organisms that evolved from a common ancestor.

cline A gradual change in some phenotypic characteristic from one population to the next.

Clovis Earliest Native American ("Paleoindian") culture of North America; technology known for large, fluted, bifacial stone projectile points used as spear points for big-game hunting.

coding DNA Sequences of a gene's DNA (also known as exons) that are coded to produce a specific protein and are transcribed and translated during protein synthesis.

codominance Refers to two different alleles that are equally dominant; both are fully expressed in a heterozygote's phenotype.

codons The sequences of three nitrogen bases carried by mRNA that are coded to produce specific amino acids in protein synthesis.

cognitive abilities Refers to the capacity of the brain to perceive, process, and judge information from the surrounding environment.

complementary bases The predictable pairing of nitrogen bases in the structure of DNA and RNA, such that adenine and thymine always pair together (adenine and uracil in RNA) and cytosine and guanine pair together.

cribra orbitalia Porosity in the eye orbits due to anemia caused by an iron-deficient diet, parasitic infection, or genetic disease.

crossing-over The process by which homologous chromosomes partially wrap around each other and exchange genetic information during meiosis.

cultural anthropology The study of modern human societies through the analysis of the origins, evolution, and variation of culture.

cultural dating Relative dating methods that are based on material remains' time spans.

culture Learned behavior that is transmitted from person to person.

cytoplasm The jellylike substance inside the cell membrane that surrounds the nucleus and in which the organelles are suspended.

cytosine One of the nitrogen bases that make up DNA and RNA; it pairs with guanine.

data Evidence gathered to help answer questions, solve problems, and fill gaps in scientific knowledge.

deciduous dentition Also known as baby teeth or milk teeth, this is the first set of teeth, which form in utero and erupt shortly after birth.

deme A local population of organisms that have similar genes, interbreed, and produce offspring.

demic diffusion A population's movement into an area previously uninhabited by that group.

demography The study of a population's features and vital statistics, including birth rate, death rate, population size, and population density.

dendrochronology A chronometric dating method that uses a tree-ring count to determine numerical age.

de novo mutation A mutation that occurs in the egg or sperm of a parent or in the fertilized egg that develops in the mother; a "new" mutation that is less subject to natural selection than genetic variation inherited from the parents.

dental caries A disease process that creates demineralized areas in dental tissues, leading to cavities; demineralization is caused by acids produced by bacteria that metabolize carbohydrates in dental plaque.

dental formula The numerical description of a species' teeth, listing the number, in one quadrant of the jaws, of incisors, canines, premolars, and molars.

deoxyribonucleic acid (DNA) A double-stranded molecule that provides the genetic code for an organism, consisting of phosphate, deoxyribose sugar, and four types of nitrogen bases.

derived characteristics Characteristics present in only one or a few species of a group.

diaphyses The main midsection, or shaft, portions of long bones; each contains a medullary cavity.

diastema A space between two teeth.

dietary plasticity A diet's flexibility in adapting to a given environment.

diploid cell A cell that has a full complement of paired chromosomes.

directional selection Selection for one allele over the other alleles, causing the allele frequencies to shift in one direction.

disruptive selection Selection for both extremes of the phenotypic distribution; may eventually lead to a speciation event.

diurnal Refers to those organisms that normally are awake and active during daylight hours.

domestication The process of converting wild animals or wild plants into forms that humans can care for and cultivate.

dominance The ability to intimidate or defeat another individual in a pairwise or dyadic encounter.

dominant Refers to an allele that is expressed in an organism's phenotype and that simultaneously masks the effects of another allele, if another one is present.

dryopithecids Early Miocene apes found in various locations in Europe.

Dryopithecus A genus of dryopithecid apes found in southern France and northern Spain.

electron spin resonance dating An absolute dating method that uses microwave spectroscopy to measure electrons' spins in various materials.

empirical Verified through observation and experiment.

endemic Refers to a characteristic or feature that is natural to a given population or environment.

endogamous Refers to a population in which individuals breed only with other members of the population.

endotoxins Toxins released by bacteria when they break down or die.

Eoanthropus dawsoni The species name given to the cranium and mandible in the Piltdown hoax.

Eosimias A genus of very small basal anthropoids from the Eocene.

epidemic An outbreak of an infectious disease in which a relatively high number of people are infected within a short period of time.

epigenetic Refers to heritable changes but without alteration in the genome.

epiphyses The end portions of long bones; once they fuse to the diaphyses, the bones stop growing longer.

epochs Divisions of periods (which are the major divisions of eras) in geologic time.

equilibrium A condition in which the system is stable, balanced, and unchanging.

eras Major divisions of geologic time that are divided into periods and further subdivided into epochs.

essential amino acids Those amino acids that cannot be synthesized in the body; they must be supplied by the diet.

eukaryotes Multicelled organisms that have a membrane-bound nucleus containing both the genetic material and specialized organelles.

euprimates The first true primates from the Eocene: the tarsierlike omomyids and the lemurlike adapids.

evolutionary biology A specialty within the field of biology; the study of the process of change in organisms.

evolutionary synthesis A unified theory of evolution that combines genetics with natural selection.

exogamous Refers to a population in which individuals breed only with nonmembers of their population.

fission track dating An absolute dating method based on the measurement of the number of tracks left by the decay of uranium-238.

fitness Average number of offspring produced by parents with a particular genotype compared to the number of offspring produced by parents with another genotype.

fluorine dating A relative (chemical) dating method that compares the accumulation of fluorine in animal and human bones from the same site.

Folsom Early Native American (immediately after Clovis) culture of North America; technology known for large, fluted, bifacial projectile points used as spear points for big-game hunting.

foraminifera Marine protozoans that have variably shaped shells with small holes.

forensic anthropology The scientific examination of skeletons in hope of identifying the people whose bodies they came from.

fossil fuel Combustible material, such as oil, coal, or natural gas, composed of organisms' remains preserved in rocks.

fossils Physical remains of part or all of once-living organisms, mostly bones and teeth, that have become mineralized by the replacement of organic with inorganic materials.

founder effect The accumulation of random genetic changes in a small population that has become isolated from the parent population due to the genetic input of only a few colonizers.

frameshift mutation The change in a gene due to the insertion or deletion of one or more nitrogen bases, which causes the subsequent triplets to be rearranged and the codons to be read incorrectly during translation.

free-floating nucleotide Nucleotide (the basic building block of DNA and RNA) that is present in the nucleus and is used during DNA replication and mRNA synthesis.

functional adaptations Biological changes that occur during an individual's lifetime, increasing the individual's fitness in the given environment.

gametes Sexual reproductive cells, ova and sperm, that have a haploid number of chromosomes and that can unite with a gamete of the opposite type to form a new organism.

gemmules As proposed by Darwin, the units of inheritance, supposedly accumulated in the gametes so they could be passed on to offspring.

gene The basic unit of inheritance; a sequence of DNA on a chromosome, coded to produce a specific protein.

gene flow Admixture, or the exchange of alleles between two populations.

gene pool All the genetic information in the breeding population.

genetic drift The random change in allele frequency from one generation to the next, with greater effect in small populations.

genome The complete set of genetic information—chromosomal and mitochondrial DNA—for an organism or species that represents all the inheritable traits.

genomics The branch of genetics that studies species' genomes.

genotype The genetic makeup of an organism; the combination of alleles for a given gene.

genus A group of related species.

geology The study of Earth's physical history.

Gigantopithecus A genus of Miocene pongids from Asia; the largest primate that ever lived.

global warming The increase in the average temperature of Earth's atmosphere in response to the greenhouse effect; a cause of climate change.

glucose-6-phosphate dehydrogenase (G6PD) An enzyme that aids in the proper functioning of red blood cells; its deficiency, a genetic condition, leads to hemolytic anemia.

grade Group of organisms sharing the same complexity and level of evolution.

growth velocity The speed with which an organism grows in size, often measured as the amount of growth per year.

guanine One of the nitrogen bases that make up DNA and RNA; it pairs with cytosine.

habitat The specific area of the natural environment in which an organism lives.

habituate Refers to the process of animals becoming accustomed to human observers.

half-life The time it takes for half of the radioisotopes in a substance to decay; used in various radiometric dating methods.

handaxe The most dominant tool in the Acheulian Complex, characterized by a sharp edge for both cutting and scraping.

haplogroups A large set of haplotypes, such as the Y chromosome or mitochondrial DNA, that may be used to define a population.

haploid cell A cell that has a single set of unpaired chromosomes; half of the number of chromosomes as a diploid cell.

haplotypes A group of alleles that tend to be inherited as a unit due to their closely spaced loci on a single chromosome.

Hardy–Weinberg law of equilibrium A mathematical model in population genetics that reflects the relationship between frequencies of alleles and of genotypes; it can be used to determine whether a population is undergoing evolutionary changes.

heme iron Iron—found in red meat, fish, and poultry—that the body absorbs efficiently.

hemoglobinopathies A group of related genetic blood diseases characterized by abnormal hemoglobin.

hemolytic anemias Conditions of insufficient iron in the blood due to the destruction of red blood cells resulting from genetic blood diseases, toxins, or infectious pathogens.

heritability The proportion of phenotypic variation in a population that is due to genetic variation across individuals rather than variation in the environmental conditions experienced by the individuals.

heteroplasmic Refers to a mixture of more than one type of organellar DNA, such as mitochondrial DNA, within a cell or a single organism's body, usually due to the mutation of the DNA in some organelles but not in others.

heterozygous Refers to the condition in which the two alleles of a pair of alleles at a single locus on homologous chromosomes are different.

homeostasis The maintenance of the internal environment of an organism within an acceptable range.

homeothermic Refers to an organism's ability to maintain a constant body temperature despite great variations in environmental temperature.

homeotic (*Hox*) genes Also known as homeobox genes, they are responsible for differentiating the specific segments of the body, such as the head, tail, and limbs, during embryological development.

hominin Humans and humanlike ancestors.

Homo erectus An early species of *Homo* and the likely descendant of *H. habilis;* the first hominin species to move out of Africa into Asia and Europe.

Homo floresiensis Nicknamed "Hobbit" for its diminutive size, a possible new species of *Homo* found in Liang Bua Cave, on the Indonesian island of Flores.

Homo habilis The earliest *Homo* species, a possible descendant of *Au. garhi* and an ancestor to *H. erectus;* showed the first substantial increase in brain size and was the first species definitively associated with the production and use of stone tools.

homologous Refers to each set of paired chromosomes in the genome.

homoplasmic Refers to nuclear DNA, which is identical in the nucleus of each cell type (except red blood cells).

homozygous Refers to the condition in which the two alleles of a pair of alleles at a single locus on homologous chromosomes are the same.

Huntington's chorea A rare genetic disease in which the central nervous system degenerates and the individual loses control over voluntary movements, with the symptoms often appearing between ages 30 and 50.

hygiene hypothesis The proposition that increasing allergies among children are the result of decreased exposure to microbes, such as those found in dirt.

hypercholesterolemia The presence of high levels of cholesterol in an organism's blood; this condition may result from the dietary consumption of foods that promote high cholesterol or through the inheritance of a genetic disorder.

hypothermia A condition in which an organism's body temperature falls below the normal range, which may lead to the loss of proper body functions and, eventually, death.

hypotheses Testable statements that potentially explain specific phenomena observed in the natural world.

hypoxia Less than usual sea-level amount of oxygen in the air or in the body.

igneous Rock formed from the crystallization of molten magma, which contains the radioisotope ^{40}K; used in potassium–argon dating.

index fossils Fossils that are from specified time ranges, are found in multiple locations, and can be used to determine the age of associated strata.

induced mutations Refers to those mutations in the DNA resulting from exposure to toxic chemicals or to radiation.

infanticide The killing of a juvenile.

intrauterine Refers to the area within the uterus.

iron deficiency anemia A condition in which the blood has insufficient iron; may be caused by diet, poor iron absorption, parasitic infection, and severe blood loss.

isotopes Two or more forms of a chemical element that have the same number of protons but vary in the number of neutrons.

karyotype The characteristics of the chromosomes for an individual organism or a species, such as number, size, and type. The karyotype is typically presented as a photograph of a person's chromosomes that have been arranged in homologous pairs and put in numerical order by size.

Khoratpithecus A genus of Miocene apes from Asia, likely ancestral to orangutans.

kin selection Altruistic behaviors that increase the donor's inclusive fitness; that is, the fitness of the donor's relatives.

Klinefelter's syndrome A chromosomal trisomy in which males have an extra X chromosome, resulting in an XXY condition; affected individuals typically have reduced fertility.

lactation The production and secretion of milk from a female mammal's mammary glands, providing a food source to the female's young.

Lamarckism First proposed by Lamarck, the theory of evolution through the inheritance of acquired characteristics in which an organism can pass on features acquired during its lifetime.

language A set of written or spoken symbols that refer to things (people, places, concepts, etc.) other than themselves.

law of independent assortment Mendel's second law, which asserts that the inheritance of one trait does not affect the inheritance of other traits.

law of segregation Mendel's first law, which asserts that the two alleles for any given gene (or trait) are inherited, one from each parent; during gamete production, only one of the two alleles will be present in each ovum or sperm.

Levallois A distinctive method of stone tool production used during the Middle Paleolithic, in which the core was prepared and flakes removed from the surface before the final tool was detached from the core.

life history The timing and details of growth events and development events from conception through senescence and death.

linguistic anthropology The study of the construction, use, and form of language in human populations.

linkage Refers to the inheritance, as a unit, of individual genes closely located on a chromosome; an exception to the law of independent assortment.

locus The location on a chromosome of a specific gene.

loph An enamel ridge connecting cusps on a tooth's surface.

Lower Paleolithic The oldest part of the period during which the first stone tools were created and used, beginning with the Oldowan Complex.

Lucy One of the most significant fossils: the 40% complete skeleton of an adult female *Au. afarensis,* found in East Africa.

macroevolution Large-scale evolution, such as a speciation event, that occurs after hundreds or thousands of generations.

macronutrients Essential chemical nutrients,

including fat, carbohydrates, and protein, that a body needs to live and to function normally.

masticatory-functional hypothesis The hypothesis that craniofacial shape change during the Holocene was related to the consumption of softer foods.

material culture The part of culture that is expressed as objects that humans use to manipulate environments.

matriline DNA, such as mitochondrial DNA, whose inheritance can be traced from mother to daughter or to son.

megafauna General term for the large game animals hunted by pre-Holocene and early Holocene humans.

meiosis The production of gametes through one DNA replication and two cell (and nuclear) divisions, creating four haploid gametic cells.

melanic Refers to an individual with high concentrations of melanin.

melanin A brown pigment that determines the darkness or lightness of a human's skin color due to its concentration in the skin.

melanocytes Melanin-producing cells located in the skin's epidermis.

menarche Refers to the onset of menstruation in an adolescent female.

Mendelian inheritance The basic principles associated with the transmission of genetic material, forming the basis of genetics, including the law of segregation and the law of independent assortment.

menopause The cessation of the menstrual cycle, signifying the end of a female's ability to bear children.

Mesozoic The second major era of geologic time, 245–66 mya, characterized by the emergence and extinction of dinosaurs.

messenger RNA (mRNA) The molecules that are responsible for making a chemical copy of a gene needed for a specific protein; that is, for the transcription phase of protein synthesis.

methylation The attachment of a methyl group, a simple chemical, to DNA at certain sites throughout the genome.

microcephaly A condition in which the cranium is abnormally small and the brain is underdeveloped.

microevolution Small-scale evolution, such as changes in allele frequency, that occurs from one generation to the next.

micronutrients Essential substances, such as minerals or vitamins, needed in very small amounts to maintain normal body functioning.

Micropithecus A genus of very small proconsulids from the Miocene, found in Africa.

microsatellites Also called *short tandem repeats* (STRs); refers to sequences of repeated base pairs of DNA, usually no more than two to six. If repeated excessively, they are often associated with neurological disorders, such as Huntington's chorea.

Middle Paleolithic The middle part of the Old Stone Age, associated with Mousterian tools, which Neandertals produced using the Levallois technique.

mitochondria Energy-producing (ATP) organelles in eukaryotic cells; they possess their own independent DNA.

mitosis The process of cellular and nuclear division that creates two identical diploid daughter cells.

monogamous Refers to a social group that includes an adult male, an adult female, and their offspring.

monosomy Refers to the condition in which only one of a specific pair of chromosomes is present in a cell's nucleus.

morphology Physical shape and appearance.

motor skills Refers to the performance of complex movements and actions that require the control of nerves and muscles.

Mousterian The stone tool culture in which Neandertals produced tools using the Levallois technique.

mutagens Substances, such as toxins, chemicals, or radiation, that may induce genetic mutations.

mutation A random change in a gene or chromosome, creating a new trait that may be advantageous, deleterious, or neutral in its effects on the organism.

natural selection The process by which some organisms, with features that enable them to adapt to the environment, preferentially survive and reproduce, thereby increasing the frequency of those features in the population.

Neolithic The late Pleistocene–early Holocene culture, during which humans domesticated plants and animals.

nocturnal Refers to those organisms that are awake and active during the night.

noncoding DNA Sequences of a gene's DNA (also known as introns) that are not coded to produce specific proteins and are excised before protein synthesis.

nondisjunctions Refers to the failure of the chromosomes to properly segregate during meiosis, creating some gametes with abnormal numbers of chromosomes.

nonheme iron Iron—found in lentils and beans—that is less efficiently absorbed by the body than is heme iron.

nonhoning canine An upper canine that, as part of a nonhoning chewing mechanism, is not sharpened against the lower third premolar.

nonmelanic Refers to an individual with low concentrations of melanin.

nonmineralized Refers to bone reduced to its organic component.

nonsynonymous point mutation A point mutation that creates a triplet coded to produce a different amino acid from that of the original triplet.

Notharctus A genus of one of the largest adapids from the Eocene.

nucleotide The building block of DNA and RNA, composed of a sugar, a phosphate group, and one of four nitrogen bases.

nucleus A membrane-bound structure in eukaryotic cells that contains the genetic material.

nutrition transition The shift in diet to one that is high in saturated fat and sugar; a cause of the global obesity epidemic.

obstetric dilemma Hypothesis pertaining to hominin mothers giving birth to a large-brained, large-bodied infant: Owing to the large brain, the birth process requires a wide pelvis, but efficient bipedalism requires a narrow pelvis.

occipital bun A cranial feature of Neandertals in which the occipital bone projects substantially from the skull's posterior.

Oldowan Complex The stone tool culture associated with *H. habilis* and, possibly, *Au. garhi,* including primitive chopper tools.

olfactory bulb The portion of the anterior brain that detects odors.

oligopithecids The earliest anthropoid ancestors in the Oligocene, found in the Fayum, Egypt.

omomyids Eocene euprimates that may be ancestral to tarsiers.

opposable Refers to primates' thumb, in that it can touch each of the four fingertips, enabling a grasping ability.

oreopithecids Miocene apes that were found in Europe.

Oreopithecus A genus of oreopithecids found in Italy that was extinct within a million years of its appearance.

Orrorin tugenensis A pre-australopithecine species found in East Africa that displayed some of the earliest evidence of bipedalism.

osteoarthritis Degenerative changes of the joints caused by a variety of factors, especially physical activity and mechanical stress.

osteoblasts Cells responsible for bone formation.

osteoclasts Cells responsible for bone resorption.

osteoporosis The loss of bone mass often due to age, causing the bones to become porous, brittle, and easily fractured.

Ouranopithecus A genus of Miocene dryopithecids found in Greece.

paleogenetics The application of genetics to the past, especially in anthropology and paleontology; the study of genetics in past organisms.

Paleoindians The earliest hominin inhabitants of the Americas; they likely migrated from Asia and are associated with the Clovis and Folsom stone tool cultures in North America and comparable tools in South America.

paleomagnetic dating An absolute dating method based on the reversals of Earth's magnetic field.

paleontology The study of extinct life-forms through the analysis of fossils.

Paleozoic The first major era of geologic time, 545–245 mya, during which fish, reptiles, and insects first appeared.

pandemic Wide regional or global spread of infectious disease.

Pangaea A hypothetical landmass in which all the continents were joined, approximately 300–200 mya.

parapithecids Anthropoid ancestors from the Oligocene, found in the Fayum, Egypt.

Parapithecus A genus of later parapithecids from the Oligocene, found in the Fayum, Egypt.

parental investment The time and energy parents expend for their offspring's benefit.

pathogen A microorganism that can cause disease.

patriline DNA whose inheritance can be traced from father to son via the Y chromosome.

pebble tools The earliest stone tools, in which simple flakes were knocked off to produce an edge used for cutting and scraping.

peptide bond Chemical bond that joins amino acids into a protein chain.

periosteal reaction Inflammatory response of the bones' outer covering due to bacterial infection or to trauma.

Perupithecus The earliest genus of a platyrrhine, dating to the early Oligocene.

personal genomics The branch of genomics focused on sequencing individual genomes.

phenotype The physical expression of the genotype; it may be influenced by the environment.

phylogeny The evolutionary relationships of a group of organisms.

physical anthropology The original term for biological anthropology.

Pithecanthropus erectus The name first proposed by Ernst Haeckel for the oldest hominin; Dubois later used this name for his first fossil discovery, which later became known as *Homo erectus*.

pleiotropy A single gene can have multiple effects.

plesiadapiforms Paleocene organisms that may have been the first primates, originating from an adaptive radiation of mammals.

point mutations Replacements of a single nitrogen base with another base, which may or may not affect the amino acid for which the triplet codes.

polarized light A kind of light used in amino acid dating because it allows amino acid changes to be observed and measured.

polyandrous Refers to a social group that includes one reproductively active female, several adult males, and their offspring.

polygenic Refers to one phenotypic trait that is affected by two or more genes.

polygynous Refers to a social group that includes one adult male, several adult females, and their offspring.

polymerase chain reaction (PCR) A technique that amplifies a small sample of DNA into a larger amount that can be used for various genetic tests.

polymorphism Refers to the presence of two or more alleles at a locus and where the frequency of the alleles is greater than 1% in the population.

polypeptide Also known as a protein, a chain of amino acids held together by multiple peptide bonds.

population genetics A specialty within the field of genetics; it focuses on the changes in gene frequencies and the effects of those changes on adaptation and evolution.

porotic hyperostosis Expansion and porosity of cranial bones due to anemia caused by an iron-deficient diet, parasitic infection, or genetic disease.

positive selection Process in which advantageous genetic variants quickly increase in frequency in a population.

postnatal stage The second stage of life, beginning with birth, terminating with the shift to the adult stage, and involving substantial increases in height, weight, and brain growth and development.

power grip A fistlike grip in which the fingers and thumbs wrap around an object in opposite directions.

preadaptation An organism's use of an anatomical feature in a way unrelated to the feature's original function.

precision grip A precise grip in which the tips of the fingers and thumbs come together, enabling fine manipulation.

prehensile tail A tail that acts as a kind of a hand for support in trees, common in New World monkeys.

prenatal stage The first stage of life, beginning with the zygote in utero, terminating with birth, and involving multiple mitotic events and the differentiation of the body into the appropriate segments and regions.

primates A group of mammals in the order Primates that have complex behavior, varied forms of locomotion, and a unique suite of traits, including large brains, forward-facing eyes, fingernails, and reduced snouts.

primitive characteristics Characteristics present in multiple species of a group.

Proconsul A genus of early Miocene proconsulids from Africa, ancestral to catarrhines.

proconsulids Early Miocene apes found in East Africa.

prokaryotes Single-celled organisms with no nuclear membranes or organelles and with their genetic material as a single strand in the cytoplasm.

propliopithecids Anthropoid ancestors from the Oligocene, found in Africa.

Propliopithecus Oligocene propliopithecid genus.

Proprimates A separate order of early primate ancestors from the Paleocene, such as the plesiadapiforms.

putrefaction The breakdown of dead tissues that results from the activity of microorganisms, especially bacteria.

racemization The chemical reaction resulting in the conversion of l amino acids to d amino acids for amino acid dating.

radiocarbon dating The radiometric dating method in which the ratio of ^{14}C to ^{12}C is measured to provide an absolute date for a material younger than 50,000 years.

radiopotassium dating The radiometric dating method in which the ratio of ^{40}K to ^{40}Ar is measured to provide an absolute date for a material older than 200,000 years.

recessive An allele that is expressed in an organism's phenotype if two copies are present but is masked if the dominant allele is present.

recombination The exchange of genetic material between homologous chromosomes, resulting from a crossover event.

regulatory genes Those genes that determine when structural genes and other regulatory genes are turned on and off for protein synthesis.

regulatory proteins Proteins involved in the expression of control genes.

replication The process of copying nuclear DNA prior to cell division, so that each new daughter cell receives a complete complement of DNA.

reproductive isolation Any circumstance that prevents two populations from interbreeding and exchanging genetic material, such as when two populations are separated by a large body of water or a major mountain range.

rhinarium The naked surface around the nostrils, typically wet in mammals.

ribonucleic acid (RNA) A single-stranded molecule involved in protein synthesis, consisting of a phosphate, ribose sugar, and one of four nitrogen bases.

ribosomal RNA (rRNA) A fundamental structural component of a ribosome.

ribosomes The organelles attached to the surface of the endoplasmic reticulum, located in the cytoplasm of a cell; they are the site of protein synthesis.

rigidity (bone) Refers to the strength of bone to resist bending and torsion.

Saadanius An early catarrhine Oligocene genus from a group of primates that gave rise to later catarrhines.

sagittal keel A slight ridge of bone found along the midline sagittal suture of the cranium, which is typically found on *H. erectus* skulls.

Sahelanthropus tchadensis The earliest pre-australopithecine species found in central Africa with possible evidence of bipedalism.

scientific law A statement of fact describing natural phenomena.

scientific method An empirical research method in which data are gathered from observations of phenomena, hypotheses are formulated and tested, and conclusions are drawn that validate or modify the original hypotheses.

sectorial (premolar) Refers to a premolar adapted for cutting.

secular trend A phenotypic change over time, due to multiple factors; such trends can be positive (e.g., increased height) or negative (e.g., decreased height).

sedimentary Rock formed when the deposition of sediments creates distinct layers, or strata.

senescence Refers to an organism's biological changes in later adulthood.

sex chromosomes The pair of chromosomes that determine an organism's biological sex.

sexual dimorphism A difference in a physical attribute between the males and females of a species.

sexual selection The frequency of traits that change due to those traits' attractiveness to members of the opposite sex.

shovel-shaped incisors A dental trait, commonly found among Native Americans and Asians, in which the incisors' posterior aspect has varying degrees of concavity.

sickle-cell anemia A genetic blood disease in which the red blood cells become deformed and sickle-shaped, decreasing their ability to carry oxygen to tissues.

single nucleotide polymorphisms (SNPs) Variations in the DNA sequence due to the change of a single nitrogen base.

sivapithecids Early Miocene apes found in Asia.

Sivapithecus A genus of Miocene sivapithecids, proposed as ancestral to orangutans.

skin reflectance Refers to the amount of light reflected from the skin that can be measured and used to assess skin color.

social learning The capacity to learn from other humans, enabling the accumulation of knowledge across many generations.

sociolinguistics The science of investigating language's social contexts.

somatic cells Diploid cells that form the organs, tissues, and other parts of an organism's body.

species A group of related organisms that can interbreed and produce fertile, viable offspring.

spontaneous mutations Random changes in DNA that occur during cell division.

stabilizing selection Selection against the extremes of the phenotypic distribution, decreasing the genetic diversity for this trait in the population.

Steno's law of superposition The principle that the lower the stratum or layer, the older its age; the oldest layers are at the bottom, and the youngest are at the top.

strata Layers of rock, representing various periods of deposition.

stratigraphic correlation The process of matching up strata from several sites through the analysis of chemical, physical, and other properties.

stressors Any factor that can cause stress in an organism, potentially affecting the body's proper functioning and its homeostasis.

structural genes Genes coded to produce particular products, such as an enzyme or hormone, rather than for regulatory proteins.

structural proteins Proteins that form an organism's physical attributes.

sun protection factor (SPF) The rating calculated by comparing the length of time needed for protected skin to burn to the length of time needed for unprotected skin to burn.

superfoods Cereal grains, such as rice, corn, and wheat, that make up a substantial portion of the human population's diet today.

synonymous point mutation A neutral point mutation in which the substituted nitrogen base creates a triplet coded to produce the same amino acid as that of the original triplet.

systematics The study and classification of living organisms to determine their evolutionary relationships with one another.

taphonomy The study of the deposition of plant or animal remains and the environmental conditions affecting their preservation.

taxonomy The classification of organisms into a system that reflects degrees of relatedness.

tectonic Refers to various structures on Earth's surface, such as the continental plates.

terrestrial Life-forms, including humans, that live on land versus living in water or in trees.

thalassemia A genetic blood disease in which the hemoglobin is improperly synthesized, causing the red blood cells to have a much shorter life span.

theory A set of hypotheses that have been rigorously tested and validated, leading to their establishment as a generally accepted explanation of specific phenomena.

thermoluminescence dating A relative dating method in which the energy trapped in a material is measured when the object is heated.

Theropithecus A genus of fossil and living Old World monkeys found in Africa; it was more diverse in the past than it is today and was one of the first monkey genera to appear in the evolutionary record.

thymine One of four nitrogen bases that make up DNA; it pairs with adenine.

tooth comb Anterior teeth (incisors and canines) that have been tilted forward, creating a scraper.

total daily energy expenditure (TDEE) The number of calories used by an organism's body during a 24-hour period.

transcription The first step of protein synthesis, involving the creation of mRNA based on the DNA template.

transfer RNA (tRNA) The molecules that are responsible for transporting amino acids to the ribosomes during protein synthesis.

translation The second step of protein synthesis, involving the transfer of amino acids by tRNA to the ribosomes, which are then added to the protein chain.

translocations Rearrangements of chromosomes due to the insertion of genetic material from one chromosome to another.

transposable elements Mobile pieces of DNA that can copy themselves into entirely new areas of the chromosomes.

treponematoses A group of related diseases (venereal syphilis, yaws, endemic syphilis) caused by the bacteria *Treponema,* which causes pathological changes most often to the cranium and tibiae.

triplets Sequences of three nitrogen bases each in DNA, known as codons in mRNA.

trisomy Refers to the condition in which an additional chromosome exists with the homologous pair.

type 2 diabetes A disease in which the body does not produce sufficient amounts of insulin or the cells do not use available insulin, causing a buildup of glucose in the cells.

uniformitarianism The theory that processes that occurred in the geologic past are still at work today.

Upper Paleolithic Refers to the most recent part of the Old Stone Age, associated with early modern *Homo sapiens* and characterized by finely crafted stone and other types of tools with various functions.

uracil One of four nitrogen bases that make up RNA; it pairs with adenine.

vasoconstriction The decrease in blood vessels' diameter due to the action of a nerve or of a drug; it can also occur in response to cold temperatures.

vasodilation The increase in blood vessels' diameter due to the action of a nerve or of a drug; it can also occur in response to hot temperatures.

victoriapithecids Miocene primates from Africa, possibly ancestral to Old World monkeys.

virulence The capacity of a pathogen to cause harm to its host; pathogens with high virulence are more likely to kill their hosts.

visual predation hypothesis The proposition that unique primate traits arose as adaptations to preying on insects and on small animals.

weaning The process of substituting other foods for the milk produced by the mother.

Wolff's Law The principle that bone is placed in the direction of functional demand; that is, bone develops where needed and recedes where it is not needed.

Y-5 Hominoids' pattern of lower molar cusps.

zygote The cell that results from a sperm's fertilization of an ovum.

GLOSSARY OF PLACE NAMES

Primary research and/or findings are noted for each place.

CHAPTER 1

Baffin Island—Franz Boas research

St. Catherines Island, Georgia—Clark Larsen research

CHAPTER 2

Galápagos Islands—Charles Darwin trip and observations

CHAPTER 6

New World (primates)

Old World (primates)

Taï Forest, Ivory Coast, West Africa—primate behavior and conservation

CHAPTER 7

Gombe, Tanzania—Jane Goodall research

CHAPTER 9

Bighorn Basin, Wyoming—*Carpolestes*

The Fayum Depression, Egypt—*Aegyptopithecus, Parapithecus, Apidium, Biretia,* oligopithecids, parapithecids, propliopithecids

Jingzhou, China—*Archicebus*

Paris Basin—*Adapis*

Rukwa Rift Basin, Tanzania—*Rukwapithecus fleaglei, Nsungwepithecus gunnelli*

Rusinga Island, Lake Victoria, Kenya—*Proconsul*

Salla, Bolivia—*Branisella*

Santa Rosa, Peru—*Perupithecus*

Saudi Arabia—*Saadanius*

Shanghuang, Jiangsu Province, China—*Eosimias*

St. Gaudens, France—*Dryopithecus*

Tuscany, Italy—*Oreopithecus*

CHAPTER 10

Afar Depression, Ethiopia—*Ardipithecus*

Allia Bay, Kenya—*Australopithecus anamensis*

Aramis, Ethiopia—*Ardipithecus kadabba* and *Ardipithecus ramidus*

Asa Issie, Ethiopia—*Australopithecus anamensis*

Awash River Valley, Ethiopia—*Ardipithecus* and *Australopithecus garhi*

Bouri, Middle Awash River Valley, Ethiopia—*Australopithecus garhi*

Burtele, Ethiopia—*Australopithecus* species unknown

Dikika, Ethiopia—*Australopithecus afarensis* and evidence of cutmarks on bones

Djurab Desert, Chad—*Sahelanthropus tchadensis*

Drimolen, South Africa—*Australopithecus robustus*

Eastern Rift Valley, Africa—*Australopithecus*

Gona River, Ethiopia—*Australopithecus garhi* tools

Hadar, Ethiopia—*Australopithecus afarensis*

Kanapoi, Kenya—*Australopithecus anamensis*

Korsi Dora, Ethiopia—*Australopithecus afarensis*

Kromdraai, South Africa—*Australopithecus robustus*

Laetoli, Tanzania—*Australopithecus afarensis*

Lake Turkana, Kenya—*Australopithecus anamensis, Orrorin tugenensis, Australopithecus (Kenyanthropus) platyops,* and *Australopithecus aethiopicus*

Lomekwi, Kenya—*Australopithecus (Kenyanthropus) platyops* and Oldowan-like cobble tools

Makapansgat, South Africa—*Australopithecus africanus*

Malapa, South Africa—*Australopithecus sediba*

Olduvai Gorge, Tanzania—various Australopithecines

Piltdown Common, East Sussex, England—Piltdown hoax

Sterkfontein, South Africa—*Australopithecus africanus*

Swartkrans, South Africa—*Australopithecus robustus*

Taung, South Africa—*Australopithecus africanus*

Tugen Hills, Kenya—*Orrorin tugenensis*

CHAPTER 11

Atapuerca, Spain—*Homo erectus*

Bodo, Middle Awash River Valley, Ethiopia—*Homo erectus* and evidence of cutmarks on bones

Bouri, Middle Awash River Valley, Ethiopia—*Homo erectus* and evidence of animal butchery

Boxgrove, England—*Homo erectus*

Buia, Eritrea—*Homo erectus*

Ceprano, Italy—*Homo erectus*

Dmanisi, Republic of Georgia—*Homo erectus*

Gona, Ethiopia—complete pelvis of *Homo erectus*

Gongwangling, China—*Homo erectus*

Gran Dolina, Spain—*Homo erectus,* evidence of animal butchery, and cutmarks on *H. erectus* bones

Ileret, Kenya—*Homo erectus*

Lake Turkana, Kenya—*Homo habilis*

Ledi-Geraru, Afar Region, Ethiopia—transitional hominin between australopithecines and *Homo*

Majuangou, China—*Homo erectus*

Mauer, Germany—*Homo erectus*

Nariokotome, Kenya—*Homo erectus*

Olduvai Gorge, Tanzania—*Homo habilis, Homo erectus,* and *Homo rudolfensis*

Olorgesailie, Kenya—Acheulian tools
Omo, Ethiopia—*Homo habilis*
Rising Star Cave, South Africa—Homo naledi
Sambungmacan, Java—*Homo erectus*
Sangiran, Java—*Homo erectus*
Sima del Elefanté, Spain—*Homo erectus*
Sterkfontein, South Africa—*Homo habilis*
Trinil, Java—*Homo erectus*
Uraha, Malawi—*Homo habilis*
Zhoukoudian, China—*Homo erectus* and evidence of fire

CHAPTER 12

Aduma, Middle Awash River Valley, Ethiopia—early modern *Homo sapiens*
Amud, Israel—Neandertal and evidence of intentional burial
Arago, France—early archaic *Homo sapiens*
Atapuerca, Spain—early archaic *Homo sapiens*
Bouri, Middle Awash River Valley, Ethiopia—early modern *Homo sapiens*
Clovis, New Mexico—Paleoindian sites
Cro-Magnon, France—early modern *Homo sapiens*
Cueva Antón, Spain—Neandertal
Cueva de los Aviones, Spain—Neandertal
Dali, China—early archaic *Homo sapiens*
Dederiyeh, Syria—Neandertal
Denisova, Russia—Denisovan
Dolni Vestonice, Czech Republic—early modern *Homo sapiens*
El Sidron, Spain—Neandertal
Engis, Belgium—Neandertal
Feldhofer Cave, Germany—Neandertal
Flores, Indonesia—*Homo floresiensis*
Folsom, New Mexico—Paleoindian sites
Fuyan Cave, south China—early modern *Homo sapiens*
Gobero, Niger—early modern *Homo sapiens*

Grimaldi Caves, Italy—early modern *Homo sapiens*
Hayonim, Israel—Neandertal
Herto, Middle Awash River Valley, Ethiopia—early modern *Homo sapiens*
Hofmeyr, South Africa—early modern *Homo sapiens*
Kabwe (Broken Hill), Zambia—early archaic *Homo sapiens*
Katanda, Congo—early modern *Homo sapiens*
Kebara, Israel—Neandertal
Kennewick, Washington—controversial Paleoindian find
Kilianstädten, Germany
Klasies River Mouth Cave, South Africa—early modern *Homo sapiens*
Kow Swamp, Victoria, Australia—early modern *Homo sapiens*
Krapina, Croatia—Neandertal and possible evidence of cannibalism
La Chapelle-aux-Saints, France—Neandertal and evidence of intentional burial
Lagar Velho, Portugal—early modern *Homo sapiens*
Lake Mungo, New South Wales, Australia—early modern *Homo sapiens*
Les Rochers de Villeneuve, France—Neandertal
Liang Bua, Indonesia—*H. floresiensis*
Lothagam, Kenya—early modern *Homo sapiens*
Marillac, France—Neandertal
Mezmaiskaya, Russia—Neandertal
Minatogawa, Japan—early modern *Homo sapiens*
Mladeč, Czech Republic—early modern *Homo sapiens*
Monte Lessini, Italy—Neandertal
Moula-Guercy, France—Neandertal and possible evidence of cannibalism
Narmada, India—early archaic *Homo sapiens*
Ngandong, Java—early archaic *Homo sapiens*

Omo, Ethiopia—early modern *Homo sapiens*
Peștera cu Oase, Romania—early modern *Homo sapiens*
Petralona, Greece—early archaic *Homo sapiens*
Předmostí, Czech Republic—early modern *Homo sapiens*
Qafzeh, Israel—Neandertal
Rochers de Villeneuve, France—Neandertal
Scladina, Belgium—Neandertal
Shanidar, Kurdistan, Iraq—Neandertal, evidence of care of the sick, and evidence of intentional burial
Sima de los Huesos, Sierra de Atapuerca, Spain—early archaic *Homo sapiens*
Skhul, Israel—early modern *Homo sapiens*
Spy, Belgium—Neandertal
Steinheim, Germany—early archaic *Homo sapiens*
Swanscombe, England—early archaic *Homo sapiens*
Tabun, Israel—Neandertal and evidence of intentional burial
Teshik Tash, Uzbekistan—Neandertal
Tianyuan Cave, China—early modern *Homo sapiens*
Vindija Cave, Croatia—Neandertal
Wadi Halfa, Egypt—early modern *Homo sapiens*
Wadi Kubbaniya, Egypt—early modern *Homo sapiens*
Zhoukoudian, Upper Cave, China—early modern *Homo sapiens*

CHAPTER 13

Çatalhöyük, Turkey—evidence of early cities
Cowboy Wash, Colorado—evidence of cannibalism
Fertile Crescent, Jordan Valley—early agricultural communities
Jericho, Israel—evidence of early cities
Levant—early plant domestication

BIBLIOGRAPHY

Abbate, E., A. Albianelli, A. Azzaroli, M. Benve-
nuti, B. Tesfamariam, P. Bruni, N. Cipriani,
R. J. Clarke, G. Ficcarelli, R. Macchiarelli,
G. Napoleone, M. Papini, L. Rook, M. Sagri,
T. M. Tecle, D. Torre, and I. Villa. 1998. A
one-million-year-old *Homo* cranium from
the Danakil (Afar) depression of Eritrea.
Nature 393: 458–460.

Abbate, E., B. WoldeHaimanot, Y. Libsekal,
T. M. Tecle, and L. Rook. 2004. *A step
towards human origins: the Buia Homo
one-million-years ago in the Eritrean Danakil
Depression (East Africa). Revista Italiana di
Paleontologia e Stratigrafia* 110.

Achilli, A., U. A. Perego, H. Lancioni, A. Olivieri,
and F. Gandini. 2013. Reconciling migration
models to the Americas with the variation of
North American native mitogenomes. *Proceedings of the National Academy of Sciences
USA* 110: 14308–14313.

Adger, N. 2007. *Climate Change 2007: Climate
Change Impacts, Adaptation and Vulnera-
bility*. Washington, DC: Intergovernmental
Panel on Climate Change.

Aerts, P. 1998. Vertical jumping in *Galago
senegalensis*: the quest for an obligate
mechanical power amplifier. *Philosophical
Transactions of the Royal Society of London B*
353: 1607–1620.

Agarwal, S. C. and S. D. Stout, eds. 2003. *Bone
Loss and Osteoporosis: An Anthropological
Perspective*. New York: Kluwer Academic/
Plenum Press.

Aiello, L. C. 2010. Five years of *Homo floresiensis. American Journal of Physical Anthropology* 142: 167–179.

Ainsworth, C. and D. MacKenzie. 2001. Coming
home. *New Scientist* 171(2298): 28–33.

Alba, D. M. 2012. Fossil apes from the
Valles-Penedes basin. *Evolutionary Anthropology* 21: 254–269.

Alberts, S. C., J. Altmann, D. K. Brockman, M.
Cords, L. M. Fedigan, A. Pusey, T. S. Stoinski,
K. B. Strier, W. F. Morris, and A. M. Broni-
kowski. 2013. Reproductive aging patterns
in primates reveal that humans are distinct.
*Proceedings of the National Academy of Sci-
ences USA* 110: 13440–13445.

Alemseged, Z., F. Spoor, W. H. Kimbel, R. Bobe,
D. Geraads, D. Reed, and J. G. Wynn. 2006. A
juvenile early hominin skeleton from Dikika,
Ethiopia. *Nature* 443: 296–301.

Allison, A. C. 2004. Two lessons from the interface of genetics and medicine. *Genetics* 166:
1591–1599.

Alvarez, W. 1997. T. rex *and the Crater of Doom.*
Princeton, NJ: Princeton University Press.

Alvesalo, K. and P. M. A. Tigerstedt. 1974.
Heritabilities of human tooth dimensions.
Hereditas 77: 311–318.

Ambrose, S. H., L. J. Hlusko, D. Kyule, A. Deino,
and M. Williams. 2003. Lemudong'o: a new
6 Ma paleontological site near Narok, Kenya
Rift Valley. *Journal of Human Evolution* 44:
737–742.

Ambrose, S. H. and J. Krigbaum. 2003. *Bone
Chemistry and Bioarchaeology. Journal of
Anthropological Archaeology*, special issue,
22(3): 193–199.

Ankel-Simons, F. 2007. *Primate Anatomy: An
Introduction*. Amsterdam, Netherlands:
Elsevier.

Anonymous. 2012. Genomics beyond genes.
Science 338: 1528.

Antón, S. C. and C. C. Swisher III. 2004. Early
dispersals of *Homo* from Africa. *Annual
Review of Anthropology* 33: 271–296.

Arbib, M. A., K. Liebal, and S. Pika. 2008.
Primate vocalization, gesture, and the evolution of human language. *Current Anthropology* 49: 1053–1076.

Armelagos, G. J. and K. N. Harper. 2005. Genomics of the origins of agriculture, part one.
Evolutionary Anthropology 14: 68–77.

Aron, J. L. and J. A. Patz. 2001. *Ecosystem
Change and Public Health: A Global Perspec-
tive*. Baltimore: Johns Hopkins University
Press.

Arsuaga, J.-L. 1997. Sima de los Huesos. *Journal
of Human Evolution* 33: 105–421.

Arsuaga, J.-L. 2010. Terrestrial apes and phylogenetic trees. *Proceedings of the National
Academy of Sciences USA* 107(suppl. 2):
8910–8917.

Arsuaga J. L., J.-M. Carretero, C. Lorenzo, A.
Gomez-Olivencia, and A. Pablos. 2015.
Postcranial morphology of the middle Pleis-
tocene humans from Sima de los Huesos,
Spain. *Proceedings of the National Academy
of Sciences USA* 112: 11524–11529.

Arsuaga, J. L., I. Martínez, L. J. Arnold, A. Aran-
buru, A. Gracia-Téllez, W. D. Sharp, R. M.
Quam, C. Falguères, A. Pantoja-Pérez, J. Bischoff, et al. 2014. Neandertal roots: cranial
and chronological evidence from Sima de los
Huesos. *Science* 344: 1358–1364.

Arsuaga, J.-L., I. Martínez, C. Lorenzo, A.
Gracia, A. Muñoz, O. Alonso, and J. Gallego.
1999. The human cranial remains from Gran
Dolina lower Pleistocene site (Sierra de Atapuerca, Spain). *Journal of Human Evolution*
37: 431–457.

Ascenzi, A., I. Biddittu, P. F. Cassoli, A. G. Segre,
and E. Segre-Naldini. 1996. A calvarium of
late *Homo erectus* from Ceprano, Italy. *Journal of Human Evolution* 31: 409–423.

Asfaw, B., W. H. Gilbert, Y. Beyene, W. K. Hart,

P. R. Renne, G. WoldeGabriel, E. S. Vrba, and T. D. White. 2002. Remains of *Homo erectus* from Bouri, Middle Awash, Ethiopia. *Nature* 416: 317–320.

Asfaw, B., T. White, O. Lovejoy, B. Latimer, S. Simpson, and G. Suwa. 1999. *Australopithecus garhi:* a new species of early hominid from Ethiopia. *Science* 284: 629–635.

Atsalis, S. and S. W. Margulis. 2006. Sexual and hormonal cycles in geriatric *Gorilla gorilla gorilla. International Journal of Primatology* 27: 1663–1687.

Ayala, F. J. 2007. Darwin's greatest discovery: design without designer. *Proceedings of the National Academy of Sciences USA* 104: 8567–8573.

Backwell, L. R. and F. d'Errico. 2001. Evidence of termite foraging by Swartkrans early hominids. *Proceedings of the National Academy of Sciences USA* 98: 1358–1363.

Bajpai, S., R. F. Kay, B. A. Williams, D. P. Das, V. V. Kapur, and B. N. Tiwari. 2008. The oldest Asian record of Anthropoidea. *Proceedings of the National Academy of Sciences USA* 105: 11093–11098.

Baker, C. 2006. *The Evolution Dialogues.* Washington, DC: American Association for the Advancement of Science.

Balter, M. 2005. Are humans still evolving? *Science* 309: 234–237.

Balter, M. 2006. Radiocarbon dating's final frontier. *Science* 313: 1560–1563.

Balter, M. 2007. Seeking agriculture's ancient roots. *Science* 316: 1830–1835.

Balter, M. 2008. Going deeper into the Grotte Chauvet. *Science* 321: 904–905.

Balter, M. 2010. Candidate human ancestor from South Africa sparks praise and debate. *Science* 328: 154–155.

Balter M .2014. Ancient infant was ancestor of today's Native Americans. *Science* 343: 716–717.

Barker, D. J. P. 1996. The origins of coronary heart disease in early life. Pp. 155–162 in C. J. K. Henry and S. J. Ulijaszek, eds. *Long-Term Consequences of Early Environment: Growth, Development and the Lifespan Developmental Perspective.* Cambridge, UK: Cambridge University Press.

Barker, D. J. P. 1998. *In utero* programming of chronic disease. *Clinical Science* 95: 115–128.

Barker, D. J. P. 1998. *Mothers, Babies, and Health in Later Life.* Edinburgh and New York: Churchill Livingstone.

Barker, D. J. P. 2001. *Fetal Origins of Cardiovascular and Lung Disease.* Oxford, UK: Taylor & Francis.

Barker, D. J. P. 2004. The developmental origins of chronic adult disease. *Acta Paediatrica* 93(suppl. 446): 26–33.

Barker, D. J. P. and D. T. Lackland. 2003. Prenatal influences on stroke mortality in England and Wales. *Stroke* 34: 1598–1602.

Barnosky, A. D., P. L. Koch, R. S. Feranec, S. L. Wing, and A. B. Shabel. 2004. Assessing the causes of late Pleistocene extinctions on the continents. *Science* 306: 70–75.

Barsh, G. S. 2003. What controls variation in human skin color? *PLoS Biology* 1: 19–22.

Bartlett, T. Q. 2009. *The Gibbons of Khao Yai: Seasonal Variation in Behavior and Ecology.* Upper Saddle River, NJ: Pearson Prentice Hall.

Bar-Yosef, O. 2006. *Kebara Cave, Mt. Carmel, Israel.* Cambridge, MA: Harvard University Press.

Bar-Yosef, O. and A. Belfer-Cohen. 1989. The origins of sedentism and farming communities in the Levant. *Journal of World Prehistory* 3: 477–498.

Bar-Yosef, O. and B. Vandermeersch. 1993. Modern humans in the Levant. *Scientific American* 268(4): 94–100.

Barzun, J. 1965. *Race: A Study in Superstition.* New York: Harper & Row.

Bass, W. M. 1984. Time interval since death: a difficult decision. Pp. 136–147 in T. A. Rathbun and J. E. Buikstra, eds. *Human Identification: Case Studies in Forensic Anthropology.* Springfield, IL: Charles C. Thomas.

Bayon, G., B. Dennielou, J. Etoubleau, E. Ponzevera, S. Toucanne, and S. Bermell. 2012. Intensifying weathering and land use in Iron Age central Africa. *Science* 335: 1219–1222.

Beall, C. M. 2014. Adaptation to high altitude: phenotypes and genotypes. *Annual Review of Anthropology* 43: 251–272.

Beall, C., K. Song, R. C. Elston, and M. C. Goldstein. 2004. Higher offspring survival among Tibetan women with high oxygen saturation genotypes residing at 4,000 m. *Proceedings of the National Academy of Sciences USA* 101: 14300–14304.

Beall, C. and A. T. Steegmann Jr. 2000. Human adaptation to climate: temperature, ultraviolet radiation, and altitude. Pp. 163–224 in S. Stinson, B. Bogin, R. Huss-Ashmore, and D. O'Rourke, eds. *Human Biology: An Evolutionary and Biocultural Perspective.* New York: Wiley-Liss.

Beall, C. M. 2001. Adaptations to altitude: a current assessment. *Annual Review of Anthropology* 30: 423–456.

Beall, C. M. 2006. Andean, Tibetan, and Ethiopian patterns of adaptation to high-altitude hypoxia. *Integrative and Comparative Biology* 46: 18–24.

Beard, C. 2004. *The Hunt for the Dawn Monkey: Unearthing the Origins of Monkeys, Apes, and Humans.* Berkeley: University of California Press.

Beard, K. C. 2002. Basal anthropoids. Pp. 133–149 in W. C. Hartwig, ed. *The Primate Fossil Record.* Cambridge, UK: Cambridge University Press.

Beard, K. C., T. Qi, M. R. Dawson, B. Wang, and C. Li. 1994. A diverse new primate fauna from middle Eocene fissure-fillings in southeastern China. *Nature* 368: 604–609.

Beattie, O. and J. Geiger. 2000. *Frozen in Time: The Fate of the Franklin Expedition.* New York: Sterling Publishing.

Beck, T. J., C. B. Ruff, R. A. Shaffer, K. Betsinger, D. W. Trone, and S. K. Brodine. 2000. Stress fracture in military recruits: gender differences in muscle and bone susceptibility factors. *Bone* 27: 437–444.

Begun, D. R. 2002. European hominoids. Pp. 339–368 in W. C. Hartwig, ed. *The Primate Fossil Record.* Cambridge, UK: Cambridge University Press.

Begun, D. R. 2003. Planet of the apes. *Scientific American* 289(2): 74–83.Begun, D. R. 2010. Catarrhine cousins: the origin and evolution of monkeys and apes of the Old World. Pp. 295–313 in C. S. Larsen, ed. *A Companion to Biological Anthropology.* Chichester, UK: Wiley-Blackwell.

Begun, D. R. 2013. The Miocene hominoid radiations. Pp. 398–416 in D. R. Begun, ed. *A Companion to Paleoanthropology.* Chichester, UK: Wiley-Blackwell.

Begun, D.R., ed, 2013. *A Companion to Paleoanthropology.* Chichester, UK: Wiley-Blackwell.

Behrensmeyer, A. K. and A. P. Hill. 1980. *Fossils in the Making: Vertebrate Taphonomy and Paleoecology.* Chicago: University of Chicago Press.

Beleza, S., A. M. Santos, B. McEvoy, I. Alves, C. Martinho, E. Cameron, M. D. Shriver, E. J. Parra, and J. Rocha. 2012. The timing of pigmentation lightening in Europeans. *Molecular Biology and Evolution* 30: 24–35.

Bellisari, A. 2013. *The Obesity Epidemic in America.* Long Grove, IL: Waveland Press.

Bellwood, P. 2005. *First Farmers: The Origins of Agricultural Societies.* Malden, MA: Blackwell.

Benefit, B. R. and M. L. McCrossin. 1995. Miocene hominoids and hominid origins. *Annual Review of Anthropology* 24: 237–256.

Bennett, M. R., J. W. K. Harris, B. G. Richmond, B. R. Braun, E. Mbua, P. Kiura, D. Olago, M. Kibunjia, C. Omuombo, A. K. Behrensmeyer, D. Huddart, and S. Gonzalez. 2010. Early hominin foot morphology based on 1.5-million-year-old footprints from Ileret, Kenya. *Science* 323: 1197–1201.

Benn Torres, J., M. B. Doura, S. O. Y. Keita, and R. A. Kittles. 2012. Y chromosome lineages in men of West African descent. *PLoS One* 7: e29687.

Benton, M. J. 2003. *When Life Nearly Died: The Greatest Mass Extinction of All Time.* London: Thames & Hudson.

Benyshek, D. C., J. F. Martin, and C. S. Johnson. 2001. A reconsideration of the origins of the type 2 diabetes epidemic among Native Americans and the implications for intervention policy. *Medical Anthropology* 20: 25–64.

Berger, L. R. 2013. The mosaic nature of *Australopithecus sediba. Science* 340: 163–164.

Berger, L. R., D. J. de Ruiter, S. E. Churchhill, P.

Schmid, K. J. Carlson, P. H. G. M. Dirks, and J. M. Kibii. 2010. *Australopithecus sediba*: a new species of *Homo*-like australopith from South Africa. *Science* 328: 195–204.

Berger, L. R., J. Hawks, D. J. de Ruiter, S. E. Churchill, P. Schmid, et al. 2015. *Homo naledi*, a new species of the genus *Homo* from the Dinaledi chamber, South Africa. *eLife*. DOI: 10.7554/eLife.09560:1-35.

Berger, L. R. and W. S. McGraw. 2007. Further evidence for eagle predation of, and feeding damage on, the Taung child. *South African Journal of Science* 103: 495–498.

Berger, S. L., T. Kouzarides, R. Shiekhatter, and A. Shilatifard. 2009. An operational definition of epigenetics. *Genes and Development* 23: 781–783.

Berger, T. D. and E. Trinkaus. 1995. Patterns of trauma among the Neandertals. *Journal of Archaeological Science* 22: 841–852.

Bermejo, M., J. D. Rodriguez-Teijeiro, G. Illera, A. Barroso, C. Vila, and P. D. Walsh. 2006. Ebola outbreak killed 5000 gorillas. *Science* 314: 1564.

Bermúdez de Castro, J. M., M. Martinón-Torres, E. Carbonell, S. Sarmiento, A. Rosas, J. van der Made, and M. Lozano. 2004. The Atapuerca sites and their contribution to the knowledge of human evolution in Europe. *Evolutionary Anthropology* 13: 25–41.

Berna, F., P. Goldberg, L. K. Horwitz, J. Brink, S. Holt, M. Bamford, and M. Chazan. 2012. Microstratigraphic evidence of in situ fire in the Acheulean strata of Wonderwerk Cave, Northern Cape Province, South Africa. *Proceedings of the National Academy of Sciences USA* 109: 1215–1220.

Berra, T. M. 2008. Charles Darwin's paradigm shift. *The* Beagle: *Records of the Museums and Art Galleries of the Northern Territory* 24: 1–5.

Berra, T. M. 2009. *Charles Darwin: The Concise Story of an Extraordinary Man.* Baltimore: Johns Hopkins University Press.

Beyene, Y., S. Katoh, G. WoldeGabriel, W. K. Hart, K. Uto, M. Sudo, M. Kondo, M. Hyodo, P. R. Renne, G. Suwa, and B. Asfaw. 2013. The characteristics and chronology of the earliest Acheulean at Konso, Ethiopia. *Proceedings of the National Academy of Sciences USA* 110: 1584–1591.

Bhattacharjee, J. K., G. R. Janssen, and T. G. Gregg. 2006. Human genealogy: how wide and deep do our genetic connections go? *American Biology Teacher* 68: 69–71.

Billman, B. R., P. M. Lambert, and B. L. Leonard. 2000. Cannibalism, warfare, and drought in the Mesa Verde region during the twelfth century A.D. *American Antiquity* 65: 145–178.

Bininda-Emonds, O. R. P., M. Cardillo, K. E. Jones, R. D. E. MacPhee, R. M. D. Beck, R. Greyner, S. A. Price, R. A. Vos, J. L. Gittleman, and A. Purvis. 2007. The delayed rise of present-day mammals. *Nature* 446: 507–512.

Bischoff, J. L., R. W. Williams, R. U. J. Rosenbauer, A. Aramburu, J. L. Arsuaga, N. García, and G. Cuenca-Bescós. 2007. High-resolution U-series dates from the Sima de los Huesos hominids yields 600 kyrs: implications for the evolution of the early Neanderthal lineage. *Journal of Archaeological Science* 34: 763–770.

Bitty E. A., S. G. Bi, J.-C. K. Bene, P. K. Kouassi, and W. S. McGraw. 2015. Cocoa farming and primate extirpation inside Cote d/Ivoire's protected areas. *Tropical Conservation Science* 8: 95–113.

Blakey, M. L. 1999. Scientific racism and the biological concept of race. *Literature and Psychology* 45: 29–43.

Bloch, J. I. and D. M. Boyer. 2002. Grasping primate origins. *Science* 298: 1606–1610.

Bloch, J. I., M. T. Silcox, D. M. Boyer, and E. J. Sargis. 2007. New Paleocene skeletons and the relationship of plesiadapiforms to crown-clade primates. *Proceedings of the National Academy of Sciences USA* 104: 1159–1164.

Blumenbach, J. F. 1775. *De Generis Humani Varietate Nativa.* Göttingen, Germany: Rosenbuschii.

Blumenbach, J. F. 1790–1828. *Decades suae craniorum diversarum Gentium, illustratae.* Göttingen, Germany: I. C. Dietrich.

Boas, F. 1912. Changes in bodily form of descendants of immigrants. *American Anthropologist* 14: 530–563.

Bocherens, H. 2009. Neanderthal dietary habits: review of the isotopic evidence. Pp. 241–250 in J.-J. Hublin and M. P. Richards, eds. *The Evolution of Hominin Diets: Integrating Approaches to the Study of Palaeolithic Subsistence.* New York: Springer.

Boesch, C. and M. Tomasello. 1998. Chimpanzee and human cultures. *Current Anthropology* 39: 591–614.

Bogin, B. 1999. *Patterns of Human Growth*, 2nd ed. Cambridge, UK: Cambridge University Press.

Bogin, B., H. Azcorra, H. J. Wilson, A. Vazquez-Vazquez, M. L. Avila-Escalante, M. T. Castillo-Burgette, I. Varela-Silva, and F. Dickinson. 2014. Globalization and children's diets: the case of Maya of Mexico and Central America. *Anthropological Review* 77: 11–32.

Bogin, B. and B. H. Smith. 2000. Evolution of the human life cycle. Pp. 377–424 in S. Stinson, B. Bogin, R. Huss-Ashmore, and D. O'Rourke, eds. *Human Biology: An Evolutionary and Biocultural Perspective.* New York: Wiley-Liss.

Bogin, B. and B. H. Smith. 2012. Evolution of the human life cycle. Pp. 515–586 in S. Stinson, B. Bogin, and D. O'Rourke, eds. *Human Biology: An Evolutionary and Biocultural Perspective,* 2nd ed. Hoboken, NJ: Wiley-Blackwell.

Bogin, B., P. Smith, A. B. Orden, M. I. Varela Silva, and J. Louky. 2002. Rapid change in height and body proportions of Maya American children. *American Journal of Human Biology* 14: 753–761.

Bond, M., M. F. Tejedor, K. E. J. Campbell, L. Chornogubsky, N. Novo, and F. Goin. 2015. Eocene primates of South America and the African origins of New World monkeys. *Nature* 520: 538–541.

Bouchard, C. 2007. The biological predisposition to obesity: beyond the thrifty genotype scenario. *International Journal of Obesity* 31: 1337–1339.

Bouzouggar, A., N. Barton, M. Vanhaeren, F. d'Errico, S. Collcutt, T. Higham, E. Hodge, S. Parfitt, E. Rhodes, J.-L. Schwenninger, C. Stringer, E. Turner, S. Ward, A. Moutmir, and A. Stambouli. 2007. 82,000–year-old shell beads from North Africa and implications for the origins of modern human behavior. *Proceedings of the National Academy of Sciences USA* 104: 9964–9969.

Bowen, M. 2005. *Thin Ice: Unlocking the Secrets of Climate in the World's Highest Mountains.* New York: Henry Holt.

Bowler, P. J. 2003. *Evolution: The History of an Idea.* Berkeley: University of California Press.

Bowler, P. J. 2005. Variation from Darwin to the modern synthesis. Pp. 9–27 in B. Hallgrimson and B. K. Hall, eds. *Variation: A Central Concept in Biology.* Burlington, MA: Elsevier Academic Press.

Bowler, P. J. 2009. Darwin's originality. *Science* 323: 223–226.

Bown, T. M. and K. D. Rose. 1987. Patterns of dental evolution in early Eocene anaptomorphine primates (Omomyidae) from the Bighorn Basin, Wyoming. *Paleontological Society Memoirs* 23: 1–162.

Brace, C. L. 2002. The concept of race in physical anthropology. Pp. 239–253 in P. N. Peregrine, C. R. Ember, and M. Ember, eds. *Physical Anthropology: Original Readings in Method and Practice.* Upper Saddle River, NJ: Prentice Hall.

Brace, C. L. 2005. *"Race" Is a Four-Letter Word: The Genesis of a Concept.* New York: Oxford University Press.

Brace, C. L., S. L. Smith, and K. D. Hunt. 1991. What big teeth you had grandma! Human tooth size, past and present. Pp. 33–57 in M. A. Kelley and C. S. Larsen, eds. *Advances in Dental Anthropology.* New York: Wiley-Liss.

Bradley, R. S. 1999. *Paleoclimatology.* San Diego: Academic Press.

Brain, C. K. 1981. *The Hunters or the Hunted? An Introduction to African Cave Taphonomy.* Chicago: University of Chicago Press.

Brain, C. K. 1993. *Swartkrans: A Cave's Chronicle of Early Man. Transvaal Museum Monographs* 8.

Bräuer, G. 2008. The origin of modern anatomy: by speciation or intraspecific evolution? *Evolutionary Anthropology* 17: 22–37.

Bribiescas, R. G. 2006. *Men: Evolutionary and Life History.* Cambridge, MA: Harvard University Press.

Bridges, P. S. 1996. Skeletal biology and behavior in ancient humans. *Evolutionary Anthropology* 4: 112–120.

Briggs, A. W., J. M. Good, R. E. Green, J. Krause, T. Maricic, U. Stenzel, C. Lalueza-Fox, P. Rudan, D. Brajkovic′, Z. Kuc′an, I. Gušic′, R. Schmitz, V. B. Doronichev, L. V. Golovanova, M. de la Rasilla, J. Fortea, A. Rosas, and S. Pääbo. 2009. Targeted retrieval and analysis of five Neandertal mtDNA genomes. *Science* 325: 318–321.

Brooke J. L., and C. S. Larsen. 2014. The nurture of nature: genetics, epigenetics, and environment in human biohistory. *American Historical Review* 119: 1500–1513.

Brown, K. 2002. Tangled roots? Genetics meets genealogy. *Science* 295: 1634–1635.

Brown, K. A. 2001. Identifying the sex of human remains by ancient DNA analysis. *Ancient Biomolecules* 3: 215–226.

Brown, P. 1992. Recent human evolution in East Asia and Australasia. *Proceedings of the Royal Society of London B* 337: 235–242.

Brown, P., T. Sutikna, M. J. Morwood, R. P. Soejono, Jatmiko, E. Wayhu Saptomo, and Rokus Awe Due. 2004. A new small-bodied hominin from the late Pleistocene of Flores, Indonesia. *Nature* 431: 1055–1061.

Brown, R. A. and G. J. Armelagos. 2001. Apportionment of racial diversity: a review. *Evolutionary Anthropology* 10: 34–40.

Bruner, E. and G. Manzi. 2007. Landmark-based shape analysis of the archaic *Homo* calvarium from Ceprano (Italy). *American Journal of Physical Anthropology* 132: 355–366.

Brunet, M., F. Guy, D. Pilbeam, H. T. Mackaye, A. Likius, D. Ahounta, A. Beauvilain, C. Blondel, H. Bocherens, J. R. Boisserie, L. De Bonis, Y. Coppens, J. Dejax, C. Denys, P. Duringer, V. Eisenmann, G. Fanone, P. Fronty, D. Geraads, T. Lehmann, F. Lihoreau, A. Louchart, A. Mahamat, G. Merceron, G. Mouchelin, O. Otero, P. P. Campomanes, M. P. De Leon, J. C. Rage, M. Sapanet, M. Schuster, J. Sudre, P. Tassy, X. Valentin, P. Vignaud, L. Viriot, A. Zazzo, and C. Zollikofer. 2002. A new hominid from the upper Miocene of Chad, Central Africa. *Nature* 418: 145–151.

Brutsaert, T. D., E. Parra, M. Shriver, A. Gamboa, J.-A. Palacios, M. Rivera, I. Rodriguez, and F. Leon-Velarde. 2004. Effects of birthplace and individual genetic admixture on lung volume and exercise phenotypes of Peruvian Quechua. *American Journal of Physical Anthropology* 123: 390–398.

Bufford, J. D. and J. E. Gern. 2005. The hygiene hypothesis revisited. *Immunology and Allergy Clinics of North America* 25: 247–262.

Buikstra, J. E. 1988. *The Mound-Builders of Eastern North America: A Regional Perspective.* Amsterdam, Netherlands: Elfde Kroon-Voordracht.

Buikstra, J. E. 2010. Paleopathology: a contemporary perspective. Pp. 395–411 in C. S. Larsen, ed. *A Companion to Biological Anthropology.* Chichester, UK: Wiley-Blackwell.

Burger, J., M. Kirchner, B. Bramanti, W. Haak, and M. G. Thomas. 2007. Absence of the lactase-persistence-associated allele in early Neolithic Europeans. *Proceedings of the National Academy of Sciences USA* 104: 3736–3741.

Burke, A. 2004. *The Ecology of Neanderthals. International Journal of Osteoarchaeology,* special issue, 14(3–4): 155–342.

Bustamente, C. D. and B. M. Henn. 2010. Shadows of early migrations. *Nature* 468: 1044–1045.

Butynski, T. M., J. Kingdon, and J. Kalina, eds. 2013. *Primates of Africa.* Vol. 2: *The Mammals of Africa.* London: Bloomsbury.

Caballero, B. and B. M. Popkin. 2002. *The Nutrition Transition: Diet and Disease in the Developing World.* London: Academic Press.

Calcagno, J. M. and A. Fuentes. 2012. What makes us human? Answers from evolutionary anthropology. *Evolutionary Anthropology* 21: 182–194.

Calcagno, J. M. and K. R. Gibson. 1991. Selective compromise: evolutionary trends and mechanisms in hominid tooth size. Pp. 59–76 in M. A. Kelley and C. S. Larsen, eds. *Advances in Dental Anthropology.* New York: Wiley-Liss.

Caldecott, J. and L. Miles, eds. 2005. *World Atlas of Great Apes and Their Conservation.* Berkeley: University of California Press.

Callaway, E. 2011. The Black Death decoded. *Nature* 478: 444–446.

Callaway, E. 2015. Crowdsourcing digs up an early human species. *Nature* 525: 297–298.

Cameron, D. W. 2004. *Hominid Adaptations and Extinctions.* Sydney: University of New South Wales Press.

Campbell, C. J., A. Fuentes, K. C. MacKinnon, M. Panger, and S. K. Bearder, eds. 2006. *Primates in Perspective.* New York: Oxford University Press.

Campbell, M.C., and S. A. Tishkoff. 2010. The evolution of human genetic and phenotypic variation In Africa. Current Biology 20:R106-R173.

Cann, R. L., M. Stoneking, and A. Wilson. 1987. Mitochondrial DNA and human evolution. *Nature* 325: 31–36.

Candela, P. B. 1942. The introduction of blood-group B into Europe. *Human Biology* 14: 413–443.

Caramelli, D., C. Lalueza-Fox, C. Vernesi, A. Casoli, F. Mallegni, B. Chiarelli, I. Dupanloup, J. Bertranpetit, G. Barbujani, and G. Bertorelle. 2003. Evidence for a genetic discontinuity between Neandertals and 24,000–year-old anatomically modern Europeans. *Proceedings of the National Academy of Sciences USA* 100: 6593–6597.

Carbonell, E., J. M. Bermúdez de Castro, J. M. Parés, A. Pérez-González, G. Cuenca-Bescós, A. Ollé, M. Mosquera, R. Huguet, J. van der Made, A. Rosas, R. Sala, J. Vallverdú, N. García, D. E. Granger, M. Martinón-Torres, X. P. Rodríguez, G. M. Stock, J. M. Vergès, E. Allué, F. Burjachs, I. Cáceres, A. Canals, A. Benito, C. Diez, M. Lozano, A. Mateos, M. Navazom, J. Rodríguez, J. Rosell, and J. L. Arsuaga. 2008. The first hominin of Europe. *Nature* 452: 465–470.

Carey, N. 2012. *The Epigenetics Revolution: How Modern Biology Is Rewriting Our Understanding of Genetics, Disease, and Inheritance.* New York: Columbia University Press.

Carlson, D. S. and D. P. Van Gerven. 1977. Masticatory function and post-Pleistocene evolution in Nubia. *American Journal of Physical Anthropology* 46: 495–506.

Carlson, E. A. 2004. *Mendel's Legacy: The Origins of Classical Genetics.* Cold Spring Harbor, NY: Cold Spring Harbor Laboratory Press.

Carlson, K. J., D. Stout, T. Jashashvili, D. J. de Ruiter, P. Tafforeau, K. Carlson, and L. R. Berger. 2011. The endocast of MH1, *Australopithecus sediba. Science* 333: 1402–1407.

Carmody, R. N., G. S. Weintraub, and R. W. Wrangham. 2011. Energetic consequences of thermal and nonthermal food processing. *Proceedings of the National Academy of Sciences USA* 108: 19199–19203.

Carmody, R. N. and R. W. Wrangham. 2009. The energetic significance of cooking. *Journal of Human Evolution* 57: 379–391.

Carroll, M. W., D. A. Matthews, J. A. Hiscox, M. J. Elmore, G. Pollakis, A. Rambut, et al. 2015. Temporal and spatial analysis of the 2014-2015 Ebola virus outbreak in West Africa. *Nature* 524: 97–101.

Carroll, S. B. 2005. *Endless Forms Most Beautiful: The New Science of Evo Devo.* New York: Norton.

Carroll, S. B. 2006. *The Making of the Fittest: DNA and the Ultimate Forensic Record of Evolution.* New York: Norton.

Carroll, S. B. 2009. *Remarkable Creatures: Epic Adventures in the Search for the Origins of Species.* Boston: Houghton Mifflin Harcourt.

Cartmill, M. 1974. Rethinking primate origins. *Science* 184: 436–443.

Cartmill, M. 1975. *Primate Origins.* Minneapolis, MN: Burgess.

Cartmill, M. 1992. New views on primate origins. *Evolutionary Anthropology* 1: 105–111.

Cartmill, M. 1996. *A View to a Death in the Morning: Hunting and Nature through History.* Cambridge, MA: Harvard University Press.

Cartmill, M. 2002. Explaining primate origins. Pp. 42–52 in P. N. Peregrine, C. R. Ember, and M. Ember, eds. *Physical Anthropology: Original Readings in Method and Practice.* Upper Saddle River, NJ: Prentice Hall.

Cartmill, M. and F. H. Smith. 2009. *The Human Lineage.* Hoboken, NJ: Wiley.

Caspari, R. 2003. From types to populations: A century of race, physical anthropology, and the American Anthropological Association. *American Anthropologist* 105: 65–76.

Caspari, R. 2009. 1918: Three perspectives on race and human variation. *American Journal of Physical Anthropology* 139: 5–15.

Caspari, R. 2010. Deconstructing race: racial thinking, geographic variation, and implications for biological anthropology. Pp. 104–123 in C. S. Larsen, ed. *A Companion to Biological Anthropology*. Malden, MA: Wiley-Blackwell.

Caspi, A., K. Sugden, T. E. Moffitt, A. Taylor, I. W. Craig, H. Harrington, J. McClay, J. Mill, J. Martin, A. Braithwaite, and R. Poulton. 2003. Influence of life stress on depression: moderation by a polymorphism in the 5-HTT gene. *Science* 301: 386–389.

Cavalli-Sforza, L. L. and F. Cavalli-Sforza. 1995. *The Great Human Diasporas*. Cambridge, UK: Perseus.

Center for Disease Control. 2008. State-specific incidence of diabetes among adults—participating states, 1995–1997 and 2005–2007. *MMWR Weekly* 57(43): 1169–1173.

Cerling, T. E., J. M. Harris, S. H. Ambrose, M. G. Leakey, and N. Solounis. 1997. Dietary and environmental reconstruction with stable isotope analyses of herbivore tooth enamel from the Miocene locality at Fort Ternan, Kenya. *Journal of Human Evolution* 33: 635–650.

Cerling, T. E., J. Quade, Y. Wang, and J. R. Bowman. 1989. Carbon isotopes in soils and paleosols as ecologic and paleoecologic indicators. *Nature* 341: 138–139.

Chaimanee, Y., O. Chavasseau, K. C. Beard, A. A. Kyaw, A. N. Soe, C. Sein, V. Lazzari, L. Marivaux, B. Marandat, M. Swe, M. Rugbumrung, T. Lwin, X. Valentin, Zin-Maung-Maung-Thein, and J.-J. Jaeger. 2012. Late middle Eocene primate from Myanmar and the initial anthropoid colonization of Africa. *Proceedings of the National Academy of Sciences USA* (in press) 109:10293-10297.

Chaimanee, Y., D. Jolly, M. Benammi, P. Tafforeau, D. Duzer, I. Moussa, and J.-J. Jaeger. 2003. A middle Miocene hominoid from Thailand and orangutan origins. *Nature* 422: 61–65.

Chaimanee, Y., V. Suteethorn, P. Jintasakul, C. Vidthayanon, B. Marandat, and J.-J. Jaeger. 2004. A new orangutan relative from the late Miocene of Thailand. *Nature* 427: 439–441.

Chaimanee, Y., C. Yamee, P. Tian, K. Khaowiset, B. Marandat, P. Tafforeau, C. Nemoz, and J.-J. Jaeger. 2006. *Khoratpithecus piriyai*, a late Miocene hominoid of Thailand. *American Journal of Physical Anthropology* 131: 311–323.

Chalmers, J. and K. C. Ho. 1970. Geographical variations in senile osteoporosis: the association with physical activity. *Journal of Bone and Joint Surgery* 52B: 667–675.

Chaplin, G. 2004. Geographic distribution of environmental factors influencing human skin coloration. *American Journal of Physical Anthropology* 120: 292–302.

Chaplin, G. and N. G. Jablonski. 2009. Vitamin D and the evolution of human depigmentation. *American Journal of Physical Anthropology* 139: 451–461.

Chatters, J. C. 2001. *Ancient Encounters: Kennewick Man and the First Americans*. New York: Touchstone.

Chatters J. C., D. J. Kennett, Y. Asmerom, B. M. Kemp, V. Polyak, A. N. Blank, P. A. Beddows, E. Reinhardt, J. Arroyo-Cabrales, D. A. Bolnick, R. S. Malhi, B. J. Culleton, P. L. Erreguerena, D. Rissolo, S. Morell-Hart, and T. W. Stafford Jr. 2014. Late Pleistocene human skeleton and mtDNA link Paleoamericans and modern Native Americans. *Science* 344: 750–754.

Check, E. 2006. How Africa learned to love the cow. *Nature* 444: 994–996.

Cheney, D. L. and R. M. Seyfarth. 1990. *How Monkeys See the World: Inside the Mind of Another Species*. Chicago: University of Chicago Press.

Cheney, D. L. and R. M. Seyfarth. 2007. *Baboon Metaphysics: The Evolution of a Social Mind*. Chicago: University of Chicago Press.

Childe, V. G. 1925. *The Dawn of European Civilization*. London: Kegan Paul.

Churchill, S. E. 1998. Cold adaptation, heterochrony, and Neandertals. *Evolutionary Anthropology* 7: 46–61.

Churchill, S. E. 2001. Hand morphology, manipulation, and tool use in Neandertals and early modern humans of the Near East. *Proceedings of the National Academy of Sciences USA* 98: 2953–2955.

Churchill, S. E., T. W. Holiday, K. J. Carlson, T. Jashashvili, M. E. Macias, S. Mathews, T. L. Sparling, P. Schmid, D. J. de Ruiter, and L. R. Berger. 2013. The upper limb of *Australopithecus sediba*. *Science* 340. DOI: 10:1126/science.1233477-1-6.

Churchill, S. E. and F. H. Smith. 2000. Makers of the early Aurignacian of Europe. *Yearbook of Physical Anthropology* 43: 61–115.

Ciochon, R. L. and G. F. Gunnell. 2002. Chronology of primate discoveries in Myanmar: influences on the anthropoid origins debate. *Yearbook of Physical Anthropology* 45: 2–35.

Ciochon, R. L. and G. F. Gunnell. 2002. Eocene primates from Myanmar: historical perspective on the origin of Anthropoidea. *Evolutionary Anthropology* 11: 156–168.

Clark, J. D., Y. Beyene, G. WoldeGabriel, W. K. Hart, P. R. Renne, H. Gilbert, A. Defleur, G. Suwa, S. Katoh, K. R. Ludwig, J.-R. Boisserie, B. Asfaw, and T. D. White. 2003. Stratigraphic, chronological and behavioural contexts of Pleistocene *Homo sapiens* from Middle Awash, Ethiopia. *Nature* 423: 747–752.

Clark, J. D. and S. A. Brandt. 1984. *From Hunters to Farmers: The Causes and Consequences of Food Production in Africa*. Berkeley: University of California Press.

Clark, J. D., J. de Heinzelin, K. D. Schick, W. K. Hart, T. D. White, G. WoldeGabriel, R. C. Walter, G. Suwa, B. Asfaw, E. Vrba, and Y. H.-Selassie. 1994. African *Homo erectus*: old radiometric ages and young Oldowan assemblages in the Middle Awash valley, Ethiopia. *Science* 264: 1907–1910.

Clarke, R. J. and P. V. Tobias. 1995. Sterkfontein Member 2 foot bones of the oldest South African hominid. *Science* 269: 521–524.

Clarke T. K., M. K. Lipton, A. M. Fernandez-Pujals, J. Starr, G. Davies, et al. 2016. Common polygenic risk for autism spectrum disorder (ASD) is associated with cognitive ability in the general population. *Molecular Psychiatry* vol. 2 1359–4184/15:1–7.

Clutton-Brock, J. 1999. *A Natural History of Domesticated Mammals*. Cambridge, UK: Cambridge University Press.

Cohen, J. M. 1992. *The Four Voyages of Christopher Columbus*. New York: Penguin.

Cohen, M. N. 1977. *The Food Crisis in Prehistory*. New Haven, CT: Yale University Press.

Cohen, M. N. 1989. *Health and the Rise of Civilization*. New Haven, CT: Yale University Press.

Cohen, M. N. 2002. Were early agriculturalists less healthy than food-collectors? Pp. 180–191 in P. N. Peregrine, C. R. Ember, and M. Ember, eds. *Archaeology: Original Readings in Method and Practice*. Upper Saddle River, NJ: Prentice Hall.

Cohen, M. N. and G. J. Armelagos, eds. 1984. *Paleopathology at the Origins of Agriculture*. Orlando, FL: Academic Press. Reprinted 2013, University Press of Florida, Gainesville.

Cohen, M. N. and G. Crane-Kramer, eds. 2007. *Ancient Health: Skeletal Indicators of Economic and Political Intensification*. Gainesville: University Press of Florida.

Colbert, E. 2007. *Field Notes from a Catastrophe: A Frontline Report on Climate Change*. London: Bloomsbury.

Collins, D. N. 2003. *Nature Encyclopedia of the Human Genome*. London: Nature.

Collins, F. S., M. Morgan, and A. Patrinos. 2003. The human genome project: lessons from large scale biology. *Science* 300: 286–290.

Conroy, G. C. 1990. *Primate Evolution*. New York: Norton.

Conroy, G. C. and H. Pontzer. 2012. *Reconstructing Human Origins: A Modern Synthesis*, 3rd ed. New York: Norton.

Cook, D. C. 2006. The old physical anthropology and the New World: a look at the accomplishments of an antiquated paradigm. Pp. 27–71 in J. E. Buikstra and L. A. Beck, eds. *Bioarchaeology: The Contextual Analysis of Human Remains*. Burlington, MA: Academic Press.

Cook, L. M., R. L. H. Dennis, and G. S. Mani. 1999. Melanic morph frequency in the peppered moth in the Manchester area. *Proceedings of the Royal Society of London B* 266: 293–297.

Cook, L. M., G. S. Mani, and M. E. Varley. 1986. Postindustrial melanism in the peppered moth. *Science* 231: 611–613.

Coon, C. S., S. M. Garn, and J. B. Birdsell. 1950. *Races: A Study of the Problems of Race Formation in Man.* Springfield, IL: Charles C. Thomas.

Cooper, C., G. Campion, and L. J. Melton III. 1992. Hip fractures in the elderly: a world-wide projection. *Osteoporosis International* 2: 285–289.

Cordain, L., B. A. Watkins, G. L. Florant, M. Kelher, L. Rogers, and Y. Li. 2002. Fatty acid analysis of wild ruminant tissues: evolutionary implications for reducing diet-related chronic disease. *European Journal of Clinical Nutrition* 56: 1–11.

Costa, D. L. and R. H. Steckel. 1997. Long-term trends in health, welfare, and economic growth in the United States. Pp. 47–89 in R. H. Steckel and R. Floud, eds. *Health and Welfare during Industrialization.* Chicago: University of Chicago Press.

Covert, H. H. 2002. The earliest fossil primates and the evolution of prosimians: introduction. Pp. 13–20 in W. C. Hartwig, ed. *The Primate Fossil Record.* Cambridge, UK: Cambridge University Press.

Cowgill, L. W., E. Trinkaus, and M. A. Zeder. 2007. Shanidar 10: A middle Paleolithic immature distal lower limb from Shanidar Cave, Iraqi Kurdistan. *Journal of Human Evolution* 53: 213–223.

Crawford, M. H. 1998. *The Origins of Native Americans: Evidence from Anthropological Genetics.* Cambridge, UK: Cambridge University Press.

Crews, D. E. 2003. *Human Senescence: Evolutionary and Biocultural Perspectives.* Cambridge, UK: Cambridge University Press.

Crews, D. E. and B. Bogin. 2010. Growth, development, senescence, and aging: a life history perspective. Pp. 124–152 in C. S. Larsen, ed. *A Companion to Biological Anthropology.* Chichester, UK: Wiley-Blackwell.

Critser, G. 2003. *Fat Land.* New York: Penguin.

Culotta, E. 2016. Likely hobbit ancestors lived 600,000 years earlier. Science 352: 1260-1261.

Daegling, D. J. 2010. Understanding skull function from a mechanicobiological perspective. Pp. 501–515 in C. S. Larsen, ed. *A Companion to Biological Anthropology.* Chichester, UK: Wiley-Blackwell.

Dagasto, M. 2002. The origin and diversification of anthropoid primates: introduction. Pp. 125–132 in W. C. Hartwig, ed. *The Primate Fossil Record.* Cambridge, UK: Cambridge University Press.

Dahlberg, A. A. 1963. Analysis of the American Indian dentition. Pp. 147–177 in D. R. Brothwell, ed. *Dental Anthropology.* New York: Pergamon Press.

DARA International. 2012. Climate Vulnerability Monitor: A Guide to the Cold Calculus of a Hot Planet. Fundación DARA International 2012. Madrid, Spain.

Darwin, C. 1859. *On the Origin of Species.* London: John Murray.

Darwin, C. 1871. *The Descent of Man and Selection in Relation to Sex.* Akron, OH: Werner.

Davies, A. G. and J. F. Oates. 1994. *Colobine Monkeys: Their Ecology, Behaviour and Evolution.* Cambridge, UK: Cambridge University Press.

Dawkins, R. 2004. *The Ancestor's Tale: A Pilgrimage to the Dawn of Civilization.* Boston: Houghton Mifflin.

Deacon, T. W. 1997. What makes the human brain different? *Annual Review of Anthropology* 26: 337–357.

Dean, C., M. G. Leakey, D. Reid, F. Schrenk, G. T. Schwartz, C. Stringer, and A. Walker. 2001. Growth processes in teeth distinguish modern humans from *Homo erectus* and earlier hominins. *Nature* 414: 628–631.

Dear, P. 2006. *The Intelligibility of Nature: How Science Makes Sense of the World.* Chicago: University of Chicago Press.

De Bonis, L., G. D. Koufos, and P. Andrews. 2001. *Hominoid Evolution and Climatic Change in Europe: Volume 2, Phylogeny of the Neogene Hominoid Primates of Eurasia.* Cambridge, UK: Cambridge University Press.

Defleur, A., T. White, P. Valensi, L. Slimak, and É. Crégut-Bonnoure. 1999. Neanderthal cannibalism at Moula-Guercy, Ardèche, France. *Science* 286: 128–131.

De Heinzelin, J., J. D. Clark, K. D. Schick, and W. H. Gilbert. 2000. *The Acheulian and the Plio-Pleistocene Deposits of the Middle Awash Valley, Ethiopia. Musée Royal de L'Afrique Centrale, Annales Sciences Geologiques* 104.

De Heinzelin, J., J. D. Clark, T. White, W. Hart, P. Renne, G. WoldeGabriel, Y. Beyene, and E. Vrba. 1999. Environment and behavior of 2.5 million-year-old Bouri hominids. *Science* 284: 625–629.

Deino, A., P. R. Renne, and C. C. Swisher III. 1998. ^{40}Ar/^{39}Ar dating in paleoanthropology and archeology. *Evolutionary Anthropology* 6: 63–75.

Delson, E. 1992. Evolution of Old World monkeys. Pp. 217–222 in J. S. Jones, R. D. Martin, D. Pilbeam, and S. Bunney, eds. *Cambridge Encyclopedia of Human Evolution.* Cambridge, UK: Cambridge University Press.

Delson, E., I. Tattersall, J. A. Van Couvering, and A. S. Brooks. 2000. *Encyclopedia of Human Evolution and Prehistory,* 2nd ed. New York: Garland.

Demeter, F., L. L. Shackelford, A.-M. Bacon, P. Duringer, K. Westaway, T. Sayavongkhamdy, J. Braga, P. Sichanthongtip, P. Khamdalavong, J.-L. Ponche, H. Wang, C. Lundstrom, E. Patole-Edoumba, and A.-M. Karpoff. 2012. Anatomically modern human in southeast Asia (Laos) by 46 ka. *Proceedings of the National Academy of Sciences USA* 109: 14375–14380.

Demment, M. W., M. M. Young, and R. L. Sensenig. 2003. Providing micronutrients through food-based solutions: a key to human and national development. *Journal of Nutrition* 133: 3879S–3885S.

Denham, T. P., S. G. Haberle, C. Lentfer, R. Fullagar, J. Field, M. Therin, N. Porch, and B. Winsborough. 2003. Origins of agriculture at Kuk Swamp in the highlands of New Guinea. *Science* 301: 189–193.

D'Errico, F., C. Henshilwood, G. Lawson, M. Vanhaeren, A.-M. Tillier, M. Soressi, F. Bresson, B. Maureille, A. Nowell, J. Lakarra, L. Backwell, and M. Julien. 2003. Archaeological evidence for the emergence of language, symbolism, and music—an alternative multidisciplinary perspective. *Journal of World Prehistory* 17: 1–70.

Derry, G. 2002. *What Science Is and How It Works.* Princeton, NJ: Princeton University Press.

DeVore, I. 1963. A comparison of the ecology and behavior of monkeys and apes. Pp. 301–339 in S. L. Washburn, ed. *Classification and Human Evolution.* Chicago: Aldine.

DeVore, I. 1965. *Primate Behavior: Field Studies of Monkeys and Apes.* New York: Holt, Rinehart and Winston.

Diamond, J. 2004. The astonishing micropygmies. *Science* 306: 2047–2048.

Diamond, J. 2005. Geography and skin color. *Nature* 435: 283–284.

Diamond, J. and P. Bellwood. 2003. Farmers and their languages: the first expansions. *Science* 300: 597–603.

Disotell, T. R. 2012. Archaic human genomics. *Yearbook of Physical Anthropology* 55: 24–39.

Dixon, R. A. and C. A. Roberts. 2001. Modern and ancient scourges: the application of ancient DNA to the analysis of tuberculosis and leprosy from archaeologically derived human remains. *Ancient Biomolecules* 3: 181–194.

Dominguez-Rodrigo, M. and T. R. Pickering. 2003. Early hominid hunting and scavenging: a zooarchaeological review. *Evolutionary Anthropology* 12: 275–282.

Dorit, R. L. 2012. Rereading Darwin. *American Scientist* 100: 21–23.

Drapeau, M. S. M. and C. V. Ward. 2007. Forelimb segment length: proportions in extant hominoids and *Australopithecus afarensis. American Journal of Physical Anthropology* 132: 327–343.

Drapeau, M. S. M. and M. A. Steeter. 2006. Modeling and remodeling responses to normal loading in the human lower limb. *American Journal of Physical Anthropology* 129: 403–409.

Dressler, W. W., K. S. Oths, and C. C. Gravlee. 2005. Race and ethnicity in public health research: models to explain health disparities. *Annual Review of Anthropology* 34: 231–252.

Dronamraju, K. R. and P. Arese. 2006. *Malaria: Genetic and Evolutionary Aspects.* New York: Springer.

Ducrocq, S. 1998. Eocene primates from Thailand: are Asian anthropoideans related to African ones? *Evolutionary Anthropology* 7: 97–104.

Dufour, D. 2010. Nutrition, health, and function. Pp. 194–206 in C. S. Larsen, ed. *A Companion to Biological Anthropology.* Chichester, UK: Wiley-Blackwell.

Dunavan, C. P. 2005. Tackling malaria. *Scientific American* 293(6): 76–83.

Dunbar, R. 1977. Feeding ecology of gelada baboons: a preliminary report. Pp. 252–273 in T. H. Clutton-Brock, ed. *Primate Ecology: Studies of Feeding and Ranging Behaviour in Lemurs, Monkeys and Apes.* London: Academic Press.

Dunsworth, H. and A. Walker. 2002. Early genus *Homo.* Pp. 419–435 in W. C. Hartwig, ed. *The Primate Fossil Record.* Cambridge, UK: Cambridge University Press.

Duren, D. L., R. J. Sherwood, A. C. Choh, S. A. Czerwinski, W. C. Chumlea, M. Lee, S. S. Sun, E. W. Demerath, R. M. Siervogel, and B. Towne. 2007. Quantitative genetics of cortical bone mass in healthy 10–year-old children from the Fels Longitudinal Study. *Bone* 40: 464–470.

Eaton, S. B., S. B. Eaton III, and L. Cordain. 2002. Evolution, diet, and health. Pp. 7–17 in P. S. Ungar and M. F. Teaford, eds. *Human Diet: Its Origin and Evolution.* Westport, CT: Bergin & Garvey.

Eckhardt, R. B. 2003. Polymorphisms: past and present. *Human Biology* 75: 559–575.

Edgar, H. J. H. and K. L. Hunley, eds. 2009. Race reconciled. *American Journal of Physical Anthropology* (Special Symposium Issue) 139: 1–102.

Edgar H. J. H. and K. L. Hunley. 2009. Race reconciled?: How biological anthropologists view human variation. *American Journal of Physical Anthropology* 139: 1–4.

Eimerl, S. and I. DeVore. 1965. *The Primates.* New York: Time-Life.

Ellis, E. C., J. O. Kaplan, D. Q. Fuller, S. Vavrus, K. K. Goldewijk, and P. H. Verburg. 2013. Used planet: a global history. *Proceedings of the National Academy of Sciences USA* 110: 7978–7985.

Ellison, P. 2001. *On Fertile Ground: A Natural History of Human Reproduction.* Cambridge, MA: Harvard University Press.

Ellison, P. T. 1994. Advances in human reproductive ecology. *Annual Review of Anthropology* 23: 255–275.

Ellison, P. T. and M. T. O'Rourke. 2000. Population growth and fertility regulation. Pp. 553–586 in S. Stinson, B. Bogin, R. Huss-Ashmore, and D. O'Rourke, eds. *Human Biology: An Evolutionary and Biocultural Perspective.* New York: Wiley-Liss.

Elton, S. 2006. Forty years on and still going strong: the use of hominin-cercopithecid comparisons in palaeoanthropology. *Journal of the Royal Anthropological Institute* 12: 19–38.

El Zaatari, S., F. E. Grine, P. S. Ungar, and J.-J. Hublin. 2011. Ecogeographic variation in Neandertal dietary habits: evidence from occlusal molar microwear texture analysis. *Journal of Human Evolution* 61: 411–424.

ENCODE Project Consortium. 2012. An integrated encyclopedia of DNA elements in the human genome. *Nature* 489: 57–74.

Epstein, P. R. and D. Ferber. 2011. *Changing Planet, Changing Health: How the Climate Crisis Threatens Our Health and What We Can Do about It.* Berkeley: University of California Press.

Ericson, P. A. 1997. Morton, Samuel George (1799–1851). Pp. 689–691 in F. Spencer, ed. *History of Physical Anthropology: An Encyclopedia.* New York: Garland.

Erikson, D. L., B. D. Smith, A. C. Clarke, D. H. Sandweiss, and N. Tuross. 2005. An Asian origin for a 10,000-year-old domesticated plant in the Americas. *Proceedings of the National Academy of Sciences USA* 102: 18315–18320.

Eriksson, J. G., T. Forsen, J. Tuomilehto, C. Osmond, and D. J. P. Barker. 2000. Early growth, adult income, and risk of stroke. *Stroke* 31: 869–874.

Eshleman, J. A., R. S. Malhi, and D. G. Smith. 2003. Mitochondrial DNA studies of Native Americans: conceptions and misconceptions of the population history of the Americas. *Evolutionary Anthropology* 12: 7–18.

Estrada-Mena, B., F. J. Estrada, R. Ulloa-Arvizu, M. Guido, R. Méndez, R. Coral, T. Canto, J. Granados, R. Rubí-Castellanos, H. Rangel-Villalobos, and A. Garcia-Carrancá. 2010. Blood group O alleles in Native Americans: implications in the peopling of the Americas. *American Journal of Physical Anthropology* 142: 85–94.

Eveleth, P. B. and J. M. Tanner. 1990. *Worldwide Variation in Human Growth,* 2nd ed. Cambridge, UK: Cambridge University Press.

Fagan, B. M. 2004. *The Great Journey: The Peopling of Ancient North America.* Gainesville: University Press of Florida.

Falk, D. 2000. *Primate Diversity.* New York: Norton.

Falk, D. 2010. Evolution of the brain, cognition, and speech. Pp. 258–271 in C. S. Larsen, ed. *A Companion to Biological Anthropology.* Chichester, UK: Wiley-Blackwell.

Falk, D., C. Hildebolt, K. Smith, M. J. Morwood, T. Sutikna, P. Brown, Jatmiko, E. W. Saptomo, B. Brunsden, and F. Prior. 2005. The brain of LB1, *Homo floresiensis. Science* 308: 242–245.

Feathers, J. K. 1996. Luminescence dating and modern human origins. *Evolutionary Anthropology* 5: 25–36.

Field, J. S., M. D. Petraglia, and M. M. Lahr. 2006. The southern dispersal hypothesis and the South Asian archaeological record: examination of dispersal routes through GIS analysis. *Journal of Anthropological Archaeology* 26: 88–108.

Feldman, M. W., R. C. Lewontin, and M.-C. King. 2003. Race: a genetic melting-pot. *Nature* 424: 374.

Fiala, N. 2008. Meeting the demand: an estimation of potential future greenhouse gas emissions from meat production. *Ecological Economics* 67: 412–419.

Finlayson, C. 2004. *Neanderthals and Modern Humans: An Ecological and Evolutionary Perspective.* New York: Cambridge University Press.

Fiorato, V., A. Boylston, and C. Knusel. 2000. *Blood Red Roses: The Archaeology of a Mass Grave from the Battle of Towton A. D. 1461.* Oxford, UK: Oxbow.

Fiorenza, L., S. Benazzi, J. Tausch, O. Kullmer, T. G. Bromage, and F. Schrenk. 2011. Molar macrowear reveals Neanderthal eco-geographic dietary variation. *PLoS One* 6: 1–11.

Fischman, J. 2005. Dmanisi find. *National Geographic Research* 207: 18–27.

Fiske, S. J., S. A. Crate, C. L. Crumley, K. Galvin, H. Lazrus, et al. 2014. *Changing the Atmosphere: Anthropology and Climate Change.* Final report on the AAA Global Climate Task Force, 117 pp. Arlington, VA: American Anthropological Association.

Flannery, K. V. 1969. Origins and ecological effects of early domestication in Iran and the Near East. Pp. 73–100 in P. J. Ucko and G. W. Dimbleby, eds. *The Domestication of Plants and Animals.* Chicago: Aldine.

Fleagle, J. G. 1999. *Primate Adaptation and Evolution,* 2nd ed. San Diego: Academic Press.

Fleagle, J. G. 2000. A century of the past: one hundred years in the study of primate evolution. *Evolutionary Anthropology* 9: 87–100.

Fleagle, J. G. 2013. *Primate Adaptation and Evolution,* 3rd ed. San Diego, CA: Academic Press.

Fleagle, J. G. and R. F. Kay, eds. 1994. *Anthropoid Origins.* New York: Plenum Press.

Fleagle, J. G. and M. F. Tejedor. 2002. Early platyrrhines of southern South America. Pp. 161–173 in W. C. Hartwig, ed. *The Primate Fossil Record.* Cambridge, UK: Cambridge University Press.

Formenty, P., C. Boesch, M. Wyers, C. Steiner, F. Donati, F. Dind, F. Walker, and B. Le Guenno. 1999. Ebola virus outbreak among wild chimpanzees living in a rain forest of Cote d'Ivoire. *Journal of Infectious Diseases* 179: S120–126.

Foster, E. A., M. A. Jobling, P. G. Taylor, P. Donnelly, R. de Knijff, R. Mieremet, T. Zerjal, and C. Tyler-Smith. 1998. Jefferson fathered slave's last child. *Nature* 396: 27–28.

Fragaszy, D., P. Izar, E. Visalberghi, E. B. Ottoni, and M. G. De Oliveira. 2004. Wild capuchin monkeys (*Cebus libidinosus*) use anvils and stone pounding tools. *American Journal of Primatology* 64: 359–366.

Frayer, D. W., M. Lozano, J. M. Bermúdez de Castro, E. Carbonell, J.-L. Arsuaga, J. Radovčić, I. Fiore, and L. Bondioli. 2012. More than 500,000 years of right-handedness in Europeans. *Laterality* 17: 51–69.

Freed, S. A. 2012. *Anthropology Unmasked: Museum, Science, and Politics in New York City.* Vol. 1: *The Putnam-Boas Era.* Wilmington, OH: Orange Frazer Press.

Freeman, A. S. and J. E. Byers. 2006. Divergent induced responses to an invasive predator in marine mussel populations. *Science* 313: 831–833.

Freeman, H. and R. D. Cox. 2006. Type-2 diabetes: a cocktail of genetic discovery. *Human Molecular Genetics* 15: R202–R209.

Frisancho, A. R. 1975. Functional adaptation to high-altitude hypoxia. *Science* 187: 313–319.

Frisancho, A. R. 1993. *Human Adaptation and Accommodation.* Ann Arbor: University of Michigan Press.

Fuentes, A. 1999. Re-evaluating primate monogamy. *American Anthropologist* 100: 890–907.

Fuller, D. Q., T. Denham, M. Arroyo-Kalin, L. Lucas, C. J. Stevens, et al. 2014. Convergent evolution and parallelism in plant domestication revealed by an expanding archaeological record. *Proceedings of the National Academy of Sciences USA* 111: 6147–6152.

Fuller, D. Q., L. Qin, Y. Zheng, Z. Zhao, X. Chen, L. A. Hosoya, and G.-P. Sun. 2009. The domestication process and domestication rate in rice: spikelet bases from the Lower Yangtze. *Science* 323: 1607–1610.

Futuyma, D. J. 2005. *Evolution.* Sunderland, MA: Sinauer Press.

Gage, T. B. 1998. The comparative demography of primates: with some comments on the evolution of life histories. *Annual Review of Anthropology* 27: 197–221.

Gage, T. B. 2010. Demographic estimation: indirect techniques for anthropological populations. Pp. 179–193 in C. S. Larsen, ed. *A Companion to Biological Anthropology.* Chichester, UK: Wiley-Blackwell.

Galik, K., B. Senut, M. Pickford, D. Gommery, J. Treil, A. J. Kuperavage, and R. B. Eckhardt. 2004. External and internal morphology of the BAR 1002'00 *Orrorin tugenensis* femur. *Science* 305: 1450–1453.

Garcia, R. S. 2003. The misuse of race in medical diagnosis. *The Chronical of Higher Education* May 9: B15.

Garrett, L. 1994. *The Coming Plague: Newly Emerging Diseases in a World Out of Balance.* New York: Farrar, Straus, and Giroux.

Garruto, R. M., C.-T. Chin, C. A. Weitz, J.-C. Liu, R.-L. Liu, and X. He. 2003. Hematological differences during growth among Tibetans and Han Chinese born and raised at high altitude in Qinghai, China. *American Journal of Physical Anthropology* 122: 171–183.

Gasperetti, M. A., and S. G. Sheridan. 2013. Cry havoc: interpersonal violence at Early Bronze Age Bab edh-Dhra'. *American Anthroplogist* 115: 388–410.

Gasperetti, M. A., and S. G. Sheridan. 2013. *Postcranial Adaptation in Nonhuman Primates.* DeKalb: Northern Illinois University Press.

Gebo, D. L., ed. 1993. *Postcranial Adaptation in Nonhuman Primates.* DeKalb: Northern Illinois University Press.

Gebo, D. L. 2002. Adapiformes: phylogeny and adaptation. Pp. 21–43 in W. C. Hartwig, ed. *The Primate Fossil Record.* Cambridge, UK: Cambridge University Press.

Gebo, D. L. 2010. Locomotor function across primates: the postcranial skeleton. Pp. 530–544 in C. S. Larsen, ed. *A Companion to Biological Anthropology.* Chichester, UK: Wiley-Blackwell.

Gebo, D. L., M. Dagosto, K. C. Beard, and T. Qi. 2000. The smallest primates. *Journal of Human Evolution* 38: 585–594.

Gebo, D. L., M. Dagasto, K. C. Beard, T. Qi, and J. Wang. 2000. The oldest known anthropoid postcranial fossils and the early evolution of higher primates. *Nature* 404: 276–278.

Gebo, D. L., M. Dagosto, X. Ni, and K. C. Beard. 2012. Species diversity and postcranial anatomy of Eocene primates from Shanghuang, China. *Evolutionary Anthropology* 21: 224–238.

Gebo, D. L., L. MacLatchy, R. Kityo, A. Deino, J. Kingston, and D. Pilbeam. 1997. A hominoid genus from the early Miocene of Uganda. *Science* 276: 401–404.

Gibbard, P. L., M. J. Head, M. J. C. Walker, and Subcommission on Quaternary Stratigraphy. 2010. Formal ratification of the Quaternary system/period and the Pleistocene series/epoch with a base at 2.58 ma. *Journal of Quaternary Science* vol. 25 (in press), pp. 96-102.

Gibbons, A. 2006. *The First Human: The Race to Discover Our Earliest Ancestors.* New York: Doubleday.

Gibbons, A. 2007. Food for thought: did the first cooked meals help fuel the dramatic evolutionary expansion of the human brain? *Science* 316: 1558–1560.

Gibbons, A. 2007. European skin turned pale only recently, gene suggests. *Science* 316: 364.

Gibbons, A. 2008. The birth of childhood. *Science* 322: 1040-1043.

Gibbons, A. 2009. A new kind of ancestor: *Ardipithecus* unveiled. *Science* 326: 36–43.

Gibbons, A. 2010. Close encounters of a prehistoric kind. *Science* 328: 680–684.

Gibbons, A. 2011. A new view of the birth of *Homo sapiens. Science* 331: 392–394.

Gibbons, A. 2012. Turning back the clock: slowing the pace of prehistory. *Science* 338: 189–191.

Gibson, R. 1990. *Principles of Human Nutrition.* Oxford, UK: Oxford University Press.

Gilbert, C. C., W. S. McGraw, and E. Delson. 2009. Plio-Pleistocene eagle predation on fossil cercopithecids from the Humpata Plateau, southern Angola. *American Journal of Physical Anthropology* 139: 421–429.

Gilbert, W. H. and B. Asfaw. 2008. Homo erectus: *Pleistocene Evidence from the Middle Awash, Ethiopia.* Berkeley: University of California Press.

Gilby, I. C., L. E. Eberly, L. Pintea, and A. E. Pusey. 2006. Ecological and social influences on the hunting behaviour of wild chimpanzees, *Pan troglodytes schweinfurthii. Animal Behaviour* 72(1): 169–180.

Gillespie, J. H. 2004. *Population Genetics: A Concise Guide,* 2nd ed. Baltimore: Johns Hopkins University Press.

Gingerich, P. D. 1976. *Cranial Anatomy and Evolution of Early Tertiary Plesiadapidae (Mammalia, Primates). University of Michigan Museum of Paleontology, Papers on Paleontology* 15.

Gingerich, P. D. 1976. Paleontology and phylogeny: patterns of evolution at the species level in early tertiary mammals. *American Journal of Science* 276: 1–28.

Gingerich, P. D. 1980. *Early Cenozoic Paleontology and Stratigraphy of the Bighorn Basin, Wyoming. University of Michigan Museum of Paleontology, Papers on Paleontology* 24.

Gingerich, P. D. 1990. Mammalian order Proprimates. *Journal of Human Evolution* 19: 821–822.

Gingerich, P. D. and G. F. Gunnell. 2005. Brain of *Plesiadapis cookei* (Mammalia, Proprimates): surface morphology and encephalization compared to those of Primates and Dermoptera. *Contributions of the Museum of Paleontology, University of Michigan* 31: 185–195.

Gingerich, P. D. 2011. Primates in the Eocene. Pp. 67–68 in T. Lehmann, and S. F. K. Schaal, eds. *The World of Time of Messell: Puzzles in Palaeobiology, Palaeoenvironment, and the History of Early Primates.* Frankfurt am Main, Germany: Senckenberg Gesellschaft fur Naturforschung.

Glass, B., M. S. Sacks, E. Jahn, and C. Hess. 1952. Genetic drift in a religious isolate: an analysis of the causes of variation in blood group and other gene frequencies in a small population. *American Naturalist* 86: 145–159.

Gluckman, P. D., M. A. Hanson, and A. S. Beedle. 2007. Early life events and their consequences for later disease: a life history and evolutionary perspective. *American Journal of Human Biology* 19: 1–19.

Godfrey, K. 2006. The developmental origins hypothesis: epidemiology. Pp. 6–32 in P. D. Gluckman and M. A. Hanson, eds. *Developmental Origins of Health and Disease.* Cambridge, UK: Cambridge University Press.

Godfrey, L. R. and W. L. Jungers. 2002. Quaternary fossil lemurs. Pp. 97–121 in W. C. Hartwig, ed. *The Primate Fossil Record.* Cambridge, UK: Cambridge University Press.

Goebel, T., M. R. Waters, and D. H. O'Rourke. 2008. The late Pleistocene dispersal of modern humans in the Americas. *Science* 319: 1497-1502.

Goldberg, K. E. 1982. *The Skeleton: Fantastic Framework.* Washington, DC: U.S. News.

Golden, B. E. 2009. Diseases of nutrient deficiencies. Pp. 141–162 in W. G. Pond, B. L. Nichols, and D. L. Brown, eds. *Adequate Food for All: Culture, Science, and Technology of Food in the 21st Century.* Boca Raton, FL: CRC Press.

Goodall, J. 1986. *The Chimpanzees of Gombe: Patterns of Behavior.* Cambridge, MA: Harvard University Press.

Goodman, A. H. 1994. Cartesian reductionism and vulgar adaptationism: issues in the interpretation of nutritional status in prehistory. Pp. 163–177 in K. D. Sobolik, ed. *Paleonutrition: The Diet and Health of Prehistoric Americans. Southern Illinois University at Carbondale, Center for Archaeological Investigations, Occasional Paper* 22.

Goodman, A. H. 2005. Three questions about race, human biological variation and racism. *Anthropology News* 46(6): 18–19.

Goodman, A. H., Y. T. Moses, and J. L. Jones. 2012. *Race: Are We So Different?* New York: Wiley-Blackwell.

Goodman, A. H. and T. L. Leatherman. 1998. *Building a New Biocultural Synthesis: Political-Economic Perspectives on Human Biology.* Ann Arbor: University of Michigan Press.

Goodman, M., C. A. Porter, J. Czelusniak, S. L. Page, H. Schneider, J. Shoshani, G. Gunnell, and C. P. Groves. 1998. Toward a phylogenetic classification of primates based on DNA evidence complemented by fossil evidence. *Molecular Phylogenetics and Evolution* 9: 585–598.

Gore, A. 2006. *An Inconvenient Truth: The Planetary Emergency of Global Warming and What We Can Do about It.* New York: Rodale Press.

Goren-Inbar, N., N. Alperson, M. E. Kislev, O. Simchoni, Y. Melamed, A. Ben-Nun, and E. Werker. 2004. Evidence of hominin control of fire at Gesher Benot Ya'aqov, Israel. *Science* 304: 725–727.

Gosman, J. H. and S. D. Stout. 2010. Current concepts in bone biology. Pp. 465–484 in C. S. Larsen, ed. *A Companion to Biological Anthropology.* Chichester, UK: Wiley-Blackwell.

Gould, S. J. 1982. Darwinism and the expansion of evolutionary theory. *Science* 216: 380–387.

Gould, S. J. 1989. *Wonderful Life: The Burgess Shale and the Nature of History.* New York: Norton.

Gould, S. J. 1992. *Ever since Darwin: Reflections on Natural History.* New York: Norton.

Gould, S. J. 1996. *The Mismeasure of Man.* New York: Norton.

Grant, P. R. and B. R. Grant. 2002. Adaptive radiation of Darwin's finches. *American Scientist* 90: 130–139.

Graves, J. L. Jr. 2004. *The Race Myth.* New York: Dutton.

Gravlee, C. C., H. R. Bernard, and W. R. Leonard. 2003. Heredity, environment, and cranial form: a reanalysis of Boas's immigrant data. *American Anthropologist* 105: 125–138.

Grayson, D. K. 2001. The archaeological record of human impacts on animal populations. *Journal of World Prehistory* 15: 1–68.

Grayson, D. K. and D. J. Meltzer. 2003. A requiem for North American overkill. *Journal of Archaeological Science* 30: 585–593.

Green, B. B., N. S. Weiss, and J. R. Daling. 1988. Risk of ovulatory infertility in relation to body weight. *Fertility and Sterility* 50: 721–726.

Green, R. E., J. Krause, A. W. Briggs, T. Maricic, U. Stenzel, M. Kircher, N. Patterson, H. Lee, W. Zhai, M. H.-Y. Fritz, N. F. Hansen, E. Y. Durand, A.-S. Malaspinas, J. D. Jensen, T. Marques-Bonet, C. Alkan, K. Prufer, M. Meyer, H. A. Burbano, J. M. Good, R. Schultz, A. Aximu-Petri, A. Butthof, B. Hober, B. Hoffner, M. Siegemund, A. Weihmann, C. Nusbaum, E. S. Lander, C. Russ, N. Novod, J. Affourtit, M. Egholm, C. Verna, P. Rudan, D. Brajkovic, Z. Kucan, I. Gusic, V. B. Doronichev, L.V. Golovanova, C. Lalueza-Fox, M. de la Rasilla, J. Fortea, A. Rosas, R. W. Schmitz, P. L. F. Johnson, E. E. Eichler, D. Falush, E. Birney, J. C. Mullikin, M. Slatkin, R. Nielsen, J. Kelso, M. Lachmann, D. Reich, and S. Paabo. 2010. A draft sequence of the Neandertal genome. *Science* 328: 710–722.

Green, R. E., A.-S. Malaspinas, J. Krause, A. W. Briggs, P. L. F. Johnson, C. Uhler, M. Meyer, J. M. Good, T. Maricic, U. Stenzel, K. Prüfer, M. Siebauer, H. A. Burbano, M. Ronan, J. M. Rothberg, M. Egholm, P. Rudan, D. Brajković, Z. Kuc'an, I. Gušic', M. Wikström, L. Laakkonen, J. Kelso, M. Slatkin, and S. Pääbo. 2008. A complete Neandertal mitochondrial genome sequence determined by high-throughput sequencing. *Cell* 134: 416–426.

Green, R. E., J. Krause, S. E. Ptak, A. W. Briggs, M. T. Ronan, J. F. Simons, L. Du, M. Egholm, J. M. Rothberg, M. Paunovic, and S. Pääbo. 2006. Analysis of one million base pairs of Neanderthal DNA. *Nature* 444: 330–336.

Greene, B. 2008. Put a little science in your life. *New York Times* June 1: 14.

Greene, M. 2005. *Jane Goodall: A Biography.* Westport, CT: Greenwood.

Gremillion, K. J. 2004. Seed processing and the origins of food production in eastern North America. *American Antiquity* 69: 215–233.

Grieco, E. M. and R. C. Cassidy. 2001. Overview of race and Hispanic origin. Pp. 1–11 in *Census 2000 Brief,* C2KBR/01-1. Washington, DC: *U.S. Census Bureau, U.S. Department of Commerce.*

Grine, F. E., R. M. Bailey, K. Harvati, R. P. Nathan, A. G. Morris, G. M. Henderson, I. Ribot, and A. W. G. Pike. 2007. Late Pleistocene human skull from Hofmeyr, South Africa, and modern human origins. *Science* 315: 226–229.

Gross, B. L., and Z. Zhao. 2014. Archaeological and genetic insights into the origins of domesticated rice. *Proceedings of the National Academy of Sciences USA* 111: 6190–6197.

Grove, L. 1962. *Now It Can Be Told: The Story of the Manhattan Project.* New York: Harper.

Grün, F. and B. Blumberg. 2006. Environmental obesogens: organotins and endocrine disruption via nuclear receptor signaling. *Endocrinology* 147: S50–S55.

Grün, R. 1993. Electron spin resonance dating in paleoanthropology. *Evolutionary Anthropology* 2: 172–181.

Grün, R. 2006. Direct dating of human fossils. *Yearbook of Physical Anthropology* 49: 2–48.

Guatelli-Steinberg, D. 2010. "Growing planes": incremental growth layers in the dental enamel of human ancestors. Pp. 485–500 in C. S. Larsen, ed. *A Companion to Biological Anthropology.* Chichester, UK: Wiley-Blackwell.

Guatelli-Steinberg, D., A. Stinespring-Harris, D.J. Reid, C.S. Larsen, D.L. Hutchinson, and T.M. Smith. 2014. Chronology of linear enamel hypoplasia formation in the Krapina Neanderthals. Paleoanthropology 2014:431-445, DOI: 10.4207/PA.2014.ART84.

Guatelli-Steinberg, D., C. S. Larsen, and D. L. Hutchinson. 2004. Prevalence and the duration of linear enamel hypoplasia: a comparative study of Neandertals and Inuit foragers. *Journal of Human Evolution* 47: 65–84.

Guatelli-Steinberg, D., D. J. Reid, T. A. Bishop, and C. S. Larsen. 2005. Anterior tooth growth periods in Neandertals were comparable to those of modern humans. *Proceedings of the National Academy of Sciences USA* 102: 14197–14202.

Gunnell, G. F. and K. D. Rose. 2002. Tarsiiformes: evolutionary history and adaptation. Pp. 45–82 in W. C. Hartwig, ed. *The Primate Fossil Record.* Cambridge, UK: Cambridge University Press.

Gunnell, G. F. and M. T. Silcox. 2010. Primate origins—the early Cenozoic fossil record. Pp. 275–294 in C. S. Larsen, ed. *A Companion to Biological Anthropology.* Chichester, UK: Wiley-Blackwell.

Haeckel, E. 1874. *The Evolution of Man.* 2 vols. Akron, OH: Werner.

Haeckel, E. 1889. *The History of Creation: Or the Development of the Earth and Its Inhabitants by the Action of Natural Causes.* New York: D. Appleton.

Haile-Selassie, Y. 2001. Late Miocene hominids from the late Awash, Ethiopia. *Nature* 412: 178–181.

Haile-Selassie, Y., B. Asfaw, and T. D. White. 2004. Hominid cranial remains from upper Pleistocene deposits at Aduma, Middle Awash, Ethiopia. *American Journal of Physical Anthropology* 123: 1–10.

Haile-Selassie, Y., B. M. Latimer, M. Alene, A. L. Deino, L. Gibert, S. M. Melillo, B. Z. Saylor, G. R. Scott, and C. O. Lovejoy. 2010. An early *Australopithecus afarensis* postcranium from Woranso-Mille, Ethiopia. *Proceedings of the National Academy of Sciences USA* (in press) 107: 12121-12126.

Haile-Selassie, Y., G. Suwa, and T. D. White.

2004. Late Miocene teeth from Middle Awash, Ethiopia, and early hominid dental evolution. *Science* 303: 1503–1505.

Haile-Selassie, Y. and G. WoldeGabriel. 2009. Ardipithecus kadabba: *Late Miocene Evidence from the Middle Awash, Ethiopia.* Berkeley: University of California Press.

Hallgrímsson, B. and B. K. Hall. 2005. *Variation: A Central Concept in Biology.* Burlington, MA: Elsevier Academic Press.

Halligan, J.J., M.R. Waters, A. Perrotti, I.J. Owens, J.M. Feinberg, et al. 2016. Pre-Clovis occupation 14,550 years ago at the Page-Ladson site, Florida, and the peopling of the Americas. Science Advances 2:e1600375: 1-8..

Hamada, Y. and T. Udono. 2002. Longitudinal analysis of length growth in the chimpanzee. *American Journal of Physical Anthropology* 118: 268–284.

Hardy, K., S. Buckley, M. J. Collins, A. Estalrrich, D. Brothwell, L. Copeland, A. García-Tabernero, S. García-Vargas, M. de la Rasilla, C. Lalueza-Fox, R. Huguet, M. Bastir, D. Santamaría, M. Madella, J. Wilson, Á Fernández Cortés, and A. Rosas. 2012. Neanderthal medics? Evidence for food, cooking, and medicinal plants entrapped in dental calculus. *Naturwissenschaften* 99: 617–626.

Harlow, H. F. and M. K. Harlow. 1965. Social deprivation in monkeys. *Scientific American* 207(5): 136–146.

Harmand, S., J. E. Lewis, C. S. Feibel., C. J. Lepre, S. Prat, A. Lenoble, et al. 2015. 3.3-Million-year-old stone tools from Lomekwi 3, West Turkana, Kenya. *Nature* 521: 310–315.

Harper, G. J. and D. E. Crews. 2000. Aging, senescence, and human variation. Pp. 465–505 in S. Stinson, B. Bogin, R. Huss-Ashmore, and D. O'Rourke, eds. *Human Biology: An Evolutionary and Biocultural Perspective.* New York: Wiley-Liss.

Harris, E. E. and D. Meyer. 2006. The molecular signature of selection underlying human adaptations. *Yearbook of Physical Anthropology* 49: 89–130.

Harris, J. M. and T. D. White. 1979. *Evolution of the Plio-Pleistocene African Suidae. Transactions of the American Philosophical Society* 69(2): 1–128.

Harrison, G. A. 1982. Lifestyles, well-being and stress. *Human Biology* 54: 193–202.

Harrison, G. A. 1993. *Human Adaptation.* Oxford, UK: Oxford University Press.

Harrison, G. G. and S. Hamide. 2009. Overweight, obesity, and related diseases. Pp. 129–139 in W. G. Pond, B. L. Nichols, and D. L. Brown, eds. *Adequate Food for All: Culture, Science, and Technology of Food in the 21st Century.* Boca Raton, FL: CRC Press.

Harrison, T. 2002. Late Oligocene to middle Miocene catarrhines from Afro-Arabia. Pp. 311–338 in W. C. Hartwig, ed. *The Primate Fossil Record.* Cambridge, UK: Cambridge University Press.

Harrold, F. B. 1980. A comparative analysis of Eurasian Paleolithic burials. *World Archaeology* 12: 195–211.

Hart, D. and R. W. Sussman. 2009. *Man the Hunted: Primates, Predators, and Human Evolution.* Expanded edition. Jackson, TN: Westview Press.

Hartwig, W. C., ed. 2002. *The Primate Fossil Record.* Cambridge, UK: Cambridge University Press.

Haslam, M., A. Hernandez-Aguilar, V. Ling, S. Carvalho, I. de la Torre, A. DeStefano, A. Du, B. Hardy, J. Harris, L. Marchant, T. Matsuzawa, W. McGrew, J. Mercader, R. Mora, M. Petraglia, H. Roche, E. Visalberghi, and R. Warren. 2009. Primate archaeology. *Nature* 460: 339–344.

Havill, L. M., M. C. Mahaney, L. A. Cox, P. A. Morin, G. Joslyn, and J. Rogers. 2005. A quantitative trait locus for normal variation in forearm bone mineral density in pedigreed baboons maps to the ortholog of human chromosome 11q. *Journal of Clinical Endocrinology and Metabolism* 90: 3638–3645.

Hawkes, K. 2003. Grandmothers and the evolution of human longevity. *American Journal of Human Biology* 15: 380–400.

Hawkes, K., J. F. O'Connell, N. G. Blurton Jones, H. Alvarez, and E. L. Charnov. 1998. Grandmothering, menopause, and the evolution of human life histories. *Proceedings of the National Academy of Sciences USA* 95: 1336–1339.

Hawks, J. 2012. Longer time scale for human evolution. *Proceedings of the National Academy of Sciences USA* 109: 15532–15532.

Hawks, J., E. T. Wang, G. M. Cochran, H. C. Harpending, and R. K. Moyzis. 2007. Recent acceleration of human adaptive evolution. *Proceedings of the National Academy of Sciences USA* 104: 20753–20758.

Hay, R. L. and M. D. Leakey. 1982. The fossil footprints of Laetoli. *Scientific American* 246(2): 50–57.

Head, M. J., P. Gibbard, and A. Salvador A. 2008. The Tertiary: a proposal for its formal definition. *Episodes* 31: 248–250.

Heeney, J. L., A. G. Dalgleish, and R. A. Weiss. 2006. Origins of HIV and the evolution of resistance to AIDS. *Science* 313: 462–466.

Henry, A. G., A. S. Brooks, and D. R. Piperno. 2011. Microfossils in calculus demonstrate consumption of plants and cooked foods in Neanderthal diets (Shanidar III, Iraq; Spy I and II, Belgium). *Proceedings of the National Academy of Sciences USA* 108: 486–491.

Henshilwood, C. S., F. d'Errico, K. L. van Niekerk, Y. Coquinot, Z. Jacobs, S.-E. Lauritzen, M. Menu, and R. García-Moreno. 2011. A 100,000-year-old ochre-processing workshop at Blombos Cave, South Africa. *Science* 334: 219–222.

Hernandez-Aguilar, R. A., J. Moore, and T. R. Pickering. 2007. Savanna chimpanzees use tools to harvest the underground storage organs of plants. *Proceedings of the National Academy of Sciences USA* 104: 19210–19213.

Higham, T., C. B. Ramsey, I. Karavanic, F. H. Smith, and E. Trinkaus. 2006. Revised direct radiocarbon dating of the Vindija G1 upper Paleolithic Neandertals. *Proceedings of the National Academy of Sciences USA* 103: 553–557.

Hill, W. C. O. 1972. *Evolutionary Biology of the Primates.* London: Academic Press.

Hlusko, L., N. Do, and M. C. Mahaney. 2007. Genetic correlations between mandibular molar cusp areas in baboons. *American Journal of Physical Anthropology* 132: 445–454.

Hodges, G. 2015. First Americans. *National Geographic* 227(1): 124–137.

Holden, C. 2004. The origin of speech. *Science* 303: 1316–1319.

Holliday, T. W. 1997. Body proportions in late Pleistocene Europe and modern human origins. *Journal of Human Evolution* 32: 423–447.

Holloway, R. L., D. C. Broadfield, and M. S. Yuan. 2004. *The Human Fossil Record, Volume 3: Brain Endocasts, The Paleoneurological Evidence.* Hoboken, NJ: Wiley-Liss.

Holman, D. J., M. A. Grimes, J. T. Achterberg, E. Brindle, and K. A. O'Conner. 2006. The distribution of postpartum amenorrhea in rural Bangladeshi women. *American Journal of Physical Anthropology* 129: 609–619.

Hudjashov, G., T. Kivisild, P. A. Underhill, P. Endicott, P. Sanchez, J. J. Sanchez, A. A. Lin, P. Shen, P. Oefner, C. Renfrew, R. Villems, and P. Forster. 2007. Revealing the prehistoric settlement of Australia by Y chromosome and mtDNA analysis. *Proceedings of the National Academy of Sciences USA* 104: 8726–8730.

Huijbrets, B., P. De Wachter, L. S. N. Obiang, and M. E. Akou. 2003. Ebola and the decline of gorilla *Gorilla gorilla* and chimpanzee *Pan troglodytes* populations in Minkebe Forest, north-eastern Gabon. *Oryx* 37: 437–443.

Hunley, K. L., G. S. Cabana, D. A. Merriwether, and J. C. Long. 2007. A formal test of linguistic and genetic coevolution in native Central and South America. *American Journal of Physical Anthropology* 132: 622–631.

Hunley, K. L., J. E. Spence, and D. A. Merriwether. 2008. The impact of group fissions on genetic structure in native South America and implications for human evolution. *American Journal of Physical Anthropology* (in press) 135: 195–205.

Huss-Ashmore, R. 2000. Theory in human biology: evolution, ecology, adaptability, and variation. Pp. 1–25 in S. Stinson, B. Bogin, R. Huss-Ashmore, and D. O'Rourke, eds. *Human Biology: An Evolutionary and Biocultural Perspective.* New York: Wiley-Liss.

Huss-Ashmore, R., J. Schall, and M. Hediger. 1992. *Health and Lifestyle Change.* Philadelphia: Museum Applied Science Center for Archaeology, University of Pennsylvania.

Huxley, R. 2007. *The Great Naturalists.* New York: Thames & Hudson.

Ice, G. H. and G. D. James. 2012. Stress and human biology. Pp. 459–512 in S. Stinson, B. Bogin, and D. O'Rourke, eds. *Human Biology: An Evolutionary and Biocultural Perspective,* 2nd ed. Hoboken, NJ: Wiley-Blackwell.

Institute of Vertebrate Paleontology and Paleoanthropology. 1980. *Atlas of Primitive Man in China.* Beijing, China, and New York: Science Press of the People's Republic of China and Van Nostrand Reinhold.

Irish, J. D., D. Guatelli-Steinberg, S. S. Legge, D. J. de Ruiter, and L. R. Berger. 2013. Dental morphology and the phylogenetic "place" of *Australopithecus sediba. Science* 340. DOI: 10.1126/science.1234598-1-4.

Irvine, W. 1955. *Apes, Angels, and Victorians.* New York: McGraw-Hill.

Isaac, G. L. 1977. *Olorgesailie: Archeological Studies of a Middle Pleistocene Lake Basin in Kenya.* Chicago: University of Chicago Press.

Itan, Y., B. L. Jones, C. J. E. Ingram, D. M. Swallo, and M. G. Thomas. 2010. A worldwide correlation of lactase persistence phenotype and genotypes. *BMC Evolutionary Biology* 10: 36.

Jablonka, E. and M. J. Lamb. 2005. *Evolution in Four Dimensions: Genetic, Epigenetic, Behavioral, and Symbolic Variation in the History of Life.* Cambridge, MA: MIT Press.

Jablonski, N. 2002. Fossil Old World monkeys: the late Neogene radiation. Pp. 255–299 in W. C. Hartwig, ed. *The Primate Fossil Record.* Cambridge, UK: Cambridge University Press.

Jablonski, N. G. 2004. The evolution of human skin and skin color. *Annual Review of Anthropology* 33: 585–623.

Jablonski, N. G. 2006. *Skin: A Natural History.* Berkeley: University of California Press.

Jablonski, N. G. and G. Chaplin. 2000. The evolution of skin coloration. *Journal of Human Evolution* 39: 57–106.

Jablonski, N. G. and G. Chaplin. 2002. Skin deep. *Scientific American* 287(4): 50–55.

Jablonski, N. G. and G. Chaplin. 2010. Human skin pigmentation as an adaptation to UV radiation. *Proceedings of the National Academy of Sciences USA* 107(suppl. 2): 8962–8968.

Jablonski, N. G., M. G. Leakey, C. Kiarie, and M. Anton. 2002. A new skeleton of *Theropithecus brumpti* (Primates: Cercopithecidae) from Lomekwi, West Turkana, Kenya. *Journal of Human Evolution* 43: 887–923.

Jacob, T., E. Indriati, R. P. Soejono, K. Hsu, D. W. Frayer, R. B. Eckhardt, A. J. Kuperavage, A. Thorne, and M. Henneberg. 2006. Pygmoid Australomelanesian *Homo sapiens* skeletal remains from Liang Bua, Flores: population affinities and pathological abnormalities. *Proceedings of the National Academy of Sciences USA* 103: 13421–13426.

Jaeger, J.-J., K. C. Beard, Y. Chaimanee, M. Salem, M. Benammi, O. Hlal, P. Coster, A. A. Bilal, P. Duringer, M. Schuster, X. Valentin,

B. Marandat, L. Marivaux, E. Metais, O. Hammuda, and M. Brunet. 2010. Late middle Eocene epoch of Libya yields earliest known radiation of African anthropoids. *Nature* 467: 1095–1098.

Jaeger, J.-J. and L. Marivaux. 2005. Shaking the earliest branches of anthropoid primate evolution. *Science* 310: 244–245.

James, G. 2010. Climate related morphological variation and physiological adaptations in *Homo sapiens.* Pp. 153–166 in C. S. Larsen, ed. *A Companion to Biological Anthropology.* Chichester, UK: Wiley-Blackwell.

Janmaat, K. R. L., S. D. Ban, and C. Boesch 2013. Chimpanzees use long-term spatial memory to monitor large fruit trees and remember feeding experiences across seasons. *Animal Behaviour* 86: 1183–1205.

Jannmaat, K. R. L., L. Polansky, S. D. Ban, and C. Boesch. 2014. Wild chimpanzees plan their breakfast time, type, and location. *Proceedings of the National Academy of Sciences USA* 111: 16343–16348.

Jantz, L. M. and R. L. Jantz. 1999. Secular change in long bone length and proportion in the United States, 1800–1970. *American Journal of Physical Anthropology* 110: 57–67.

Jantz, R. L. and M. K. Spradley. 2014. Cranial morphometric evidence for early Holocene relationships and population structure. Pp. 472–491 in D. W. Owsley and R. L. Jantz, eds. *Kennewick Man: The Scientific Investigation of an Ancient American Skeleton.* College Station: Texas A&M University Press.

Johnston, W. R. 2015. Statistics on the 2014-2015 West Africa Ebola outbreak. http://www.johnstonarchive.net/policy/westafrica-ebola.html.

Jolly, A. 1985. *The Evolution of Primate Behavior.* New York: Macmillan.

Jones, M. 2003. Ancient DNA in pre-Columbian archaeology: a review. *Journal of Archaeological Science* 30: 629–635.

Jungers, W. L., S. G., Larson, W. Harcourt-Smith, M. J. Morwood, T. Sutikna, R. Due Awe, and T. Djubiantono. 2009. Descriptions of the lower limb skeleton of *Homo floresiensis. Journal of Human Evolution* 57: 538–554.

Kaestle, F. A. 1995. Mitochondrial DNA evidence for the identity of the descendants of the prehistoric Stillwater Marsh populations. Pp. 73–80 in C. S. Larsen and R. L. Kelly, eds. *Bioarchaeology of the Stillwater Marsh: Prehistoric Human Adaptation in the Western Great Basin. Anthropological Papers of the American Museum of Natural History* 77. New York: American Museum of Natural History.

Kaestle, F. A. 2010. Paleogenetics: ancient DNA in anthropology. Pp. 427–441 in C. S. Larsen, ed. *A Companion to Biological Anthropology.* Chichester, UK: Wiley-Blackwell.

Kaestle, F. A. and K. A. Horsburgh. 2002. Ancient DNA in anthropology: methods, applications, and ethics. *Yearbook of Physical Anthropology* 45: 92–130.

Kaestle, F. A., R. A. Kittles, A. L. Roth, and E. J. Ungvarsky. 2006. Database limitations on the evidentiary value of forensic mitochondrial DNA evidence. *American Criminal Law Review* 43: 53–88.

Kaestle, F. A., J. G. Lorenz, and D. G. Smith. 1999. Molecular genetics and the Numic expansion: a molecular investigation of the prehistoric inhabitants of Stillwater Marsh. Pp. 167–183 in B. E. Hemphill and C. S. Larsen, eds. *Prehistoric Lifeways in the Great Basin Wetlands: Bioarchaeological Reconstruction and Interpretation.* Salt Lake City: University of Utah Press.

Kaifu, Y., H. Baba, F. Aziz, E. Indriati, F. Schrenk, and T. Jacob. 2004. Taxonomic affinities and evolutionary history of the early Pleistocene hominids of Java: dento-gnathic evidence. *American Journal of Physical Anthropology* 128: 709–726.

Kalaydjieva, L., B. Morar, R. Chaix, and H. Tang. 2005. A newly discovered founder population: the Roma/Gypsies. *BioEssays* 27: 1084–1094.

Kappeler, P. M. and C. P. van Schaik. 2006. *Cooperation in Primates and Humans: Mechanisms and Evolution.* New York: Springer.

Kappelman, J. 1993. The attraction of paleomagnetism. *Evolutionary Anthropology* 2: 89–99.

Kappelman, J., M. C. Alcicek, N. Kazanci, M. Schultz, M. Ozkul, and S. Sen. 2008. First *Homo erectus* from Turkey and implications for migrations into temperate Eurasia. *American Journal of Physical Anthropology* (in press) 135:110–116.

Karavanic, I. and F. H. Smith. 1998. The middle/upper Paleolithic interface and the relationship of Neanderthals and early modern humans in the Hrvatsko Zagorje, Croatia. *Journal of Human Evolution* 34: 223–248.

Katzenberg, M. A. 2008. Stable isotope analysis: a tool for studying past diet, demography, and life history. Pp. 413–441 in M. A. Katzenberg and S. R. Saunders, eds. *Biological Anthropology of the Human Skeleton,* 2nd ed. New York: Wiley-Liss.

Kay, R. F., C. Ross, and B. A. Williams. 1997. Anthropoid origins. *Science* 275: 797–804.

Kay, R. F. 2015. New World monkey origins. *Science* 347: 1068–1069.

Keesing, F., L. K. Belden, P. Daszak, A. Dobson, C. D. Harvell, R. D. Holt, P. Hudson, A. Jolles, K. E. Jones, C. E. Mitchell, S. S. Myers, T. Bogich, and R. S. Ostfeld. 2010. Impacts of biodiversity on the emergence and transmission of infectious diseases. *Nature* 468: 647–652.

Keith-Lucas, T., F. J. White, L. Keith-Lucas, and L. G. Vick. 1999. Changes in behavior in free-ranging *Lemur catta* following release in a natural habitat. *American Journal of Primatology* 47: 15–28.

Kelley, E. A. and R. W. Sussman. 2007. An academic genealogy on the history of American field primatologists. *American Journal of Physical Anthropology* 132: 406–425.

Kelley, J. 2002. The hominoid radiation in Asia. Pp. 369–384 in W. C. Hartwig, ed. *The Primate Fossil Record*. Cambridge, UK: Cambridge University Press.

Kelly, R. L. 2003. Maybe we know when people first came to North America; and what does it mean if we do? *Quaternary International* 109–110: 133–145.

Kemp, B. M., R. S. Malhi, J. McDonough, D. A. Bolnick, J. A. Eshleman, O. Rickards, C. Martinez-Labarga, J. R. Johnson, J. G. Lorenz, E. J. Dixon, T. E. Fifield, T. H. Heaton, R. Worl, and D. G. Smith. 2007. Genetic analysis of early Holocene skeletal remains from Alaska and its implications for the settlement of the Americas. *American Journal of Physical Anthropology* 132: 605–621.

Kemper, S. 2013. No alpha males allowed. *Smithsonian* 44(5): 38–43.

Kenneally, C. 2007. *The First Word: The Search for the Origins of Language*. New York: Viking.

Kennedy, G. 2003. Palaeolithic grandmothers? Life history theory and early *Homo. Journal of the Royal Anthropological Institute* 9: 549–572.

Kennedy, G. 2005. From the ape's dilemma to the weanling's dilemma: early weaning and its evolutionary context. *Journal of Human Evolution* 48: 123–145.

Kennedy, K. A. R. 2000. *God-Apes and Fossil Men: Paleoanthropology in South Asia*. Ann Arbor: University of Michigan Press.

Kennedy, K. A. R., A. Sonakia, J. Chiment, and K. K. Verma. 1991. Is the Narmada hominid an Indian *Homo erectus? American Journal of Physical Anthropology* 86: 475–496.

Kettlewell, H. B. D. 1973. *The Evolution of Melanism*. Oxford, UK: Oxford University Press.

Kevles, B. H. 2006. *The Reluctant Mr. Darwin: An Intimate Portrait of Charles Darwin and the Making of His Theory of Evolution*. New York: Norton.

Keyser, A. W. 2000. The Drimolen skull: the most complete australopithecine cranium and mandible to date. *South African Journal of Science* 96: 189–197.

Khoury, M. J., R. Millikan, J. Little, and M. Gwinn. 2004. The emergence of epidemiology in the genomics age. *International Journal of Epidemiology* 33: 936–944.

Kim, U.-K., E. Jorgenson, H. Coon, M. Leppert, N. Risch, and D. Drayna. 2003. Positional cloning of the human quantitative trait locus underlying taste sensitivity to phenylthiocarbamide. *Science* 299: 1221–1225.

Kimbel, W. H. and L. K. Delezene. 2009. "Lucy" redux: a review of research on *Australopithecus afarensis. Yearbook of Physical Anthropology* 52: 2–48.

Kimbel, W. H., D. C. Johanson, and Y. Rak. 1994. The first skull and other new discoveries of *Australopithecus afarensis* at Hadar, Ethiopia. *Nature* 368: 449–451.

Kimbel, W. H., Lockwood, C., Ward, C., Leakey, M., Rak, Y. & Johanson, D. (2006). Was *Australopithecus anamensis* ancestral to *A. afaraensis*? A case of anagenesis in the hominin fossil record. *Journal of Human Evolution* 51: 134–152.

Kimbel, W. H., Y. Rak, and D. C. Johanson. 2004. *The Skull of* Australopithecus afarensis. New York: Oxford University Press.

King, T. E., G. R. Bowden, P. L. Balaresque, S. M. Adams, M. E. Shanks, and M. A. Jobling. 2007. Thomas Jefferson's Y chromosome belongs to rare European lineage. *American Journal of Physical Anthropology* 132: 584–589.

Kirch, P. V. 2005. Archaeology and global change: the Holocene record. *Annual Review of Anthropology* 30: 409–440.

Kirk, S. F., T. L. Penney, and T.-L. F. McHugh. 2011. Characterizing the obesogenic environment: the state of the evidence with directions for future research. *Obesity Reviews* 11: 109–117.

Kitchen, D. M. 2003. Alpha male black howler monkey responses to loud calls: effect of numeric odds, male companion behaviour and reproductive investment. *Animal Behaviour* 67: 125–139.

Klaus, H. D., C. S. Larsen, and M. E. Tam. 2009. Economic intensification and degenerative joint disease: life and labor in postcontact north coast, Peru. *American Journal of Physical Anthropology* 139: 204–221.

Klein, R. G. 2009. *The Human Career: Human Biological and Cultural Origins*, 3rd ed. Chicago: University of Chicago Press.

Klepinger, L. L. 2006. *Fundamentals of Forensic Anthropology*. Hoboken, NJ: Wiley-Liss.

Klitz, W., C. Brautbar, A. M. Schito, L. F. Barcellos, and J. R. Oksenberg. 2001. Evolution of the CCR5 delta 32 mutation based on haplotype variation in Jewish and northern European population samples. *Human Immunology* 62: 530–538.

Koch, M., S. Wedmann, C. Labandeira, and J. Hamlin. 2011. Fossil bugs (Insecta: Heteroptera) of Messel and the Green River Formation (USA)—Are there any connections? Pp. 89-90 in T. Lehmann and S. F. K. Schaal, eds. *The World of Time of Messel: Puzzles in Palaeobiology, Palaeoenvironment, and the History of Early Primates*. Frankfurt am Main, Germany: Senckenberg Gesellschaft für Naturforschung.

Koenigswald, W., J. Habersetzer, and P. D. Gingerich. 2011. Morphology and evolution of the distal phalanges in primates. Pp. 91–94 in T. Lehmann and S. F. K. Schaal, eds. *The World at the Time of Messel: Puzzles in Palaeobiology, Palaeoenvironment, and the History of Early Primates*. Frankfurt am Main, Germany: Senckenberg Gesellschaft für Naturforschung.

Kolbert, E. 2007. *Field Notes from a Catastrophe: A Frontline Report on Climate Change*. London: Bloomsbury.

Kolman, C. J. 2006. Anthropological applications of ancient DNA: problems and prospects. *American Antiquity* 71: 365–380.

Komlos, J., ed. 1994. *Stature, Living Standards, and Economic Development: Essays in Anthropometric History*. Chicago: University of Chicago Press.

Kordos, L. and D. R. Begun. 2002. Rudabanya: a late Miocene subtropical swamp deposit with evidence of the origin of the African apes and humans. *Evolutionary Anthropology* 11: 45–57.

Kramer, A. 2002. The natural history and evolutionary fate of *Homo erectus*. Pp. 140–154 in P. N. Peregrine, C. R. Ember, and M. Ember, eds. *Physical Anthropology: Original Readings in Method and Practice*. Upper Saddle River, NJ: Prentice Hall.

Krause, J., C. Lalueza-Fox, L. Orlando, W. Enard, R. E. Green, H. A. Burbano, J.-J. Hublin, C. Hänni, J. Fortea, M. de la Rasilla, J. Bertranpetit, A. Rosas, and S. Pääbo. 2007. The derived *FOXP2* variant of modern humans was shared with Neandertals. *Current Biology* 17: 1908–1912.

Krause, J., L. Orlando, D. Serre, B. Viola, B. Prufer, M. P. Richards, J.-J. Hublin, C. Hanni, A. P. Derevianko, and S. Pääbo. 2007. Neanderthals in central Asia and Siberia. *Nature* 449: 902–904.

Krause, K. W. 2009. Pathology or paradigm shift? Human evolution, *ad hominem* science, and the anomalous hobbits of Flores. *Skeptical Inquirer* 33(4): 31–39.

Krech, S. III. 1999. *The Ecological Indian: Myth and History*. New York: Norton.

Krogman, W. M. and M. Y. Iscan. 1986. *The Human Skeleton in Forensic Medicine*, 2nd ed. Springfield, IL: Charles C. Thomas.

Kunimatsu, Y., M. Nakatsukasa, Y. Sawada, T. Sakai, M. Hyodo, H. Hyodo, T. Itaya, H. Nakaya, H. Saegusa, A. Maxurier, M. Saneyoshi, H. Tsujikawa, A. Yamamoto, and E. Mbua. 2007. A new late Miocene great ape from Kenya and its implications for the origins of African great apes and humans. *Proceedings of the National Academy of Sciences USA* 104: 19220–19225.

Kuzawa, C. W. 1998. Adipose tissue in human infancy and childhood: an evolutionary perspective. *Yearbook of Physical Anthropology* 41: 177–209.

Laitman, J. T. and I. Tattersall, eds. 2001. *Homo erectus newyorkensis. The Anatomical Record* 262(1).

Lake, A., T. B. Townshend, and S. Alvanides. 2010. *Obesogenic Environments*. Hoboken, NJ: Wiley-Blackwell.

Lamason, R. L., M.-A. P. K. Mohideen, J. R. Mest, A. C. Wong, H. L. Norton, M. C. Aros, M. J. Jurynec, X. Mao, V. R. Humphreville, J. E. Humbert, S. Sinha, J. L. Moore, P. Jagadeeswaran, W. Zhao, G. Ning, I. Makalowska, P. M. McKeigue, D. O'Donnell, R. Kittles, E. J. Parra, N. J. Mangini, D. J. Grunwald, M. D. Shriver, V. A. Canfield, and K. C. Cheng. 2005. SLC24A5, a putative cation exchanger, affects pigmentation in zebrafish and humans. *Science* 310: 1782–1786.

Lambert, D. M. and C. D. Millar. 2006. Ancient genomics is born. *Nature* 444: 275–276.

Lambert, D. M. and L. Huynen. 2010. Face of the past reconstructed. *Nature* 463: 739–740.

Lambert, J. E. 1999. Seed handling in chimpanzees (*Pan troglodytes*) and redtail monkeys (*Cercopithecus ascanius*): implications for understanding hominoid and cercopithecine fruit-processing strategies and seed dispersal. *American Journal of Physical Anthropology* 109: 365–386.

Lambert, J. E., C. A. Chapman, R. W. Wrangham, and N. L. Conklin-Brittain. 2004. Hardness of cercopithecine foods: implications for the critical function of enamel thickness in exploiting fallback foods. *American Journal of Physical Anthropology* 125: 363–368.

Lambert, P. M., ed. 2000. *Bioarchaeological Studies of Life in the Age of Agriculture: A View from the Southeast*. Tuscaloosa: University of Alabama Press.

Lambert, P. M. 2002. The archaeology of war: a North American perspective. *Journal of Archaeological Research* 10: 207–241.

Lambert, P. M. 2009. Health versus fitness: competing themes in the origins and spread of agriculture. *Current Anthropology* 50: 603–608.

Lander, E. S. 2011. Initial impact of the sequencing of the human genome. *Nature* 470: 187–197.

Langergraber, K. E., K. Prüfer, C. Rowney, C. Boesch, C. Crockford, K. Fawcett, E. Inoue, M. Inoue-Muruyama, J. C. Mitani, M. N. Muller, M. M. Robbins, G. Schubert, T. S. Stoinski, B. Viola, D. Watts, R. M. Wittig, R. W. Wrangham, K. Zuberbühler, S. Pääbo, and L. Vigilant. 2012. Generation times in wild chimpanzees and gorillas suggest earlier divergence times in great ape and human evolution. *Proceedings of the National Academy of Sciences USA* 109: 15716–15721.

Langdon, J. H. 2005. *The Human Strategy: An Evolutionary Perspective on Human Anatomy*. New York: Oxford University Press.

Lanham, U. 1973. *The Bone Hunters*. New York: Columbia University Press.

Larsen, C. S., ed. 2015. *The Antiquity and Origin of Native North Americans*, Second Edition. New York: Garland Publishing.

Larsen, C. S. 1994. In the wake of Columbus: native population biology in the postcontact Americas. *Yearbook of Physical Anthropology* 37: 109–154.

Larsen, C. S. 1995. Biological changes in human populations with agriculture. *Annual Review of Anthropology* 24: 185–213.

Larsen, C. S. 1997. *Bioarchaeology: Interpreting Behavior from the Human Skeleton*. Cambridge, UK: Cambridge University Press.

Larsen, C. S. 2000. *Skeletons in Our Closet: Revealing Our Past through Bioarchaeology*. Princeton, NJ: Princeton University Press.

Larsen, C. S. 2002. Bioarchaeology: the lives and lifestyles of past people. *Journal of Archaeological Research* 10: 119–166.

Larsen, C. S. 2003. Animal source foods and human health during evolution. *Journal of Nutrition* 133: 1S–5S.

Larsen, C. S. 2003. Equality for the sexes in human evolution?: Early hominid sexual dimorphism and implications for mating systems and social behavior. *Proceedings of the National Academy of Sciences USA* 100: 9103–9104.

Larsen, C. S., ed. 2010. *A Companion to Biological Anthropology*. Chichester, UK: Wiley-Blackwell.

Larsen, C. S., D. L. Hutchinson, M. J. Schoeninger, and L. Norr. 2001. Food and stable isotopes in La Florida: diet and nutrition before and after contact. Pp. 53–81 in CS Larsen, ed. *Bioarchaeology of Spanish Florida: The Impact of Colonialism*. Gainesville: University Press of Florida.

Larsen, C. S. and P. L. Walker. 2010. Bioarchaeology: health, lifestyle, and society in recent human evolution. Pp. 379–394 in C. S. Larsen, ed. *A Companion to Biological Anthropology*. Chichester, UK: Wiley-Blackwell.

Larsen, C. S., R. M. Matter, and D. L. Gebo. 1998. *Human Origins: The Fossil Record*, 3rd ed. Prospect Heights, IL: Waveland Press.

Larsen, C. S. and T. C. Patterson. 1997. Americas: paleoanthropology. Pp. 69–74 in F. Spencer, ed. *History of Physical Anthropology: An Encyclopedia*. New York: Garland.

Larsen, E. 2005. Developmental origins of variation. Pp. 113–129 in B. Hallgrímson and B. K. Hall, eds. *Variation: A Central Concept in Biology*. Burlington, MA: Elsevier Academic Press.

Larson, G., U. Albarella, K. Dobney, P. Rowley-Conway, J. Schibler, A. Tresset, J.-D. Vigne, C. J. Edwards, A. Schlumbaum, A. Dinu, A. Balacsecu, G. Dolman, A. Tagliacozzo, N. Manaseryan, P. Miracle, L. Van Wijngaarden-Bakker, M. Masseti, D. G. Bradley, and A. Cooper. 2007. Ancient DNA, pig domestication, and the spread of the Neolithic into Europe. *Proceedings of the National Academy of Sciences USA* 104: 15276–15281.

Larson, G., D. R. Piperno, R. G. Allaby, M. D. Purugganan, L. Andersson, et al. 2014. Current perspectives and the future of domestication studies. *Proceedings of the National Academy of Sciences USA* 111: 6139–6146.

Larson, S. 2010. Did australopiths climb trees? *Science* 338: 478–479.

Lassek, W. D. and S. J. C. Gaulin. 2006. Changes in body fat distribution in relation to parity in American women: a covert form of maternal depletion. *American Journal of Physical Anthropology* 131: 295–302.

Latham, R. 1982. *The Travels of Marco Polo*. New York: Viking.

Lau, E. M., C. Cooper, C. Wickham, S. Donnan, and D. J. Barker. 1990. Hip fracture in Hong Kong and Britain. *International Journal of Epidemiology* 19: 1119–1121.

Leakey, M. 1984. *Disclosing the Past: An Autobiography*. Garden City, NY: Doubleday.

Leakey, M. G., C. S. Feibel, I. McDougall, and A. Walker. 1995. New four-million-year-old hominid species from Kanapoi and Allia Bay, Kenya. *Nature* 376: 565–571.

Leakey, M. G., F. Spoor, F. H. Brown, P. N. Gathogo, C. Kiarie, L. M. Leakey, and I. McDougall. 2001. New hominin genus from eastern Africa shows diverse middle Pliocene lineages. *Nature* 410: 433–440.

Leakey, M. G., F. Spoor, M. C. Dean, C. S. Feibel, S. C. Antón, C. Kiarie, and L. N. Leakey. 2012. New fossils from KoobiFora in northern Kenya confirm taxonomic diversity in early *Homo*. *Nature* 488: 201–204.

Lebatard, A.-E., D. L. Bourlès, P. Duringer, M. Jolivet, R. Braucher, J. Carcaillet, M. Schuster, N. Arnaud, P. Moniè, F. Lihoreau, A. Likius, H. T. Mackaye, P. Vignaud, and M. Brunet. 2008. Cosmogenic nuclide dating of *Sahelanthropus tchadensis* and *Australopithecus hahrelghazali*: Mio-Pliocene hominids from Chad. *Proceedings of the National Academy of Sciences USA* 105: 3226–3231.

Lee, S.-H. and M. H. Wolpoff. 2003. The pattern of evolution in Pleistocene human brain size. *Paleobiology* 29: 186–196.

Lee-Thorp, J. 2002. Hominid dietary niches from proxy chemical indicators in fossils: the Swartkrans example. Pp. 123–141 in P. S. Ungar and M. F. Teaford, eds. *Human Diet: Its Origin and Evolution*. Westport, CT: Bergin & Garvey.

Lee-Thorp, J. and M. Sponheimer. 2006. Distributions of biogeochemistry to understanding hominin dietary ecology. *Yearbook of Physical Anthropology* 49: 131–148.

Lee-Thorp, J. A., M. Sponheimer, and N. J. van der Merwe. 2003. What do stable isotopes tell us about hominid dietary and ecological niches in the Pliocene? *International Journal of Osteoarchaeology* 13: 104–113.

Leidy, L. E. 1994. Biological aspects of menopause: across the lifespan. *Annual Review of Anthropology* 23: 231–253.

Lemons, D. and W. McGinnis. 2006. Genomic evolution of Hox gene clusters. *Science* 313: 1918–1922.

Leonard, W. R. 2002. Food for thought: dietary change was a driving force in human evolution. *Scientific American* December: 106–115.

Leonard, W. R. 2012. Human nutritional evolution. Pp. 251–324 in S. Stinson, B. Bogin, and D. O'Rourke, eds. *Human Biology: An Evolutionary and Biocultural Perspective*, 2nd ed. Hoboken, NJ: Wiley-Blackwell.

Lepre, C. J., and D. V. Kent. 2015. Chronostratigraphy of KNM-ER 3733 and other Area 104 hominins from Koobi Fora. *Journal of Human Evolution* 86: 99–111.

Levy, S. 1994. *The Antibiotic Paradox: How Miracle Drugs Are Destroying the Miracle*. New York: Plenum Press.

Lewin, R. 1988. *Bones of Contention: Controversies in the Search for Human Origins.* New York: Touchstone.

Lewis, S. L. and M. A. Maslin. 2015. Defining the Anthropocene. *Nature* 519: 171–180.

Lewontin, R. C. 1972. The apportionment of human diversity. *Evolutionary Biology* 6: 381–398.

Libby, W. F. 1952. *Radiocarbon Dating.* Chicago: University of Chicago Press.

Lieberman, D. E. 2007. Homing in on early *Homo. Nature* 449: 291–292.

Lieberman, L., R. C. Kirk, and A. Littlefield. 2003. Perishing paradigm: race—1931–1999. *American Anthropologist* 105: 110–113.

Lieberman, L. S. 2006. Evolutionary and anthropological perspectives on optimal foraging in obesogenic environments. *Appetite* 47: 3–9.

Little, B. B., P. H. Buschang, M. E. P. Reyes, S. K. Tan, and R. M. Malina. 2006. Craniofacial dimensions in children in rural Oaxaca, southern Mexico: secular change, 1968–2000. *American Journal of Physical Anthropology* 131: 127–136.

Little, M. A. 2010. Franz Boas's place in American physical anthropology and its institutions. Pp. 55–85 in M. A. Little and K. A. R. Kennedy, eds. *Histories of American Physical Anthropology in the Twentieth Century.* Lanham, MD: Rowman & Littlefield.

Little, M. A. and P. W. Leslie. 1999. *Turkana Herders of the Dry Savanna: Ecology and Biobehavioral Response of Nomads to an Uncertain Environment.* Oxford, UK: Oxford University Press.

Little, M. A. and R. W. Sussman. 2010. History of biological anthropology. Pp. 13–38 in C. S. Larsen, ed. *A Companion to Biological Anthropology.* Chichester, UK: Wiley-Blackwell.

Liu, W., C.-Z. Jin, Y.-Q. Zhang, Y.-J. Cai, S. Xing, X.-J. Wu, X.-J. Cheng, H. Cheng, R. L. Edwards, W.-S. Pan, D.-G. Qin, Z.-S. An, E. Trinkaus, and X.-Z. Wu. 2010. Human remains from Zhirendong, south China, and modern human emergence in east Asia. *Proceedings of the National Academy of Sciences USA* 107: 19201–19206.

Liu, W., M. Martinon-Torres, Y.-J. Cai, S. Xing, and H.-W. Tong. 2015. The earliest unequivocally modern humans in southern China. *Nature* 526: 696–700.

Livingstone, F. B. 1958. Anthropological implications of sickle cell gene distribution in West Africa. *American Anthropologist* 60: 533–562.

Livingstone, F. B. 1962. On the non-existence of human races. *Current Anthropology* 3: 279.

Livingstone, F. B. 1967. *Abnormal Hemoglobins in Human Populations.* Chicago: Aldine.

Livingstone, F. B. 1971. Malaria and human polymorphisms. *Annual Review of Genetics* 5: 33–64.

Livingstone, F. B. 1973. *Data on the Abnormal Hemoglobins and Glucose-6-Phosphate Dehydrogenase Deficiency in Human Populations, 1969–1973. Museum of Anthropology, University of Michigan, Technical Reports* 3, *Contributions in Human Biology* 1.

Livingstone, F. B. 1985. *Frequencies of Hemoglobin Variants: Thalassemia, The Glucose-6-Phosphate Hydrogenase Deficiency, G6PD Variants, and Ovolocytosis in Human Populations.* Oxford, UK: Oxford University Press.

Lock, M. and P. Kaufert. 2001. Menopause, local biologies, and cultures of aging. *American Journal of Human Biology* 13: 494–504.

Lockwood, C. A., W. H. Kimbel, and D. C. Johanson. 2000. Temporal trends and metric variation in the mandibles and dentition of *Australopithecus afarensis. Journal of Human Evolution* 39: 23–55.

Londo, J. P., Y.-C. Chiang, K.-H. Hung, T.-Y. Chiang, and B. A. Schaal. 2006. Phylogeography of Asian wild rice, *Oryza rufipogon,* reveals multiple independent domestications of cultivated rice, *Oryza sativa. Proceedings of the National Academy of Sciences USA* 103: 9578–9583.

Long, J. C., J. Li, and M. E. Healy. 2009. Human DNA sequences: more variation and less race. *American Journal of Physical Anthropology* 139: 23–34.

Long, J. C. and R. A. Kittles. 2003. Human genetic diversity and the nonexistence of biological races. *Human Biology* 75: 449–471.

Loomis, W. F. 1967. Skin-pigment regulation of vitamin-D biosynthesis in man. *Science* 157: 501–506.

Lordkipanidze, D., T. Jashashvili, A. Vekua, M. S. Ponce de Leon, C. P. E. Zollikofer, G. P. Rightmire, H. Pontzer, R. Ferring, O. Oms, M. Tappen, M. Bukhsianidze, R. Agusti, R. Kahlke, G. Kiladze, B. Martinez-Navarro, A. Mouskhelishvili, M. Nioradze, and L. Rook. 2007. Postcranial evidence from early *Homo* from Dmanisi, Georgia. *Nature* 449: 305–310.

Lordkipanidze, D., M. S. Ponce de Leon, A. Margvelashvili, Y. Rak, G. P. Rightmire, A. Vekua, and P. E. Zollikofer. 2013. A complete skull from Dmanisi, Georgia, and evolutionary biology of early *Homo. Science* 342: 326–331.

Louwe Kooijmans, L. P., Y. Smirnov, R. S. Solecki, P. Villa, and T. Weber. 1989. On the evidence for Neandertal burial. *Current Anthropology* 30: 322–326.

Lovejoy, C. O., G. Suwa, S. W. Simpson, J. H. Matternes, and T. D. White. 2009. The great divides: *Ardipithecus ramidus* reveals the postcrania of our last common ancestors with African apes. *Science* 326: 100–106.

Lwanga, J. S., T. T. Struhsaker, P. J. Struhsaker, T. M. Butynski, and J. C. Mitani. 2011. Primate population dynamic over 32.9 years at Ngogo, Kibale National Park, Uganda. *American Journal of Primatology* 73: 997–1011.

Lyell, C. 1830–33. *Principles of Geology.* London: Murray.

Lynch, M. and B. Walsh. 1998. *Genetics and Analysis of Quantitative Traits.* Sunderland, MA: Sinauer.

Macdougall, D. 2008. *Nature's Clocks: How Scientists Measure the Age of Almost Everything.* Berkeley: University of California Press.

Maddox, B. 2002. *Rosalind Franklin: The Dark Lady of DNA.* New York: HarperCollins.

Madrigal, L., B. Ware, R. Miller, G. Saenz, M. Chavez, and D. Dykes. 2001. Ethnicity, gene flow and population subdivision in Limon, Costa Rica. *American Journal of Physical Anthropology* 114: 99–108.

Madrigal, L. and J. Willoughby. 2010. Ongoing evolution in humans. Pp. 207–221 in C. S. Larsen, ed. *A Companion to Biological Anthropology.* Chichester, UK: Wiley-Blackwell.

Malone, N., A. H. Wade, A. Fuentes, E. P. Riley, M. Remis, and C. J. Robinson. 2014. Ethnoprimatology: critical interdisciplinarity and multispecies approaches in anthropology. *Critique of Anthropology* 34: 8–29.

Malthus, T. R. 1798. *An Essay on the Principle of Population.* Reprinted 2004, ed. Philip Appleman. New York: Norton.

Manson, J. H., S. Perry, and A. R. Parish. 1997. Nonconceptive sexual behavior in bonobos and capuchins. *International Journal of Primatology* 18: 767–786.

Maples, W. R. and M. Browning. 1994. *Dead Men Do Tell Tales.* New York: Doubleday.

Marcus, G. F. and S. E. Fisher. 2003. *FOXP2* in focus: what can genes tell us about speech and language. *Trends in Cognitive Sciences* 7: 257–262.

Marks, J. 1994. Black, white, other. *Discover* December: 32–35.

Marks, J. 1995. *Human Biodiversity: Genes, Race, and History.* New York: Aldine de Gruyter.

Marks, J. 1996. Science and race. *American Behavioral Scientist* 40: 123–133.

Marlar, R. A., B. L. Leonard, B. M. Billman, P. M. Lambert, and J. E. Marlar. 2000. Biochemical evidence of cannibalism at a prehistoric Puebloan site in southwestern Colorado. *Nature* 407: 74–78.

Marquez, S., K. Mowbray, G. J. Sawyer, T. Jacob, and A. Silvers. 2001. New fossil hominid calvaria from Indonesia—Sambungmacan 3. *Anatomical Record* 262: 344–368.

Marshak, S. 2012. *Earth: Portrait of a Planet,* 4th ed. New York: Norton.

Marshall, G. A. 1968. Racial classifications: popular and scientific. Pp. 149–166 in M. Mead, T. Dobzhansky, E. Tobach, and R. E. Light, eds. *Science and the Concept of Race.* New York: Columbia University Press.

Martin, D. L. and D. W. Frayer, eds. 1997. *Troubled Times: Violence and Warfare in the Past.* Amsterdam: Gordon and Breach.

Martin, D. L., R. P. Harrod, and V. R. Perez, eds. 2012. *The Bioarchaeology of Violence.* Gainesville: University Press of Florida.

Martin, L. 1985. Significance of enamel

thickness in hominoid evolution. *Nature* 314: 260–263.

Martin, N., L. Eaves, and D. Loesch. 1982. A genetic analysis of covariation between finger ridge counts. *Annals of Human Biology* 9: 539–552.

Martin, R. A. 2004. *Missing Links: Evolutionary Concepts and Transitions through Time.* Sudbury, MA: Jones and Bartlett.

Martin, R. D. 1990. *Primate Origins and Evolution: A Phylogenetic Reconstruction.* London: Chapman & Hall.

Martin, R. D. 1993. Primate origins: plugging the gaps. *Nature* 363: 223–234.

Masters, J., M. Gamba, and F. Génin. 2013. What's in a name? Higher level taxonomy of the prosimian primates. Pp. 3–9 in J. Masters and F. Genin, eds. *Leaping Ahead: Advances in Prosimian Biology.* New York: Springer.

Mayor, A. 2001. *The First Fossil Hunters: Paleontology in Greek and Roman Times.* Princeton, NJ: Princeton University Press.

Mayr, E. 1942. *Systematics and the Origin of Species.* New York: Columbia University Press.

Mayr, E. 1970. *Populations, Species, and Evolution.* Cambridge, MA: Harvard University Press.

Mayr, E. 2004. 80 years of watching the evolutionary scenery. *Science* 305: 46–47.

McBrearty, S. and A. S. Brooks. 2000. The revolution that wasn't: a new interpretation of the origin of modern human behavior. *Journal of Human Evolution* 39: 453–563.

McCalman, I. 2009. *Darwin's Armada: Four Voyages and the Battle for the Theory of Evolution.* New York: Norton.

McCarthy, J. J., O. F. Canziani, N. A. Leary, D. J. Dokken, and K. S. White. 2001. *Climate Change 2001: Impacts, Adaptations, and Vulnerability.* Cambridge, UK: Cambridge University Press.

McCorriston, J. 2000. Wheat domestication. Pp. 158–174 in K. Kiple and C. Ornelas, eds. *Cambridge World History of Food and Nutrition.* New York: Cambridge University Press.

McDade, T. W., J. Rutherford, L. Adair, and C. W. Kuzawa. 2009. Early origins of inflammation: microbial exposures in infancy predict lower levels of C-reactive protein in adulthood. *Proceedings of the Royal Society of London B* 277: 1129–1137.

McDougall, I., F. H. Brown, and J. G. Fleagle. 2005. Stratigraphic placement and age of modern humans from Kibish, Ethiopia. *Nature* 433: 733–736.

McGovern, P. E. 2003. *Ancient Wine: The Search for the Origins of Viniculture.* Princeton, NJ: Princeton University Press.

McGraw, W. S. 2010. Primates defined. Pp. 222–242 in C. S. Larsen, ed. *A Companion to Biological Anthropology.* Chichester, UK: Wiley-Blackwell.

McGraw, W. S., and L. R. Berger. 2014. Raptors and primate evolution. *Evolutionary Anthropology* (in press) 22:280–293.

McGraw, W. S., C. Cooke, and S. Shultz. 2006. Primate remains from African crowned eagle (*Stephanoaetus coronatus*) nests in Ivory Coast's Taï Forest: implications for primate predation and early hominid taphonomy in South Africa. *American Journal of Physical Anthropology* 131: 151–165.

McGraw, W. S. and K. Zuberbühler. 2008. Socioecology, predation, and cognition in a community of West African monkeys. *Evolutionary Anthropology* 17: 254–266.

McGraw, W. S., K. Zuberbühler, and R. Noe, eds. 2007. *Monkeys of the Taï Forest: An African Primate Community.* Cambridge, UK: Cambridge University Press.

McGrew, W. C. 1998. Culture in nonhuman primates. *Annual Review of Anthropology* 27: 301–328.

McGrew, W. C., L. F. Marchant, and T. Nishida. 1996. *Great Ape Societies.* Cambridge, UK: Cambridge University Press.

McHenry, H. M. 2002. Introduction to the fossil record of human ancestry. Pp. 401–405 in W. C. Hartwig, ed. *The Primate Fossil Record.* Cambridge, UK: Cambridge University Press.

McHenry, H. M. and K. Coffing. 2000. *Australopithecus* to *Homo*: Transformations in body and mind. *Annual Review of Anthropology* 29: 125–146.

McKee, J. K. 1996. Faunal evidence and Sterkfontein Member 2 foot bones of early hominid. *Science* 271: 1301.

McKee, J. K. 2003. *Sparing Nature: The Conflict between Human Population Growth and Earth's Biodiversity.* New Brunswick, NJ: Rutgers University Press.

McKee, J. K., F. E. Poirier, and W. S. McGraw. 2005. *Understanding Human Evolution,* 4th ed. Upper Saddle River, NJ: Pearson Prentice Hall.

McKee, J. K., P. W. Sciulli, C. D. Fooce, and T. A. Waite. 2003. Forecasting global biodiversity threats associated with human population growth. *Biological Conservation* 115: 161–164.

McPHerron, S. P., Z. Alemseged, C. W. Marean, J. G. Wynn, D. Reed, D. Geraads, R. Bobe, and H. A. Béarat. 2010. Evidence for stone-tool-assisted consumption at Dikika, Ethiopia. *Nature* 466: 857–860.

Meltzer, D. J. 1993. Pleistocene peopling of the Americas. *Evolutionary Anthropology* 1: 157–169.

Meltzer, D. J. 2009. *First Peoples in a New World: Colonizing Ice Age America.* Berkeley: University of California Press.

Mercader, J., H. Barton, J. Gillespie, J. Harris, S. Kuhn, R. Tyler, and C. Boesch. 2007. 4,300-year-old chimpanzee sites and the origins of percussive stone technology. *Proceedings of the National Academy of Sciences USA* 104: 3043–3048.

Mercader, J., M. Panger, and C. Boesch. 2002. Excavation of a chimpanzee stone tool site in the African rainforest. *Science* 296: 1452–1455.

Merriwether, D. A. 2007. Mitochondrial DNA. Pp. 817–830 in D. H. Ubelaker, ed. *Handbook of North American Indians.* Washington, DC: Smithsonian Institution Press.

Meyer, C., C. Lohr, D. Gronenborn, and K. W. Alt 2015. The massacre mass grave of Schoneck-Kilianstadten reveals new insights into collective violence in Early Neolithic Central Europe. *Proceedings of the National Academy of Sciences USA* 112: 11217–11222.

Meyer, M., J.-L. Arguago, C. de Filippo, S. Nagel, A. Aximu-Petri, et al. 2016. Nuclear DNA sequences from the Middle Pleistocene Sima de los Huesos hominins. *Nature* 531: 504–507.

Meyer, M., J.-L. Arsuaga, C. de Filippo, S. Nagel, A. Aximu-Petri, B. Nickel, I. Martinez, A. Gracia, J. M. de Castro, E. Carbonell, J. Kelso, K. Prufer, and S. Paabo. 2016. Nuclear DNA sequences from the Middle Pleistocene Sima de los Huesos hominins. *Nature* 531: 504–508.

Mielke, J. H., L. W. Konigsberg, and J. H. Relethford. 2006. *Human Biological Variation.* New York: Oxford University Press.

Miller, E. R., G. F. Gunnell, and R. D. Martin. 2005. Deep time and the search for anthropoid origins. *Yearbook of Physical Anthropology* 48: 60–95.

Minugh-Purvis, N. 2002. Neandertal growth: examining developmental adaptations in earlier *Homo sapiens.* Pp. 154–173 in P. N. Peregrine, C. R. Ember, and M. Ember, eds. *Physical Anthropology: Original Readings in Method and Practice.* Upper Saddle River, NJ: Prentice Hall.

Mitani, J. C., J. Call, P. Kappeler, R. Palombit, and J. Silk, eds. 2012. *The Evolution of Primate Societies.* Chicago: University of Chicago Press.

Mittermeier, R. A. 2000. Foreword. Pp. xv–xxiii in P. Tyson, ed. *The Eighth Continent: Life, Death, and Discovery in the Lost World of Madagascar.* New York: HarperCollins Publishers.

Moffat, A. S. 2002. New fossils and a glimpse of evolution. *Science* 295: 613–615.

Molleson, T. 1994. The eloquent bones of Abu Hureya. *Scientific American* 271(2): 70–75.

Molnar, S. 2005. *Human Variation: Races, Types, and Ethnic Groups.* Upper Saddle River, NJ: Prentice Hall.

Montagu, A. 1964. Natural selection and man's relative hairlessness. *Journal of the American Medical Association* 187: 356–357.

Monteiro, C. A., E. C. Moura, W. L. Conde, and B. M. Popkin. 2004. Socioeconomic status and obesity in adult populations of developing countries: a review. *Bulletin of the World Health Organization* 82: 940–946.

Moore, J. A. 1999. *Science as a Way of Knowing: The Foundations of Modern Biology.* Cambridge, MA: Harvard University Press.

Moorehead, A. 1969. *Darwin and the Beagle.* New York: Penguin Books.

Rasmussen, D. T. 2002. The origin of primates. Pp. 5–9 in W. C. Hartwig, ed. *The Primate Fossil Record*. Cambridge, UK: Cambridge University Press.

Rasmussen, M., S. L. Anzick, M. R. Waters, P. Skoglund, M. DeGiorgio, T. W. Stafford Jr., S. Rasmussen, I. Moltke, A. Albrechtsen, S. M. Doyle, G. D. Poznik, V. Gudmundsdottir, R. Yadav, A. S. Malaspinas, S. S. White, M. E. Allentoft, O. E. Cornejo, K. Tambets, A. Eriksson, P. D. Heintzman, M. Karmin, T. S. Korneliussen, D. J. Meltzer, T. L. Pierre, J. Stenderup, L. Saag, V. M. Warmuth, M. C. Lopes, R. S. Malhi, S. Brunak, T. Sicheritz-Ponten, I. Barnes, M. Collins, L. Orlando, F. Balloux, A. Manica, R. Gupta, M. Metspalu, C. G. Bustamante, M. Jakobsson, R. Nielsen, and E. Willerslev. 2014. The genome of a late Pleistocene human from a Clovis burial site in western Montana. *Nature* 506: 225–229.

Rasmussen, M., X. Guo, Y. Wang, K. E. Lohmueller, S. Rasmussen, et al. 2011. An Aboriginal Australian genome reveals separate human dispersals into Asia. *Science* 334: 94–98.

Rasmussen, M., M. Sikora, A. Albrechtsen, T. S. Korneliussen, J. V. Moreno-Mayer, et al. 2015. The ancestry and affiliations of Kennewick Man. *Nature* 523: 455–458.

Reich, D., N. Patterson, D. Campbell, A. Tandon, S. Mazieres, N. Ray, et al. 2012. Reconstructing Native American population history. *Nature* 488: 370–374.

Reilly, P. R. 2006. *The Strongest Boy in the World: How Genetic Information Is Reshaping Our Lives*. Cold Spring Harbor, NY: Cold Spring Harbor Laboratory Press.

Relethford, J. H. 1995. Genetics and modern human origins. *Evolutionary Anthropology* 4: 53–63.

Relethford, J. H. 1997. Hemispheric difference in human skin color. *American Journal of Physical Anthropology* 104: 449–457.

Relethford, J. H. 1998. Genetics of modern human origins and diversity. *Annual Review of Anthropology* 27: 1–23.

Relethford, J. H. 2001. Absence of regional affinities of Neandertal DNA with living humans does not reject multiregional evolution. *American Journal of Physical Anthropology* 115: 95–98.

Relethford, J. H. 2001. *Genetics and the Search for Modern Human Origins*. New York: Wiley-Liss.

Relethford, J. H. 2002. Apportionment of global human genetic diversity based on craniometrics and skin color. *American Journal of Physical Anthropology* 118: 393–398.

Relethford, J. H. 2003. *Reflections of Our Past: How Human History Is Revealed in Our Genes*. Boulder, CO: Westview Press.

Relethford, J. H. 2004. Global patterns of isolation by distance based on genetic and morphological data. *Human Biology* 76: 499–513.

Relethford, J. H. 2007. Population genetics and paleoanthropology. Pp. 621–641 in W. Henke

and I. Tattersall, eds. *Handbook of Paleoanthropology: Volume 1. Principles, Methods and Approaches*. Berlin: Springer.

Relethford, J. H. 2009. Race and global patterns of phenotypic variation. *American Journal of Physical Anthropology*. 139: 16–22.

Relethford, J. 2010. The study of human population genetics. Pp. 74–87 in C. S. Larsen, ed. *A Companion to Biological Anthropology*. Chichester, UK: Wiley-Blackwell.

Relethford, J. H. 2011. *Human Population Genetics*. Hoboken, NJ: Wiley-Blackwell.

Remis, M. J. 2000. Preliminary assessments of the impacts of human activities on gorillas (*Gorilla gorilla gorilla*) and other wildlife at Dzanga-Sangha Reserve, Central African Republic. *Oryx* 34: 56–64.

Remis, M. J. 2001. Nutritional aspects of western lowland gorilla diet during seasonal fruit scarcity at Bai Hokou, Central African Republic. *International Journal of Primatology* 22: 807–835.

Renfrew, C. and K. Boyle. 2000. *Archaeogenetics: DNA and the Population Prehistory of Europe*. Cambridge, UK: McDonald Institute Monographs.

Reno, P. L., R. S. Meindl, M. A. McCollum, and C. O. Lovejoy. 2003. Sexual dimorphism in *Australopithecus afarensis* was similar to that of modern humans. *Proceedings of the National Academy of Sciences USA* 100: 9404–9409.

Repcheck, J. 2003. *The Man Who Found Time: James Hutton and the Discovery of the Earth's Antiquity*. Cambridge, MA: Perseus Publishing.

Reynolds, V. 2005. *The Chimpanzees of the Budongo Forest: Ecology, Behavior, and Conservation*. New York: Oxford University Press.

Richard, A. F. 1985. *Primates in Nature*. New York: W. H. Freeman.

Richards, G. D. 2006. Genetic, physiologic and ecogeographic factors to variation in *Homo sapiens: Homo floresiensis* reconsidered. *Journal of Evolutionary Biology*. 19: 1744–1767.

Richards, M. 2003. The Neolithic invasion of Europe. *Annual Review of Anthropology* 32: 135–162.

Richards, M., P. Pettitt, E. Trinkaus, F. Smith, M. Paunovic, and I. Karavanic. 2000. Neanderthal diet and Vindija and Neanderthal predation: the evidence from stable isotopes. *Proceedings of the National Academy of Sciences USA* 97: 7663–7666.

Richards, M. P. and E. Trinkaus. 2009. Isotopic evidence for the diets of European Neanderthals and early modern humans. *Proceedings of the National Academy of Sciences USA* 106: 16034–16039.

Richards, M. P., R. Jacobi, J. Cook, P. B. Pettitt, and C. B. Stringer. 2005. Isotope evidence for the intensive use of marine foods by late upper Paleolithic humans. *Journal of Human Evolution* 49: 390–394.

Richmond, B. G. 2007. Biomechanics of

phalangeal curvature. *Journal of Human Evolution* 53: 678–690.

Richmond, B. G., D. R. Begun, and D. S. Strait. 2001. Origin of human bipedalism: the knuckle-walking hypothesis revisited. *Yearbook of Physical Anthropology* 44: 70–105.

Richmond, B. G. and W. L. Jungers. 2008. *Orronin tugenensis* femoral morphology and the evolution of hominin bipedalism. *Science* 319: 1662–1665.

Ridley, M. 2004. *Evolution*. Malden, MA: Blackwell Science.

Ridley, M. 2006. *Francis Crick: Discoverer of the Genetic Code*. New York: HarperCollins.

Riehl, S., M. Zeidi, and N. J. Conard. 2013. Emergence of agriculture in the foothills of the Zagros Mountains of Iran. *Science* 341: 65–67.

Rightmire, G. P. 1990. *The Evolution of* Homo erectus. Cambridge, UK: Cambridge University Press.

Rightmire, G. P. 1998. Human evolution in the middle Pleistocene: the role of *Homo heidelbergensis*. *Evolutionary Anthropology* 6: 218–227.

Rightmire, G. P. 2009. Middle and later Pleistocene hominins in Africa and southwest Asia. *Proceedings of the National Academy of Sciences USA* 106: 16046–16050.

Rightmire, G. P. 2010. Origins, evolution, and dispersal of early members of the genus *Homo*. Pp. 341–356 in C. S. Larsen, ed. *A Companion to Biological Anthropology*. Chichester, UK: Wiley-Blackwell.

Riley, E. P. 2007. The human-macaque interface: conservation implications of current and future overlap and conflict in Lore Lindu National Park, Sulawesi, Indonesia. *American Anthropologist* 109: 473–484.

Riley, E. P., and A. Fuentes. 2011. Conserving social-ecological systems is Indonesia: human-nonhuman primate interconnections in Bali and Sulawesi. *American Journal of Primatology* 73: 62–74.

Robbins, A. M., M. M. Robbins, N. Gerald-Steklis, and H. D. Steklis. 2006. Age-related patterns of reproductive success among female mountain gorillas. *American Journal of Physical Anthropology* 131: 511–521.

Robbins, L. H. 1974. *The Lothagam Site*. Michigan State University Anthropological Series 1(2).

Roberts, M. B., C. B. Stringer, and S. A. Parfitt. 1994. A hominid tibia from middle Pleistocene sediments at Boxgrove, UK. *Nature* 369: 311–313.

Roberts, R. G. and M. I. Bird. 2012. *Homo* "incendius." *Nature* 485: 586–587.

Rodman, P. S. 1999. Whither primatology?: The place of primates in contemporary anthropology. *Annual Review of Anthropology* 28: 311–339.

Faria, N. R., R. do Socorro da Silva Azevedo, M. U. G. Kraemer, R. Souza, M. S. Cunha, S. C. Hill, et al. 2016. Zika virus in the Americas:

early epidemiological and genetic findings. *Science* 352: 345–349.

Roebroeks, W., M. J. Sier, T. Kellberg Nielsen, D. De Loecker, J. M. Parés, C. E. S. Arps, and H. J. Mucher. 2012. Use of red ochre by early Neandertals. *Proceedings of the National Academy of Sciences USA* 109: 1889–1894.

Roff, D. A. 1992. *The Evolution of Life Histories: Theory and Analysis.* New York: Chapman and Hall.

Rolland, N. 2004. Was the emergence of home bases and domestic fire a punctuated event?: A review of the middle Pleistocene record in Eurasia. *Asian Perspectives* 43: 248–280.

Rosas, A., C. Martínez-Maza, M. Bastir, A. Garcia-Tabernero, C. Lalueza-Fox, R. Huguet, J. E. Ortiz, R. Julià, V. Soler, T. de Torres, E. Martínez, J. C. Cañaveras, S. Sánchez-Moral, S. Cuezva, J. Lario, D. Santamaría, M. de la Rasilla, and J. Fortea. 2006. Paleobiology and comparative morphology of a late Neandertal sample from El Sidrón, Asturias, Spain. *Proceedings of the National Academy of Sciences USA* 103: 19266–19271.

Rose, K. D. 1994. The earliest primates. *Evolutionary Anthropology* 3: 159–173.

Rose, K. D. 2006. *The Beginning of the Age of Mammals.* Baltimore: Johns Hopkins University Press.

Rosenberg, K. and W. Trevathan. 2002. Birth, obstetrics and human evolution. *British Journal of Obstetrics and Gynaecology* 109: 1199–1206.

Rosenberg, K. R. 1992. The evolution of modern human childbirth. *Yearbook of Physical Anthropology* 35: 89–124.

Rosenberg, K. R. and W. Trevathan. 2003. The evolution of human birth. *Scientific American* 13(2): 81–85.

Roseman, C. C. 2004. Detecting inter-regionally diversifying natural selection on modern human cranial form using matched molecular and morphometric data. *Proceedings of the National Academy of Sciences USA* 101: 12824–12829.

Rosenzweig, C., D. Karoly, M. Vicarelli, P. Neofotis, Q. Wu, G. Casassa, A. Menzel, T. Root, N. Estrella, B. Seguin, P. Tryjanowski, C. Liu, S. Rawlins, and A. Imeson. 2008. Attributing physical and biological impacts to anthropogenic climate change. *Nature* 453: 353–358.

Ross, C. F. 2000. Into the light: the origin of anthropoidea. *Annual Review of Anthropology* 29: 147–194.

Ross, C. F. and R. F. Kay, eds. 2004. *Anthropoid Origins: New Visions.* New York: Kluwer Academic/Plenum.

Rossie, J. B., X. Ni, and K. C. Beard. 2006. Cranial remains of an Eocene tarsier. *Proceedings of the National Academy of Sciences USA* 103: 4381–4385.

Rougier, H., I. Crevecoeur, C. Beauval, C. Posth, Flas et al. 2016. Neandertal cannibalism and Neandertal bones used as tools in northern Europe. Nature Scientific Reports 6:29005/ DOI: 10.1038/srep29005.

Rougier, H., S. Milota, R. Rodrigo, M. Gherase, L. Sarcina, O. Moldovan, J. Zilhao, S. Constantin, R. G. Franciscus, C. P. E. Zolliker, M. Ponce de Leon, and E. Trinkaus. 2007. Pestera cu Oase 2 and the cranial morphology of early modern Europeans. *Proceedings of the National Academy of Sciences USA* 104: 1165–1170.

Rowe, N. 1996. *The Pictorial Guide to the Living Primates.* Charlestown, RI: Pogonias.

Roy, S. R., A. M. Schiltz, A. Marotta, Y. Shen, and A. H. Liu. 2003. Bacterial DNA in house and farm barn dust. *Journal of Allergy Clinical Immunology* 112: 571–578.

Rubin, G. M. 2001. Comparing species. *Nature* 409: 820–821.

Rudwick, M. J. S. 1997. *Georges Cuvier, Fossil Bones, and Geological Catastrophes: New Translations and Interpretations of the Primary Texts.* Chicago: University of Chicago Press.

Rudwick, M. J. S. 2005. *Bursting the Limits of Time: The Reconstruction of Geohistory in the Age of Revolution.* Chicago: University of Chicago Press.

Ruff, C. B. 1991. Climate and body shape in hominid evolution. *Journal of Human Evolution* 21: 81–105.

Ruff, C. B. 1993. Climatic adaptation and hominid evolution: the thermoregulatory imperative. *Evolutionary Anthropology* 2: 53–60.

Ruff, C. B. 1994. Morphological adaptation to climate in modern and fossil hominids. *Yearbook of Physical Anthropology* 37: 65–107.

Ruff, C. B. 2002. Variation in human body size and shape. *Annual Review of Anthropology* 31: 211–232.

Ruff, C. B. 2005. Mechanical determinants of bone form: insights from skeletal remains. *Journal of Musculoskeletal and Neuronal Interactions* 5: 202–212.

Ruff, C. B. 2006. Gracilization of the modern human skeleton. *American Scientist* 94: 508–514.

Ruff, C. B. 2008. Biomechanical analyses of archaeological human skeletons. Pp. 183–206 in M. A. Katzenberg and S. R. Saunders, eds. *Biological Anthropology of the Human Skeleton,* 2nd ed. Hoboken, NJ: John Wiley & Sons.

Ruff, C. B. and M. L. Burgess. 2015. How much more would KNM-WT 15000 have grown? *Journal of Human Evolution* 80: 74–82.

Ruiz-Pesini, E., D. Mishmar, M. Brandon, V. Procaccio, and D. C. Wallace. 2004. Effects of purifying and adaptive selection on regional variation in human mtDNA. *Science* 303: 223–226.

Ryan, T. M. and C. N. Shaw. 2015. Gracility of the modern *Homo sapiens* skeleton is the result of decreased mechanical loading. *Proceedings of the National Academy of Sciences USA* 112: 372–377.

Sabeti, P. C., S. F. Schaffner, B. Fry, J. Lohmueller, P. Varilly, O. Shamovsky, A. Palma, T. S. Mikkelsen, D. Altshuler, and E. S. Lander.

2006. Positive natural selection in the human lineage. *Science* 312: 1614–1620.

Samson, M., F. Libert, B. J. Doranz, J. Rucker, C. Liesnand, C. M. Farber, et al. 1996. Resistance to HIV-1 infection in Caucasian individuals bearing mutant alleles of the CCR-5 chemokine receptor gene. *Nature* 382: 722–725.

Sankararaman, S., S. Mallick, M. Dannemann, K. Prüfer, J. Kelso, S. Pääbo, N. Patterson, and D. Reich. 2014. The genomic landscape of Neanderthal ancestry in present-day humans. *Nature* 507: 354–357.

Santé-Lhoutellier, V., T. Astruc, P. Marinova, E. Greve, and P. Gatellier. 2008. Effect of meat cooking on physicochemical state and in vitro digestibility of myofibrillar proteins. *Journal of Agricultural Food Chemistry* 56: 1488–1494.

Sapolsky, R. M. 2004. Of mice, men, and genes. *Natural History* May: 21–24, 31.

Sapolsky, R. M. 2004. Social status and health in humans and other animals. *Annual Review of Anthropology* 33: 393–418.

Sapolsky, R. M. 2005. The influence of social hierarchy on primate health. *Science* 308: 648–652.

Sapolsky, R. M. 2006. Social cultures among nonhuman primates. *Current Anthropology* 47: 641–656.

Sardi, M. L., P. S. Novellino, and H. M. Pucciarelli. 2006. Craniofacial morphology in the Argentine center-west: consequences of the transition to food production. *American Journal of Physical Anthropology* 130: 333–343.

Sattenspiel, L. and D. A. Herring. 2010. Emerging themes in anthropology and epidemiology: geographic spread, evolving pathogens, and syndemics. Pp. 167–178 in C. S. Larsen, ed. *A Companion to Biological Anthropology.* Chichester, UK: Wiley-Blackwell.

Saunders, M. A., M. F. Hammer, and M. W. Nachman. 2002. Nucleotide variability in G6pd and the signature of malarial selection in humans. *Genetics* 162: 1849–1861.

Savolainen, P., Y. Zhang, J. Luo, J. Lundeberg, and T. Leitner. 2002. Genetic evidence for an East Asian origin of domestic dog. *Science* 298: 1610–1613.

Scheinfeldt, L. B., S. Soi, and S. A. Tishkoff. 2010. Working toward a synthesis of archaeological, linguistic, and genetic data for inferring African population history. *Proceedings of the National Academy of Sciences USA* 107(suppl. 2): 8931–8938.

Schmitz, R. W. 1997. Neandertal (Feldhofer Grotte). Pp. 710–711 in F. Spencer, ed. *History of Physical Anthropology: An Encyclopedia.* New York: Garland.

Schmitz, R. W., D. Serre, G. Bonani, S. Feine, F. Hillgruber, H. Krainitzki, S. Pääbo, and F. H. Smith. 2002. The Neandertal type site revisited: interdisciplinary investigations of skeletal remains from the Neander Valley, Germany. *Proceedings of the National*

Academy of Sciences USA 99: 13342–13347.

Schoenemann, P. T. 2006. Evolution of the size and functional areas of the human brain. *Annual Review of Anthropology* 35: 379–406.

Schoeninger, M. J. 2010. Diet reconstruction and ecology using stable isotope ratios. Pp. 445–464 in C. S. Larsen, ed. *A Companion to Biological Anthropology.* Chichester, UK: Wiley-Blackwell.

Schroeder, L., J.E. Scott, H.M. Garvin, M.F. Laird, M. Dembo, D.Radovcic, L.R. Bergr, D.J. de Ruiter, and R.r. Acikermann. 2016. Skull diversity in the Homo lineage and the relative position of *Homo naledi. Journal of Human Evolution* http://dx.doi.org/10.1016/j.jhevol.2016.09.014.

Schultz, A. H. 1969. *The Life of Primates.* New York: Universe.

Schurr, T. G. 2000. Mitochondrial DNA and the peopling of the New World. *American Scientist* 88: 246–253.

Schurr, T. G. 2004. The peopling of the New World. *Annual Review of Anthropology* 33: 551–583.

Schurr, T. G. and S. T. Sherry. 2004. Mitochondrial DNA and Y chromosome diversity and the peopling of the Americas: evolutionary and demographic evidence. *American Journal of Human Biology* 16: 420–439.

Schwartz, J. H. 1999. *Sudden Origins: Fossils, Genes, and the Emergence of Species.* New York: Wiley.

Schwartz, J. H. and I. Tattersall. 2000. The human chin revisited: what is it and who has it? *Journal of Human Evolution* 38: 367–409.

Schwartz, J. H. and I. Tattersall. 2002. *The Human Fossil Record, Volume One: Terminology and Craniodental Morphology of Genus* Homo *(Europe).* New York: Wiley-Liss.

Schwartz, J. H. and I. Tattersall. 2003. *The Human Fossil Record: Volume Two, Craniodental Morphology of Genus* Homo *(Africa and Asia).* New York: Wiley-Liss.

Schwartz, J. H. and I. Tattersall. 2005. *The Human Fossil Record, Volume Four: Craniodental Morphology of Early Hominids (Genera* Australopithecus, Paranthropus, Orrorin) *and Overview.* Hoboken, NJ: Wiley-Liss.

Scott, E. C. 2004. *Evolution vs. Creationism: An Introduction.* Westport, CT: Greenwood Press.

Scott, G. R. and C. G. Turner II. 1997. *The Anthropology of Modern Human Teeth: Dental Morphology and Its Variation in Recent Human Populations.* Cambridge, UK: Cambridge University Press.

Scrimshaw, N. S. and E. B. Murray. 1988. The acceptability of milk and milk products in populations with a high prevalence of lactose intolerance. *American Journal of Clinical Nutrition* 48(suppl): 1083–1159.

Seager, R., Y. Kushnir, C. Herweijer, and N. Naik. 2005. Modeling of tropical forcing of persistent droughts and pluvials over western North America. *Journal of Climate* 18: 4068–4091.

Segalen, L., J. A. Lee-Thorp, and T. Cerling. 2007. Timing of C_4 grass expansion across sub-Saharan Africa. *Journal of Human Evolution* 53: 549–559.

Seiffert, E. R. 2006. Revised age estimates for the later Paleogene mammal faunas of Egypt and Oman. *Proceedings of the National Academy of Sciences USA* 103: 5000–5005.

Seiffert, E. R. 2012. Early primate evolution in Afro-Arabia. *Evolutionary Anthropology* 21: 239–253.

Seiffert, E. R., E. L. Simons, W. C. Clyde, J. B. Rossie, Y. Attia, T. M. Bown, P. Chatrath, and M. E. Mathison. 2005. Basal anthropoids from Egypt and the antiquity of Africa's higher primate radiation. *Science* 310: 300–304.

Selinus, O. 2005. *Essentials of Medical Geology: Impacts of the Natural Environment on Public Health.* Amsterdam, Netherlands: Elsevier Academic Press.

Semaw, S. 2000. The world's oldest stone artefacts from Gona, Ethiopia: their implications for understanding stone technology and patterns of human evolution between 2.6–1.5 million years ago. *Journal of Archaeological Science* 27: 1197–1214.

Semaw, S., P. Renne, J. W. K. Harris, C. S. Feibel, R. L. Bernor, N. Fesseha, and K. Mowbray. 1997. 2.5-Million-year-old stone tools from Gona, Ethiopia. *Nature* 385: 333–336.

Semino, O., G. Passarino, P. J. Oefner, A. A. Lin, S. Arbuzova, L. E. Beckman, G. De Benedictis, P. Francalacci, A. Kouvatsi, S. Limborska, M. Marcikiae, A. Mika, B. Mika, D. Primorac, A. S. Santachiara-Benerecetti, L. L. Cavalli-Sforza, and P. A. Underhill. 2000. The genetic legacy of Paleolithic *Homo sapiens sapiens* in extant Europeans: a Y chromosome perspective. *Science* 290: 1155–1159.

Senut, B., M. Pickford, D. Gommery, P. Mein, K. Cheboi, and Y. Coppens. 2001. First hominid from the Miocene (Lukeino Formation, Kenya). *Comptes Rendus* 332: 137–144.

Sereno, P. C., E. Garcea, H. Jousse, C. M. Stojanowski, J.-F. Saliège, A. Maga, O. A. Ide, J. K. Knudson, A. M. Mercuri, T. W. Stafford, T. G. Kaye, C. Giraudi, I. M. N'siala, E. Cocca, H. M. Moots, D. B. Dutheil, and J. P. Stivers. 2008. Lakeside cemeteries in the Sahara: 5,000 years of Holocene population and environmental change. *PLoS One* 3(8): e2995. DOI: 10.1371/journal.pone.0002995.

Serre, D., A. Langaney, M. Chech, M. Teschler-Nicola, M. Paunovic, P. Mennecier, M. Hofreiter, G. Possnert, and S. Paabo. 2004. No evidence of Neandertal mtDNA contribution to early modern humans. *PLoS Biology* 2(3). DOI: 10.1371/journal.pbio.0020057.

Shackelford, L. L. 2007. Regional variation in the postcranial robusticity of late upper Paleolithic humans. *American Journal of Physical Anthropology* 133: 655–668.

Shah, S. 2016. Pandemic: Tracking Contagions, from Cholera to Ebola and Beyond. Sarah Crichton Books, New York.

Shang, H., H. Tong, S. Zhang, F. Chen, and E. Trinkaus. 2007. An early modern human from Tianyuan Cave, Zhoukoudian, China. *Proceedings of the National Academy of Sciences USA* 104: 6573–6578.

Shapiro, H. L. 1962. *The Pitcairn Islanders.* New York: Simon & Schuster.

Shapiro, H. L. 1974. *Peking Man: The Discovery, Disappearance and Mystery of a Priceless Scientific Treasure.* New York: Simon & Schuster.

Sharpe, T. 2015. The birth of the geological map. *Science* 347: 230–231.

Shea, J. J. 2003. Neandertals, competition, and the origin of modern human behavior in the Levant. *Evolutionary Anthropology* 12: 173–187.

Shea, J. J. 2006. Interdisciplinary approaches to the evolution of hominid diets. *Evolutionary Anthropology* 15: 204–206.

Shen, G., T.-L. Ku, H. Cheng, R. L. Edwards, Z. Yuan, and Q. Wang. 2001. High-precision u-series dating of locality 1 at Zhoukoudian, China. *Journal of Human Evolution* 41: 679–688.

Shen, G., W. Wang, Q. Wang, J. Zhao, K. Collerson, C. Zhou, and P. V. Tobias. 2002. U-series dating of Liujiang hominid site in Guangxi, Southern China. *Journal of Human Evolution* 43: 817–830.

Shen, G., X. Gao, B. Gao, and D. E. Granger. Age of Zhoukoudian *Homo erectus* determined with $^{26}A/^{10}Be$ burial dating. *Nature* 458: 198–200.

Shendure, J. and J. M. Akey. 2015. The origins, determinants, and consequences of human mutations. *Science* 349: 1478–1483.

Shipman, P. 2001. *The Man Who Found the Missing Link.* New York: Simon & Schuster.

Shipman, P. 2002. Hunting the first hominid. *American Scientist* 90: 25–27.

Shipman, P. 2002. *The Evolution of Racism: Human Differences and the Use and Abuse of Science.* Cambridge, MA: Harvard University Press.

Shipman, P. 2003. We are all Africans. *American Scientist* 91: 496–499.

Shirley, N. R., R. J. Wilson, and L. M. Jantz. 2011. Cadaver use at the University of Tennessee's Anthropological Research Facility. *Clinical Anatomy* 24: 372–380.

Sholtis, S. and K. Weiss. 2005. Phenogenetics: genotypes, phenotypes, and variation. Pp. 499–523 in B. Hallgrimson and B. K. Hall, eds. *Variation: A Central Concept in Biology.* Burlington, MA: Elsevier Academic Press.

Shoshani, J., C. P. Groves, E. L. Simons, and G. F. Gunnell. 1996. Primate phylogeny: morphological vs. molecular results. *Molecular Phylogenetics and Evolution* 5: 102–154.

Shreeve, J. 1994. Terms of estrangement. *Discover* 15(11): 56–63.

Shreeve, J. 2015. Mystery man. *National Geographic* 228(4): 30–56.

Shriver, M. D., E. J. Parra, S. Dios, C. Bonilla,

H. Norton, C. Jovel, C. Pfaff, C. Jones, A. Massac, N. Cameron, A. Baron, T. Jackson, G. Argyropoulos, L. Jin, C. J. Hoggart, P. M. McKeigue, and R. Kittles. 2003. Skin pigmentation, biogeographical ancestry and admixture mapping. *Human Genetics* 112: 387–399.

Shultz, S., R. Noe, W. S. McGraw, and R. I. M. Dunbar. 2004. A community-level evaluation of the impact of prey behavioural and ecological characteristics on predator diet composition. *Proceedings of the Royal Society of London B* 271: 725–732.

Sicherer, S. H., A. Muñoz-Furlong, and H. A. Sampson. 2003. Prevalence of peanut and tree nut allergy in the United States is determined by means of a random digit dial telephone survey: a 5-year follow-up study. *Journal of Allergy Clinical Immunology* 112: 1203–1207.

Sievert, L. L. 2006. *Menopause: A Biocultural Perspective*. Newark, NJ: Rutgers University Press.

Sigmon, B. A. and J. S. Cybulski, eds. 1981. Homo erectus: *Papers in Honor of Davidson Black*. Toronto: University of Toronto Press.

Simons, E. L. 1972. *Primate Evolution: An Introduction to Man's Place in Nature*. New York: Macmillan.

Simons, E. L. 1990. Discovery of the oldest known anthropoidean skull from the Paleogene of Egypt. *Science* 247: 1567–1569.

Simons, E. L. 1995. Skulls and anterior teeth of *Catopithecus* (Primates: Anthropoidea) from the Eocene. *Science* 268: 1885–1888.

Simons, E. L. and P. C. Ettel. 1970. *Gigantopithecus. Scientific American* 222(1): 77–85.

Simons, E. L. and T. Rasmussen. 1994. A whole new world of ancestors: Eocene anthropoideans from Africa. *Evolutionary Anthropology* 3: 128–139.

Simons, E. L., E. R. Seiffert, T. M. Ryan, and Y. Attia. 2007. A remarkable female cranium of the early Oligocene anthropoid *Aegyptopithecus zeuxis* (Catarrhini, Propliopithecidae). *Proceedings of the National Academy of Sciences USA* 104: 8731–8736.

Simpson, G. G. 1944. *Tempo and Mode of Evolution*. New York: Columbia University Press.

Simpson, G. G. 1967. *The Meaning of Evolution*. New Haven, CT: Yale University Press.

Simpson, S. W. 1996. *Australopithecus afarensis* and human evolution. Pp. 3–28 in C. R. Ember, M. Ember, and P. Peregrine, eds. *Research Frontiers in Anthropology*. Needham, MA: Simon & Schuster.

Simpson, S. W. 2002. *Australopithecus afarensis* and human evolution. Pp. 103–123 in P. N. Peregrine, C. R. Ember, and M. Ember, eds. *Physical Anthropology: Original Readings in Method and Practice*. Upper Saddle River, NJ: Prentice Hall.

Simpson, S. W. 2010. The earliest hominins. Pp. 314–340 in C. S. Larsen, ed. *A Companion to Biological Anthropology*. Chichester, UK: Wiley-Blackwell.

Simpson S. W. 2013. Before *Australopithecus*: the earliest hominins. Pp. 417–433 in D. R. Begun, ed. *A Companion to Paleoanthropology*. Chichester, UK: Wiley-Blackwell.

Simpson, S. W., J. Quade, N. E. Levin, R. Butler, G. Dupont-Nivet, M. Everett, and S. Semaw. 2008. A female *Homo erectus* pelvis from Gona, Ethiopia. *Science* 322: 1089–1092.

Simpson, S. W., L. Kleinsasser, J. Quade, N. E. Levin, W. C. McIntosh, N. Dunbar, S. Semaw, and M. J. Rogers. 2015. Late Miocene hominin teeth from the Gona Paleoanthropological Research Project. *Journal of Human Evolution* 81: 68–82.

Skinner, M. M., N. B. Stephens, Z. J. Tsegai, A. C. Foote, N. H. Nguyen, T. Gross, et al. .2015. Human-like hand use in *Australopithecus africanus. Science* 347: 395–399.

Slocombe, K. E., and K. Zuberbühler. 2006. Food-associated cells in chimpanzees: Responses to food types or food preferences? *Animal Behaviour* 72: 989–999.

Smail, J. K. 2002. Remembering Malthus: a preliminary argument for a significant reduction in global human numbers. *American Journal of Physical Anthropology* 118: 292–297.

Smith, B. D. 1992. *Rivers of Change: Essays on Early Agriculture in North America*. Washington, DC: Smithsonian Institution Press.

Smith, B. D. 1995. *The Emergence of Agriculture*. New York: Scientific American Library.

Smith, B. D. 2001. Documenting plant domestication: the consilience of biological and archaeological approaches. *Proceedings of the National Academy of Sciences USA* 98: 1324–1326.

Smith, B. D. and M. A. Zeder. 2013. The onset of the Anthropocene. *Anthropocene* 4: 8–13.

Smith, B. H. 1989. Dental development as a measure of life history in primates. *Evolution* 43: 683–688.

Smith, B. H. 1991. Dental development and the evolution of life history in the Hominidae. *American Journal of Physical Anthropology* 86: 157–174.

Smith, B. H. 1993. The physiological age of KNM-WT 15000. Pp. 195–220 in A. Walker and R. Leakey, eds. *The Nariokotome* Homo erectus *Skeleton*. Cambridge, MA: Harvard University Press.

Smith, B. H. 1994. Ages of eruption of primate teeth: a compendium for aging individuals and comparing life histories. *Yearbook of Physical Anthropology* 37: 177–231.

Smith, F. H. 2002. Migrations, radiations and continuity: patterns in the evolution of middle and late Pleistocene humans. Pp. 437–456 in W. C. Hartwig, ed. *The Primate Fossil Record*. Cambridge, UK: Cambridge University Press.

Smith, F. H. 2010. Species, population, and assimilation in later human evolution. Pp. 357–378 in C. S. Larsen, ed. *A Companion to Biological Anthropology*. Chichester, UK: Wiley-Blackwell.

Smith, F. H., A. B. Falsetti, and S. M. Donnelly. 1989. Modern human origins. *Yearbook of Physical Anthropology* 32: 35–68.

Smith, F., I. Janković, and I. Karavanić. 2005. The assimilation model, modern human origins in Europe, and the extinction of Neandertals. *Quaternary International* 137: 7–19.

Smith G. J. D., D. Vijaykrishna, J. Bahl, S. J. Lycett, M. Worobey, O. G. Pybus, S. K. Ma, C. L. Cheung, J. Raghwani, S. Bhatt, J. S. M. Peiris, Y. Guan, and A. Rambaut. 2009. Origins and evolutionary genomics of the 2009 swine-origin H1N1 influenza A epidemic. *Nature* 459: 1122–1126.

Smith, S. L. 2004. Skeletal age, dental age, and the maturation of KNM-WT 15000. *American Journal of Physical Anthropology* 125: 105–120.

Smith, T. M., A. J. Olejniczak, L. B. Martin, and D. J. Reid. 2005. Variation in hominoid molar enamel thickness. *Journal of Human Evolution* 48: 575–592.

Smith, T. M., A. J. Olejniczak, D. J. Reid, R. J. Ferrell, and J.-J. Hublin. 2006. Modern human molar enamel thickness and enamel-dentine junction shape. *Archives of Oral Biology* 51: 974–995.

Smuts, B. B., D. L. Cheney, R. M. Seyfarth, R. W. Wrangham, and T. T. Struhsaker, eds. 1987. *Primate Societies*. Chicago: University of Chicago Press.

Snodgrass, J. J., M. V. Sorensen, L. A. Tarskaia, and W. R. Leonard. 2007. Adaptive dimensions of health research among indigenous Siberians. *American Journal of Human Biology* 19: 165–180.

Soficaru, A., C. Petrea, A. Dobos, and E. Trinkaus. 2007. The human cranium from the Pestera Cioclovina Uscata, Romania. *Current Anthropology* 48: 611–619.

Spencer, F. 1990. *Piltdown: A Scientific Forgery*. London: Oxford University Press.

Spencer, F., ed. 1997. *History of Physical Anthropology: An Encyclopedia*. New York: Garland.

Spencer, F. 1997. Piltdown. Pp. 821–825 in F. Spencer, ed. *History of Physical Anthropology: An Encyclopedia*. New York: Garland Publishing.

Speth, J. D. 2005. News flash: negative evidence convicts Neanderthals of gross mental incompetence. *World Archaeology* 36: 519–526.

Sponheimer, M., B. H. Passey, D. J. de Ruiter, D. Guatelli-Steinberg, T. E. Cerling, and J. A. Lee-Thorp. 2006. Isotopic evidence for dietary variability in the early hominin *Paranthropus robustus. Science* 314: 980–981.

Spoor, F., M. G. Leakey, P. N. Gathogo, F. H. Brown, S. C. Anton, I. McDougall, C. Kiarie, F. K. Manthi, and L. N. Leakey. 2007. Implications of new early *Homo* fossils from Ileret, east of Lake Turkana, Kenya. *Nature* 448: 688–691.

Stafford, N. 2007. The other greenhouse effect. *Nature* 448: 526–528.

Stanford, C. B. 1995. Chimpanzee hunting behavior and human evolution. *American Scientist* 83(3): 256–263.

Stanford, C. B. 2001. *The Hunting Apes.* Princeton, NJ: Princeton University Press.

Stanton, W. 1960. *The Leopard's Spots: Scientific Attitudes toward Race in America, 1815–59.* Chicago: University of Chicago Press.

Steadman, D. W. 2003. *Hard Evidence: Case Studies in Forensic Anthropology.* Upper Saddle River, NJ: Prentice Hall.

Stearns, S. C. 1992. *The Evolution of Life Histories.* New York: Oxford University Press.

Stearns, S. C., S. G. Byars, D. R. Govindaraju, and D. Ewbank. 2010. Measuring selection in contemporary human populations. *Nature Reviews Genetics* 11: 611–622.

Steckel, R. H., J. C. Rose, C. S. Larsen, and P. L. Walker. 2002. Skeletal health in the Western Hemisphere from 4000 B.C. to the present. *Evolutionary Anthropology* 11: 142–155.

Steegmann, A. T. Jr. 2007. Human cold adaptation: an unfinished agenda. *American Journal of Human Biology* 19: 218–227.

Steele, D. G. and J. F. Powell. 1993. Paleobiology of the first Americans. *Evolutionary Anthropology* 2: 138–146.

Steinfeld, H., P. Gerber, T. Wassenaar, V. Castel, M. Rosales, and C. de Haan. 2006. *Livestock's Long Shadow: Environmental Issues and Options.* Rome, Italy: Food and Agriculture Organization of the United Nations.

Stevens, N. J., E. R. Seiffert, P. M. O'Connor, E. M. Roberts, M. D. Schmitz, C. Krause, E. Gorscak, S. Ngasala, T. L. Hieronymus, J. Temu. 2013. Palaeontological evidence for an Oligocene divergence between Old World monkeys and apes. *Nature* 497: 611–614.

Stevenson, J. C., M. A. Grimes, and P. M. Stevenson. 2004. Reproductive measures, fitness, and migrating Mennonites: an evolutionary analysis. *Human Biology* 76: 667–687.

Stewart, T. D. 1977. The Neanderthal skeletal remains from Shanidar Cave, Iraq: a summary of findings to date. *Proceedings of the American Philosophical Society* 121: 121–165.

Stewart, T. D. 1979. *Essentials of Forensic Anthropology.* Springfield, IL: Charles C. Thomas.

Stiner, M. C. 2001. Thirty years on the "Broad Spectrum Revolution" and paleolithic demography. *Proceedings of the National Academy of Sciences USA* 98: 6993–6996.

Stini, W. A. 1995. Osteoporosis in biocultural perspective. *Annual Review of Anthropology* 24: 397–421.

Stinson, S. 2000. Growth variation: biological and cultural factors. Pp. 425–463 in S. Stinson, B. Bogin, R. Huss-Ashmore, and D. O'Rourke, eds. *Human Biology: An Evolutionary and Biocultural Perspective.* New York: Wiley-Liss.

Stinson, S., B. Bogin, R. Huss-Ashmore, and D. O'Rourke, eds. 2000. *Human Biology: An Evolutionary and Biocultural Perspective.* New York: Wiley-Liss.

Stinson, S., B. Bogin, and D. O'Rourke, eds. 2012. *Human Biology: An Evolutionary and Biocultural Perspective,* 2nd ed. Hoboken, NJ: Wiley-Blackwell.

Stinson, S., B. Bogin, D. O'Rourke, and R. Huss-Ashmore. 2012. Human biology: an evolutionary and biocultural perspective. Pp. 3–22 in S. Stinson, B. Bogin, and D. O'Rourke, eds. *Human Biology: An Evolutionary and Biocultural Perspective,* 2nd ed. Hoboken, NJ: Wiley-Blackwell.

Stocker, T. F., D. Qin, G. K. Plattner, M. Tignor, S. K. Allen, J. Boschung, A. Nauels, Y. Xia, V. Bex, and P. M. Midgley, eds. 2013. *Climate Change 2013: The Physical Science Basis. Contribution of Working Group I to the Fifth Assessment Report of the Intergovernmental Panel on Climate Change.* New York: Cambridge University Press.

Stocking, G., ed. 1974. *The Shaping of American Anthropology, 1883–1911: A Franz Boas Reader.* New York: Basic Books.

Stokstad, E. 2003. The vitamin D deficit. *Science* 302: 1886–1888.

Stokstad, E. 2004. Forest loss makes monkeys sick. *Science* 305: 1230–1231.

Stone, A. C. 2000. Ancient DNA from skeletal remains. Pp. 351–371 in M. A. Katzenberg and S. R. Saunders, eds. *Biological Anthropology of the Human Skeleton.* New York: Wiley-Liss.

Stone, L., P. F. Lurquin, and L. L. Cavalli-Sforza. 2007. *Genes, Culture, and Human Evolution: A Synthesis.* Malden, MA: Blackwell.

Stoneking, M. 1993. DNA and recent human evolution. *Evolutionary Anthropology* 2: 60–73.

Storz, J. F. 2010. Genes for high altitudes. *Science* 329: 40–41.

Stott, R. 2003. *Darwin and the Barnacle: The Story of One Tiny Creature and History's Most Spectacular Scientific Breakthrough.* New York: Norton.

Stott, R. 2012. *Darwin's Ghosts: The Secret History of Evolution.* New York: Spiegel & Grau.

Strachan, D. P. 1989. Hay fever, hygiene, and household size. *British Medical Journal* 299: 1259–1260.

Street, M., T. Terberger, and J. Orschiedt. 2006. A critical review of the German Paleolithic hominin record. *Journal of Human Evolution* 51: 551–579.

Strickland, S. S. and P. S. Shetty. 1998. *Human Biology and Social Inequality.* Cambridge, UK: Cambridge University Press.

Strier, K. B. 1994. Myth of the typical primate. *Yearbook of Physical Anthropology* 37: 233–271.

Strier, K. B. 2007. *Primate Behavioral Ecology,* 3rd ed. Boston: Allyn & Bacon.

Strier K. B. 2011. *Primate Behavioral Ecology,* 4th ed. Boston: Pearson/Prentice Hall.

Strier, K. B. 2010. Primate behavior and sociality. Pp. 243–257 in C. S. Larsen, ed. *A Companion to Biological Anthropology.* Chichester, UK: Wiley-Blackwell.

Strier, K. B. and J. P. Boubli. 2006. A history of long-term research and conservation of northern muriquis (*Brachyteles hypoxanthus*) at the Estacao Biologica de Caratinga/ RPPN-FMA. *Primate Conservation* 20: 53–63.

Strier, K. B., J. P. Boubli, F. B. Pontual, and S. L. Mendes. 2006. Human dimensions of northern muriqui conservation efforts. *Ecological and Environmental Anthropology* 2: 44–53.

Stringer, C. and R. McKie. 1998. *African Exodus: The Origins of Modern Humanity.* New York: Henry Holt.

Stringer, C. B., J. C. Finlayson, R. N. E. Barton, Y. Fernández-Jalvo, I. Cáceres, R. C. Sabin, E. J. Rhodes, A. P. Currant, J. Rodríguez-Vidal, F. G. Giles-Pacheco, and J. A. Riquelme-Cantal. 2008. Neanderthal exploitation of marine mammals in Gibraltar. *Proceedings of the National Academy of Sciences USA* 105: 14319–14324.

Strum, S. C. and L. F. Fedigan. 2000. *Primate Encounters: Models of Science, Gender, and Society.* Chicago: University of Chicago Press.

Susman, R. L. 1994. Fossil evidence for early hominid tool use. *Science* 265: 1570–1573.

Susman, R. L. 1998. Hand function and tool behavior in early hominids. *Journal of Human Evolution* 35: 23–46.

Susman, R. L. 2004. *Oreopithecus bamboli:* an unlikely case of hominidlike grip capability in a Miocene ape. *Journal of Human Evolution* 46: 105–117.

Susman, R. L. 2005. *Oreopithecus:* still apelike after all these years. *Journal of Human Evolution* 49: 405–411.

Susman, R. L., J. T. Stern, and W. L. Jungers. 1984. Arboreality and bipedality in Hadar hominids. *Folia Primatologica* 43: 113–156.

Susser, E., J. B. Kirkbride, B. T. Heijmans, J. K. Kresovich, L. H. Lumey, and A. D. Stein. 2012. Maternal prenatal nutrition and health in grandchildren and subsequent generations. *Annual Review of Anthropology* 41: 577–610.

Sussman, R. W. 2014. *The Myth of Race: The Troubling Persistence of an Unscientific Idea.* Cambridge, MA: Harvard University Press.

Sussman, R. W. and P. A. Garber. 2007. Primate sociality. Pp. 636–651 in S. Bearder, C. J. Campbell, A. Fuentes, K. C. Mackinnon, and M. Panger, eds. *Primates in Perspective.* New York: Oxford University Press.

Sussman, R. W., P. A. Garber, and J. M. Cheverud. 2005. Importance of cooperation and affiliation in the evolution of primate sociality. *American Journal of Physical Anthropology* 128: 84–97.

Sutikna, T., M. W. Tocheri, M. J. Morwood, E. W. Saptomo, Jatmiko, R. D. Awe, et al. 2016. Revised stratigraphy and chronology for *Homo floresiensis* at Liang Bua in Indonesia. *Nature* 532: 366–369.

Suwa, G., R. T. Kono, S. Katoh, B. Asfaw, and Y. Beyene. 2007. A new species of great ape from the late Miocene epoch in Ethiopia. *Nature* 448: 921–924.

Suwa, G., R. T. Kono, S. W. Simpson, B. Asfaw, C. O. Lovejoy, and T. D. White. 2009. Paleobiological implications of the *Ardipithecus ramidus* dentition. *Science* 326: 94–99.

Swallow, D. 2003. Genetics of lactase persistence and lactose intolerance. *Annual Review of Genetics* 37: 197–219.

Swindler, D. R. 1998. *Introduction to the Primates*. Seattle: University of Washington Press.

Swisher, C. C. III, W. J. Rink, S. C. Anton, H. P. Schwarcz, G. H. Curtis, A. Suprijo, and S. Widiasmoro. 1996. Latest *Homo erectus* of Java: potential contemporaneity with *Homo sapiens* in Southeast Asia. *Science* 274: 1870–1874.

Swisher, C. C. III, G. H. Curtis, and R. Lewin. 2000. *Java Man*. New York: Scribner.

Sykes, B. 2001. *The Seven Daughters of Eve: The Science That Reveals Our Genetic Ancestry*. New York: Norton.

Szalay, F. S. 1975. *Approaches to Primate Paleobiology. Contributions to Primatology* 5. Basel, Switzerland: S. Karger.

Szalay, F. S. and E. Delson. 1979. *Evolutionary History of the Primates*. New York: Academic Press.

Szalay, F. S., A. L. Rosenberger, and M. DaGosto. 1987. Diagnosis and differentiation of the order Primates. *Yearbook of Physical Anthropology* 30: 75–105.

Tabor, E., ed. 2007. *Emerging Viruses in Human Populations*. Amsterdam, Netherlands: Elsevier.

Takai, M., F. Anaya, N. Shigehara, and T. Setoguchi. 2000. New fossil materials of the earliest New World monkey, *Branisella boliviana*, and the problem of platyrrhine origins. *American Journal of Physical Anthropology* 111: 263–281.

Tamm, E., T. Kivisild, M. Reidla, M. Metspalu, D. G. Smith, C. J. Mulligan, C. M. Bravi, O. Rickards, C. Martinez-Labarga, E. K. Khusnutdinova, S. A. Fedorova, M. V. Golubenko, V. A. Stepanov, M. A. Gubina, S. I. Zhadanov, L. P. Ossipova, L. Damba, M. I. Voevoda, J. E. Dipierri, R. Villems, and R. S. Malhi. 2007. Beringian standstill and spread of Native American founders. *PLoS One* 9: e829.

Tang, H., T. Quertermous, B. Rodriguez, S. L. R. Kardia, X. Zhu, A. Brown, J. S. Pankow, M. A. Province, S. C. Hunt, E. Boerwinkle, N. J. Schork, and N. J. Risch. 2005. Genetic structure, self-identified race/ethnicity, and confounding in case-control association studies. *American Journal of Human Genetics* 76: 268–275.

Tanner, J. M. 1978. *Fetus into Man: Physical Growth from Conception to Maturity*. Cambridge, MA: Harvard University Press.

Tanno, K.-I. and G. Wilcox. 2006. How fast was wild wheat domesticated? *Science* 311: 1886.

Tattersall, I. 1995. *The Fossil Trail*. New York: Oxford University Press.

Tattersall, I. 2007. Madagascar's lemurs: cryptic diversity or taxonomic inflation. *Evolutionary Anthropology* 16: 12–23.

Taubes, G. 2008. The bacteria fight back. *Science* 321: 356–361.

Taylor, R. E. 1995. Radiocarbon dating: the continuing revolution. *Evolutionary Anthropology* 4: 169–181.

Taylor, R. E. 2002. Dating archaeological materials. Pp. 15–35 in P. N. Peregrine, C. R. Ember, and M. Ember, eds. *Archaeology: Original Readings in Method and Practice*. Upper Saddle River, NJ: Prentice Hall.

Taylor, R. E. and M. J. Aitken. 1997. *Chronometric Dating in Archaeology*. New York: Plenum Press.

Teaford, M. F., P. S. Ungar, and F. E. Grine. 2002. Paleontological evidence for the diets of African Plio-Pleistocene hominins with special reference to early *Homo*. Pp. 143–166 in P. S. Ungar and M. F. Teaford, eds. *Human Diet: Its Origin and Evolution*. Westport, CT: Bergin & Garvey.

Teleki, G. 1973. *The Predatory Behavior of Wild Chimpanzees*. Bucknell, PA: Bucknell University Press.

Templeton, A. 2002. Out of Africa again and again. *Nature* 416: 45–51.

Templeton, A. 2005. Haplotype trees and modern human origins. *Yearbook of Physical Anthropology* 48: 33–59.

Teshler-Nicola, M., ed. 2006. *Early Modern Humans at the Moravian Gate: The Mladeč Caves and Their Remains*. New York: Springer.

Thalmann, O., B. Shapiro, P. Cui, V. J. Schuenemann, and S. K. Sawyer. 2013. Complete mitochondrial genomes of ancient canids suggest a European origin of domestic dogs. *Science* 342: 871–874.

The 1000 Genomes Project Consortium. 2015. A global reference for human genetic variation. *Science* 526: 68–74.

Theunissen, B., L. T. Theunissen, and E. Perlin-West. 2006. *Eugène Dubois and the Ape-Man from Java: The History of the First Missing Link and Its Discoverer*. Berlin, Germany: Springer.

Thompson, J. L., G. E. Krovitz, and A. J. Nelson. 2003. *Patterns of Growth and Development in the Genus* Homo. Cambridge, UK: Cambridge University Press.

Thompson, L. 2010. Climate change: the evidence and our options. *Behavior Analyst* 33: 153–170.

Thompson, L. G., H. H. Brecher, E. Mosley-Thompson, D. R. Hardy, and B. G. Mark. 2009. Glacier loss on Kilimanjaro continues unabated. *Proceedings of the National Academy of Sciences USA* 106: 19770–19775.

Thompson, L. G., E. Mosley-Thompson, M. E. Davis, K. A. Henderson, H. H. Brecher, V. S. Zagorodnov, T. A. Mashiotta, P.-N. Lin, V. N. Mikhalenko, D. R. Hardy, and J. Beer. 2002.

Kilimanjaro ice core records: evidence of Holocene climate change in tropical Africa. *Science* 298: 589–593.

Thomson, K. 2011. Jefferson's old bones. *American Scientist* 99: 200–203.

Thorne, A. G. and M. H. Wolpoff. 2003. The multiregional evolution of humans. *Scientific American* 2: 46–53.

Thuiller, W. 2007. Climate change and the ecologist. *Nature* 448: 550–552.

Tianyuan, L. and D. A. Etler. 1992. New middle Pleistocene hominid crania from Yunxian in China. *Nature* 357: 404–407.

Tidwell, J. 2004. Requiem for a primate. *Zoogoer* 33(5): 8–15.

Tishkoff, S. A., F. A. Reed, A. Ranciaro, B. F. Voight, C. C. Babbitt, J. S. Silverman, K. Powell, H. M. Mortensen, J. B. Hirbo, M. Osman, M. Ibrahim, S. A. Omar, G. Lema, T. B. Nyambo, J. Ghori, S. Bumpsted, J. K. Pritchard, T. B. Wray, and P. Deloukas. 2006. Convergent adaptation of human lactase persistence in Africa and Europe. *Nature Genetics* 39: 31–40.

Tishkoff, S. A., R. Varkonyi, N. Cahinhinan, S. Abbes, G. Argyropoulos, G. Destro-Bisol, A. Drousiotou, B. Dangerfield, G. Lefranc, J. Loiselet, A. Piro, M. Stoneking, A. Tagarelli, G. Tagarelli, E. H. Touma, S. Williams, and A. G. Clark. 2001. Haplotype diversity and linkage disequilibrium at human G6pd: recent origin of alleles that confer malarial resistance. *Science* 293: 455–462.

Tobias, P. V. 1967. *The Cranium and Maxillary Dentition of* Zinjanthropus (Australopithecus) boisei. Cambridge, UK: Cambridge University Press.

Tobias, P. V. 1997. Dart, Raymond A. (1893–1988). Pp. 314–315 in F. Spencer, ed. *History of Physical Anthropology: An Encyclopedia*. New York: Garland.

Tobias, P. V. 1997. Taung. Pp. 1022–1025 in F. Spencer, ed. *History of Physical Anthropology: An Encyclopedia*. New York: Garland.

Tocheri, M. W., C. M. Orr, S. G. Larson, T. Sutikna, Jatmiko, E. W. Saptomo, R. A. Due, T. Djubiantono, M. J. Morwood, and W. L. Jungers. 2007. The primitive wrist of *Homo floresiensis* and its implications for hominin evolution. *Science* 317: 1743–1745.

Tomasello, M. and J. Call. 1994. Social cognition in monkeys and apes. *Yearbook of Physical Anthropology* 37: 273–305.

Toth, N. and K. Schick, eds. 2007. *The Oldowan: Case Studies into the Earliest Stone Age*. Bloomington, IN: Stone Age Institute.

Trevathan, W. 2015. Primate pelvic anatomy and implications for birth. *Philosophical Transactions of the Royal Society of London B* 370. DOI: 10.1098/rstb2014.0065.

Trinkaus, E. 1983. *The Shanidar Neandertals*. New York: Academic Press.

Trinkaus, E. 2005. Early modern humans. *Annual Review of Anthropology* 34: 207–230.

Trinkaus, E. 2006. Modern human versus

Neandertal evolutionary distinctiveness. *Current Anthropology* 47: 597–620.

Trinkaus, E. 2007. European early modern humans and the fate of the Neandertals. *Proceedings of the National Academy of Sciences USA* 104: 7367–7372.

Trinkaus, E., O. Moldovan, S. Milota, A. Bilgar, S. Sarcina, S. Athreya, S. Bailey, R. Rodrigo, G. Mircea, T. Higham, C. Ramsey, and J. van der Plicht. 2003. An early modern human from the Pestera cu Oase, Romania. *Proceedings of the National Academy of Sciences USA* 100: 11231–11236.

Trinkaus, E. and P. Shipman. 1993. Neandertals: images of ourselves. *Evolutionary Anthropology* 1: 194–201.

Trinkaus, E. and P. Shipman. 1994. *The Neandertals: Of Skeletons, Scientists, and Scandal.* New York: Vintage.

Trinkaus, E. and J. Svoboda. 2006. *Early Modern Human Evolution in Central Europe: The People of Dolni Vestonice and Pavlov.* New York: Oxford University Press.

Tubiello, F. N. and G. Fischer. 2007. Reducing climate change impacts on agriculture: global and regional effects of mitigation, 2000–2080. *Technological Forcasting and Social Change* 74: 1030–1056.

Tung, T. A. 2011. *Bioarchaeology of Wari Imperialism.* Gainesville: University Press of Florida.

Turner, C. G. II. 1991. *The Dentition of Arctic Peoples.* New York: Garland Publishing.

Ubelaker, D. H. 2010. Issues in forensic anthropology. Pp. 412–426 in C. S. Larsen, ed. *A Companion to Biological Anthropology.* Chichester, UK: Wiley-Blackwell.

Ubelaker, D. H. and H. Scammell. 1992. *Bones: A Forensic Detective's Casebook.* New York: Edward Burlingame.

Ugan, A. 2005. Does size matter?: Body size, mass collecting, and their implications for understanding prehistoric foraging behavior. *American Antiquity* 70: 75–89.

Ulijaszek, S. J. 2008. Seven models of population obesity. *Angiology* 59: S34–S38.

Ulijaszek, S. J., F. E. Johnston, and M. A. Preece. 1998. *The Cambridge Encyclopedia of Human Growth and Development.* Cambridge, UK: Cambridge University Press.

Ulijaszek, S. J. and H. Lofink. 2006. Obesity in biocultural perspective. *Annual Review of Anthropology* 35: 337–360.

Ulijaszek, S. J. and L. M. Schell. 1999. The future of urban environments. Pp. 311–322 in L. M. Schell and S. J. Ulijaszek, eds. *Urbanism, Health and Human Biology in Industrialised Countries.* Cambridge, UK: Cambridge University Press.

Underdown, S. and S. J. Oppenheimer. 2016. Do patterns of covariation between human pelvis shape, stature, and head size alleviate the obstetric dilemma. *Proceedings of the National Academy of Sciences USA* 113. DOI: 10.1073/pnas.15175224113.

Ungar, P. and P. Lucas. 2010. Tooth form and function in biological anthropology. Pp. 516–529 in C. S. Larsen, ed. *A Companion to Biological Anthropology.* Chichester, UK: Wiley-Blackwell.

Ungar, P. S., F. E. Grine, and M. F. Teaford. 2006. Diet in early *Homo:* a review of the evidence and a new model of adaptive versatility. *Annual Review of Anthropology* 35: 209–228.

Ungar, P. S. and M. Sponheimer. 2011. The diets of early hominins. *Science* 334: 190–193.

Ungar, P. S. and M. F. Teaford. 2002. *Human Diet: Its Origin and Evolution.* Westport, CT: Bergin & Garvey.

United Nations Human Settlements Programme. 2005. *2005 Annual Report.* Nairobi, Kenya: UN-HABITAT.

U.S.–Venezuela Collaborative Research Project and N. S. Wexler. 2004. Venezuelan kindreds reveal that genetic and environmental factors modulate Huntington's disease age of onset. *Proceedings of the National Academy of Sciences USA* 101: 3498–3503.

Vahakangas, K. 2004. Ethical aspects of molecular epidemiology of cancer. *Carcinogenesis* 25: 465–471.

Van Arsdale, A. P. and M. H. Wolpoff. 2012. A single lineage in early Pleistocene *Homo:* size variation continuity in early Pleistocene *Homo* crania from East Africa and Georgia. *Evolution* 67: 841–850.

Van den Bergh, G. D., Y. Kaifu, I. Kurniawan, R. T. Kono, A. Brumm, E. Setiyabudi, F. Aziz, and M. J. Morwood. 2016. *Homo floresiensis*-like fossils from the early Middle Pleistocene of Flores. *Nature* 534: 245–248.

Van Schaik, C. and C. D. Knott. 2001. Geographic variation in tool use on Neesia fruits in orangutans. *American Journal of Physical Anthropology* 114: 331–342.

Van Schaik, C. P., M. Ancrenaz, G. Borgen, B. Galdikas, C. D. Knott, I. Singleton, A. Suzuki, S. S. Utami, and M. Merrill. 2003. Orangutan cultures and the evolution of material culture. *Science* 299: 102–105.

Varea, C., C. Bernis, P. Montero, S. Arias, A. Barroso, and B. Gonzalez. 2000. Secular trend and intrapopulational variation in age at menopause in Spanish women. *Journal of Biosocial Science* 32: 383–393.

Vekua, A., D. Lordkipanidze, G. P. Rightmire, J. Agusti, R. Ferring, G. Maisuradze, A. Mouskhelishvili, M. Nioradze, M. P. de Leon, M. Tappen, M. Tvalchrelidze, and C. Zollikofer. 2002. A new skull of early *Homo* from Dmanisi, Georgia. *Science* 297: 85–89.

Veltman, J. A. and H. G. Brunner. 2012. De novo mutations in human genetic disease. *Nature Reviews Genetics* 13: 565–575.

Vignaud, P., P. Duringer, H. T. Mackaye, A. Likius, C. Blondel, J.-R. Boisserie, L. de Bonis, V. Eisenmann, M.-E. Etienne, D. Geraads, F. Guy, T. Lehmann, F. Lihoreau, N. Lopez-Martinez, C. Mourer-Chauvire, O. Otero, J.-C. Rage, M. Schuster, L. Viriot, A. Zazzo, and M. Brunet. 2002. Geology and paleontology of the upper Miocene Toros-Menalla hominid locality, Chad. *Nature* 418: 152–155.

Villa, P. 1992. Cannibalism in prehistoric Europe. *Evolutionary Anthropology* 1: 93–104.

Villanea, F.A., D. A. Bolnick, C. Monroe, R. Worl, R. Cambra, A. Leventhal, and B. M. Kemp 2013. Evolution of a specific O allele (01vG542A) supports unique ancestry of Native Americans. *American Journal of Physical Anthropology* 151: 649–657.

Villmoare, B., W. H. Kimbel, C. Seyoum, C. J. Campisano, E. N. DiMaggio, J. Rowan, D. R. Braun, J. R. Arrowsmith, and K. E. Reed. 2015. Early *Homo* at 2.8 Ma from Ledi-Geraru, Afar, Ethiopia. *Science* 347: 1352–1359.

Visalberghi, E., D. Fragaszy, E. Ottoni, P. Izar, M. G. de Oliveira, and F. R. D. Andrade. 2007. Characteristics of hammer stones and anvils used by wild capuchin monkeys (*Cebus libidinosus*) to crack open palm nuts. *American Journal of Physical Anthropology* 134 (in press) : 132:426-444.

Visalberghi, E., M. Haslam, N. Spagnoletti, and D. Fragaszy. 2013. Use of stone hammer tools and anvils by bearded capuchin monkeys over time and space: construction of an archeological record of tool use. *Journal of Archeological Science* 40(8): 3222–3232.

Vogel, G. 2016. Experts fear Zika's effects may be even worse than thought. Science 352: 1375-1376.

Voland, E., A. Chasiotis, and W. Schiefenhövel, eds. 2005. *Grandmotherhood: The Evolutionary Significance of the Second Half of Female Life.* New Brunswick, NJ: Rutgers University Press.

Volpato, V., R. Macchiarelli, D. Guatelli-Steinberg, I. Fiore, L. Bondioli, and D. W. Frayer. 2012. Hand to mouth in a Neandertal: right-handedness in Regourdou 1. *PLoS One* 7: e43949.

Von Koenigswald, G. H. R. 1952. *Gigantopithecus blacki* von Koenigswald, a giant fossil hominoid from the Pleistocene of Southern China. *Anthropological Papers of the American Museum of Natural History* 43(4): 293–325.

Voris, H. K. 2000. Maps of Pleistocene sea levels in Southeast Asia: shorelines, river systems and time durations. *Journal of Biogeography* 27: 1153–1167.

Wagner, G. 1996. Fission-track dating in paleoanthropology. *Evolutionary Anthropology* 5: 165–171.

Wagner, G. A. 1999. *Age Determination of Young Rocks and Artifacts: Physical and Chemical Clocks in Quarternary Geology and Archaeology.* New York: Springer-Verlag.

Walker, A. and R. Leakey. 1993. *The Nariokotome* Homo erectus *Skeleton.* Cambridge, MA: Harvard University Press.

Walker, A. and P. Shipman. 1996. *The Wisdom of the Bones: In Search of Human Origins.* New York: Knopf.

Walker, A. and P. Shipman. 2005. *The Ape in the Tree: An Intellectual and Natural History of Proconsul.* Cambridge, MA: Belknap Press.

Walker, A. and M. Teaford. 1989. The hunt for *Proconsul. Scientific American* 260(1): 75–82.

Walker, J., R. A. Cliff, and A. G. Latham. 2006. U-Pb isotopic age of the StW 573 hominid from Sterkfontein, South Africa. *Science* 314: 1592–1594.

Walker, P. L. 2001. A bioarchaeological perspective on the history of violence. *Annual Review of Anthropology* 30: 573–596.

Walsh, P. D. 2015. Protecting apes could backfire. *New York Times* September 27: 5.

Wang, E. T., G. Kodama, P. Baldi, and R. K. Moyzis. 2006. Global landscape of recent inferred Darwinian selection for *Homo sapiens. Proceedings of the National Academy of Sciences USA* 103: 135–140.

Ward, C., M. Leakey, and A. Walker. 1999. The new hominid species *Australopithecus anamensis. Evolutionary Anthropology* 7: 197–205.

Ward, C. V., M. G. Leakey, and A. Walker. 2001. Morphology of *Australopithecus anamensis* from Kanapoi and Allia Bay, Kenya. *Journal of Human Evolution* 41: 255–368.

Ward, S. C. and D. L. Duren. 2002. Middle and late Miocene African hominoids. Pp. 385–397 in W. C. Hartwig, ed. *The Primate Fossil Record.* Cambridge, UK: Cambridge University Press.

Washburn, S. L. and I. DeVore. 1961. The social life of baboons. *Scientific American* 204: 62–72.

Waters, M. R. and T. W. Stafford Jr. 2007. Redefining the age of Clovis: implications for the peopling of the Americas. *Science* 315: 1122–1126.

Watson, J. D. 1980. *The Double Helix: A Personal Account of the Discovery of the Structure of DNA.* New York: Norton.

Watson, J. D. 2005. *Darwin: The Indelible Stamp.* Philadelphia: Running Press.

Watson, J. D. and F. H. C. Crick. 1953. Molecular structure of nucleic acids: a structure for deoxyribonucleic acid. *Nature* 171: 964–969.

Weaver, T. D. 2003. The shape of the Neandertal femur is primarily the consequence of a hyperpolar body form. *Proceedings of the National Academy of Sciences USA* 100: 6926–6929.

Weaver, T. D. 2009. The meaning of Neandertal skeletal morphology. *Proceedings of the National Academy of Sciences USA* 106: 16028–16033.

Webb, S. G. 2006. *The First Boat People.* Cambridge, UK: Cambridge University Press.

Weiner, J. 1994. *The Beak of the Finch: A Story of Evolution in Our Time.* New York: Knopf.

Weiner, J. S. and K. P. Oakley. 1954. The Piltdown fraud: available evidence reviewed. *American Journal of Physical Anthropology* 12: 1–7.

Weinstein, K. J. 2007. Thoracic skeletal morphology and high-altitude hypoxia in Andean prehistory. *American Journal of Physical Anthropology* 134: 36–49.

Weiss, E., M. E. Kislev, and A. Hartmann. 2006. Autonomous cultivation before domestication. *Science* 312: 1608–1610.

Weiss, K. M. 1995. *Genetic Variation and Human Disease: Principles and Evolutionary Approaches.* Cambridge, UK: Cambridge University Press.

Weiss, K. M. 2010. Seeing the forest through the gene-trees. *Evolutionary Anthropology* 19: 210–221.

Weiss, K. M. and A. V. Buchanan. 2003. Evolution by phenotype: a biomedical perspective. *Perspectives in Biology and Medicine* 46: 159–182.

Weiss, K. M. and A. V. Buchanan. 2010. Evolution: what it means and how we know. Pp. 41–55 in C. S. Larsen, ed. *A Companion to Biological Anthropology.* Chichester, UK: Wiley-Blackwell.

Weiss, K. M. and D. M. Parker. 2013. Will you stop bugging me? Malaria and the evolutionary challenge that won't go away. *Evolutionary Anthropology* 22: 46–51.

Weiss, M. L. 2000. An introduction to genetics. Pp. 47–85 in S. Stinson, B. Bogin, R. Huss-Ashmore, and D. O'Rourke, eds. *Human Biology: An Evolutionary and Biocultural Perspective.* New York: Wiley-Liss.

Weiss, M. L. and J. Tackney. 2012. An introduction to genetics. Pp. 53–98 in S. Stinson, B. Bogin, and D. O'Rourke, eds. *Human Biology: An Evolutionary and Biocultural Perspective,* 2nd ed. Hoboken, NJ: Wiley-Blackwell.

Westaway, M. C., and D. Lambert. 2014. First Australians: origins. Pp. 2787–2800 in C. Smith, ed. *Encyclopedia of Global Archaeology.* New York: Springer Science.

White, T. D. 2001. Once were cannibals. *Scientific American* 265(2): 58–65.

White, T. D. 2002. Earliest hominids. Pp. 407–417 in W. C. Hartwig, ed. *The Primate Fossil Record.* Cambridge, UK: Cambridge University Press.

White, T. D. 2006. Early hominid femora: the inside story. *Comp-tes Rendus Palevolution* 5: 99–108.

White, T. D. 2006. Human evolution: the evidence. Pp. 65–81 in J. Brockman, ed. *Intelligent Thought: Science versus the Intelligent Design Movement.* New York: Vintage.

White, T. D., B. Asfaw, D. DeGusta, H. Gilbert, G. D. Richards, G. Suwa, and F. C. Howell. 2003. Pleistocene *Homo sapiens* from Middle Awash, Ethiopia. *Nature* 423: 742–747.

White, T. D., B. Asfaw, Y. Beyene, Y. Haile-Selassie, C. O. Lovejoy, G. Suwa, and G. WoldeGabriel. 2009. *Ardipithecus ramidus* and the paleobiology of early hominids. *Science* 326: 75–86.

White, T. D. and P. A. Folkens. 2005. *The Human Bone Manual.* Burlington: Elsevier Academic.

White, T. D., G. Suwa, and B. Asfaw. 1994. *Australopithecus ramidus,* a new species of early hominid from Aramis, Ethiopia. *Nature* 371: 306–312.

White, T. D., G. Suwa, W. K. Hart, R. C. Walter, G. Wolde-Gabriel, J. de Heinzelin, J. D. Clark, B. Asfaw, and E. Vrba. 1993. New discoveries of *Australopithecus* at Maka in Ethiopia. *Nature* 366: 261–267.

White, T. D., G. Suwa, S. Simpson, and B. Asfaw. 2000. Jaws and teeth of *Australopithecus afarensis* from Maka, Middle Awash, Ethiopia. *American Journal of Physical Anthropology* 111: 45–68.

White, T. D., G. WoldeGabriel, B. Asfaw, S. Ambrose, Y. Beyene, R. L. Bernor, J.-R. Boisserie, B. Currie, H. Gilbert, Y. Haile-Selassie, W. K. Hart, L.-J. Hlusko, F. C. Howell, R. T. Kono, T. Lehmann, A. Louchart, C. O. Lovejoy, P. R. Renne, H. Saegusa, E. S. Vrba, H. Wesselman, and G. Suwa. 2006. Asa Issie, Aramis and the origin of *Australopithecus. Nature* 440: 883–889.

White, T. D., C. O. Lovejoy, B. Asfaw, J. P. Carlson, and G. Suwa. 2015. Neither chimpanzee nor human, *Ardipithecus* reveals the surprising ancestry of both. *Proceedings of the National Academy of Sciences USA* 112: 4877–4884.

White House Task Force on Childhood Obesity Report to the President. 2010. *Solving the Problem of Childhood Obesity within a Generation.* Washington, DC: Executive Office of the President of the United States.

Whiten, A. 2005. The second inheritance system of chimpanzees and humans. *Nature* 435: 60–63.

Whiten, A., J. Goodall, W. C. McGrew, T. Nishida, V. Reynolds, Y. Sugiyama, C. E. G. Tutin, R. W. Wrangham, and C. Boesch. 1999. Cultures in chimpanzees. *Nature* 399: 682–685.

Whiten, A., K. Schick, and N. Toth. 2009. The evolution and social transmission of percussive technology: integrating evidence from paleaeoanthropology and primatology. *Journal of Human Evolution* 57: 420–435.

Wild, E. M., M. Tescler-Nicola, W. Kutschera, P. Steier, E. Trinkaus, and W. Wanek. 2005. Direct dating of early upper Paleolithic human remains from Mladeč. *Nature* 435: 332–335.

Wiley, A. S. and J. S. Allen. 2009. *Medical Anthropology: A Biocultural Approach.* New York: Oxford University Press.

Willcox, G. 2013. The roots of cultivation in southwestern Asia. *Science* 341: 39–40.

Williams, S. R. 2006. Menstrual cycle characteristics and predictability of ovulation in Bhutia women in Sikkim, India. *Journal of Physiological Anthropology* 25: 85–90.

Wilson, E. O. 1975. *Sociobiology: The New Synthesis.* Cambridge, MA: Harvard University Press.

Wilson, E. O. 2006. *From So Simple a Beginning: Darwin's Four Great Books [Voyage of the H.M.S. Beagle, The Origin of Species, The Descent of Man, The Expression of Emotions in Man and Animals].* New York: Norton.

Wilson, E. O. 2016. The global solution to extinction. *New York Times* March 13: 7.

Winchester, S. 2001. *The Map That Changed the World: William Smith and the Birth of Modern Geology.* New York: HarperCollins.

WoldeGabriel, G., Y. Haile-Selassie, P. R. Renne, W. K. Hart, S. H. Ambrose, B. Asfaw, G. Heiken, and T. White. 2001. Geology and paleontology of the late Miocene Middle Awash valley, Afar rift, Ethiopia. *Nature* 412: 175–177.

WoldeGabriel, G., T. D. White, G. Suwa, P. Renne, J. de Heinzelin, W. K. Hart, and G. Heiken. 1994. Ecological and temporal placement of early Pliocene hominids at Aramis, Ethiopia. *Nature* 371: 330–333.

Wolfe, N. D., C. P. Dunavan, and J. Diamond. 2007. Origins of major human infectious diseases. *Nature* 447: 279–283.

Wolpoff, M. H. 1996. *Human Evolution.* New York: McGraw-Hill.

Wolpoff, M. H. 1999. *Paleoanthropology,* 2nd ed. New York: McGraw-Hill.

Wolpoff, M. H. 2006. *Neandertals on Our Family Tree.* Denver, CO: John Wesley Powell Memorial Lecture, Southwestern and Rocky Mountain Division of the American Association for the Advancement of Science.

Wolpoff, M. H. and R. Caspari. 1997. *Race and Human Evolution: A Fatal Attraction.* New York: Simon & Schuster.

Wolpoff, M. H., B. Senut, M. Pickford, and J. Hawks. 2002. *Sahelanthropus* or 'Sahelpithecus'. *Nature* 419: 581–582.

Wolpow, N. 2015. Meet the woman who helped discover a new species of human. *Refinery29.* http://www.refinery29.com/2015/09/93844/hannah-morris-homo-discovery#.hr2fv4:1g0m.

Wood, A. R., T. Esko, J. Yang, S. Vedantam, T. H. Pers, S. Gustafsson, et al. 2014. Defining the role of common variation in the genomic and biological architecture of adult human height. *Nature Genetics* 46: 1173–1186.

Wood, B. 1997. The oldest whodunnit in the world. *Nature* 385: 292–293.

Wood, B. 2002. *Palaeoanthropology:* hominid revelations from Chad. *Nature* 418: 133–135.

Wood, B. 2006. A precious little bundle. *Nature* 443: 278–280.

Wood, B. 2010. Systematics, taxonomy, and phylogeny: ordering life, past and present. Pp. 56–73 in C. S. Larsen, ed. *A Companion to Biological Anthropology.* Chichester, UK: Wiley-Blackwell.

World Health Organization. 2013. Chronic diseases and health promotion. http://www.who.int/chp/en/.

Wrangham, R. and R. Carmody. 2010. Human adaptation to the control of fire. *Evolutionary Anthropology* 19: 187–199.

Wrangham, R. and D. Peterson. 1996. *Demonic Males: Apes and the Origins of Human Violence.* Boston: Mariner.

Wrangham, R. W. 2009. *Catching Fire: How Cooking Made Us Human.* New York: Basic Books.

Wrangham, R. W. 1999. Evolution of coalitionary killing. *Yearbook of Physical Anthropology* 42: 1–30.

Wynn, T. 2002. Archaeology and cognitive evolution. *Behavioral and Brain Sciences* 25: 389–438.

Xia, W., S. He, A. Liu, and L, Xu. 2008. Epidemiological study of hip fracture in Beijing, China. *Bone* 43: S13.

Yong, E. 2015. 6 tiny cavers, 15 odd skeletons, and 1 amazing new species of ancient human. *Atlantic Monthly.* http://www.theatlantic.com/science/archive/2015/09/homo-naled i-rising-star-cave-hominin/404362/.

Yudell, M. 2014. *Race Unmasked: Biology and Race in the 20th Century.* New York: Columbia University Press.

Yudell, M., D. Roberts, R. DeSalle, and S. Tishkoff. 2016. Taking race out of human genetics. *Science* 351: 564–565.

Yusupova, G., L. Jenner, B. Rees, D. Moras, and M. Yusupov. 2006. Structural basis for messenger RNA movement on the ribosome. *Nature* 444: 391–394.

Zalasiewicz, J., C. N. Waters, A. D. Barnosky, A. Cearreta, M. Edgeworth, E. C. Ellis, et al. 2015. Colonization of the Americas, 'Little Ice Age' climate, and bomb-produced carbon: their role in defining the Anthropocene. *Anthropocene Review* 2: 117–127.

Zalmout, I. S., W. J. Sanders, L. M. MacLatchy, G. F. Gunnell, Y. A. Al-Mufarreh, M. A. Ali, A.-A. H. Nasser, A. M. Al-Masari, S. A. Al-Sobhi, A. O. Nadhra, A. H. Matari, J. A. Wilson, and P. D. Gingerich. 2010. New Oligocene primate from Saudi Arabia and the divergence of apes and Old World monkeys. *Nature* 466: 360–365.

Zeder, M. A. 1994. After the revolution: post-Neolithic subsistence strategies in northern Mesopotamia. *American Anthropologist* 96: 97–126.

Zeder, M. A. 1999. Animal domestication in the Zagros: a review of past and current research. *Paleorient* 25: 11–25.

Zeder, M. A. 2000. The goats of Ganj Dareh: identification of the earliest directly dated domestic animals. *Science* 287: 2254–2257.

Zeder, M. A. 2006. Central questions in the domestication of plants and animals. *Evolutionary Anthropology* 15: 105–117.

Zeder, M. A. 2008. Domestication and early agriculture in the Mediterranean Basin: origins, diffusion, and impact. *Proceedings of the National Academy of Sciences USA* 105: 11597–11604.

Zeder, M. A., D. G. Bradley, E. Emshwiller, and B. D. Smith. 2006. *Documenting Domestication: New Genetic and Archaeological Paradigms.* Berkeley: University of California Press.

Zhivotovsky, L. A., P. A. Underhill, C. Cinnioglu, M. Kayser, B. Morar, T. Kivisild, R. Scozzari, F. Cruciani, G. Destro-Bisol, G. Spedini, G. K. Chambers, R. J. Herrera, K. K. Yong, D. Gresham, I. Tournev, M. W. Feldman, and L. Kalaydjieva. 2004. The effective mutation rate at Y chromosome short tandem repeats, with application to human population-divergence time. *American Journal of Human Genetics* 74: 50–61.

Zhu, R. X., K. A. Hoffman, R. Potts, C. L. Deng, Y. X. Pan, B. Guo, C. D. Shi, Z. T. Guo, B. Y. Yuan, Y. M. Hou, and W. W. Huang. 2001. Earliest presence of humans in northeast Asia. *Nature* 413: 413–417.

Zhu, R. X., R. Potts, F. Xie, K. A. Hoffman, C. L. Deng, C. D. Shi, Y. X. Pan, H. Q. Wang, G. H. Shi, and N. Q. Wu. 2004. New evidence on the earliest human presence at high northern latitudes in northeast Asia. *Nature* 431: 559–562.

Zilhão, J. and E. Trinkaus. 2002. *Portrait of the Artist as a Child: The Gravettian Human Skeleton from the Abrigo do Lagar Velho and Its Archeological Context. Trabalhos de Arqueologia* 22. Lisbon, Portugal: Instituto Portugues de Arqueologia.

Zilhão, J., D. E. Angelucci, E. Badal-Garcia, F. D'Errico, F. Daniel, L. Dayet, K. Douka, T. F. G. Higham, M. J. Martínez-Sánchez, R. Montes-Bernárdez, S. Murcia-Mascarós, C. Pérez-Sirvent, C. Roldán-Garcia, M. Vanhaeren, V. Villaverde, R. Wood, and J. Zapata. 2010. Symbolic use of marine shells and mineral pigments by Iberian Neandertals. *Proceedings of the National Academy of Sciences USA* 107: 1023–1028.

Zimmer, C. 2006. *Smithsonian Intimate Guide to Human Origins.* Washington, DC: Smithsonian Books.

Zimmer, C. 2006. A fin is a limb is a wing: how evolution fashioned its masterworks. *National Geographic* 210(5): 111–135.

Zimmet, P., K. G. M. M. Alberti, and J. Shaw. 2001. Global and society implications of the diabetes epidemic. *Nature* 414: 782–787.

Zollikofer, C. P. E. and M. S. Ponce de León. 2010. Reconsidering Neanderthal birth: Tabun mom, Kebara dad, Mezmaiskaya baby, and the consequences. *American Journal of Physical Anthropology* Supplement 50, 252.

Zuberbühler, K. 2003. Referential signaling in non-human primates: cognitive precursors and limitations for the evolution of language. *Advances in the Study of Behavior* 33: 265–307.

PERMISSIONS ACKNOWLEDGMENTS

PHOTO CREDITS

Front Matter: Page ii: H Lansdown/Alamy Stock Photo; p. vi: Courtesy of the author; ix: Victor Thompson, University of Georgia; p. x (top): Photo12/UIG/Getty Images; (bottom): Anup Shah/Getty Images; p. xi (top): Juniors Bildarchiv GmbH/Alamy Stock Photo; (bottom): Chris Fitzgerald/CandidatePhotos/The Image Works; p. xii: Sune Wendelboe/Getty Images; p. xiii: CBS via Getty Images; p. xiv: Leonello Calvetti/Science Photo Library/Getty Images; p. xv (top): Edward E. Chatelain; (bottom): © Adriadne Van Zandbergen/Africa Image Library; p. xvvi: Garrreth Bird; p. xvii: © 2003 Photographer P. Plaily/E. Daynès/Eurelios; p. xviii: TTstudio/Shutterstock; p. xix: VCG/VCG via Getty Images; p. xxxi: Clark Larsen.

Chapter 1: Page 2: Victor Thompson, University of Georgia; p. 6 (a): Bettmann/Getty Images; (b): Pasquale Sorrentino/Science Source; (c): Leslie Moore; (d): Horacio Villalobos/Corbis/Getty Images; p. 8: Courtesy of American Philosophical Society; p. 9: Courtesy of American Philosophical Society; p. 10 (a): Giuseppe Vercellotti; (b): Jochen Tack/Alamy;(c-d): Barbara Piperata; (e): Daniel Herard/Science Source; (f): Penelope Breese/Getty Images; p. 14 (top): © The Trustees of the British Museum; (bottom): Photoshot; p. 15: Blend Images/Alamy Stock Photo; p. 17(top): AKG/Science Source; (bottom): Tim Graham/Getty Images; p. 19: Forensic Anthropology Center, The University of Tennessee, Knoxville; p. 20 (top): Wolfgang Kaehler/Getty Images; (bottom): Getty Images; p. 23: W. Perry Conway/Getty Images.

Chapter 2: Page 24: Photo12/UIG/Getty Images; p.26 (both): Bettmann/Getty Images; p. 27 (b): Tim Graham/Getty Images; (c): Miguel Castro/Science Source; (d): Kevin Schafer/Getty Images; (e): Tim Graham/Getty Images; (f): Tim Graham/Getty Images; p. 28 (top): Classic Image/Alamy; (bottom): Scottish National Portrait Gallery; p. 29 (top): Stephen Marshak; (bottom): Hulton Archive/Getty Images; p. 30 (top a): Granger Collection; (top b): Omikron/Science Source; (bottom a): Bettmann/Getty Images; (bottom b):

Wikimedia, pd; p. 31: Time Life Pictures/Getty Images; p. 33 (a): Bettmann/Getty Images; (b): Fred Ramage/Getty Images; p. 34: SPL/Science Source; p. 36: Publiphoto/Science Source; p. 39(a): David Ball/Getty Images; (b): Mary Evans/Science Source; (d): Hulton Archive/Getty Images; (bottom): Wikimedia, pd; p. 40 (background image): Granger Collection; (1): Granger Collection; (2): Mary Evans Picture Library; (3 top): Classic Image/Alamy; (3 bottom): Manfred Gottschalk/Alamy Stock Photo; (4): Carl de Souza/AFP/Getty Images; (4): © Desmond Fitz-Gibbon; (5): Wikimedia, pd; (6): Bettmann/Getty Images; p. 42: De Agostini Picture Library/Bridgeman Art Library; p. 43 (a): From Catalogue of Ernst Benary; image © Copyright Board of Trustees of the Royal Botanic Gardens, Kew; (b): Field Museum/Getty Images; p. 45 (top): Getty Images; (bottom both): Science Source; p. 46: California Institute of Technology; (b-c): Eye of Science/Science Source; p. 48 (a): Bettmann/Getty Images (c): Omikron/Science Source; (d): Science Source; p. 50: CDC/Frederick A. Murphy.

Chapter 3: Page 54 (author): Courtesy of Clark Spencer Larsen; (chimp): Anup Shah/Getty Images; (dna): Benjamin Albiach Galen/Shutterstock; p. 57 (b): M.I. Walker/Science Source; (c): Eye of Science/Science Source; 58 (a): M. I. Walker/Science Source; (b): Michael Abbey/Science Source; (c): Visuals Unlimited; (d): Biophoto Associates/Science Source; (e-1): Michael Abbey/Science Source; (e-2): SPL/Science Source; (f): Jim Zuckerman/Getty Images; (bottom a): CNRI/Science Source; (bottom b): Steve Gschmeissner/Science Source; (bottom c): Eye of Science/Science Source; p. 59 (chromosomes): Biophoto Associates/Science Source;(camel): Richard Nowitz/National Geographic Image Collection; (guinea pig): Corbis; (salamander): dpa picture alliance archive/Alamy Stock Photo; (house fly): Nigel Cattlin/Science Source; (apple): Dionisvera/Shutterstock; (potato): Joe Gough/Shutterstock; (petunia): Roy Morsch/Getty Images; (algae): JP Nacivet/Getty Images;(lemur): Millard H. Sharp/

Science Source; (colubus monkey): Mark boulton/Science Source; (orangutan): Gudkov Andrey/Shutterstock; p. 60: Biophoto Associates/Science Source; p. 61: Keith R. Porter/Science Source; p. 63 (right): Addenbrookes Hospital/Science Source; (left a): L. Willatt/Science Source; (left b): Biophoto Associates/Science Source; p. 67: Steve Gschmeissner/Science Source; p. 68: Krzysztof Odziomek/Shutterstock; p. 73 (a): Clouds Hill Imaging Ltd./Getty Images; (b): Dr. Fred Hossler/Visuals Unlimited; p. 78 (a): John Radcliffe Hospital/Science Source; (b): Bettmann/Getty Images.

Chapter 4: Page 88: Juniors Bildarchiv GmbH/Alamy Stock Photo; p. 91 (b): Kevin Schafer/Getty Images; (c): Mark Boulton/Science Source; p. 92(a): Scott T. Smith/Getty Images; (b): Colin Keates/Getty Images; (c): Somchai Som/Shutterstock; (d): Jonathan Blair/Getty Images; (e): Andre Mueller/Shutterstock; (f): Courtesy of Smithsonian Institution. Photo by J. Hamlin; p. 95 (top): J. Terrence McCabe, University of Colorado; (bottom): James P. Blair/Getty Images; p. 96 (a): Trinity College Library, Cambridge; (b): Genetics Society of America; p. 99: Zuzana Egertova/Alamy Stock Photo; p. 100 (a): W. Perry Conway/Corbis; (b): Jane Burton/Getty Images; (c): Anthony Bannister/Science Source; (d): Eye of Science/Science Source; p. 103 (a): PhotoCuisine RM/Alamy Stock Photo; (b): Envision/Getty Images; p. 104: Stephen Frink Collection/Alamy; p. 105 (top): Michael Wilmer Forbes; Tweedie/Science Source; (bottom both): Roger Tidman/Getty Images; p. 109: Dr. Gopal Murti/Science Source; p. 111 (a); Reuters/Mike Hutchings; (b): Science Source; p. 116 (top): Conor Caffrey/Science Source; (bottom): Acey Harper/Time Life Pictures/Getty Images.

Chapter 5: Page 124: Chris Fitzgerald/Candidate Photos/The Image Works; p. 126: Bettmann/Getty Images; p. 127 (all): Reprinted by permission of the New York Public Library/Art Resource; p. 128: Bettmann/Getty Images; p. 131: Paul D. Stewart/Science Source; p. 132: David M. Phillips/Science Source; p. 133: Heleen/Toddlertoes/Getty Images; p. 136 (top a): SPL/Science Source; (bottom a):

Neil Borden/Science Source; (bottom b): Gwen Robbins, Appalachian State University; p. 138 (both): Barbara Piperata; p. 139: Biophoto Associates/Getty Images; p. 141: Andrew Aitchison/Getty Images; p. 143: Sonya Farrell/Getty Images; p. 150: Topical Press Agency/Getty Images; p. 151: Cynthia Beall; p. 154: David Turnley/Getty Images; p. 157: Robert Wallis/Getty Images; p. 162: AP Photo/Bill Kostroun.

Chapter 6: Page 166: Sune Wendelboe/Getty Images; p. 173 (b): (c) Kennan Ward 2017; (c): Rich Reid/Getty Images; p. 174: Sergey Uryadnikov/Shutterstock; p. 175: Theo Allofs/Getty Images; p. 176 (a): Robert Ross/Getty Images; (b): Noah Dunham; (bottom): Elliotte Rusty Harold/Shutterstock; p. 177: Kornelius Kupczik, Max Planck Institute of Evolutionary Anthropology; p. 178 (all): William K. Sacco; p. 179 (top, both): William K. Sacco; (bottom): Norbert Rosing/National Geographic/Getty Images; p. 180 (top): Martin Harvey/Getty Images; (lemur): kungverylucky/Shutterstock; (macaque): Petr Malyshev/Shutterstock; (gibbon): nattanan726/Shutterstock; (orangutan):Edwin Butter/Shutterstock; (chimpanzee): apple2499/Shutterstock; (man): racorn/Shutterstock; p. 184 (loris): Martin Harvey/Getty Images; (tarsier): Cheryl Ravelo/Reuters; (lemur): Kevin Schafer/Getty Images;(indri): Wolfgang Kaehler/Getty Images; (aye-aye): Nigel J. Dennis; (tamarin): Charles Krebs/zefa/Getty Images; (spider monkey): Herbert Kehrer/Getty Images; p. 185 (colobus): Kevin Schafer/Getty Images; (mandrill): DLILLC/Getty Images; (gibbon): Anup Shah/Getty Images; (orangutan): Corbis; (man): Corbis; p. 186 (top): marcophotos/Getty Images; (bottom): *Brevity* © 2006. Dist. By ANDREWS MCMEEL SYNDICATION. Reprinted with permission; p. 188: Clark S. Larsen; p. 189 (red berry): Photo used by the kind permission of Zeping Yang; (grape): Michael McMurrough/Alamy; (hackberry): Celtis sinensis. Photo by Kenpei. May 20, 2007; http://creativecommons.org/licenses/by-sa/3.0/deed.en; (pine): Sunnyfrog/Dreamstime.com; (sparkleberry): USDA; (acorn nut): Andykazie/Dreamstime.com; (magnolia): Buch/Dreamstime.com; (china berry): Melia azedarach. Photo by Paolo Fisicaro. April 29, 2007. http://creativecommons.org/licenses/by-sa/3.0/deed.en; (mulberry): Morus alba. 2007. Photo by Jean-Pol Grandmont. http://creativecommons.org/licenses/by-sa/3.0/deed.en; (myrtle): Lenta/Dreamstime.com; (fig): Mcerovac/Dreastime.com; (hickory): riekephotos/Shutterstock; (cabbage palm leaves): Natphotos/Getty Images; (laurel cherry): REDA &CO srl/Alamy Stock Photo; (dogwood): Stevem Russell Smith Photos/Dreamstime; (cabbage palm fruit nut): Elenaray/Dreamstime; (quince): Dionisvera/Dreamstime; p. 190: (a): Ryan M. Bolton/Shutterstock; (b): Photo Researchers/Getty Images; (c): Hugh Lansdown/Shutterstock; (d): John Warburton-Lee Photography/Alamy Stock Photo; p. 191 (both): Courtesy of the Division of Fossil Primates at Duke University, Elwyn L. Simons. (c) 2015, Division of Fossil Primates at Duke University. All Rights Reserved; Courtesy of the Division of Fossil Primates at Duke University, Elwyn L. Simons. (c) 2015, Division of Fossil Primates at Duke University. All Rights Reserved; p. 192 (top a): Mint Images/Frans Lanting/Getty Images; (top b): David Haring/Getty Images; (top c): David Haring/DUPC/Getty Images; (bottom a): Roland Seitre/Minden Pictures; (bottom

b): EcoPrint/Shutterstock; (bottom c): Ann & Steve Toon/Nature Picture Library; p. 194 (top left): Ann Kakaliouas, Whittier College; (bottom left): Nature Picture Library/Alamy Stock Photo; (right): Kevin Schafer/Getty Images; p. 195 (a): Art Wolfe/Science Source; (b): Theo Allofs; (c): Gavriel Jecan; (d): AppStock/Shutterstock; (e): Tim Laman/Getty Images; (f): Art Wolfe/Science Source; (g): Tom Brakefield/Getty Images; (h): Nevada Wier/Getty Images; p. 197: Luciano Candisani/Minden Pictures/Getty Images; p. 198 (a): Roy Toft/National Geographic Image Collection; (b): Michael Nichols/National Geographic Image Collection; (c): D. Robert & Lorri Franz; (d): Martin Harvey/Alamy Stock Photo; (e): Adam Jones/Science Source; p. 199: Dane Jorgensen/Shutterstock; p. 200: Pascal Goetgheluck/Science Source.

Chapter 7: Page 206: CBS via Getty Images; p. 213 (a): Manoj Shah/Getty Images; (b): Tadashi Miwa/Getty Images; p. 214: Ian C. Gilby; p. 217: Photo credit: Jane Goodall Institute www.janegoodall.org; p. 218 (left): Martin Harvey/Alamy; (right): Susanne Shultz; (bottom): © Klaus Zuberbuhler; p. 219 (left and center): (c) Scott McGraw from McGraw et al. (2006), "Primate remains from African crowned eagle (Stephanoaetus coronatus) nests in Ivory Coast's Taï Forest: Implications for primate predation and early hominid taphonomy in South Africa." *American Journal of Physical Anthropology*, 131: 151-65. Copyright (c) 2006 Wiley-Liss, Inc.; (right): Mark Bowler/Alamy; p. 220: Photo by Etsuko Nogami, provided by Primate Research Institute, Kyoto University. Matsuzawa, T. Humle, T., and Sugiyama, Y. 2011 "The Chimpanzees of Bossou and Nimba," Springer; p. 221 (a): Clark S. Larsen; (b): Dr. Paco Bertaloni; p. 223 (top): Matthew Hamilton/Dreamstime.com; (center): Roland Seitre/Nature Picture Library; (bottom): Alison A. Zak; p. 224: Dawn Kitchen; p. 225 (a): David Tipling/Getty Images; (b): MHGallery/Getty Images; p. 226 (top): imageBroker/Alamy; (bottom): Alison Jones/DanitaDelimont.com Danita Delimont Photography/Newscom; p. 227: Yukiko Shimooka; p. 228: Susan Kuklin/Science Source.

Chapter 8: Page 231: Photo © 1996 David L. Brill, humanoriginsphotos.com; p. 232: Leonello Calvetti/Science Photo Library/Getty Images; p. 234 (top): Courtesy of American Philosophical Society; (inset): Bettmann/Getty Images; p. 235: Wikipedia, pd; p. 236 (a): Reuters; (b): Henry Romero/Reuters; (c): Science Photo Library/Alamy; (d): Tom Bean; (e): Wolfgang Kaehler/LightRocket/Getty Images; (f): Naturfoto Honal/Getty Images; (g): James L. Amos/Getty Images; (h): Tom Bean; (i): Philip Gould/Getty Images; (j): Darwinius Massillae 2009. Jens L. Franzen, Philip D. Gingerich, Jörg Habersetzerl, Jørn H. Hurum, Wighart von Koenigswald, B. Holly Smith; http://creativecommons.org/licenses/by-sa/2.5/deed.en; p. 239: © 1985 David L. Brill, humanoriginsphotos.com; p. 242 (a): John Reader/Science Source; (b): "The Fossil Footprint Makers of Laetoli," © 1982 by Jay H. Matternes; p. 244 (left): Kenneth Garrett/National Geographic Creative; (center both): Professor David Lordkipanidze, Georgian National Museum; (bottom): © 2007 Photographer P. Plailly/E. Daynès/Eurelios/Look at Science. Reconstruction Elisabeth Daynès Paris; p. 245 (all): © 2007 Photographer P. Plailly/E. Daynès/Eurelios/Look at Science. Reconstruction Elisabeth Daynès Paris; p. 249: History of Medicine/National Institute of Health,

pd; p. 250: British Library, London, UK/© British Library Board. All Rights Reserved/Bridgeman Images; p. 251: Courtesy of the Croation Natural History Museum; p. 252 (c) 1985 Jay H. Matternes; p. 253 (a,b,i,n): Peter A. Bostrom; (c): John Reader/Science Source; (d): Kenneth Garrett/Getty Images; (e): Javier Trueba/Madrid Scientific Films/Science Source; (f): Martin Land/Science Source; (g): Alfredo Dagli Orti/The Art Archive at Art Resource, NY; (h): World Museum of Man, 2004; (j): Sheila Terry/Science Source; (k): Martin Land/Science Source; (l) Pascal Goetgheluck/Science Source; (m): Steven Alvarez/National Geographic Image Collection/Getty Images; (o): DEA Picture Library/De Agostini/Getty Images;(p,q): Werner Forman/Art Resource, NY; (r): Bettmann/Getty Images; (s): Visions of America/Universal Images Group/Getty Images; p. 254 (top): Lion Man Statuette-photo by Thomas Stephan © Ulmer Museum, Ulm, Germany; (a,b): Gianni Dagli Orti/The Art Archive at Art Resource, NY; (c): akg-images; (d): David Muench; (e): David J. & Janice L. Frent Collection/Getty Images; p. 256: Sergieie/Shutterstock; p. 259 (left): National Archives; (right): AP Photo; p. 260: Trevor Dumitry, Stanford University; p. 262: James O. Hamblen; p. 266: Photo Quest LTD/Getty Images; p. 267: Getty Images; p. 268 (left): iStock/Getty Images; (right): Aedka Studio/Shutterstock; p. 269: Guenter Guni/istockphoto/Getty Images.

Chapter 9: Page 272: Edward E. Chatelain; p. 274: Chronicle/Alamy Stock Photo; p. 278 (both): Original art by Mark Klingler; copyright: Carnegie Museum of Natural History; p. 279 (all): William K. Sacco; p. 281 (left): Xijun Ni/Chinese Academy of Science; (right); Paul Tafforeau/ESRF and Xijun Ni/Chinese Academy of Sciences; p. 283 (top): John Kappelman; (bottom): Duke University Lemur Center; p. 284: Nancy Perkins, Carnegie Museum of Natural History; p. 285: Seiffert et al. (2005). "Basal anthropoids from Egypt and the antiquity of Africa's higher primate radiation." *Science* 310: 300-304. Copyright © 2005, AAAS; p. 289: Takai et al. (1996). "New specimens of the oldest fossil platyrrhine. Branisella boliviana, from Salla, Bolivia." *American Journal of Physical Anthropology* 99:301-314. Copyright © 1996, Wiley-Liss, Inc.; p. 291 (both): Martin Harvey/Getty Images; p. 296 (a): Alan Walker; (c): © 1992 Jay H. Matternes; p. 298 (a): Courtesy of and © of Eric Delson; (b): William K. Sacco; (bottom): David Pilbeam; p. 299: Courtesy of and © of Eric Delson; p. 300 (from top to bottom): Alan Walker; Courtesy of and © of Eric Delson; David Pilbeam; Courtesy of and © of Eric Delson; p. 302: © The New Yorker Collection 2006 Charles Barsotti from cartoonbank.com. All rights reserved.

Chapter 10: Page 308: © Adriadne Van Zandbergen/Africa Image Library; p. 310: Bettmann/Getty Images; p. 311 (top): Adrienne I. Zihlman, Adapted from A. Zihlman, The Human Evolution Coloring Book; (bottom) © David L. Brill, www.humanoriginsphotos.com; p. 312 (a): Pixoi Ltd/Alamy Stock Photo; (b): Luca Zanetti/laif/Redux; (c): Bruce Peter/agefotostock.com; (d): Ramin Talaie/Corbis/Getty Images; (e): Eric Vandeville/Gamma-Rapho/Getty Images; (f): BSIP/UIG/Getty Images; p. 314 (top): Martin Harvey/Gallo Images/Getty Images; (bottom): William K. Sacco; p. 315 (both): William K. Sacco; p. 317 (from left to right): Picture Post/Hulton Archive/Getty Images; Bettmann/Getty Images; Photo ©

1985, David L. Brill, www.humanoriginsphotos. com; p. 320: Wikimedia, pd; p. 322: iStock/Getty Images Plus; p. 324 (b): Philippe Bourseiller/Getty Images; (c): Jeffrey K. McKee, Ohio State University; p. 325 (a): MPFT; (b): Patrick Robert/Corbis/ Getty Images; (c): Publiphoto/Science Source; p. 327 (top): © Naci Kahn/Institute of Human Origins, Arizona State University; (bottom left): Photo Credit: (c) 2003 Tim D. White; (bottom right): Cover Image: © 2009 Jay H. Matternes. From *Science* 18 December 2009: Vol. 326. no. 5960. Copyright © AAAS; p. 328 (1): © 2002, David L. Brill, www.humanoriginsphotos.com; (2): Photo Credit: (c) 1994 Tim D. White; (3): © 1995, David L. Brill, www.humanoriginsphotos. com; p. 329 (4 left): Photo Credit: (c) 2009 Tim D. White; (4 right): Image © 2009 Jay H. Matternes. From: Lovejoy et al. "The Great Divides: Ardipithecus ramidus Reveals the Postcrania of Our Last Common Ancestors with African Apes." Science 2 October 2009: Vol. 326. no. 5949, pp. 73, 100-106. Copyright © AAAS; (5): Photo Credit: Suwa et al. The Ardipithecus Ramidus Skull and Its Implications for Hominid Origins. *Science* 2 October 2009:Vol. 326. no. 5949, 68, 68e1-68e7. Reprinted with permission from AAAS; p. 330 (top): Mauricio Antón; (bottom): Photo Credit: (c) 2009 C.O. Lovejoy et al. Ardipithecus ramidus and the Paleobiology of Early Hominids. *Science* 2 October 2009:Vol. 326. no. 5949, pp. 64, 75-86. Copyright (c) 2009 AAAS; p. 331 (top left): MPFT; (both): Photo credit © 2003 Tim White; p. 333: Kenneth Garrett/National Geographic Image Collection; p. 334 (a): © 1985 David L. Brill, www.humanoriginsphotos.com; (b): Zeresenay Alemseged/Science Source; (c): Yohannes Haile-Selassie, Liz Russel, Cleveland Museum of Natural History. Used with permission from the Proceedings of the National Academy of Science. "An early Australopithecus afarensis postcranium from Woranso-Mille, Ethiopia," Yohannes Haile-Selassie et al., PNAS, 6 July 2010: Vol. 107 no. 27, Fig. 1. Anatomically arranged elements of KSD-VP-1/1; p. 336 (top): William H. Kimbel, Ph.D; (bottom): J. Reader/Science Source; p. 337: Fred Spoor; courtesy of National Museums of Kenya; p. 339: © 1999 David L. Brill, www. humanoriginsphotos.com; p. 340 (top): Photo by Curtis Marean. ©Dikika Research Project; (center): Polaris/Newscom; (bottom a, b): Photo credit (c) 1999: © Tim D. White; (bottom c): Photo credit: Permission of G. Richards & B. Plowman; p. 341 (all): Stout et al. 2010. "Technological variation in the earliest Oldowan from Gona, Afar, Ethiopia." *Journal of Human Evolution* 58 (2010) 474-491. Copyright © 2010, Elsevier; p. 342 (both): Marion Kaplan/Alamy Stock Photo; p. 343: Diana Walker/Time & Life Pictures/Getty Images; p. 344 (bottom): © David L. Brill, www. humanoriginsphotos.com; p. 345 (top left): Photo by W. David Fooce, Cover, American Journal of Physical Anthropology, January 2003, volume 120. Copyright © 2003 Wiley-Liss; (top right): Mark Harris/Getty Images; (bottom left): © David L. Brill, www.humanoriginsphotos.com; (bottom right): Photo by Brett Eloff, courtesy of Lee Berger and the University of Witwatersrand; p. 346 (Australopithecus platyops): Fred Spoor; courtesy of National Museums of Kenya; (afarensis skeleton): © 1985 David L. Brill, www.humanoriginsphotos. com; (deyiremeda): Cleveland Museum of Natural History. Yohannes Haile-Selassie, Luis Gibert, Stephanie M. Melillo, Timothy M. Ryan, Mulugeta

Alene, Alan Deino, Naomi E. Levin, Gary Scott and Beverly Z. Saylor, New species from Ethiopia further expands Middle Pliocene hominin diversity. *Nature* 28, May 2015, Vol.521, Ext.Data Fig.5. doi:10.1038/nature14448. ©2015 Macmillan Publishers Limited. All rights reserved; p. 347 (africanus skull): © Jeffrey Schwartz, University of Pittsburgh; (garhi): © David L. Brill, www. humanoriginsphotos.com; (aethiopicus): © David L. Brill, www.humanoriginsphotos.com; (boisei): © David L. Brill, www.humanoriginsphotos. com; (robustus): © David L. Brill, www.humanoriginsphotos.com; (sediba): Photo by Brett Eloff courtesy of Lee Berger and the University of Witwatersrand.

Chapter 11: Page 352: Garrreth Bird; p. 354: Naturalis Biodiversity Center, Leiden; p. 355:Naturalis Biodiversity Center, Leiden, the Netherlands; p. 356 (a, c): © David L. Brill, www. humanoriginsphotos.com; (b): John Reader/ Science Source; p. 357 (both): © David L. Brill, www.humanoriginsphotos.com; p. 358: © David L. Brill, www.humanoriginsphotos.com; p. 359 (a): Lee R Berger, John Hawks Darryl J de Ruiter, Steven E Churchill.Peter Schmid,Lucas K Delezene,Tracy L Kivell, Heather M Garvin, Scott A Williams, Jeremy M DeSilva, Matthew M Skinner, Charles M Musiba, Noel Cameron, Trenton W Holliday, William Harcourt-Smith, Rebecca R Ackermann Markus Bastir Barry Bogin, Debra Bolter, Juliet Brophy,Zachary D Cofran,Kimberly A Congdon, Andrew S Deane, Mana Dembo, Michelle Drapeau, Marina C Elliott, Elen M Feuerriegel, Daniel Garcia-Martinez, David J Green, Alia Gurtov Joel D Irish , Ashley Kruger, Myra F Laird Damiano Marchi, Marc R Meyer, Shahed Nalla, Enquye W Negash, Caley M Orr, Davorka Radovcic, Lauren Schroeder, Jill E Scott, Zachary Throckmorton, Matthew W Tocheri, Caroline VanSickle, Christopher S Walker, Pianpian Wei,Bernhard Zipfel Homo naledi, a new species of the genus Homo from the Dinaledi Chamber, South Africa. September 10, 2015. eLife 2015;4:e09560. DOI: http://dx.doi. org/10.7554/eLife.09560 ©2015, Berger et at. CC BY 4.0; (b): Stefan Fichtel/National Geographic Creative; p. 361 (top): Dave Ingold; (bottom): Photo by Elen Feuerriegel/©University of the Witwatersrand; p. 363(top left): © 1985 David L. Brill, www.humanoriginsphotos.com; (top right): © Donald Johanson, Institute of Human Origins, Airzona State University; (bottom both): Human Origins Program at the National Museum of Natural History, Smithsonian Institution. Photo by Chip Clark; p. 364 (top): National Museum of Kenya; photo by Alan Walker; (bottom): © 1985 David L. Brill, www.humanoriginsphotos.com; p. 365:Image by Matthew Bennett, Bournemouth University. Bennett et al. "Early Hominin Foot Morphology Based on 1.5-Million-Year-Old Footprints from Ileret, Kenya," *Science* 27 February 2009: vol. 323, no. 5918, pp. 1197-1201. Copyright © 2009, AAAS; p. 366 (top): Photo © 2001 David L. Brill, www.humanoriginsphotos. com; (bottom): Photo Credit: (c) Tim D. White; p. 367 (top): Courtesy of and © National Museum of Tanzania & Eric Delson (photo by C. Tarka); (bottom): Photo Credit: © Tim D. White; p. 370: Lordkipanidze et al. "A Complete Skull from Dmanisi, Georgia, and the Evolutionary Biology of Early Homo." *Science* `8 October 2013: 342 (6156), 326-331. Copyright © 2013 AAAS; p. 371: Milford Wolpoff; p. 372: Philippe Plailly/Science Source; p.

373:© David L. Brill, www.humanoriginsphotos. com; p. 374 (all): Javier Trueba/Madrid Scientific Films/Science Source; p. 377 (both): © David L. Brill, www.humanoriginsphotos.com; p. 378 (both): Photo credit: © Tim D. White; p. 379: © 1995 Jay H. Matternes; p. 382: Courtesy Michael Chazen; p. 383:Photo © 1996 David L. Brill, www. humanoriginsphotos.com; p. 385: John Reader/ Science Source.

Chapter 12: Page 390 (left): © 2003 Photographer P. Plaily/E. Daynès/Eurelios; p. 392 (top): LVR—LandesMuseum, Bonn; (bottom): National Institute of Health/Wikimedia, pd; p. 396 (Swanscombe): Dr. Jeffrey H. Schwartz; (Steinheim): Courtesy of Staatliches Museum fur Naturkunde; (Petralona): Milford Wolpoff; (Dali): Courtesy of Dr. Xinzhi Wu; (Narmada): Courtesy of Dr. K. A. R. Kennedy, Cornell University and the University of Allahabad, India; (Ngandong): Milford Wolpoff; (Bodo): Photo Credit © Tim D. White; (Kabwe): John Reader/Science Source; (Arago): © David L. Brill, www.humanoriginsphotos.com; (Atapuerca): Javier Trueba, Madrid, Scientific Films/Science Source; p. 397: (top): John Reader/Science Source; (bottom): Milford Wolpoff; p. 398: Javier Trueba/Madrid Scientific Films/Science Source; p. 399 (a-c): Javier Trueba/ Madrid Scientific Films/Science Source; (d): Photo credit: © Tim D. White; p. 400 (a): Courtesy of Dr. K. A. R. Kennedy, Cornell University and the University of Allahabad, India; (b): Courtesy of and © of Eric Delson; p. 401 (a): © David L. Brill, www.humanoriginsphotos.com; (b): Milford Wolpoff; (c): Courtesy of Staatliches Museum fur Naturkunde; (d): Javier Trueba, Madrid, Scientific Films/Science Source; p. 402: Ira Block/ National Geographic/Getty Images; p. 403 (top): © 1985 David L. Brill, www.humanoriginsphotos. com; (bottom): Georg Kristiansen/Alamy Stock Photo; p. 404 (all): Photo credit and copyright by Dr. Erik Trinkaus; p. 405: Tamisclao/Shutterstock; p. 406 (top): © David L. Brill, www. humanoriginsphotos.com; (a): Photo credit: © Tim D. White; (b): © 1999 Henry Gilbert, Berkeley; p. 407 (top): John Reader, Science Source/ Science Source; (bottom a): Granger Collection; (bottom b): © S. Entressangle, E. Daynes/Look at Sciences; Reconstruction Elisabeth Daynes, Paris; p. 408 (top): John Reader/Science Source; (bottom): Milford Wolpoff; p. 411: © David L. Brill, www.humanoriginsphotos.com; p. 413: Musée de l'Homme de Neandertal; p. 414: Photo by David W. Frayer; p. 415 (left): Javier Trueba, Madrid, Scientific Films/Science Source; (right): Photo credit and copyright by Dr. Erik Trinkaus; p. 417 (a): Jeff Pachoud/Getty Images; (b): AP Photo/ Jean Clottes; (c, all): © 1985 David L. Brill, www. humanoriginsphotos.com; p. 419: Reuters/Patrick Price; p. 420 (Herto Reconstruction): © 2005 Jay H. Matternes; (Kabwe skull): Courtesy of Milford Wolpoff; (cleaver and mark): Photo credit: © Tim D. White; p. 421 (Herto skull): © David L. Brill, www.humanoriginsphotos.com; (skull bones and cutmarks): Photo credit: © Tim D. White; p. 423 (a): Ira Block/National Geographic Image Collection; (b): Milford Wolpoff; (bottom): Milford Wolpoff; p. 424 (a-b): © Mike Hettwer; (bottom): © David L. Brill, www.humanoriginsphotos. com; p. 425 (a-b): Clark S. Larsen; p. 426 (cave): Reuters; (reconstruction): © 2007 Photographer P. Plailly/E. Daynès Eurelios/Look at Sciences/ Reconstruction Elisabeth Daynès, Paris; (skulls): Photograph courtesy of Peter Brown; p. 427 (a-b):

Courtesy of and © of Eric Delson; p. 428 (left): Zilhão, J. & Trinkaus, E. (2002) 'Portrait of the Artist as a Child. The Gravettian Human Skeleton from the Abrigo do Lagar Velho and its Archaeological Context'. Instituto Português de Arqueologia. Photo by José Paulo Ruas; (right): Photo by Milford Wolpoff. Wolpoff et al. 2004, "Why not the Neandertals?" *World Archaeology* 36(4): 527-546. Copyright © 2004 Routledge; p. 429 (a-b): © David L. Brill, www.humanoriginsphotos.com; p.430: Courtesy of and © of Eric Delson; p. 431: Zhang, S., F. d'Errico, L.R. Backwell, Y. Zhang, F. Chen,and X. Gao. Ma'anshan cave and the origin of bone tool technology in China. *Journal of Archaeological Science*, January 2016, Vol 65, pp.57-69. DOI: 10.1016/j.jas.2015.11.004 Copyright © 2015 Elsevier Ltd. All rights reserved; p. 438 (top): Alan Thorne/epa/Newscom; (bottom): Milford Wolpoff; p. 439: Ira Block/National Geographic Image Collection; p. 440 (a): Chase Studio/Science Source; (b): Leland C. Berment; p. 441 (a-b): by James C. Chatters.

Chapter 13: Page 444: TTstudio/Shutterstock; p. 446 (a): Cartoon by Ron Therien www.cartoonstock.com; (b): Corbis; p. 447 (a): Illustration Copyright © 2013 Nucleus Medical Media, All rights reserved. www.nucleusinc.com; (b): Christopher Stojanowski; p. 449: Photo by John Doebly; p. 452 (a): blickwinkel/Alamy; (b): Courtesy Elizabeth Lee, ©Catalhoyuk Research Project; p. 453: Corbis RF; p. 458 (a): Paul Walker. From Walker 1989. "Cranial injuries as evidence of violence in prehistoric Southern California." *American Journal of Physical Anthropology.* 80:313-323. Copyright © 1989, Wiley-Liss, Inc.; p. 458 (b): George Milner; (c): Courtesy of Penn Museum, image # 78138; (d): Malin Holst; p. 459: China Photos/Getty Images; pp. 460-461: Christian Meyer, Christian Lohr, Detlef Gronenborn, and Kurt W. Alt. The massacre mass grave of Schöneck-Kilianstädten reveals new insights into collective violence in Early Neolithic Central Europe *PNAS* 2015, Vol.112, no.36, 11217-11222; published ahead of print August 17, 2015, doi:10.1073/pnas.1504365112; p. 464: Gianni Dagli Orti/Getty Images; p. 465: Peter Johnson/Corbis/Getty Images; p. 469: Clark Larsen/Mark Griffin; p. 470: Desmond Boylan/Reuters; p. 471 (top): Clark Spencer Larsen; (bottom): Tracy K. Betsinger; p. 472 (a): Clark Spencer Larsen; (b): Donald J. Ortner, Smithsonian Institution; (c): Science Source; p.474:Barry Stark. From Larsen. 1994. In the wake of Columbus: Postcontact Native population biology of the Americas. *Yearbook of Physical Anthropology* 37:109-154. © Wily-Liss; p. 475 (top): David Scharf/Science Source; (bottom a): Clark Spencer Larsen; (bottom b): Mark C. Griffin. From Larsen 1994. In the wake of Columbus: postcontact Native population biology of the Americas. Yearbook of Physical Anthropology 37:109-154. Copyright © 1994 Wiley-Liss, Inc.; p. 476: (microwear): Clark Spencer Larsen; (crowding): Haagen Klaus, Utah Valley University; (lipping): Haagen Klaus, Utah Valley University; (vertebrae TB): Donald J. Ortner, Smithsonian Institution; (DJD vertebrae): Haagen Klaus, Utah Valley University; p. 477 (DJD knee): Haagen Klaus, Utah Valley University; (Cribra orbitalia): Donald J. Ortner, Smithsonian Institution; (Enamel hypoplasias): Daniel Temple, UNC Wilmington; (Dental caries): Daniel Temple, UNC Wilmington; (Porotic hyperostosis): Haagen Klaus, Utah Valley University; (Syphilis tibia): Donald J. Ortner, Smithsonian Institution; (Periostitis tibia): Haagen Klaus, Utah Valley University; (Ulnar fracture): Haagen Klaus, Utah Valley University; p. 478 (a): Eye of Science/Science Source; (b): yabchikova-Voisin/Science Source.

Chapter 14: Page 481: NASA; p. 482: VCG/VCG via Getty Images; p. 485: Photo courtesy of Lonnie Thompson; p. 486: Image by Janell Strouse; p. 487: Ellen Mosley-Thompson; p. 488 (a): Robb Kendrick/Getty Images; (b): NASA, Robert Simmon; based on data by the Tropospheric Emission Monitoring Internet Service (TERMIS); p. 489: PhotoQuest/Getty Images; p. 490: luoman/istockphoto/Getty Images; p. 491 (a): Kevin Schafer/zefa/Getty Images; (b): Jacob Silberberg/Getty Images; p. 492: Brian Harris/Alamy Stock Photo; p. 499 (a): BSIP SA/Alamy; (b): Science Source; (c): Dennis Kunkel Microscopy, Inc./Visuals Unlimited, Inc.; (d): Hannah Gal/Science Source; p. 500:Darwin Dale/Visualphotos.com/Science Source.

TEXT CREDITS

Chapter 2: Page 43 (Figure 2.17b): Greg Mercer, Figure, "Seven Pairs of Contrasting Traits." © The Field Museum, #GN91263d. Reprinted with permission.

Chapter 3: Page 65 (Anthro Matters 3.1): Maanasa Raghavan, et al. Figure from "Genomic evidence for the Pleistocene and recent population history of Native Americans," *Science*, Vol. 349, August 21, 2015. Copyright © 2015, The American Association for the Advancement of Science. Reprinted with permission from AAAS.

Chapter 4: Page 104 (Figure 4.9A-D): Mark Ridley: Figure from *Evolution*, p. 77. Copyright © 2004 by Blackwell Science Ltd., a Blackwell Publishing Company. Reproduced with permission of Blackwell Publishing Ltd.; Page 110 (Figure 4.19): Jen Christiansen: Figure: Malaria Cycle, originally printed in "Tackling Malaria" by Claire P. Dunavan, *Scientific American*, Vol. 293, No. 6, Dec. 2005, p. 79. Reprinted by permission.

Chapter 5: Page 140 (How Do We Know, Figure 1): John Lamphear: Map from "Aspects of 'Becoming Turkana': Interactions and Assimilation Between Maa- and Ateker-Speakers" from *Being Maasai: Ethnicity in East Africa*, ed. Thomas Spear and Richard Waller, Ohio University Press, 1993. Reprinted with permission of Ohio University Press, Athens, Ohio (www.ohioswallow.com); Page 149 (Figure 5.16A): George Chaplin: Figures modified from N.G. Jablonski, *Skin: A Natural History*. 2006 © G. Chaplin. Reprinted by permission.

Chapter 6: Page 199 (Figure 6.30): Bruce Latimer: Figure: Ape and human pelvis mechanics. Reprinted by permission.

Chapter 8: Page 256 (Figure 8.21B): R.H. Towner: Figure: Box 4. Constructing Chronologies from "Archaeological Dendrochronology in the Southwestern U.S.", *Evolutionary Anthropology*, p. 73. Copyright © 2002, Wiley-Liss, Inc. Reprinted with permission of Wiley-Liss, Inc., a subsidiary of John Wiley & Sons, Inc.; Page 261 (Figure 8.24A): BioArch: Figure: Amino Acid Dating from "Amino Acid Racemization." Reprinted by permission; Page 261 (Figure 8.24B): Philip L. Stein and Bruce M. Rowe: Figure 11-13: "The Geomagnetic Reversal Time Scale" from *Physical Anthropology, 9th Edition*, p. 280. Copyright © 2006, The McGraw-Hill Companies. Reprinted by permission.

Chapter 9: Page 293 (Figure 9.19): Laurie Grace: Figure: Map of Miocene Ape Fossil Localities, originally printed in "Apes" by D.R. Begun, *Scientific American*, Vol. 289, No. 2, 2003, p. 77. Reprinted by permission; Page 305 (Figure 9.28): Reprinted from *Current Biology*, Vol. 8, No. 16, Caro-Beth Stewart and John R. Disotell, "Primate Evolution – In and Out of Africa", pp. 582-588, Copyright © 1999 Elsevier Science Ltd., with permission from Elsevier.

Chapter 10: Page 311 (Figure 10.2): "Olduvai Gorge", p. 61 from *The Human Evolution Coloring Book, 2nd Edition* by Adrienne Zihlman. Copyright © 1982, 2000 by Coloring Concepts, Inc. Reprinted by permission of HarperCollins Publishers; Page 332 (Figure 10.23): Figure from "Australopithecus garhi: A New Species of Early Hominid from Ethiopia", Berhane Asfaw, et al., *Science*, Vol. 284, April 23, 1999, p. 634. Copyright © 1999, The American Association for the Advancement of Science. Reprinted with permission from AAAS; Page 335 (Figure 10.28):Figure from "Did australopiths climb trees?" by Susan Larson. *Science* Vol. 338. Pp. 478-479. Copyright © 2010, The American Association for the Advancement of Science. Reprinted with permission from AAAS.

Chapter 11: Page 360 (How Do We Know, Figure 1): Ewen Callaway, Figure from "Crowdsourcing digs up an early human species," *Nature*, Vol. 525, September 17, 2015. Copyright © 2015 Nature Publishing Group. Reprinted by permission from Macmillan Publishers Ltd.

Chapter 12: Page 412 (Figure 12.29): Reprinted from *Journal of Archaeological Science*, Vol. 26, No. 6, June 1999, Hervé Bocherens, et al., "Palaeoenvironmental and Palaeodietary Implications of Isotopic Biogeochemistry of Last Interglacial Neanderthal and Mammal Bones in Scladina Cave (Belgium)," pp. 599-607, Copyright © 1999 Academic Press, with permission from Elsevier; Page 439 (Figure 12.53): Theodore G. Schurr: Figure 2, pg. C-1 from "The Peopling of the New World: Perspectives from Molecular Anthropology." Reprinted, with permission, from the *Annual Review of Anthropology*, Volume 33, © 2004 by Annual Reviews. www.annualreviews.org.

Chapter 13: Page 350 (Figure 13.5B): Bruce D. Smith: Figure "The approximate time periods when plants and animals were first domesticated" from *The Emergence of Agriculture*, p. 13, 1998. Reprinted by permission; Page 357 (Figure 13.9): Colin Renfrew and Paul Bahn: Figure drawn by Annick Boothe. From *Archaeology: Theories, Methods and Practice* by Colin Renfrew and Paul Bahn, Thames & Hudson Inc., New York. Reprinted by permission of the publisher; Page 468 (Figure 13.16): Roberto Osti: Figure "Bones of the Postcontact Indians" from "Reading the Bones of La Florida" by Clark S. Larsen, *Scientific American*, Vol. 282, No. 6, p. 84. Reprinted by permission of Roberto Osti Illustrations; Page 473 (Figure 13.22): Clark S. Larsen: Figure 3.2 "Percentage of teeth affected by dental caries in eastern North America" from *Bioarchaeology: Interpreting Behavior from the Human Skeleton*, p. 69, Cambridge University Press, 1997.

INDEX

Mexico, *36*, 36–37, 452, 475, 488, 500
Meyer, Christian, 460
Meyer, Matthias, 398
Mezmaiskaya, 432
microcephaly, **425**
microevolution, **92,** *93*
Micrographia (Hooke), *30*
micronutrients, 151–52, **152,** *153*, 154
Micropithecus, **292**
microsatellites, **81,** 129
Middle Awash Valley, 231, 268, 325–26, *326, 327,*
    328, *328,* 340, *340,* 341, 369, 377, 417, *421*
Middle East, 119
Middle Paleolithic culture, **409**
Middleton, James, 249
migrations
    of anthropoids, *290,* 290–91
    of modern humans, 65, *436,* 436–41
        to Australia and Pacific Islands, *436, 437,*
            437–38, *438*
        to the Western Hemisphere (first
            Americans), 438–41, *439, 440, 441*
Miguelón (Atapuerca 5), 398
millet, 473
Minatogawa, 425
minerals, *153*
Miocene epoch, *246, 267,* 275
    hominins in, 349
    primates in, 292, *293, 294–95, 296, 297,* 300,
        301, 319
    temperature change in, *266, 267, 267*
Mission Santa Catalina, *4, 4*
Miss Waldron's red colobus monkey, 195
mitochondria, **56, 60,** *61*
mitochondrial DNA (mtDNA), 60, 66
    human evolution and, 432
    of Native Americans, 68, *439,* 439–40
    of native Australians, 438
    social structure in, *118*
    spread of agriculture and, 120
mitosis, **62,** *66,* 66–67, *67,* 85, 132, *132*
Mladec skulls, 425, 427
modern humans
    biocultural variation in, 434–35, *435*
    body shape of, 496, *496*
    chimpanzees' genetic closeness to, 186, *186*
    evolutionary lineages of, 394–95, *395*
    face morphology of, 462
    genetic variation in, *433,* 433–35, *435*
    grooming among, *213*
    height of, 82, *137,* 137–38, 496, *496*
    life history of (*see* life history of humans)
    life span of, 209, 494, *494*
    material culture of, 217, 220
    migrations of, *436,* 436–41
        to Australia and Pacific Islands, *436, 437,*
            437–38, *438*
        to the Western Hemisphere (first
            Americans), 438–41, *439, 440, 441*
    Neandertals' genetic relationship to, 434–35,
        435
    racial categorization of (*see* race concept)
    skeletal structure of, 394, 427–28, *428,* 476–77
    skin color of, *124*
    skull morphology of, *393,* 393–94, *477*
    teeth of, 445–46, *446,* 462–64, *476*
    see also Homo sapiens: early modern
molars
    of australopithecines, 344
    bilophodont, **177,** 216
    fossil pig, *252*
    of *Homo erectus,* 354
    of primates, *171,* 177, *178*
    Y-5, **177,** *178,* 186–87, 199, 292

Mongol migrations, 118
Mongoloid race, 127, *127*
monkeys
    brain morphology of, *181*
    evolution of, 193, 301, *304,* 304–5, *305*
    New World (*see* New World monkeys)
    Old World (*see* Old World monkeys)
    predators of, *218–19*
    taxonomy of, 183, 186
    teeth of, 177, *177, 178, 179*
monogamous, **210,** 210–11
monosomy, **72**
Monte Lessini, 432
Moore, Leslie, *6*
Morgan, Thomas Hunt, 43, *45, 46*
morphology, **20**
Morwood, Michael, 425
Mosley-Thompson, Ellen, *486,* 487
moth, peppered, 101, *104,* 104–5, *105, 106,* 107, 485
motor skills, **133,** 302–3
Moula-Guercy cave, *406, 406*
mouse lemur, 182, 190
Mousterian tools, *253,* **409,** *411*
Moyà-Solà, Salvador, 302, 303
mRNA (messenger RNA), *75,* **76,** *98*
mtDNA, *see* mitochondrial DNA (mtDNA)
Müller, Paul, 500
Mulligan, Connie, 84, 440
multiple endocrine neoplasia, type 2, *49*
Multiregional Continuity evolutionary model,
    394–95, *395,* 432, 433, *433,* 434, 435, 442
Mungo, Lake, 438, *438*
muriquis, 196–97, *197*
muscles, masticatory, 199, *200,* 318, *318,* 462, 500
mutagens, **100**
mutations, **45,** *46,* 97, *98, 99,* 99–100, *100, 108,*
    108–9, 120, 122, 440, 501
    de novo, **64**
    frameshift, **99**
    induced, **100**
    point, **99**
    spontaneous, **100,** *100*
Muybridge, Eadweard, *20*
Mycobacterium tuberculosis, 500

Nagasaki, 258, *259*
nails, 275
Napier, John, 172, 356
Nariokotome Boy, 363–64, *364,* 367, 370
Narmada, 400, *400*
nasal apertures of Neandertals, 407–8, *408*
Native Americans, 404
    blood types of, *115,* 115–16
    European contacts with, 3–4, *4,* 117
    evolutionary change in, 3–4, *7*
    genomic record of, 65, *65*
    haplogroups of, 68, *69,* 438–39, *439,* 440
    mtDNA of, 68, *439,* 439–40
    Paleoindians *vs.,* **441,** *441*
    as race, 127, *127*
    shovel-shaped incisors of, **438,** *439*
    skin color of, 129
    type 2 diabetes among, 159–60
    Y chromosomes of, 440
natural selection, **26,** 35, 39, 43, 45, 88, 101, 120,
    122
    in animals (peppered moth), 101, *104,* 104–5,
        105, 106, 107
    in humans (abnormal hemoglobins and malaria
        resistance), *107,* 107–9, *108, 109, 110, 111,*
        111–13, *112*
    lactase persistence and, 94–95, *95*
    patterns of, 101, *104*
    sickle-cell anemia and, 90

Navajo, 440
nDNA (nuclear nDNA), 60, *60,* 432
Neandertals, 431–32
    in Asia, 401, *402,* 402–4, *403, 404*
    body shape of, *407,* 407–9, *408, 409, 410*
    brain size of, 401
    burials by, 412–13, *413*
    cannibalism of, 405–6, *406*
    diet of, 410–12, *412*
    in Europe, 401, 404–7, *405, 406, 407*
    face morphology of, 407–8, *408*
    height of, 409, *409*
    hunting by, 409–12, *411, 412*
    intelligence of, 409, 416
    interbreeding between early modern *Homo*
        sapiens and, 432–33
    Krapina, 249–50, *251,* 404–6, *405, 406,* 412,
        460
    limb bones of, 408
    modern humans' genetic relationship with,
        434–35, *435*
    mtDNA of, 438
    nasal aperture of, 407–8, *408*
    reconstructions of, *390*
    skeletons of, 391–92, *392,* 401–3, *403, 404,*
        406–7, *407,* 418–19
    skull of, 391–92, *392, 409,* 443
    speech ability of, 413–14, *414*
    symbolism used by, 415–16, 431
    teeth of, 401, 403–4, *405,* 412, 414, *414*
    tool use and technology of, 403–4, 409–10, *411*
    violence of, 456
Neel, James V., 159
Neolithic demographic transition, 456
Neolithic period, **447,** 488
Neolithic tools, *253*
neonatal period, 132, 142
neural tube defects, 154
neurodevelopmental disorders, 82
neurofibromatosis, type 2, *49*
New Guinea, *421,* 433, 452
New South Wales, 438
New World monkeys, 193–94, *194*
    distribution of, *169*
    evolution of, 275, *289,* 289–91, *290, 291*
    residence patterns of, 210
    teeth of, 177, *177*
Ngandong, Java, 397, *397,* 400, *400*
Ni, Xijun, 281
Nile River, 282, 489
Nile Valley, 462
nitrogen dioxide, 488
nocturnal adaptation, **174,** *294*
noncoding DNA, **77,** 77–78, 97
nondisjunctions, **72**
nonheme iron, **474**
nonhoning canine teeth, **11,** *12–13,* 314, *314*
nonhoning chewing, 11, *12–13,* 14, 21, 310–11, *312,*
    314, 314–15, *315,* 318, 318–19
nonmelanic form, 101, **104,** 104–5, *105, 106*
nonmineralized bone, **136**
non-radiometric dating, 260–61, *261, 262*
nonsynonymous point mutations, **99**
nonvocal communication, *227,* 227–28, *228*
North America
    agriculture in, 452, 454–55
    East Asian migrations to, 438–41, *439, 440,*
        441
    native populations of (*see* Native Americans)
northern muriquis, 196–97, *197*
Notharctus, **279**
NR3C1 gene, 85
Nubia, 462, *463*
nuclear DNA (nDNA), 60, *60,* 432